Reflections of Eminent Economists

B'H

For Naomi, Avi, Marc and Tova,
and Elki, Batya, Chanoch, Devora, Ephraim, Ayala and Jacob

To my wife, Noreena Ramrattan,
to my children – Devi and her husband Arjun, Shanti, Hari and Rani –
and to my grandchildren – Soham and Lakshmi

Reflections of Eminent Economists

Edited by

Michael Szenberg

Distinguished Professor of Economics, Lubin School of Business, Pace University, USA and Editor-in-Chief, The American Economist

Lall Ramrattan

Instructor, University of California, Berkeley Extension, USA

Foreword by Kenneth J. Arrow

Edward Elgar

Cheltenham, UK • Northampton, MA, USA

Published by
Edward Elgar Publishing Limited
Glensanda House
Montpellier Parade
Cheltenham
Glos GL50 1UA
UK

Edward Elgar Publishing, Inc.
136 West Street
Suite 202
Northampton
Massachusetts 01060
USA

A catalogue record for this book
is available from the British Library

Library of Congress Cataloguing in Publication Data

Reflections of eminent economists/edited by Michael Szenberg, Lall Ramrattan;
foreword by Kenneth J. Arrow.
p. cm.
Includes bibliographical references and index.
1. Economists—Biography. I. Szenberg, Michael. II. Ramrattan, Lall,
1951– .
HB76.R44 2004
330'.092'2—dc22

2004042266

ISBN 1 84376 628 0 (cased)

Printed and bound in Great Britain by MPG Books Ltd, Bodmin, Cornwall

Contents

Contributors

Irma Adelman, Professor, Graduate School, University of California at Berkeley.

Bela Balassa was Professor of Political Economy, Johns Hopkins University, and consultant to the World Bank.

Carolyn Shaw Bell, Katharine Coman Professor of Economics, Emerita, Wellesley College.

Barbara R. Bergmann, Professor Emeritus, American University.

Mark Blaug, Professor, University of Exeter.

Martin Bronfenbrenner was Kenan Professor of Economics, Emeritus, Duke University.

Graciela Chichilnisky, UNESCO Professor of Mathematics and Economics, Professor of Statistics, Columbia University. Director, Program on Information and Resources (PIR) and Director, Columbia Consortium for Risk Management (CCRM).

Richard A. Easterlin, Professor of Economics, University of Southern California.

Ronald G. Ehrenberg, Irving M. Ives Professor of Industrial and Labor Relations and Economics, Cornell University, and Director of the Cornell Higher Education Research Institute.

Victor R. Fuchs, Henry J. Kaiser, Jr Professor, Emeritus, Stanford University, and Research Associate National Bureau of Economic Research.

Roger W. Garrison, Professor of Economics, Auburn University.

Eli Ginzberg was Professor, Presidential Adviser and Director of Revson, Director, Conservation of Human Resources, Columbia University.

Aron Gottesman, Assistant Professor of Finance, Lubin School of Business, Pace University.

Edward M. Gramlich, Member, Board of Governors of the Federal Reserve System, former Dean of the School of Public Policy, and Professor of Economics, University of Michigan.

Everett E. Hagen was Professor of Economics, Emeritus, Massachusetts Institute of Technology.

G.C. Harcourt, Emeritus Reader in the History of Economic Theory, University of Cambridge. Emeritus Fellow, Jesus College, Cambridge and Professor Emeritus, University of Adelaide.

E. Malinvaud, Professor of Economics, College of France, Paris.

Harry M. Markowitz, 1991 Nobel laureate, former Marvin Speiser Distinguished Professor of Finance and Economics, Baruch College, City University of New York, and Consultant, Dawa Securities Trust Co.

Allan H. Meltzer, the Allan H. Meltzer University Professor of Political Economy, Carnegie Mellon University and Visiting Scholar, American Enterprise Institute.

Geoffrey H. Moore was Director, Center for International Business Cycle Research, Columbia University.

Walter Y. Oi, Elmer B. Milliman Professor of Economics, University of Rochester.

Mark Perlman, University Professor of Economics, Emeritus, University of Pittsburgh.

Lall Ramrattan, Instructor, University of California, Berkeley Extension.

Kurt W. Rothschild, Professor Emeritus, University of Linz.

F.M. Scherer, Roy E. Larsen Professor of Public Policy and Management, John F. Kennedy School of Government, Harvard University.

Julian L. Simon was Professor of Business Management, University of Maryland, at College Park.

Michael Szenberg, Distinguished Professor of Economics, Lubin School of Business, Pace University and Editor-in-Chief, *The American Economist*.

Hirofumi Uzawa, Professor of Economics, University of Tokyo.

Sir Alan Walters, Vice Chairman and Director of AIG Trading Group and Director of Idea Limited and Chairman of Counter Cyclical Investment Fund, and former economic adviser to the Prime Minister of Britain, Margaret Thatcher.

Foreword

Kenneth J. Arrow

We are indebted to Michael Szenberg's persuasive powers in eliciting the self-analyses of economists in this and in two preceding volumes. Their existence performs (at least) two functions: interest in their own right as the expressions of a specially capable set of humans outside their technical achievements, and material for the future historian of economic thought.

The writers in this and the earlier volumes constitute a very broad representation of the leaders of economic thought in the last thirty years and more. Being an economist imposes reasonably severe constraints on beliefs, policy positions, and the attitudes towards the fundamental questions that might be said to constitute a 'life philosophy.' Whether these constraints operate by selection or indoctrination, I will leave for those more qualified to judge. But within those constraints, we find a wide variety of self-expressions. As I have observed my colleagues over many years, I find, for example, that their underlying motivations vary greatly. Some enjoy the use of specific tools that they have learned or developed. Some enjoy attempting to resolve intellectual puzzles. Others have strong policy views and visions of social rights and wrongs and engage in analyses designed to reinforce those views. Some are mainly interested in self-advancement, in outdoing others in novelty and distinction. Others have had a saintly or perhaps priestly attitude; the development of economics by whomever and however was the goal.

As may not surprise an economist, motivations do not necessarily affect outcomes; what matters is their strength and the reward system of the academic world. I have known excellent work to be performed by individuals who were concerned about their fidelity to science and also by those whose concern was their own advancement.

Just as diversity in motivation and ideology is compatible with development in economics (or any other science), so is diversity in methodology. Indeed, variety in methodology is positively beneficial. To continue the economic metaphor, there are large gains from trade from a variety of approaches. The most obvious example is the falsity of the empirical–theoretical dichotomy. The roles of empirical evidence in stimulating theory and of theory in guiding empirical inquiry are by now commonplaces as they were not fifty years ago. The increasing tendency to join these approaches in a single paper is to be applauded. What is not always recognized, though, is that the differences have roots in personality differences, to be identified in part with 'life philosophies.'

To turn to a different aspect of these self-analyses, many, perhaps most, put great emphasis on the presence of some outstanding teacher or teachers. Indeed, not only in these volumes but in the history of economic thought, we have narratives based on some great original scholar who inspires and teaches disciples. Thus, Marshall trained many economists, most notably, Pigou, Keynes and Robertson, and other economists whose reputations have survived less well. Keynes in turn stimulated his own even more devoted followers – Kahn, Joan Robinson and Meade. At Vienna, Carl Menger's teaching was received by Wieser, Böhm-Bawerk and Schumpeter (a pretty formidable trio).

But in a world of publication, influence is not confined to the classroom. Marshall himself drew on John Stuart Mill, who, to the best of my knowledge, never faced a class; and Mill, of course, followed, even slavishly, the work of David Ricardo, not a professor but a retired businessman. W. Stanley Jevons, who certainly is one of the original figures of neoclassical economics, was essentially self-taught. Léon Walras had an economist father; but he seems to have spent his youth trying to find some other occupation; and his work reflects no great influence from his father (though he did use one of his technical terms as a form of piety). Francis Edgeworth, Irving Fisher, Vilfredo Pareto and Knut Wicksell all seem to have acquired their economic knowledge by reading, and they did not have many students whom they inspired. Paul Samuelson was as student at one of the two most important centers of economic research in the United States at the time. Yet I find it hard to detect the influence of his teachers in the central part of his work, though he did have very fruitful contacts with fellow-students. Even in Keynes's case, many of those who most contributed to the further development of his doctrines were not students of his but other economists who were influenced by his writings: the names of Harrod, Hicks, Kaldor and Lerner spring immediately to mind, not to mention the many American followers from Alvin Hansen on.

It would be interesting to examine the essays collected in this and earlier volumes in the same series to see what proportion ascribe a dominant role to one or a few professors and to what extent an outside observer would agree that the professor was in fact influential in the writer's work.

This remark leads back to one made at the beginning of this Foreword – that these essays will be of use to a historian of economic thought. To what extent are essays of this kind reliable evidence? On factual matters, one's memory is not infallible, as I have had occasion to learn to my embarrassment. Do we really know the motives which led us into economics or into our particular research directions? From a practical viewpoint, should we interview elderly scholars about their career and research choices? Recently, one author put out an examination of the development of economics since World War II. The book is full of scholarly apparatus. He went into archives and cited them. But he did not interview anyone, even though many of those whom he discusses are still alive. Was this because he felt that the interviews would be self-serving?

I am not so pessimistic. I believe it was Wordsworth who wrote, 'Poetry is emotion recollected in tranquility.' That means the poetry is not conveying fully the original emotion, but it does not mean that we don't learn a good deal, more indeed, than we could from the incoherent expressions of a less tranquil time. We are certainly learning one thing from the essays – what the writer thinks today. But more than that, we get one privileged insight, not the whole truth (which is always unknowable), but one perspective which could not be obtained from any other source than the author.

For these insights, the budding economist as well as the historian of thought should be grateful.

Preface and acknowledgements

The purpose of this volume is to relate positive and negative autobiographical phenomena as perceived with reflections by eminent economists. Thus, this book is intended for those individuals who are fascinated by scholars' lives, personalities and morals. The collection of essays in this volume offers us details about wise and accomplished lives. The essays contain elements characteristic of great literature – pathos and wit, pain and humor. Examining the essayists' reflections here affords us the opportunity to explore the question of what makes distinctive and exciting scholarship, as well as probe the criteria for excellence. Further, as a reviewer of a recent book notes, 'autobiography is a source for understanding the social history of a discipline.'[1]

We are grateful for the help of a number of individuals in the preparation of this volume. We are especially indebted to Kenneth Arrow, who penned the Foreword, and to the contributors of this collection. We thank them for their congenial partnership. I feel an immeasurable debt of gratitude towards Victor R. Fuchs, a participant in this book. It was only his readiness to meet with me in the New York offices of the National Bureau of Economic Research and to overrule my disseration 'sponsor' (who found excuses to delay reading my chapters for six to eight months) that made it possible for me to move ahead. The words of the 'sponsor' still ring in my head: 'If Victor Fuchs says it is good then go ahead.' I know that my life would have been less without him. Here I witnessed in practice the Talmudic teaching that 'the highest wisdom is kindness.' We extend special thanks to Alan Sturmer, the acquisitions editor of Edward Elgar Publishing, and to Edward Elgar himself for their enthusiastic support of this book. I asked my collaborator, Lall Ramrattan, to join me as the co-editor for this work. Observers of the scientific enterprise note that joint authorship is increasing,[2] and I have been very fortunate in this since Lall and I, on the basis of a single telephone conversation and without meeting each other, decided to hitch ourselves together four years ago in order to advance our modest scientific wagon. Even though Lall and I reside on opposite coasts of the United States, our productive and joyful team effort unites us. I am immensely grateful to him since the collaboration, besides maximizing the differential between the returns and costs of publishing, brings reflection and conversation of a kind that single authorship cannot provide.

I cannot imagine writing without the help of friends. Friends who provide solace, advice, and are always there to listen include my colleagues and co-workers at Lubin – Lew Altfest, Walter G. Antognini, Jeannine Arrigo, Peter Hoefer, Surendra Kaushik, Matt Morey, Jouahn Nam, James Russell, Joseph Salerno, Nicola Simpson, Lynette Wailoo, Diana Ward, Berry Wilson and Carmen Urma. I also wish to thank Aron Gottesman and P.V. Viswanath for their invaluable critiques of the work as it passed through successive stages and for their literary sensibilities and their warmth. The librarians of Pace University – Elisabeth Birnbaum, Michelle Fanelli and Lucy Gonzales – were unfailingly enthusiastic and supportive.

I received encouragement, advice and labor on this volume from Andrea Pascarelli, the editorial assistant of the Center for Applied Research, and from Hema Gajaraj, my devoted graduate research assistant. They both have lightened many a task. Sandy Franklin, an MBA Lubin alumna and a freelance editor, has been very supportive of my efforts. She is a marvel of humor, understanding and generosity of spirit. The last three books benefited tremendously from her professional rigor.

My deep thanks also to the members of the Executive Board of the Honor Society in Economics for being a steady source of support: Professors Mary Ellen Benedict, James Bradley Jr, Kristine L. Chase, Robert R. Ebert, William D. Gunther, Shirley Johnson-Lans, Charles F. Phillips Jr and Robert S. Rycroft.

Again I acknowledge with gratitude the continuing assistance, both intellectual and material, and the encouragement for this and my other scholarly quests of Arthur L. Centonze, Dean of the Lubin School of Business, Pace University.

My children Naomi and Avi, their spouses Marc and Tova, and my grandchildren Elki, Batya, Chanoch, Devora, Ephraim, Ayala and Jacob fill my life and my wife's life with wonder and joy. For me, children offer a tremendous sense of pride, accomplishment and renewal, not the least because most of my family perished during the Holocaust.

M.S.

I would like to thank my family – my wife Noreena, and my children: Devi and her husband Arjun, Shanti, Hari and Rani, and my grandchildren Brian and Sabrina – for their patience and understanding for allowing me the time I put into this work. There are many teachers that have molded my methodological perspective in economics that I wish to thank as well. I particularly thank the late Alan Coddington for my positive economic outlook, and Thomas Vietorisz for his teaching of other philosophical methods. I want also to acknowledge the unselfish recommendation of Professor Charles Baird of California State University, Hayward for recommending Roger Garrison instead of himself to cover the Austrian perspective in this volume. Last but not least, I wish to thank Michael Szenberg, who was overly generous to bring me on board of this project. I consider myself lucky that he chose me instead of his so many other capable friends.

L.B.R.

NOTES

1. Evelyn L. Forget, review of *Passion and Craft: Economists at Work*, ed. Michael Szenberg (Ann Arbor: University of Michigan Press, 1999), *Review of Social Economy*, **59** (1) (March 2003), 112.
2. Michael Szenberg, 'Intellectual Collaborative Experiences, Editorial Note,' *The American Economist*, **40** (Fall 1996), 3–4.

'No bird soars too high, if he soars with his own wings.'

William Blake

Introduction

Aron Gottesman, Lall Ramrattan and Michael Szenberg

While the topic of this book is ostensibly the reflections of leading economists, a thorough reading will convince you that this book is fundamentally a fascinating record of prodigious achievement and lives well lived, even in the face of devastating odds. The essays in this book reveal the degree to which events and experiences during the lives of our authors – all luminaries in economics – molded their career paths, worldviews, and philosophies.[1]

To employ a metaphor, this book is a veritable journey into some of the finest minds of the twentieth century, all of which are in the possession of individuals that we classify as 'economists.' During the course of reading this book, you will soar across the globe, across time (or at least the past 100 years or so), and across the very foundations of modern economic theory, ideas, applications and thoughts.

The insights provided in these essays are priceless, not only in the domain of economics but also from many other angles. You will explore economic ideas, lessons learnt after years of experience, political and religious convictions, lineage, influences, geography, thoughts on war and peace, and career paths. All of these topics are explored in the context of the history of the world, of the United States, and of economics over the past century. We only have a limited amount of space in this introduction; hence, we can do little more than whet your appetite for the delights that await you. But we are sure you will be motivated to open the portals and explore the minds of these leading economists more closely as they describe their life experiences in their own words.

Our essayists trade in ideas. Consider Barbara Bergmann, who applied microsimulation to macroeconomic methods, was touched by discrimination against African Americans and women, and wrote several books about race and gender, or Bela Balassa, who attached great value to personal freedoms and advocated economic liberalization. Carolyn Shaw Bell describes discovering that the 'typical family' is actually in the minority. Sir Alan Walters ponders the secrets of statistics for policy aims. Harry Markowitz uses Hume's ideas as exemplar in portfolio theory. E. Malinvaud discusses the appeal of economics as a normative science, challenging the positive viewpoint. Victor Fuchs explains why economists should recognize the role of integrative systems beyond the market and government, while G.C. Harcourt relates the political economy to politics and religion. And this is the tip of the iceberg!

Are you interested in exploring our essayists' lineage to attempt to resolve conclusively whether it was nature or nurture that led to their successes? If so, you can travel back in time to 1905 and observe the participation of Martin Bronfenbrenner's father in the seizure of Odessa by the revolting sailors of the Black Sea Fleet, or see Everett Hagen's Norwegian parents meet on an immigrant ship steaming towards the United States. Of course, we cannot ignore Schumpeter's accidental role in the marriage of Irma Adelman's parents.[2] And did you know that Graciela Chichilnisky's father was Eva Peron's physician when Peron died?

Is geography your pastime? Our native-born American essayists are diverse, ranging from Mark Perlman, born in Wisconsin, to F.M. Scherer, born in Ottawa, Illinois. But our contributors also include Mark Blaug, who attended Stuyvesant High School in New York City, and Julian Simon, whose first clear memory is downstairs in Grandma Simon's old-fashioned hardware store in Newark, New Jersey – and who can still recall a character named 'Bupkiss' Barnhart? We also follow Walter Oi, who was legally blind, as he leaves UCLA and travels on the Union Pacific bound for the University of Chicago, accompanied by his brother. And while many of our essayists were born in the United States, many were not. For example, Graciela Chichilnisky was born in Buenos Aires; E. Malinvaud in Limoges, France; G.C. Harcourt in Melbourne, Australia; and Kurt Rothschild in Vienna between the world wars (and between the Freudians and the Adlerians). Irma Adelman was born in Cernowitz, Romania, while Bela Balassa was born in Budapest. Hirofumi Uzawa was born in Yonago, in Tottori Prefecture, in the region known in Japan as the 'Region in the Shadow of the Mountains,' while Sir Alan Walters, who later advised Margaret Thatcher, was born in a Leicester slum.

Do issues of war and peace engage your mind? If so, consider that Richard Easterlin was a deck officer on a US Navy cruiser, while Julian Simon was a deck officer aboard a destroyer. Eli Ginzberg did a four-year stint in the Pentagon; Mark Perlman fought in the US Army; Victor Fuchs enlisted in the Army Air Corps; Roger Garrison took a commission in the Air Force during the Vietnam era; and Sir Alan Walters volunteered for the British Army at age 17. F.M. Scherer's experience is particularly engaging: he describes himself as a 'thoughtful peacenik,' and notes that he attended Counter-Intelligence Corps school after basic training, participated in the Harvard Business School's Weapons Acquisition Research Project following the 1957 launch of the

Sputnik, and vigorously disagreed with John F. Kennedy's 'missile gap' arguments, relegating himself to a pariah status in Pentagon circles.

Are you still unsure what you want to be when you grow up? You'll be relieved to learn that many of our essayists shared your problem. An overwhelming majority of our essayists describe events beyond their control or expectations that led them to economics. Allan Meltzer writes of a generation that was attracted to economics as a discipline that can be used to improve welfare, and perceives economics as a policy science, not a branch of applied mathematics. Everett Hagen suggests that one chooses to study economics, as opposed to other fields that study the 'human animal and his society,' because one has a 'guarded interest' in humans. Geoffrey Moore originally planned to work in the field of poultry husbandry before switching to agricultural economics. Eli Ginzberg, who served every president from Roosevelt to Reagan, explains why he was lucky there was no competent course in microeconomics during his studies. F.M. Scherer, a future chief economist of the FTC, was initially rejected by Harvard Business School, while Julian Simon explains how he achieved a grade of 'A' in philosophy at Harvard College. And Mark Perlman describes difficulties fitting into the *Genossenschaft* at Cornell through failing the 'level of mediocrity test.'

Are you a history buff? The field of economics is thoroughly intertwined with events in history. So too are the lives of our economists, as the ivory tower offers no protection from the changing tides of history. You will learn how a *coup d'état* in Argentina led Graciela Chichilnisky to study at MIT, and why career choices meant little to Kurt Rothschild after Hitler invaded Austria. You will discover that following the Holocaust in Europe, Irma Adelman fought in Israel's war of independence, and also spent time in Vietnam during the events of 1963. You will learn that 26 February 1936 was an important date for Hirofumi Uzawa: on that date, a group of rebellious young army officers headquartered next to his middle school attacked the official residence of the Japanese prime minister, the Diet, and other strategic locations (they were later crushed). Martin Bronfenbrenner, who witnessed the post-World War II economic miracle of Japan many years later, describes being investigated during the period of McCarthyism, while Mark Blaug reveals how his encounter with McCarthyism strengthened the case against socialism. For Bela Balassa, the memorable date was 23 October 1956. Balassa participated in the Hungarian Revolution and was a member of a committee that took over the Ministry of Construction; when the Soviets regained Budapest, Budapest lost Balassa, who eventually arrived at Yale.

On the topic of history, have you ever wondered how technology was diffused in economics in the twentieth century? Then you must read how Walter Oi used Frieden calculators to invert a matrix using the Doolittle method, and how Allan Meltzer ran regressions on a (rented) calculator. Irma

Adelman describes programming in machine language before the days of FORTRAN. In his essay, Harry Markowitz describes how he toiled to develop a programming language – designated SIMSCRIPT – in order to simulate economic models. Also, Roger Garrison explains how he wrote a program in BASIC to solve the 'Knight's Tour of the Board' problem. These programming attempts are representative of the way algorithmic thinking has slipped into economics over time.

Are you interested in cross-fertilization from other sciences? Graciela Chichilnisky chose mathematics in order to understand social issues. To Chichilnisky, 'mathematics seemed clearer and easier' than philosophy and sociology, and could 'be applied to resolve social problems.' Ronald G. Ehrenberg came to economics from mathematics and physics. This was an easy transition for him as he thought math and physics were hard, and economics allowed him to apply his training in calculus.

Finally, our essays are rich with life and economics lessons that our economists acquired through decades of experience. Some brief examples: Richard Easterlin touches on the values of the economics profession. Graciela Chichilnisky shares her experience as to how women can survive and thrive in academia. Allan Meltzer shows how to motivate major policy changes. Mark Perlman provides practical guidance as to what an economics department should be, as well as how to create an academic journal. F.M. Scherer explains why he believes that one requires all three of the techniques that Schumpeter uses to distinguish a 'scientific' economist – history, statistics and theory. Edward Gramlich compares the state of the field of policy economics today to its state in the 1960s. Sir Alan Walters describes how he received more from his fellow students than from faculty. Martin Bronfenbrenner relays what he 'needed and acquired' at Chicago and Minnesota. Geoffrey Moore provides fascinating insight into the principles and practices at the National Bureau of Economic Research (NBER). Carolyn Shaw Bell reveals political arguments that make her cringe, and also provides an enlightening discussion of the responsibility economists have to the general public. Barbara Bergmann used economics to create a more humane world. Victor Fuchs, influenced by his family and great teachers (von Mises, Burns, Bergson, Stigler and Becker), has great 'Respect for tradition combined with rejection of dogma.'

Why read these reflections of leading economists? Of what possible benefit are life histories, and even philosophies, to an aspiring economist? Our preliminary response is that even a purist will find this book interesting as a narrative of the history of economics. This book sets examples from great achievers for the generality of economic students to learn from, but not necessarily to imitate or follow. As Cardozo wrote, 'Often a liberal antidote of experience supplies a sovereign cure for a paralyzing abstraction built upon a theory.'[3] In our opinion, the most efficient mechanism through which a novice can bootstrap experience is through reading the experiences of others. This volume of essays is rich in descriptions of life experiences.

Additionally, we hope that these essays provide a lesson to our young (and not so young) readers on the usefulness of reflection, the importance of which has been deliberated extensively before. From the Physiocratic School to modern essays in academic journals, reflections on economics have been continuous.[4] Let's briefly review the Aristotelian and Kantian perspectives.[5]

From an Aristotelian point of view, reflection enables the economist to grasp things that are far removed from the senses. Through reflection, an economist is able to make universal judgments, adding wisdom to the discipline. Of course, to obtain well-formed Aristotelian arguments, we should not have doubts about our premises. One can postulate self-evident truths with these reflections where the readers will want to have a conversation with the authors.[6] From a Kantian point of view, reflection is a state of mind. As economists, we always compare states; indeed students are taught comparative static analysis at an early stage. How can students compare equilibria? According to Kant, all judgments and all comparisons cannot proceed without reflections. Reflections are of two types – logical and transcendental. Logical reflection is a mere comparison, for example the intersection of the demand and supply curves. Mostly, it is a mechanical exercise where students solve for price and quantity in terms of slope and intercept parameters. Even mathematical software can achieve this in a logical manner.

Kant proceeds from the logical to the transcendental reflection. He introduced four dualisms – appearances vs reality, intuitions vs concepts, *a priori* vs empirical, and inner vs outer. Through this dualism, we attain concepts in our mind. Reality is represented as appearances and understanding. Assume that objects affect our mind and produce sensations. When we think about objects, through these representations, we attain an understanding that objects are thoughts, and we are concepts. When we pay attention to the relationships of these concepts, we are reflecting transcendentally. The word 'transcendence' suggests that we are bridging from pure reasoning.[7]

Some of our essayists identify the lenses through which they reflect – be they scientific, religious, or metaphysical. Others explain how they wrestle with ideas, and how they decide that some are worthy of further development, while others are not. The authors invite us to share their experiences to allow us to learn from their few failures and to build on their many successes. Artie Shaw, the great clarinetist, who was at home with both jazz and classical music, had this to say:

> Maybe twice in my life I reached what I wanted to. (In the piece of music 'These Foolish Things') at the end, the band stops and I play a little cadenza. That cadenza

– no one can do it better. Let's say it is five bars. That's a very good thing to have done in a lifetime. An artist should be judged by his best, just as an athlete is. Pick out one or two best things and say, 'That's what he did: all the rest was rehearsal.'

The enjoyment we continue to receive from these essays is considerable and continuing. We hope you experience similar satisfaction as you embark on your journey.

NOTES

1. Indeed, one observation that will be evident as you read this book is that regardless of the years that our essayists have attained, their ideas and attitudes remain youthful. This recalls the anecdote of a Hasidic Rabbi – in Yiddish, a *Rebbe* – surrounded by thousands of disciples whose sexton failed to procure the necessary wine required for a religious ritual. Panic ensued, until the *Rebbe* rose and declared: 'I know a youth who can obtain the wine from a nearby town!' and retired to his private quarters, ostensibly to make the necessary arrangements. After several hours, the *Rebbe* reappeared with the required wine. The disciples whispered busily among each other: 'Who is this youth that saved the day?' Finally, one disciple boldly inquired: '*Rebbe*, we see the wine, but who is the youth?' The *Rebbe* beamed and answered: 'I am the youth.' In the words of Aldous Huxley, 'The secret of genius is to carry the spirit of the child into old age.'' The author of the Foreword to this book, Nobel laureate Kenneth Arrow, also possesses this quality. At a June 2000 Conference on Biblical Economics in Jerusalem, Michael Szenberg observed how Kenneth Arrow arrived first to every session, sat in the front row, and remained engaged in the seminars throughout.
2. Not to be confused with F.M. Scherer's self-description as 'an accidental Schumpeterian.'
3. *Paradoxes of Legal Science* 1928,125.
4. Reflection is distinct from perception. Reflection is the connection of an object with its name, genus, quality, action and other entities, while perception is knowledge other than reflection. These two concepts are not easy to separate. In everyday life, reflection can be organized around forces that are natural, intuitive and rational. We can distinguish between the theoretical and empirical, universal and particular, mind and thought, and intentions.
5. Of the major reflective modes, the natural method can be traced to Aristotle. Aristotle might apply natural reasoning in economics as follows: If the individual is a natural unit of economics investigation, the family, which is a grouping of individuals, will be the next important unit, and so on until we reach society. Aristotle holds that the mind takes its content from nature as well. On the physical side, he holds that things once disturbed tend to return to their original place. David Hume advanced the study of the content of the human mind. The mind can be compared to a receiver that accepts impressions. Ideas are formed in the mind through faint association of impressions. Adam Smith was impressed by Hume's idea of the self-interested person. But when Hume put two self-interested people in a marketplace, he expected conflicts, not harmonious resolution. Impressed with Newton's Law of Gravity, Smith wanted to replicate something like that for the social sciences. His mind came up with the idea of a spectator, a concept that extols the idea of self-interest, and integrates it with the market system.
6. Aristotle gave us premises to back up our arguments. He did not instruct us to build certainty into the premises. Descartes improved on Aristotle by introducing some rationality into the premises by his famous statement *cogito ergo sum* (I think therefore I am). Since the denier exists, it is impossible to deny his existence. Kant offered the synthetic *a priori*, which introduced facts into our premises.
7. Austrian economics is also peppered with Kantian ideas. It traces all economic causes to the action axiom (AA). The Austrians pay special attention to *Gedankenexperiment*, or mental experiment in economics through the *ceteris paribus* assumption. They hold things constant

to enable comparative analysis, which would not be possible otherwise, as the economist, unlike the physical scientist, does not have a laboratory. While this methodology is not quantitative, it does predict direction of change, not magnitude or percentage of change. For Austrian economists, the term 'predict' is synonymous with 'explain' but not 'forecast.' For example, if demand increases, prices will go up, *ceteris paribus*, but we cannot forecast what quantity the producers will offer in the future.

1. My life philosophy*

Irma Adelman

Writing my intellectual autobiography is an assignment which I have long postponed, primarily out of fear. Such a retrospective self-appraisal would inevitably make me stand naked in front of myself, influence the rest of my career and impart a sense of, it is to be hoped, premature, semi-closure. A gentle reminder by the editors has now made me grit my teeth, lay my trepidations aside, and begin.

I was born in Cernowitz, Romania, in March 1930. Amusingly enough, Joseph Schumpeter had played an unwitting role in my parents' marriage. My mother was a law student at the University of Cernowitz while Schumpeter was teaching there. She was being courted by my father, a businessman ten years her senior. She decided to reject his suit, took her qualifying exam in economics from Schumpeter, and returned to her home town. A few months later, she was informed that Schumpeter had lost her examination paper, and that she would have to take the exam again. She returned to Cernowitz, was met by my father who, in his sorrow at being rejected by her, had shaved his head and lost about fifteen pounds. Her heart went out to him and she reversed her decision.

FORMATIVE INFLUENCES

The formative influences on my life and values were my parents, my early education, and the trauma of World War II. My mother, a very attractive, intelligent and vivacious woman, never got to practice law. My father claimed that her working would ruin his credit rating and the quota on Jewish lawyers imposed by the Romanian government in the 1930s meant that by choosing to practice she would take bread out of the mouth of a Jewish male *pater familias*. So she concentrated her boundless energy and ambition on me, a single child. She was determined (poor woman) that I would be as attractive as possible given my original, rather unpropitious, endowments and that I would have the career that circumstances had conspired to rob her of. Her

*This chapter first appeared in *The American Economist*, **34**(2), Fall 1990, 3–19.

efforts imbued me with a view of the perfectibility of individuals and society that have dominated my teaching and research.

My father was a socialist businessman, a not unusual paradox among East European Jewish businessmen at the time. He had been studying at the University of Kiev, in the Ukraine, when the Russian Revolution broke out, and was a Zionist Menshevik, a socialist reformer. When the Bolsheviks won, he fled to Romania. He had been scheduled to be shot, but the officer in charge of the firing squad turned out to be a friend of my uncle's and enabled him to escape. From my father I gained my commitment to social reform, my compassion for the poor, and my sense of outrage at social conditions that generate mass poverty and mass deprivation.

Despite being Jewish, my early education in Romania was at a French Catholic nuns' school, Notre Dame de Sion. The Jews are said to own 'guilt' and the Catholics to have a lifetime lease on it. My early education therefore left me with a mammoth sense of primordial guilt, that was later reinforced by the guilt of the survivor of the Holocaust. The expiation of this guilt through the only mechanism it can be expiated – service to humanity – has been a primary driving force in my life.

World War II left an indelible mark, even though I escaped comparatively unscathed. My father had had the foresight and courage to leave Romania in 1939 for Palestine, so that the entire nuclear family survived intact. The main impact of the war on me was the wrenching break in personal attachments involved in becoming a refugee, and the experience of mass religious hatred. I remember my father telling me when I was six that I might be reviled for being Jewish, but that I should be proud of this fact. Since I knew not what being Jewish was, and had been taught by the nuns that pride is sin, this talk left me totally bewildered. The war imbued me with a sense of rootlessness, a suspicion of mass ideologies, a sense of the impermanence of any state, a lack of attachment to possessions, and a sense of personal worthlessness. It also induced a sense of belonging nowhere and everywhere that is the mark of the cosmopolitan, and a feeling of 'There but for the grace of God go I' towards the less fortunate, akin to Rawls's initial state of ignorance. On the positive side, I learned that the only thing one can rely on is one's human capital – one's knowledge, skills and character – because all else can be taken away at the bellow of a demagogue. My later fascination with stochastic shocks, with nonlinear dynamics, and sociopolitical view of economic development also have their roots in my World War II experience.

There was never any doubt in my mind that I had to become an intellectual. It was my only comparative advantage (I was an uncoordinated, roly-poly and cross-eyed youngster), and my parents and worldview had predisposed me to see in education my only potential for achieving a moderately stable and socially productive life. After finishing high school in Palestine and fighting in the Israeli war of independence, I enrolled in 1949 as an undergraduate at the University of California at Berkeley. I chose business administration with a minor in public administration not because of my interest in these subjects – had I let myself pursue my own inclinations I would have studied French and German literature and art history – but rather because of my perception of the primary needs of the nascent State of Israel, the furthering of whose interests I was dedicated to. But this was not to be! Shortly after coming to Berkeley, I met my husband, an American physics PhD candidate, fell in love, married and stayed. In making the decision to marry and stay, I felt very guilty at putting my personal happiness ahead of my duty to Israel, whom I felt I was betraying by not returning there.

I sailed through undergraduate school, shifted to economics in graduate school, and obtained my PhD six years after having entered as an undergraduate. My graduate education was sadly lacking. At the time, Berkeley was very weak in economic theory and in mathematical training. Robert Dorfman was the only ray of light in the graduate program and I shudder to think what I would have become had I not been able to benefit from his tutelage. I supplemented the graduate program in economics by taking courses in statistics, mathematics, and in agricultural economics. Here, together with Arnold Zellner, Zvi Griliches and Yair Mundlak, I learned my econometrics from George Kuznets. I also benefited greatly from the influence of my husband, Frank Adelman, who taught me a view of scientific method involving a continual iterative interaction between theory, and experimental or statistical 'stylized facts' that is natural to applied physicists but still not to economists.

RESEARCH

From the perspective of a historian of doctrine, the research process appears planned *a priori*; from the perspective of the author, it appears as a series of unplanned choices that are guided by personal interest and a sense of the importance of the issues, and are made in response to opportunities, both external and self-generated. Although both perspectives are correct, I shall adopt the latter in this narrative.

My early research was eclectic, but there were a few common threads arising from my values and early personal experiences: concern with dynamics, both cyclical and long run; concern with stochastic processes; and concern with aggregation procedures. 'The Dynamic Properties of the Klein Goldberger Model', 'Business Cycles, Endogenous or Stochastic?', 'A Stochastic Analysis of the Size Distribution of Firms', my first book, and my work on hedonic index numbers (1961) were all facets of these concerns.

There were also some methodological predilections, which have stayed with me throughout my entire career, and which reflect my scientific predispositions: a view of the world as an interdependent system; a view of the world as real and of scientific research as holding up a (it is to be hoped, non-distorting) mirror to it; and an inner compulsion to contribute to the elucidation of real-world issues that affect the welfare of a large proportion of the world's population.

The Klein–Goldberger paper arose when my husband, a physicist, one day expressed a desire to try programming a simple problem and asked whether there was anything in economics that might be suitable. I suggested the Klein–Goldberger model. This was before the days of FORTRAN (1955): all programming was in machine language. I remember spreading out a large sheet of paper on the floor, with a map of the computer memory, and keeping track of the location of individual variables after every operation. Nevertheless, when we ran the problem, there was only one error in the code! After we finished the computer runs, my husband taught me a valuable lesson. He said: 'Now it's up to you to milk the results.' The writing of the paper was excruciating: we composed it jointly and fought over every word in every sentence, finishing only one or two paragraphs per night. This paper, which confirmed the Frisch hypothesis of the random origin of business cycles, has been identified as one of the best 20 articles in *Econometrica*, and achieved the status of a 'classic' in business cycles and in simulation of economic systems.

My first book, *Theories of Economic Growth and Development* (Stanford Press, 1961), was originally written as the development-theory section of an undergraduate text on economic development joint with L. Mears and A. Pepelassis. The publisher, McGraw-Hill, objected that my section was at a more advanced level than the rest of the book and insisted that it be taken out. I then revised it, making the text more lucid, but, when it came to seeking a publisher, I became racked with doubt. It seemed to me that the book contained little that was original, and that when I was describing the interactions of sociocultural and institutional features of societies with their economic development I did not know what I was talking about. So, for a few months after finishing the revision, I held the manuscript. But this troubled me. Paul Baran, my then colleague at Stanford, noticed that I was upset and asked me why. When I blurted out my concerns, he said: 'It's all very simple, Irma. Let the market decide! Send the book to a few publishers, and see whether they take it.' Amusing advice from the then only Marxist economist teaching at an American university …

This book, with its associated doubts, set the stage for one of my consistent lines of research: how the economic growth of nations is affected by and, in turn, affects economic and political institutions, and sociocultural structures and values: and how institutions and economic structures and choices affect the diffusion of benefits from economic and institutional change. I felt the need to understand these processes better and to base my understanding on empirically generated hypotheses and stylized facts. This is the line of research with which Professor Cynthia Taft Morris became associated.

I first met Cynthia Taft Morris in Washington DC in the summer of 1962, when we were both Research Associates at the Brookings Institution. We both had just moved to Washington, following, like the biblical Ruth, our husbands' careers, and were both a little disoriented by the need to build new professional bases for ourselves. Our work together that summer was the beginning of a lifetime friendship and association. After the summer, Cynthia Morris combined teaching at American University with part-time work at the Agency for International Development (AID), in the research division headed by Hollis Chenery. And I started teaching at Johns Hopkins University, in Baltimore, and was brought by Hollis Chenery into his research division with a vague mandate to roam through the AID files and find something researchable. I found the AID country reports – monographs generated by AID offices in the field as annual reports on their respective countries. This was before the days of general data banks; indeed, even before the days of published comparable figures on per capita GNP! The reports were variable in quality and reliability, but had undergone some vetting before being sent to Washington, and, at least in principle, were uniform in coverage. They were treasure-troves of up-to-date information concerning political and sociocultural country situations together with quantitative and descriptive information on industry, agriculture, investment and international trade. Naturally, the information had to be cross-checked, especially for political bias and lack of comparative experience with other developing countries, but nevertheless offered an invaluable starting point. I became very excited about the potential of these country reports for generating information usable in research on interactions of economic, social and political facets of economic development. Also, in reading psychological literature, I had come across the use of factor analysis. This technique seemed to offer an ideal statistical vehicle for exploratory research on interactions about which there were no validated theories. I asked Cynthia Morris whether she would be interested in collaborating with me on this project. And so, *Society, Politics, and Economic Development – A Quantitative Approach* (Johns Hopkins Press, 1967) was born.

A word about our professional collaboration may be in order: Cynthia Morris had had polio as a teenager and has been on crutches ever since. As a result, her mobility has been limited. She therefore informed me early in our collaboration that she did not wish to be involved in presenting papers at conferences, professional meetings, etc.; that task would be up to me.

Unfortunately, her less visible role has led the profession to underestimate her contributions to our joint work.

In 1965, when the major work on *Society, Politics, and Economic Development* was done, it occurred to us that it would be interesting to see how applicable the hypotheses generated by this research on contemporary development were to the historical development process during the period of the Industrial Revolution. This research was especially appealing to Cynthia Morris, whose training was as an economic historian with a strong institutional bent. She then started working on gathering comparable information on 23 countries for the period 1850–1914. In 1972, I met Herman Wold, at a talk on the methodology of partial least squares and, more generally, on soft modelling that he gave at the World Bank. I got very excited by his philosophy and approach, rare among mainstream statisticians, to which I resonated. Ever since finishing *Society, Politics, and Economic Development*, I had been looking for distribution-free methods of melding partial prior specification with sample information. (While my philosophy was Bayesian, there were two reasons I could not go the strict Bayesian route: I did not want to specify a specific prior distribution, especially with the type of discrete, ranked data that characterized my work on interactions between social, political and institutional features of societies and their development patterns. I also wanted to deal with interdependent systems, and this is still difficult with present Bayesian techniques.) Herman Wold's approach seemed to be the answer. I started working with him in the early stages of the development of the partial least squares approach, and through him became aware of the work of Svante Wold, on disjoint principal components models. It is this latter approach that Cynthia Morris and I used in our historical work. Little did we know, when we started this research in 1965, that it would be 23 years before our historical work could culminate in a book describing what role institutional and political forces had played in inducing the very diverse economic responses of individual countries to the challenges and opportunities offered by the early Industrial Revolution in Great Britain! Our book, *Comparative Patterns of Economic Development, 1850–1914* (Johns Hopkins Press) appeared only in 1988. In this book, I finally succeeded in persuading Cynthia Morris to put her name as first author, both as a means of reflecting our relative contributions to this work and as a means of partially rectifying the general misconceptions about her contributions to our past joint research.

Of course, during the 23 years that it took to complete this book, there were several detours on the way. The most important was our joint and my separate work on income distribution in developing countries. In 1969, the Agency of International Development came under fire from the US Congress for not paying enough attention to the spread of benefits from its projects. (It would appear that international junkets by Senators and Congressmen have some uses!) Cynthia and I were asked to undertake a study of the breadth of participation, both economically and politically, by developing countries' populations in the development process. The result was *Economic Growth and Social Equity in Developing Countries* (Stanford Press, 1973). While generally taken as having confirmed Kuznets's U-hypothesis, our results confirmed a J-hypothesis. We found that the share of income accruing to the poor first declines rapidly, then less rapidly, and then, depending on the policy choices made, either levels off (the J) or starts increasing (the U). Politically, as the indigenous middle class and urbanization increase, and as education and communication improve, the influence on policy of non-elite groups starts extending to the middle class and to workers in the modern sector. But we found that the greater political participation of these groups does not redound to the benefit of the poor. Indeed, the middle class benefits at the expense of both the poor and the rich.

We were deeply shocked by our findings. Up to then we had believed in the benign view of economic development offered by modernization scholars and in the trickle-down hypothesis imbuing mainstream writings on economic development. Were it not for the function-free statistical technique we adopted for our study, and were it not for our inductive empirical approach, we would have adopted an *a priori* specification confirming the modernization-cum-trickle-down theories. We would then have ascribed the poor statistical fit to poor data and small sample size. It is also fortunate that we undertook an arduous effort to obtain direct information on income distribution, despite the virtual lack of published studies. Of over 200 books and more than 1000 articles on individual countries published in the previous ten years, we found income-distribution information in only one – Samuel Barber's study of South Africa – for 1948! We found a list, prepared by the United Nations Statistical Office, of income distribution studies in developing countries that had been carried out but had not been published, and then proceeded to use the leverage of AID field offices to obtain the studies themselves. We were also fortunate to find the comparative study by Christian Morrisson, written as his PhD dissertation, with income-distribution estimates for Sub-Saharan African countries. These data, though of lesser reliability than the data for the more developed countries, played a critical role in generating the initial decline of the income share of the poorest. We submitted our report to AID and then did not publish the results for two years since we feared that our findings would be used as an argument to curtail resources for foreign assistance rather than redirect resources to more poverty-oriented projects and programs. We felt free to publish our findings only after we were convinced they would do no harm: by 1973 the decline in foreign assistance was already under way and new evidence concerning increasing urban unemployment despite rapid growth was making it clear that all was not well with the development process.

Our findings in this book led to the second major strand in my work: that dealing with income distribution and poverty, both descriptively and from a policy viewpoint. Two articles, 'On the State of Development Economics' and 'Development Economics – A Reassessment of Goals', summarize the effect my shock had on my research. In the former I argued that the fundamental failure of development economics had its roots in several methodological deficiencies: the failure to take a sufficiently broad systems approach; the failure to monitor results adequately; the pervasive search for panaceas and for simplicity and simple guidance rules: and insufficient humility and insufficient professionalism in our approach to development. In the latter article, I argued that the goals of development should become the creation of the social and material conditions for the realization of human potential by all. This goal should replace the goal of self-sustained growth: rather, growth should be viewed as an instrument for the achievement of poverty reduction – a goal to which I referred as 'depauperization'. Mark Blaug (1985) calls this paper my most readable and controversial article.

I joined the World Bank in 1971 and started a research program aimed at seeing whether an approach to economic development policy exists that would spread more of the benefits of development to the poor. This was genuinely an open question, since the history of the early phases of the Industrial Revolution in developed countries had also exhibited a decrease in the share of income accruing to the poor. It seemed to me that finding such an approach would require generating a computer laboratory in which experiments with policies and programs could be carried out and evaluated. This laboratory should represent how economic actors interact in an actual economy, portray the governmentally set rules for markets and behavior, incorporate all the instruments for intervention and all the variables that are important in mediating the impact of the economy, of governments, and of the rest of the world on the poor. Having seen how the simple (simplistic?) *a priori* models that identified single-cause development prime-movers or bottlenecks had led the development-policy-formulating community into advocating a seriously flawed development process, I rejected the methodology of specifying a two- or three-sector model with one or two classes of actors, solving it for its comparative statics implications, and then basing policy recommendations on these findings. Rather, I argued for building a complex but realistic computer model and then simplifying it *a posteriori*, on the basis of sensitivity experiments. This returned me to the methodology of digital simulation, introduced into economics by my first major published article, on the Klein–Goldberger model. I asked Sherman Robinson, who was then an assistant professor at Princeton, to join me in this research. (I had first met Sherman Robinson when, as a PhD candidate at Harvard, he asked me for the *Society, Politics, and Economic Development* data for use in his dissertation.

When he finished, he sent me a copy of his dissertation, and I was impressed with him.)

We first thought that the appropriate model structure for our research on income distribution would be offered by a Johansen model. But it then became clear that, since our purpose was to model structural change and large-program interventions, a model like Johansen's, that is expressed in linear rates of growth, might miss effects that are of the same order of magnitude as the impacts of the experiments themselves. Sherman Robinson suggested that we change our formulation to solving for the levels of the endogenous variables rather than, as in the Johansen model, for their rates of change. And so, the first large-scale computable general equilibrium model (CGE) was born. The model was quite large (it contained over 3000 endogeneous variables); mixed neoclassical and structuralist features; incorporated non-homogeneities in investment and government behavior; had an endogenous demand for money; two loanable funds markets (one official and one unorganized); two policy regimes (a tight-money regime with fixed money supply and rationing, and a loose-money regime with fixed interest rates); and some elements of industrial organization within sectors (four firm or farm sizes, with different behavior rules and different credit and foreign exchange access by large firms). The model was applied to South Korea, a country for which we both had a feeling. The initial reactions to our model specification were skeptical. Our critics contended that we would never be able to solve the model, and that, even if we were able to solve it, we would not be able to understand what was going on in the model. We proved them wrong, however, on both counts. Our book, *Income Distribution Policy in Developing Countries: The Case of Korea* (Stanford Press), finished in 1975, appeared in 1978. In it, we were able to identify the important policy variables, explain how the model worked, and gain a feeling for the relative importance of different policy interventions. (The first general presentation of the model was in 1973, at a World Congress of the Econometric Society, in Toronto. There we met with John Whalley, then a graduate student writing his dissertation with Herbert Scarf, and he asked us many questions about solution techniques, and about the feasibility of solving other than toy-models. The first written reports on the model were in 1973 and the first publication, giving our rather pessimistic policy conclusions based on our comparative statics experiments, was in 1975, as part of my paper calling for a shift in emphasis away from economic growth, and towards poverty alleviation as the major goal of development policy.)

In the policy experiments we performed with our CGE model we found that policy interventions aimed at increasing the equality of the size distribution of income were very difficult. Of the roughly 3000 endogenous variables in the model only two, rural–urban migration and the agricultural terms of trade, had a perceptible impact. The size distribution of income was exceedingly stable –

even large-scale programs produced effects that altered only the second decimal of the Gini coefficient. Most interventions altered the incidence of poverty (i.e. the functional distribution of income), especially between the rural and urban poor and near poor, without changing the relative magnitude of poverty (i.e. the size distribution of income). In the absence of changes in the distribution of assets or institutions affecting the access of the poor to factor and commodity markets, only changes in development strategy, equivalent to large packages of mutually coordinated programs, could alter the relative magnitude of poverty by engendering the right kind of economic growth. Absolute poverty was easier to reduce than relative poverty. This conclusion was confirmed by our dynamic experiments and is consistent with the conclusions from models for different countries, with different closure rules, and different structural specifications (Adelman and Robinson, 1988).

After the book was finished, Sherman Robinson joined the World Bank and shifted to work on industrialization and trade with generic CGE models. He simplified the specification of the Korea CGE model, based on the intuition gained from our sensitivity and policy experiments; improved the solution algorithm; improved the trade specification; and based the model calibration explicitly, rather than only implicitly, on the Social Accounting Matrix (SAM) accounting framework. His work did a great deal to disseminate the use of CGE models among academic researchers and in the policy-planning community. Amusingly enough, however, with the currently renewed interest in the impact of IMF-inspired structural adjustment programs on the poor in debt-ridden developing countries, many of the monetary, macroeconomic, industrial-organization, and credit-allocation mechanisms that he ripped out of the Korea CGE model, in an effort to arrive at a simpler generic model, are being reintroduced into CGEs of the 1980s, one by one.

I continued my work on income-distribution policy and, becoming increasingly discouraged about the potential for policy impact on development assistance and on development policy after the two oil shocks, increasingly turned to non-policy work on institutions in development and economic history.

In 1977, I was invited to hold the Cleveringa chair at Leyden. This was a chair established by the Queen of the Netherlands to commemorate the resistance of Leyden University, led by Cleveringa, a law professor, to the Nazi order to fire all Jewish professors. The chair was to deal with some issue affecting human rights, be staffed by a social scientist on a one-year basis, and rotate between a Dutch and a foreign professor. I was the fourth holder of the chair, the second economist after Tinbergen. In my inaugural address, 'Redistribution Before Growth – A Strategy for Developing Countries' (Martinus Nijhoff, 1978) I advocated asset redistribution before, rather than after, improvements in the asset's productivity: land reform before improvements in agricultural productivity and mass primary education before a major push on industrialization. Asset redistribution before improvements in productivity would enable growth-promoting measures to go hand in hand with equity-improving measures, thereby greatly enhancing the potential for improving the lot of the poor through economic development. The profession has accepted the call for increased emphasis on primary education while ignoring the call for land reform as unrealistic. In 'Beyond Export-Led Growth' (*World Development*, 1984) I advocated a temporary shift during the low-growth-in-world-income-and-trade period of the 1980s towards agricultural development in an open trade regime as a mechanism for accelerating domestic industrialization and increasing equity (the ADLI strategy). I used the generic CGE model of Korea developed by Sherman Robinson to demonstrate the superiority of this strategy in a low-growth world environment over export-led growth.

At the same time, Cynthia Morris and I intensified our work on economic history. After finishing the historical book in 1988, we felt that we had enough insight into the complex interactions that determined the diversity of country responses to the industrial revolution in Great Britain to be able to specify a simultaneous equation partial least squares model of nineteenth-century economic development using Herman Wold's statistical methodology (Adelman, Lohmoller and Morris, 1988). We are now working on a monograph comparing historical and contemporary development patterns.

POLICY WORK

My policy work started early in my career, and I have always felt that it offered both the motivation and new insights for my research. My first involvement with policy started by accident. In 1963, AID in Washington received an urgent request from its Vietnam office for a statistician who would design a rural income-expenditure survey in the Delta. I did not quite understand why this was so urgent, but was eager to travel so I volunteered. When I came to Saigon, I was struck by two things: the Vietnamese population did not seem to be committed to the war and the security situation was much worse than depicted by either military or diplomatic communications from Saigon. I reasoned that, with incorrect information, correct decisions could not be made in Washington, and, with the arrogance of youth, started on a one-woman fact-finding mission. My starting point was why the Vietnamese population was not committed to the war. I soon realized that an important part of the answer was that, with existing tenurial conditions, the rural population had a large positive incentive to keep a low level of military activity going: due to the war, most of the landlords had left the rural areas, and rents had not been collected for as much as three years. At existing rents, pacification would mean an indebtedness of about 1.5 years' output! This led me to argue for a US-supported land reform of the land-to-the-tiller variety as a higher-probability alternative than the military approach to ending the war. Buying all the land of the Delta at market prices from the landlords would cost only about half the then military annual budget! Upon returning from Saigon, I spent much of my effort for about three months peddling this view to the policy establishment. I gained a hearing, but, alas, the military approach prevailed. Many years later I met the director of the Saigon AID mission again and asked him why the consumption-expenditure survey had been such a high-priority item. His answer: 'The country may be burning but Washington still wants to know: what's GNP?' – a sad, but accurate, comment on bureaucracies.

My work in development planning started early, has given me some insight into methods of policy formulation and a great deal of personal and professional satisfaction. In the 1950s and 1960s, work in economic development was by and large non-technical except in one area – that of development planning. This area, which started with Tinbergen's formulation of planning and his hierarchic view of state–economy interactions, offered scope for the use of all techniques of econometrics and operations research. The technical part of my soul could therefore find satisfaction in this branch of work. That period also offered scope for the influential foreign adviser. Both coincided in my work on South Korea's Second Five Year Plan, summarized in *Practical Approaches to Development Planning – Korea's Second Five Year Plan* (Johns Hopkins Press, 1969).

My involvement in Korea started fortuitously. I was sitting in the office of a friend at AID in the summer of 1964, and he was complaining that his boss (Hollis Chenery) wanted him to go to South Korea, whereas he wanted to go to Turkey. I said: 'I'll go!' I went under AID auspices in early 1965, wrote a critical report on the institutional set-up for planning in Korea, and came home, expecting never to return. To my great surprise, my recommendations were implemented, and I was called back to assist with the work on the plan. We would end up using all the econometric and operations research techniques then known to formulate investment, credit and foreign exchange allocation for the next five year plan. The plan, initiated in 1967, involved a shift towards export-led growth, after a 50 percent devaluation to realign exchange rates, substantial reductions in tariffs and in the scope of protection to reduce distortions, and a doubling of interest rates to reduce inflation and increase savings. The shift towards export-led growth was a natural recommendation for an economy with highly developed human resources (a level of education three times the average for an economy of its per capita income); a very small internal market (per capita income in 1965 was about $70): and a very poor natural resource base (hence high import coefficients).

I was not sensitive at the time to income distribution issues, but the plan worked out very well for poverty too, tripling the incomes of the poor in ten years, because of the very egalitarian distribution of assets. Korea had had two major land reforms in the early 1950s, and had universal primary education. In 1972, I received a presidential decoration from President Park, the Order of the Bronze Tower, for my work on the Second Five Year Plan. The citation reads:

> With deep interest in the wellbeing of the Korean people, Mrs. Irma Adelman, the professor at Northwestern University, has devoted her efforts with superb competence to the economic development of the Republic of Korea and thereby greatly contributed towards attaining the goals of economic self-sufficiency pursued by the Government of the Republic of Korea. Her valuable donation and service has gained for her the appreciation and admiration of the Korean people.

But when, in 1973, President Park turned from benevolent dictator to oppressive despot, torturing and jailing the opposition, I felt I had to resign from any advisory role in South Korea, after checking with my previous Korean co-workers that my resignation, would not place them in jeopardy.

My final direct involvement with policy came in 1971, when I joined the World Bank. A paper summarizing the findings of my work with Cynthia Morris on income distribution and development was circulating as a working paper at the Bank. McNamara's speech writer, who was looking for material on this subject, came across the paper and used it as background for McNamara's Chile speech. This was the speech that signaled a change in Bank policy toward emphasis on poverty alleviation in lending to developing countries.

With my change of emphasis in development policy towards income distribution and poverty, I lost all popularity with planning agencies in developing countries themselves. For a while, I was popular with international agencies with a poverty orientation: the ILO and the World Bank, in particular. But as their interest shifted towards debt and trade problems, this policy involvement stopped as well. Whatever policy influence I now have is indirect: through my academic research and policy writings.

CAREER ISSUES

So far, I have not touched on how the particular issues affecting professional women – discrimination; handling the multiple demands of home, child and career; and managing two careers – impinged on my life and career. I hit discrimination against women for the first time when I got my PhD, in 1955. I was totally unprepared for this. I was a foreigner to the United States, and I had not realized that, like democracy in ancient Greece, the Horatio Alger myth characterizing the United States as an open, mobile society did not apply to American women. In the 1950s, discrimination against women in US academia was incredible. I had graduated from a top institution, at the top of my class, in a period of high demand for college teachers. Nevertheless, when it came to entering the job market, no one would waste a recommendation on a low-probability hire. At the time, openings were not advertised, and were publicized only through a network of personal contacts. When I applied for a teaching position at San Francisco State, the chairman suggested that I might look for a position in a local private high school! In the end, Berkeley hired me on a one-year appointment as a teaching associate – a position routinely given to third-year graduate students who have passed their field examinations. Then came six years, all on one-year, non-tenure-ladder appointments, at Berkeley, Mills College (a local private elite women's college, where I became aware of the many phenomena described in Betty Friedan's *Feminine Mystique*), and Stanford. By then I had published my first book, the Klein–Goldberger article, two other articles on business cycles, my articles on sampling and hedonic index numbers, and my article on the use of Markov chains to predict the long-run size distribution of firms. The quantity and quality of my publications would have been sufficient to earn me a solid promotion to tenure in any first rate institution, had I been male. And still, I had no foot on the tenure ladder ... The hardest thing during this period was to keep from getting bitter. I thank my lucky stars that I had the maturity to realize that, if I were to allow the process to make me bitter, the world would have won its fight against me, regardless of the ultimate professional outcome. I forbade myself the making of invidious comparisons with males, and ordered myself to consider myself as part of a Cairns-type non-competing group. And yet, had the process continued much longer, I would not have been able to hold out against being corroded by bitterness. Still, I was fortunate: I was employed continuously, at first-rate institutions, and worked with excellent colleagues, with whom I interacted on a par. My work relationships with my colleagues and students were easier than those of males: women are used to interacting as equals with more senior males, my assistant professor colleagues did not consider me a threat, and the educator–maternal role with students came easily.

Then, I got a break: my husband became bored with his position at the Livermore Laboratory, and obtained a more challenging position in Washington, DC. I used the Hungarian Connection (from Tibor Scitovsky, at Berkeley, to George Jaszy, at Johns Hopkins) to indicate my availability, and was offered a regular Associate Professorship at Hopkins, at the princely salary of $10000 a year, a 60 percent increase on my previous salary at Stanford. We moved, I met Cynthia Morris, started being exposed to policy through Hollis Chenery at AID, and could use my tenured status to engage in longer-term, riskier research which culminated in the Adelman–Morris publications. Still, salary discrimination continued. When I complained to my chairman at Hopkins about the lack of a raise for three years despite high productivity, I was told to solicit alternative offers, as indication of my opportunity cost. Within a week, I obtained two offers, one from Maryland at 60 percent higher salary, and one from Northwestern, at 80 percent higher salary. The Northwestern position looked especially attractive, because there was an active interdisciplinary group in economic development, and because several of my would-be colleagues, George Dalton, Karl de Schweinitz and Jonathan Hughes, shared my broad-ranging institutional interests. My husband found a satisfactory position in Chicago, and, in 1966, we moved.

I was very happy at Northwestern. I liked the department, my colleagues, the size of the school, the quality of the students, the attitude of the administration and, last but not least, the computer center. I continued my collaboration with Cynthia Morris, and would have happily stayed at Northwestern except for my husband's work situation. His position at a research lab in Chicago proved to be unrewarding – so, again, we had to move. We spent a very happy year in 1971 at the Center for Advanced Studies in Behavioral Sciences, in Palo Alto. Influenced by Vietnam, my husband tried during this year to switch from defense physics to work on urban social-science problems. We worked on a model of urban politics, which incorporated many novel features, but was only published in book chapters and conference proceedings. We hoped that, at the end of the year, we would be able to find joint teaching positions. But our timing was wrong: 1972 was the beginning of the academic recession, and departments were even more than usual concerned with credentialling. I tried to get us hired as a package deal, and almost succeeded at Cornell. But, in the end, my husband's end of the deal fell through.

After the year at the Center, we moved to Washington once again. I took a job at the World Bank, my husband continued his work on the urban book, and we continued the search for joint positions. For one year, I was the major breadwinner in the family. I then learned how heavy the psychological burden of being the major breadwinner actually is. I would wake up in the middle of the night in a cold sweat, wondering what would happen to the family if I were to suffer an incapacitating accident, or be fired. I now know that what I was trying to do was wrong, even had it succeeded: my husband should have gotten a job on his own merits rather than as part of a package deal. I felt inadequate for being unable to give him what he wanted (a professorial position in the social sciences) and he resented my efforts and support, though asking for them. When I gave up, he found a position in his old career within a week! I did not know whether to laugh or cry.

At the end of the year at the World Bank, I took a professorial position at Maryland. Maryland was a commuter campus, and this meant that both students and faculty only came there for a purpose, retreating to home or office in Washington in between. I missed the college atmosphere typical of non-urban campuses, such as Berkeley, Stanford, or Northwestern. My husband and I were both working too hard and had no energy left to build a social life. We started drifting apart, interacting only on the level of practical problems or when going to an event at the Kennedy Center. Finally, the inevitable happened: we separated and, in 1980, divorced.

When we separated, I became a free agent, and when Berkeley's Department of Agriculture and Resource Economics inquired about my potential interest, I jumped at the opportunity. My work on poverty had made me realize the importance of agricultural development, and I was painfully aware how little I knew about agriculture, and how much more difficult agricultural development was than industrialization. I hoped that through exposure to my colleagues' work I might learn about agricultural economics, agricultural technology, and about the physical bases of agriculture. I have not been disappointed. Since joining the Department in 1979, I have learned a great deal about these issues, but I still have a great deal more to learn. Indeed, I expect agriculture–industry interactions and patterns of agricultural development to be a focus of my research in the coming years.

Thus, my response to the twin problems of discrimination against women and two careers was high geographic mobility. I once counted that we had owned more houses than cars! We moved whenever a Pareto-optimal move was possible, and alternated in initiating moves.

My female students occasionally ask me: 'When is a good time to have a child, if I want to also have a career?' My answer is: 'Either in graduate school or once tenure is assured.' (As a result, I wind up with a fair number of pregnant dissertation advisees …) I myself had chosen a different timing, which did not make my early career any easier. Our son was born in 1958, when I had a very precarious hold on an academic career. The most difficult parts about melding childrearing with career were the tremendous physical stamina it required, the constant guilt at not being a full-time mother, and the constant anxiety that something might happen to him while I was at work. At the time, day care facilities were very few and of dubious quality. Therefore, for the first ten years of his life, I had live-in help. After that, I had day-help, at first five days a week, then two, then one. He was an easy child, intelligent, energetic, charming, and with a great sense of humor. Our relationship has remained close, though there have been a few rocky patches in the last ten years.

In July of 1995 I took early retirement. I had not intended to retire, but the University offered senior faculty an irresistible package of financial inducements. I have been appointed 'Professor in the Graduate School', which gives me an office, access to secretarial services, library and computer facilities, and requires me to continue interacting with students on a one-to-one basis. Since retiring I have started work on a book on Korea and another one updating the work in *Society, Politics and Economic Development* to the 1990s. I have also started work on environmental issues, particularly on environmental accounting.

Like all autobiographies, my story is, fortunately, still unfinished. However, I do not anticipate many new departures; just a deepening of old lines of research and a continuation of my present, satisfying, personal and professional life-style.

But then, who knows?

REFERENCES

Adelman, Irma, 'A Stochastic Analysis of the Size Distribution of Firms', *Journal of the American Statistical Association*, pp. 893–904, 1959.

Adelman, Irma and Frank L. Adelman, *The Dynamic Properties of the Klein–Goldberger Model*, pp. 596–625, 1959.

Adelman, Irma, 'Business Cycles – Endogenous or Stochastic?', *Economic Journal*, pp. 783–96, 1960.

Adelman, Irma and Zvi Griliches, 'On an Index of Quality Change', *Journal of the American Statistical Association*, pp. 535–48, 1961.

Adelman, Irma, *Theories of Economic Growth and Development*, Stanford University Press, Palo Alto, 1964.

Adelman, Irma and Cynthia Taft Morris, *Society, Politics, and Economic Development: A Quantitative Approach*, Johns Hopkins, Baltimore, 1967.

Adelman, Irma, *Practical Approaches to Development Planning: Korea's Second Five Year Plan*, Johns Hopkins Press, Baltimore, 1969.

Adelman, Irma and Cynthia Taft Morris, *Economic Growth and Social Equity in Developing Countries*, Stanford Press, Palo Alto, 1973.

Adelman, Irma and Sherman Robinson, 'A Non-Linear. Dynamic, Microeconomic Model of Korea: Factors Affecting the Distribution of Income in the Short Run', *Discussion Paper 36, Research Program in Economic Development*, Princeton University, 1973.

Adelman, Irma and Laura D'Andrea Tyson, 'A Regional Microeconomic Model of Jugoslavia: Factors Affecting the Distribution of Income in the Short Run', *Development Research Center*, World Bank, 1973, mimeographed.

Adelman, Irma, 'On the State of Development Economies', *Journal of Development Economics*, pp. 3–5, 1974.

Adelman, Irma, 'Development Economics – A Reassessment of Goals', *American Economic Review*, pp. 302–9, 1975.

Adelman, Irma and Sherman Robinson, *Income Distribution Policy in Developing Countries: The Case of Korea*, Stanford University Press, Palo Alto, 1978.

Adelman, Irma, *Redistribution Before Growth – A Strategy for Developing Countries*, Martinus Nijhoff, The Hague, 1978.

Adelman, Irma, 'Beyond Export-Led Growth', *World Development*, vol. 12, pp. 937–49, 1984.

Adelman, Irma, *A Poverty Focussed Approach to Development Policy*, pp. 49–65, Transactions Books, New Brunswick and Oxford, 1986.

Adelman, Irma, Jan-Bernd Lohmoller and Cynthia Taft Morris, 'A Latent Variable Regression Model of Nineteenth Century Economic Development', *Giannini Foundation Working Paper No. 439*, University of California, Berkeley, 1988.

Adelman, Irma and Sherman Robinson, 'Macroeconomic Adjustment and Income Distribution: Alternative Models Applied to Two Economies', *Journal of Development Economics*, 1988.

Blaug, Mark, *Great Economists since Keynes: An Introduction to the Lives and Works of One Hundred Modern Economists*, Wheatsheaf Books, Hemel Hempstead, 1985.

Morris, Cynthia Taft and Irma Adelman, *Comparative Patterns of Economic Development, 1850–1914*, Johns Hopkins Press, Baltimore, 1988.

2. My life philosophy*

Bela Balassa

My life philosophy can be described at three levels. At one level it means that I try to make the best of any situation, whatever the circumstances. This goes from writing my first paper on economics in English while I was deported from Hungary between 1951 and 1953 to rebuilding my professional life after a serious cancer operation in August 1987.

At another level, my life philosophy refers to the importance I attach to personal freedoms, including the freedom of economic opportunity. In fact, I was exhilarated to find on arriving in the United States in April 1957 that as a foreigner I had no handicap in competing at the university and later for jobs.

Finally, my attachment to economic freedoms has led me to espouse a liberal economic philosophy, in the European sense. This philosophy has influenced my views on economic policies in developed, socialist and developing countries alike. But more about this later.

A BRIEF LIFE HISTORY

I was born on 6 April, 1928 in Budapest. My father was an officer in the Hungarian army, which meant high social standing on a very small income. Nonetheless, I was sent to the best schools and the education I received at the Cistercian Gymnasium remained a major asset throughout my professional life.

Having finished high school in 1946, I simultaneously enrolled at the Law and Political Science Faculty of the University of Budapest and at the Foreign Trade Academy, completing both with honors. At the University, my interest soon turned to economics. I was much influenced in this by my mentor, Professor István Varga, with whom I worked at the University as well as at an Institute he directed. This work, but not our relationship, ended in 1949 when Varga was pensioned under the Stalinist regime. In view of the changes at the University, it appeared safer for me to write my doctoral dissertation on sampling theory rather than on economics.

*This chapter first appeared in *The American Economist*, **33**(1), Spring 1989, 16–23.

With my newly minted doctorate, I went to the Construction Trust in Miskolc, the third largest Hungarian city, as a planner in May 1951. I soon became known to the director, József Bondor, who wanted to appoint me as head of planning. Then came, however, deportation from Budapest (which remained my domicile) for people of a particular social or political background, of whom I was considered to be one. While I was not in Budapest on the night the deportation was to take place, when next day I appeared at Police Headquarters armed with a laudatory letter from Bondor, this was rejected and I was summarily taken to the train just before it departed for the eastern part of Hungary.

There followed three months of working in the cotton fields, a crop that represented a misuse of land in Hungary's climatic conditions. Fortunately, my parents were living and working on our land in the western part of Hungary, hence they escaped deportation, and I was allowed to join them, while being confined to their village. I soon got a job as head of finances in an alcohol factory and stayed there until it was discovered that as a deportee I was not to do intellectual work.

The next year and a half was a period that greatly strengthened my physique through work in the fields, in the forest and in construction. It also brought a deepening of my intellectual interests. István Varga provided me with books on economics (Keynes was proscribed at the time in Hungary). I tried my hand at writing papers on economics, including comparisons of Karl Marx and John Stuart Mill as well as Marx and Keynes; the former subsequently saw the light of day in a revised form.[1] My first published paper in English was also on John Stuart Mill.[2]

During the deportation, I learnt Italian (to read Pirandello and to listen to the Italian radio), in which I was helped by eight years of Latin in the Gymnasium. I also acquired a life-long taste for music, in particular opera (I still remember chancing upon *Pelléas et Mélisande* on the radio and recognizing it immediately for what it was).

Deportation came to a sudden end in June 1953 under the first Nagy government. By that time, József Bondor was heading a large construction trust in Sztalinváros (subsequently renamed Dunaujváros) and he hired me to be organizer of the trust, later to become what might be called business manager. This was a unique opportunity since few former deportees were able to return to their old, or equivalent, jobs.

There followed a very pleasant period of three years. Interesting work, including considerable travel to the enterprises supervised by the trust, and weekends in Budapest, on a relatively high income. I also wrote two books, both of them on the construction industry.

There was a fly in the ointment, however. I had nowhere to go, in terms of advancement, because of my social background. Thus, at 28 years of age, I had an excellent job without any possibility for further advancement.

On 23 October 1956 the Revolution broke out. With four engineers, I became member of a committee that took over the Ministry of Construction and I was also to teach economics at the University with my mentor, István Varga.

At the Ministry, we started to think how to proceed. On 2 November, we called the prime minister's office and asked for a meeting over the weekend. We were told that the prime minister wanted to rest for the first time in weeks and we should see him on Monday. It was too late; on Sunday, 4 November Russian troops regained Budapest. The rest is history.

On 18 November, I left Budapest for Austria, where I arrived by travelling successively on truck, bicycle and boat. It was the last night before the lake froze and I spent it under some cornstalks on the Austrian side of the border.

Armed with a letter of introduction from István Varga, I went to Vienna, where I visited the Institute for Economic Research. I met there Professor Gottfried Haberler, spending his sabbatical in Vienna, who helped me to write an application to the Rockefeller Foundation. Haberler became a fatherly friend who cheered me on in my subsequent career.

I received one of the Foundation's postgraduate grants for Hungarian refugees and applied to Yale for graduate studies in economics. Haberler advised me to go to the United States and to choose Yale over the Institute for Graduate Studies in Geneva from where I received an invitation. My reason for selecting Yale among American universities was that Willy Fellner, a friend of István Varga, taught there. It turned out to be a good choice, and Fellner became a guiding light in my studies and, subsequently, my daughter's godfather.

From Vienna, I went to Salzburg and then to Frankfurt, where I wrote and lectured on the Hungarian economy in German, a language that has since been largely pushed out by English and French. However, I had little chance to shore up my knowledge of economics although I badly needed it.

I had a curious background in economics, having been taught successively by a member of the German historical school, a follower of Veblen and Commons (István Varga), and a Marxist. I had no access to books published after the war and never read Chamberlin or Joan Robinson. I knew practically no microeconomics and Keynes was my only source for macroeconomics.

It should not be surprising that on reading Samuelson's introductory textbook, I found it very advanced. I consoled myself that since my interest was in international economics, I did not have to know the theoretical chapters …

LIFE IN THE UNITED STATES

It was with such naiveté that I arrived at Yale on 1 April 1957. Then came the cold shower and an understanding of what was required of me. Fortunately Keynes helped in the macro course and in May I successfully passed the examinations for the second semester.

In the summer, I took courses in microeconomics and in statistics at the Harvard summer school. As luck would have it, I had as my professor of microeconomics Franco Modigliani, the later Nobel Prize winner, whose rapid-fire Italian-accented English I understood better than my American fellow students. Statistics was taught by a young professor with a French-sounding name, Louis Lefeber. One day, however, I read on his lips that he was counting the number of students in Hungarian. Thus, I also found a Hungarian connection at Harvard.

Returning to Yale, I completed a full year of studies and passed the comprehensives with distinction, an honor I shared with Sidney Winter, who is now a professor at Yale. At Yale, I specialized in international economics. I learned the subject by myself as I had an impossible teacher, a visitor for the year, in whose class I took only half a page of notes. But, going through the readings, I developed lecture notes myself that I used two years later when I began teaching.

But first the dissertation had to be written. My original intention was to write the thesis on economic integration. But I wanted to write what became my first book in English on the *Hungarian Experience in Economic Planning* (1959). Having finished the book in about six months and having it accepted for publication by the Yale University Press, the idea occurred to me to use it as a dissertation. This was agreed to, and a committee was set up with the membership of Willy Fellner, Lloyd Reynolds and Robert Triffin, who accepted the finished product. It received the Addison Porter prize from Yale University.

This meant that I completed the requirements for the PhD in economics in less than two years and in June 1959 I received the degree. My children would like to have this certified as a world record but they have yet to contact the Guinness outfit to receive confirmation.

I stayed on at Yale as assistant professor to teach international trade and microeconomics, where my notes from Modigliani's course were of great help. I continued at Yale the following year, although I received an invitation from MIT, in the hope that I could teach the PhD course in international economics (at the time I was teaching the course in the masters' program in international economic administration). This occurred soon afterwards, when I returned from year's leave at Berkeley. I was accompanied there by my wife, the former Carol Levy, a graduate student in international relations, whom I married in June 1960. She received her PhD at Johns Hopkins and has become an international economist with the Office of the US Trade Representative.

Before going to Berkeley, I finished my book on *The Theory of Economic*

Integration (1961), which was translated into Spanish, Portuguese, Japanese and Czech, and seems to have remained the standard book in the field. At Berkeley, I embarked on a large research project that became my *Trade Prospects for Developing Countries* (1964), also published in Spanish and Portuguese.

I edited *Changing Patterns in Foreign Trade and Payments* (1964), with two subsequent editions (1970 and 1978). I also gave a series of lectures at the Centro de Estudios Monetarios Latinoamericanos that were published under the title *Economic Development and Integration* (1965) simultaneously in English and Spanish.

After my return to Yale as associate professor, I wrote chiefly on international economics. Then came, in rapid succession, a paper on purchasing power parity;[3] the introduction of the concept of 'revealed' comparative advantage;[4] a paper on effective protection,[5] simultaneously with Max Corden and Harry Johnson; the introduction of the concepts of intra-industry vs inter-industry trade and horizontal vs vertical specialization;[6] and a new method for measuring trade creation and trade diversion.

My next large research project was at the Council on Foreign Relations, where I directed a group of studies on international trade policy. They were published under the title *Studies in Trade Liberalization* (1967), while my own book on the subject appeared under the title *Trade Liberalization among Industrial Countries: Objectives and Alternatives* (1967). When these books were published, I was already at Johns Hopkins, where I was appointed Professor of Political Economy in 1966.

There came a period of dual existence as professor at Johns Hopkins and consultant to the World Bank over the next 21 years. I found this arrangement, combining teaching at Hopkins with research and policy advising at the World Bank, a happy one. Each of the two institutions may have benefited as my experience at the World Bank helped my teaching of international trade, development policy and comparative systems at Hopkins, while keeping up with the economic literature for my teaching helped my work at the Bank.

THE DEVELOPMENT EXPERIENCE

At the World Bank I divided my time between my own research, research and policy advising, and advising developing countries. I particularly enjoyed the last as it meant applying economic principles to practical situations. My first experience was in the Dominican Republic, followed by advising in Argentina, Chile, Mexico, Venezuela, Portugal, Turkey, Egypt, Morocco, Tunisia, Korea and Taiwan.

My advice to developing countries was impregnated by my liberal economic philosophy. I advocated liberalizing trade and reducing state interventions in economic life. This came at a time when a dirigiste philosophy still held sway. Acclaimed writers like Gunnar Myrdal, Raul Prebisch and Hans Singer called for import protection and state intervention.

In the older generation, Gottfried Haberler alone espoused a liberal economic philosophy in the development field. In 1966, when I wrote my first paper on development, I was practically alone with such a philosophy among economists of my generation. At the World Bank also, protection and state intervention were the order of the day.

Things changed slowly in subsequent years as more and more economists recognized the need for import liberalization and for reducing the extent of state interventions. Changes occurred also at the World Bank, which came to be regarded as one of the mainstays of a liberal economic philosophy in development.

In 1969 I was asked for the first time to head a Bank economic mission. This led to the preparation of a report under the title *Policies for Economic Growth in Portugal* (1970). There followed a hiatus of nearly a decade, but afterwards I led a Bank mission every two years. The reports of three of my missions: *Industrial Development Strategy in Thailand* (1980); *Turkey: Industrialization and Trade Strategy* (1982); and, originally written in French, *Morocco: Industrial Incentives and Export Promotion* (1984), were published by the Bank; two, *Tunisia: Industrial Sector Report* (1986) and *Development Strategy in Venezuela* (1988), remained confidential.

At the World Bank, I also directed several research projects. The findings of the first of these projects appeared under the title *The Structure of Protection in Developing Countries* (1971), also published in Spanish; those of the second were published under the title *Development Strategies in Semi-Industrial Economies* (1982). Other research projects on Western Africa and on export incentives resulted in articles and short monographs.[7]

Over the years, my country advisory reports and comparative papers were published successively in several volumes. They include *Policy Reform in Developing Countries* (1977), translated into Chinese and Spanish; *The Newly Industrializing Countries in the World Economy* (1981), translated into French and Spanish; and *Change and Challenge in the World Economy* (1985).

'The Process of Industrial Development and Alternative Development Strategies' was the subject of my Frank D. Graham Memorial Lecture at Princeton,[8] while the topic of my V.K. Ramaswami Memorial Lecture in New Delhi was 'Policy Making for Economic Development.'[9] International trade and economic development incorporated my work on the 'stages approach' to comparative advantage[10] and again, on policy responses to external shocks.[11]

My teaching also increasingly moved in the direction of development economics. On the graduate level, I continued with my international economics course but added a new course on development policies and programming. Subsequently, I also taught a graduate course on the theory of development.

My interests in development again came to the fore when I joined the Institute for International Economics as a visiting fellow while on sabbatical from Johns Hopkins. My first project there, carried out with three outstanding Latin American economists, was to write a book entitled *Toward Renewed Economic Growth in Latin America* (1986), simultaneously published in English, Spanish and Portuguese, in which the adoption of an outward-oriented development strategy with less government intervention was recommended. I stayed on at the Institute on a part-time basis afterwards, leading to the publication of *Adjusting to Success: Balance of Payments Policy in the East Asian NICs* with John Williamson (1987), translated into Chinese.

THE FRENCH CONNECTION

For centuries, Hungarians looked to Paris as the center of the universe. Apart from French culture, they were attracted to the French political philosophy, and they regarded France as a counterweight to Germany (after World War II it was said in newspapers that Hungarians now look to Moscow, but this was not taken seriously).

My own interest in France goes back to reading French literature while in high school. It was followed by the preparation of an anthology of French poetry – in the original and in Hungarian translation – during my first year at the University. From François Villon onwards, all major French poets were represented in the anthology.

Not surprisingly, after arriving in the United States, I soon explored possibilities to visit France. The opportunity presented itself in 1959 when I obtained travel documents to go to France in the summer. Although I did some travelling, I spent most of my time in Paris, which has become my favorite city. I had an office at the Institut d'Economie Appliquée, which published one of my first papers in its journal.[12]

In 1960, I spent my honeymoon in France, with a sidetrip to Italy. We visited friends of my wife whom she had met under the Experiment in International Living Program a few years earlier. At 18 years of age, she wrote on the application form that she liked to play tennis and was chosen by a family that had a tennis court – a rare case in France. They became her French family, who subsequently also acquired a swimming pool.

I was well received by Carol's French family and we went back there every year; first by ourselves and later with our children, Mara, born in 1970, and Gabor, born in 1972. We stayed with the family that originally welcomed

Carol; Aymé Bernard, now 94, an amazingly intelligent and knowledgeable man, and his charming wife. We also developed lifelong friendships with people of our age who had summer homes on the same property. And we bought a house there ourselves in 1985, helped by a dollar worth 9.50 French francs at the time, as one of our friends moved to the château of his deceased parents.

But France was not all vacation for me. In 1963 I spent a sabbatical semester in Paris at CEPREL, a research institute, where I studied French planning. This led to the publication of a paper entitled 'Whither French Planning?',[13] where I correctly predicted its demise following entry into the Common Market. In another paper, 'Planning in an Open Economy',[14] I emphasized the incompatibility of planning and full participation in international trade.

Paris was not only a place of intellectual pursuits for me. It was also a culinary delight. After exploring many bistros with my wife and discussing their merits with my friends, it was suggested that I write a culinary guide. This I did under the title *A Primer in Culinary Economics or How to Maximize the Culinary Utility of the Dollar in Paris*. The first edition, prepared in 1969, covered 20 restaurants with one page each; the subsequent seven editions figured 25 restaurants with two pages each. The eighth edition of the guide also appeared in print.[15]

In 1970 I returned to Paris on sabbatical to teach at the Université de Paris IX (Dauphine). I also started writing on the French economy and in 1979 the French translation of my paper 'The French Economy under the Fifth Republic, 1958–1978'[16] received the Prix Rossi of the Académie des Sciences Morales et Politiques, which gave me the title Lauréat de l'Institut. In subsequent years, I wrote annually a paper for the French review *Commentaire*, the English versions of which were published in *The Tocqueville Review*.

In my papers, I emphasized the need to liberalize the French economy, which has been the direction taken in subsequent years. I also called for improving competitiveness, using the exchange rate and incentives to investment activity, as well as to research and development, as instruments.

At the same time, I started teaching mini courses in France. I began at the Institut d'Etudes Politiques (customarily called Sciences-Po) and continued at the Université de Paris I (Sorbonne-Panthéon) and at the Université de Clérmont-Ferrand. My subjects were international trade and development economics.

In 1984, I travelled to Kiel in Germany to receive the Bernhard Harms Prize in International Economics at the Institute for World Economics of the University of Kiel. My prize lecture was entitled 'The Economic Consequences of Social Policies in the Industrial Countries,'[17] a subject that is of particular importance for France. In fact, my paper was translated into French.

MY HUNGARIAN RELATIONS

I did not return to Hungary between 1956 and 1968. During this period my mother died in an automobile accident but my father was still alive; he died in 1988.

In 1968, I was invited officially to Budapest. I gave a public lecture at the Karl Marx University of Economics that was chaired by two former ministers. The lecture was announced in the Communist Party newspaper and was well attended.

In subsequent years, I returned to Hungary at least once a year to lecture and to participate in conferences. On these occasions I usually met with the Ministers of Planning and of Finance and had discussions with leading academic and governmental economists. I published several papers in Hungarian economic journals, which also appeared in English.[18]

In my discussions and papers I emphasized the need for continuing with the reform effort and for carrying out adjustment measures to reduce Hungary's large external debt. The taking of such measures was unfortunately postponed until a much larger adjustment effort has become necessary.

My trips to Hungary provided opportunities to meet with relatives and friends. Apart from seeing my father, I particularly cherished the meetings with my economist friends and with my former co-workers in Dunaujváros, for whom my visit provided an occasion to get together.

Every two years I took my children to Hungary to visit Budapest and to spend a few days at Lake Balaton, where my father joined us. My wife also came with us when her work permitted.

My children very much enjoyed these trips. While they had no common language with my father (the children speak English and French and my father Hungarian, German and Italian), they were linked by strong feelings that obviate the need for verbal communication. In fact, just like the yearly stays in France, the trips to Hungary became part of my children's life.

EPILOGUE AND PROLOGUE

This is an epilogue, as my 30-year career in economics described here came to an end with my cancer operation of 5 August 1987. It is also a prologue because it describes my activities as they have developed after the operation.

On 30 July 1987 I was diagnosed as having neck and head cancer. This came as a complete surprise. Not only did I not have any warning signs, but I had a complete physical check-up in June. Also, I gave up the sporadical smoking of my youth a long time ago and was a moderate consumer of alcohol.

The cancer was very far advanced. I overheard an intern saying that I was at the very limit where an operation was still possible. In fact, because of the advanced stage of the cancer, I was admitted to the Johns Hopkins University Hospital on an emergency basis and was operated on two days later. It involved removing part of my jaw, my palate and part of my tongue. It necessitated putting a piece of steel in my jaw and transplanting a flap from my left breast. My neck was also operated on and I often have the feeling of having a collar inside it.

The operation, which took 13 hours, was performed by Dr John Price, an outstanding surgeon at the Johns Hopkins Hospital, who considers it his masterwork. I spent five weeks at the hospital, partly because of pneumonia I contracted there. During my stay I had the daily visits of my wife and children, whose support has been of immense benefit since the operation.

My wife and daughter also often accompanied me on daily visits for radiotherapy to the Johns Hopkins Hospital over a seven-week period. On other visits friends and students drove me there. The radiotherapy necessitated removing one-third of my teeth, fortunately from the back of my mouth. It also gave me dryness of the mouth that requires use of artificial saliva on a regular basis.

I cannot swallow and have to take nourishment through a gastro-ostomy tube. I was also given a tracheostomy tube that was removed in December 1987 but reinstated a few days afterwards, as I developed a life-threatening breathing problem. It is scheduled to be removed by the first anniversary of my operation.

My inability to swallow brings to an end my writing of the culinary guide and removes one of the pleasures of life. Because of the danger of infection around the tube I cannot swim either, thus ending another of my pleasures: daily swimming of a kilometer, which I rarely ever missed. Also, movement in my left arm is impaired so that I have some difficulty in putting on a coat.

More importantly for my professional career, my speech is impaired. This brings to an end leading Bank missions to developing countries, creates difficulties in day-to-day contacts, and does not permit me to lecture. I have continued directing a dissertation seminar at Johns Hopkins and next year I am to give a graduate seminar on development policies, relying on notes distributed to the students and having students make presentations.

Nevertheless, following the operation I started anew my professional life. At the World Bank I completed the report on Venezuela that was referred to above. I also finished a book, written with Luc Bauwens, on *Changing*

Patterns of Trade in Manufactured Goods: An Econometric Investigation (1988), and collected comparative papers and country advisory reports written between 1985 and 1987 in a volume entitled *New Directions in the World Economy* (1989). Furthermore, I wrote several papers on varied subjects in development.

My work at the World Bank involves writing papers and commenting on papers written by others as well as reports by the economics staff. Also, I was given responsibility for reviewing submissions to the new Working Paper series at the Bank.

I continue part time at the Institute for International Economics. Following my operation, I completed, with Marcus Noland, a book on *Japan in the World Economy* (1988). I also started work on a Pacific project that deals with the developing countries of the area. And I am organizing a conference on *Europe 1992* to examine the measures to be taken to complete the internal market of the European Community.

I am also resuming travel, although this is made difficult by having to carry cans of liquid food and a variety of paraphernalia necessary for mouth care that requires about an hour a day. Consultations at the OECD and OECD Development Centre in June will be followed by trips to Middlebery, Geneva and New York to deliver papers. In fact, the papers will be read by my wife while I will intervene in the discussion stage.

The continuation of these activities will depend on future developments regarding my health. At the time of the operation, I was told that the probability of recurrence of the cancer was 80 percent. This probability, however, declines rapidly as time progresses. It is 50 percent one year after the operation and 35 percent two years later. I sometimes feel as if I am living on borrowed time.

NOTES

1. 'Karl Marx and John Stuart Mill', *Weltwirtschaftliches Archiv*, Band 83, Heft 2 (1959), pp. 147–55. (This and all papers cited below were written by the author.)
2. John Stuart Mill and the Law of Markets', *Quarterly Journal of Economics*, May 1959, pp. 263–74.
3. 'The Purchasing Power Parity Doctrine: A Reappraisal', *Journal of Political Economy*, December 1964, pp. 584–96.
4. 'Trade Liberalization and "Revealed" Comparative Advantage', *Manchester School*, May 1965, pp. 99–121.
5. 'Tariff Protection in Industrial Countries: An Evaluation', *Journal of Political Economy*, December 1965, pp. 573–94.
6. 'Trade Creation and Trade Diversion in the European Common Market', *Economic Journal*, March 1967, pp. 1–21.
7. Cf. e.g. 'The "Effects Method" of Project Evaluation', *Oxford Bulletin of Economics and Statistics*, November 1976, pp. 219–32 and 'Export Incentives and Export Growth in Developing Countries: An Econometric Investigation' (with E. Voloudakis, P. Fylaktos and

S.T. Suh), Washington, DC, World Bank Development Research Department Discussion Paper No. 159, February 1986.
8. *Essay in International Finance*, No. 141, December 1980.
9. *Indian Economic Review*, forthcoming.
10. 'A "Stages Approach" to Comparative Advantage', in *Economic Growth and Resources*, Vol. 4: National and International Issues (Irma Adelman, ed.), London, Macmillan, 1971, pp. 121–56.
11. 'The Newly-Industrializing Developing Countries After the Oil Crisis', *Weltwirtschaftliches Archiv*, Band 117, Heft 1 (1981), pp. 142–94.
12. 'La théorie de la firme socialiste', *Economie Appliquée*, July–December 1959, pp. 535–70.
13. *Quarterly Journal of Economics*, November 1965, pp. 537–54.
14. *Kyklos*, 1966 (3), pp. 383–410.
15. *The Tocqueville Review*, 1986/87, pp. 377–415.
16. *Revue Economique*, November 1979, pp. 939–71.
17. Institute for World Economics at the University of Kiel, June 1984.
18. Cf. e.g. 'The Economic Reform in Hungary', *Economica*, February 1970, pp. 1–22; 'The Economic Reform in Hungary Ten Years After', *European Economic Review*, December 1978, pp. 245–68, and 'The "New Growth Path" in Hungary', *Banca Nazionale del Lavoro, Quarterly Review*, December 1985, pp. 347–77.

3. Thinking about economics*

Carolyn Shaw Bell

The way I think about economics consists of things I learned years ago before knowing anything about economics as well as all the ways I have been learning since. I find that my way of thinking, which I assert is 'thinking like an economist,' applies to a wide range of issues and concerns in my life. But I do not, repeat NOT, agree one whit with some definitions of economics as an all-powerful way of thinking which can be applied to solve any problem in life, obviating the need for any other field like sociology or psychology or managerial decision-making.

What then is economics all about, to me? The first economic issue of which I was aware may very well have shaped my entire career, a good bit of it concerned with definitions and data. I grew up in Framingham, Massachusetts, then a relatively small town dominated by the Dennison Manufacturing Company, where my father was an executive. Although Framingham was more than just a 'company town,' many of its high-school graduates found employment in the Dennison's office or factory jobs and the thriving retail sector supported by Dennison paychecks included food stores in several districts and a flourishing 'downtown' with hardware stores, national chain outlets, specialty shops, a few restaurants, banks and movie theaters.

At home, I was used to my parents discussing things I didn't fully understand and so was able to reply, with some assurance, when a fifth-grade teacher, in the depression of 1930, asked me if I had heard anything about Dennison's plans for continued operation. 'Oh yes,' I offered, having no idea what I was talking about, 'I heard my father say they would fire about five hundred people,' and made appropriate noises as the teacher shook her head in dismay. When I repeated my tale at home my father's reaction was considerable, and he was by nature more silent than not. 'Carolyn! The Dennison Company did NOT fire anyone. We had to let 500 people go!'

It took some years before I realized that my father's anger with me masked his very real dismay, and that unemployment created by the company was a tragic and unavoidable event. What I learned from the incident was that being 'fired' was different from being 'let go', although the distinction between

*This chapter first appeared in *The American Economist*, **42**(2), Spring 1998, 18–33.

voluntary and involuntary unemployment took longer to understand. I also learned not to repeat my father's remarks about his business, although I found my curiosity growing about his business, and what 'the depression' meant. Unfortunately these lessons were not accompanied by any encouragement at home to ask questions, at least not about distressing things. At the same time I was taught that questions could be answered by looking things up: my parents had bought a wonderful set of *Compton's Pictured Encyclopedia* for my older sister and brother, and I was the one who sat down and read it, as well as looking things up. I learned that the big leather-covered dictionary on the library table in our living room was also for looking things up, and I learned that some books had an index in the back which was enormously helpful.

As for school, US history was required by the Commonwealth of Massachusetts of all high-school graduates, and I was fortunate in having a teacher who used the requirement as a minimum and set his students to exploring in all kinds of ways. He was the first person I met who talked about primary sources and why they were essential to any serious study; and how we could add to the bare bones of the text if we pursued, on our own, other books than an encyclopedia. I did a paper for that course on money, and learned about the things that have been used as money in different cultures and at different times. That was easy to understand, and I grasped the notion that anything could be money as long as people accepted it and used it in exchange or trade, or, most simply, 'as money.' I remember getting hung up on banking, and why 'credit' was different from 'money' and yet it wasn't. It was Mr Lundberg who told me that the paper I tried to write about the first Bank of the United States was not a history paper but an economics paper, and when I asked if there were books about economics he recommended Adam Smith's *The Wealth of Nations*. So I read it.

It was a wonderful read, and I remember becoming completely absorbed in the parts I understood. Without anyone to warn me, I had great difficulties because I didn't know the difference between English and American, nor the difference between eighteenth-century and twentieth-century terminology. I never did find out, while I was reading it, that 'corn' was wheat and since I knew the corn my father grew in his vegetable garden was special it was impossible for me to understand the corn laws and much of the argument about tariffs. I also did not grasp Adam Smith's use of the term 'stock' meaning inventory or asset, so I equated it comfortably with corporate stock. How did I know about that? My father's position in the Dennison Manufacturing Company made him a stockholder, and he explained how purchasing stock enabled lots of people to become part owners of a company. But despite these obstacles along the way, I reveled in Adam Smith and became a firm believer in the division of labor, limited primarily by the size of the market, the labor theory of value, and much more. And there is a lot of history in the *Wealth of Nations* which I enjoyed because it spoke of people and issues I'd already read about and I became aware of how different points of view about an event or a course of events can lead to quite different historical accounts.

At Christmas time of that year my older brother came home from college, bringing with him Taussig's *Principles of Economics* (1913), the required reading in his first-year course. So I read that, and was astonished at how stodgy it was, compared to Smith. I was learning to distinguish between books written as texts and books written about subjects. The upshot was that I knew my first year in college would include a course in economics, and so it came to pass. My undergraduate education was nourished by a famous and short-lived set of beginning books known as the Princeton Series. I can't remember any of the authors but I do know that the text on price analysis was still useful in graduate school, as were a couple of others on what I later recognized as micro fields. The discussion of macro issues was highly institutional, as I recall (this was 1937–38) and I learned a lot of history about the banking system, market regulation and anti-trust, as well as Ricardo's theory of international trade, the operations of the gold standard, and the current disarray in most economies of the world.

As an honors graduate I wrote a thesis on mercantilism and its resemblance to the systems of autarky then developing in Germany. I learned a lot about economic planning under fascism and systems of bilateral trade. By then I had learned to drive, and the trip from my home to Cambridge enabled me to use the collection of early writers at the Harvard Graduate School of Business Administration – I knew that primary sources would provide me with the best understanding of mercantilism. So I read Thomas Mun, Edward Misselden, Josiah Child, Davenant and I was particularly delighted with Sir William Petty and Gregory King, and their heroic attempts to put a value on the wealth and income of their country.

For the greatest gift my undergraduate economics department gave me was devoting our senior seminar to reading J.M. Keynes's *General Theory of Employment, Interest and Money* (1936). We were joined by one or more of the faculty each week, as we struggled through each chapter. The faculty was reading the journal literature, which helped them somewhat to interpret for us, but mostly it was a situation in which the difference in confusion between professor and student was not very great.

That early introduction to the *General Theory*, however, was of enormous value to me in the years to follow, because I became accustomed to the idea of aggregates and particularly aggregate demand, and comfortable with the notion of sticky wages and a variety of reasons for saving. As for the propensity to consume, it made sense the way Keynes explained it although it took many more years before I realized what he was about in setting forth his General Law of the propensity to consume.

When Keynes wrote 'The fundamental psychological law, upon which we are entitled to depend with great confidence both *a priori* from our knowledge of human nature and from the detailed facts of experience, is that men are disposed, as a rule and on the average, to increase their consumption as their income increases, but not by as much as the increase in their income' (Keynes, p. 96), I believed him. Not just about the functional relationship between spending and income – I believed that there was a 'psychological law.' It seemed clear to me that psychology scholars could develop special knowledge useful to economists. (I was still reveling in the notion of specialization and the division of labor.)

But as well as my immersion in economics, I was enthralled by the sheer abundance of ideas around me. Like many other undergraduates at an excellent college of liberal arts, I was joyously overwhelmed with reading philosophy, history, English criticism, international law, and by the general wonder of knowledge itself. I had freedom of the stacks in a library whose riches lured me to endless hours in my carrel; I was taking courses which presented me with new ways of thinking, not just new knowledge. I experimented with all sorts of interdisciplinary majors, and wound up concentrating on economics through a sheer fluke of course registration (and, of course, the invitation to do honors work).

By the time I graduated, Europe had been at war for almost two years and the United States economy was already adjusting to war demands. Learning that my training in economics could qualify me for a job that wasn't purely clerical or administrative, I promptly took off for Washington, DC, aided by a phone call from my father to one of his colleagues, then on leave from the Dennison Company to assist in setting up newly formed war agencies. Through him I was referred to the Office of Price Administration and there I entered the next stage of learning about economics, from 1941 to 1945.

The first lesson was about how economic theory could be applied. Price control was a matter of analyzing particular markets to learn how supply and demand were out of balance; I could almost use the diagrams from my undergraduate textbook to illustrate the problem with fluid milk (and the myriad local markets, each posing a different situation) or scrap metal (where markets for different metals also differed widely) or pepper or other imports where prices shot up by several hundred percent and forecasting future shortages became easy. I also realized how well Keynes's general theory, or his way of looking at the economy, applied to the situation. There was clearly an enormous expansion of aggregate demand from the requirements of the armed forces and the lend-lease program, and the pressures on firms to retool and hire far exceeded the ability of the economy to increase supplies. It was not just a matter of using idle capacity; it meant moving manpower among industries and areas of the country, building new capacity like shipyards and aluminum plants and also closing firms and creating shortages. I learned to distinguish between aggregate demand and total civilian demand, total supply and aggregate civilian supplies, and I discovered that with effective price controls a disequilibrium solution could persist.

The other lesson I learned has remained with me for all of my professional life, and that is an appreciation of the remarkable efficiency of the market system. This became clear from the attempts by one war agency after another to enact rules or orders forcing buyers and sellers to act in ways other than those identified by the market solution. For example, firms needing scarce supplies were given priority ratings to assure delivery. But the simple A, B, C system of rating had to be revised as new requirements were discovered by war agencies developing new weapons. So A was supplanted by Al and A2 and so on, and fairly soon a priority rating of B2 meant no supplies at all. And the priority system gave way to a system of direct allocation, and that didn't work because nobody knew, precisely, how much of a given scarce material there was anyway.

The lesson was spelled out in detail during my brief stint with the rationing program for new cars when production was stopped in 1942. I had the job of dealing with Congressional pressure, in correspondence and otherwise, on the agency. This pressure was for two ends: getting a car for a particular constituent who 'really needed an automobile in his work' or getting a job for another 'whose knowledge of the automobile industry comes from his thirty years' service on Main Street in the Metropolis Automobile Agency.' Again, simple rules of dividing up the existing supply became more and more complicated and we in Washington knew that the local boards charged with actually carrying out the rules were not at all consistent in their decisions, subject as they were not only to differing local situations but differing local political pressures.

Most of my time with OPA in Washington was in Ken Galbraith's office; he was then Price Administrator, second in command to Leon Henderson. As the legal regulations became more and more complex I realized the acuity of Ken's perception that the easiest prices to administer were those already administered by a handful of firms in markets that could not faintly be called competitive. Price control could work for aluminum, sugar, tin and other commodities produced mostly by a very few firms, but it was enormously cumbersome and saddled with dreadfully complex legal regulations for men's shirts, furniture, or dry cleaning services. In Galbraith's first postwar book, *A Theory of Price Control* (1952), he elaborated on these and other market characteristics which shape if not dictate the success of market regulation.

I also concluded, on the basis of Washington OPA experience, that it is foolish to suspect 'the government' or Federal agencies or the Washington establishment of conspiracy. I served as recorder to the committee planning the General Maximum Price Regulation, in secrecy during the months of February and March in 1942. We met after hours, and I took careful notes which I later transcribed at home before tumbling into bed well after midnight. I came to work as soon after six as possible, to feed my notes into the copier (hectograph? mimeo? I don't remember) and send them off in sealed envelopes, marked 'CONFIDENTIAL' by special messenger. The price freeze was to be one of a seven-point (maybe there were nine) attack on inflation. OPA's announcement was to be coordinated with a new system of farm price supports to be announced simultaneously by the Agriculture Department, some action by the Treasury Department, a new policy for the Manpower Administration, and so on. The whole thing would be announced in a major speech by the President; I remember long discussions about how much explanation of price control should be in the speech or if it should consist of general exhortation. There was to be, in short, a conspiracy among several Federal agencies on a common course of action. But it never came off. It proved impossible to get coordination even of the messages to be sent to the public by the new program, much less coordination of agency activity. Personal jealousies, pride of place, foot dragging in some places and refusal to consider a new policy in others all conspired to make inter-agency conspiracy impossible.

Of course there were successful conspiracies during World War II. Of course many of the plans for military buildup and deployment were kept secret. Of course the activity surrounding the development of atomic weapons was a conspiracy. But for these and other cases no *general* conspiracy involving several different agencies was required. The conspirers had firm control over the activities to be kept secret. So firm, in fact, that two years later in California, when the regional OPA prepared an order preventing dairy farmers in the area of Hanford, Washington from raising prices, we were all furious at a countermanding order by the Washington OPA to leave the Hanford area alone. Our colleagues in the capitol didn't know why, only that the White House had decreed hands off. But watching the attempts of top administrators to secure cooperation on a program establishing an anti-inflation economic policy convinced me that the popular bugbear 'Big Government' is just a bogeyman, invented to scare children from looking under the bed.

'Government' in the sense of a monolithic activity, directed and programmed to one purpose or even to a set of complementary purposes, may exist in some countries or some epochs, but it does not exist in Washington, DC. I find the term 'government' to be very badly misused, especially when it comes to economic affairs. I cringe when state or local officials urge constituents to vote for a new bridge or recreation program on the grounds that 'Anyway, the government will pay for most of it, so it doesn't cost us here in Metropolis very much.' I also cringe when electioneering drives people to say they are against 'big government' or they are 'against bureaucrats.' Most of all, I suppose, I deplore the data which list the amount of tax revenue provided to Washington by the residents of a given state or county or city to show how little the people 'get back in exchange.' Government in this country exists at three major levels: Federal, state and municipal, together with a number of assorted other political entities, including school districts, counties, watershed authorities and so on. It is difficult to make any flat statement about 'government' that holds true for each of these entities.

Aside from these two major lessons from my wartime experience, I learned a lot both in Washington and in San Francisco, where I joined the regional office of OPA (which extended over the Pacific states plus Arizona, New Mexico and Nevada), and worked on three different types of cases, each of which taught me about the limits to economic analysis.

There regularly crossed my desk appeals from a particular firm to have its ceiling price lifted or adjusted; I did the analysis according to an established format and my recommendation was rarely overturned by higher authority. If a manufacturer of, say, work gloves, wrote that his costs had gone up to the point where he would stop producing without price relief, I investigated by asking for cost data, volume of total sales and sales of the particular item under consideration and overall profit and loss statements for several previous years. The idea was that if the firm's overall profit level was in line with previous figures, and the increased costs were real, a price adjustment could be given to cover marginal costs, that is, the rise in costs since the ceiling price had been established. (The same principles were followed with a slightly more complicated analysis if the firm's entire line was threatened.) The firm had also to establish that its product was 'essential to the war effort' and this usually meant showing existing or potential contracts with a military procurement agency or a buyer whose output went to such markets.

These were fun to do, and I learned a lot of extraneous information. I thoroughly approved of the methodology, which of course came straight out of my Princeton Series textbook on price analysis, and was fascinated by the relationship between accounting data and economic theory. I thought OPA was doing a good job of keeping justifiable price increases to a minimum. Then I met the price specialist for the garment trades and textile industries. The 'trade' or 'price' specialist came from business and typically had years of experience with sellers at different market levels. Thus, our office had a fish specialist as well as a food specialist, and my mentor was the textiles and garment trade specialist, Sherwood Levy. He was highly knowledgeable, totally committed to what OPA was trying to do, loved to talk with the price economists, and spent hours at his desk conferring with visiting business executives, whom he sent away without a hope of obtaining the freedom from price control they'd expected from a 'trade specialist' as opposed to those ivory-tower economists or brash young lawyers.

Sherwood introduced me to the notion of price lines and price points, and explained with gusto what the relevant numbers were for almost any item you could mention. Men's shirts or socks, which of course sold by the dozen, were manufactured to sell in a very few price lines. Women's underwear was sold in separate price lines. Give Sherwood a retail price and he would tell you the wholesale price and the probable manufacturer's selling price. As Sherwood explained, patiently but firmly, that my solution to the work-glove manufacturer's rising cost problem simply would not do. Just as patiently I demurred that if the new price covered his variable costs he would naturally continue producing. Why not? 'Because,' said Sherwood, 'he couldn't sell gloves at a price of $17.08 a dozen. Nobody sells gloves at that price. He'll simply drop the line unless you let him go up to the next level, $18.50.' I persisted and Sherwood countered with predictions of how buyers would behave. 'Standard weight men's work-gloves at $17.08? Whoever heard of that? What is this guy trying to sell?'

That particular order went out, signed by the regional price administrator, allowing a price rise from $15.95 to $17.08 and, sure enough, the work-gloves completely disappeared. I think the procurement agency involved eventually located a supplier with previously approved prices much above our petitioner's request. So I came to believe in the existence of 'trade practices' which operated in the market with a powerful force unrecognized by economics. True, one could speak of market imperfections, and solutions in a less than purely competitive market. But these were almost irrelevant, or over-elaborate accounts of what was going on. Supply and demand took effect not sensitively, as portrayed in minute detail in a geometric diagram or a mathematical equation, but crudely, pulled this or that way by price lines, 'customary practices,' and other selling conditions. Economic analysis still had powerful things to say, and I thought it would be more acceptable if economists recognized the strength of institutional factors, which so clearly shaped the actual transactions signaled by supply and demand. Sherwood agreed that government could, if it worked hard enough at dreaming up ever new and complex regulations, change or even overturn trade practices, but he impressed me with the enormous costs that would result. Simpler to accept the vagaries of actual markets rather than try to impose 'market' solutions calculated by pure analysis. Sherwood Levy knew about transaction costs, and taught me what he knew, long before the formal economic theory appeared in Coase's classic article.

But California also demonstrated that if trade practices could be tolerated in some cases they had to change in others. Fresh seafood in San Francisco and elsewhere on the Pacific Coast was both a delicacy and a staple, with ceiling prices set for individual retailers by their own prices in effect on 1 April 1942, the date of the General Maximum Price Regulation. That was fine for salmon or gray sole, but crabs, the fresh-caught fresh-cooked marvel of sellers along Fishermen's Wharf, were not sold by the pound. Crabs sold for a dollar a piece, or $1.50 for a larger size, or $2.25 for a giant and so on. Now price control cannot work under these conditions. Economic analysis, after all, determines two variables, equilibrium price and equilibrium quantity. A given dollar price had to be associated with a given *quantity*, not number of units. Clearly without setting a price per pound for crabs, prices would soar even more than they already had.

The West Coast office had authority to set prices on a number of items including fresh foodstuffs and the chief price economist for the office, Earl Rolph (on leave from the Economics Department at the University of California in Berkeley), proposed a regional price order which would not only give all sellers the same ceiling prices, but would apply to fresh and cooked crab, per pound. The uproar from the 'industry' – fishermen, wholesalers, retailers, restaurants – was immediate and prolonged. Over and over again we heard 'Nobody will catch crab if you insist on doing this.' 'We'll all be put out of business!' 'Your average housewife isn't going to like this one little bit!' And threateningly, 'We'll see what my Congressman has to say about this!' I remember sitting at my desk watching Earl farther down the room, ensconced with three or four burly fisherfolk or their customers. The back of Earl's neck would grow red. Then it would get redder. Making an excuse to walk by his desk I was impressed at the serenity of his facial expression as he patiently argued the case for changing the customary trade practices for Pacific crab.

In fact, the order went out, tradition and custom went by the board, and years later when my husband and I traveled to San Francisco and walked on Fishermen's Wharf, I pointed with some awe to all the dollar prices posted over live crab, cooked crab, by the pound. A living answer to the question 'What did you do in the war, Mommy?' What I learned from my years doing price control was a lot about market imperfections, along with my overwhelming conviction that the market's job of coordinating, providing information and getting goods from supplier to user could not possibly be bettered by any system of regulation. I didn't learn much price theory but I did learn a lot about the limits of price theory based on the competitive model. And, since the summer before I went to Washington I had taken Edward Chamberlin's course in graduate micro theory at Harvard, I learned that the more sophisticated and to me far more realistic model of monopolistic competition wasn't much good either in making price controls (or rationing, or allocation, or any other form of administrative rule design) work in an economy as complex and totally involved in markets as that of the United States. Along the way I also picked up an interest in accounting (well, all those firms asking for price increases had to submit detailed cost data along with the financials of profit and loss and balance sheets which meant that I had to learn, fast, how to read and evaluate such statements).

And then I went to the London School of Economics, in January of 1946, and three years later received the PhD in economics, with a thesis discussing how real firms put real technological change into effect. England immediately after World War II (and all too soon after the precipitate end of lend-lease) was a sad and sorry country, people with pinched faces and cold bare hands jammed into their pockets on a gray wet dismal February morning, people looking drawn and tired on the tube, people whose lot didn't seem to improve much from 1946 to 1949. Most of them had horrible teeth, or wore dentures, and when I went for a routine checkup to a local dentist he spent a good bit of time admiring the minor fillings I'd had in the States. War damage was highly visible, from the plots in central London barred off by fences and warning signs to those showing new growth of London Pride, that scarlet flower that shot up on dismal locations; from the still standing buildings sliced through from top to bottom so you could see half a stairway or a fireplace against one wall and a window with shattered glass in another to the acreage of bare lots in the City, with only an occasional standing structure. The children looked wonderful, though, all rosy cheeked, with stout little bodies and active limbs, running around with all the energy in the world. I realized almost immediately that although World War II had visited enormous damage and depredation on both physical and human capital in England, it had also brought about a revolutionary redistribution of real income. With children, you couldn't tell rich from poor: they all looked healthy and were healthy … no bad teeth among them! Food rationing had provided extra nutrients for children, and price control had made milk and bread, potatoes and greens, widely available.

I had already begun to interpret what I observed in terms of economic concepts and analysis – in short, to think like an economist. When the papers reported strikes by the coal miners, and then a concerted refusal to work overtime on Saturdays, and everyone knew that coal not only fueled British industry and homes but was also a major export, the reaction was mostly ideological. Some said 'Shoot the bastards' and others said 'Good for them! Standing up for their rights!' The government offered higher wages, the miners obstinately took the weekend off, and I added another example of a backward-bending supply curve to the one that had been provided by the native folk at Dakar, who, when enlisted to help unload the ships for the African invasion in 1943, worked very hard for a week but once paid, took off for their home villages, since they had earned enough to live happily for months. Only dropping the wage brought new workers to the docks. But the case of the British miners was of a different sort: money wages were irrelevant because civilian supplies had been so drastically curtailed.

And so some smart Whitehall official, who I'm sure must have been an economist and most likely a woman, got supplies of cookware, bed linens, tea kettles, cups and saucers shipped to the mining towns and villages. The supply problem was instantly solved – once the miners (and their wives) had something on which to spend their wages, the incentive to earn more by working more reappeared.

One reason I started to think like an economist was my plunging into economic history and the development of economic thought. My tutor, Ronnie Edwards, insisted that I read widely in both: historically the major technological change occurred in England during the Industrial Revolution, and what did I know about that, beyond James Watt and the spinning jenny, and the power loom? Not much in March of 1946, but I plowed through *Tours in England and Wales* (Young, 1932) Samuel Smiles' stories of entrepreneurs, and all the economists writing in the early 1800s whose names had not survived, like those of Malthus, Ricardo and Mill. I enjoyed it all, and the chapter in my thesis reviewing the literature on technological change is indeed complete. Along with this immersion in British history and economics, I was also reading Schumpeter on innovation, and working with my tutor on his project of learning more about British efforts to stimulate technological change with cooperative research arrangements among firms in the same industry or with a common interest in material or technology. We traveled to interview and tour the firms in hosiery, machine tools, chemicals, publishing and others, and along the way I learned how English industrialists differed from their US counterparts, so that I felt comfortable two years later when I set out to interview firms for my own research.

Formal learning at LSE was very much a matter of choice and chance. I was 'set up' (that is obviously slang of the period because it is not natural to my current vocabulary; it means enormously pleased and proud but not faintly showing pleasure or pride) to be invited to attend the Robbins's seminar, where the faculty and a select few graduate students met weekly to discuss everything under the sun from elasticity to the multiplier. I found my tutor's seminars, where a British business executive discussed his firm and his decision-making before an audience of economists some of whom were trying to understand and some of whom were determined to criticize, lively and thought-provoking. I was awed at the British ability to speak: the undergraduates whom I met talked miles around me and other Americans … they were literate, articulate, clever, quick on their feet, and, besides, they had that accent which sounded to me like total certainty. And of course I learned a lot in the Graduate Common Room, and in the local pub, from my peers doing economics or anthropology or political science.

As for 'LSE economics,' Robbins's definition of the field as the study of how to allocate scarce resources among competing ends seemed obviously correct to me. A great deal of nonsense has been written about this definition as a spurious attempt to create a 'value-free' economics, as if there could possibly be such a thing. To me, it merely illustrated once again the well-known principle of division of labor: economists could concentrate on the allocation problem, leaving it up to philosophers, politicians, voters, or whomever to determine the ends or uses for the scarce resources. Economics occupied a middle ground, with consumers' preferences or utility functions setting the assumptions of choice theory at one end and the engineering functions determining the limits of production theory at the other. Like my earlier lessons, the considerable discussion of the scope and method of economics at LSE colored my later work. I thought it essential to be clear about what economics was and why we were doing it, at the same time that I was learning economics. It was good for me that happened, for such discussions have not occupied the profession to any extent since the late 1940s.

I also learned about the British class system: where everyone knew what class s/he was and that was that. Earlier in my own country I had grown up knowing that I lived on the right side of the railroad tracks and I think people's perception of sociological classifications, as of economic specifications or religious dogma, probably occurs at a very early age. Only children don't know what they are learning, and it becomes as close to inbred as can be. When I became an economist, I mused upon the fact that almost everyone in the United States, when asked, replied that he or she was middle class. And they meant middle income, too. I took it to be a Good Thing, one of the ways in which my country was a bit more democratic than England, and not until much later did I come to realize that one reason this response existed was that nobody really knew the facts. Very few people knew how their own yearly income compared to that of others. Figures weren't published (for the very good reason that they weren't collected in the first place), and what people had to go on was their perception of people around them, and of people whose life styles (although that term appeared decades later) differed significantly from theirs. Later on, when data about incomes became abundant, people had other problems of perception and understanding, ranging from pure disbelief ('if they only ask 60000 people how can they possibly get the facts about 180 million?') to confusion between income, wealth, money and earnings.

So as a card-carrying professional economist, I joined the faculty at Wellesley College. My first marriage had failed, and the need to be as much of a full-time parent to my two-year-old daughter as possible meant to me teaching, at least in the short run, to give me some flexibility over my working hours. In 1951 Wellesley College faculty, burdened with classes six days a week and giving six courses a term, were shamefully low-paid; except for a few senior professors or those with private means, everyone held two jobs. I was rescued from poverty by Ken Galbraith, who found me various projects for the Social Science Research Council, and my training as an economist continued. It seems laughable to think of research, given that kind of teaching load, but I had been appointed to teach British economic history, accounting, and something called consumer economics and just doing course preparations required getting acquainted with library resources and text supplements. After I remarried, my income rose sufficiently to quit the Harvard job, and I spent even more time pursuing my new interests.

First was the economics of consumption. I disapproved thoroughly of 'consumer economics' on the basis of every textbook I read. They were puerile in style and thought, asking students to prepare 'ideal' budgets for a variety of cases, they posed loaded questions about the value of advertising and the need for grade labeling; they were, in short, dreadful and I refused to admit this body of prejudice, misinformation and ninth-grade arithmetic into my field of economies. The entire field was, perhaps, a caricature of the normative judgments which I believed firmly were no part of the economist's toolbox. On the other hand, I had a class to meet. So began an exploration of two fields on which I concentrated heavily for almost 20 years. One was to explore consumer expenditures and saving, and I became acquainted with the wealth of existing survey data.

Wellesley's economics department has been blessed with scholars from the late nineteenth century. Katharine Coman, widely recognized by her peers, founded the department and as perhaps the first economic historian in this country did extensive research. Prominent in the founding of the American Economic Association, she wrote the first article in the first issue of the *American Economic Review* (Coman, 1911). And she entered subscriptions, for the Wellesley College library, to each economic periodical as it was created and ordered state and Federal reports on industry, banking, railroads, labor legislation, and all the rest. The collection of early works surpasses that in many universities and I had it all to myself. Not only did I devour every major study of income, expenditure, and saving from the Massachusetts study in 1875 carried out by Carroll Wright, who became the first administrator of the Bureau of Labor Statistics to those in 1950, but I also began learning about survey methodology and statistical analysis as fields of their own.

At the same time I tried to explore, with equal attention, the field of marketing and market research, at least as it applied to consumer goods and services. It had long seemed obvious to me that microeconomic analysis had a major omission. The consumer choice problem could be solved, and the consumer's income allocated according to rational decision-making rules and preferences. But economics didn't have anything to say about how the consumer went out and bought the things s/he had decided on. Equally, the producer decision problem could be solved: that level of production where marginal cost equaled marginal revenue would prove best for the firm with a variety of complications applicable for imperfect competition, innovation, and so forth. But economics had nothing to say about how the product, whatever it was, got from the firm to the buyer. Yet there was a whole sector of industry in the US economy known as distribution, there were Census data on retailing, wholesaling, and the distributive trades that weren't mentioned in economic analysis. The undergraduate course I evolved dealt with all these approaches to consumption and marketing and exposed students to the wealth of data and sources available in the business world as well as in economic journals. One unforeseen result was the number of very bright young women choosing marketing as a career, some to hold senior executive positions. And I still think economists err in giving so little attention to marketing and merchandising.

However, as an economist I realized that the standard micro model didn't really work: the pretense that the retailer sold a 'service' with its own costs failed to describe discounting, supermarkets, shopping malls, franchising and other innovations of the 1950s and 1960s. I developed a theory of retailing as a form of monopolistic competition, and was delighted that Chamberlin's model fitted so well. But I didn't know enough to submit a journal article, and so my analysis languished in a book which had some success as a text (Bell, 1967). That was also where I outlined my new knowledge about innovation in consumer goods industries gathered from field studies in the early 1960s, and explored the notion that consumers must also innovate when they adopt new products. Looking back, it is obvious that most of this book belonged as separate articles submitted to several different economic journals. When I first reappeared on the Cambridge scene, both Chamberlin and Galbraith had encouraged me to prepare an article from my dissertation and so my critique of the omissions in Schumpeter's theory had appeared in *The Quarterly Journal of Economics* (Bell, 1951). It has been widely quoted, although I abandoned the field because of the demands of my teaching. But after that I lacked any planned research agenda and wrote for publication when I thought I had something to say.

For example, before the book on consumer choice and marketing appeared, I wrote a small paper (Bell, 1960) using data from my husband's retail business to illustrate his understanding and sophisticated use of the elasticity of demand; he was also amiable when I acquainted him with this new term. Faced with potential competition from new outlets offering deep discounts, he had considered how far to discount his own prices in return, by calculating not the additional sales revenue from the potential prices but the changes in his gross margin which would result. His analysis imitated that of the textbook and came out with the same solutions – only in his business, with the costs of his merchandise determined by his suppliers, it was gross margin and not total sales that was the relevant variable.

Along with marketing, I developed my accounting course into something of a hybrid. Wellesley students, especially those majoring in economics, were keen workers and elegant thinkers; when I assigned a text used in graduate schools of business they promptly solved all the problems. I added some material on the structure of the national income accounts, which of course originate in the business accounting records of firms, and course attendance still throve. So we studied managerial decision-making, and, as economists, found cost accounting much more fun than financial analysis.

If I despaired that economists were neglecting merchandising, I was vastly amused by the general ignorance among economists about fairly simple accounting theory. A case in point was the controversy over whether real firms used marginal costing or maximized profits according to theory, and a well-publicized study purporting to show that full costing and rules of thumb were the way in which US business firms operated. If the researchers had learned cost accounting, they would have discovered that accountants' incremental costs are very much like marginal costs, and that accountants and managers know very well that pricing at less than full costs is preferable to discontinuing production, as long as prices cover variable costs in the short term. And neither my students nor I persuaded any of my colleagues to abandon their favorite examples of 'fixed' costs – rent and depreciation – since both could vary when space was paid for by a percentage of sales and equipment was leased, not owned.

A small contribution to the *American Economic Review* (Bell, 1960) came when I could no longer put up with the nonsensical version of accounting presented in most elementary texts; I wrote on depreciation and distinguished for the text writers the difference between expenses and expenditures, as well as the fallacy in identifying depreciation as a source of capital investment. Things have improved since that article, although I still think more economists should learn more accounting, particularly cost accounting and managerial decision-making. Some economic policies are more likely to be acceptable if they are designed with an eye to accounting rules, for example the investment tax credit, whose impact on current spending by firms depends on rulings by the accounting profession. The immediate result of the *AER* article was an invitation from Paul Samuelson to change the treatment of accounting in the sixth edition of his influential text, so I suppose my contribution to economic thought must include preventing some unknown number of economics students from referring blithely to 'depreciation as a source of investment.'

In the same way, my knowledge of patterns of consumption expenditure and of marketing stimulated a critique in the *American Economic Review* (Bell, 1968) of Baumol's distinction between the 'technologically progressive' sector and that of slow growth. Again, my article was picked up by others. Its insistence that measuring productivity in a 'service' activity like composing, cutting hair, or piloting a plane differs substantively from measuring productivity in an activity with a physical output like mining, farming, or manufacturing still holds true, although efforts to develop proxies for physical output have been fairly successful in some areas, like banking, insurance and certain government programs. But the major thrust of that article, that technological change in some sectors requires innovation by consumers equal to, or exceeding, that by producers has not been generally accepted.

Both then and now I have wished that more economists would take the time to explain productivity in education. Not merely because it is fashionable from time to time to bash college faculty for how little they do, and easy to recommend a doubling of the teaching load in order to cut costs. An economist, especially one as devoted to teaching as everyone on the faculty at Wellesley College was and presumably still is, can demonstrate better than most why such solutions are ineffective. To calculate faculty productivity requires first that there be a definition of faculty output. It presumably has something to do with a difference in students' knowledge or skills before and after faculty teaching. It might even be called 'education.' One can elaborate and sketch a production function with several inputs including laboratory equipment, library resources, faculty time in and out of the classroom, staff assistance, and so on. But any teacher will add to this list 'and student effort.' In fact, of course, education requires *student* input, hard work spent learning. And since faculty do not and cannot control student *learning*, it is quite absurd to expect them to be able to increase their productivity.

Although as a child I had thought teaching was the last thing on earth I would ever want to do, I found at Wellesley that I thoroughly enjoyed what I was doing. Wellesley students were extremely bright and well prepared, and the college grew more selective as its deserved reputation for excellence rose. Faculty salaries and workload became competitive and young colleagues joining us from big universities began to say that a senior seminar at Wellesley worked at a higher level than many graduate courses. As for economics, it had long been a strong department ranking in the first four or five choices of undergraduate majors. Our commitment to teaching meant that every one on the economics faculty taught the first-year course, which we believed to be our most influential offering. By the 1970s very few students graduated from Wellesley without studying economics for at least one term.

It was fairly early on that I learned, however, that 'teaching' is the wrong verb – nobody can teach anyone anything, all we can do is help others learn. My ideas about how best to help people learn economics stemmed first from my observation that most professional economists spend a lot, if not most, of their time talking, and therefore that students could learn by talking economics. Accordingly, my classes consisted sometimes of general uproar with people offering analysis, criticism, new facts or insights, sharp contradictions, and the occasional clarification or provocation from me. I cultivated all sorts of ways in which to encourage such open discussion and discovered that it led to real learning. And although some Wellesley students shunned my courses because they knew they would be forced to talk, others thrived. One result: a woman holding a PhD in economics is more likely to have a BA from Wellesley than from any other undergraduate institution, allowing for size of the student body. Unfortunately, the vitally important undergraduate degree is often scanted in public knowledge; I have more than once chided a newspaper reporter or editor for noting that a newly appointed official has a Harvard Law degree but not a Wellesley economics degree. This neglect appears more often with women than with men, whose undergraduate degree is far more frequently noted.

Taken for granted in my teaching, as in my life, has been the knowledge that a woman can do everything that a man can do, except for biological functions, and so Wellesley students escaped the nonsense that economics is a man's field. My daughter grew up knowing that little boys can do everything little girls can do except have babies, and that little girls can do everything little boys can do except make babies. The economics of this, of course, means that the labor market or the supply of human resources expands significantly with the disappearance of discrimination or misguided notions of 'natural' abilities or preferences among women instead of among individuals. And although I reveled in seeing a young woman change from being a student to becoming a young economist, I remained committed to liberal arts education as my primary loyalty. When a brilliant student who'd done well in graduate school and seemed headed for economic research dropped everything and went to divinity school I was delighted, as I was by the young business executive, whose firm had paid for her MBA, who quit her job to write poetry and give successful classes in public schools developing fifth- and sixth-grade awareness of poetry. Nonetheless, my work consisted in helping people learn economics, and quite often they helped me in my learning as well.

One case took place in the 1960s. After the race riots of the mid-1960s I led a seminar on the economics of the ghetto, and focused the students' attention on small local areas, studied by means of the data in the Census tracts, using the Census of 1960 and the mid-decade updates. Students pored over the data for urban Census tracts, differing only by race but otherwise comparable in median income, age and sex distribution, and other variables. Their analysis showed, over and over again, a much wider distribution of income in the minority tracts than in the white. And of course over the next 20 years the ghettos became pockets of highly concentrated poverty as the middle- and upper-income blacks moved out. I counted my own personal success in the comments of two black students in the course who came to me at its end and confessed they'd elected it planning to sneer at the 'middle-aged white lady who'd never lived in a ghetto' but had been astonished at the depths of their own ignorance revealed by the data from the Census and other statistical sources. But a more tangible result was a monograph *The Economics of the Ghetto* (Bell, 1974) which, unbelievably, failed to sell because of a corporate merger. Some 10000 volumes languished on the shelf, real-life examples of frozen assets, unable to move during negotiations. And since it was a trade book, it didn't sell the next year because it was 'out of date.'

By this time I had also begun writing Op Ed articles in the *Wall Street Journal*, the *New York Times*, the *Los Angeles Times*, and also to present testimony before Congressional committees. I thought it important to try to explain technical points that people needed to understand in order to consider policy actions, and I dealt with a wide range of issues. I became known as a woman economist (and we were more rare then than now), although I continually maintained that I was a professional economist who happened to be a woman. But that is another story, of some complexity. What amazed me was how easy it was to become 'famous.' I'd been invited to speak at a Washington conference in the late 1960s, and had planned an attack on those who were then arguing that women's unemployment should probably be discounted, since it was less important than that of men. I wrote to three economics reporters urging them to cover the conference and promising I would name names in my criticism (including the then Secretary of the Treasury). They came, they referred to me in print as a 'nationally known economist' and my public career was launched.

Much of my work has been concerned with clarifying definitions and data, as in the late 1960s and early 1970s when I became irritated with the treatment of women's employment in the popular press, the economic journals, and policy discussions in Washington. The general assumption throughout was that women's earnings were supplemental to family income, that women's employment was a function of husband's earnings and the presence of children, and that policy should be developed for the typical family which consisted of a man supporting a wife at home and two children. Contradictory evidence existed for all these, but it was buried in the fine print and in the tables at the back of government releases. For example, the unemployment rate for married men was always shown as an indicator of the severity of joblessness. I pointed out that there were some millions of married women whose earnings supported the family, and other millions who were household heads in the absence of a husband. At one public event where I spoke, mentioning some of these facts, I was complimented later by the then Secretary of Labor. He was astonished at my findings and asked with great respect about my research. I gave him the page number (way at the back) of the Department of Labor periodical which regularly reported the data.

Part of the problem was the insistence on one simple model, ignoring all the actual data. Thus the assumption that women were married and their work was necessarily supplemental to the 'male provider' omitted the group of respectable single women, numbering millions, who had never married and had always held jobs and who, in growing numbers, sometimes supported their elderly parents. As the divorce rate soared (or gained more public awareness) all sorts of sloppy thinking appeared suggesting that women's employment threatened the family, or that the children of working mothers were destined for poor grades in school and later delinquency. None of these were, of course, supported by data.

The 'single mother on welfare' phenomenon was a separate case, although in 1973 (Bell, 1973) I had identified this group as posing a major, and growing, economic problem and in 1980 (Bell, 1980) I published the first quantitative analysis calling attention to the increase of poverty among children. At a time when the number of children was dropping at the end of the baby boom, and the number and percentage of people in poverty was also dropping, the absolute number of poor children was on the rise, and drew little public notice despite the efforts of many. I thought getting the facts out would help solve the problem, but it's not that easy. People continue believing economic myths long after they have been shattered.

It was early in the 1970s that I was asked by Eileen Shanahan, then economics reporter for the *New York Times* about the typical family consisting of a man supporting a wife and two children. 'How typical is this?' asked Eileen, and I had to tell her that I didn't know; nor did anyone. But it set me working.

First, I went through all the published data in an effort to extract more than the conventional tabulations showed. The result was published in the *Eastern Economics Journal* in 1974 (Bell, 1974). Although I knew that I had made every allowance possible for incomplete data, and that my assumptions were extremely conservative, I was nevertheless terrified at my finding that fewer than 10 percent of the families fitted the definition of what was thought to be typical. Adding all the cases where the husband's income supported a wife and children still kept the number of such families below 25 percent. (Of course, nobody could contradict me because they didn't have any hard data either.) But I knew that actual numbers, not estimates, were already available to BLS from the income data of its annual supplement to the Current Population Survey. So my next step was to talk with friends at the Bureau, and try to persuade them to present a new tabulation. This finally happened in 1976.

With accurate counting, the 'typical family' was in fact a minority. Although television shows and the famous children's reading series about

Dick and Jane relied on the man supporting a wife and two children, such families accounted for 7 percent of the total when they were first counted. When BLS notified me (they mailed me a printout) of this before issuing their press release, I was elated and thought instantly 'How can I spread the word?' Not, you note, how can I use this in a scholarly article, replete with references to labor market analysis and income theory, but how can I change popular thinking? My solution was to call the editor of *Newsweek*'s feature, 'My Turn,' and ask her how many families she thought consisted of a man supporting a wife and two children. 'Oh, at least half, is it sixty percent?' When I quoted my figures she gasped, and agreed instantly to publish a column, which I duly submitted (Bell, 1977). It got a lot of attention, given that the readership of *Newsweek* vastly exceeds that of the *AER* or any other economic journal. But I also thought it a more useful presentation, in that all kinds of people, not just economists, became acquainted with the facts.

I have been amused by the way in which this news, about the demise of the typical family, has spread. Some two or three years after my *Newsweek* article it was fairly common to learn of a speaker or a newly published article about some piece of 'research' which had established that the 'typical family' no longer existed. Since I had thought getting the facts straight, and spreading the word as widely as possible, were both far more important than getting 'credit,' I never objected. All the same I was impressed when Professor Mary Ann Glendon, now of Harvard Law School, tracked me down because she knew that the earliest published mention of this fact was under my name. She telephoned apologetically; she had been quite unable, she said, to find any other bibliographic record and could I give her the name of the scholarly publication I had written, so that she could footnote it accurately? I told her my story and she joined in glee over having *Newsweek* cited in a *Law Review* footnote.

Much of my published work has presented available data cast in new forms, or asking different questions. My central interest continues to be income, and the distribution of income among people. Thus when a special volume of research on the economic implications of the minimum wage was being put together I contributed an analysis of the income provided by minimum wage workers (Bell, 1981), the second such analysis to appear in a literature replete with research about the employment effect of such wages. It was criticized because it did not replicate the methodology of the first researcher, who used simulated income data, but I preferred the more awkward facts of the Current Population Survey of real people living in real families.

I fault economists for not being sufficiently concerned with the basic data and the way they are collected, rather than with the measurement of income change, income inequality, poverty measures and all the rest. Whether the data are suitable for such analyses is rarely discussed. Primarily I disagree with the overwhelming agreement on using the family or household as the central unit of analysis. Income originates, after all, in production, and very few productive efforts consist of family activity. I have made the point repeatedly; aside from the Flying Wallendas and a very few farms or firms, *families* do not get paychecks; individuals do. Earning income as an individual follows from the fact that, absent illegal slavery, wages paid for labor belong to the worker. As for the ownership of capital, the basic unit again is the individual although a wide variety of arrangements for combining individuals, including joint ownership trusts, and common property exist. That individuals live together and share their incomes is, of course, undisputed but adds nothing to the *economic* analysis of income.

In addition, the wide use of survey data has also not led to as much enlightenment as it should. Surveys by definition take snapshots of the situation at one point in time; the findings of a survey two months, two years, or two decades later, since they refer to a different set of people altogether, can only be compared to those earlier in a limited way. That median or mean incomes in one year are higher than those of a previous year does not allow us to say anything about how incomes have risen for any individual or any group of individuals. On the other hand, for the individual, income change over time brings probably the most significant economic events possible. It follows that data from longitudinal surveys should be more frequently used and that longitudinal studies should be designed, funded, carried through and analyzed.

Finally, the other major defect in the economists' tacit agreement to use the family or household as a unit of analysis is its failure to acknowledge human development. All economists lived in other families when they were children than they did when they first studied economics, or when they became professionals in the field. Each of us moves from one family situation to another during our lifetime, or has our family situation change around us. Consequently it seems obvious to me that the individual is the only stable unit which exists: maximizing the household utility function or the family lifetime income stream, seems absurd on the face of it.

When you add to this kind of analysis the facts about change in US families over the past generation, it is beyond me why economists continue to present stories and models and data showing family income or anything else. Family *composition* today includes a broader variety of types than previously: single-parent families, two-generation families with an adult child caring for adult parents or other relatives, couples with no children, married couples with children from one, two, or more previous marriages, and same-sex couples with or without children but with the same kind of commitment and attitude (and economic behavior) as those 'related by blood, marriage, or adoption,' to quote the Census definition of a family. Average family size has dwindled over time, although to birth, death and adoption have been added the changes when adult children move out or move back in. The first published volume of findings from the Panel Study of Income Dynamics (Morgan et al., 1974) emphasized that changes in family composition and labor force participation dominated all other variables in explaining changes in, or the level of, family income over time and, of course, labor force participation for a *family* is itself a matter of composition. This finding is still true, and my most recent article (Bell, 1996) contains yet another presentation of the harmful effects of ignoring it. And the dynamics of change for one family consists of decisions and actions by one or more *individuals*. All this rich behavior is specifically and purposely ignored by the sterile approach of the so-called New Household Economists, but it has also been overlooked by more mainstream analysts.

So what is my philosophy of economics? That this particular specialty provides clues to understanding human activities and human events which are best studied with empirical data. That an economist should know as much about primary sources and methodology of data collection as about theory or history. That economists, all of them, share a teaching responsibility, a duty to explain for general public understanding what they know or have discovered about how an economy works and in particular about how to design or evaluate economic policy. That, although economists do not provide a value-free science, they do at least try hard to separate out value questions from those of pure analysis. An economist has no more knowledge of the 'best' choice between a little more unemployment or a little more inflation than anyone else. We may be able to suggest which is the more likely *outcome* in a given situation, but our preference for one over the other should carry no more weight than our preference for green olives over black.

I am not averse to stating my own economic preferences or my value judgments. Every individual has some capacity to produce, to be useful, to do something useful; personal development consists largely in exploring and developing such capacities. It follows that I think each of us should be economically independent, that is, able to earn wages by working or being productive in some way. Of course one must allow for temporary difficulties or disabilities, and the emergencies whose burdens should be shared, not individually borne. I believe that no person, man or woman, has the right to bring another person into the world unless the parent is financially and emotionally ready and able to support the new human being and raise it alone, if necessary. I think most of us are born with a rich inheritance of human capital although inequalities exist, and I think that each of us has a duty to provide society with a return on the capital it has invested in us. I think more effort can be useful in improving the design of societal and governmental institutions but I hope the basic social culture of my country continues to keep the individual central to its thinking and its policy decisions.

I think these statements sound like economics, and are couched in economic terms because that is the way I think. That's what I meant back in the beginning of this piece, explaining my title of thinking like an economist.

At the same time I have always been fascinated by the readiness with which many people contradict or attempt to refute statements by economists. We lack the respect automatically granted to, say, nuclear physicists or molecular biologists when they talk about their fields. Nobody thinks to argue a biochemist's explanation of the primordial soup or a physicist's of gravitational force, but equally factual or explanatory statements about the size of the average Federal income tax, the number of workers laid off in recent months, or the effect of a change in Federal Reserve policy will be greeted with frank disbelief or a condescending divulgement of TRUTH. I think this attitude on the part of the public springs partly from the enormous amount of jargon and misinformation now current in the daily press and other media. I used to tell my students 'Try to write dull! don't use colorful adjectives to describe economic variables!' but the admonition has never been heard by those writing for the printed page, where the dollar 'is beaten down' by the yen or mark, where municipal bonds 'stage a rally,' the price index 'plunges' and wages 'stagnate.' What is 'strong' about the dollar exchange rate and what is 'stagnant' about unchanged incomes? Nobody ever explains. By contrast, an economist describing these events relies wholly on extremely precise definitions and the rigorous application of equally precise concepts. On balance, it is probably much easier to teach economists how to be journalists than to expect journalists to learn economics.

I have also argued that the professional has a responsibility to the general public, which is very poorly carried out if at all, to help people understand economic facts or economic reasoning. There is no excuse for people *still* talking about 'the elderly living on fixed incomes' given that since 1972 when Social Security payments were indexed the elderly have been the one group in the populace assured of changing incomes in response to changing prices. There is no excuse for people counting only the costs of immigration and not the contributions of workers, of new skills, of added output and added taxes. There is no excuse for a Presidential candidate to say, and his audience to applaud, that people are working because they have to work to pay Federal taxes; the bulk of taxes are levied on income. Comparative advantage and the benefits of the division of labor, limited only by the size of the market, is no more difficult to comprehend today than when I read Adam Smith years ago. People can understand with proper explanation how universal health insurance can lead to lower costs and how anything less can lead to perverse outcomes. The ramifications of 'there's no such thing as a free lunch' should be more familiar: attendance soars at state colleges and universities because students and their parents believe they cost less than private IHLs, and like other taxpayers know little about the subsidies they are providing to people whose incomes would provide a much greater contribution to the cost of their education.

Above all, economists should tell people how they can find out for themselves, they can urge people to buy *The Statistical Abstract of the United States* and to lobby their public libraries to subscribe to as many reliable basic data sources as possible. With more and more such information available on the Internet, people should be set free from the limitations of what politicians or lobbyists or pundits tell them.

REFERENCES

Bell, Carolyn Shaw, 'A Critique of the Schumpeterian Theory' (under my former name of Carolyn Shaw Solo), *Quarterly Journal of Economics*, **LXV**:3 (August 1951).

———, 'Economics and Depreciation Accounting,' *American Economic Review*, **L**:1 (March, 1960).

———, 'On the Elasticity of Demand at Retail,' *American Journal of Economics and Sociology*, **XX**:1 (October 1960).

———, *Consumer Choice in the American Economy*, New York, Random House, 1967.

———, 'Macroeconomics and Unbalanced Growth,' *American Economic Review*, **LVIII**:4 (September, 1968).

———, 'Age, Sex, Marriage, and Jobs,' *The Public Interest*, #30 (Winter 1973).

———, 'Working Women's Contribution to Family Income,' *Eastern Economic Journal*, **I**:2/3 (Summer 1974).

———, *The Economics of the Ghetto*, New York, Western Publishing Company, 1974.

———, 'Let's Get Rid of Families!' *Newsweek, My Turn*, May 1977.

———, 'Economic Data, Policy-Making and the Law,' *Boston College Law Review*, **XXI**:5 (July 1980).

———, 'Minimum Wages and Personal Income,' *The Economics of Legal Minimum Wages* (ed. Simon Rottenberg), Washington, DC, American Enterprise Institute for Public Policy Research, 1981.

———, 'Data on Race, Ethnicity, and Gender: Caveats for the User,' *International Labor Review*, Vol. 135 (1996, No. 5).

Coman, Katharine, 'Some Unsettled Problems of Irrigation,' *The American Economic Review*, **I**:1 (March 1911).

Galbraith, John Kenneth, *A Theory of Price Control*, Cambridge, Harvard University Press, 1952.

Keynes, John Maynard, *The General Theory of Employment Interest and Money*, New York, Harcourt Brace, 1936.

Morgan, James, and Katherine Dickinson, Jonathan Dickinson, Jacob Benus and Greg Duncan, *Five Thousand American Families – Patterns of Economic Progress*, Ann Arbor, Michigan, The University of Michigan Press, 1974.

Smiles, Samuel, *The Huguenots*, 1876, *Self Help*, 1881, *Lives of the Engineers* (5 vols), 1904.

Taussig, F.W., *Principles of Economics*, New York, The Macmillan Company, 1913.

Young, Arthur, *Tours in England and Wales (Selected from The Annals of Agriculture, 1792–1808),* London, London School of Economics and Political Science, No. 14 in Series of Reprints on Scarce Tracts in Economic and Political Science, 1932.

4. Pushing for a more humane society

Barbara R. Bergmann

Like most economists, I came to the profession not through any great interest in the actual economy itself. Rather, I enjoyed studying and creating models of simple processes that might or might not resemble what goes on in the actual economy – a form, really, of recreational mathematics. However, as time went on, I became interested as well in working on issues of race, gender and poverty in the economy, and the social policy questions these issues raised. I have been able to use my standing as an economist, and even a bit here and there of my economics training, to write on these matters, and, I hope, to make a contribution to the eventual achievement of a more humane world.

I was born in 1927 in the Bronx. I became an atheist at age four, when I failed to receive a minor favor I had prayed for and believed I deserved. It then occurred to me that nobody was up there listening. I became a feminist (a person who believes in working toward the equality of women and men) at age five, when it became obvious to me that you needed your own money to be an independent person, which was what I wanted to be when I grew up.

My grandparents had come to the United States from Eastern Europe in the huge wave of immigration prior to 1914, fleeing anti-Semitism. Neither of my parents stayed in school through high school, because their families needed the money they could earn. One of my mother's sisters had been sent to work at seven, and never learned to read and write. But for my generation there were better hopes. We were expected by our parents to integrate seamlessly into American life and succeed financially. The hope for a boy was that he would become a lawyer or a doctor, and the hope for a girl was that she would marry a lawyer or a doctor. We were encouraged to look forward to going to college, which was realistic, because New York City provided tuition-free public colleges, a prestigious one for boys and a lesser one for girls. We were pressed very hard to do well in school.

My father was a union typesetter and earned a good wage of $50 a week all through the Great Depression of the 1930s, so we were not in want. However, the unemployment rate was about 25 percent, and the terrible state of much of the populace was obvious, even to a child in elementary school. I had two male cousins who were about ten years older than I was, and who were unable to find jobs after they left high school. Their pride and morale were destroyed.

When World War II came, they were taken into the army, and that experience, plus the jobs they found in the prosperous post-war economy, saved them.

My most vivid single memory of the depression is of a middle-aged man who walked into our neighborhood one day carrying a violin, a bow, and a battered wooden folding chair. He set the chair on the sidewalk outside our apartment house, sat down, and played several pieces. People listening through open windows in the apartments above threw down pennies. After he had picked up the coins, he made an announcement in a loud voice: he said he would give the violin, the bow, and the chair to anyone who would get him a job. It was the inclusion of the chair that I found, and still find, most poignant.

My childhood during the Great Depression left me a strong believer in having government provide help when people face problems either beyond their power to control, as was the case during the depression, or because they have made improvident choices, or because they have legitimate needs that they cannot supply out of their own resources. There was a brief period, when I was about 17, when I became very vain about my own intelligence and prospects. I hated the idea that the riches I felt sure to earn during my glorious future career might be taxed away by the government and transferred to those less talented and less hardworking than I. It was a brief spasm of immaturity and selfishness, and soon passed off. I have been left of center in my politics ever since.

But I never became a devotee of Marxism, or an advocate of getting rid of capitalism. That I probably owe to the teacher I had in the sixth grade of my Bronx public school. She was a Communist, and a fanatical admirer of Stalin's Russia. That was obvious, even to a 12-year-old, because she dragged Russia into our lessons on all subjects on the slightest pretext.

The New York World's Fair went on that year, and our class was taken to visit it. The most popular exhibit was put on by General Motors, showing the marvelous capitalist world of the future, an auto-dominated landscape, all in miniature, through which one rode, seated on a moving sofa. The Russians also had a huge exhibit at the fair, and our teacher saw to it that our class spent much of our time there. In one corner of each room of the Russian exhibit building was a mammoth piece of agricultural equipment. As I recall it, most of the rest of the space was devoted to the iconography of Stalin. He was depicted in paintings, in bas reliefs, in busts and in full-length statues. In addition, there were plates and cups with Stalin's picture, spoons with his picture on the bowl, and other spoons with his picture on the handle. The exhibit was both disgusting and boring. Spending a school year in the class of that teacher inoculated me for life against admiring any such regime, and taught me to beware of fanatics.

Even today, among many of the academic people I know, 'capitalism' is a term of opprobrium, and they attribute to capitalism everything bad that happens. A lot of what is bad does come from capitalism, but that can be corrected by appropriate government regulations, and by the generous government provision of important services and safety nets. But a lot of what is good and indispensable comes from capitalism too.

From high school, I applied to MIT, but was rejected, probably because the alumnus who interviewed me thought my stated ambition to become an engineer was ridiculous. I won a scholarship to Cornell University, where I majored in mathematics. While in college, I read Gunnar Myrdal's book *An American Dilemma*, which presented in painful detail the racial regime that at that time prevailed in the southern part of the United States. Myrdal's book told how African Americans could not eat in most restaurants, except perhaps outside the back door, or buy a seat in movie theaters, except perhaps in the balcony. It told how, at the peril of his life, a black man had to address all white men as 'boss', and how he would customarily be addressed as 'boy'. It told how blacks were not allowed to vote. And it told how any white could kill any black, without fear of legal consequences. Of course, it told about the pervasive discrimination by race in access to jobs that was part and parcel of the Southern states' racial regime. Myrdal's book sparked a lasting interest in race discrimination, which was later extended to an interest in sex discrimination.

I graduated with a BA in 1948, and went back to living with my mother in New York. She was quite angry at me for not having 'caught' a husband, and told me so frequently. Women used to say at that time, quite matter-of-factly, and without overt resentment, 'It's a man's world.' My mother didn't like that fact, but she felt that for a successful life one had to conform. As she said to me, 'You're nothing without a man.' I resented it, though, and it strengthened my feminist propensities.

I had graduated in the midst of the first post-World War II recession, and jobs were scarce. I had two other strikes against me in finding one. In those days, there was discrimination against Jews, and the want ads were segregated by sex under 'Help Wanted, Male' and 'Help Wanted, Female'. All of the latter were for maids, department store salesladies and clerical workers. I looked for a job for months in the male category, never getting a nibble. In desperation, I took a job in the female category, typing names and addresses, but couldn't endure the boredom for more than two days. (People ask me whether I myself have ever been discriminated against. My answer is, 'Of course, from beginning to end.') Luckily, I had applied for a job with the federal government, and that finally came through. I was taken in on the lowest professional rung at the New York office of the Bureau of Labor Statistics, where I was part of the unit that answered inquiries from the public.

After a year I was the head of the inquiries unit. At BLS I found that race discrimination was not confined to the South. There was just one black employee at the New York City office at that time. His name was Harvey Purdy, and he was the lowest person on the office totem pole – he ran the mimeograph machine and distributed the mail. Our unit had a vacancy, and I got Harvey appointed to it. But it was decreed that he couldn't sit with the rest of us, where the members of the public who came into our office could see him. He had to sit next door in the stock room, where we kept the spare copies of publications, and take inquirers' phone calls. He didn't hold the job long. It was decreed that somebody else was to have that job, and Harvey had to go back to the mimeograph machine. I tried to get the unit that surveyed wages to take him on, but its head said that cooperation with our survey was voluntary, and businessmen wouldn't want to be giving wage information to the likes of Harvey. That was in 1950. When I was working in Washington in 1962, by which time the civil rights movement had been in progress for a decade and was in full flower, I happened to visit the people in the wage survey branch in the central office of BLS. I told them Harvey's story, expecting that they would say that such things were no longer tolerated. To my surprise, these very nice people told me, in a matter-of-fact way and with no sign of guilt or regret, that they still 'needed' to follow the same practice.

By and large, the people who worked for the Bureau of Labor Statistics were able and conscientious. The experience of working there left me with a good impression of government employees and government operations, and of the capabilities of government agencies. Many years later, in the early 1980s, while teaching at the University of Maryland, I was writing a monthly column for the *New York Times* Sunday business section. I wrote in one of them that a lot of government workers were capable and hard-working people. The young *Times* editor who went over my columns said I should omit that. His impression was entirely opposite: government employees were stupid and loafed all the time. He could see them leaning on their shovels as he rode to work every day. This anti-government attitude was starting at that time to become widespread. Based on my own experience with BLS, and later with other government agencies, I believe it is in many cases based on false impressions. Unfortunately, it feeds the reluctance to use government as a means of providing needed services.

While I was working for the BLS in New York, an economist came into the office looking for data and we got into friendly conversation. He asked me whether my job left time for 'doing my own work.' I told him I hadn't the vaguest idea what he meant, and he said he was talking about the economic research he assumed I would be wanting to do. He said I ought to apply to graduate school, and after thinking it over, I did. My BLS boss wrote a letter of recommendation saying I was 'a young lady of culture and refinement.' I don't know whether that helped or hurt my chances, but probably thanks to my math degree I was admitted to Harvard.

At Harvard, my future work was most influenced by Guy Orcutt, who introduced economists to computer simulation. Later, when teaching at the University of Maryland, which provided extraordinarily free access to a mainframe computer, I co-authored a book entitled *A Microsimulated Transactions Model of the United States Economy*, in which simulated individuals, businesses, governments and banks make trades of commodities and capital instruments for money. The model went beyond traditional methods of dealing with macroeconomy, in which equations with macro variables are constructed on the basis of loose verbal analogies to supposedly valid microeconomic equations. Given the amount of pain and suffering inflicted by recessions, macroeconomics is the most important field of economic study, and deserves more rigorous methods. Microsimulation provides rigor, realism and an ability to incorporate complexities revealed by more empirical investigations into the workings of business.

I remember fondly three then-famous professors at Harvard whose reputations have since vanished. Alvin Hansen was the leading expositor of Keynesian macroeconomics, and a strong voice for vigorous government action to keep the economy on an even keel. I still share his hope that economics could be used for human betterment. I much appreciated Gottfried Haberler's crystal-clear writing style and have tried hard to emulate it. Edward Chamberlin was the author of *The Theory of Monopolistic Competition*, an attempt to get away from the never-never land of perfect competition, and to describe the messier and more complex real-world phenomena of product differentiation and oligopoly.

Chamberlin was also a pioneer in experimental economics. He had the students in his class run a market experiment, making deals with each other. The average price usually turned out to be different than the price that would equalize supply and demand. The lesson I took from Chamberlin's market experiment was that theory, no matter how seemingly persuasive, no matter how clever and logically tight, no matter how revered by generations of economists, might well provide a misleading picture of the actual functioning of the economy and needed to be confronted by observation.

That lesson of skepticism I was able to apply to Gary Becker's theory that race and sex discrimination in employment, if ever they appeared, could not long persist. He claimed that any employer who discriminated would be driven out of business by competitors who didn't discriminate, who would be able to hire labor cheaper, and produce the product at a lower price, drawing away all the customers of the discriminating employer. Becker's theory, neat but totally negated by the facts, gained wide acceptance among economists, and continues to be quoted with approval today. Most economists are not capable of seeing that wage setting and other employment practices were and are affected by societal systems of status differences, whether in the brutally harsh regime of the pre-civil rights southern United States as described by Myrdal, or in the subtler regimes of race and sex favoritism that are still in force everywhere today. They are trained to explain all business behavior on the basis of simple profit maximization.

In my book *The Economic Emergence of Women* I used actual examples of discriminatory behavior derived from the records of lawsuits against large employers that had been brought under the Civil Rights Act as evidence that it did indeed exist. (As I write this in 2003, evidence of still-existing sex discrimination is being provided by lawsuits against Morgan Stanley, a leading Wall Street firm, and Walmart, the largest employer of women in the United States.) It has been customary among economists to brand that kind of evidence 'anecdotal', and of no consequence. My own view is that true anecdotes may well contain more valuable information about the state of things in the world than do economists' theories, which are by and large nothing but (possibly untrue) stories made up by economists sitting in their offices, with no factual input whatever.

More generally, as time has gone on, I have come to believe that the methodology of advancing economic science needs radical revision. Economics fails to advance because we economists have cut ourselves off from doing any real observing. When we decide to work on some topic – the rate of interest, consumers' saving behavior, foreign exchange rates, business behavior in setting prices or wages or making investments – we don't try to look around the world to see what is actually going on. Instead, we retire to our studies and think up some simple version of what might be going on. There is an 'empirical' side to economic research but it is very underdeveloped. We don't actually observe people dealing with the matters we are interested in, or, God forbid, ask them what they think they are doing, and how they make their decisions. Rather, we look at some numbers that have been generated or at least influenced by their activities and try to see whether those numbers are consistent with the theory we have thought up. Actually, we don't look at the numbers themselves, but at computed summaries of them ground out by a regression program.

I believe economists should do more survey research, and should adopt anthropological methods: become participant observers of business behavior. I regret that I have not had the courage or entrepreneurship to try to start a group of economists and students who would go out and observe business behavior and write up what they found. I am glad to see that there is some movement in the profession in that direction, led by Alan Blinder, who had done survey work on price setting, Truman Bewley, who has interviewed employers about wage setting, and David Card and Alan B. Krueger, who looked to see the effects on fast-food employment of rises in the minimum wage. All of them have found behavior not predicted by standard theories.

Aided and abetted by my husband, a microbiologist who cheerfully shared household chores and child care, I have been able to produce a series of books on issues of social policy mostly concerning race and gender. *The Economic Emergence of Women* explains why sex roles have changed so greatly in the last century, and what policies are needed to accommodate that revolution, surely ranking with the French Revolution in importance in human affairs. *In Defense of Affirmative Action* explains why discrimination and exclusion by race and sex won't go away without quotas. *Saving Our Children from Poverty: What the United States Can Learn from France* shows what a country that is determined to give every child a decent upbringing and education can do, and what the budgetary cost of doing it in the United States would be. I teamed up with an artist to put together *Is Social Security Broke?: A Cartoon Guide to the Issues*. The answer to the question, contrary to what the politicians of both parties have been saying, is that Social Security is not broke, and does not now need fixing. The most recent book I have published, *America's Child Care Problem: The Way Out*, labels subsidized child care as one of the country's chief unmet needs, and proposes a $50 billion a year program of government subsidies and quality regulations.

My next project is a book on single mothers, now 20 percent of all American mothers. The book will discuss the history of the treatment of single mothers, why their numbers are increasing, and what must be done to enable these mothers and their children to live a decent life. The answer, I will suggest, is not a return to sub-poverty-level cash payments on condition that these mothers refrain from paid work. Rather, it is the establishment of programs (open to all, in which single mothers can take part without stigma) providing health care, good-quality child care, and access to higher education. All of these are services which most single mothers cannot finance out of their own earnings. In other words, I am advocating that the United States, which currently devotes 30 percent of GDP to public expenditure, become more like France which devotes 45 percent, and Sweden which devotes 60 percent. That doesn't look very probable now, and I'm not counting on living long enough to see it happen. But as long as I can, I'm trying to keep doing work that nudges that good cause along.

REFERENCES

Bennett, Robert and Barbara R. Bergmann, *A Microsimulated Transactions Model of the United States Economy*, Baltimore: Johns Hopkins University Press, 1985.

Bergmann, Barbara R., *The Economic Emergence of Women,* New York: Basic Books, 1986.

Bergmann, Barbara R., *In Defense of Affirmative Action,* New York: Basic Books, Inc., 1996.

Bergmann, Barbara R., *Saving Our Children From Poverty: What the United States Can Learn From France*, New York: Russell Sage Foundation, 1996.

Bergmann, Barbara R., *Is Social Security Broke?: A Cartoon Guide to the Issues* (cartoons by Jim Bush), Ann Arbor, MI: University of Michigan Press, 2000.

Chamberlin, Edward, *The Theory of Monopolistic Competition; A Re-Orientation of the Theory of Value*, Cambridge, MA: Harvard University Press, 1962.

Helburn, Suzanne and Barbara R. Bergmann, *America's Child Care Problem: The Way Out*. New York: Palgrave St Martin's Press, 2002.

Myrdal, Gunnar, with the assistance of Richard Sterner and Arnold Rose, *An American Dilemma: The Negro Problem and Modern Democracy*, New York: Harper & Brothers, 1944.

5. Not only an economist – autobiographical reflections of a historian of economic thought*

Mark Blaug

I owe the decision to study economics to the influence of the writings of Henry George and Karl Marx. In 1944 I was 17 years old and attending Peter Stuyvesant High School in New York City. I enrolled for a course in commerce, and in the last week of the term the teacher took some of the better students, who included me, to a special lecture at a nearby Henry George School. The lecture was an explanation of why the unrestrained growth of land rentals had produced poverty, wars, and all the other ills of modern civilization. Henry George had long ago provided both the diagnosis of the evil and the treatment that would cure it: a single confiscatory tax on ground rent! At the end of the lecture, we were all presented with free copies of Henry George's *Progress and Poverty*, which I duly read without understanding much of it. But years later, when I finally studied the Ricardian theory of differential rent, I did have a moment of excitement at discovering the true source of George's theory.

THE INFLUENCE OF MARXISM

I was intrigued by *Progress and Poverty* but I was not entirely convinced. But shortly afterwards, during my first year at New York University, I became friendly with some left-wing students who introduced me first to the pamphlets of Lenin and Stalin and later to the weightier tomes of Marx and Engels. I was completely bowled over by these writings and within a matter of months became a Marxist, that is, an avowed follower of Marx.

When I now try to recall just what it was about Marxist writings that converted me so quickly, I think it was a combination of qualities that says as much about me as about Marxism. First, it was the aura of the absolute conviction of possession of the truth that radiated from every page of the

*This chapter first appeared in *The American Economist*, **38**(2), Fall 1994, 12–27.

writings the leading Marxists, accentuated in the case of Lenin and Stalin by their dogmatic and abusive tone towards their intellectual opponents. Second, it was the encyclopaedic range of Marxist theory, the sense that here was a universal science of society and indeed a philosophy of history as well as a philosophy of nature; whether it was the latest political election result, or the causes of the French Revolution, or the overthrow of the matriarchy in ancient Greece, or why Rembrandt was so partial to chiaroscuro, or why Beethoven's last piano sonata Op. 102 consisted of only two movements, or what Goethe meant by the ending of *Faust*, it could all be explained by Marxism. I was always a bit of a smart alec when I was young and Marxism was made to order for me: it allowed me to pontificate on every subject with a cock-sureness that suited me perfectly.

Marxism taught me economic determinism, that is, the idea that economic interests and economic forces are the foundations of all social and political conflicts. It followed that economics is the queen of all social sciences because everything is ultimately reducible to economics. Within six months of becoming a Marxist, I had therefore decided that I had to master economics. I took my first course in economics in my second year of university and I keenly remember finding it a rather taxing subject. I am glad that I can still remember my own difficulties in learning economics because it has made me a better teacher as a result.

Even all this does not fully account for my attraction to Marxism. The real appeal of Marxism for me was its conceptual apparatus, its intricate jargon of special terms and categories, its endless Talmudic distinctions between 'base' and 'superstructure,' between 'modes of production' and 'relations of production,' between 'strategies' and 'tactics' of social action, between the 'contradictions' and the 'unity of opposites' of social and economic systems, and so on. Once one had commanded the technical language, adherence to Marxism created an entire subculture of discourse in which, literally, one could only be understood by other Marxists. In short, Marxism gave me my first glimpse of the culture of scholarship, an intellectual community that feeds upon itself.

I did not remain a purely intellectual Marxist. I joined the American Communist Party, attended political meetings and participated in party demonstrations. I did this reluctantly because I was never much of a joiner but, nevertheless, I went through a brief period of genuine political activity. It was brief because my natural rebelliousness soon got me thrown out of the Communist Party. As the war drew to a close in 1945, the question of the continued occupation of Germany by Allied troops came to the fore as a political issue. Earl Browder, the President of the American Communist Party, endorsed President Roosevelt's recommendation of post-war military conscription so as to allow American troops to be stationed permanently in

Germany. This was regarded as heresy by some members of the Communist Party and when Stalin came out against Roosevelt's policy, Browder's fate was sealed: he was deprived of his presidency and expelled from the Party. In a flash, he became *persona non grata*. A few of the communist students at college collected a petition on Browder's behalf, which I signed after due consideration. I was called before a Party tribunal and, having failed to repent, was promptly expelled. From that moment on, a large number of friends and acquaintances in the Party refused, not just to speak to me, but even to recognize me when they met me in the street. To those who have never been a member of a conspiratorial or quasi-conspiratorial group, the speed with which Party members will ostracize a heretic is hard to believe. In retrospect, and given the total political insignificance of the American Communist Party in 1945, the experience seems ludicrous but at the time it proved to be a harrowing awakening to the realities of left-wing politics.

Although I ceased to be a card-carrying member of the Communist Party in 1945, it took me at least another seven to eight years to shake off all the blinkers that Marxism leaves behind. Between 1945 and 1952 I travelled gradually but irreversibly away from communism. I well remember the effect of reading *The God That Failed. Six Studies in Communism* (1950) by Arthur Koestler, Ignazio Silone, André Gide, Richard Wright, Louis Fischer and Stephen Spender, all writers who had at one time been 'fellow-travelers.' Even after all these years, I can still recall the awful feeling of having shared the disillusionment of these famous communist converts. It is curious how far one can go in abandoning previous beliefs without making the final jump to non-belief. The moment for me was the abortive East German 'revolution' in the summer of 1952 when the people of East Berlin came close to throwing off the Soviet-imposed government of East Germany. I had visited East Berlin as a tourist in May 1952 and had seen evidence of seething resentment against the regime. When I returned to London, I read accounts of the outbreak and its suppression by Soviet tanks in the communist press. I had always recognized that communist papers are capable of telling lies but I had previously closed my eyes to the extent to which they carry their lying. The disillusionment of a 'true believer,' such as I had been, comes in the final analysis like a cold shower after a hot bath.

When I think of some of the things that I believed when I was a communist and that I expounded passionately and with a sense of total conviction, I blush to the roots of my hair. I can remember, for example, how I defended the Stalinist version of the Moscow Trials, namely that Trotsky living in Paris and Mexico City had orchestrated a vast conspiracy of sabotage inside the Soviet Union that even infected the Soviet military hierarchy – and this despite reading Arthur Koestler's *Darkness at Noon*, which I brushed aside as bourgeois propaganda. It has made me suspicious ever since of beliefs strongly held and has helped me to be more tolerant than I am naturally inclined to be. Whenever I now pronounce that so-and-so is absolutely true, I always say quietly to myself, 'yes, just like the Moscow Trials.'

I dropped communism like an old coat thrown off, but Marxism took longer to discard. In some sense, the great themes of exploitation, alienation and inequality haunt me still. Of course, the more economics I learned, the less Marxian economics I believed in. I could soon see that Marx's grasp of the economic problems of running a socialist society was ludicrous: he really thought that it would present no more than an accounting problem rather like a corner grocery store writ large. Moreover, most of Marx's economic predictions were palpably awry and it was perfectly clear that he himself was deeply disappointed at the time of his death by the failure of the proletariat to overthrow capitalism. But it still took me many years to perceive the profound, central fallacy at the core of Marxian economics, a fallacy which even today is not acknowledged by Marxists and even ex-Marxists. It is a most interesting fallacy and it is so cleverly hidden away in *Capital* that not one in a thousand readers ever notices it. It is the idea that there is a uniform rate of surplus value in every industry in the economy, that in short every dollar of wages paid out yields capitalists an identical number of dollars of profit, irrespective of whether these wages are earned in agriculture digging ditches or in the oil industry refining oil. This is a most improbable assumption but there is no way of demonstrating that it is false because the rate of surplus value is neither an observable nor a behavioral variable in a capitalist economy: no one strives to minimize or maximize it; it is truly a ghost in the machine. Marx was well aware of this phenomenon but, in the eagerness to disguise the arbitrariness of his assumption he reified value and surplus value and spoke repeatedly of the capitalist system striving to increase the rate of surplus value; this is something that individual capitalists cannot do and in any case have no incentive to do. Nevertheless, Marx simply had to assume a uniform rate of surplus value because without it his claim that labor alone creates surplus value would have fallen to the ground.

Many modern Marxist economists, at least in Western countries, no longer believe in the labor theory of value and its corollary, the labor theory of surplus value. Even so, to the extent that they remain Marxists they continue to believe that capitalism is grounded on the exploitation of labor. By 'exploitation,' they mean simply that workers do not own the means of production and hence are denied the profits that result from employing labor in the production of saleable goods. Their argument is therefore that there is a fundamental injustice in capitalism, an injustice residing in the fact that workers do not own and owners do not work. It is fascinating to me to see how far such 'analytical Marxists,' as they call themselves, have abandoned all varieties of consequentialism in appraising capitalism and have instead opted for moral judgements based on the ethical meaning of social relationships in a capitalist system. In other words, they ask: is it fair that most of us have to work for a living, while a small minority can live without working? (to which of course the only answer is that it is exceedingly unfair), instead of asking whether the consequences of capitalism in generating unprecedented economic growth could be obtained without an unequal and hence unfair distribution of private property. In other words, we can agree that capitalism is not an edifying system: it is crass, brutal and morally reprehensible but it does deliver the goods and in the final analysis it is the goods that we want!

THE McCARTHY EXPERIENCE

I doubt whether it would have taken me so many years to throw off the weight of Marxism if it had not been for an encounter in 1952 with the spectre of McCarthyism. McCarthy was riding high in 1952, the product of the anti-communist hysteria that held America in its grip at the height of the cold war. And it was a hysteria as the following story will show. I had graduated from Queens College of the City University of New York in 1950 and was in the midst of my preliminary year for the PhD at Columbia University when Arthur D. Gayer, the chairman of the economics department at Queens College, was killed in an automobile accident. The department looked around for someone to take over his courses in the middle of the semester and since I had worked for him as a research assistant, I was asked whether I would have a go. And so I suddenly found myself teaching a full load of courses in microeconomics, consumer economics and marketing, a subject I had never studied. I can remember being so nervous about my first lectures that I literally memorized them in their entirety the night before giving them.

I was just getting on top of all this teaching when the Un-American Activities Committee, chaired by Senator Joseph McCarthy, arrived in New York city to investigate communism in the New York City college system. They called on three well-known professors to appear before them in order, no doubt, to ask them the familiar questions: 'Are you now or have you ever been a member of the Communist Party?' All three refused to cooperate with the committee, pleading the First and Fifth Amendment to the Constitution, which prohibits witnesses from incriminating themselves. Despite the fact that all three were tenured professors, they were promptly and summarily dismissed by their employer, the City University of New York. One of these three professors was Vera Shlakman, Professor of Labor Economics at Queens College, a former teacher of mine and, at that point in time, a colleague. She was the president of the Teachers' Union, a left-wing professional union of college teachers in the New York City area, and was herself left-wing and, for all I knew, a fellow-traveler. But having been taught by her, I knew that she was scrupulously impartial and leaned over backwards not to indoctrinate her students. A number of students organized a petition to the President of Queens College demanding Vera Shlakman's reinstatement but, by the by-laws of the college, student petitions could not be submitted to a higher authority without an endorsing signature of at least one faculty member. The students went right through the economics department, which then numbered 40 professors, associate professors, assistant professors, and lowly tutors like myself, without encountering one person willing to endorse the petition. At the end of the line, they came to me and because of my personal regard for Professor Shlakman, and because I could not bear the thought of being pusillanimous, I signed the petition. Within 24 hours, I received a curt note from President Thatcher of Queens College (odd that I should remember his name after 40 years!) informing me that, unless I resigned forthwith, I would be dismissed, and black-listed for future employment.

For a day or two, I contemplated a magnificent protest, a statement that would ring down the ages as a clarion call to individual freedom, that would be read and recited for years to come by American high-school students – and then I quietly sent in my letter of resignation.

I was now at my wits' end. I had planned to apply for a scholarship to begin working on my doctoral dissertation and had been relying on my teaching salary from Queens College to carry me through the application period. I was broke and depressed by the entire experience when suddenly the telephone rang to inform me that I had been offered a grant by the Social Science Research Council to enable me to go abroad to write my PhD thesis: clearly, there were people here and there behind the scenes lending assistance to victims of McCarthyism.

In the curious way that every disaster in my life has always in due course turned into a blessing, there now began what I quickly realized were the best two years in my life. I had picked a topic, the rise and fall of the school of David Ricardo in nineteenth-century economic opinion, that turned out to be even more promising than I had imagined.[1] I also discovered that scholarly research was my true *métier*. I took a room within a stone's throw of the British Museum Reading Room in London and lived the life of a medieval monk, reading and writing as much as 18 hours a day, seven days a week. My early efforts were sent off to my doctoral supervisor, George Stigler, then at Columbia University, whose acerbic but acute comments were just what I needed to spur me on. Two years later I was back in New York with a completed thesis and the undeniable pleasure of witnessing the final downfall of Senator McCarthy on television.

In the summer of 1954, I was interviewed for a post as Assistant Professor at Yale University. On my interview committee was William Fellner, who later became one of my mentors. In the course of the interview, I felt impelled to explain how I had lost my previous teaching position at Queens College. I always remember how Fellner cut me off, saying: 'We don't want to hear about that. This is a private college and what transpired at a public university a few years ago is of no concern to us.' I never had a better demonstration of Milton Friedman's thesis that a free market, by multiplying the number of probable employers, is more likely to secure liberty for the individual than a socialist system in which the state is a monopsonist.

It is difficult nowadays to convey the extraordinary atmosphere of the McCarthy era in which one was likely to be stabbed in the back by one's best friends and in which everyone was literally looking for 'reds under their beds' every night. In my youth I had innocently believed that intellectuals would always stand up for ideas against the powers that be but, as a result of the McCarthy experience, I lost whatever respect I ever had for intellectuals and academics. With enough social pressure, they will capitulate to McCarthy, Hitler, Stalin, Sadam Hussein, or anyone else with the power of the army and police behind them.

By the time I started teaching at Yale in 1954, I had shaken off almost all of my old communist beliefs, and when Kruschev delivered his famous anti-Stalin speech in 1956, I had the quiet satisfaction of having all my new beliefs confirmed out of the horse's mouth. In the next few years, I moved steadily to the right but I never became as maniacally anticommunist as many ex-communists. I remained, and probably still remain, politically schizophrenic: rather right-wing on questions of economic policy, such as privatization, deregulation, trade union legislation and the like, but fiercely left-wing on questions of social policy, such as welfare payments, unemployment compensation, positive discrimination in favor of women, blacks and gays, the right to abortion, legalization of soft drugs, and so forth. My right-ward journey was halted by Reagan and Thatcher. Living in England in the 1980s, I was increasingly appalled by the blatant use of mass unemployment to counter inflation and was amazed that the persistence of double-digit unemployment was tolerated by the British electorate for a decade or more. I was struck by the way Mrs Thatcher managed to persuade voters, financial journalists and even many economists that the costs of inflation are always greater than the costs of unemployment, which I believe to be blatantly false for single-digit inflation but double-digit unemployment rates, which indeed was the prevailing scenario throughout most of the 1980s.[2] The Falklands War was bad enough but her failure to attack the unemployment problem, or even to admit that it was a problem, made me as left-wing on macroeconomic questions as I had long been on social questions. Thanks to Mrs Thatcher I came back to a more or less consistent belief in capitalism, yes, but capitalism tempered by Keynesian demand management and quasi-socialist welfarism.

THE FLIRTATION WITH FREUD

Even as I fell under the spell of Marx, I also succumbed to the siren call of Freud. In the summers of 1944, 1945 and 1946, I worked as a waiter in upstate New York hotels – the so-called 'Borsht Belt' – and many of my guests were psychiatrists and psychoanalysts. It didn't take long before I was deeply immersed in the writings of Freud and Freudians and thrilled by the power of Freudian theory to explain everything, a power which of course reminded me of the style of Marx. I still recall vividly being absolutely entranced by Freud's *Interpretation of Dreams*, the sense that something as inherently mysterious as dreams could be accounted for in a rational manner. I yielded, too, to the enormous rhetorical power of Freud, who, whatever one may think of him as a scientist, was a great literary artist. Freudianism stayed with me insidiously much longer than Marxism. But gradually, over the years, I became increasingly aware of how self-fulfilling and self-justifying were many of the key concepts of psychoanalytic theory and how characteristic was the unwillingness of analysts to submit Freudian ideas to an empirical test. I now think that virtually the whole of Freudian theory is a tissue of mumbo-jumbo and that psychoanalysis as a therapeutic technique is not very different from Chinese brain-washing. But this was a view that came to me only slowly and not without a certain measure of personal experience with psychoanalysis.

In the wonderful poem, 'In Memory of Sigmund Freud,' every line of which I ought to quote, W.H. Auden concludes:

> If often he was wrong and at times absurd
> To us he is no more a person
> Now but a whole climate of opinion,
> Under whom we conduct our differing lives
> Like weather he can only hinder or help …

Not so: he can only hinder and does!

WHY BOTHER WITH THE HISTORY OF ECONOMICS?

Ever since my childhood, I have been a voracious reader. When I was young, I read to escape, and later reading a book a day became a habit which I could not shake off. A non-stop reader has a comparative advantage in a subject like the history of economic thought, and in that sense intellectual history, at least for me, a form of self-indulgence. Within a year of arriving at Yale University in 1954, I was asked to take over William Fellner's graduate course in the history of economic thought for no better reason than that I was the only person on the faculty anxious to teach it. And so, at the tender age of 27, I found myself teaching a compulsory course in the history of economics to postgraduate students at one of America's foremost institutions of higher education. Yale in those years admitted some twenty to thirty hand-picked graduate students in economics and in the next few years my students numbered at least a dozen or so names who later became well-known academic economists. I was so nervous about teaching the course that I over-prepared myself: within a few years I had collected thousands of pages of notes, notes that were eventually to become my only well-known book, *Economic Theory in Retrospect* (1962).

In the introduction of the book, I claimed that all historians of economic thought are either 'relativists,' or 'absolutists': they either believe that all past doctrines are more or less faithful reflections of the historical circumstances in which they are created or that past ideas are largely the result of the internal logical development of the subject, being almost always mistaken in the light of later thinking. I announced myself an unapologetic absolutist and poked fun at relativists throughout the book. This is not a point of view I now hold, having been upstaged over the years by even more strident upholders of the 'Whig interpretation of history.' When I witness the attempt of many commentators in recent years to reproduce the great ideas of the past in modem dress, particularly in one or another mathematical model, I realize that absolutism carried to its logical extreme deprives the history of ideas of all *raison d'être*: far from imparting an appreciation of the past, it actually destroys historical understanding by condemning all thinkers down the ages to live now and to think as we do.

Be that as it may, my youthful absolutism was the product of three forces. Firstly, the discipline of economics was never so confident as it was in the late 1950s and early 1960s: we *knew* that general equilibrium theory was the last word in theoretical elegance, that input–output analysis and linear programming would soon make it not just elegant but operational, and that 'the neo-classical synthesis' had successfully joined Keynesian macro-economics to Walrasian microeconomics; in short, that economics was one church and that the full truth was at any moment to be revealed to us. If ever one were going to take an absolutist view of the history of economic ideas, 1960 was just the right date to bring it off. Second, I was deeply influenced by Schumpeter's *History of Economic Analysis* (1954), and Schumpeter was of course a peculiar but nevertheless adamant absolutist. Reinforcing the influence of Schumpeter was the influence of both the writings and the personality of George Stigler, my doctoral supervisor.[3] He had a reputation for destroying students but I always got along very well with him. I like aggressive, assertive people and when George Stigler said that something you had written was nonsense, he produced so many crushing reasons to back up his judgment that you could not but be grateful that he had condescended to criticize you. Also he was one of the few really funny men that I have ever known: his sense of humor was wicked and even vicious and I loved it. I found myself imitating his lecture style and of course his writing style but I have never been able to match his biting footnotes.

Whenever I met him in later years, I regressed immediately to the status of a young graduate student ingratiating himself with a senior figure. In fact, I was a bit scared of him, particularly as our political views were a thousand miles apart and I once or twice inadvertently expressed opinions that were abhorrent to him. My most touching memory of him is a day in 1960 when he introduced me in Chicago to Frank Knight, his doctoral supervisor in the 1930s. I watched him talking to Frank Knight with the same deference that I showed him and I suddenly realized that he too could not address an elderly teacher of Knight's renown as an equal, no more than I could relate to him as an equal. There is something very stirring in the idea of the successive generations of teachers and pupils passing down 'the lamp of knowledge.'

But apart from Schumpeter and Stigler, it was my students at Yale who would have driven me to absolutism whatever its intellectual merits. The history of economic thought was a compulsory graduate course in the 1950s but these students were typical American graduate students: they wanted to learn the tools and techniques of modern economics and to hell with such scholarly subjects as economic history and the history of economic thought. I was aware from the moment the course began that I had to sell the history of economics as somehow relevant to these young Turks. No wonder then that I taught the subject by emphasizing the filiation of purely analytical concepts and continually emphasizing the modernity, and sometimes lack of modernity, of the ideas of the past.

The very task of working so hard to put over the history of economics as a legitimate subject for intellectual inquiry eventually soured me on the subject altogether. By the time I left America in 1962, I was more or less determined to work instead in applied economics. But eventually; after a holiday from the history of economic thought for a decade, I came back to it again in the 1970s as my first, and ultimately last, love. In the final analysis, I find nothing as intellectually satisfying as the history of ideas. I have never been able to grasp how one can understand any idea without knowing where it came from, how it evolved out of previous ideas. As soon as I learned calculus, I had to find out how Newton invented it, how Leibniz invented it independently, how they argued over the right calculus notation and just what was meant by the concept of a derivative. And one reason I have never really understood Einstein's general theory of relativity, despite repeated attempts to learn it, is that late-nineteenth-century physics is too difficult for me, so that I can't follow how Lorenz almost got as far as Einstein did. Great theories, in economics as in other subjects, are path-dependent, to use popular recent jargon in economic history, that is, it is not possible to explain their occurrence without considering the corpus of received ideas which led to the development of that particular new theory; had the body of received ideas been different we would have arrived at a different theory at the culmination of that development. In other words, without the history of economics, economic theories just drop from the sky; you have to take them on faith. The moment you wish to judge a theory, you have to ask how they came to be produced in the first place and that is a question that can only be answered by the history of ideas.

I understand very well why historians of economic thought figure so little in the pecking order of economists. But it does mean that economics is for most economists an almost wholly unintellectual subject. In the face of ideas, many economists are simply philistines, like troglodytes listening to a Beethoven quartet and asking why the four players seem to be unable to bow in unison.

THE ECONOMICS OF EDUCATION

In 1962, I left America to spend a year in Paris on a research scholarship to continue my investigations of the nineteenth-century cotton industry. At the end of that year I reached the promotion barrier at Yale: after six years as an assistant professor an American university must either promote you to an associateship, which carries tenure, or dismiss you. Yale refused to promote me on the grounds that they had no need of a senior professor specializing in the history of economic thought and I therefore found it necessary to look elsewhere for a new appointment. When I now thought of returning to the United States, my heart sank. I realized that despite 20 years in America, I had never ceased to think of myself as a European. America was too crass, too commercialized for me, and I had never entirely given up the condescending feeling of a cultured European for those vulgar Americans. A nation in which 'the life of the whole of one sex is devoted to dollar-hunting, and of the other to breeding dollar-hunters,' as John Stuart Mill put it, or, in Oscar Wilde's words, 'a country that has passed straightway from barbarism to decadence without the intervening phase of civilization.' I made up my mind to move to Britain, a country in which I had lived as a boy during World War II and had lived in again as a student working on my doctoral dissertation.

I began making applications for a number of vacancies at British universities but there was little expansion in the academic job market in 1962 and I soon realized that I might well fail to find a job before the year was out. By a fluke I bumped into Lionel Elvin, the Director of the University of London Institute of Education, who told me that they had been unable to fill a vacancy in the economics of education because this was a new field in Britain.

I had never heard of something called 'the economics of education' and decided to inform myself. This did not take long because the subject was indeed little researched in 1962. I took the bull by the horns and wrote to Lionel Elvin, admitting that I was a novice in the economics of education, but asking whether the Institute would hire me on a temporary basis for a year or two. They agreed to do so and those two years turned, much to my amazement and theirs, into 23 years! I mention all this only to emphasize the role of accident in life. I have read dozens of involved explanations of how people make occupational choices or marital choices, for that matter, but when investigated closely and in detail it often appears that it was pure chance that A became a chemist and B a lawyer, or that A married B and C married D.

The Institute was a postgraduate teacher training college and the bulk of my students were teachers seeking to upgrade themselves. My teaching load at the Institute was light; my administrative duties were equally light because the Department of Economics at the Institute numbered only two or at most three; and for the first time I was able to give myself almost wholly to writing and research. The lack of economists to talk to would have been painful but for the fact that the London School of Economics was just down the street. I soon became a visiting lecturer at LSE and divided my time between the two institutions.

The world of education was a wholly new milieu for me: it was much softer than the world of economics; very few educationists paid much attention to empirical evidence in supporting their assertions and many arguments degenerated into a clash of value judgments. I was not at first prepared for the unmitigated hostility with which educationists viewed all economists who they regarded at best as cost-cutters and at worst as fascist swine. The sway of fashion was even worse in education than in economics and, while the center of gravity of the political spectrum in education was well to the left of what it was in economics, when educationists were right-wing they made Milton Friedman look like a loony left-winger.

It did not take me long to become an enthusiastic advocate of human capital, and I was certainly the first to venture to make rate-of-return calculations for educational investment in Britain. For about a decade, roughly from 1965 to 1975, I proselytized on behalf of human capital theory and I, like all enthusiasts, outperformed my adversaries at least quantitatively. But then this God failed, as had Marxism and Freudianism before. In 1976, I published a long post-mortem whose title says it all: 'Human Capital theory: A Jaundiced Survey'. It said, not that human capital theory is wrong, but that it is thin and unproductive despite its early promise, and unable to vanquish its principal competitor, the screening hypothesis, credentialism, the diploma disease, call it what you will. I came in the end to think that human capital theory vastly exaggerates the role of cognitive knowledge in the undoubted economic value of education. What really accounted for the economic and even the social and political role of education in the modernization process was what educational psychologists call 'the affective behavioral traits' that formal education imparts; that is, the effect of schooling in shaping the values and attitudes of students; what employers really value about education is not so much what educated workers know than how educated workers behave. This insight has far-reaching implications for questions of vocational training, for aspects of educational planning and even for problems in the financing of education. Eventually, I married up my notions of the incomplete employment contract, requiring the monitoring of effort and the screening and signaling problem that characterizes the hiring and promotion of workers with my new conception of the economic value of education. But by the late 1970s, I found myself repeating this message over and over again in different contexts without the slightest visible effect on either educational circles or the treatment of education by economists and, as a consequence, became bored by the very topic.

Indeed, it seemed to me then, and it still seems to me now, that education is more plagued than most subjects by a sense of *déjà vu*, an endless merry-go-round in which every question or argument recurs every ten or twenty years, frequently in identical form. I could give many examples of this phenomenon, but let me cite just one: I began advocating student loans in higher education, preferably financed by a graduate tax throughout working life, in the late 1960s; although this was already old hat in the US by then, it remained right up to the 1980s in Britain an outrageous and extremely unpopular idea. I came very close to the centers of power in British education, first under Labour in the early 1970s and then under the Tories in the early 1980s, but was never successful in selling the idea to those who could have implemented it. I gave it up in disgust around 1982 but since then the argument has been carried on more ably by other British economists but again to no real avail! When the Conservative government under Mrs Thatcher in 1988 finally adopted a very modest student loan scheme, conceived as a personal debt repayable in 15 years, no reference whatsoever was made to 20 years of writings on the subject, and the British economic profession swallowed the proposal without a murmur of criticism. To this day it is not generally recognized by politicians that the finance of higher education is an economist's issue *par excellence*.

I spent a good deal of time during my years at the Institute of Education on leave in Asia and Africa as an educational consultant for various UN agencies, such as UNESCO, UNECAFE, ILO and the World Bank. I participated in economic missions to six underdeveloped countries in tropical Africa, South and South-east Asia. I lived in India for six months writing a book on graduate unemployment and worked in Thailand and Indonesia for a year, working for the Ford Foundation. At first, I learned a lot about development economics and the role of economic advice to Third World governments, but diminishing returns to learning soon set in and I found myself repeating more or less everything I had said in the last country I had worked in. I started out as a do-gooder, anxious to help lift the downtrodden masses of the Third World from the squalor in which they lived. But as time passed, I found myself more and more inclined to agree with Peter Bauer that aid to developing countries does more harm than good. The whole business of UN aid missions and advice to Third World governments on what to do or not to do in economic policy was a gigantic charade. The governments in question simply wanted aid or World Bank loans but could not get it unless they could show they had consulted the best advice they could obtain. Instead of buying that advice from the international consultancy industry, which did in fact happen in technical fields like oil drilling or hydraulic engineering, they went to the UN agencies to secure the services of freelance consultants like myself, who soon learned which side their bread was buttered on – always the underside of course – and did well by doing good, at least for a while until the song they were singing at that moment went out of fashion.

I became more and more cynical about the Third World ministers and politicians I had to work with who exploited me and other economists like myself to get the aid they wanted, while lining their own pockets with the leavings of that aid. The amount of corruption and political hypocrisy that I witnessed in every country I worked in eventually turned me against the entire development consultancy business. Getting out was easy: all one did was to say something that Third World governments did not want to hear; by saying it often enough, one could be assured of not being rehired.

The bee in my bonnet was simple enough: down with higher education and up with primary schooling! In my view, all these countries, and particularly those in Africa, overspent outrageously on free higher education, which the government officials of the moment had of course themselves enjoyed, and underspent equally outrageously on the primary schooling of the rural poor. Another bee in my bonnet was the wastefulness of formal vocational schooling at the secondary level, not to mention the vocationalization of the primary and secondary school curriculum, which was simply the old fallacy that the cognitive knowledge of students was what made education so economically valuable. Underlying both of these mistaken policies was a technique of educational planning called the manpower-requirements approach, which was input–output analysis inappropriately applied to the matching of educated workers to different occupational slots in individual industries. I spent ten years or more attacking the manpower-requirements approach to educational planning but to no avail, at least in the Third World. The fact of the matter is that the approach, being entirely in terms of physical quantities and involving no prices – 'priceless economics,' as someone called it – is so easy to understand and hence so politically irresistible that the manpower-requirements approach remains to this day the principal technique for the planning of education and training in the Third World.

One of the great lessons imbibed from my years as a Third World adviser was the hopeless inconsistencies involved in marrying the objective of socialism with that of development and modernization. Every government I ever worked for was to some extent committed to socialism but also wanted to modernize and to imitate America, Japan, Britain, etc. They would wax eloquent about the need for indigenous entrepreneurship but would stamp on everyone who made money, particularly by selling shoddy goods to ordinary people in the so-called 'informal sector'. In short, they never could accept the rugged individualism and the consequent inequalities that rapid economic growth inevitably entails but, nevertheless, they could not abandon the objective of growth and development. They utterly failed to understand the 'causes of the wealth of nations,' which whatever they are, are not the immediate eradication of unearned incomes and perfect equality in the distribution of earnings.

It is ironic that practically every one of the economic mission reports that I helped to write in the 1970s was commissioned by a government headed by a dictator who was overthrown either as soon as the report was delivered or shortly thereafter: a UNESCO World Experimental Literacy Project mission to Iran headed by the Shah in 1964 and 1976; a ILO World Employment Programme Mission to Ethiopia headed by Haile Selassie in 1972; a ILO World Employment Comprehensive Mission to the Philippines headed by President Ferdinand Marcos in 1973; a ILO World Employment Comprehensive Mission to the Sudan headed by President El Nimeiry in 1975; a ILO World Employment Programme Mission to Lesotho headed by King Moshoeshoe in 1976; a UNDP Mission to Buthan headed by King Wanghuk in 1981; a UNDP Mission to Brunei headed by Sultan Bolkiah in 1983; and a World Bank Mission to China headed by Dang Xiao Ping in 1983. With the exception of Buthan, Brunei and China, all the other countries are now governed by other leaders, often in violent opposition to those to whom I and my team-mates delivered our reports. So much for the notion that economists have an influence on the policies of foreign governments!

THE METHODOLOGY OF ECONOMICS

As the 1970s passed by, I turned increasingly towards the methodology or philosophy of economics as a subject of abiding interest. Actually, this had been my interest all along but I had never realized it. It started of course with my early infatuation with Marxism, or rather with my gradual disillusionment with Marxism. In my last year as an undergraduate at Queens College I took a seminar course in the philosophy of the social sciences with Donald Davidson (who, I learned later, was an eminent philosopher of science). Davidson knew that there were a number of young Marxists in the class (remember this was 1949) and his way of dealing with Marxism was gently to ridicule it. Thus, when I trotted out the three laws of Hegelian dialectics (the change of quantity into quality, the unity of opposites, the negation of the negation) as the master-key to unlock all doors, he topped it with Herbert Spencer's 'law' of evolution: evolution is a change from a state of relatively indefinite, incoherent homogeneity to a state of relatively definite coherent heterogeneity. 'That neatly explains absolutely everything,' Davidson said, and with a shock I realized that was just as true of the laws of dialectics: they explained everything, which was just like explaining nothing.

Davidson asked us to read Carl Hempel's 'The Function of General Laws in History' (1942), which argues that any valid explanation of a historical phenomenon like, say, the French Revolution must necessarily invoke some universal empirical hypothesis or of which this is said to be a particular instance; if it fails to do so, it is merely a pseudo-explanation. This is what later came to be called 'the covering-law model of scientific explanation': to explain a thing is to 'cover' it under some universal law. I can still recall more than 40 years later how this article hit me like a thunder-clap; it is probably one of the dozen or so essays that has left a permanent mark on my thinking. I suddenly realized that I had been employing pseudo-explanations for years without realizing that they were untenable because they involved alleged covering laws of which I nor anyone else had any knowledge. A covering law for revolutions? Yes, we had all read Crane Brinton's *Anatomy of Revolution* (1938), which collected some general features of revolutions, based on a sample of three, but these hardly amounted to universal laws or even universally applicable characteristics. In short, no one had ever really explained the French Revolution of the Russian Revolution except in a purely *ad hoc* way.

By the time I had come to work on my doctoral dissertation, I had somehow absorbed Popperian falsificationism without ever reading Popper. Some of it I acquired from Milton Friedman's classic essay 'The Methodology of Positive Economics' (1953), which, without mentioning Popper, presents a sort of vulgar, Mickey Mouse Popperianism. Some of it filtered down from remarks and asides in Stigler's essays on the history of economic thought. When I started teaching in Yale in 1954, I soon became friendly with Tjalling Koopmans, partly because he was an amateur composer and I had just started playing the cello, so we talked about music, and partly because we were both Dutch and enjoyed speaking Dutch together. Our interests in economics were totally different, but when he started working on the second of his *Three Essays on the State of Economic Science* (1957), which is all about methodology, we talked about Friedman's essay and then for the first time I became entirely persuaded by predictionism, that is, the idea that theories must ultimately be judged by the accuracy of their prediction. When I published my first professional paper in 1956, 'The Empirical Content of Ricardian Economics,' it was shot through by predictionism, but, nevertheless, I still had read no Popper. Indeed, I can remember like yesterday the first moment I finally decided to read Popper.

In 1962, while living in Paris, I strolled into a bookshop one Friday afternoon and saw a copy of Karl Popper's *The Open Society and Its Enemies* (1945), which, as everyone knows, is a study of Plato, Hegel and Marx as three great enemies of the open society, I went home and started reading it as soon as I had finished dinner. I read all night, all day Saturday, and, after falling asleep reluctantly, finished the book on Sunday. I can safely say that no book before and no book since has excited me more. It was literally like drinking a whole bottle of champagne at a single sitting.[4] Not only did it slay Plato and Hegel, both of whom I had always regarded as monsters of the right, but it made short shrift of Marx for committing the 'apocalyptic fallacy,' the game of predicting doomsday some day in the indefinite fume. At the same time, it offered a philosophy of science, falsificationism, and a convincing argument against political revolutions, on the grounds that we lack the knowledge totally to transform society, but that we can and should reform society on a piecemeal basis.

I then sat down and read everything that Popper had ever written. I became a through-and-through Popperian and although I now think that there are exaggerations in Popper – there is no such thing as induction; there is a fundamental asymmetry between verification and falsification; methodology is normative and has nothing to do with the history of science – I remain to this day an unregenerate Popperian. I think that I learnt from Popper how to write about complex issues in clear, unadorned, Saxon English and indeed found myself almost copying his style word for word.[5] When I arrived in London in 1952 to work on my doctoral thesis, I was thrilled to learn that Popper was teaching a weekly seminar at the London School of Economics in the philosophy of science. I was given permission to audit the course but imagine my surprise when I soon saw that Popper was a Prussian-style teacher of the old school, a walking embodiment of all the arrogant intolerance that he preached against in his books. There was a cruel joke about Popper that went around the London School of Economics, invented apparently by one of his students: '*The Open Society by One of Its Enemies* is what he should have called his book. *The Open Society by a Closed Mind* would have been an even better title.' Ah well, Beethoven, the greatest composer that ever lived, was a dreadful man and so was Wagner, and Goethe, and Tolstoy – and I am not very nice myself!

BEFORE ECONOMICS THERE WAS PHILOSOPHY

I have never regretted my youthful decision to become an economist but there have been moments when I wished I had studied philosophy. In one sense philosophy is where I started and philosophy seems to be where I am ending up. But where I started was not so much philosophy in general as a particular kind of philosophy, namely, theology. The question of the existence of God was the first philosophical question I ever asked, and answered, and it interests me still. I was brought up as an orthodox Jew, achieved pantheism by the age of 12, agnosticism by the age of 15, and militant atheism by the age of 17, from which I have never wavered. Indeed, I seem to become more militant about my atheism the longer I live and it taxes all my tolerance nowadays to keep a civil tongue in my head when I argue with arch believers, which I am afraid I love to do, love too much to do.

It all started when one of my uncles gave me a Bible at the age of 12, not noticing that it included the New as well as the Old Testament. Being a non-stop reader, who devoured any book that I could lay my hands on, I naturally read the New Testament of whose very existence I had never heard. I was immediately enthralled by the story of Jesus and reinforced it by reading Ernest Renan's *Life of Jesus*, a romanticized nineteenth-century biography of Jesus as a humanized prophet of old. This account I thought had to be true but all my relatives told me that it was not true. I argued with them and was sent to a rabbi to be corrected. He soon persuaded me that Jesus could not be the son of God, because the central intelligence that created the universe does not have children nor could he be the Messiah because when the Messiah has come to this world, the lamb will lie down with the lion, swords will be turned into plowshares, and nations shall no longer war with one another. Have swords turned into plowshares? Have nations ceased to war with one another? Well then. That struck me as a thoroughly convincing argument.

Perhaps the beautiful story of Jesus as set down in the Gospels was false, but what about the story of the Buddha, the next account of a god that I read. That struck me as an equally beautiful story. But again, I was told, by relatives and friends, that the story of the Buddha could not be true. All these beautiful stories, the story of Moses and Joseph and David in the Old Testament, the story of Jesus in the New Testament, the story of Buddha in the Mahayama texts of Buddhism, must all be true, I thought because they were so beautiful, and yet equally they must all be false because they contradicted each other. In one leap, I ceased to believe in any authorized religion and became a

Spinozean pantheist, without of course ever having heard of Spinoza. When we fled Holland after the German invasion of 1940 and my parents sent my elder brother and me to a boarding school in England, the headmaster of the school was a Christian Scientist and he tried to convert me to Christian Science. This introduced me to unauthorized deviant religious sects and for several years I was a regular little pest to adults because I never left off asking them questions about their religious beliefs, not to learn but to persuade them to drop the argument of design, or the argument of first cause, or the argument of ultimate purpose as fallacious arguments for the existence of God. As for the historicity of Jesus, I had a dozen clever reasons for demonstrating that his existence was no better established than that of King Arthur or Robin Hood. I am afraid that this is a weakness I have never really learned to overcome. To this day I cannot resist trying to argue with a fundamentalist, whether Christian, Jewish, Islamic or Hindu, even though I know it to be a hopeless undertaking. I am an infernal optimist and always believe, against all evidence, that rational argument will eventually win out.

I like to describe myself as a religious person, meaning that not a day goes by but I ponder the great questions: is there order in the universe?; does it mean anything?; are we here for a purpose? These are good questions but to answer them by God or Church is to insult the profundity of the questions. One reason that I took to Marxism in my teens like a duck takes to water is that its atheism suited me down to the ground. One reason that I took to the writings of Popper, when I eventually read them, is not that Popperianism equals atheism but that Popperian falsification is perfectly suited to atheism. Show me what events, if they occurred, would imply that God does not exist. None, of course; the existence of God is a matter of faith. Well, then, it makes no difference whether we believe or do not believe in the existence of God. A difference that makes no difference is no difference! QED.

FROM POPPER TO LAKATOS

Sometime in the late 1960s, while I was teaching regularly at the LSE, I met Imre Lakatos, Popper's successor to the professorship in logic and philosophy of science at LSE. Imre, in the few years that I knew him (he died in 1974), was someone of whom I became extremely fond. In the course of the student troubles at LSE in 1968, he emerged as a fearless and yet sympathetic critic of the students, making merciless fun of their radical chic, which he was entitled to do as someone who had spent years in a Hungarian prison as a 'right-wing deviationist' before escaping to the West in 1956. He had a marvelous sense of humor[6] and we took to each other almost as soon as we met. He knew no economics but was becoming interested in economics as a field of application for his methodological views, inspired by one of his PhD students, Spiro Latsis, who was indeed the first to apply Lakatos's ideas to economics. In 1974, Imre organized a conference in Greece, which was to bring together physicists, economists and philosophers of science in the attempt to develop some case studies in his own 'methodology of scientific research programmes.' A month before the conference was to take place, he died suddenly. Spiro Latsis went on to hold the conference as a memorial to Imre and it proved to be, for myself and for many others, the conference of a lifetime. In economics, there were great men like Lionel Robbins, John Hicks, Terence Hutchison, Herbert Simon and Axel Leijonhufvud. In philosophy, there were giants like Carl Hempel, Adolf Grünbaum and Paul Feyerabend. It was intellectually exciting; it was held in Nafplion, a beautiful site in Greece; and it was lavishly financed by John Latsis, Spiros Latsis's father, who gave us all a glimpse of the style to which we would have loved to have become accustomed.

Arguments about the relationship between Popper and Lakatos have raged on ever since 1974. I regard Lakatos as, say, 80 percent Popper and 20 percent Kuhn, emphasizing different things but conveying essentially the same methodology as that of Popper. When Neil de Marchi and I organized a second Nafplion conference in Capri in 1989, I was taken aback by the hostility that so many of the economists at the conference expressed for the ideas of Lakatos and Popper. Much of that hostility was directed at Lakatos's insistence that scientific research programs should ultimately be judged by the number of novel predictions that they generate. This criterion proved to be too much to stomach for most of the participants who realized that its implication was to cast doubt on virtually the whole of what passes nowadays as neoclassical economics.

Gradually, since the 1950s, and at an accelerating rate in recent years, economics has become ever more formalistic, that is, almost exclusively concerned with analytical rigor at the expense of policy relevance, taking on ever more the appearance of a kind of social mathematics rather than an empirical social science. Economists have sometimes been accused of physics-envy, but that is an utterly misleading accusation. Anyone who knows modern physics will testify that physicists care about experimental evidence, about bringing their theories into conformity with the experimental evidence, and very little about rigoros theorems and analytical lemmas. What economists really suffer from is mathematics-envy. Consider general equilibrium theory, the most prestigious type of economic theory, practiced only by the professional front-runners of the subject. Here is a theory with absolutely no empirical content. Having 'proved' the existence, uniqueness and local stability of multimarket, general equilibrium what have we learned about the economy? Absolutely nothing. No physicist would ever think that general equilibrium theory raised interesting questions, but a mathematician would of course find it perfect grist for his mill. Some modern practitioners of general equilibrium theory even justify it as fulfilling Adam Smith's age-old promise of demonstrating the tendency of 'the invisible hand' of competition to harmonize private and social interests. This assertion is not only a travesty of intellectual history but an utter misunderstanding of the significance of competition as a social process occurring in real time and ensuring technical dynamism and cost minimization in an economy based on private enterprise; an end-state theory like Walrasian general equilibrium theory is simply irrelevant to it.

What strikes me most about economics after 45 years of studying the subject is the high regard that general equilibrium theory continues to enjoy, despite its failure to realize its own objectives, and the persistent neglect of technical progress as a topic of economic investigation. Economic historians have in recent years finally begun to open the black box of technical change, but economic theorists continue to study economic growth as if it were all the result of capital accumulation and the growth of the labor force, mere quantitative increment in the factors of production. There is a central figure in twentieth-century economics that perfectly reflects this overemphasis on Walrasian general equilibrium theory combined with the underemphasis of technical progress, namely, Joseph Schumpeter. The curious fact about him is how much he himself admired Walrasian theory as the pinnacle of intellectual achievement in economics and, on the other hand, how his own original contributions to economics owed little if anything to the Walrasian inspiration; indeed, if truth be told, they clashed with it. In my younger days, I did not rate highly Schumpeter's theory of entrepreneurship and its associated treatment of innovations, but since then I have come to regard *The Theory of Economic Development* (1911), the product of a 28-year-old economist, as one of the seminal works of twentieth-century economics, on a par with Fisher's *Theory of Interest* or Keynes's *General Theory*. The insight that process innovations are only one kind of innovation and probably much less important in economic growth than product innovations or organizational innovations was an insight of genius.[7] And so was Schumpeter's recognition that bank credit played an essential role in the promotion of entrepreneurship and was not just a financial appendage to machine-driven factory production. It is true that Schumpeter glamorized entrepreneurship and almost reduced it to the heroism of outstanding individuals but, nevertheless, he said more about economic progress under capitalism than any economist since Marx. (What a sad comment on the last hundred years of economics theorizing!) He also recognized that Pareto optimality, perfect competition, static efficiency, and all that – the much-praised first and second Fundamental Theorems of Welfare Economics, inspired by general equilibrium theory – have no practical import because we actually appraise market structures by means of the standards of workable competition, dynamic efficiency and technical dynamism: that's what Adam Smith meant by the invisible hand of competition, not the equality of the marginal rate of substitution in consumption with the marginal rate of transformation in production.

An alarming manifestation of sterile formalism in much current economics is the popularity of post-modernist strictures on the very idea of methodology as a set of prescriptive norms. Economics, Donald McCloskey has told us, is nothing more than a species of persuasive rhetoric, not really different from literary criticism and aesthetics. Certain 'thick' methodological rules – speak softly, listen to your opponents, give reasons for your conclusions – were all right, but the 'thin' methodology of Popper and Lakatos was somehow ruled out as illegitimate. That this is a hopelessly inconsistent position seemed never to have occurred to him or his acolytes.

Without turning Popper or Lakatos into gurus whose writings may not be questioned, I would insist that the valid core of their contribution is the notion that economics must aspire to address real-world economic problems and that this aspiration is best satisfied by the production of theories with empirically refutable implications. That is not to say that every analytical concept that fails to meet that requirement must be instantly discarded, but simply that we must strive to make falsifiable predictions and certainly must never rest satisfied with an economic theory until it has been confronted by empirical evidence. Technical puzzle-solving as a game to be played for its own sake is not to be held out as an ideal to students, the way in which it is at the moment.

Throughout my professional career as an economist, I have admired Milton Friedman's style of doing economics while detesting his political views, and admired Paul Samuelson's political views while disliking the type of economics he practices. Between that Scylla and Charybdis, I seem condemned forever to remain.

NOTES

1. When I published my thesis as *Ricardian Economics* (1958), I thought that Ricardo, the rigorous theorist, was an admirable figure, so much that I named my eldest son after him. But over the years I came to identify Ricardo's 'telescopic' tendency to collapse the long run into the short run as if there was no transition period as the abiding vice of orthodox economics.
2. The economics of inflation has interested me ever since my days as a graduate student at Columbia University. One of my teachers was Arthur F. Burns, who taught me macroeconomics tinged with great skepticism about the theories of John Maynard Keynes. Burns was one of the four examiners in my doctoral oral examination (the other three being Abram Bergson, John Maurice Clark and Karl Polanyi). Burns asked me what was wrong with inflation, a strange question in 1952 when the American inflation rate was 1 percent. Whatever answer I gave him – unfair to creditors, costly to wage-earners and pension receivers, a tax on saving, and the like – he refuted with a counter-example. Within ten

minutes, he reduced me to gibberish and made me feel two feet tall. My heart sank as I realized that I had certainly failed his part of the oral. When I was finally told that I had passed over-all, I apologized to him for my poor performance on the inflation question. He patted me on the shoulder familiarly, saying: 'That's all right, my boy, better men than you have flunked that question.' I ran home and read myself blue in the face on the question of inflation, swearing that I would never fail that question again.

3. Of all my Columbia University teachers, James Angela, Arthur Burns, William Vickrey, John Maurice Clark, Abram Bergson, Ragnar Nurkse and Karl Polanyi, I recall vividly only the last because he introduced me to general economic history, made me read books I had never heard of (like Malinowski's *Argonauts of the Western Pacific*) and taught me how easy it is to concoct 'laws' of history – Polany's categories were 'reciprocity' and 'redistribution' and in these terms he described just about all pre-market economies in history. I did not believe the central thesis of *The Great Transformation* (1944), but it was congenial 'bourgeois Marxism' and immensely stimulating.
4. *Favorite Books*. This is a Victorian parlor game which I love to play: (1) favorite novel: Homer's *Odyssey*; (2) favorite poem: Stephen Spender, 'I Think Continually of Those Who Were Truly Great'; (3) favorite drama: Arnold Strindberg, *The Father*; (4) favorite military history: William Prescott, *The Conquest of Mexico*; (5) favorite history of ideas: Arthur Koestler, *The Sleepwalkers*; (6) favorite philosophical work: Alfred Ayer, *Language, Truth and Logic*; (7) favorite anthropological study: Malinowsky as above; (8) favorite political study: Popper's *Open Society*; etc.; this is a game without end; it is made difficult because second choices are not allowed.
5. A similar stylistic inspiration nearer to home was Joan Robinson, whose economic writings I first encountered as a student; they continued to fascinate me in later years. I read every word that she ever wrote and her language – verbal algebra peppered with homely colloquialisms – attracted me as much as her political views repelled me. She was always very rude to me when we met – after the Cambridge controversies on capital theory she regarded me as an enemy – but I did not mind. It's hard enough to be a brilliant woman in a male-dominated profession like economics, but to be a brilliant woman in the homophilial atmosphere of the Cambridge economics department must have been maddening.
6. One of my favorite Lakatos stories has all the flavor of a great Jewish joke. He told us that he was brought up in a small Hungarian village. When he came home at the age of seven with his first report card, he had As in all subjects except physical education in which he received a C. His mother beat him black and blue in punishment and the next year, he brought home a report car with As in all subjects including physical education (this was already funny enough, half way through the story, because he was a physical runt and unlikely to have ever excelled in sports). His mother always told him that she hoped that he would one day be a professor at the University of Cambridge, a university that for some unknown reason she regarded as the pinnacle of academic achievement. Imre escaped from Hungary in 1956, and fled to England, and, lo and behold, obtained a scholarship to study the history of mathematics at Cambridge. He completed his doctorate (later published as *Proofs and Refutations*) and was appointed on the strength of it as temporary lecturer at Cambridge. He wrote to his mother still living in Hungary to tell her the news and she wrote back: 'Yes, but why didn't they make you a professor?'
7. I have personal reasons for appreciating the importance of product innovations. My father manufactured raincoats in Holland in the 1930s. A Swede transformed the business in 1932 inventing the poplin raincoat; before that raincoats were always made of artificial rubber. My father found himself with thousands of unsalable rubber raincoats in 1933, the depth of the Great Depression in the Netherlands, and faced bankruptcy. Everyone in the industry thought that the new fad of poplin raincoats would not last, but my father, being a pessimist, was convinced that rubber coats would never again be demanded, so he offered his entire stock at a penny a piece to C&A, the leading clothing store in Amsterdam. They were so impressed by his boldness that they gave him an order for poplin raincoats if he could learn to manufacture them. He went to Sweden, poached a tailor and a cutter, and filled the order. That led to more orders and still more orders and by 1935, he was the Raincoat King of the Netherlands and a self-made millionaire. His good fortune did not last very long because in

1940, the Germans invaded Holland and we lost it all. When this rags-to-riches story started, I was six years old; when it ended, I was 12. In short, I have good reasons to think that new products can make a difference.

6. Instead of a philosophy of life*

Martin Bronfenbrenner

Like everyone else, I have mused at times on the universal aspects of universality, among philosophical issues of equal pith and moment. But the results of these musings, in their present state of disorganization randomly walking, are unworthy of the impressive title 'Philosophy of Life.' So I propose to substitute some autobiographical snapshots, plus a few scattered observations on the state of the world and of our discipline – which, you remember, Carlyle has dignified with the title of 'pig philosophy.'

AUTOBIOGRAPHICAL NOTES

There was once a book, whose title I have forgotten, which someone reviewed acidly in some journal. The reviewer called the author a pedantic ass for citing so many obscure unknowns with difficult names. And lo! I was a case in point, one of perhaps half a dozen! So I had best be modest in my autobiographical section, as befits an obscure unknown with a difficult name.

I was conceived in the golden age of the middle classes, an age cut short by World War I before I was born. I was also a 'comparative-systems diaper baby,' in the same sense that certain third-generation Marxists are 'Red diaper' ones. My father, before being born again as a respectable and indeed eminent bacteriologist and immunologist, had been a student leader of the Social Revolutionary Party at the University of Odessa in the Old Country, where the Bronfenbrenners were friends and perhaps relatives of the Bronsteins, whose best-known product was Leon Trotsky. In the disappointing uprising of 1905 – for which see the Eisenstein movie, *Battleship Potemkin* – Father had helped the revolting sailors of the Black Sea Fleet seize the city of Odessa. Subsequently he spent a couple of years underground, before escaping first to France and then to the US (The Czarist *Okhrana* was less efficient than its successor, the KGB, and no visa was necessary to enter the US). My mother, better known as the historian of science Martha Ornstein, unfortunately died while I was young; the Ornsteins had come to the US about

*This chapter first appeared in *The American Economist*, **32**(2), Fall 1988, 3–10.

1890 to enable their sons to avoid service in the Austro-Hungarian Army. She believed in the causes of woman suffrage and evolutionary (not Marxian) socialism; had she lived, she could have been a New Deal Democrat. I also had two paternal uncles and a paternal grandmother. One uncle was non-political in principle, which had not saved him from being beaten up in *pogroms* and later condemned to death several times by several contending armies in the Russian Civil War (1918–20); the other was an anarchist. My grandmother was a good Bolshevik, possibly a Stalinist. (I never met a paternal aunt, who would die in the defense of Leningrad against the Nazis.) So I became interested as a boy in the issues which separated my relatives, both from each other and from most of the neighbors wherever we lived – in Pittsburgh, in Boston, in New York, or in St Louis. The depression, arriving when I was a senior in high school, heightened my interests in 'dangerous thoughts.'

But why economics, rather than history or politics or sociology or activism? A number of reasons, none of them good. As a child, I had been a neighborhood sissy, unable to give orders and unwilling to receive them; I could not follow in my father's footsteps. My undergraduate college, Washington University in St Louis, then had a weak spot in its economics faculty. I had been an interscholastic and intercollegiate debater on a wide variety of economic issues, without benefit of formal instruction in the subject. My background made me a star in economics classes. I was not only appreciated and awarded prizes, but came to believe I knew as much as some of my teachers, and was therefore God's gift to economics! (I still think I knew as much as these teachers, but explain the fact differently now.) Had I had better and 'tougher' teachers, I'm sure I would never have gone on in economics, especially in view of a mathematics allergy that dated back to the third grade. And finally, there were no jobs, or so I thought, when I took my undergraduate degree in 1934 at the ripe old age of 19. Graduate school, since my family could afford it, seemed like 'any port in a storm.'

The decision for graduate work in economics over unemployment in St Louis involved no commitment to 'intellectual eminence and scholarship sublime.' My ambition was to become a serious economic journalist and editorial writer, possibly even a columnist on economic matters, after fortifying myself with a good MA or perhaps even a doctorate if the depression lasted long enough. Teaching and research? Well, maybe, if I forgot how to write, or missed out on journalistic connections. Definitely a second choice; checkers, if I couldn't do chess.

Of the eight or ten graduate schools to which I had applied – and to none of which I imparted the heresies of the last paragraph – only Chicago had offered me financial aid. So it was there I went, despite the warnings of my Washington University teachers about the horrendous ogres I should find in residence as teachers.

The Chicago ogres were, it turned out, somewhat over-rated in the fire-breathing department. True, I would in any normal year have flunked out in my first year, but that term the chief and unavoidable ogre (Jacob Viner) was wasting his sweetness on the desert air of Washington, DC, and I accepted the advice to utilize this unearned respite by getting myself 'a little potted calculus' and a good undergraduate course in economic theory before facing him and the other big guns of the Chicago Department.

As a result, my principal traumas at Chicago were not its big guns – not even Professor Viner[1] – but my fellow students. There were *four* (4!) future Nobel Prize economists roaming the halls of the Social Science Building in those years (1934–38). If I underestimated some of these, I overestimated certain others who have thus far received less professional recognition than the Big Four. Most impressive of all was Paul Samuelson, still technically an undergraduate and somewhat younger than myself, but well on his way to becoming the Liszt or the Paganini of twentieth-century economic gymnastics.

Of course I had much to learn from any half-way decent graduate faculty in economics. In fact, I learned much of it at Chicago (and at Minnesota, where I spent the summer of 1937). Some of the things I needed and acquired:

1. Some revival of confidence. (I still enjoy quoting Paul Douglas: 'You needn't be as good as Samuelson to get along in economics.')
2. Respect for 'the theoretical mechanics of the price system' (Frank Knight) as an intellectual construct, as compared with 'that social-work twaddle' (Henry Simons's characterization of the warmed-over labor institutionalism I had brought with me from St Louis).
3. The ease of paving the road to Hell with good intentions in economic policy (Simons again). The frequent limitation of many policy proposals to 'Me (and My Gang) for Dictator!' (Knight again).
4. Realization that economics was neither 'cut and dried' nor 'all in Marshall' (or anyone else). That it was evolving and developing, especially in the empirical direction. That it was a worthy enterprise to join the procession (Henry Schultz and Paul Douglas), even when it leads to alternatives for 'free enterprise' (Oskar Lange).
5. That academic life can be more than a consolation prize for not 'mattering' in the Real World. But also, that racial, religious and ideological quotas made Ivory Towers difficult to climb (Schultz at Chicago, Arthur Marget at Minnesota).

By the time I took my degree in 1939 (with an undistinguished thesis under Schultz[2] on the monetary theories of the Lausanne School) I had accumulated a little teaching experience at the University itself and elsewhere in 'Chicagoland.' I was a pretty good undergraduate teacher, especially for those fortunate students who needed no teaching at all.[3] Also, I liked teaching too well to search actively for a journalistic post – although of course if journalism had sought me, things would have been different!

The ashes of my journalistic ambitions have been on balance handicaps in my later work. Despite the pressures of scholarship, I still write pretty well (for an economist, that is). But I remain impatient with both logical rigor and factual detail. (The last-named failing would of course disqualify me as an 'investigative reporter.') I retain a certain willingness to jump to conclusions, and then to change my mind, more quickly than one should as a reliable spokesman for any partisan viewpoint; I sympathize deeply with Judge Robert Bork, crucified and rejected in 1987 as a Supreme Court nominee for certain law-review opinions of a dozen years before. And finally, I flit hither and yon in economics, and sometimes beyond economics, before attaining expertise in any topic. Doubtless I shall end, if I live long enough, 'knowing nothing about everything,' as against the specialist's 'knowing everything about nothing.' In the meantime, I have entitled my selected essays *Keizaigaku Tokorodokoro*, which I believe to be the Japanese translation of 'Here and There in Economics.'

Thus far I have mentioned no 'Japanese' interests, and for good reason. Such interests were in fact infinitesimal.'[4] But Pearl Harbor naturally developed my Japan-consciousness at the same time that it propelled the country into World War II.

At that time (1941–42) I had been, I thought, broadening myself by bureaucratic experience in the Treasury and the Federal Reserve system, but the broadening process did not extend to matters international. Actually, my most important lesson from this venture – a lesson often confirmed later – was that I was poorly adapted to work in a hierarchical organization, civil or military. I had not learned, and still do not know, how to adjust to an ass as superior officer. How does one report to an ass on technical matters beyond his asinine understanding, or communicate through such an ass with the higher authorities 'upstairs,' who may or may not be equally asinine? Remember, it must all be done without revealing one's awareness of anyone's asininity, especially the asininity of one's immediate superior. (One's occasional asinine chair-monster, dean-monster, or president-monster can easily be evaded among the nooks and crannies of the ivory tower.)

But back to Pearl Harbor and its consequences: World War II was a 'popular' war, meaning that one's draft-dodging had best be done in uniform, and that the 4-F or 'unfit for service' classification was a mark of shame, not a stroke of good fortune. My state of nearsightedness and mal-coordination, I believed, might get me killed or disabled in basic training, or possibly assigned to permanent latrine duty or office routine after I survived. Of such as I, along with more conventional cowards, are draft-dodgers made, both in and out of uniform. As for me, I qualified academically for the Japanese-language program of the Naval Training School (Oriental Languages) on the University of Colorado campus nestled under the Rocky Mountain foothills at Boulder. I volunteered, I was accepted, and there I was (late January 1943, at 15° below zero). Technically I was an apprentice seaman, but if I performed satisfactorily I would be commissioned an officer. Statistically speaking, I would be 'promoted from the ranks' as evidence against the Navy's reputation for elitist gentility in its officer corps.

Language School was 18 months of intensive Hell. Brute memory, for which I had lost a childhood aptitude, was the principal component. All in all, it was the most unpleasant educational experience I had ever had. (One little detail: a four-hour examination every Saturday morning!) My performance was mediocre but passable, and I lived largely for the periodic 'breaks' during which I could try to read and write economics again. Many of my classmates cracked psychologically under the strain, but I only swayed sufficiently to graduate two or three months behind schedule. My Ensign's commission, incidentally, had been held up by a foretaste of what we now call McCarthyism. I was one of the '85 club' of 85 Boulder students with relatives in Axis-occupied lands, or (in my case) something called 'premature anti-Fascism' on their records. As an offset, contact with my Japanese teachers – many of them refugees from Japanese militarism – immunized me permanently from the racist attitudes pervading the American forces in what was a 'race war' to a much greater extent than we like to admit.

Graduation came about the time of the Normandy landings in Europe. My first assignment was to the Advanced Naval Intelligence School in New York. Then came the Navy Department in Washington and finally Pearl Harbor itself, primarily as a translator of captured documents and secondarily as a POW (prisoner of war) interrogator. The translation was deadly stuff, economically significant insofar as it involved Japanese modifications of US designs in response to Japanese wartime shortages. POW interrogation was fun. Far from torturing or maltreating prisoners 'like in the movies,' I got along better with them than with my superior officers, and gave them most of my rations of beer and tobacco. (I drink only moderately, and smoke not at all.) I was assigned prisoners who had worked in factories of which we had aerial photographs. As an economist, and therefore an expert on factory production, I was instructed to ask questions whose answers might help the Air Force assign priorities for future pinpoint bombing. The prisoners cooperated without question – we treated them considerably more humanely than the Japanese Army and Navy had done – and perhaps my questions might have been useful had the war lasted longer. Pearl Harbor, of course, was thousands of miles behind the battle lines, but there was a widespread rumor that we were being saved for the invasion of Japan's southern island of

Kyushu, scheduled for November 1945. (This was to take place simultaneously at three widely separated beaches on that large island; Kagoshima, the Naples of Japan, was where rumor had me headed.)

But in August 1945 the atom bombs fell, the Soviets entered the war, and Japan surrendered. For admittedly selfish reasons, therefore, I am less opposed than most of my friends to nuclear warfare as compared with the 'conventional' varieties. After the Japanese surrender, I did indeed go to Kyushu, but as a member of a forlorn Civil Censorship Detachment wandering about the northern half of the island in search of a more definite assignment. It was on these travels that I was bitten by the 'Japan bug' from which I have never recovered. Forty-odd years later, Japan remains 'Good to the Last Drop' even though 'the last drop' falls far short of the first ones.

Japan's appeal was not a matter of serenity, geishas and Mt Fuji. There was no serenity about immediate postwar Japan; girls calling themselves 'geishas' were mostly something else; my first view of Fuji was from an aircraft carrier headed back to the US. What was it then, this peculiar appeal? Mainly, I think, being a highly privileged observer of a society in flux – turning itself inside out, under an Occupation mild enough to transform wartime hatred into a temporary wave of good feeling. (By the same token, contemporary China is a more interesting place than today's complacent Japan!) And second, going back to 1945, the realization that language-school Japanese was good for something, so that my investment of time and effort (over and above the Navy's estimated investment of 27000 pre-inflation dollars per Japanese language officer) was not a complete waste.

I had of course learned that bygones were bygones and bad investments bad investments. One took one's losses and started over; one did not pour good money after bad. I was advised again and again, by colleagues I respected, to 'forget all that Japan stuff' in favor of following the current fads of the scholarly journals to professional recognition as a mainstream economist. Perhaps I should even have taken their well-meaning advice, but 'economic principles' sometimes make better sense on the blackboard than under one's own skin.

Having been fortunate enough to wangle repeated revisits to Japan, I have found them paying unanticipated dividends, of which I mention four:

1. A box seat at the 'economic miracle' --- whose 'miraculous' nature and significance I somehow failed to recognize until it had already happened! (Had the Japanese taken my advice, they would neither have subsidized heavy and technical industries, come 'up-market' in their price and quality policies, nor tolerated the inflationary accompaniment of their 'income-doubling' plans. Had the miracle occurred at all, it would have been slower than it was, and run more quickly into foreign resentment.)

2. A certain recognition as a specialist, if not precisely an expert, in Japanological economics or economic Japanology. This came to include an increasingly important teaching field, which tolerant colleagues in other departments have sometimes let me expand into general Japanese history at an advanced undergraduate level.
3. A post-retirement teaching position in a School of International Studies at a Japanese private university, Aoyama Gakuin in Tokyo, which is evolving from a pre-war 'mission school' into a full-fledged institution of learning.
4. And most important of all, my wife Teruko. She is a civilian veteran of both strafing from the air, at her wartime job in an airplane-parts plant, and the fire-bombing of her home city – Yokohama, in May 1945. After my first marriage became a casualty of wartime separation, I met Teruko on my second trip to Japan in 1949–50. I was disguised as a tax economist and revenue estimator; she was a trade-union activist and a student of Western-style dramatic art. After a difficult courtship and a long separation, we were married in Madison, Wisconsin, late in 1951. She has been an ideal wife (and psychiatric nurse) for a problem husband, as I found out under the related strains of McCarthyism and periodic psychological depression. She has also learned some economics in spite of herself; originally well to my political Left in economic policy, she has moved well beyond me on the Right, to the dismay of two children who grew up protesting this and that in the late 1960s and early 1970s.

After people settle into domestic routine, their lives tend to become dull and uninteresting – sometimes even to themselves. In my case, the years since 1951 have been spent on campuses and in airplanes between campuses, so I am no exception to the general tendency. Few people, I am sure, are interested in how I became first enchanted and then disenchanted with Keynesianism, how my concern with the alleged maldistribution of income and wealth became weathered down to a desire for safety nets for those at the very bottom of those distributions, how I tried to 'modernize' Marxian economics, or how I struggled to reconcile general theories of economic growth with the special case of Japan. But a few points have involved 'philosophy of life' issues during the past generation.

First among these is the 'scoundrel time' of McCarthyism, during which I was investigated by several 'security' and 'intelligence' agencies. My closest approaches to conviction (or even indictment) for anything at all came when I resigned my Naval Reserve commission in 1947, ostensibly as 'over-age for my rank,' and when I cut short a leave of absence in Japan 'under fire' in 1950. This near-immunity I may owe largely to luck; what the Navy had against me was not what the Civil Service Commission had against me, and neither was what SCAP (the Occupation of Japan) had against me. Had the various 'Bronfenbrenner' files been unified and combined, as they may be today, I might have been in real trouble on the principle of 'where there's this much smoke, there must be some fire.' Eventually I made and kept a New Year's resolution never to apply for any position requiring a security clearance. Meanwhile I never had occasion to 'take the Fifth Amendment' or to have a passport denied. I was, in short, a very small fish indeed – perhaps a sub-minnow.

Once, in 1955 I believe, I was asked to 'name names' among my former associates. I am ashamed to confess that I did so, 'covering myself' (or so I thought) by adding that I knew nothing of anyone's Communist Party membership or present political position, and that to my best knowledge none of these people had ever committed a seditious act. But one of them, a California medical researcher named Bill Sherwood, whom I had known at Chicago, committed suicide two years later on the eve of a re-investigation of his own case.

So far as I know, my academic superiors were not informed of these problems of mine.[5] The troubles I anticipated never eventuated. I did not even, for any long period, consciously take a low profile or moderate my policy positions. (Some of my students have wondered whether McCarthyism had amputated my intellectual backbone; I not only hope but believe that they are wrong.)

What McCarthyism (and its successor, the John Birch Society) actually did was to keep me voting New Deal Democrat for some years after my economic-policy views had drifted away from Keynesian orthodoxy. Better to be a free man under Keynesian inflation or neo-Cambridge 'incomes policies,' I thought, than in jail under free enterprise! More generally, what does one do when one's best friends within the profession are on the other side of some important policy questions, and when one's policy allies include a significant minority of unsavory characters with whom one would rather avoid association? My solution has been to follow principles and ignore associations; I am not sure I can recommend it for others.

A dozen years after disgrace and alcohol had silenced both 'Our Joe' and his numerous imitators in the Wisconsin State Legislature, the universities faced similar pressures again – this time from the Left, in the so-called student revolts. It had taken disgrace and death to end McCarthyism. Ending the military draft, withdrawal from Viet Nam, co-ed dormitories, the erosion of academic standards – and a dose of postwar unemployment! – sufficed to scuttle the student revolt. At that time, as a senior professor at Carnegie-Mellon University, I took a stronger stand against student activism than I had dared take at Wisconsin against McCarthy. I felt and stated that, in hiring junior faculty members from outside, we should investigate who had and who had not been involved in physical violence on the campuses from which they came, and reject out of hand those who had been so. And also, that we should warn other universities against the extremists in our own student body – speaking, of course, as individuals and not as representatives of the university. Such steps should not have been matters of academic freedom, but might of course have become so in practice. I still think I was right in this position, and later observed with some horror the influences of Vietnam-era appointees in other departments. (Economics has been fairly effective in isolating direct-action extremists in a few 'Red ghetto' departments here and there; as a result, 'political economy' courses, springing up outside economics departments, have tended toward emotional propaganda devoid of analytical content.)

Having located myself at several different institutions at various points in time, I cannot dispute my reputation as one of the more volatile and nomadic members of our profession, with overtones of unreliability and being difficult to deal with. I have indeed moved too much, and some of my lateral moves have been mistakes. But in every case I was pulled rather than pushed, and I claim to have avoided some mistakes worse than any I actually made. Also, precisely because of my Jewish ancestry, I have deliberately refrained from haggling about money, fringe benefits and so on. When I felt myself treated unfairly and received an attractive offer from outside, I have tended to accept it, sometimes with too little concern about leaping from frying pans into fires. In terms of Albert Hirschman's *Exit, Voice, and Loyalty*, hindsight suggests that I overplayed the first and underplayed the third. Duke University, however, was the exception. In my 13 years at Duke, I was happy to be there, and I would have been happy to see the children enrolled there; in the event, they chose to go away from home; but Duke does a remarkably good job of satisfying faculty and student body otherwise than at the expense of each other.

ADDITIONAL MATERIALS

Much my substitute for any formal 'philosophy of life' has already been interspersed with the autobiographical notes just completed. The result is a kind of club sandwich, I hope digestible – readable, I mean. But there are postscripts I want to add.

C.P. Snow was right to speak of the Western world's *Two Cultures*, the humanistic and the scientific. And Paul Samuelson was more than half right to point out that economics is most unusual among our scholarly disciplines in combining the two cultures and providing room for both scientists and humanists. But Samuelson may be less than 100 percent right, because I think he forgets three points:

1. Economists are not born but made.
2. There are two separate and disparate streams of recruits into economics, one from more exclusively humanistic branches of learning, and the other from more exclusively scientific ones.
3. Within economics, members of these two streams engage in competitive coexistence, more competitive on balance than coexistential.

With only so many 'loaves and fishes' to go round – graduate fellowships, prestigious chairs, Nobel prizes – there has arisen a certain rivalry between our 'humanists' and our 'scientists' about their division. At the beginning of twentieth century, the rivalry was muted, because *The Economist as Preacher* – George Stigler's title – had things pretty much his own way. 'The economist as preacher' (or social philosopher, or historian of economic institutions) was the profession's first-class citizen. The occasional 'economist as applied mathematician' (or statistician) was the second-class citizen if not the outcast or what we have more recently come to call the 'weirdo.' By the time I ventured out of the woodwork, in the 1930s, the balance was being redressed; the formation of the Econometric Society in 1933 was a benchmark. Although basically a humanist by preference, I thought the change was desirable, and supported it in some small way. (Had I known how far the change would go I should surely have got out of economics while the getting out was good, if indeed I had ever entered at all!) For now the balance is reversed. To see economics as a branch of applied mathematics (or applied statistics, or applied computerology) makes one a first-class citizen, while 'the economist as preacher' is exiled to Academic Siberia at places like *Elmer Gantry*'s Terwilliger College 'with standards equal to the better high schools.' I have been thinking wishfully for a generation that this trend too had gone far enough, had reached its peak, and would reverse itself next year or the year after. Thus far I have been egregiously wrong.

Many budding economists share my experience of having thought themselves God's gifts to economics, and then being deflated to something considerably less. How one should react to such psychological trauma I do not know, but have advised students along the following pessimistic lines:

1. The profession has plenty of room, even 'need' for mediocrity. (If agencies want PhDs for high-school-level hack work, some graduate schools will meet the demand.)
2. Forget about 'not failure, but low aim, is crime.' If your deficiencies consign you to the lower levels, adjust accordingly – even when others no better qualified (but better connected!) make it to the topmost heights.
3. Don't try to make a marginal dissertation mediocre, either by expansion or by mathematization. Don't let 'landmark' dissertations (*Canada's*

Balance, *Monopolistic Competition*, *Economics of Control*, *Foundations of Economic Analysis*) scare you into a writing block. If your subject is the dog tax in your home county, just do whatever you can with it.

4. Melancholia is to professional work, including economics, as black lung is to coal mining. Many people of course escape, but you should assume you will eventually get it. Finish graduate work and get your first job quickly, so that you can relax and take it easy if depression hits you. Pick your family and friends, if you can, with an eye to their prowess at psychiatric nursing. If worst comes to worst, you may even have to see a psychiatrist.

Teaching, at or below the undergraduate level, is a common fate, often involuntary, for economists at some stage in their careers. Economists should therefore rid themselves, if they can, of the notion that such teaching is below their dignity, even if their 'average students' belong in universities only to the limited extent that deaf-mutes belong in the Metropolitan Opera.

Teaching relatively small groups of self-starting superior students – who, I have said, do not really need to be taught – demands different skills (subject-matter enthusiasm and facility) than does the keeping of thundering herds of Yahoos reasonably awake and happy for 50 or 75 minutes at a time. Some great university teachers can do both at once; among my professional acquaintances, Walter Heller and Abba Lerner came closest to doing so. Others are content to concentrate on one group, letting the other shift largely for itself. Admitting myself an intellectual snob and lecturing on that basis, I came at Duke to combine the best of two worlds – high student 'ratings,' small undergraduate classes.

But was it ethical to fob off average students so largely on one's colleagues? My 'other' chairman at Duke – I held a secondary lectureship in history – said that it was. I said that it was not. It conformed, I thought, to my comparative advantage; many teachers, perhaps most, prefer students who come to be entertained and who ask no searching questions; and finally, the reward structure for teaching concentrates at most institutions on one's performance in the big classes, through which research time is opened up for one's colleagues.

Nineteen Eighty Four has come and gone; it was my retirement year at Duke. But the problem Orwell raises has not really gone away. (The Orwell model must be modified to whatever extent new generations of nuclear weaponry make continuous long-range nuclear warfare obsolete.) Independently of Orwell, I agree that contemporary military technology, with its premia on speed and secrecy and its 'unbearable' cost, combined with electronic surveillance and data-banking, put the liberal society at increasing disadvantage. This disadvantage is not only against illiberal foreign powers, but also against private armies and professional guerilla groups within its own borders.[6] I therefore fear we may be headed for at least a modicum of dictatorship with civil rights at least suspended. The regime may, if all goes well, permit liberal ideas to hibernate in isolated spots (ivory towers included).

As early as World War II I had feared that civilian control might not be given up after hostilities had lasted for a few more years; in the event, the Nazi collapse and the atom bombs proved me not wrong but irrelevant. I thought the same in the Viet Nam War, here the American war effort collapsed instead. And so it may be indefinitely, or at least until technology changes back in favor of the ordinary citizen. Nevertheless it behooves more of us, I fear, to keep escape hatches open than now seem willing to make the investment. (We could use potential American Solzhenitsyns, capable of teaching junior high school physics and math in small towns and writing 'for the drawer' while waiting for the next thaw.)

I close by rewarding your patience with a parody on Gilbert and Sullivan's *Patience*:

> If this old fud expresses himself in words
>   too deep for *me*,
> What an extraordinarily deep old fud
>   this deep old fud must be!

NOTES

1. Professor Viner was a hard grader, but meticulously fair. He also called on students in class, to cross-examine them with the technique of a prisoner-of-war interrogator. I was afraid of him, but never felt I deserved better than the mediocre grades he gave me. He did, however, scare me away from his principal teaching field of international economics. (Paradoxically, this has become my own principal teaching field in Japan, after a crash course of self-education on my part.) Shortly before his death (in 1970), Viner expressed to a colleague of mine regrets at having discouraged students by the harshness of his grading and classroom manner. Scenting a message meant for myself, I wrote Viner to assure him that I deserved no better grades than he had given me. His reply: 'Are you sure? I thought I had given you As.' As for classroom manner, some critics claim I have learned more from Viner than I am willing to admit. Certainly the aimless flounderings of 'the average student' still lead me to recall Viner's methods of handling such oafs at Chicago half a century or more ago.
2. Professor Schultz himself had died during the preceding autumn, in an automobile accident on California's Pacific Coast Highway.
3. This is an exaggeration of a sort. What can a teacher do for a student 'who does not need teaching?' He can make it worth such a student's while to attend class and stay awake. He can encourage such a student to go on to more advanced levels of study. He can slow such students down when, in their haste, they neglect the fundamentals. And he can be a wall off which such students can bounce ideas, both orally and in writing.
4. My father had got his professional start in America, well before I was born, as research assistant to the great Japanese bacteriologist Hideyo Noguchi in the study of the trypanosome of syphilis. I recall meeting the Great Man shortly before he left for Africa to study the etiology of yellow fever, which would kill him in 1928. Later I had read his biography (by Gustav Eckstein), an unhelpful introduction to 'things Japanese.'

5. An exception from the early 1960s: speaking at Morehead, Minnesota, I mentioned my grandmother's service in the Red Army during the Russian Civil War. (She was a nurse, and had headed a military orphanage.) Certain Morehead citizens came to Minneapolis and complained to the President of the University of Minnesota about hiring professors without investigating their grandmothers! President Meredith Wilson of Minnesota did not inform me of this incident; when I found out about it by the grapevine, I apologized to President Wilson for involving him in such a stupid waste of time.
6. I have tried to spell out and support these ideas in 'The Liberal Economist in the Directed Economy,' *Southern Economic Journal* (April 1980).

7. Sex and the Ivy League

Graciela Chichilnisky*

Life is strange. Since childhood I have followed a peaceful and enjoyable inner path, which later developed into a matching professional and family life. I felt in harmony with my goals, and able to achieve what is important. Playing 'tomboy', I was attracted to masculine arenas and accomplishments, and never thought of myself as a woman. I always enjoyed good challenges, which to me are the spice of life. Yet somewhere along this path I met uncontrollable external forces, full of sound and fury, and had to experience first-hand the stormy transition of women's roles at the turn of the twenty-first century. I joined Columbia University in 1977. For me, Columbia has become a challenge to meet, and the road to merge my internal and external lives: my personal values with my public life.

TWO REFLECTIONS

My first reflection from my professional experience in academia is that for a woman to survive and to thrive she must learn to turn negative responses into positive resources. This is a perverse reversal of the Pavlovian response. I call this, for short, 'turning dung into fertilizer.' I truly believe it is one of the most important elements for women's success and happiness. It is a wonderful recipe for dealing with the 'glass ceiling,' a well-known and somewhat cruel situation where the more you succeed, the more you get punished. Think of it this way – energy is energy, and simply changing the sign of the response one receives from negative to positive allows one to use all the energy received constructively, and turn it into a survival tool. In mathematical terms, this is 'life modulo two.' It is the absolute value of the response that counts, not the sign.

For women who are at the frontier, there is one positive feature of the strategy of transforming 'dung into fertilizer.' When using negative responses as fertilizer, one never runs out of resources.

*The author has posted an unabridged version of this chapter on her website: www.chichilnisky.com.

The second reflection is simpler yet, and perhaps more fundamental. It is that the only genuine source of happiness in life is the feeling of being useful to others. Nothing else does the job. This is true for anybody. It is not achievement or success; it is not money. It is this feeling of being useful that counts. This is why the issues of sex and the Ivy League are important to me, and below I explain why.

BORN IN BUENOS AIRES AFTER WORLD WAR II

I was born in Buenos Aires at the end of World War II, into a warm and loving family of Jewish intellectuals who fled the Russian pogroms at the turn of the twentieth century and immigrated to Argentina to build a future. I was the second child of a wonderful and very prominent man, Salomon Chichilnisky, who built many hospitals in Argentina and a large part of its national health system as the Secretary of Health in Juan Peron's government and beyond. My father was the physician of Eva Peron when she died. He started life carrying loads in the docks in the port of Buenos Aires to support his parents, brothers and sisters. Against all odds he became a medical doctor and the first Jew to become a chaired professor at the School of Medicine of the University of Buenos Aires, in neurology. He eloped with my mother, Raquel Gavensky, whom everybody called 'Duke.' My mother was a child from a wealthy fur-exporting family, and was as beautiful as she was intelligent and kind, 25 years younger than my father. Both were wonderful. They died while I was in my thirties.

DISCOVERING MATHEMATICS AND EDUARDO JOSE

Attending high school in Buenos Aires, at an advanced all-girls school called Instituto Nacional de Lenguas Vivas, I discovered that Jews were not really welcome. Being the first in the class did not help. I always worked hard and had the best grades, but somehow I could never make it to the position of raising the flag in the morning's convocation on the school's old patio, a position that is given to the best students. There was always something missing. Finally, when all excuses were gone, in my last year in that school there came a day when without doubt I was the only one that could raise the flag in an important school event. I was full of pride as my illusion was finally to be fulfilled. Suddenly, hours before the event, the schoolmistress found that there was a small spot on my white uniform. I called my mother at home and she rushed to school with another fresh uniform and gave it to the headmistress. However, after she was gone the schoolmistress discovered to my surprise that there was a small button missing in the second uniform. My wonderful mother then brought another button, but when she came back for the second time, they had put me in a small room to wait for her and somehow nobody could steer her to where I was. There she stood with the button as I waited for her in another room in the school, and we never met. In the meantime, the ceremony unfolded and my mother stood there watching as someone else raised the flag. This was the last time I could have done this act at the school. My mother thought that I had done something wrong by being kept away in this manner – and so did several others, who knew that it was my turn to raise the flag. The suspicion has lingered in the school since then, and I learned first-hand what it means to 'blame the victim' – without of course knowing those exact words at the time.

In my junior year at high school I started taking courses informally at the University of Buenos Aires. Initially, I tried Philosophy and Sociology, because I always thought that those were the main topics facing humankind and the areas where more progress was needed, namely in human and social organization. However, I gave up these topics quickly in favor of Mathematics – Mathematics seemed clearer and therefore easier – with the idea of going back to social issues later on. I wanted to do Mathematics that would be applied to resolve social problems. I thought that studying Mathematics first would give me a control of the 'technology' that economists use to validate their theories and their policies. I felt it was important to 'control the technology' – rather than 'be controlled by it' – since many economists appear to fear the mathematical foundations of economics and adopt theories or policies based on what they learn from others' mathematical models. I always liked the idea of creating my own mathematical models, rather than adopting somebody else's. Mathematics was a pleasure to learn. I think of it as the natural language that the brain uses to communicate with itself.

My first child, Eduardo Jose, was born in Buenos Aires at about the time I finished high school. Eduardo Jose was a healthy, happy, beautiful and loving baby who grew up to become my best friend and ally. He is now a professor of neurobiology at the Salk Institute of the University of California in San Diego, where he lives with his wife Sascha and baby Ariella. While in retrospect Eduardo Jose had a hard life, born in Buenos Aires and growing up in the US with little money and while his mother was completing two PhD degrees, he was the greatest source of pleasure and sense of accomplishment for me. It is true that children are the greatest pleasures in life.

A MILITARY *COUP* LED TO MIT

Just as I was about to start college in Buenos Aires, there was a *coup d'état* and a military junta took over Argentina and closed down the University. The students demonstrated against their actions. A notable American mathematician from MIT, Warren Ambrose, a founder of modern geometry, was at that time a visiting professor at the University of Buenos Aires. He was hit and hurt by the military police when they closed down the campus and after this incident decided to go back to MIT and take some of the brightest PhD students he met in Buenos Aires with him. I had not started college yet, nor did I know much English, but through the college courses I had taken informally Ambrose and others recommended me as a 'special student' to the Mathematics Department at MIT. I became a special PhD student without having gone to college, with the task of proving myself in the first year of graduate studies in order to be accepted as a regular student. Thus in 1967 I moved with baby Eduardo Jose to Boston, where I started my 'test year' at MIT.

My adviser at MIT was the excellent and late mathematician Norman Levinson, a specialist in ordinary differential equations, and a kindly man who wished well. He recommended that I should give all of this up. He told me that being a woman, a single woman with a small child, and having to compete with PhD students in a top Mathematics department when I had not even gone to college myself, was an impossible task. He recommended that I move instead to Boston University to study a lesser subject such as computers. However, the Ford Foundation generously provided me with a scholarship, and I completed my first year of PhD courses at the graduate program in Mathematics ranked first in the class, thus becoming officially a PhD student at MIT. Eduardo Jose, now almost two years old, lived with me through this process, sharing a room in Cambridge Massachusetts. The hardship of this enormous effort solidified our bond. During this period Ambrose had many PhD students at MIT, from Argentina and elsewhere, some of whom became my friends, such as Alberto Baider, now a professor at the City University in New York, and Ahmad Chalabi, who since then has become a leader of the Iraqi opposition to Saddam Hussein and the founder in 1992 of the Iraqi National Congress in London. Reversing Norman Levinson's expectations was an eye-opener. This period fortified my will and my belief that hard work can conquer almost all. It was the beginning of my view that women need a 'reverse Pavlovian' response to succeed. After that record of success, I was accepted also at UC Berkeley, where I completed my PhD in Mathematics in 1971.

UC BERKELEY – JERRY MARSDEN, MORRIS HIRSCH AND STEVE SMALE

My PhD adviser at UC Berkeley was Jerrold Marsden, a prominent Canadian mathematician who specializes in fluid dynamics. Other mentors included well-known mathematicians Stephen Smale and Morris Hirsch. My PhD dissertation was on ‘Group Actions on Spin Manifolds’ and appeared in the *Bulletin of the American Mathematical Society* in 1972. It was accepted with great reviews by the editor and the referees, who I think were Schlomo Sternberg, a great mathematician and friend who became years later the Chairman of the Mathematics Department at Harvard University, and a great physicist, Roger Penrose of Oxford University. The topic was very attractive, and established a pattern in my life, dealing with the intersection of two fields that rarely come together: in this case, algebraic topology and physics. I used this to explore the possible ‘shape’ of a universe in which there was a conservation of ‘spin angular momentum’. This dissertation dealt with questions such as the finiteness of the universe and its global geometrical structure, an area that has continued to be very fashionable years later. Given the positive response it had, it was tempting to continue that path. While at UC Berkeley I worked also for the cause of women students who had a hard time, with small children – like myself – and created the first US university child care center within the UC Berkeley campus, with the help of the United Automobile Workers Association, a child care center that Eduardo Jose himself attended at the time. I understand this center is still working and has been imitated at other universities.

PhD IN MATHEMATICS AND CREATING BASIC NEEDS

Towards the end of my studies at UC Berkeley, my father became very ill and I started commuting to Buenos Aires to see him. He was 70 years old. To support this expensive traveling I started working in Argentina part-time – in particular while completing my PhD in Mathematics, I took a job as a Director of Modeling at Fundacion Bariloche, located in the beautiful resort town of the same name in the south of Argentina, with high mountains surrounding a huge blue lake. My job was to create a mathematical model of the world economy, which was later called the Bariloche Model. I was collaborating with an interdisciplinary team of prominent Latin American scientists, including geologists, sociologists, population experts, computer scientists, political scientists and economists. Their aim was to rebut the Club of Rome’s Limits to Growth vision of a world in which developing countries could not, and should not, grow because otherwise they would exhaust the earth’s resources. In the Bariloche model, I created the concept of ‘development based on the satisfaction of basic needs.’ This led to my first two publications in Economics, ‘Economic Development and the Satisfaction of Basic Needs,’ published in 1977, and in 1976 *Catastrophe or New Society: A Latin American*

World Model, a book co-authored with the Bariloche team. Both of these publications introduced basic needs into the literature and implemented it empirically with data from five continents. The name itself was created in those publications, and the concept of basic needs became my first real contribution to economics – a somewhat radical concept at the time, which was nevertheless adopted subsequently by 166 nations in 1987 at the Earth Summit of Rio de Janeiro, which voted it as the cornerstone of efforts to define sustainable development. Basic needs is now officially part of the Brundtland Commission's definition of sustainable development, but at the time I had to threaten to resign my job in Bariloche because the rest of the team wanted the model to focus on GDP maximization rather than on satisfaction of basic needs, as I wanted. Maximizing GDP was not, in my view, the main goal of development for the world economy, nor the way to use the earth's resources wisely. I won, and basic needs became the trademark for the Bariloche model, igniting interest and controversy around the world. Eventually basic needs penetrated the United Nations system and the World Bank, becoming a world standard in re-thinking fair and sustainable economic development.

The great and late mathematician and economist Tjalling Koopmans and William Nordhaus, his distinguished Yale colleague, gave the Bariloche model and basic needs a very supportive reception, organizing an entire meeting at the International Institute for Applied Systems Analysis (IIASA) in Vienna, Austria in 1976. After that Koopmans became a strong supporter and Nordhaus, also very supportive, wrote at the time an article, 'Global Modelling from the Bottom Up' which commended the Bariloche model and its goal of satisfying basic needs as a unique combination of 'radical thinking with state of the art technical expertise.'

BACK TO ARGENTINA AND A SECOND PhD

After completing a PhD in Mathematics at UC Berkeley, I went back to Buenos Aires in 1972 where I was appointed as a Member of the Presidential Cabinet of Banco Central of Argentina, the country's monetary authority. This high-level position would allow me to build a career in economic policy with political influence in Argentina, as my father had done. I took this job during a period of democratic presidential rule, and the career path seemed very attractive. Yet I saw first hand how decisions on monetary policy were made, and how little we knew about it all. It was then that I decided I wanted to go back as originally planned to the social sciences, and study economics to understand fully the role of markets, particularly international markets, which I considered key.

I received a scholarship from the Central Bank of Argentina to obtain a second PhD, this time in economics, and was accepted both at Yale University and at UC Berkeley. I decided to go back to Berkeley, where I obtained officially a PhD in Economics in 1976. During this period, while I was completing my second PhD, my father died in Buenos Aires. This was heartbreaking. My mother joined me in Berkeley, where we lived with my son Eduardo Jose for some time. But she was heartbroken and homesick, and went back to Buenos Aires, where she herself died about six years after my father.

This period, when I lost my father and then my mother, was the worst part of my life. Adding to the pain, the legal system in Argentina prevented me from visiting my parents towards the end because at the time the law gave all rights to the father for the traveling of the child. This meant that I could not travel to Buenos Aires unless I left Eduardo Jose in Berkeley – which was impossible. My father and mother died without seeing Eduardo Jose again, their dearest grandchild. This taught me a bitter lesson – at that time in Argentina, marriage gave men undue rights over a woman's life and made it more difficult to take care of one's children. This strengthened my commitment to do what I could so that future women would not face similar situations.

HARVARD UNIVERSITY AND KENNETH ARROW

In 1974, I left Berkeley to go to Harvard University, with a masters degree in Economics but before completing an official PhD in Economics. At Harvard I was to work as a research associate with Kenneth Arrow on an Office of Naval Research (ONR) grant. Kenneth Arrow became an important mentor for me. The research position at Harvard involved collaborating also with Peter Kalman, an excellent economist and friend from the State University of New York at Stoney Brook, who sadly died prematurely a few years later. At the time I went to Harvard I had successfully finished all my courses and PhD exams, and also completed a first draft of a PhD dissertation in Economics that I produced for Gerard Debreu, my PhD adviser at Berkeley.

As a foreign woman and a single mother, I started to face bewildering circumstances in the submission of my second PhD dissertation. This led me eventually to abandon all the research done in the first dissertation I wrote in economics and to write, two years later, while I was teaching at Harvard and after publishing several articles, a third and completely different PhD dissertation. This was the second dissertation I wrote in economics, and the third PhD dissertation I wrote in my life. In 1976, while I was teaching at Harvard, I was awarded officially a PhD in Economics with Gerard Debreu as my main adviser.

While it is hard enough to compete with men in academic research, obtaining credit for what one has accomplished proved to be much more difficult. Achievement in academia is often 'word of mouth' and based on colleagues' voluntary references, which is less objective and more difficult to measure. I would like to cite a book, *The Outer Circle*, where some of these findings were substantiated by the co-authors, several sociologists who included Jonathan Cole. *The Outer Circle* documents that academic citations in scientific publications are consistently biased against women. Cole and his co-authors found that men resist giving women the credit in the form of citations for prior or related work, while these citations are in reality the 'currency' for academic recognition, and the basis for measuring academic achievement. There is even a book on 'citation indices' that measure this form of achievement. Men, according to *The Outer Circle*, successfully deny women credit for their work in the form of much lower or less appropriate academic citations. In my case it became so pronounced that Geoffrey Heal called it a 'conspiracy of silence.' People would often replicate my work without, however, giving me acknowledgement in the form of citations. This problem exists today and in my case it has only become worse as my work has become better known.

TEACHING AT HARVARD AND TRAVELING TO BARILOCHE

By 1976 I became a lecturer at Harvard, where I taught Mathematical Economics. During the time I was there, from 1974 to 1978, I published some of the defining work in my career, in particular the work on the Bariloche model and basic needs, 'Development Patterns and the International Order' in *Journal of International Affairs*, the book *Catastrophe or New Society*, and the work that introduced Hilbert spaces in optimal growth theory, 'Non Linear Analysis and Optimal Economic Growth,' in *Journal of Mathematical Analysis and its Applications* and solved outstanding problems of duality in that area, as well as some of my best work on international trade, 'Terms of Trade and Domestic Distribution: Export led growth with Abundant Labor Supplies,' *Journal of Development Economics*, in which I showed that export-led growth can backfire as a foundation for growth in a country with abundant labor supply and must be replaced by policies that shore up domestic markets.

Towards the end of that period I also published my work on international aid or transfers, and on topology and social choice. The latter demonstrates the intrinsic geometrical structure of the paradoxes of social choice, and found a resolution to the social choice paradox. It is an area that Kenneth Arrow had initiated many years ago while he was a PhD student at Columbia University, closing a cycle in the development of the subject.

UNITED NATIONS AND PHILIPPE DE SEYNES

Towards the end of the period at Harvard I received a visit by M. Philippe de Seynes, a Frenchman who had just left his post as Under Secretary General for Economic and Social Affairs at the United Nations to lead the 'Project on the Future' of the United Nations Institute for Training and Research in New York, UNITAR. Philippe was an important figure in international diplomacy, and an admirable man. He thought that my concept of basic needs was the way forward, and encouraged me to produce further work in that area, but like me he thought it needed international market underpinnings. Hired by him, I started my official career as UN adviser running UNITAR's international research projects starting in 1976 for about ten years. My work with UNITAR was based on the fame that the basic needs concept had achieved and the value that the Bariloche model had in pursuing the development strategies for the Third World.

COLUMBIA, NED PHELPS AND BOB MUNDELL

At the end of the period at Harvard, I met two wonderful economists from Columbia University: Ned Phelps, a friend of Kenneth Arrow, and Robert Mundell, both of whom recruited me successfully as an associate professor at Columbia University starting in the fall of 1977. At that time I almost took a job as a researcher at the Bell Labs of AT&T, and was also offered, by Professor Harold Shapiro who later became President of the University of Michigan, a position as Associate Professor in their Economics Department.

However, Columbia University attracted me at the time because of the proximity to the United Nations in New York, and because of the first-class people I met there. Robert Mundell is a warm man and one of the most original and incisive thinkers I have ever met, and Ned Phelps is equally warm – an extraordinarily distinguished economist in a class all of his own. My instincts were right, because there are truly wonderful people at Columbia.

SUSSEX, ESSEX AND GEOFFREY HEAL

I joined the Columbia faculty in the fall of 1977, and during 1978 I spent part of the year working also at the Harvard Institute for International Development (HIID) in continuation of the growing research project I directed then for the United Nations and UNITAR, called Technology Distribution and North–South Relations. In expanding this project to Europe, I started a collaboration with Dr Sam Cole of the University of Sussex Science

Policy Research Unit, a specialist in the MIT Limits to Growth model, who joined me as a co-director of a larger UNITAR project which then included a team of interdisciplinary researchers in four continents. This project acquired a large projection in the United Nations organization and had a major impact on policy, leading to discussions and resolutions related to basic needs, export-led growth and international aid, supported by an excellent team of researchers.

In England I also met Geoffrey Heal, a Cambridge University economic theorist who had recently become the Chair of the Economics Department of the University of Sussex. This turned out to be a defining event in my life, because several years later in 1983 Geoff Heal joined Columbia University as a professor in the Business School; soon he and I became prolific co-authors and Geoffrey eventually became the father of my second child, my daughter Natasha Sable, who was born in New York in 1987.

UNITED NATIONS, WORLD BANK AND OPEC

By 1978 I was promoted as a tenured associate professor at Columbia, a year after arriving at the University, and in 1980 became a tenured full professor of economics at Columbia. During late 1979 and 1980 I accepted the Keynes Chair at the Economics Department University of Essex, living in England during a period of leave from Columbia University and returning to Columbia in 1981. During this period I also worked at the International Institute for Applied Systems Analysis (IIASA) and acted as an adviser to OPEC in several wonderful summers spent in Vienna, at the World Bank in Washington DC, and the United Nations in Geneva. Both the World Bank and the United Nations were naturally aligned and very interested in my concept of basic needs and in using mathematical and economic modeling to make it operational in economic terms. In Geneva the International Labor Office (ILO) of the United Nations started an entire research effort based on basic needs in a number of countries. Basic needs took off as a paradigm for alternative development. I also advised the World Bank on trade policy and on international aid during that period. At OPEC in Vienna, I created a model of the world economy where the role of their organization was seen in an integrated international market framework – showing how high oil prices could eventually backfire for their organization ('Non-Conflicting Oil Pricing in the Long Run,' *OPEC Review*, 1983). This period was full of insights in theoretical and policy terms, and eventually led to the publication of two books, *The Evolving International Economy* and *Oil and the International Economy*, both co-authored with Geoffrey Heal, which are discussed below.

SOUTH TRADE: EXPORT-LED GROWTH

While initially I had great difficulties publishing my work – it was considered too mathematical and too 'different' – at the end of the 1970s my list of publications started to grow fast, and from 1980 on my research and publications took on a life of their own.

In addition to mathematical economics, one angle that greatly interested me due to my work at Bariloche and the United Nations was to see the world divided into a North and a South, two regions that were in two very different stages of development. The North represents the nations that have already completed the Industrial Revolution, while the South is in the midst of a change from agricultural to industrial societies. Coincidentally, the geography of the planet is such that the industrial countries are indeed mostly in the northern hemisphere and the developing nations in the southern hemisphere, which explained the North–South divide. I thought this divide was pregnant with explanatory power. In particular I thought it could be used to explain the dynamics of the world economy. I focused on two policies that I thought were misguided and could be improved: one was the emphasis on international aid as the most important way to resolve poverty and other developing nations' problems. The second was the emphasis on recommending developing nations to specialize in resource-intensive or labor-intensive exports as the main policy to accelerate economic growth. Both policies seemed wrong to me, and I looked for ways to model what I thought were the main issues, to explain them mathematically in order to offer alternatives. In 'Term of Trade and Domestic Distribution: Export Led Growth with Abundant Labor' (*Journal of Development Economics*, 1981), I created a model of international trade that in time became an alternative to the existing models created by Heckscher–Ohlin and by Ricardo – and ended up being called my North–South model.

At that point in time, international trade was modeled either as a Heckscher–Ohlin world, consisting of two countries trading with each other who differ only in the relative proportions of capital and labor, or modeled as a Ricardian world where the two countries differ in technological productivity in two sectors. In each case the differences (factor proportions or technologies) were used to explain why countries trade with each other, and why they benefit from trade.

My view was different. I thought that the world was divided into two regions that were in two different stages of development. In one region, the 'South,' labor was abundant in the sense of the great late economist Arthur Lewis, namely very 'elastic' labor supplies, and technologies were quite different in terms of factor use across the two sectors. I described this by saying that the South had 'dual technologies' and 'abundant labor.' In the North, matters are different. The economy is more homogeneous, in the sense that factor use is similar across the two sectors, and labor supply is fixed as in the Heckscher–Ohlin world. In sum, my southern region was close to Arthur Lewis's model of a developing economy, while my northern region was closer to a Heckscher–Ohlin model of an economy. My North–South model represented a world where Heckscher–Ohlin trade with Arthur Lewis.

I felt that seeing a world where trade occurs between such different nations has tremendous explanatory power. Such a world is quite different from one where trade occurs between equals (as in Ricardo or in Heckscher–Ohlin). I was right in the sense that the results I obtained in the North–South model on classic topics, such as trade policies or transfers, were radically different from the results that other economists had obtained up to that point.

My work in international trade quickly became well known, particularly my models of export-led growth and of transfers, and it started to take over my life. While the attention it received was flattering, the results created a lively controversy in the US as well as in Europe, and some hostility as well. The work on export-led growth was considered heresy by those who advocated growth for developing countries based on exports, and particularly exports of labor-intensive products. In a way, they were right in considering my work heresy. I was advocating economic growth based on strengthening domestic markets, while the 'export-led growth' vision saw the engine of growth for developing countries in the industrialized world, with the domestic economy being mostly a source of cheap labor. This to me was a neocolonialist way of looking at the economy of a developing country – and one that was dated and could not succeed in the modern world.

ANOTHER HERESY: INTERNATIONAL AID AND TRANSFERS

My 1980 results on transfers ('Basic Goods, the Effects of Commodity Transfers and the International Economic Order') were somewhat unsettling because they turned on its head common wisdom with respect to international aid. International aid was considered to be, at the time, the leading solution to the increasing North–South wealth differential. In the late 1970s and early 1980s, great economists such as Wassily Leontief were advocating international aid in their United Nations projects as a solution to close the gap between the North and the South. In my view, this was once again looking at developing nations as dependent on the industrial countries, and not the engine of their own growth.

Earlier, great economists such as John Stuart Mill, John Maynard Keynes and Wassily Leontief himself had anticipated that aid could help the donor more than it helps the receiver, due to the effect of market forces after the gift.

While those classic economists had shown this to be a possibility, Paul Samuelson and his student Robert Mundell had argued that this effect was more of a 'curiosum' than real, that in well-behaved stable markets aid always ends up benefiting the receiver, as it is intended to do. Their arguments view market forces as benign. My work, however, showed the opposite. I showed that international aid that ends up benefiting the donor and hurting the receiver is a standard phenomenon. It happens in well-behaved, competitive and *stable* markets, and in markets that have unique equilibrium. It is not a curiosum. Markets are not that benign. This is something that Paul Samuelson and Robert Mundell said could never happen. This work appeared in the 1980 article in the *Journal of Development Economics*, 'Basic Goods, the Effects of Commodity Transfers and the International Economic Order,' and led to a lively controversy for several years. My 1980 article dealt with what has been called the 'transfer paradox' – it refers to the fact that market forces can subvert the intentions of international aid, because a donor can end up better off than the receiver of the gift due to market forces.

My contribution to this classic issue was looking at a world with three or more trading nations – while Samuelson and Mundell had restricted their work to worlds with no more than two countries. Here is where my mathematics helped – by allowing me to attack a more complex but more realistic problem while other economists shied away from this because of the intrinsic mathematical difficulties.

In the debate that ensued, many articles were written about the results on transfers and the export-led work, and eventually, in the early 1980s, two separate issues of the *Journal of Development Economics*, then edited by Lance Taylor at MIT, were dedicated to comments on these two results. One double volume of the *Journal of Development Economics* (vol. 15, nos 1, 2 and 3) was dedicated to comments on the results on export-led growth, and a second issue of the *Journal of Development Economics* (vol. 13, nos 1 and 2) was dedicated to the work on transfers. The debate was heated to the point that UNITAR, which was funding my research, received a letter from one of my colleagues calling my results 'dangerous' and untrue. Eventually, however, everybody accepted the validity of my results on transfers, particularly after an excellent geometrical article published in 1983 by John Geanakoplos and Geoffrey Heal, 'A Geometrical Explanation of the Transfer Paradox in Stable Markets' that made the points transparent and easy to grasp.

Here is the point: transfers alter market prices. After the gift, the donor country has fewer resources but their market value goes up so the country ends up richer than before. The opposite happens to the receiver; this is the competitive market at work. The results on export-led growth were also accepted although there was some debate because the dynamical system I used was more complex than that used frequently in trade theory.

FITEL AND NATASHA IS BORN

In December 1985 I took a short leave from Columbia and started a company called FITEL with a group of friends who included Geoffrey Heal, Eduardo Jose and Jeff Bezos, who since then has become the Founder and CEO of Amazon.com. I became FITEL's Chairman and CEO, and raised $6 million in investment that I transformed into a $30 million corporate valuation in two years. The company was ahead of its time. It offered financial services to support international trading of securities, services which only recently has the industry started to imitate. Based on state-of-the-art electronic technology, FITEL created the first global electronic network offering global processing and communications – one that preceded the Internet and the World Wide Web – facilitating communications and matching of securities trades between the US, Europe and Japan. I created the software, developed it and marketed the services, and led successfully as CEO a group of about 60 people in three continents. FITEL became a very profitable and well-known company. With offices in New York, London and Tokyo, it offered me a shelter against the hostility at Columbia, a way to succeed without being punished.

In the midst of this development, my daughter Natasha Sable was born in New York in August 1987. In my eyes, Natasha was the most beautiful and happy baby ever known. She was born sufficiently apart from my first child Eduardo Jose that I had forgotten the rigors of motherhood. Natasha's fate was to travel widely since birth, and when she was one year old she had her birthday party in a plane to Tokyo. Eventually the pressures of motherhood led me to sell my stake in the company, which is now a successful communications provider in Japan, and dedicate myself to care for Natasha for a year. Today Natasha is 15 years old and has fulfilled my wildest dreams as a daughter. She is currently in Buenos Aires, Argentina, with my sister Tamara and her two children – and with their father Torcuato Di Tella, who is a prominent Latin-American sociologist currently serving as Minister of Culture in the newly elected democratic government of President Kirschner.

INCREASING RETURNS AND OIL IN THE INTERNATIONAL ECONOMY

Following this period in the late 1980s, I started the study of trade with increasing returns to scale, a topic that became rather popular years later, and published several articles and two more books, *The Evolving International Economy* published by Cambridge University Press in 1993, and *Oil and the International Economy* published by Oxford University Press in 1996, both co-authored with Geoffrey Heal.

The Evolving International Economy focused on the theory and policy of international trade in a world divided into industrial and developing nations, a world in which increasing returns to scale were achieving increasing importance. The book was an outgrowth of the Bariloche model for me, because it integrated the North–South issues in the context of international markets. In the Bariloche model there were no international markets – while this book was all about them.

This book led to many insights and policy predictions, some of which are still unfolding today. For example, we predicted that increasing returns to scale sectors are the first to 'boom' when the market upswings, and the first to 'bust' with lows in the business cycle. Indeed, telecommunications and airspace industries showed extravagant growth in the dot.com boom while many firms in these sectors became bankrupt in today's long downswing. The recent article, 'Volatility in the Knowledge Economy,' co-authored with Olga Gorbachev in 2003, validates this fact. The data show that in the telecommunications industry alone, 87.9 percent of the firms went bankrupt between 2000 and 2003. This was our prediction, and it has come to pass.

Our book also predicted an increasing wealth differential between the North and the South as long as such trade policies persisted, emphasizing decreasing returns exports from the South and increasing return exports from the North – a wealth gap that unfortunately has come to pass also. The book called for an end to the resource exports policies in developing nations, proposing to strengthen internal markets as an alternative policy. I stand behind those recommendations now more than ever.

The second book during this period, *Oil and the International Economy*, published in 1991, focused on oil as the single most strategic resource exported by developing countries. It pointed out that oil is a 'double-edged sword' for those nations. We showed data validating that developing countries that export oil do not grow more than those that import it; they grow less. This was a surprising finding at the time, but has become almost common knowledge since then. We explained that exports of resources, principally petroleum, could be a curse rather than a blessing. This policy-based book also contains theoretical models showing the increased wealth divide that would occur between North – the industrial nations which export under increasing returns to scale conditions – and South – the developing nations that export mostly resources and labor-intensive products with decreasing returns to scale.

At the end of the 1980s, a number of articles on trade and increasing returns to scale showed that increasing returns to scale on their own explain why countries trade – to benefit from increased markets. I used this to explain (in 'Traditional Comparative Advantages and Increasing Returns to Scale: NAFTA and the GATT,' 1994) the emergence of 'trading blocks' and the extent to which trading blocks with increasing returns can be viewed as a step towards the liberalization of trade rather than a step towards isolation and trade wars between trading blocks.

TOPOLOGY AND SOCIAL CHOICE – SOCIAL DIVERSITY

A stroke of luck led me in 1977 to find a geometric explanation for the mysterious 'social choice paradox' that Kenneth Arrow had presented in the 1950s as part of his own PhD dissertation at Columbia. This finding led to a complete resolution for the first time for the 'social choice paradox,' namely to a set of conditions which are both necessary and sufficient for a resolution of the social choice paradox that Arrow had found. My insight identified the problem as being geometrical in nature, using algebraic topology tools as I had done in 1977 with my PhD dissertation in Mathematics. In economic terms I was able to demonstrate that the problem of social choice could be viewed simply as one derived from excessive social diversity. There is a precise degree of social diversity that allows a solution to the social choice paradox. Beyond that, there is no solution.

Social diversity of course is a good feature of the economy – as it allows gains from trade. But my results showed that there is a limit, that beyond a certain point it renders voting systems dysfunctional.

These new results were very satisfactory for me. While I had worked with Kenneth Arrow and greatly respected his brain and his wonderful results, in truth, I could never understand the 'structure' of his paradox of social choice, which he had presented in a combinatorial fashion. Arrow's combinatorial results were unclear to me. The entire literature following Arrow's lead was combinatorial, while I could only 'see' geometrical structures and spatial representations.

The breakthrough for me occurred in 1977, while I was advising the United Nations and after a seminar that I presented at the Bell Labs, in a division led by Elizabeth Bailey who was interested in hiring me at that point. I came upon a response to a question by Robert Willig, now at Princeton, which led me to the creation of a topological explanation for the problems of social choice. This led eventually to my article 'Social Choice and the Topology of Spaces of Preferences' published in an MIT journal edited by the great late mathematician Gian Carlo Rota, *Advances in Mathematics*, in 1980, and to a number of other articles that used the first result to explain a lot of what had been unclear in the field. New results emerged that could not be obtained before, I suspect, because the right mathematical infrastructure was not available until then. Somewhat unexpectedly, Rota himself was a great specialist in combinatorial mathematics.

As a follow-up to this discovery, I published another mathematics article, 'Intersecting Families of Sets and the Topology of Cones in Economics' in 1994, in the leading mathematics journal, *Bulletin of the American Mathematical Society*, edited at that time by the excellent mathematician Richard Palais. Here I showed, somewhat surprisingly, that the basic structure of the most important forms of resource allocation was connected with that of the social choice paradox that Kenneth Arrow had pioneered. The same mathematical structure was also the cause of problems of market equilibrium as well as the 'core' in game theory. Surprisingly, the common root of all these problems is the issue of when sets intersect, and in economic terms this measures once again social diversity. This is the key issue in finding a solution to market equilibrium, for social choices and for game solutions.

In this work I showed with Geoffrey Heal the first necessary and sufficient conditions for the existence of social choice rule ('Necessary and Sufficient Conditions for a Resolution of the Social Choice Paradox,' *Journal of Economic Theory*, 1983). Later on, somewhat surprisingly, I extended on my own these earlier results to create the first necessary and sufficient conditions for the existence of market equilibrium, the core and social choice – the same conditions in the three cases. I called these conditions 'social diversity' and also 'limited arbitrage'; these conditions have a mathematical expression as a 'topological invariant' that measures the extent of social diversity. Social diversity holds the key. Beyond a certain point, it prevents the economy from reaching market equilibrium, a core solution or social choice rules. Otherwise, the economy has all three properties. This theory validated the key role of diversity in allowing markets to function, and gains from trade, while at the same time limiting most forms of resource allocation beyond a certain point.

TOPOLOGY AND INNOVATION

The initial insights to resolve the social choice problem were followed up in a series of several articles in the *Journal of Mathematical Economics*, *Economic Letters* and in *Social Choice and Welfare*. Later on in 1986 I published necessary and sufficient conditions for the resolution of the paradox in *Journal of Economic Theory* with Geoffrey Heal. To everyone's surprise, my 1980 discovery focused on a topological 'obstruction' that has to be removed for appropriate voting to be possible. This 'obstruction' is an object from algebraic topology – the area of my first work in mathematics where I looked at the geometry of the universe. The 'obstruction' I discovered measures the degree of 'social diversity' of the population. This concept was developed in some detail many years later in 1993, as discussed below.

More recently I refined this work with the introduction of a 'topological invariant' that decides when there is a solution to three problems simultaneously: the existence of market equilibrium, social choice and the core of a game. It is called an 'invariant' because it does not depend on numerical measurements but rather on geometrical or topological shapes. This is important in economics or in other social choices where numerical measurements are often unreliable.

These findings convinced me that topology, and more particularly algebraic topology, is an ideal tool for the social sciences. This is a point I had already made in a lecture I gave at Harvard University, 'On the Foundations of Political Economy,' organized by a great economist and friend, Amartya Sen, in 1990. Since then a journal has emerged on the topic, *SocioTopology*, created in 2002, in which I act as an editor. I was not alone, therefore, in thinking that algebraic topology is a 'tool of choice' for the social sciences.

My newly created 'topological invariant' is based on the homology of a 'nerve' defined by a family of sets naturally associated to the economy. This mathematical construct was never used before in economics and appeared in my 1993 article in the *Bulletin of the American Mathematical Society*. The concept turned out to be too advanced for the mathematical tool kit of most economists so far, and it has not been widely used yet.

The 1980 results on social choice are some of my best-known work (together with basic needs and the global trading of carbon emissions permits) possibly because Arrow is an arbiter of this area and he is more flexible and open-minded than most. My work on trade is perhaps more widely known, as the number of mathematical economists is much smaller than the number of international economists. Yet the mathematical sophistication of the field of international trade is lower than that of mathematical economics, and technological innovation in international trade is generally less well received. This could be considered somewhat of an understatement.

NORTH–SOUTH TRADE AND THE GLOBAL ENVIRONMENT

Soon after the results of 'Intersecting Families of Sets and the Topology of Cones in Economics' appeared in *Advances in Mathematics*, I published in 1994 'North–South Trade and the Global Environment' in the *American Economic Review* (*AER*). Paul Milgrom of Stanford University, a great economist and a friend, acted as an editor and showed tremendous patience and intelligence in dealing with the innovation in that piece. The *AER* is of course a leading journal in economics, and my new article develops and generalizes my earlier work on international trade, clarifying the linkages between global markets and the problem of the global environment. This link underlies my earlier work in the Bariloche model and on basic needs. The thesis of this new article is that difference in property rights for resources explains trade between nations. Since then this has become well known and accepted. In March 2003 I gave a series of lectures to a group of students from several Danish universities and other Scandinavian countries at the University of Southern Denmark; to my surprise, all were familiar with my 1994 results, which they took almost to be 'common knowledge' within the environmental literature.

The 1994 *American Economic Review* articles 'North–South Trade and the Global Environment,' and its earlier 1993 'twin' for the case of renewable resources, 'North–South Trade and the Dynamics of Renewable Resources,' in *Structural Change and Economic Dynamics*, show that differences in property rights for environmental resources predict why nations trade, and how. The North, the industrial countries, hold their resources as private property, while developing nations in the South treat resources as common property or even 'open access'. I showed that this difference in property rights regimes between the North and the South by itself explains why those countries that are not particularly rich in natural resources end up exporting resources to others which have more. It also explains the low international prices for resources. This creates overconsumption of resources and lack of technological innovation in energy within the North, and overexploitation of resources and poverty in the South. It is the main cause of today's global environmental problems.

Overuse of the 'global commons' leads to global warming, which is a result of excessive consumption of fossil fuels. It also leads to the biodiversity loss associated with the destruction of forests and watersheds ecosystems to grow cash crops or graze animals, in both cases for the international market. Export-led policies based on resources, under these conditions, benefit nobody. This article is an evolution of my first article in international trade, and it shows that differences in property rights result in apparent 'abundance' of labor and resources in the South.

A solution to the problem would be reached by improving property rights regimes in the South, so that markets can operate more efficiently. However, it is difficult to change property rights on land or on petroleum. It may be easier to define property rights on the output of production, which is the environment, rather than on the inputs, which are the resources themselves. Changing the rights to use the global environment may be easier than changing property rights on land.

This leads to limits on emissions and allocating global rights to emit, potentially trading these rights globally. In a nutshell: this is the creation of global emissions markets.

I made this recommendation to Timothy Wirth, Undersecretary of the US

Department of State, and Larry Summers, Undersecretary of the US Treasury, in 1996 and 1997. Tim Wirth took this recommendation as the US position in the United Nations global climate negotiations. This in turn led to the Kyoto Protocol, which incorporates both limits on emissions by industrial countries and the beginning of the rights to trade them. This was contained in the Protocol, parts of which I wrote directly at the 1997 Tokyo Meeting of the Parties to the United Nations Framework Convention on Climate Change (UNFCCC), working with Raul Estrada Oyuela, the Argentinian diplomat who was the chief negotiator of the Kyoto Protocol for the UNFCCC and its creator.

ENVIRONMENTAL MARKETS: EQUITY AND EFFICIENCY

The recent book *Environmental Markets: Equity and Efficiency*, published by Columbia University Press and co-authored with Geoffrey Heal, documents the evolution of my work on the area of emission markets. It also documents the intense debate that ensued when we showed, with Geoffrey Heal and David Starrett in the early 1990s, that there is a connection between equity and efficiency in markets with privately produced public goods – such as the carbon composition of the planet's atmosphere. The book captures the entire debate incorporating articles from OECD economists as well as from Raul Estrada Oyuela himself, the author of the Kyoto Protocol.

This book began the study of markets with privately produced public goods, which I view as the most important markets in the twenty-first century. Examples of such goods are knowledge and the environment. They represent the most important trends in the world economy. These markets behave differently from the classical markets with private goods. In these markets the distribution of property rights matters for efficiency. Efficiency and equity are linked. These are the markets of the future.

Back at Columbia I felt that the hostility had become relentless. I asked for the help of the Faculty Affairs Committee of the University Senate, who produced a favorable report recommending improvements in my teaching and my salary, but led to no action. After exhausting all internal remedies, in 1991 I filed a claim with the New York Equal Employment Opportunity Commission (EEOC). In 1992 I filed a class action suit in the Federal Court for gender discrimination in salary and promotion on behalf of all faculty women. This case was eventually settled in 1995, and in addition to my settlement agreement, four other women faculty at Columbia were offered significant salary increases.

Meanwhile, starting in 1992, I spent a few years as a visitor to the excellent Stanford Institute for Theoretical Economics during the summers, and in 1994 and 1995 I was also Visiting Professor at Stanford University, teaching in their Economics Department and also in the School of Engineering, Department of Operations Research, where I was invited by a distinguished mathematician Curtis Eaves.

Also in 1993 and 1994 I was offered by the United Nations Educational and Scientific Organization (UNESCO) an academic chair called the UNESCO Chair, in recognition of my 20 years of service to the United Nations community. This Chair could be held either at Stanford University or at Columbia, depending on my choice. Jorge Werthein, a political scientist from Stanford then in charge of UNESCO's office in New York and an Argentinian colleague, communicated this decision to me. Eventually this Chair was endowed to me at Columbia and in 1995 I became the UNESCO Professor of Mathematics and Economics at Columbia University. This was a singular honor since there are few chairs of that type endowed by UNESCO across the world. Columbia's Administration committed funding, space and resources for the Chair and administrative support of its activities including a program of academic visitors and students, and collaboration with other universities in South Africa and South America.

Around early 1996, I was also made Professor of Statistics in addition to my position of Professor of Economics. I was already part of the faculty of Columbia's School of International Affairs as well as the Political Science Department. Around that time also, Columbia University released a long-anticipated salary equity report that resulted in disclosing irregularities and led to salary adjustments for four other female professors. An article, 'Equal Job, Equal Pay' in the university's newspaper *Columbia Spectator* of 12 February 1996 reported that 'problematic areas for women faculty at Columbia' were 'detected' and that 'women were concentrated in the lower professional ranks.' The article concluded: 'Until such a time where salaries and promotions are granted solely on a merit-only basis, the University must make every effort to discover the reason behind these discrepancies and to reverse past discrimination practices.'

AXIOMS FOR SUSTAINABLE DEVELOPMENT AND ENDOGENOUS RISKS

Starting in 1992, I had the privilege of working at Stanford University with great colleagues such as Paul Milgrom, Masaiko Aoki, Kenneth Arrow, David Starrett, Curtis Eaves, Joe Stiglitz, Peter Hammond, Paul Davies and many others. Walt Heller and Ross Starr from UC San Diego were great colleagues and friends who supported me particularly through the process of putting together the book *Markets, Information, and Uncertainty* that I published with

Cambridge University Press in 1999 with original contributions from many of the best economic theorists in the US, in honor of Kenneth Arrow's seventieth birthday. This followed a conference that I had organized at Columbia University in 1992 to celebrate this event. The conference was packed and continued very late into the evening with enormous participation by the audience, as fitted Kenneth Arrow's warm and engaging personality as well as his extraordinary life's work. It was a heartwarming event followed by a party that Ken himself described as one of the most enjoyable celebrations he had.

While at Stanford in 1993, Kenneth Arrow organized a workshop on inequality and asked me to produce an article for presentation in it. He specifically wanted 'original' articles and not 'run of the mill' work. I took him at his word, and this led to my article 'What is Sustainable Development?' where I tackle a difficult problem – the definition of the concept of sustainable development in a way that is operational and yet truthful to its meaning. To achieve this aim, I introduced in this article two axioms that require equal treatment for the present and the future generations. This imitated the process that was followed by Von Neumann and Morgenstern in their theory of choice under uncertainty. Like them, too, through a representation theorem, I identified all the preferences that satisfy the axioms. The preferences that emerge from this process are unusual – indeed, never seen before – a combination of discounted sums of utilities with a long-term factor and I called them 'sustainable preferences.' In mathematical terms, sustainable preferences are a mix of 'countably additive' with 'purely finitely additive' measures. The classical calculus of variations on which much of modern economics and mathematics is based – does not work for these new types of functionals. It must be reworked to accommodate such types of maximizing functions. Some of this work has been done, but much remains open.

AXIOMS FOR SUSTAINABLE DEVELOPMENT AND CATASTROPHIC RISKS

The purpose of the article 'What is Sustainable Development?' (*Land Economics*, 1997) was to define economics in a way that treats the present and the future in a more balanced way than in most of economic theory. Economics often treats the future by 'discounting' it. Therefore any project with gains in the future and costs today is given a low value. Discounting the welfare of the future inevitably leads to a bias against any form of development that has long-term goals, such as sustainability. This explains why our economic policies are, on the whole, not sustainable.

At the time, in 1993, economists were seeking a definition of sustainability that was as 'rigorous' and workable as that used in optimal growth theory, where the future is exponentially discounted. Taking a somewhat bold step that led to some friction, I introduced the two axioms 'no dictatorship for the present' and 'no dictatorship for the future.' Then I identified all the preferences that satisfy these axioms.

My article, 'What is Sustainable Development?', initially met with great skepticism by Kenneth Arrow and by Peter Hammond, both of whom thought that what I was trying to achieve was mathematically impossible. Peter Hammond helped refine the ideas with his friendly but critical stance. Arrow's great mind sought first errors and logical flaws, and gave me a really hard time, but eventually he became convinced and indeed very supportive of the concept of sustainable preferences. So did Geoffrey Heal, who investigated further its properties in a book entitled *Valuing the Future*, published recently by Columbia University Press.

This work led to a completely new way of seeing 'time' in economics. I used it subsequently to treat the economics of risks in an analogue mathematical fashion. This led to a number of pieces on 'catastrophic risks.' Small-and large-probability events are treated axiomatically in a more even-handed fashion than allowed by the Von Neumann–Morgenstern axioms and their expected utility theory that is the foundation of game theory. In 2000, I published 'An axiomatic approach to choice under uncertainty with catastrophic risks' (*Resource and Energy Economics*), where I proved that Von Neumann's expected utilities are insensitive to small-probability events and characterized all utilities that satisfy my axioms. These are a new type of utilities – a convex combination of 'expected utility' with purely finitely additive measures that represent concern for small-probability events. These utilities have never appeared before in economics (or elsewhere) and their optimization requires a different treatment, leading to different results. Expected utility theory leads to a number of contradictions pointed out in the so-called 'Allais paradox,' which finds inconsistencies between the way people choose under uncertainty in reality and in expected utility theory. My axioms corrected that. In doing so I identified a new way to treat catastrophic risks – namely small-probability events with large consequences, in a way that tallies with the observed evidence, and resolves Allais's paradox.

As part of this research program I wrote with Geoffrey Heal an article, 'Global Environmental Risks' (published in the *Journal of Economic Literature* in 1998). Here we introduced the idea that, as humans now dominate the planet, they themselves pose the largest risks to our species. We have evolved to the point where we are our own worst enemy. This led me to introduce a theory of endogenous risks, a name that afterwards was also used by others in a somewhat different context, and to establish several existence theorems in financial markets with such risks, published in the book

Mathematical Economics (three volumes) published with Edward Elgar in 1998. Some of these results appeared in 'Markets with Endogenous Uncertainty: Theory and Policy' (*Theory and Decision*, 1996), which led to the Leif Johansen award at the University of Oslo. As part of this program I also created a new type of financial instruments called 'catastrophe bundles' – a mix of securities and insurance – and proved that they can hedge against unknown risks. 'Catastrophic Bundles Can Deal with Unknown Risks' was published in *Best's Review* in 1996, and 'Managing Unknown Risks: the Future of Global Reinsurance' appeared in *The Journal of Portfolio Management* in 1998.

COLUMBIA'S PROGRAM ON INFORMATION AND RESOURCES

In 1994 I became the Director of Columbia University's Program on Information and Resources (PIR), a program in which Geoffrey Heal acted as Deputy Director. In a short period of time, about two and a half years, PIR raised millions of dollars of research funding from public agencies such as the National Science Foundation, the United Nations (UNESCO, UNDP) and the UN Foundation, as well as private foundations such as the Sloan Foundation, the Turner Foundation, and several reinsurance companies. PIR focused on interdisciplinary work on the global environment and on risk management. These are areas that Geoff Heal and myself pioneered at Columbia and which fit well with my work going back to Bariloche.

PIR created a series of books on the global environment published by Columbia University Press. Together with an excellent geologist, Dr Christopher Barton of the US Geological Survey, we created the Columbia Center for Risk Management with $1.5 million in funding from several leading reinsurance companies including Swiss Re, Center Solutions and Willis Faber. Many students and prestigious academic visitors gathered around PIR. Raul Estrada Oyuela, the creator of the Kyoto Protocol, was a PIR Visiting Professor for a year, teaching at Columbia Law School, and we had a series of distinguished lectures on the global environment with the participation of some of the most important figures in the world – among others, the extraordinary scientists Lynn Margulis of Boston University and Ilyas Prygogin, the IBM executive Ralph Gomory, the biologist Thomas Lovejoy of the Smithsonian Institution and Peter Raven, the environmentalist who is the Director of the Missouri Botanical Gardens. The Director General of UNESCO, Federico Mayor, and Pierre Lasserre, a French marine biologist in charge of UNESCO's environmental division, visited us and provided additional resources and support towards the formation of a network of like-minded universities around the world, particularly in South America and South Africa.

Since its beginnings in 1994, PIR became my intellectual home at Columbia University, and to a certain extent also that of many students and visiting faculty who joined us. Its concept was unique at the time – and still seems unique now – as it was interdisciplinary in nature and dedicated to global issues, particularly those related to pressing problems of the global environment. We created a version of the GREEN model of the OECD, which we adapted to study the implications of global trading of emissions rights. This is a topic in which PIR advised the US government, the United Nations and the OECD. From these studies Geoff Heal and I recently published a book called *Environmental Markets, Equity and Efficiency* in 2001.

While at PIR I published a large number of scientific articles and books, from 1994 to 1999, some of which were jointly with Geoffrey Heal, encompassing economics, mathematics and mostly focused on the global environment, financial markets, social choice and international trade.

PIR AND THE UNESCO CHAIR

Since its foundation in 1994, Columbia had supported PIR in various ways, providing its office space, matching research funds, and additional administrative resources. As part of the December 1995 agreement to settle the earlier lawsuit, Columbia promised additional support to PIR in various ways, including additional office space and administrative resources. Separately, the Chair that UNESCO had wanted to endow at Stanford or at Columbia, providing seed funding for this purpose, fit well the themes of PIR, and UNESCO decided to endow its seed resources to PIR so that the Chair's activities themselves became part of PIR. In 1995, Columbia University committed a continuing permanent support of $50 000 a year for me at PIR, to support research in the general research areas of the UNESCO Chair. Eventually, however, PIR became part of a larger effort, the Earth Institute, directed by a new person, Peter Eisenberger, who had a different perspective, coming as he did from the physical rather than the social sciences. The Earth Institute now included the Lamont Doherty Earth Observatory, directed also by Peter Eisenberger.

KNOWLEDGE REVOLUTION

One of the most interesting and thought-provoking areas of research being conducted at PIR was the 'Knowledge Revolution.' We created this term to describe the rapid period of change of the last few years during which knowledge is gradually replacing capital as the most important input of production. To put an imprint in our contributions I trademarked the term 'Knowledge Revolution' and started the process of trademarking also 'Biosphere and Society,' publishing a number of articles and conducting empirical research in these two areas. To study the Knowledge Revolution, we developed mathematical models of a new type of markets. These are markets with 'privately produced public goods,' and 'knowledge' is one of those goods, as are many environmental goods.

The transforming global trend that I call the 'Knowledge Revolution' is similar in scope to that which took place when capital replaced land as the most important input of production. This was the transition from agricultural to industrial societies, and was called the Industrial Revolution. The analogy is clear.

The topic, and the research on markets with privately produced public goods, led to a number of research projects that were funded by the Sloan Foundation as well as by the Italian Academy at Columbia University and were supported partly by Columbia resources.

Several articles were published in this period highlighting public policy issues that were the results coming from those models. One of the main policy issues was the importance of property rights regimes on knowledge. In parallel with the historical debate on the ownership of capital when it became the most important input of production after the Industrial Revolution, property rights on knowledge are probably the most significant policy issue after the Knowledge Revolution. At PIR we developed a proposal to replace patents by (compulsory) licenses that must be traded within competitive markets, which received much attention at the time.

THE GLOBAL ENVIRONMENT AND PETER EISENBERGER

In the summer of 1996 Columbia created the Earth Institute, and recruited as its leader Peter Eisenberger, a prominent physicist from Princeton University who joined the Columbia faculty in September 1996, holding a chaired position in Earth and Environmental Sciences as well as the position of Vice-Provost for the Earth Institute. Eisenberger had previously created and successfully led Princeton University's Materials Institute, and was clearly a most distinguished and interesting scientist. The Earth Institute had the same domain of expertise and subject matter of PIR. Indeed, the Earth Institute was itself what PIR was supposed to have grown into. To his credit, Peter Eisenberger soon realized that PIR was the exact focus of the efforts of the

Earth Institute, and adopted Geoffrey Heal and myself as natural collaborators in administrative and intellectual ways, while at the same time attempting to keep a very close and indeed symbiotic relationship with Vice-Provost Mike Crow. While not an expert on the global environment himself, Peter was clearly an intellectual powerhouse and adept at building institutions. It was heartening to observe the appreciation that he expressed intellectually for PIR's work as well as the administrative plans and fund-raising efforts of PIR. Eisenberger and Heal were soon collaborating closely in the Earth Institute Academic Committee, and I was not far behind, as a member of the Committee myself. We successfully did fund raising together, organized major conferences, 'Managing Planet Earth', the 'Reuters Forum,' 'Non Linear Dynamics, Natural Hazards and Risk Management' and 'From Kyoto to Buenos Aires: Technology Transfer and Emissions Trading,' and although I was effectively demoted by Peter's position, I had gained a powerful scientist and organizer as an ally. The situation was once again reversed, and towards the end of 1998 we managed to turn another piece of 'dung into fertilizer.'

During this period I presented to a large audience at the 1996 World Bank yearly meetings a proposal which we initiated at PIR for the creation of an International Bank for Environmental Settlements, or IBES, a global institution that would have as a mandate to derive value from the world's environmental assets without destroying them. The IBES would be self-financed, and would use as its source of funding the most valuable assets of the planet, our environmental resources.

I proposed this institution to update the Bretton Woods institutions created by Keynes and Meade after World War II, when I was born. They include the World Bank and the IMF among others, and were created to replace war by trade and succeeded beyond anyone's imagination. International trade between nations has grown four times more than actual world economic product in the world since then.

The Bretton Woods institutions are based on resource-intensive patterns of development that they enforce in developing countries, leading to deep environmental destruction. My proposal instead is to rely on knowledge-intensive development which is less damaging to the global environment. The Bretton Woods institutions have outlived their usefulness, becoming the victims of their own extraordinary success.

The International Bank for Environmental Settlements (IBES) was meant to provide and implement a regulatory environment and a liquidity source for the trading of emission rights on a global scale, as the SEC does in the US, offering also loans and options to facilitate 'reversible' policies. The IBES could also commercialize (via licensing) the use of the knowledge encoded in the developing countries' biodiversity to the benefit of those countries. This IBES proposal attracted great interest by the Global Environmental Facility related to the World Bank, and by the United Nations as a whole, and I wrote in 1996 a book published by the United Nations Educational and Scientific Organization (UNESCO) and the United Nations Development Program (UNDP), which was marketed by them over the world to make this proposal a reality: *Development and Global Finance: The Case for an International Bank of Environmental Settlements*. The IBES is still work in progress.

PIR AND NEW YORK COURT'S INJUNCTION OF MARCH 2000

Suddenly, in June 1999, Peter Eisenberger resigned his position as Vice-Provost for the Earth Institute and Director of the Lamont Doherty Laboratory, for reasons of health and for 'matters of principle.' He had an open-heart surgery operation that left him out of action for several months. We were all shocked at this unexpected development. When Eisenberger left, the Earth Institute Academic Committee was folded up, removing me from participating. In March 2000 the New York Supreme Court provided an injunction that forced Columbia University to stop dismantling PIR's offices, its equipment, research documents and data, and requiring that they preserve the status quo respecting the Settlement Agreement of 1995, until further order of the Court, and stop forthwith any further destruction of the PIR offices or materials. In response to the Court's injunction, two years later, in 2002, Columbia and I entered into an agreement that replaced the old PIR offices by a corresponding suite of offices in another building, where PIR is operating at present. In February 2003, the UNESCO Chair itself was reinstated by Provost Jonathan Cole. According to Provost Cole my title is UNESCO Professor of Mathematics and Economics and Professor of Statistics, as well as Director of the Program of Information and Resources and the Columbia Consortium for Risk Management.

LYME DISEASE

Having had the luck of being healthy all my life, in the summer of 1998 I had strange symptoms that were later confirmed to be Lyme Disease, a bacterial disease which is endemic in the eastern US, transmitted through ticks in forests or meadows. This serious disease often starts with fever, extreme tiredness and arthritis, and eventually leads to heart failure, neurological damage, meningitis, loss of memory and eventually dementia and death. Although I started several treatments in 1998, after a few months of completing each treatment, the disease would re-establish itself, each time worse than before. This was frightening. In the fall of 1999, the Chief of the Lyme Disease Center of New York's Lennox Hill Hospital, Dr Argyros, found that I had reached an advanced stage of Lyme disease, the last stage, and a condition that soon incapacitated me and took several years to eradicate. After a long and determined battle, in 2002 I was declared cured, although this disease in general can be recurrent.

In the period after 1998 I was unable to teach or work as usual, although I was able to be productive otherwise in areas where writing and thinking were key, particularly during the recurrent periods in which the disease was in temporary remission. I published a large amount of work, participated when possible in conferences, and the enforced physical limitations almost paradoxically allowed me to carry out more thinking and research than ever. I understand that this is the case with others as well, and the British physicist Stephen Hawking is an extreme and famous example. My teaching during the period was sporadic since the disease would go up and down, and when I was not well I could not stand properly, walked with a limp, and was often unable to raise my arm or write, in addition to having the memory lapses, blurred vision, and extreme tiredness and lack of body strength that characterize this disease.

NATASHA AND CROSS-BORDER EXCHANGE

The Lyme disease made everything more difficult and together with the lawsuit made this period of my life quite challenging. It also took a toll on my family life. I separated from Geoffrey Heal and eventually my lovely and happy daughter Natasha became a victim of the situation, with serious consequences for her feelings and her socialization. This took an unexpected and dangerous turn of events in the fall of 2001, threatening her life. In order to support Natasha and myself while I was unable to teach, I made an effort to increase my consultancy work – which is standard for economists and is in fact encouraged by the University in its Faculty handbook – when possible. With a few friends we started a company that followed the successful footsteps of FITEL in the Internet Age, called Cross Border Exchange, which started operating in 2000. This was very interesting and rewarding, and more accommodating than teaching at Columbia, with a flexible time schedule adapted to my physical restrictions and the ups and downs of the disease.

Life does not stop throwing new challenges. In the fall of 2001 there was a particularly dangerous incident that threatened Natasha's life, and the Board of Directors of Cross Border Exchange agreed that I had to give her my first priority as needed. Over time, as I overcame the disease, I went back to teaching full time at Columbia, devoting more time to Natasha than ever while she was successfully completing her second year of high school and gradually becoming better. Natasha is an extraordinary child and worth every second of the time I am able to invest in her. Dedicating myself to her also made me feel useful, a great bonus in what is otherwise a difficult situation. More 'dung into fertilizer.'

WHAT IS DEMOCRACY AND GLOBALIZATION?

At present I am writing on a subject that brings together several strands of my previous work: democracy and its importance in social evolution. This is based on solid scholarship but addressed to a general readership. It was motivated by the looming global conflict between the West and the Muslim worlds.

Our species now dominates the planet. Humans or their close genetic relatives have lived on earth for four million years. However, only recently has human activity reached a level at which it affects fundamental processes such as global temperatures, the planet's water mass, and the complex web of species that make up life on earth. We have progressed to the point of becoming our own worst enemy.

The challenge now is to find paths of social evolution that allow us to reap the benefits of the breathtaking achievements in science that are not matched by our laggard social skills. Social evolution and organization are the key to our ultimate success or extinction as a species.

Elsewhere in my scientific work, I have shown that populations that have a majority of genes that are dominant are condemned to extinction. In other words – in a changing world, survival of the species requires a diverse gene pool rather than genetic dominance by majorities.

Change is more intense and widespread than ever, and social evolution has become perhaps more important for survival than genetical evolution. Democracy, a widely accepted and admired principle to allocate resources in society, depends on the protection of minorities to avoid the Tyranny of the Majority as viewed by Alexis de Tocqueville in *Democracy in America*. Dominant majorities condemn a society to extinction in the same way that a dominant majority of genes condemns a population to extinction.

Starting from the work on sustainable development and choice under uncertainty with catastrophical risks, I define axiomatically democracy as the lack of dictatorships of all kinds and identify all the political processes that satisfy this axiom. Through a representation theorem I show that they are a combination of a 'rule of the majority' and the 'protection of minorities.' In my view, this is what democracy means. This is my latest finding, to be published in articles and also as a book.

Separately at PIR we are doing empirical work with a bright Columbia PhD student Olga Gorbachov, 'Volatility in the Knowledge Economy,' showing that increasing returns to scale sectors – such as communications, airspace and most of the 'new economy sectors' involving services and knowledge – grow faster than the rest when the economy expands, and shrink faster than the rest when the economy contracts. This fits well with the findings of my earlier book, *The Evolving International Economy*, and explains that globalization can be a destabilizing force – since a larger part of the modern industrial economy has increasing returns to scale. The results have a theoretical underpinning as well – and explain why nations benefit from trade – and also when globalization is a positive force for all involved – when exports involve increasing returns sectors for all involved. Then, international trade that enlarges one's market makes all countries more productive and efficient, and everybody better off.

TURNING DUNG INTO FERTILIZER

What remain therefore are my family and my public persona. This is my relationship with others. Turning 'dung into fertilizer' here means that the best I can do in this situation is to be positive towards myself and useful to others. Enjoy my life, give love to my family and those close to me, be productive and, most importantly, try to be useful to others.

I believe that 'Sex and the Ivy League' is an important topic. In the era of the knowledge revolution, universities play an important role in the marketplace of ideas. Old-fashioned systems and discipline are holding us back – but eventually change must take place and we must adapt to what society needs. This is what society needs: to make up for the change that is taking place in the comparative advantage of the two genders, compensating for the genetical mix we have inherited from the Stone Age. The comparative advantage that men have had over the ages, namely brawn, is becoming less important than knowledge and social skill. Here women have no handicap. Social evolution has to catch up with genetic evolution, and make up for the fact that our brains and bodies through human evolution do not fully reflect the needs of today's world.

'Sex and the Ivy League' is a critical topic because the 'glass ceiling' is an important problem for the cause of women. While we hear every day of sexual discrimination and harassment at all levels, the glass ceiling is a key for women. The problem right now is at the top, where more role models are needed. Women are able to enter in the lower ranks, but not able to go all the way up. The higher they go, the more discrimination they face. This is where I believe my two reflections could help most. And it is where a somewhat bewildering but exhilarating future awaits us all: a future of gender equity at all levels. A dream world where one can create, produce, succeed and be useful without being punished for it. Dear readers, men and women alike, I hope to meet you there.

PUBLICATIONS

Articles

'Group Actions on Spin Manifolds,' *Transactions of the American Mathematical Society*, Vol. 172, October 1972, 307–15.

'Economic Development and Efficiency Criteria in the Satisfaction of Basic Needs,' *Applied Mathematical Modeling*, Vol. 1, No. 6, September 1977, 290–97.

'Nonlinear Functional Analysis and Optimal Economic Growth,' *Journal of Mathematical Analysis and Applications,* Vol. 61, No. 2, 15 November 1977, 504–20.

'Development Patterns and the International Order,' *Journal of International Affairs*, Vol. 31, No. 2, Fall/Winter 1977, 275–304.

'Social Choice and the Topology of Spaces of Preferences,' *Advances in Mathematics*, Vol. 37, No. 2, August 1980, 165–76.

'Basic Goods, the Effects of Commodity Transfers and the International Economic Order,' *Journal of Development Economics*, Vol. 7, December 1980, 505–19.

'Terms of Trade and Domestic Distribution: Export Led Growth with Abundant Labor Supply,' *Journal of Development Economics*, Vol. 8, 1981, 163–92.

'Social Aggregation Rules and Continuity,' *Quarterly Journal of Economics*, May 1982, 337–52.

'Trade and Development in the 1980s: Report to the Secretary General of UNCTAD', (with G.M. Heal), United Nations, Geneva, November 1982.

'Structural Instability of Decisive Majority Rules,' *Journal of Mathematical Economics*, Vol. 9, 1982, 207–21.

'The Topological Equivalence of the Pareto Condition and the Existence of a Dictator,' *Journal of Mathematical Economics*, Vol. 9, 1982, 223–33.

'Necessary and Sufficient Conditions for a Resolution of the Social Choice Paradox' (with G. Heal), *Journal of Economic Theory*, Vol. 31, No. 1, October 1983, 68–87.

'Social Choice and Game Theory: Recent Results with a Topological Approach,' *Social Choice and Welfare* (eds P.K. Pattanaik and M. Salles), Amsterdam, North-Holland, 1983, Ch. 6, 79–102.

'The Transfer Problem with Three Agents Once Again: Characterization, Uniqueness and Stability,' *Journal of Development Economics*, Vol. 13, 1983, 237–48.

'Non-Conflicting Oil Pricing Policies in the Long Run,' *OPEC Review*, Vol. VII, No. 4, 1983, 330–56.

'North–South Trade and Export-Led Policies,' *Journal of Development Economics*, Vol. 15, 1984, 131–60.

'Patterns of Power' (with G. Heal), *Journal of Public Economics*, Vol. 23, 1984, 333–49.

'Terms of Trade, Domestic Distribution and Export-Led Growth: A Rejoinder to Rejoinders,' *Journal of Development Economics*, Vol. 15, 1984, 177–84.

'The Transfer Problem in Stable Markets: A Rejoinder to Rejoinders,' *Journal of Development Economics*, Vol. 16, 1984, 319–20.

'International Trade in Resources: A General Equilibrium Analysis,' *Environmental and Natural Resource Mathematics, American Mathematical Society*, Short Course, Eugene, Oregon, 1984, *Proceedings of the American Mathematical Society*, Vol. 32, 75–125, 1985, and G.M. Heal (ed.), *Critical Writings in the Economics of Exhaustible Resources*, Cheltenham, UK and Brookfield, US, Edward Elgar, 1993.

'A General Equilibrium Theory of North–South Trade,' Chapter I, Vol. II in *Equilibrium Analysis*, Essays in Honor of Kenneth J. Arrow (eds W. Heller, D. Starrett and R. Starr), Cambridge, Cambridge University Press, 1986, 3–56.

'Topological Complexity of Manifolds of Preferences,' Chapter 8, *Essays in Honor of Gerard Debreu* (eds W. Hildenbrand and A. Mas Colell), Amsterdam, North-Holland, 1986, 131–42.

'North–South Trade and Basic Needs,' *International Journal of Development Planning Literature*, Vol. 4, No. 4, 1989, 180–221.

'On the Mathematical Foundations of Political Economy,' Invited Political Economy Lecture, Harvard University, 22 March 1990, in *Contributions to Political Economy, Cambridge Journal of Economics*, Vol. 9, 1990, 25–41.

'Social Choice and the Closed Convergence Topology,' *Social Choice and Welfare*, Vol. 8, 1991, 307–17.

'On Strategic Control,' *Quarterly Journal of Economics*, February 1993, 285–90.

'How NAFTA Can Improve Trade,' *Journal of Commerce*, Washington, DC, 16 April 1993.

'Competitive Equilibrium in Sobolev Spaces Without Bounds on Short Sales' (with Geoffrey Heal), Working Paper No. 79, Institute for Mathematics and its Applications, University of Minnesota, June 1984, *Journal of Economic Theory*, Vol. 59, No. 2, April 1993, 364–84.

'Global Environmental Risks' (with G.M. Heal), *Journal of Economic Perspectives*, Special Issue on the Environment, Vol. 7, No. 4, Fall 1993, 65–86.

'The Abatement of Carbon Emissions in Industrial and Developing Countries: Commentary', presented at OECD Conference on The Economics of Climate Change, 14–16 June 1993, *OECD: The Economics of Climate Change* (ed. T. Jones), 1994, 159–70.

'North–South Trade and the Dynamics of Renewable Resources,' *Structural Change, and Economic Dynamics*, Oxford University Press, Vol. 4, No. 2, December 1993, 219–48.

'Intersecting Families of Sets and the Topology of Cones in Economics,' *Bulletin of the American Mathematical Society*, Expository and Research Papers, Vol. 29, No. 2, October 1993, 189–207.

'Who Should Abate Carbon Emission? An International Perspective' (with G.M. Heal), *Economics Letters*, Spring 1994, 443–9.

'Arbitrage, Gains from Trade and Social Diversity: A Unified Perspective on Resource Allocation,' Invited Lecture, American Economic Association Yearly Meeting, Boston, January 1994, *American Economic Review*, Papers and Proceedings, Vol. 84, No. 2, May 1994, 427–34.

'North–South Trade and the Global Environment,' *American Economic Review*, Vol. 84, No. 4, September 1994, 851–74.

'Traditional Comparative Advantages vs Increasing Returns to Scale: NAFTA and the GATT,' in *International Problems of Economic Interdependence* (eds M. Baldassarri, M. Di Matteo and R. Mundell), New York, St Martin's Press, 1994,

161–97.

'Limited Arbitrage is Necessary and Sufficient for the Existence of a Competitive Equilibrium With or Without Short Sales,' *Economic Theory*, Vol. 5, No. 1, January 1995, 79–108.

'The Green Golden Rule' (with G. Heal and A. Beltratti), *Economic Letters*, Vol. 49, No. 2, August 1995, 175–80.

'Markets for Tradeable CO_2 Emission Quotas Principles and Practice,' Economics Department Working Paper No. 153, Organization for Economic Co-operation and Development (OECD), Paris 1995; published as Chapter 10 of *Topics in Environmental Economics* (eds M. Boman et al.), Dordrecht, Kluwer Academic Publishers, 1999.

'The Evolution of a Global Network: A Game of Coalition Formation,' *Journal of International and Comparative Economics*, Vol. 4, 1995, 179–97.

'The Economic Value of the Earth's Resources,' invited perspectives article, *Trends in Ecology and Evolution* (TREE), 1995–96, 135–40.

Chapter 55 in *Leading Economist Ponder the Publication Process*, ed. George B. Shepherd, Glen Ridge, NJ, Thomas Horton and Daughters, 1995, 56–66.

'The Greening of the Bretton Woods,' *Financial Times*, 10 January 1996, 8.

'Catastrophe Bundles Can Deal With Unknown Risk,' *Best's Review*, February 1996, 44–48.

'Individual Risk and Mutual Insurance' (with D. Cass and H.M. Wu), *Econometrica*, Vol. 64, No. 2, March 1996, 333–41.

'Development and Global Finance: The Case for an International Bank for Environmental Settlements (IBES),' United Nations Educational, Scientific and Cultural Organization (UNESCO) and United Nations Development Programme (UNDP), Office of Development Studies, Discussion Paper No. 10, September 1996.

'Markets and Games: A Simple Equivalence among the Core, Equilibrium and Limited Arbitrage,' *Metroeconomica*, Vol. 47, No. 3, October 1996, 266–87.

'Limited Arbitrage is Necessary and Sufficient for the Existence of a Competitive Equilibrium,' *Journal of Mathematical Economics*, December 1996 (Working Paper No. 9596-15, revised April 1996, Columbia University).

'On the Existence and the Structure Pseudo-equilibrium Manifold' (with G. Heal), *Journal of Mathematical Economics*, Vol. 26, 1996, 171–86.

'Trade Regimes and GATT: Resource-Intensive vs Knowledge-Intensive Growth,' *Economic Systems* merged with *Journal of International Comparative Economics*, Vol. 20, 1996, 147–81.

'Market Arbitrage, Social Choice and the Core,' *Social Choice and Welfare*, Vol. 14, No. 2, 1997, 191–210.

'Property Rights and the Dynamics of North–South Trade,' Chapter 8, in *Agriculture, Trade and the Environment: Discovering and Measuring the Critical Linkages* (eds M. Bredahl, N. Ballenger, J. Dunmore and T. Roe), Boulder, Colorado, Westview Press and Oxford, HarperCollins, 1996, 97–110.

'A Robust Theory of Resource Allocation,' *Social Choice and Welfare*, Vol 13, 1996, 1–10.

'Actions of Symmetry Groups,' *Social Choice and Welfare*, Vol. 13 No. 3, 1996, 357–64.

'An Axiomatic Approach to Sustainable Development,' *Social Choice and Welfare*, Vol. 13, No. 2, 1996, 231–57.

'Markets with Endogenous Uncertainty: Theory and Policy,' *Theory and Decision*, Vol. 41, 1996, 99–131.

'What is Sustainable Development?,' *Land Economics*, November 1997, Vol. 73, No. 4, 467–91.

'A Topological Invariant for Competitive Markets,' *Journal of Mathematical Economics*, Vol. 28, 1997, 445–69.

'Development and Global Finance: The case for an International Bank for Environmental Settlements,' Chapter 13 in *Sustainability and Global Environmental Policy: New Perspectives* (eds A.K. Dragun and K.M. Jakobsson), Cheltenham, UK and Lyme, US: Edward Elgar, 1997, 249–78.

'Market Arbitrage, Social Choice and the Core,' *Social Choice and Welfare*, Vol. 14, 1997, 161–98.

'The Knowledge Revolution,' *New Economy*, Institute for Public Policy Research (IPPR), London, 1997, 107–11.

'Limited Arbitrage is Necessary and Sufficient for the Existence of an Equilibrium,' *Journal of Mathematical Economics*, Vol. 28, 1997, 470–79.

'The Geometry of Implementation: A Necessary and Sufficient Condition for Straightforward Games' (with G.M. Heal), *Social Choice and Welfare*, Vol. 14, 1997, 259–94.

'Economics Returns from the Biosphere,' *Nature*, Vol. 391, 12 February 1998, 629–30.

'The Knowledge Revolution and its Impact on Consumption and Resource Use,' 1998 Human Development Report, United Nations Development Program (UNDP), New York, 1998.

'Topology and Invertible Maps,' *Advances in Applied Mathematics*, Vol. 21, 1998, 113–23.

'The Economics of Global Environmental Risks,' *International Yearbook of Environmental and Resource Economics*, Vol. II (eds T. Tietenberg and H. Folmer), Cheltenham, UK and Northampton, US, Edward Elgar, 1998, 235–73.

'Trade Regimes and GATT: Resources Intensive versus Knowledge Intensive Growth,' Chapter 10 in A. Levy-Livermore (ed.), *Handbook on the Globalization of the World Economy*, 226–49, Edward Elgar, Cheltenham, UK, Northampton, US, 1998.

'Smooth Infinite Economies' (with Y. Zhou), *Journal of Mathematical Economics*, Vol. 29, No. 1, 1998, 27–41.

'Global Environmental Risks' (with G.M. Heal), Chapter 12 in *Sustainability: Dynamics and Uncertainty* (eds G. Chichilnisky, G.M. Heal and A. Vercelli), Dordrecht, Kluwer Academic Publishers, 1998, 23–46.

'Managing Unknown Risks: the Future of Global Reinsurance' (with G.M. Heal), *The Journal of Portfolio Management*, Summer 1998, 85–91.

'The Knowledge Revolution,' *The Journal of International Trade & Economic Development*, London, Routledge, Vol. 7, No. 1, 1998, 39–54.

'A unified treatment of finite and infinite economies: limited arbitrage is necessary and sufficient for the existence of equilibrium and the core' (with G.M. Heal), *Economic Theory*, Vol. 12, 1998, 163–76.

'The Economics of Environmental Risks,' Chapter 7 in *The International Yearbook of Environmental and Resource Economics 1998/1999: A Survey of Current Issues* (eds Tom Tietenberg and Henk Folmer), New Horizons in Environmental Economics, Cheltenham, UK and Northampton, US: Edward Elgar, 255–78.

'Existence and Optimality of a General Equilibrium with Endogenous Uncertainty,' Chapter 5 in *Markets, Information and Uncertainty* (ed. G. Chichilnisky), New York, Cambridge University Press, 1999, 72–96.

'A Unified Perspective on Resource Allocation: Limited Arbitrage is Necessary and

Sufficient for the Existence of a Competitive Equilibrium, The Core and Social Choice,' *Topology and Markets* (ed. G. Chichilnisky), American Mathematical Society and the Fields Institute for Research in Mathematical Sciences, 1999, 31–69.

'Intergenerational Choice: A Paradox and a Solution,' *Topology and Markets* (ed. G. Chichilnisky), American Mathematical Society and the Fields Institute for Research in Mathematical Sciences, 1999, 99–110.

'Catastrophe Futures: Financial Markets for Unknown Risks,' *Markets Information, and Uncertainty* (ed. G. Chichilnisky), Cambridge, University of Cambridge Press, 1999, 120–40.

'Equity and Efficiency in Environmental Markets: Global Trade in Carbon Dioxide Emissions,' *Environmental Markets Equity and Efficiency* (eds G. Chichilnisky and G.M. Heal), Columbia University Press, 2000, 46–7.

'An Axiomatic Approach to Choice Under Uncertainty with Catastrophic Risks,' *Resource & Energy Economics*, Vol. 22, No. 3, July 2000, 221–31.

'Catastrophical Risk,' *Encyclopedia of Environmetrics*, Vol. 1 (eds Abdel El-Shaarawi and Walter W. Piegorsch), 2002, Chichester, UK, John Wiley & Sons, 274–79.

'Volatility in the Knowledge Economy' (with O. Gorbachev), September 2003, to appear.

Books

Catastrophe or New Society? A Latin American World Model (co-author), International Development Research Center, Ottawa, Canada, 1976: translation of *Catastrofe o Nueva Sociedad?*, Fundacion Bariloche, 1976; translation into Japanese by Diamond, Inc, Tokyo, 1977.

Un Monde Pour Tous: Le Modèle Mondial Latino-Americain, Paris, Presses Universitaires de France, 1977.

Grenzen des Elends, Frankfurt am Main, S. Fischer Verlag, 1977.

The Evolving International Economy (with G. Heal), Cambridge, Cambridge University Press, 1986.

Oil in the International Economy (with G. Heal), Oxford, Clarendon Press, 1991.

Development and Global Finance: The Case for an International Bank for Environmental Settlements, United Nations Development Program, Discussion Series No. 10 and United Nations Educational & Scientific Organization, 1996–97.

Markets, Information, and Uncertainty, New York, Cambridge University Press, 1999.

Sustainability, Dynamics and Uncertainty (with G. Heal, and S. Vercelli), Dordrecht, Boston and London, Kluwer Academic Publishers, 1998, 2001.

Mathematical Economics, Volumes I, II and III, Cheltenham, UK and Northampton, US, Edward Elgar, 1998.

Topology and Markets, American Mathematical Society and The Fields Institute for Mathematical Sciences, Toronto, Canada, 1999.

Environmental Markets: Equity and Efficiency, Economics for a Sustainable Earth Series, Columbia University Press, 2001.

What is Democracy?, in progress.

8. The story of a reluctant economist*

Richard A. Easterlin

I was not a reluctant economist at the start. In the beginning, economics opened up a new and exciting world. The Keynesian revolution was in full swing, and like other graduate students, I was caught up in it. The message of the revolution was new and straightforward – major depressions and staggering unemployment were not an inevitable evil of industrialization. Societies had the power through public policy to prevent and correct serious depressions.

Today disillusionment with this message prevails. But it is not the failures of the Keynesian revolution that have made me into a reluctant economist. As a teacher of introductory macroeconomics, I am still more Keynesian than my younger colleagues. Rather, my reluctance stems from a research philosophy forged at the hands of my mentor, Simon Kuznets, the third Nobel laureate in economics. In a field where theory was and is the be-all and end-all of intellectual accomplishment, Kuznets taught that the touchstone of achievement is insight into empirical reality. Moreover, other social sciences might, along with economic theory, contribute to one's understanding. It was some years before first-hand experience was to make me a true believer of this philosophy – and that is the story of a reluctant economist.

STUMBLING INTO ECONOMICS

Most young people today have a good idea of their prospective work – only about 6 percent of high-school seniors respond 'don't know' when asked 'what kind of work do you think you will be doing when you are 30 years old?' (Bachman et al., 1988). My problem was that I liked almost everything I studied – English, math, history, foreign languages – perhaps natural sciences least, but even that was not bad. I loved to read. Throughout my high-school years, I was one of today's 6 percent 'don't knows.' What followed was a trial-and-error period that led me eventually to economics. The path to

*This chapter first appeared in *The American Economist*, **41**(2), Fall 1997, 11–21.

economics was shaped partly by my own choices, but even more by factors beyond my control.

The simple model of occupational choice puts the expected rate of return in the forefront of job choice. To my generation, reared within memory of the Great Depression, income and job security were extremely important. In my personal experience, however, this factor operated largely to rule out certain choices, most notably, a youthful ambition to be a writer. But it left open a wide array of options that appeared to my limited knowledge to have quite acceptable returns.

In fact, it was events beyond my control, along with personal preferences, that led me eventually to economics. The external events were World War II; government policies with regard to the draft, officers' college training programs, and GI benefits; and an extremely strong post-World War II labor market for young adults due to the combination of rapid growth of aggregate demand and unprecedentedly small numbers of labor force entrants. Ultimately, I was to realize that these forces had shaped not only my personal experience, but that of my entire generation. This revelation provided powerful confirmation for me of the insights that economics could provide into the forces shaping our lives, and led eventually to a research monograph on population and labor force that put the post-World War II boom in the perspective of past long-term swings in the economy (Easterlin, 1968).

In retrospect, these exogenous forces provided a succession of opportunities for me to explore my interests, with personal preferences determining where I ended up. I tried engineering, and didn't like it. I served as a deck officer on a US Navy cruiser, and didn't like it – although such a career had, in fact, been a serious aspiration when I was young. I tried farming and didn't like it. I studied for an MBA degree (the combination of business and engineering was said to reap a rich harvest), and didn't like it. But, incidental to the MBA program, I was required to take economics. Finally I had discovered what I liked.

Why did economics appeal? The analytical requirements suited my abilities, but this was true too of engineering and business. In the case of economics, however, these analytical abilities were being applied to the solution of urgent social problems. My interest in these problems had been nurtured by outstanding history and English teachers in a large New York City public high school. Though I didn't realize it at the time, these teachers were forming interests that would help shape my future.

Should economic models of occupational choice give more attention to preferences? Some say no, that individual differences in tastes tend to cancel out, and economics is, after all, interested only in group behavior. But this argument ignores factors that systematically affect group preferences as a whole. Today, when schools eliminate programs in the musical and fine arts, they are eliminating opportunities for young people to explore and develop such interests and to come in contact with possible role models in the arts. It is hard to believe that this will not affect adversely group preferences for the arts. When the media and adults make the legal profession and politicians the butt of contemptuous jokes, isn't it likely that this will affect the willingness of young people to pursue such careers? It seems likely that more systematic attention to the study of preference formation might enhance the economic modeling of occupational choice.

One lesson from this job search process might be noted, namely, failed choices sometimes turn out well. The romantic aspirations of my youth to go to the Naval Academy were frustrated while I was in high school by failing a physical exam. The subsequent opportunity to experience navy life demonstrated that it was not for me. Moreover, if I had had my way, when I did go into the navy I would have been an aircraft carrier pilot. My father, however, forced me to opt for engineering. If I'd had free choice, I probably wouldn't be writing this now. Similarly, when I decided to study for an MBA degree, my first choice was Harvard. Had I gone there instead of being turned down, I would probably never have made it into economics. At Penn, where the economics department was in the business school, the switch from an MBA to economics was easy. I'm not sure what this means for the theory of revealed preference, but it certainly seems that *ex post* outcomes can be much different from those envisaged *ex ante*. Based on my personal labor market experience, the knowledge on which choices are based is highly imperfect, and there's a lot of 'learning-by-doing' that goes into finding the niche where one's abilities and interests match job requirements.

SOCIALIZATION INTO ECONOMICS

Economic analysis starts from the assumption of given preferences. Yet a little reflection by economists on their graduate school experience should disabuse them of this notion. For graduate school not only teaches subject matter; it teaches the values of the economics profession – what are the important subjects of economic research, the status hierarchy of the profession, which individuals are the proper role models. Graduate training *is* indoctrination.

Subject matter first, because this is what sold me on economics. I have already noted the heady atmosphere when I was a graduate student. There were the superb theoretical synopses and extensions of Keynes in Lawrence Klein's *Keynesian Revolution*, J.R. Hicks's LM–IS analysis, and Paul Samuelson's multiplier–accelerator interactions. There were the insights into the Great Depression in Alvin Hansen's *Fiscal Policy and Business Cycles*, the classic statement of the secular stagnation thesis. Moreover, as a graduate economics instructor, I had the opportunity to choose and use Paul

Samuelson's brilliant introductory text when it first appeared. By comparison with the other texts then available, it was a quantum advance. It brought the Keynesian revolution into the classroom. And it was written in a way that conveyed persuasively to students the new power of economics to work for human betterment.

I was much taken with economic theory, micro as well as macro, partly by the pure pleasure of theory for theory's sake, partly by the new conception it provided of the world about me. I was lucky to be taught by two excellent micro-theorists, Sidney Weintraub and Melvin Reder (the latter regretfully lasted only one year at Penn).

Two major methodological innovations in economics were under way at this time, the development of mathematical economics and econometrics. Penn, however, was then a backwater of graduate economic study, and my exposure to these subjects was limited. Moreover, I had had a full dose of math in undergraduate engineering, and though I liked it and did well, its novelty had worn off. So the mathematical feature of these developments did not appeal to me as it did to some from non-engineering backgrounds.

Because Penn was a backwater, its graduate program included some courses not usually offered in graduate economics. One such course, of which I was a beneficiary, was in central banking, offered by a gifted teacher and practitioner, Karl Bopp. This course helped teach me respect for historical perspective (it traced the evolution of central banking in Western Europe and the United States), and provided an insider's knowledge of contemporary monetary policy, complementing the knowledge of fiscal policy developed in Keynesian analysis.

And then there was my education in the values of the economics profession. I learned that economics is the queen of the social sciences. I learned that theory is the capstone of the status hierarchy in economics. I learned the brand names whose research I was to revere and respect. I learned that tastes are unobservable and never change. I learned that subjective testimony and survey research responses are not admissible evidence in economic research. I learned that what was then called 'institutional economics' (Commons, Veblen, etc.) was beyond the pale, as were other social sciences more generally. I learned that there is a mere handful of economics journals really worth publishing in, and that articles in inter- or extra-disciplinary journals count for naught. I learned that economic measurement as then practiced by the National Bureau of Economic Research was to be denigrated as 'measurement without theory.'

It was years before I could shake off some of the tastes that graduate economics education had inculcated, and begin to think for myself. Some I have never overcome; thus, I still hold the regard of economists above that of other social scientists.

SOCIALIZATION BEYOND ECONOMICS

At Penn, Simon Kuznets was a remote figure. He came in one afternoon a week to teach a graduate class and meet with his few thesis students. The courses he offered were in economic development, business cycles and statistics; curiously, there were none that related to his pioneering research on national income. Kuznets's appointment was not in the economics department, but in the even weaker statistics department, and he participated hardly at all in the affairs of either, or in those of the university. Most of his time was spent on research off campus or at his home, with occasional visits to the National Bureau of Economic Research in New York.

I took two courses from Kuznets, one in statistics, which chiefly conveyed a strong skepticism toward the field and urged the use of simple, understandable methods, and one in economic development, which was essentially a course in general economic history. This development course too transmitted a strong sense of skepticism, not, however, toward economic history, but toward economic theory. Kuznets's basic point was simple: the 'givens' of economics – technology, tastes and institutions – were the key actors in historical change, and hence most economic theory had, at best, only limited relevance to understanding long-term change. In his view, what was then called 'development theory' – even the widely hailed work of Schumpeter – lacked concrete empirical reference.

I was impressed by Kuznets's intellect, as were graduate economics students generally, but these courses did not make me into a Kuznetsian. Rather, it was chiefly what Kuznets wrote. As a graduate student, I collaborated on several studies of national income with Raymond T. Bowman, the economics department chairman and a great admirer of Kuznets. Thanks largely to Bowman's urging, I also did a thesis under Kuznets's direction, on conceptual aspects of the measurement of economic growth. As a result of these two lines of work, I read virtually everything that Kuznets had written on national income and economic growth. It was this reading that demonstrated for me the scope, depth and brilliance of Kuznets's mind.

Kuznets believed that insight into other times and places started, not from economic theory, but from knowledge of the facts, especially quantitative facts. It is typical of Kuznets that one of his rare speculative pieces, 'Towards a Theory of Economic Growth' (1955), is mostly devoted to summarizing the facts that growth theory must explain. In the present age of endogenous technical change and the 'new' growth theory, this article remains well worth reading.

Kuznets also believed that it was important to know the scholarly literature of specialists in the study of other times and places. As work on my dissertation led to a growing interest in economic development and away from macroeconomic policy, Kuznets channeled me into an interdisciplinary seminar on South Asia, where I came into contact with scholars engaged in humanistic and social science research on India, and came to know some leading Indian scholars, such as N.V Sovani. He also encouraged my tutelage in the literature of economic history by Daniel Thorner, himself an eminent scholar of Indian economic history.

It was my good fortune that Kuznets and sociology professor Dorothy S. Thomas, a renowned demographer, were starting a collaborative research project just as I was finishing graduate school. Thomas's period of graduate work in sociology at Columbia had overlapped Kuznets's in economics, and like Kuznets she had been strongly influenced by Wesley C. Mitchell. The Kuznets–Thomas project reflected this heritage. It aimed to use the United States decennial censuses from 1870 to 1950 to develop estimates of internal migration, labor force and income by states (Kuznets and Thomas, 1957, 1960, 1964). I was invited by Kuznets to do the income estimates as well as estimates of manufacturing activity.

This three-year project affected my development in two ways. For one thing, it gave me my first practical experience in economic measurement. I learned first hand what had already been clear from Kuznets's writings, that there is no measurement without theory (Kuznets, 1948ab). I also came to respect the mission of the National Bureau of Economic Research as originally conceived by Wesley Mitchell. This was to build a broad quantitative base of economic measures that would further the 'cumulation of economic knowledge' (Burns, 1948; Kuznets, 1947, 33–4). In my personal experience, the value of this philosophy is demonstrated by the fact that in economic history the most often cited work of mine is still my estimates of state income done as part of the Kuznets–Thomas project.

But these notions about the importance of economic measurement ran strongly against the tide of mainstream economics. I can still remember the shock and sense of betrayal I felt one day when George Stigler, himself an NBER staff member and eventual Nobel laureate, opined that a doctoral dissertation providing historical estimates of the US balance of payments was not appropriate for a Columbia University PhD in economics.

The other effect of the Kuznets–Thomas project was to introduce me to the field of demography. My mentor here (with Kuznets's encouragement) was Dorothy Thomas, who in numerous coffee-klatches during the project expounded on the field and its practitioners, and who forced me to attend meetings of the Population Association of America and observe and meet real demographers. Thanks largely to her influence, I acquired an education in a field outside of economics, one with quite different values. In demography, careful measurement is extolled, and those who develop techniques for making something out of fragmentary data are highly regarded. In graduate study in demography, a course in techniques of measurement is the central part of the core. In economics, there has never been a methodology of measurement, and it is doubtful that a course in measurement could even make it into the graduate economics curriculum as an elective, if there were anyone with the temerity to propose it.

Demographers also place high value on establishing the factual record, exemplified for me at the time by a number of now-classic studies associated with Princeton's Office of Population Research (Davis, 1951; Durand, 1948; Kirk, 1946; Taeuber, 1958). Such work is customarily dismissed by economists as purely descriptive. To me, however, the demographer's respect for facts resonated with the goals of Wesley Mitchell's National Bureau of Economic Research.

I do not wish to imply that my appreciation of demography was an overnight thing. The first draft of my paper analyzing the causes of the American baby boom (Easterlin, 1968, ch. 4) was replete with the usual arrogant economist's jibes at demographic research. On reading this draft, Dorothy Thomas took me aside and said, 'Look, Dick, this paper would not have been possible without all the prior demographic research that it builds on – why not be more charitable?' I realized how right she was, and changed the tone completely. One benefit, beyond my personal education, was that the paper, when published, attracted favorable attention from demographers and established my credentials in the field.

In addition to demography, I became increasingly involved in the discipline of economic history, a field that at the time was dominated by historians. The welcome extended by both historians and demographers to the incursion of economists in their fields has always been a source of wonder to me, because my own discipline of economics has hardly reciprocated.

The situation in economic history, however, was different from that in demography. The field was astir with the potentials of the 'new' economic history, whereby economists aspired to re-write history through the application of economic theory and econometrics to historical problems. I am regarded as a member of this school, and I do feel that these tools contribute to historical study. But I also believe that the traditional approach of historians was of great value, and I regret very much that they have now largely been driven from the field. Indeed, I have long felt that my early work on state income estimates would have been better if I had known more traditional American economic history. It sometimes seems these days as if the new economic history is more interested in using historical data to test economic hypotheses than in using economics to understand history. To my mind the field would have been richer if it had followed Kuznets's agenda for a comparative worldwide study of the economic growth of nations based on measurement and *multi*disciplinary theory (Kuznets, 1949).

In any event, my experience in both demography and economic history did much to further my socialization beyond economics. Training in economics has always been chock-full of requirements that leave little time to gain an appreciation of other disciplines. This is bad enough, but most aspiring economists are indoctrinated in the view, as I was, that such knowledge is not even necessary, and are taught to look on other disciplines with contempt. I was lucky that both the period of my dissertation training and my early postgraduate years provided a serious counter to this. I wish that such an opportunity were more generally available to young economists today.

THE MAKING OF A RESEARCH PHILOSOPHY

Several years ago I was the chair of the department's recruitment committee for newly minted PhDs. In this capacity I had the opportunity to read abstracts of dissertations from a large number of students from the nation's leading graduate economics departments, an experience that reveals a lot about the discipline.

Model-building is the name of the game. Empirical reality enters, if at all, chiefly in the form of 'stylized facts.' Econometrics, though a formal course requirement everywhere, plays a surprisingly small part in economic research – showing up in perhaps one dissertation in five. There is no such thing as descriptive dissertations or theses devoted to the measurement of economic magnitudes. Although topics in disciplines other than economics are not uncommon, there is little or no use of the work done in the other disciplines.

From what has gone before, it will be clear that this is a philosophy that makes me uncomfortable. I see the point of departure of research as some empirical problem, such as the American baby boom and bust. One is likely to have some theoretical preconceptions about causation, but the first step is to establish facts, both quantitative and qualitative. These facts will inform the investigator more fully about what needs to be explained, and may also suggest new possibilities regarding causation. Economic theory enters by providing a systematic framework for theorizing, but other disciplines may suggest relevant causal factors that need to be included, and supply relevant facts. Simple empirical methods provide an initial check on the consistency of theory and data; more rigorous methods are used largely to formalize one's conclusions. Qualitative evidence such as subjective statements of the actors, as found in social science surveys or the materials of historical research (diaries, letters, etc.) should be consistent with the model.

This is not the usual approach to economic research, nor do I have any illusions that it will become more common. And it was not the approach that

I started with. But it is one that has helped me to understand a little bit about the world in which I live.

There is hypothesis-testing in this approach, but a finding of support for a hypothesis is not the end of the research. The goal is to explain reality, and typically this involves more than one hypothesized causal factor. With regard to occupational choice, for example, there is a substantial economics literature hypothesizing that job choice is determined by prospective returns. The goal of this literature is to establish the validity of this hypothesis. If, however, one's research goal is to explain observed job choices in a particular place in a particular period of time, it is likely that expected returns will prove to be only one factor at work, and not necessarily the most important. Thus, although expected returns have demonstrably played a part in the changing occupational choices of American college students in recent decades, the most dramatic change – the shift towards business careers – appears to have been driven chiefly by a marked change in life goals of the young (Easterlin, 1995).

I have emphasized above the importance of instruction by the data, and the interaction between empirical study and hypothesis formulation and testing. Let me illustrate from my early experience in the study of long swings or 'Kuznets cycles.' Then, as now, there was the issue of whether such fluctuations were real or simply a statistical artifact. To study these swings I assembled a vast number of time series from widely different sources – population and its components, commodity output of various types, capital stock, labor force and employment, building permits, patents, land sales and prices, financial series, new incorporations, international trade and payments. Some series were annual, many were confined to the intermittent dates of the population and industrial censuses. The time spans differed widely. I also knew (or learned about) possible causal relationships among various subsets of these series from work by others not only on long swings, but also on building cycles, urban growth, immigration and the like. Ultimately it was the consistency in movements among a wide variety of series, many of which were fragmentary, and the consistency of these movements with theoretical expectations that convinced me of the reality of long swings, and led to the formulation of a broad model of economic–demographic interactions during long swings (Easterlin, 1968, chs 1–3). Perhaps someone else might have more quickly conceived such a model *a priori* and tested it with the few long annual time series available. For me, it took quite a few years immersed in data and various causal speculations to arrive at what was a satisfactory solution of this empirical problem.

The notion of 'instruction by the data' has its pitfalls. The biggest is that the pursuit of data becomes an end in itself and an excuse for postponing serious analysis. To avoid this, data collection and analysis should proceed in tandem, not in sequence.

Concern for empirical relevance has guided my teaching as well as my research. I have taught and still teach courses ranging from introductory macroeconomics for undergraduates to the history of economic development for graduates. At the undergraduate level, I believe emphasis on empirical relevance helps students to acquire respect for economics and to appreciate its value to society. At the graduate level, I believe such emphasis is important in enabling students to understand the limitations as well as the value of economics.

LETTING GO OF ECONOMIC THEORY (MAINSTREAM VERSION)

It is hard to overcome the preconceptions indoctrinated by graduate economics training. In the early years of my career, I sought faithfully to explain childbearing behavior on the basis of income and prices, and to eschew appeal to preferences. I was also a devoted follower of the doctrine that behavior is always the result of deliberate choice. Reality led me to retreat from both views.

Fixed preferences went first. The empirical problem was the American baby boom and bust from the end of World War II through the 1960s. If children are a 'normal good,' how does one explain the marked rise and subsequent fall in childbearing in a period when income trends sharply upward? 'Prices' won't do it – the opportunity cost of young women, the factor stressed most in the economics literature, was demonstrably higher during the baby boom than the baby bust.

The answer came ultimately from sociology via the concept of economic socialization. One's notions of a desirable living level are initially formed from one's personal experiences while growing up. The parents of the baby boom came from the economically deprived environment of the Great Depression and World War II; the parents of the baby bust came from the economically affluent post-World War II period. Even with incomes and prices the same for the two sets of parents, one would expect differences in the willingness to have children, because of differences in the material aspirations they had formed as they grew up. The parents of the baby boom with low material aspirations and good income prospects felt relatively affluent; their children, the parents of the baby bust, with much higher aspirations relative to incomes, felt poorer and less able to have children. Thus, by recognizing the role of changing material aspirations (preferences) along with growth of income, a plausible interpretation was suggested of the baby boom and bust, one that proved consistent with the evidence (Easterlin, 1980).

The issue of deliberate choice in demographic behavior first arose when I sought to understand the shift from high to low family size that occurs in the course of what demographers call the 'demographic transition.' Like most economic demographers today, I had assumed that throughout history fertility behavior was the result of conscious choice (cf. Schultz, 1981). I had already been made uncomfortable when chided by my colleague and friend at Penn, demographer John Durand, about the relevance of a deliberate choice model to the observed fertility of permanently or partially sterile women, but I thought I could get by on the grounds that quantitatively this was not very important. Matters became much worse, however, when I was confronted with a large body of survey research data in the demographic literature indicating that prior to the demographic transition most couples in developing countries reported that they did not deliberately limit family size. This implied that observed fertility behavior in these societies was what demographers call 'natural' or unregulated fertility. Moreover, by the use of an ingenious and innovative technique developed by demographers Ansley Coale and James Trussell (1974, 1975), a persuasive case was made that natural fertility had also been the common condition in the historical experience of the developed countries prior to the shift to low fertility. Eventually, aided by colleagues at Penn, I arrived at an explanation of these pre-transition conditions consistent with economic theory and rational behavior – an explanation that incorporated the demographers' concept of natural fertility (Easterlin, 1978; Easterlin, Pollak and Wachter, 1980; Easterlin and Crimmins, 1985). But the result led me to recognize that the mechanisms underlying observed fertility–income patterns in pre-transition societies might have nothing to do with deliberate household decisions about family size, and reflect, instead, social norms or physiological relationships. Thus, variations in fertility in pre-transition societies might result from variations in breastfeeding behavior that arose, not from interest in or even awareness of the effect of breastfeeding on family size, but simply from different societal conceptions of the link between breastfeeding and the health of mother and child. In such circumstances, fertility was being determined, not by conscious choice, but inadvertently by household decisions directed towards other objectives.

Recently, some economists have sought to bring the subject of mortality, as well as fertility, under the dominion of the theory of household choice (see, for example, Schultz, 1981 and the survey by Behrman and Deolalikar, 1988). The leading empirical problem with regard to mortality is the amazing decline that has occurred in both developed and developing areas over the past century (this decline is the other component of the demographers' demographic transition). The suggested explanation is straightforward: health is the product of conscious household decisions. Growth in income associated with economic development induces an improvement in the quantity and quality consumed of food, clothing, shelter, medical care, etc., and this, in time, improves health and reduces mortality.

I cannot plead innocence of this view; at one time I used it explicitly to infer, in the absence of direct measures of mortality, the probable course of American mortality in the nineteenth century (Easterlin, 1977). As in the case of fertility, however, the more I studied the literature outside of economics, the more I was led to question such a simple economic model. Before the latter part of the nineteenth century, households, governments and those in the healing arts had little knowledge of how to prevent or treat disease, a situation that prevails even today in large parts of the Third World (Caldwell et al., 1989). In such circumstances, actions by households or others to prevent or treat disease – however well-intentioned – were largely ineffective. It was not until the growth of epidemiological knowledge and the validation of the germ theory of disease in the middle and latter parts of the nineteenth century that truly effective action started to become possible (Easterlin, 1996, chap. 6). The leadership in implementing this knowledge was provided, not by households, but by public entrepreneurs, the leaders of the new public health movement. Initially, in the mid- and latter part of the nineteenth century the focus of the public health movement was on water and sanitation measures to clean up the environment, measures that significantly reduced mortality independently of household decisions. As time went on and knowledge continued to grow, the emphasis of public health officials shifted towards measures to assure a purer food supply, and education of the public in personal hygiene, maternal and child care practices, good nutrition and the importance of immunization. This new knowledge made it possible for the first time for households generally to make informed decisions to prevent disease. Eventually, as the continuing advance in knowledge led to the development of chemotherapy in the 1930s and thereafter, the medical profession became equipped with drugs that made possible an effective response to household demands for the cure of disease.

Thus, as knowledge has advanced, the determination of health and mortality has been brought increasingly within the province of human control. Today in developed societies deliberate household decisions, along with those of medical practitioners and governments, can improve health and reduce mortality. But this was not always true; nor is it true even today in large parts of the Third World.

Letting go of the preconceptions of economic theory did not come easily. It was brought about chiefly by two fundamentals instilled in me by Kuznets. One was taking an empirical problem as the point of departure for research. The other was respect for the evidence accumulated by specialists on the subject – in the case of fertility and mortality, chiefly that of demographers, public health specialists, historians and anthropologists. Survey evidence that demonstrated the widespread absence in time and space of deliberate control of family size had to be accepted as reflecting empirical reality, and a plausible model had to explain such behavior. Regrettably, many economists define such observations away by dismissing subjective testimony as inadmissible (Easterlin, 1986). Had I not had the benefit of schooling in demography, I would have missed out on an opportunity better to understand observed behavior. Similarly, in regard to mortality, evidence had to be recognized on the immense advance in knowledge regarding the control of communicable disease, and the key role of public entrepreneurship in implementing this new knowledge. Economists' insistence on starting with household choice put the cart before the horse.

One reason why most economists start with the theory of household choice is that its relevance to behavior in contemporary developed societies has been well demonstrated. As mentioned earlier, my own model of the American baby boom and bust employs the theory of household choice, although expanded to allow for systematic variation in preferences. Similarly, in the low-mortality regime of the United States today, understanding household choices regarding life style and health care utilization help provide insights into American health and mortality differentials and trends. Thus, with regard to both fertility and mortality there has developed in recent decades a substantial literature focused on the developed countries, and especially the United States, in which the theory of household choice plays a central role. Unfortunately, this literature has become the point of departure for economic research on fertility and mortality in other times and places. In effect, a theoretical predisposition has become the starting point of research, rather than empirical study of other societies. Such empirical work is readily available in the scholarly work of other social scientists and area specialists, but economists have been taught to dismiss such work and trust to the wisdom of economic theory. As a result, economics approaches the study of other times and places through glasses tinted by preoccupation with the study of contemporary American society. This is not the way Simon Kuznets would have had it. By word and example, Kuznets taught a respect for facts, and for other social sciences.

As I have indicated, making the break with the assumption of given preferences wasn't easy. But once made, the effects ramified. The relative income model used to explain the baby boom and bust was based on recognition that one's material aspirations were shaped in important part by one's material environment. Previously, I had confidently assumed that higher income and greater subjective welfare go hand in hand. But the relative income model implied that a generation raised under more affluent circumstances would, as a result, have higher material aspirations – in short, that aspirations varied directly with society's income. Thus the positive effect on material welfare of income growth would be negated by the adverse effect of increased aspirations. Subjective testimony on personal happiness provides striking confirmation of this expectation: as per capita income grows over time, subjective welfare remains unchanged, despite a marked growth in material possessions (Easterlin, 1974, 1996, ch. 10). Again, mainstream economics has spared itself confrontation with the evidence by its dogmatic rejection of subjective testimony on well-being – this, despite a large research literature in psychology and sociology pointing to the meaningfulness of such measures. At the present, hypothesis-testing in economics regularly incorporates collateral evidence such as prices and wages; one can perhaps hope that in time the bounds of admissible evidence will come to embrace as well measures devised in psychology and sociology relating to circumstances such as expectations, values and subjective feelings. Although such factors are sometimes posited in economic models, evidence relating directly to them is almost never considered.

In the study of subjective well-being, as in my work on demographic topics, I again learned the value of research in disciplines outside of economics. My work on subjective well-being was initiated in 1970–71 while I was a fellow at the Center for Advanced Study in the Behavioral Sciences. This fellowship provided an opportunity for extended contact with scholars in psychology and sociology who introduced me to relevant work in these fields. Thus, during my career, I have been fortunate to have the opportunity for serious contact with scholars and work outside of economics – first in demography and history, then in sociology and psychology – that taught me at first-hand the value of Kuznets's stress on the relevance to reality of social science generally, not just economic theory.

AN HISTORICAL PERSPECTIVE

We live today in the midst of two great revolutions that are sweeping the world and have changed human life forever. The Industrial Revolution of the late eighteenth century marked the onset of modern economic growth, a phenomenon that has raised material living levels by tenfold or more among the leaders in the process. The mortality revolution that started in the late nineteenth century has already more than doubled life expectancy at birth in many parts of the world. Together, these revolutions portend as early as a half-century hence a world largely freed from hunger and starvation, and from enormously high rates of infant and child mortality (Easterlin, 1996).

The origins of these revolutions lie in the development and growth of natural science since the late seventeenth century. Scientific knowledge grew earliest in the fields of mechanics, astronomy, chemistry and electricity, and had its payoff in widespread and continuing improvements in methods of production that raised productivity and per capita income. Scientific knowledge came later in the biological and medical fields, and because of this, the mortality revolution, based on new methods of disease control, started later than modern economic growth. The factor input and institutional requirements of the mortality revolution are less than those for modern economic growth, and because of this, the mortality revolution has spread more rapidly.

Thus, a new world is being erected on the advances in natural science. This world is richer and healthier, but it is also much more complex and incredibly interdependent. It is a world of staggering new problems – abrupt shifts in political power as modern technology spreads, new environmental concerns arising from the side-effects of this technology, and internal conflict within nations between gainers and losers in economic growth.

Ultimately, the solution to such problems depends on the newly emerging social sciences. I am an economist because I believe that economics is essential to understanding the world and that the framework of economic theory enables one to think systematically about many interrelationships. Indeed, the first major payoff to the advance of social science knowledge was, as I have noted, the insights of the Keynesian revolution into one of the major new problems of economic growth, mass unemployment. It is unfortunate that the profession of economics has retreated from this belief in the ability of economic science to help us control our destiny, because the need for relevant research is greater today than ever before.

But economics alone is not enough – and this is why I am a reluctant economist. We cannot comprehend the world about us without knowledge of the facts and insights provided by the other social sciences. Economics is a starting point, but only a starting point, in the application of social science to the world's problems. As I reflect on my own philosophy, instilled by Kuznets and molded by experience, it boils down to a few words – it is good to be an economist; it is better to be a social scientist.

REFERENCES

Bachman, Jerald G., Lloyd D. Johnston and Patrick M. O'Malley, 1988. *Monitoring the Future: Questionnaire Responses from the Nation's High School Seniors*. Ann Arbor, MI: University of Michigan, Institute for Social Research.

Behrman, Jere R. and Anil B. Deolalikar, 1988. 'Health and Nutrition' in H. Chenery and T.N. Srinivasan (eds). *Handbook of Development Economics*, I, Amsterdam: Elsevier Science Publishers, 631–711.

Burns, Arthur F., 1948. *The Cumulation of Economic Knowledge*. Annual Report. New York: National Bureau of Economic Research.

Caldwell, John, Sally Findley, Pat Caldwell, Gigi Santow, Wendy Cosford, Jennifer Braid and Daphne Broers-Freeman, 1988 (eds). *What We Know About the Health Transition: The Cultural, Social, and Behavioural Determinants of Health*, 2 vols.

Canberra, Australia: Australian National University Health Transition Centre.
Coale, Ansley J. and T. James Trussell, 1974. 'Model Fertility Schedules: Variations in the Age Structure of Childbearing in Human Populations.' *Population Index*, 40:2 (April), 185–258.
———, 1975. 'A New Method of Estimating Standard Fertility Measures from Incomplete Data.' *Population Index*, **41**, 182–210.
Davis, Kingsley, 1951. *The Population of India and Pakistan*. Princeton: Princeton University Press.
Durand, John D., 1948. *The Labor Force in the United States, 1890–1960*. New York: Social Science Research Council.
Easterlin, Richard A., 1968. *Population, Labor Force, and Long Swings in Economic Growth: The American Experience*. New York: Columbia University Press.
———, 1974. 'Does Economic Growth Improve the Human Lot?' in Paul A. David and Melvin W. Reder (eds), *Nations and Households in Economic Growth: Essays in Honor of Moses Abramovitz*, New York: Academic Press, Inc.
———, 1977. 'Population Issues in American Economic History: A Survey and Critique,' in Robert E. Gallman (ed), *Recent Developments in the Study of Business and Economic History: Essays in Honor of Herman E. Krooss*, Greenwich, CT: Johnson Associates. 131–58.
———, 1978. 'The Economics and Sociology of Fertility: A Synthesis,' in Charles Tilly (ed.), *Historical Studies of Changing Fertility*, Princeton: Princeton University Press, 57–133.
———, 1980. *Birth and Fortune: The Impact of Numbers on Personal Welfare*, New York: Basic Books; 2nd edn, Chicago: University of Chicago Press, 1987.
———, 1986. 'Economic Preconceptions and Demographic Research: A Comment,' *Population and Development Review*, **12**:3 (September), 517–28.
———, 1995. 'Preferences and Prices in Choice of Career: The Switch to Business, 1972–1987.' *Journal of Economic Behavior and Organization*, **27**:1 (June), 1–34.
———, 1996. *Growth Triumphant: The Twenty-first Century in Historical Perspective*. Ann Arbor, MI: University of Michigan Press.
——— and Eileen M. Crimmins, 1985. *The Fertility Revolution: A Supply–Demand Analysis*. Chicago: University of Chicago Press.
———, Robert A. Pollak and Michael L. Wachter, 1980. 'Toward a More General Economic Model of Fertility Determination: Endogenous Preferences and Natural Fertility,' in Richard A. Easterlin (ed.), *Population and Economic Change in Developing Countries*, Chicago: University of Chicago Press for NBER, 81–140.
Kirk, Dudley, 1946. *Europe's Population in the Interwar Years*. Geneva: League of Nations.
Kuznets, Simon, 1947. 'Economic Growth Measurement,' *Journal of Economic History*, VII, Supplement, 10–34.
———, 1948a. 'National Income: A New Version,' *Review of Economics and Statistics*, **30**,151–97.
———, 1948b. 'On the Valuation of Social Income – Reflections on Professor Hicks's Article,' *Economica*, **15**, 1–16, 116–31.
———, 1949. 'Suggestions for an Inquiry into the Economic Growth of Nations,' in Universities National Bureau Committee for Economic Research, *Problems in the Study of Economic Growth*, No. 1 (mimeographed), 3–20.
———, 1955. 'Toward a Theory of Economic Growth,' in Robert Lekachman (ed.), *National Policy for Economic Welfare at Home and Abroad*, New York: Doubleday, 12–77.

———, 1966. *Modern Economic Growth: Rate, Structure, and Spread*. New Haven, CT: Yale University Press.

Kuznets, Simon and Dorothy S. Thomas (eds), 1957, 1960, 1964. *Population Redistribution and Economic Growth, United States, 1870–1950*, Vols I, II and III, Philadelphia: American Philosophical Society.

Schultz, T. Paul, 1981. *Economics of Population*. Reading, MA: Addison-Wesley.

Taeuber, Irene B., 1958. *The Population of Japan*. Princeton: Princeton University Press.

9. My life and economics*

Ronald G. Ehrenberg

I. INTRODUCTION

Age 51 is a bit early to be writing a retrospective about one's career as an economist and one's life. This is especially true for me since I am not on track to win a Nobel Prize, to be admitted to the National Academy of Science, or even to be elected a Fellow of the Econometric Society. Nonetheless, as I write this essay during the fall of 1997, I look back on the 28 years I have spent as a PhD economist and see a record of accomplishment of which I am proud and a number of messages worth conveying to budding economists. Moreover, because I became the Vice-President for Academic Programs, Planning and Budgeting at Cornell in the spring of 1995 and am unsure when, or if, I will return to the faculty, taking the time to sum up my career to date may well help me to decide the directions in which I want it to go in the future.

I hope that a number of messages come through to you in this essay. They are that we all are products of our environment and experiences, that family, friends and students mean much more in the long run than all of the publications on one's vita, that committing oneself to a single institution can be overwhelmingly satisfying, and that famous economists are not spared from adversity and must learn to cope with life's problems just as everyone else does. However, I am getting ahead of myself, so let's start at the beginning.

II. MY EARLY YEARS

I was born in New York City in April of 1946. The defining event of my early life occurred around age four when an uncle and aunt took me upstate to a lake for a weekend vacation. Without going into the details, which I vividly remember to this day, I almost drowned. When I regained consciousness after being saved, someone told me I had almost died.

Out of this experience I developed a fear of death (which I fortunately later outgrew) and, since as a four-year-old I viewed death as the ultimate failure, a

*This chapter first appeared in *The American Economist*, **43**(1), Spring 1999, 9–18.

fear of failure. I became driven to avoid failure, and since unexpected events could always occur that might frustrate my efforts, everything I did had to be completed as soon as possible. This drive to quickly achieve things was a major motivating force for the first 40 years of my life. This drive was reinforced by my being a first child and the only grandchild for five years on my mother's side of the family. The hopes and aspirations of my grandparents, parents, and four uncles and aunts all rested with me during those early years.

III. MY SCHOOL AND COLLEGE YEARS

I grew up in a Jewish family in which my parents were both secondary school teachers. Their choice of occupation, made during the depression years, was motivated by a desire for financial security as well as by the belief in the fundamental importance of education. They were hard-working people whose life revolved around work and family; however, there was little discussion in our house of the social values that Judaism teaches that have shaped the careers of many other economists from Jewish backgrounds.

I benefited from what at the time may have well been the best public school system in the country, the New York City public schools. Public school teachers during the 1950s and early 1960s were drawn predominantly from the upper tail of the female talent distribution. They loved learning and they conveyed this love to their students. Education was also seen as a vehicle for upward mobility. Bright students were not held back in the name of 'equity.' I remember one teacher giving me a present of a book written in French after I achieved a ninth grade reading level while in fourth grade – she clearly felt I needed an additional challenge. Sadly, I never achieved any facility in foreign language, and this lack of language talent would, in large part, as we shall see, explain where I went to graduate school.

Junior high school went rather quickly for me because at that time the way the New York City schools coped with bright students was to group them together and compress three years of work into two. Given my need to achieve things quickly, this suited me perfectly.

I attended Stuyvesant High School, one of the preeminent public high schools in the nation. Specializing in math and science, it drew students from all over New York City and these students were admitted based on scores in a competitive examination that was very much akin to an SAT examination. My high-school years were probably the most intellectually challenging and competitive ones of my life, and I ultimately graduated in the top fifth of the class with a love of mathematics. Calculus thrilled me because it had so many applications to real-world problems and I wanted to major in mathematics in college.

Which college would I attend? Finishing in the top fifth of a class in which 99 percent of the students went on to college was an achievement to be proud of, but it was not an outstanding enough accomplishment for Harvard or Yale. While I was admitted to Cornell's College of Arts and Sciences for the class of 1966, this was prior to the compact between the federal government and the selective private institutions that led these institutions to adopt needs-blind admission and need-based financial aid policies. Public school teachers' salaries were still relatively low in the early 1960s and, with two sisters at home, my parents could not afford to send me to Cornell. So, off to Harpur College (which later became SUNY-Binghamton) I went.

Harpur College in the early 1960s was a truly elite public liberal arts college. It was the sole liberal arts college in the SUNY system at the time, and with only 400 students in each class, could be highly selective. Its motto was 'Let Each Achieve All That He Is Capable of Being,' and we surely did that. My rough count from my alumni directory is that over 50 of my classmates received PhDs (I ignore here all of the classmates who went into 'lesser' occupations such as medicine, law, or business). My experiences at Harpur, which included meeting the woman who became my wife in 1967, have tied me closely to that institution and made me a strong supporter of high-quality public higher education.

I wish I could say that I was destined to be an economist, but in truth I 'fell' into it.[1] I started as a mathematics major in college, but when calculus turned to advanced calculus (now called 'real analysis'), math became proving theorems rather than a tool to solve real-world problems. Furthermore, I found it quite unsettling to be given five questions in an exam, to be able to answer only one and parts of a few others correctly, but still to be awarded an A in the class.[2] A change of course was called for and I switched to physics.

Physics made extensive use of calculus and I enjoyed studying it until I came to a concept that I didn't understand in a fourth semester course. I asked the professor to re-explain the concept; he replied that he didn't understand my question, and then he also gave me an A in the class. I was devastated; how could I be doing A work if I didn't understand something? So I quit the study of physics and looked for another major.

If there was an engineering major at Harpur, I might well have become an engineer. However, there wasn't. The only other disciplines that I perceived made extensive use of mathematics were accounting and economics. I looked at the introductory accounting text and then the introductory economics text. The latter was an edition of Paul Samuelson's famous text. The decision was easy; I switched to economics.

My first three courses in economics with Robert Melville, Al Carlip and John LaTourette (later a college president) made me feel like I was in heaven. The Kennedy/Johnson tax cut of the early 1960s had just taken place and the economy was growing. Economists believed they could 'control' the macroeconomy. Microeconomics was logical and easy to understand for anyone, such as myself, who understood calculus, and could be used to figure out the solution to virtually any resource allocation program. I became an economics major.[3] Only years later did I learn how imprecise our discipline actually is and how limited is our ability to 'control' anything.

The most important influence on me at Harpur was Gene Silberberg, who at the time was a new assistant professor from Purdue, and who is now a professor at the University of Washington and author of a leading mathematical economics text. Plagued with a fear of failing if I went on for a PhD, my response was to think of becoming a high-school mathematics teacher instead. Gene threatened to 'kick me in the face' if I did. I was a coward, and off to PhD study I went.

Gene also gave me a valuable piece of advice. He told me that during my career I would meet people like Hugo Sonnenshein and that if I used them as my comparison group I would never be happy. I had no idea at the time who Hugo was. After graduate school, he turned out to be the person who attracted me to the faculty of the University of Massachusetts and was my colleague there for two years. Hugo, of course, was a leading economic theorist and editor of *Econometrica* and now is the president of the University of Chicago. Gene's advice has served me well, however, because no matter how good one is at what one does, invariably there is always someone better. If you make your comparison group that one person, rather than all the people you are better than, you are dooming yourself to be unhappy.

IV. GRADUATE SCHOOL YEARS

Harpur College was not a household word in the mid-1960s and, given my basic insecurity about my abilities, I was not sure that I could 'hack it' at the very best graduate programs in economics. So I crossed the top five off of my list and applied to the next ten. Fellowship money was readily available at all top institutions, thanks to the National Defense Education Act Fellowship program, which provided funding for three years, including summers, of PhD study. Many graduate programs in economics still required proficiency in one or two foreign languages to receive a PhD, but some had eliminated all language requirements and instead required proficiency in mathematics. Given my lack of language ability, my decision rule for which graduate school to attend was simple: choose the highest rated program among the set of programs that provided the most years of fellowship support and had no language requirement. On that basis, which had nothing to do with the economists on the faculty, I enrolled at Northwestern University.

Having made my decision based on absolutely no relevant information, I am happy to report that Northwestern was *ex post* a wonderful place to study economics. The faculty emphasized rigorous analytical training. Economic models were to be used to derive testable empirical implications and then the theory tested.

My dissertation addressed whether an increase in the overtime premium would be an effective way to reduce employers' usage of overtime hours and expand employment. It was very much a typical Northwestern dissertation for that time and had the following properties. First, a dynamic model of optimizing behavior was developed and equilibrium obtained using either the calculus of variations or optimal control theory. Next, comparative static or comparative dynamic analyses were conducted to derive testable propositions and careful econometric estimation undertaken using 'frontier' econometric methods to test the implications of the theory. Finally, the resulting estimates were used to analyze a policy issue and the implications for public policy drawn. To this day, I try to impress upon my graduate students the need to demonstrate modeling and econometric skills, as well as substantive interest in policy problems, in their dissertations.

I learned several other things during my graduate school years, which influenced both how I treated my students and the lessons that I conveyed to them. First, much of what I absorbed in graduate school in theory and econometrics classes later showed up in various strands of my applied research throughout the years. I repeatedly stress to students that individuals who apply lessons from one area of economics to problems in another area often can make major contributions to the latter.

Second, while searching for a dissertation topic, Dale Mortensen suggested to me that I write to Robert Solow at MIT and ask for a copy of an unpublished paper of Solow's that Dale thought I would find interesting. I did; Solow wrote back that he didn't have any spare copies (this was during the 'stone age' and pre-copiers), but he suggested that I might look at another topic that he thought would be interesting to think about. I followed his advice and my dissertation resulted. More importantly, I was touched that such a distinguished economist (later a Nobel Prize winner) would respond to a letter from a mere graduate student at a much lesser institution. As a result, throughout my career I have tried to emulate Bob's behavior and I promptly respond to letters (and now email messages) from faculty and students from around the world, regardless of the stature of the institutions at which they are located.

Third, after I thought about Solow's topic for a while, which led me to a paper by Sherwin Rosen, perhaps the leading labor theorist of his generation, I developed an idea for a dissertation based on Rosen's paper and took it to one of the faculty members in the Northwestern department. He told me it wouldn't work. I was crushed, but since I had no other ideas, I continued to pursue the topic. My efforts led to an article in the *American Economic Review*, while I was still a graduate student, a dissertation that I completed in four years, and ultimately three other articles and two books. This experience taught me never to tell a student 'it won't work,' and I encourage students to pursue their interests regardless of my priors about their likely success.

Fourth, Robert Eisner arranged for me to spend the summer after graduate school at the Council of Economic Advisors. My experiences at the Council transformed my career as I learned that economics is much more than an intellectual exercise and that economists really do have a lot to say about public policy. It was my good luck to work there with Michael Moskow (now President of the Chicago Fed) and Marvin Kosters (now a senior fellow at the American Enterprise Institute). They taught me, by example, that 'high-priced' senior economists should shelter their 'low-priced' junior colleagues from the pressures that the senior people face. Their example has made life a lot more pleasant for all of the graduate research assistants who worked with me during my career.

Finally, my success in graduate school, coupled with a booming academic market, meant there were many faculty positions that awaited me after my graduate career. Northwestern was an up-and-coming department and the faculty saw in me a potential placement at a better department, that would enhance the Northwestern department's reputation. My pleas that I would prefer to go to a less competitive and more teaching-oriented environment were not heard, and they made contacts for me at the very best departments. I wound up having to choose among positions at more than ten different major research universities.

Graduate students today faced with a weak job market probably would think me very lucky. In fact, contrary to what we teach our students, more alternatives are not always better than fewer, especially if none of them are the type of job one really wants. I hit an information overload and could not make a rational choice. Ultimately I accepted a position at Berkeley but concluded several months later that I needed to take a year off to regroup and decide what I really wanted to do. I spent that year teaching at Loyola University of Chicago and wrote the equivalent of a second dissertation (without any faculty advisers this time), which ultimately led to a second *American Economic Review* paper and another book.

Objectively, the faculty at Northwestern were trying to help me to get a position that, in their view, would be the best place for me to start my career. Their evaluation of what would be 'best,' however, was based on the assumption that the 'track' that they were on was the best one for me. While I have wound up on that 'track' myself, I never assume that my career path is best for all my graduate students and I never push them towards jobs that they don't really want. Many of them are now happily situated in the nonacademic sector and at 'lesser' institutions. While their career choices have not necessarily maximized my 'prestige' in the profession, most are very happy doing what they are doing.

V. MY LIFE AT CORNELL

I moved from Loyola University to the University of Massachusetts after a year, and four years later, in 1975, moved to Cornell University. I have spent the last 23 years teaching undergraduates and graduates at Cornell, conducting research on labor market and educational issues, and now serving as an academic administrator. I have been fortunate enough to be associated with the National Bureau of Economic Research during much of this time, which means that when I was young I was regularly exposed to the very best senior people in my field and, now that I am older, I get to meet all the upcoming young stars. I have interacted regularly with people in Washington but, save for six months in the early 1970s, I never was able to spend any extended period of time there in a policy position. I had many opportunities to do so, but these conflicted with my wife's career or my sons' schooling. I have never regretted doing what I perceived was best for my family as a whole.

My career at Cornell has been a wonderful one. I have had the freedom to address a wide range of interesting policy-related problems at the federal, state and institutional levels and to think and write about fundamental issues that our society confronts. I've been lucky to have a large number of wonderful colleagues and one, Bob Smith, and I wrote the first modern labor economics textbook in the early 1980s. It is now in its sixth edition and is still the bestseller in its field. This book, which was designed specifically for our students at Cornell and stresses the usefulness of labor market economics for social policy analysis, has influenced the way that a generation of students think about labor market issues. This influence is the real reward for 'nonprinciples' textbook writers.

I am now marking my 28th year as a publishing economist. Throughout the years my graduate students have had a hard time believing the early insecurities that I claim I felt, the dry periods that I claim I experienced when nothing seemed to go right, and the fears I claim I often felt during much of my career that I never would generate another research idea. They look at my long publication record and question if I am lying. But I repeatedly tell them these stories anyway to emphasize to them that their 'heroes' are mortals and that the fears that they are feeling are not unique. Most of my research has been co-authored with my students and my contacts with these students, and the other students whose dissertations I have supervised, have been among the most rewarding parts of my professional life. Many of these students have been female and I've learned from them (and they from me) that mentors do not have to be of the same gender.

The love and foundation of my life has been my wife, Randy, and our marriage has now passed the 30-year mark. In addition to love and support, I also get research ideas from her descriptions of the issues that she has faced as a teacher, a school principal, and now an assistant superintendent of schools. We have co-authored three papers together and I have also co-authored a paper with our older son. He is still angry at me because I put my name first on that paper and only first authors get the citations in the Social Science Citation Index.

My family's life has not been without its trials. Most recently, our oldest son was diagnosed with a malignant brain tumor in 1990, while he was a junior at Cornell. For over a year, his younger brother, my wife and I helped him cope with multiple surgeries, chemotherapy and radiation therapy, as he battled an illness whose prognosis was highly uncertain. Cornell and my colleagues were wonderful to us all during that period and I became an ardent supporter of the Family and Medical Leave Act and of legislation that prevents insurance companies from denying anyone health insurance coverage. Happily we are now over six years post-treatment and the 1996 Memorial Day weekend marked the simultaneous graduation of my older son from Georgetown Law School and his younger brother from Cornell. My older son is currently employed in Washington, DC and my younger son is a second-year law student at Michigan.

In 1987, Cornell made me the first Irving M. Ives Professor at the University. Ives was a United States Senator, the founder of Cornell's School of Industrial and Labor Relations, and the co-author of the first state employment discrimination law in the United States, New York's Ives–Quinn Act, which predated the Civil Rights Act by 20 years. Since I have devoted a good deal of my career to analyzing the effects of social legislation, I have always felt an affinity to Ives and I was greatly honored that Cornell chose to associate my name with his.

As I neared age 50 in 1995, the age at which my close friend Dan Hamermesh's research suggested that any economist's chance of continuing to publish in major economic journals is close to zero, it was natural for me to question the direction that my career would go.[4] I had been teaching classes in, and doing research on, university behavior and the economics of higher education for over a decade. I had been active on Cornell University faculty/administrative committees dealing with economic issues, feeling that this was a way that I could use my professional expertise to repay Cornell for all that it had done for both me and my family. When I was asked to serve as Vice-President for Academic Programs, Planning and Budgeting at the University, I felt that I really had no choice but to accept. While I miss having the freedom to allocate my time that comes with being a professor, I am enjoying the opportunity to help guide this great institution through very difficult financial times.

VI. MY CONTRIBUTIONS TO ECONOMICS[5]

Some labor economists have developed theoretical models that now bear their names. Others have similarly derived econometric specifications that carry their names. Still others have developed important econometric methods that subsequently have been named after them. Examples that come quickly to mind here are the 'Lazear' model of mandatory retirement, the 'Mincer' earnings equation, and Jim Heckman's 'Heckit' procedure to deal with sample selection bias. I, however, have neither a theoretical model, an empirical specification, nor an econometric procedure named after me. Rather, my claim to 'fame' is that I have spent a career conducting empirical analyses that have been designed to influence the public policy debate in a wide variety of labor market and educational areas. I also have devoted substantial effort to analyzing whether compensation policies are designed in a way that provides agents with incentives to perform in 'desirable' manners and have been especially interested in whether such incentives exist in the public, nonprofit and regulated sectors of our economy.

My earliest strand of research, which continues up to this date, focused on analyzing the impact of social insurance programs and protective labor legislation. As noted above, my dissertation dealt with whether raising the overtime premium from time and a half to double time would be an effective way of stimulating employment growth. This was quickly followed by the first study to analyze, in the context of a formal job search model, the labor market effects of varying unemployment insurance (UI) benefit levels. The study, conducted jointly with Ron Oaxaca, took a model of job search that had been developed by one of my dissertation advisers, Dale Mortensen, to explain the unemployment–inflation tradeoff and used this model to provide an econometric structure to analyze the effects of changing UI benefit levels on unemployed workers' durations of unemployment and post-unemployment wages. One can view longer spells of unemployment as a social cost of higher benefit levels and higher post-unemployment wages as a social benefit of higher UI benefit levels. Hence, analyses of the magnitude of both relationships is important.

During my career, I have analyzed a variety of other labor market programs and legislation. These include studies of the effects of minimum wages on the educational attainment of children from different family income classes, whether mandated social benefits, such as unemployment insurance or retirement benefits are paid for by workers in the form of lower wages, how the (now abolished) social security student benefit program influenced college-going and labor market behavior of children of social security recipients, whether comparable worth programs in the public sector would lead to a decline in female employment in the public sector, and whether advance notice requirements when workers are about to be replaced, such as those mandated under the WARN legislation, influence displaced workers' probabilities of unemployment, duration of unemployment if unemployment occurs, and post-unemployment earnings. In perhaps my major work to date on labor market policies, I wrote a book for the Brookings Institution in 1994 that addressed how free trade agreements, such as NAFTA and the European Economic Community, influence, and are influenced by, social insurance programs and protective labor legislation.

A second strand of my research has focused on public sector, nonprofit and regulated labor markets. Using models of consumer demand, including those that allowed for habit-formation (which I had learned about in graduate economic theory courses), in 1973 I was the first economist to estimate systems of demand equations for employees in the public sector. The estimated wage elasticities that were derived from these equations provided estimates of the 'market constraints' that limit the wage demands of unionized public employees and thus provided support for allowing public employees the right to bargain over their wages.

The estimated responsiveness of public employment levels to grants from other levels of government that I obtained from these models provided estimates of what has become known as the 'displacement' or 'fiscal substitution' effects of federal 'public employment' programs – programs that provide funding to state and local governments to expand their employment levels. Twenty years later, I used similar analytic frameworks to estimate how research universities react to changes in the number of graduate students for which the federal government provides financial support and how local school districts react to changes in state aid for education. In each of these cases, my interest was in showing that institutional responses to changes in external funding are often quite different than the funders may have anticipated.

My interest in public sector, regulated and nonprofit labor markets led me to conduct studies of how institutions in the public sector influence labor market outcomes. In particular, I have analyzed whether having a professional city manager led to lower public sector wages and whether the effects of public sector unions on wages and productivity depended upon the structure of public sector bargaining in the area. I also analyzed whether the substitution of different types of nurses in hospitals in response to changes in their relative wages depended upon whether the hospitals were public, private nonprofits or private for-profits and, in a book written at the end of the 1970s, I analyzed how the structure of regulated industries influences the wages of workers in these industries. This latter study grew out of my participation in a regulatory case before the New York State Public Service Commission, and from this case I learned that the standards of 'refereeing' in the 'real world' when 'big' dollars are at stake are often much stricter than those used by academic journals.

Economists tend to believe that 'actors' in economic systems respond to incentives. However, I have always wanted to know if incentives actually are structured in ways to encourage actors to perform in ways that 'principals' consider desirable and, if they are, whether such incentives have desired effects on behavior. As a result, I have looked at local governments and analyzed whether incentives for 'performance' could be inferred from the structure of compensation for city managers, police chiefs and fire chiefs. Similarly, I analyzed whether the compensation of local building trade union leaders was related to the compensation gains that they won for their members. This latter study required me (actually a student of mine) to collect considerable data from union records, and throughout my career I have stressed to my students that the best research often arises from people putting considerable effort into generating new data, or combining existing data from a wide variety of sources.

Since both my parents and my wife were involved in elementary and secondary education, it was natural that I should be interested in issues that arise in this sector. I have studied the compensation and mobility of school superintendents to see if there are incentives operating to encourage them to maximize the amount students learn and to serve as responsible fiscal managers. I have also studied how sick leave provisions in teacher contracts influence teachers' absenteeism, students' absenteeism and students' test score performance. Both of these studies involved major data collection efforts and included surveys of local school districts in New York State.

Concern for enhancing the public debate about affirmative action policies in teacher hiring recently led me to conduct several studies that analyzed whether the match of teachers and students by race, gender and ethnicity had any effect on how much students learned or on teachers' attitudes towards their students.[6] While others have often shied away from addressing such socially sensitive issues, I have appreciated the freedom that tenured faculty at major research universities have to dispassionately address controversial important social issues and continually have exercised this freedom.

As I began to get involved with faculty governance at Cornell, it was also natural for me to think about how my skills as an economist could enhance my participation on faculty committees. When Cornell's financial aid costs began to rise at a rapid rate in the early 1980s, I developed a model of how a selective university should allocate a limited financial aid budget across different categories of accepted applicants, given a specified objective function, and then showed how one could estimate the parameters necessary to actually implement such a model. The model, which was nothing more than a simple discriminating monopsonist model, provided the intellectual underpinnings for what has since become known as 'preferential packaging' in the undergraduate financial aid community. Many universities now regularly estimate, for different groups of their accepted applicants, how sensitive the decisions of admitted applicants to enroll are to the levels of financial aid provided and vary the package of grant and loan aid that they offer to individuals with identical levels of financial need. My research on this subject was followed by studies of how colleges students' grades and graduation probabilities are influenced by their employment while in college, whether the high tuitions charged by selective private colleges and law schools are warranted in terms of the postgraduate educational and labor market outcomes that they yield for their graduates, and whether African-American students are better off if they attend historically black colleges or universities (HBCUs) instead of other institutions of higher education.

My evolving interest in higher education led me to analyses of the academic labor market and how the types of financial support doctoral students receive for graduate school influence their completion probabilities and times to degree. I have also studied whether reductions in tenure probabilities influence the salaries that universities must pay for faculty and, analogously, how faculty salary levels affect their turnover probabilities. The latter study grew out of my service on the AAUP committee that annually collects data on faculty salaries from American colleges and universities and was another example of how I have combined service (this time to the profession) and research during my career. More recently, I have analyzed the determinants of doctoral program rankings and have also written about the future of higher education, from the perspective of an economist.

It is worth emphasizing that my research has often been fun to conduct and to lecture about, as well as intellectually stimulating. Two specific examples illustrate this point. First, my interest in compensation policies led me to try to test the theory of tournaments that had been developed by Ed Lazear and Sherwin Rosen, among others, in the early 1980s. To do so, I needed to find an environment in which the prizes for winning were specified *a priori*, measures of individual output were available and estimates of the relationship between output and input could be inferred. After bemoaning the fact that such data were not available for any 'real-world' situation. I realized that professional golf tournaments provided a perfect natural experiment. I wrote two papers on the incentive effects of the prize structure in professional golf and when I lectured about these papers in various venues, the audience was always very attentive.

Second, after Gary Becker's household allocation of time models had been used to analyze the determinants of an individual's investments in health, which in turn imply the determinants of an individual's expected length of life, as well as to analyze the determinants of an individual's decision to commit suicide, which in turn imply the determinants of the individual's actual length of life, I joked with a colleague at a party that the next extension would be to analyze a multi-lifetime utility function (which permitted utility after death) to derive implications about the life-cycle pattern of participation in religious activities. As my Catholic colleague and I began to think about this topic, we discovered that there was a considerable serious research by sociologists and psychologists that addressed religious behavior. We then set out to develop a simple household allocation of time model that could explain all of the observed empirical regularities about religious behavior that other social scientists had found, as well as to provide new testable implications. What began as a joke wound up as two very serious papers in the *Journal of Political Economy* and the start of what 20 years later is now a growing subfield of research on the economics of religion.

While I have always considered the research I have produced to be of great interest, I realized after a while that it is difficult for one's own research to have a major impact on either the profession or public policy. So I began organizing conferences in which I would bring together groups of researchers working on similar topics and then publish the proceedings of these conferences as symposia in journals or as books. Among the conferences that I organized and saw through to publication have been ones dealing with whether compensation policies mattered, whether raising the minimum wage would be desirable, contemporary policy issues in education, gender and family issues in the workplace, and the role of race and gender in American education. I believe that the impact of each of these collections has been far greater than anything I could have done individually.

As I look back with considerable pride at my long publication record and at the wide variety of interesting issues on which I have worked, I am almost ashamed to admit that I never had a 'research program,' or long-term research plan, as many of my colleagues did. Rather, the topics on which I have worked typically arose from discussions with family members or colleagues, and from ideas for research that I got from reading the *New York Times*, *Business Week* and the *Chronicle of Higher Education*. I was also fortunate enough to attain a sufficient level of stature in the profession so that, after a while, people often asked me to write review papers on particular topics. A number of such 'commissioned papers' often led me to develop the ideas for new independent research and a series of subsequent papers.

VII. ECONOMISTS WHO HAVE MADE A DIFFERENCE IN MY CAREER AND LIFE

A number of economists have played important roles in my career and my life. I have already mentioned some. In this concluding section, at the risk of alienating people whom I inadvertently have left out, I want to mention a few more.

While I was a graduate student, one of my dissertation advisers, Frank Brechling, introduced me to Dan Hamermesh, who was then a graduate student at Yale working on a similar topic. Over a 30-year period Dan and I became close colleagues and friends, although we have never been at the same institution and have written only one short paper together. For years, until my research productivity declined when I moved into academic administration, we regularly exchanged drafts and commented on each other's work. We have shared each other's happiness and family hardships. Every economist needs to have a professional friend like Dan.

When I was in graduate school, everything I learned about unions came from a book written by Albert Rees titled *The Economics of Trade Unions*. I was introduced to Al, who was then a professor at Princeton, when he came to Northwestern to give a seminar. Al, who later was Provost at Princeton and then President of the Sloan Foundation, invited me to Princeton, where I met Orley Ashenfelter, and some 15 years later, Al also funded a major research project/conference of mine. His son Dan was one of my PhD students and I am delighted that I could repay Al for what he meant to my career by serving as a mentor for Dan.

Orley Ashenfelter is 'my' Hugo Sonnenshein (see section III). Once I realized that I could never be as prominent as Orley, rather than feeling bad about myself I relaxed and learned everything that I could from him. Orley showed me that one can model the determinants of labor market institutions, as well as their impacts, in rigorous analytical frameworks. He also hired me as a consultant to work with him in Washington for six months at the US Department of Labor, which solidified my interest in policy-related research and led me to teach courses at Cornell for a decade on evaluation research methods.

I have already mentioned how Bob Eisner obtained a position for me at the Council of Economic Advisors after I completed graduate school. If this was not enough, Bob always praised me when, after graduate school, he would hear a paper of mine at a professional meeting. I cannot even begin to express how much such praise from an economist, who later became President of the American Economic Association, meant to me. I try to remember to always behave in a similar manner to my former students. I have also unabashedly adopted the externality framework that Bob has used for years when he explains the rationale for wage subsidy programs in my own writings on government interventions in labor markets.[7] Bob spent virtually his whole career at Northwestern University and, by example, taught me the importance of committing oneself to a single institution.

I once went up to Sherwin Rosen, after listening to a seminar of his, and commented that any one of his papers was deeper than the sum of everything that I had written in my life.

Sherwin replied that I had it all wrong. He said that he and I pursued different types of research, that the research that I pursued was equally important as what he was doing and that what I did, I did exceedingly well. His words of praise were very important to me and encouraged me to keep on my chosen path, even though the economics profession often seemed to value theory and econometric innovations more than empirical research.

A best unnamed noted economist once told me that I would never have a major effect on public policy because I always sought to understand how policies are actually working rather than to pursue a political agenda. As such, he told me that liberals consider me conservative, conservatives consider me liberal and neither group trusts me. When I told this story to Henry Aaron, for many years head of the Brookings Institution Economic Studies Program, Hank replied that the noted economist had it all backwards. He said that the profession understood that I had no 'axe to grind' and thus my research was taken very seriously. I appreciated Hank's words very much, as well as his efforts to involve me more closely in Brookings activities.

In the mid-1980s I ruptured a disk in my back and had back surgery, but the pain persisted. For a number of years I was preoccupied with pain and my professional productivity suffered. The fear of failure which had dominated my early life came back and I was convinced that my career was over. Out of the blue came a call from Dan Newlon, the Director of the National Science Foundation Economics Program, inviting me to become a member of the NSF Panel on Economics. Dan's invitation was the push that I needed to stop feeling sorry for myself and I was able to redirect myself back to my work and my life. When my son's illness, which I have described above, struck my family several years later, I was in a much better emotional position to cope with it.

Walter Oi's accomplishments as an economist are extraordinary, all the more so because he has been blind throughout most of his career. Walter has been a friend and mentor to many labor economists of my generation. When my son permanently lost three-quarters of his vision as a result of his illness, I took him to Rochester to meet Walter. This visit helped him to understand that physical limitations need not limit one's intellectual accomplishments.

Finally, about a decade ago, Charles Clotfelter of Duke invited me to join him to work on a book on the economics of higher education. His invitation is what firmly set me on the professional course that I am on today. We have also become close friends. The best part of being an academic economist is meeting people like Charlie. For, as I said in the introduction, family, friends and students mean much more in the long run than all the publications on one's vita.

VIII. POSTSCRIPT

I loved being a senior central administrator at Cornell. To paraphrase the words of James Freedman, one of the best parts of my job was that I was able to raise very fundamental issues with my colleagues in the administration and on the faculty and to force them to think about these issues. They did not always respond to these issues in the way that I personally would have preferred, but I had the satisfaction of knowing that the University was seriously thinking about these issues.[8]

I had agreed that I would serve in my administrative position for either three or five years. By the third year I had accomplished many things in my role and all of my faculty and administrative colleagues were appreciative of my contributions to the University. However, I found myself getting increasingly frustrated about the nature of my position because I did not always have access to the resources that I needed to finalize projects upon which I had been working, and because my position in the administrative hierarchy excluded me from discussions on some major issues that faced the University in which I felt my input would have been useful. As a result, in July of 1998, at the end of my third year as a vice-president at Cornell, I returned to my faculty position and established and became first Director of the Cornell Higher Education Research Institute.[9]

NOTES

1. However, I was born the week that John Maynard Keynes died.
2. To this day, some math professors persist in giving impossible exams in similar courses and then grading on curves.
3. Albert Einstein is reputed to have found economics more difficult than physics. This difference in our perceptions may be best understood as a difference in comparative advantage. My guess is that Einstein had a big absolute advantage over me in both subjects.
4. See Sharon Oster and Daniel Hamermesh, 'Age and Productivity Among Economists,' *Review of Economics and Statistics* (February 1998).
5. Readers interested in citations to my writings can check my web page, <www.ipr.cornel. edu/ RGEspage/RonsHome.HTML>. My publications are grouped there both chronologically and by subject.
6. In an effort to get something named after me, throughout one of these papers I used the abbreviation RGE to refer to race, gender and ethnicity effects. Sadly, to date, no one has

caught on that these are my initials and the abbreviation is not yet widely used.

7. Another rationale for government was provided to me long ago by Chicago labor economist Arnold Weber (who was later president of both the University of Colorado and of Northwestern), who remarked that 'the invisible hand is all thumbs in the labor market.'
8. See James O. Freedman, *Idealism and Liberal Education* (Ann Arbor, MI, University of Michigan Press, 1996).
9. For a description of what my years as an administrator taught me about the use, and uselessness of economic analysis in academic administration, see Ronald G. Ehrenberg, 'Adam Smith Goes to College: An Economist Becomes An Academic Administrator,' *Journal of Economic Perspectives*, **13** (Winter 1999).

10. Education and its consequences: my philosophy of life*

Victor R. Fuchs

'Philosophy,' wrote Stanley Cavell (1979), is 'the education of grownups.' This essay recounts my 'education' in a broad sense, including the impact of family, religion, schooling, the Army, business and fellow economists. The reader will discern the effects of this education in my views about economics, research, teaching and politics.

FAMILY

Family has always been a major influence on my life. My parents, despite the problems of their marriage, gave me great love and attention. Although their families' circumstances made it impossible for either of them to finish high school, they respected learning and were pleased that both their children pursued academic careers. My brother was my closest companion in childhood and has been a loyal friend and critic since then. Our parents' strong social concerns undoubtedly played a role in our choice of fields and our approach to research: the social sciences applied to problems of social policy.

As a child, I was frequently visiting or being visited by my grandparents (immigrants from Austria and Poland), and dozens of aunts, uncles and cousins who would crowd into our apartment in the Bronx to celebrate birthdays, graduations and holidays. At times these visits conflicted with more urgent matters such as a baseball game or a chance to meet girls, but on balance the many hours spent with different generations contributed much to my development and sense of identity.

For the past 45 years my wife has been my dearest friend, my most enthusiastic supporter, my most valuable critic. I am constantly amazed at her ability to nurture our family and my career while pursuing her own.

Our children and their spouses have added another dimension of love and understanding and each of them has taught me a great deal. They share with me their knowledge of other fields, they sensitize me to different perspectives,

*This chapter first appeared in *The American Economist*, **37**(2), Fall 1993, 17–24.

and they provide windows into the next generation. Our grandchildren are a source of inspiration and I hope that they will appreciate my research on the problems of children (1992) and women's quest for economic equality (1989).

To move from the specific to the general, why is family so important? One reason is because it is our first experience with an 'integrative system.' This has been defined by Kenneth Boulding (1968) as a system that 'involves such things as status, identity, love, hate, benevolence, malevolence, legitimacy – the whole raft of social institutions which defines roles in such a way that you do things because of what you are and because of what I am.' Economists in particular need to be aware that the market (exchange) and government (threat) are not the only institutions available to allocate resources and distribute income. Families, religious communities, professions and other integrative systems are of crucial importance in some societies and can continue to serve vital functions even in our own.

RELIGION

Boulding believes that religion is necessary for social science and for the social scientist because it is part of the whole experience of life (Silk, 1976, p. 176). I am not sure about the 'necessary,' but for me it was certainly helpful. Having been born Jewish, I had an early sense of being part of a long historical process, and a feeling of kinship with some of the most extraordinary individuals the world has ever known. I also inherited an ethical code of great power and goodness and a tradition of study with the object of improving both oneself and the world. While still quite young, I was deeply impressed by the injunction 'It is not incumbent on you to complete the task, but neither are you free to desist from it' (Mishna, Avot 2:21).

My early exposure to Judaism was unexceptional: a smattering of Hebrew language and an introduction to Jewish history and law; Passover seders; occasional attendance at synagogue; and Bar Mitzvah at age 13. Even this limited involvement, however, left me with an awareness of some fundamental questions about the human enterprise, questions that would not surface in my secular education until much later. For me it is the questions religion asks, more than the answers given, that make it such a valuable part of the human experience.

During adolescence and early adulthood I drifted away from formal connections with Judaism. In my mid-thirties, however, I was introduced to the ideas of Rabbi Mordecai Kaplan (Kaplan, 1934), the founder of the Reconstructionist movement, and from then on my engagement with Judaism and my appreciation of religion grew stronger. Kaplan, a professor at the

Jewish Theological Seminary, redefined Judaism as an evolving civilization in which religion plays a central but not exclusive role, and he sought to reconcile that religion with democracy and science. He developed a humanistic theology, repudiated the concept of the 'chosen people,' and pressed for the removal of all gender distinctions in ritual, prayer and practice. Respect for tradition combined with rejection of dogma ('The past has a vote but not a veto') sounded right to me then and still does 35 years later.

Kaplan believed that the principal function of religion is to inculcate faith in the possibility of human improvement. This tempered optimism is congenial to me and much to be preferred over yearning for unrealizable utopias or wallowing in nihilistic pessimism. It does not, however, provide an adequate preparation for the tragic side of life, and in recent years I have become more sensitive to the fact that not all problems have solutions.

SCHOOLING

Perhaps the most noteworthy aspect of my schooling is the fact that it was interrupted three times. When I was 16 I left high school for a semester in order to accompany my father on a business trip to South West Africa (now Namibia); from ages 19 to 22 I was in military service; and after World War II I spent four years in business before beginning graduate work. In each instance I returned to school with my desire and ability to learn enhanced by the interruption. I do not recommend such breaks for everyone, but neither should they be shunned or deplored.

A favorite subject in school was history, possibly because I had a good memory and that was frequently all that was needed to do well. Also, I have always been curious about what people do and why they do it. Mathematics was another favorite subject, and I regret that I did not pursue it in greater depth. In my elementary school, classes typically consisted of about 40 students with one teacher and no aides. Most of my fellow students were Jewish, while the principal and most of the teachers were Irish. Today large classes and the absence of 'role models' are blamed for poor performance, but that can only be part of the story. Our school, backed by strong support from parents, was able to start many of my classmates on paths to professional and academic careers.

In high school I was an indifferent student, perhaps because I entered at age 12 or because the school had 10000 students (all boys), or for other reasons. I started college (New York University) without any well-defined career goal; business administration seemed moderately interesting and was the path of least resistance. Two professors of economics, Jules Backman and Paul Studenski, made a strong impression on me; indeed, Backman's influence was a major reason why I eventually chose economics as a career. He was a lively, stimulating teacher, and although we often disagreed, I was never bored.

THE ARMY

In January 1943, shortly before my nineteenth birthday, I enlisted in the Army Air Corps. After a brief period of basic training, I was sent to Bowdoin College for a program in premeteorology. This meant heavy doses of math and physics, along with excellent courses in history and literature. The humanities were probably added more for the benefit of underemployed humanities professors than for the would-be meteorologists; but these courses have served me well throughout my life. One professor in particular, the poet Robert P.T. Coffin, had a great influence through his detailed critiques of my weekly essays on literary and historical subjects. Coffin gave me confidence in my writing and inspired me to improve.

At the end of my year at Bowdoin, the Air Corps announced that it had no need for additional meteorologists; my knowledge of math and physics was to be put to use in a program at Yale University that trained communications officers. At Yale we were given an interesting blend of theoretical work in electrical engineering and practical assignments such as building a radio transmitter and a receiver. These practical tasks taught me two lessons about education: (1) the right incentives can work miracles (I have always been extremely inept in the mechanical arts), and (2) the ability to pass a test is no guarantee that one has learned anything of lasting value (today I have trouble programming my VCR).

After receiving my commission, I was selected for further training in cryptographic security and then sent to the Aleutian Islands to help run an Air Corps message center. My facility with simple statistics led to a promotion and appointment as personnel officer of a communications squadron with over a thousand men located in a dozen detachments throughout Alaska and the Aleutian Islands. At the age of 21, with no previous training or experience in personnel work, I had to deal with a wide range of tasks, including classification and assignment, promotion, training, transfers, and rotation back to the mainland.

The Army experience showed me the potential benefits to young people of immersion in a structured environment and exposure to new settings and new ways of thought and action. I learned that young people are capable of assuming much more responsibility and accomplishing much more than peacetime society normally demands or allows. Given our current domestic problems, why don't we draw on the World War II experience to create new opportunities for work and training for millions of bored, frustrated and alienated young men and women?

BUSINESS

Upon discharge from the Army in 1946, I planned to enroll at Yale as an undergraduate, but a combination of family circumstances resulted in my joining my father in the small but successful firm that he had started many years before. He was an international broker, dealing with buyers and sellers of raw furs all over the world. The job required the technical ability to assess the value of fur pelts, as well as a general understanding of business and finance. International exchange rates were in a chaotic state, with blocked sterling accounts selling at great discounts that varied daily. Several business trips abroad taught me much about other cultures, and made me aware of the differences and similarities in human behavior. I also learned the value of reputation by observing how merchants in distant lands who had never met my father trusted him with large amounts of money and valuable shipments of furs.

While employed in the fur business, I studied at New York University at night to earn my BS in business administration and then continued to take occasional graduate courses. I recall in particular the lectures of Ludwig von Mises, which reinforced my view that a centrally controlled command economy could not function effectively. Another von Mises, Richard, had even more influence on me through his book, *Positivism* (1956). My attempts to write clearly and succinctly, and my belief that clear writing and clear thinking are closely linked, derive in large measure from that book.

Business was interesting and financially rewarding, but ultimately unsatisfying. It seemed like an exciting game, but something less than a fully adult activity. When my wife graduated from college in 1950, she went to work and I started graduate school at Columbia.

ECONOMICS

At that time, Columbia did not have a highly selective admissions policy; this was fortunate for me, given my rather unconventional education. The graduate student body was so large that there were over 100 enrolled in the basic statistics course given by Fred C. Mills. This course had limitations, unknown to me at the time, but his enthusiasm for the practical uses of statistics was stimulating. Ragnar Nurkse's lectures on international economics were notable for their clarity, but his views on exchange rate equilibrium ran counter to my experience in business. Other professors who made a lasting impression included Arthur F. Burns with his incisive critique of Keynesian theory, Karl Polanyi with a sweeping survey of general economic history, Abram Bergson who provided a solid introduction to Soviet economics, and most of all, George Stigler. His erudition, wit and incisive approach to economic questions continued to inspire me long after my graduate training.

After two years of course work at Columbia, without any particular concentration or focus, I began a dissertation on the economics of the fur industry. I was eager to apply some of my newly acquired tools and concepts in an attempt to understand the industry's intense cyclical fluctuations and the implications of its highly atomistic structure (Fuchs, 1957). This was a poor choice of subject from the point of view of professional recognition, but I enjoyed the research and was able to complete it expeditiously while holding down a full-time position as an instructor at Columbia.

Curiosity was a key factor for me then and has been ever since. Many graduate students seem to have difficulty finding a dissertation topic because they are insufficiently curious. High intelligence and good work habits are not enough to sustain a lifetime of scholarship in the absence of curiosity.

ECONOMIC RESEARCH

As an assistant professor I worked on a variety of subjects in industrial organization, including location of industry (Fuchs, 1962). After Columbia decided not to give me tenure, I spent two years on the staff of the Ford Foundation's program in Economic Development and Administration. This position provided an opportunity to interact with many of the finest minds in the profession; it gave me a clearer view of what was already being done in economics and a chance to think about what needed to be done.

In order to pursue my own research, I left the Foundation in 1962 to join the staff of the National Bureau of Economic Research (then exclusively in New York City). The time spent at the Bureau was like a late and extended post-doctoral experience. Many Bureau scholars helped me, but by far the greatest influence was that of Gary Becker. His seriousness of purpose, willingness to take chances, and determination to carry on in the face of skepticism provided excellent lessons for this would-be scholar.

The atmosphere at the Bureau reinforced my already revealed predilection for empirical research, but I have great respect for economists who begin their attack on a problem from the side of theory. As Goethe said, 'whatever we call a "fact" is already theory' (quoted by Richard von Mises, 1956, p. 101). My respect for theorists diminishes, however, if they believe that the solution to real-world problems can be found purely through deduction, or if their models are neither motivated by nor motivate empirical research. For me the best answer to the choice between theory and empiricism was given by Alfred North Whitehead. When asked 'Which are more important, facts or ideas?', the philosopher reflected for a while, then replied: 'Ideas *about* facts' (italics in original) (Price, 1954).

My first major study at the NBER concerned production and productivity in the service industries (1968, 1969). As a result of this work I became fascinated with the post-industrial society that was evolving in the United States and subsequently in other developed countries. The service industry project aroused my interest in health and medical care (1972, 1974a, 1986a); this aspect of my career has recently been reviewed by Joseph Newhouse (1992). My research on issues of family (1983) and gender (1974b, 1986b) also stemmed from this source.

In 1968, after several years of full-time research, I accepted a joint appointment as Professor of Economics at the CUNY Graduate Center and Professor of Community Medicine at the newly created Mount Sinai School of Medicine. Mount Sinai's president, George James, and Hans Popper, the leading intellectual force at the school, were determined to build a new kind of medical school on three foundations instead of the traditional two of basic sciences and clinical work. The third would emphasize the health of populations and would draw on biostatistics, epidemiology, the behavioral and social sciences, and other disciplines. The effort was only partially successful. The physicians at Mount Sinai were mostly quite capable and some were outstanding. As a group, however, they suffered from a limitation found in many medical school faculties: an excessive parochialism that limited their ability to transcend their specialty in analysis of a problem. Some economists appear to suffer from the same disease.

The faculty at the CUNY Graduate Center included several distinguished scholars, but there was minimal contact across disciplines, and I found that limiting. The students were not the most highly qualified, but what they lacked in their undergraduate preparation they compensated for with hard work and enthusiasm. Many have gone on to highly productive careers as professional economists in academia, government and business. This experience, plus the earlier one with the large class at Columbia that produced many fine scholars, has left me skeptical about highly selective admissions policies.

A fellowship (1972–73) at the Center for Advanced Study in the Behavioral Sciences at Stanford, California was significant in several respects. During that year I wrote *Who Shall Live? Health, Economics, and Social Choice*, the first of my books addressed to a general audience. Since then much of my writing has been for the general reader, or for specialized audiences (such as physicians) who are not trained in economics. I find this work challenging and rewarding; the need to write clearly and simply forces me to consider and reconsider assumptions and conclusions in economics that might otherwise be accepted too readily. Thomas Henry Huxley (1863) once observed 'Some experience with popular lecturing has convinced me that the necessity of making things plain to uninstructed people was one of the very best means of clearing up the obscure corners in one's own mind.'

My year at the Center for Advanced Study in the Behavioral Sciences also led to my moving to Stanford University, where I have had stimulating colleagues and students and a marvelous opportunity to indulge my interests in multidisciplinary approaches to social problems. The presence of Kenneth Arrow provides a particular strength; his brilliance in economics is matched by the depth and range of his interests in a wide variety of subjects.

I was again a fellow at CASBS in 1978–79, and I also have benefited from two opportunities to be a scholar-in-residence at the Rockefeller Foundation Center at Bellagio, Italy. In explaining to a group from outside academia the value of multidisciplinary centers such as CASBS and the Rockefeller Bellagio center, I drew an analogy with the puzzle of the nine dots. The dots are arranged in a square, made up of three sets of three dots each. The task is to connect all the dots with a single line without retracing any line and without lifting the pencil from the paper. The puzzle can only be solved by going outside the limits of the nine dots and coming back in at an angle. For me, that is what such centers offer – an opportunity to move outside one's customary limits, whether they be the limits of one's discipline, one's environment, or one's mode of thought, and to come back in on an angle in order to solve a problem.

When people ask me what I work on and I mention subjects like health, the family, or gender, they often respond 'That doesn't sound like economics.' They fail to distinguish between economic *problems* and the economic *perspective*. Unemployment, productivity and poverty are examples of economic problems. They involve what Polanyi called the 'substantive' economy. Economists probably know more about economic problems than anyone else, but many other disciplines, e.g., engineering, law and psychology, may be needed to deal effectively with them. The economic perspective, by contrast, is unique to economics. It is a way of thinking about problems that can be applied in many areas such as fertility, health, or education, as well as those problems called 'economic.' It is our mode of thought, not the object of that thought, that most distinguishes economists from other investigators.

In my experience in dealing with physicians, natural scientists, lawyers and other professionals, the economic perspective provides significant insights to a wide variety of problems. Although we are criticized for our failure to make unemployment or poverty disappear, we should not underestimate the power of our analytical concepts. We can often illuminate problems and identify possible solutions in ways that elude specialists with long experience in their own field.

Critical examination of economics from the margin of the discipline need not be nihilistic or destructive. Indeed, those insights which do stand up and can be made intelligible to non-economists gain strength in the process. The economic perspective alone is rarely sufficient for good policy-making, but it is usually necessary. To neglect it, to assume that resources are unlimited or that human behavior is insensitive to changes in incentives and constraints, is often an invitation to disaster.

This matter of human behavior has been central to my thinking about our subject. For me, economics is essentially a behavioral science, and the principal purpose of our research is to throw light on certain aspects of human behavior from both positive and normative points of view. Moreover, I have never believed in defining those 'certain aspects' narrowly, such as limiting them to behavior in formal markets. The behavioral approach does, however, bring to the fore some of the limitations of economists. We are, for instance, inclined to assume that individuals know what they want and that their only problem is to maximize utility through equality at the margin. In fact, one of the most difficult problems facing young (and not so young) people is to know what it is that they really want. The formation of preferences is a major human activity. A bit of folk wisdom says: 'The one thing worse than not getting what you want is getting what you want.' This probably means getting what you *thought* you wanted.

Another limitation is our tendency to ignore or decry behavior that does not conform to our view of how people ought to behave. Sometimes we are too quick to assert 'irrationality' or 'ignorance' when the deficiency may be in our model. I call that the fallacy of misplaced ignorance. If people value symbols, or are concerned about processes as well as final states, we should try to take that into account in our analysis.

OBJECTIVITY IN RESEARCH

I try to be objective in my work, but objectively speaking, complete objectivity is impossible. With respect to economic policy, values *must* enter; purely scientific descriptions of cause and effect cannot tell you whether or not a particular policy is socially desirable. Even the research that lays the basis of the cause and effect statements is not likely to be completely value free. I have some sympathy with Gunnar Myrdal's view that 'Valuations are always with us. Disinterested research there has never been, and can never be. Prior to answers there must be questions. There can be no view except from a viewpoint. In the questions raised and the viewpoints chosen, valuations are implied' (Myrdal, 1987).

But this concern about values can be carried too far. For me it is a warning to be self-conscious about what I am doing and why, and an injunction to try to avoid bias. I reject the view that all research is equally subjective and value-laden, and that all research findings are simply rationalizations for pre-selected conclusions. Perfectly objective research may be impossible, but research can be *more* objective or *less*, and our goal should be to be as objective as possible. Then, when the time comes to discuss economic policy, we should be as forthright as possible about how our policy conclusions are shaped by our values as well as by our analysis.

DIRECTING RESEARCH

From 1968 to 1978 I had administrative responsibility for a group of about two dozen NBER researchers gathered under the rubric 'Center for Economic Analysis of Human Behavior and Social Institutions.' It included programs in the family, income distribution, education, law and health. With Gary Becker providing the major intellectual stimulus, and with such forceful individuals, as James Heckman, Jacob Mincer, Richard Posner and Finis Welch on the staff, I did precious little 'directing.' And that's probably the way things should be. Our field does not (yet?) have the deep structure that warrants a massive commitment of research effort to lines laid down by a single individual. The director's main tasks are to help find money to keep the enterprise afloat, to insure the availability of space, computers, support staff, and to create an environment that amplifies the output of the individual researchers. Cooperation is a key element in the success of a research group. If the director has resources to redistribute, he or she will have a good chance of inducing the individual researchers to maximize the output of the group.

TEACHING

The longer I teach, the more challenging and complex the task appears. Most of my views are captured in a few aphorisms such as 'Less is more,' and 'There is no teaching; only learning.' Most teachers try to present too much. When organizing a course, I find it useful to ask myself 'What is it that I hope the students will keep from this course five or ten years from now?' I find that the same question needs to be repeated at the beginning of every lecture. Whenever possible, I prefer to combine lectures with discussion. For me, the case method of instruction (Warner and Fuchs, 1958) is particularly effective and rewarding. Student involvement is the key to student learning; the teacher's primary task is to motivate and facilitate that learning.

Education should be a moral as well as an intellectual experience. I believe that teachers should try, through example, precept, or mirrors, to help students realize what is best in themselves in terms of honesty, integrity, dependability and other dimensions of character. The libraries and the computer files are full of substantive knowledge; transmission of information is not the teacher's main job. The teacher who begins and ends each class on time is providing an extra lesson that may last a lifetime. When I teach the course required of majors that emphasizes writing about economic policy, I tell the students that good writing is partly a matter of character: be honest with your readers and respect their needs and abilities.

POLITICS

Politically I am a radical moderate. 'Moderate' because I believe in the need for balance, both in the goals that we set and in the institutions that we nourish in order to pursue those goals. 'Radical' because I believe that this position should be expressed as vigorously and as forcefully as extremists on the Right and Left push theirs. I value efficiency *and* justice, freedom *and* security, and the economic perspective tells me that we will often have to give up some of one goal in order to insure the partial achievement of others. Both theory and history indicate that the best way to seek multiple goals is through a balance of institutions – market, government, family and others. Those who stridently advocate reliance only on the market or only on government capture far more attention than their theories deserve. Because moderates see some merit in the arguments presented from both extremes, the moderate position runs the risk of being perceived as weak and indecisive. It need not be that way.

CLOSING NOTES

Nothing comes close to work and family in my priorities, but I do have a few 'outside' interests. Sports have always meant a great deal to me. As a boy I played virtually all team sports, including captaining a sandlot football team. Later in life I played tennis, and then switched to racquetball, which I enjoyed the most of all. Sports have taught me the importance of preparation and focus, how to be both a leader and a follower, how to win and how to lose, and, perhaps most importantly, that 'It's not over till it's over.'

In recent years problems with my back have forced me to forgo all sports except swimming. For diversion, I have turned to writing poetry – an awesome challenge to blend logic and emotion. I have also written and performed stand-up comedy; as an academic and an economist I do not have to look far for material. My interest in history and in trying to write succinctly continues; eventually I hope to summarize the history of the world – past, present, and future – in one word. I am leaning toward 'maybe.'

REFERENCES

Boulding, Kenneth. 1968. 'Economic Libertarianism,' in *Beyond Economics*. Ann Arbor, MI: University of Michigan Press.

Cavell, Stanley. 1979. *The Claim of Reason*. New York: Oxford University Press.

Fuchs, Victor R. 1992. 'America's Children: Economic Perspectives and Policy Options' (with Diane M. Reklis), *Science*, **255**, 41–46 (3 January).

——— 1989. 'Women's Quest for Economic Equality,' *Journal of Economic Perspectives*, **3** (1), 25–41 (Winter).

——— 1986a. *The Health Economy*. Cambridge, MA: Harvard University Press.

——— 1986b. 'Sex Differences in Economic Wellbeing,' Science, **232**, 459–64 (25 April).

——— 1983. *How We Live*. Cambridge, MA: Harvard University Press.

——— 1974a. *Who Shall Live? Health, Economics, and Social Choice*. New York: Basic Books.

——— 1974b. 'Recent Trends and Long-run Prospects for Female Earnings,' *American Economic Review Proceedings* (May), 236–42.

——— 1972. *Essays in the Economics of Health and Medical Care* (ed.). New York: Columbia University Press, for the National Bureau of Economic Research.

——— 1969. *Production and Productivity in the Service Industries* (ed.). New York: Columbia University Press, for the National Bureau of Economic Research.

——— 1968. *The Service Economy*. New York: Columbia University Press, for the National Bureau of Economic Research.

——— 1962. *Changes in the Location of Manufacturing in the United States Since 1929*. New Haven, CT: Yale University Press.

——— 1957. The Economics of the Fur Industry. New York: Columbia University Press.

Huxley, Thomas Henry. 1863. Preface to *Evidence As to Man's Place in Nature*. London: Williams & Norgate.

Kaplan, Mordecai. 1934. *Judaism As a Civilization*. New York: Macmillan.

Mishna. Avot.

Myrdal, Gunnar. 1987. 'Utilitarianism and Modern Economics,' in George R. Feiwell, (ed.), *Arrow and the Foundations of the Theory of Economic Policy*. London: Macmillan, 273–8

Newhouse, Joseph P. 1992. 'Distinguished Fellow: In Honor of Victor Fuchs,' *Journal of Economic Perspectives*, **6** (3), 179–89 (Summer).

Price, Lucien. 1954. *Dialogues of Alfred North Whitehead*, as recorded by Lucien Price. Boston: Little Brown.

Silk, Leonard. 1976. *The Economists*. New York: Basic Books.

von Mises, Richard. 1956. *Positivism*. New York: George Braziller, Inc.

Warner, Aaron, and Victor R. Fuchs. 1958. *Concepts and Cases in Economic Analysis*. New York: Harcourt Brace.

11. A roundabout approach to macroeconomics: some autobiographical reflections*

Roger W. Garrison

I. INTRODUCTION: SETTING THE STAGE

'Roundaboutness' is a concept featured in Austrian capital theory. Homely stories about the bare-handed catching of fish are a prelude to a discussion of the economy's capital structure. The outputs of some stages of production become inputs to others. Production takes time. The capital structure, broadly conceived, has a temporal profile – one that can be modified in response to changes in intertemporal consumption preferences and resource constraints. This was the central message of Eugen von Böhm-Bawerk (1959).

Alfred Marshall, who theorized in terms of the short period and the long period, taught us that most problems in economics stem from the ever-critical time element. I think Marshall was right on time. But I also believe that a healthy understanding of some of those problems – particularly the ones in macroeconomics – is not best facilitated by his simple short-period/long-period distinction.

Adopting Marshallian methods, John Maynard Keynes dealt with the polar extremes in the quality of expectations, casting serious doubt on the viability of a market system. In the short run, the time element itself is no problem: short-run expectations faithfully reflect reality. If the level of spending changes, the multiplier process plays itself out in a clockwork sequence of spending and earning, eventually achieving a new circular-flow equilibrium. Long-run expectations, however, are another matter. Here, the time element is a debilitating problem: these expectations, if you can call them that, are baseless. The future is shrouded in an impenetrable fog of uncertainty, leaving the current level of investment spending to be determined by unruly psychological factors – Keynes's infamous 'animal spirits.' The resultant

*Some material for this essay is drawn from the preface of *Time and Money* and from Garrison (1995a) and Garrison (2000).

circular flow will gush and ebb and even on average may not entail enough flow to fully employ the labor force.

The circular-flow framework, exercised in both its short-run and long-run modes, seems to me to be exactly the wrong framework for understanding and dealing with the time element in macroeconomics. Identifying the polar cases of 'no problem' and 'debilitating problem' doesn't get us any closer to a solution to all those intermediate cases lying between the poles. The tell-tale feature that inevitably characterizes this framework has been recognized in recent years by Robert Solow (1997) – namely the lack of any 'real coupling' (Solow's term) between the short run and the long run. In Solow's reckoning, the two runs simply divide our discipline's subject matter into (1) the problem of maintaining full employment of existing resources and (2) the determinants of economic growth.

A viable alternative to the Keynesian circular-flow framework is the Austrian means-ends framework. People employ means (investment) to achieve ends (consumption). In a capital-using economy, there is a significant time dimension separating means and ends. We realize that some production processes take more time than others. And, thinking in macroeconomic terms, we recognize that production time can increase or decrease for the economy as a whole as market conditions warrant. In the 'medium run' (a term from Solow, 2000), the problem is one of adjusting production decisions to (intertemporal) consumption preferences – a problem that Axel Leijonhufvud (1998) urges us to put back on our macroeconomic agenda. The only solution available in a decentralized economy is one involving entrepreneurial responses to changing market signals and especially to changes in the rate of interest. The time element here (Böhm-Bawerk's 'roundaboutness' of production activities) is a key variable in the system. Like other endogenous variables, it is subject to marginal adjustments in response to parametric changes. Of course, there is uncertainty. And the fog is more of a problem the farther into the future the entrepreneurs are trying to see. But still, what seems to be called for is an application of marginalism and not a contrasting of the polar cases.

At the very dawn of the Keynesian revolution, the circular-flow framework and the means – ends framework were seen as the two real live alternatives (Hicks, 1967). Marshall-*cum*-Keynes gets you one vision of the economy (plus a toolkit of policy options); Böhm-Bawerk-*cum*-Hayek gets you another vision of the economy. In the early 1930s, Friedrich A. Hayek was brought to the London School of Economics by Lionel Robbins precisely for the purpose of providing a counter to the ideas of Keynes. But Hayekian ideas proved ineffective against the Keynesian avalanche. Debate continues to this day about just why Hayek failed to review the *General Theory* (Caldwell, 1998) and just how he lost out to Keynes.

At mid-century, Hayek's business cycle theory, a theory that contained the seeds of a full-fledged capital-based macroeconomic framework, had sunk into oblivion. His books, including *Prices and Production*, which was the print version of the lectures he had delivered at LSE in 1931, were long out of print. Undergraduates of my generation – even economics majors – would never hear about Hayek, much less learn that his theory was once the principal rival of Keynes's. The index in Paul Samuelson's *Principles of Economics*, seventh edition (1967), which dominated the field at the time, refers the reader to a single footnote in an appendix on commodity and factor pricing – where Hayek is portrayed, in effect, as being on the losing side of the socialist-calculation debate.

Prices and Production didn't get back into print until 1967, when it was offered by Augustus M. Kelley as part of a reprint series. But in that year, I was a long way from reading Hayek and, in fact, a long way from studying economics. The progression of my own studies from the sinusoidal rhythms of alternating current to the cyclical fluctuations of a mixed economy was a roundabout one – hence the *double entendre* of this essay's title.

II. FLASHBACK: ELECTRICAL ENGINEERING AND ENGINEERING ECON

In January of 1967 I was completing the course requirements for a BS in Electrical Engineering. Few students could finish the course work in four years at the Missouri School of Mines and Metallurgy (now the University of Missouri at Rolla). Most took five years. I was lucky to get through in four-and-a-half – especially in view of my having completed the first two years at a junior college. Getting some early course work behind me at Joplin Junior College kept the cost of my education down. I could live at home and cover the out-of-pocket expenses with income from part-time and summer jobs. The junior college put me a little behind in terms of the applied engineering courses, but it put me way ahead in terms of mathematical skills. Martha McCormick was probably the best college-level professor of mathematics in the state.

Partly because of McCormick, along with some excellent junior high and high-school math teachers, mathematics was my strong suit. But it was McCormick herself who steered me away from it. At the time, she knew more economics than I did. She knew that even an advanced math degree did not translate into attractive employment opportunities. Her suggested alternative was an applied field – engineering. She suggested electrical engineering because that specialty made use of the most sophisticated mathematical techniques.

I was very good at textbook engineering but was a virtual non-starter in the electronics labs. Given some output specifications, I could design a circuit and determine the power requirements and the parametric values of all the elements and active components with ease – so many ohms here, so many farads there, and so many watts. If my calculations called for a few 500-ohm resistors and a couple of 30-farad capacitors, I was off to the supply room. It was a rude awakening – to say nothing of the embarrassment – to learn that a 30-farad capacitor would be about the size of a boxcar!

When I eventually acknowledged the constraints imposed by reality and could actually get the raw materials for a circuit, I had no trouble putting them all together – but only if the other students would leave me alone. Which is to say that I was no good at team work. Unfortunately, we usually had six hands working on one circuit. That was an exercise in frustration for me. Things were no better in the heavy-machinery lab, where we had only three hands working on the circuit. As a not-too-subtle safety reminder, the lab instructor had left one pair of sneakers welded to the floor – a result of an earlier student completing the circuit in an all-too-personal way. Each of us had to work with one hand behind his back. And by the way, 'behind her back' is a phrase that had little application at Rolla in the 1960s. The female population at the Missouri School of Mines could have been measured in picofarads.

Whether involving individual effort or team effort, the technical courses at MSM were given precedence over other courses – few in number – that were outside the hard sciences. I took a one-semester course in economics (both micro and macro) to fulfill the social-science requirement. I remember the Keynesian diagrammatics and recall thinking that Samuelson's rendition of the circular flow, complete with small drain spout that vented saving away from the investment pump, had something of a comic-book character to it. Neither the diagram nor the text inspired careful study of Keynes, and there was no hint of a more appealing alternative. The lectures on unemployment and business cycles were no help. I remember only that the professor ended almost every sentence with the words 'as such.' And sometimes there were two back-to-back 'as suches' – one deliberate, one subconscious.

The only other course that had any economics content at all was taught in the civil engineering department. It was called Engineering Economics – with the Economics always pronounced with a long e and usually shortened to 'Econ.' I look back at that course now with both amusement and gratitude. What does a professor of Engineering Econ do with a bunch of students who (1) have highly honed math skills but (2) have little or no appreciation for the economic aspects of engineering? The answer: confront them with a bunch of present-value problems in which the inputs and the outputs are described by high-order polynomials or by transcendental functions of one sort or another.

Then, award them an A if they can do the math. The professor in that course played right into my hands.

I do remember noticing that in many of the problems the interest rate was given. I wondered just who gave it in the real world, but it never occurred to me to ask. The professor didn't so much as hint that there were important issues here. If the rate of interest reflects the give and take of the marketplace, the resulting resource allocations will have a certain internal consistency about them. But if the interest rate is given from on high by the policy committee of the central bank, the internal consistency is in doubt and the economy may be moving along an unsustainable growth path. These issues were well beyond the scope of Engineering Econ.

I also recall that in some of the problems, the internal rate of return had to be determined. And for problems in which the given time profiles of outlays and revenues overlapped, there was an obvious possibility of multiple internal rates of return. It could turn out that the internal rates for such a project were 8 percent and 2 percent. Not much was made of such cases. But when I learned years-and-a-career-change later of the related possibility of 'technique reswitching' and of the so-called Cambridge capital controversy, I found the phenomenon less than earth-shaking and the controversy almost wholly sterile. Piero Sraffa (1960) had laid the groundwork in a book that he wrote in the 1920s but published decades later. Paul Samuelson offered a summing-up article in 1966: the relative profitabilities of two techniques (A and B) could change and then change back as the interest rate underwent a continuous decline. That is, during the decline, a profit-maximizing producer would switch from A to B and then back to A. The math was the same as in the case of multiple rates of return: set the present values of the two techniques equal to one another to find the two rates – maybe that same 8 percent and 2 percent – where the switching and reswitching take place. One technique is the more profitable between the switch and reswitch points; the other is the more profitable at all other rates. It's Engineering Econ. But the very possibility of technique reswitching, according to the Sraffians, casts grave doubt on the logical integrity of the neoclassical production function and on the validity of Böhm-Bawerk's capital theory. Eventually, Joan Robinson (1975) wrote an article on 'The Unimportance of Reswitching'; Cohen and Harcourt (2003), who have recently wondered out loud 'Whatever Happened to the Cambridge Capital Theory Controversies?' still see deep and unresolved issues here. My own take on the controversy appears as 'Waiting in Vienna' (1979).

III. DISRUPTING EVENTS AND CHANGING INTERESTS

During the summers of my undergraduate years, I had work experiences that gave me a taste of the real world of engineering. I worked one summer for the Eagle Picher Company in Galena, Kansas. The Galena facility, located along a stretch of the original Route 66, processed lead and zinc for the company's battery division. The work there was a little too real-world for me. I don't think I would have made a very good production engineer.

I worked another summer for the Kansas City Power and Light Company. There I learned first hand about the perversities of rate-of-return regulation that had recently been dubbed the Averch–Johnson effect. This form of regulation creates incentives for the firm to pad its capital base so that higher total profits fall within the allowed rate of return. Most of my time at KCPL was spent doing Engineering Econ – using present-value calculations to show that a well-insulated all-electric home was more cost efficient than the more conventional homes that used both electricity and natural gas. A low rate of interest favored the all-electric option because of its large up-front insulation costs.

After graduating from the Missouri School of Mines, neither my work experiences nor my one interview trip (to IBM in Poughkeepsie, New York) counted for anything. The Vietnam war was in full swing, and I was registered at one of Missouri's more draconian draft boards. My older brother (and only sibling) had received his draft notice just before graduating from the Kansas City Art Institute. Jim was in a training trajectory that would eventually land him in Vietnam. My options were limited. MSM in the 1960s was no Berkeley. Engineering students tended to be neither protesters nor draft dodgers. But many of them, including me, were risk minimizers. I chose to take a commission in the Air Force, preferring four years in that branch of the service to two years in the Army. On receiving the commission in San Antonio, Texas in April of 1967, I was assigned to an electronics-countermeasures lab at Griffiss AFB in Rome, New York. I became a systems engineer, traveling to Texas, California, and elsewhere in the continental US to monitor contracts for the development of radar-jamming systems and the like.

At Griffiss there was some in-house capability, including a state-of-the-art mainframe computer. General Electric was still in the process of debugging the new computer and hence invited the researchers at Griffiss to use it for any and all purposes in order to identify still more bugs. Computer time became a free good, and given the demands of the limited war on military personnel in the Mohawk Valley, I had plenty of free time to exercise the computer. On my own I decided to learn to program in BASIC, which at the time was a new computer language. I was motivated by my interest in mathematical puzzles. An article on BASIC in *Aviation Week*, a very popular magazine at Air Force labs, claimed that the new language deserved credit for its user friendliness, but that it was not at all adept at 'problem recognition.' For instance, BASIC could never be used, according to the article, to solve the problem known as the 'Knight's Tour of the Board.'

I had never heard of the Knight's Tour, but my *AW*-reading colleagues had. They explained that the Knight must move around the chess board, starting where a Knight always starts, moving like a Knight always moves, and landing on each square once and only once. It sounded like a challenge. Could I write a program in BASIC to generate a successful Knight's Tour? My attempt at a solution was literally my first program in BASIC. Undoubtedly I produced a very inefficient and graceless piece of programming. But I had the compensating advantage of unlimited computer time. I could set the program to running late on a Friday afternoon and return on Monday morning to see if a solution had emerged from my remote consol. Eventually, one did. The computer typed out an eight-by-eight matrix of numbers from 1 through 64, showing the trail of a successful tour. I streamlined the program and was able to get a solution in five to fifteen minutes. Before I grew tired of this puzzle, my program found some twenty-odd solutions, never finding the same one twice. And it found one solution where the Knight's 64th position was within a Knight's move of its initial position – closing the path and giving me a Knight's Tour from any starting point. I don't know what the state of knowledge of the Knight's Tour was at the time, although the *Aviation Week* article indicated that there were only a handful of solutions. I never tried to publish the program to demonstrate the 'problem-recognition' qualities of BASIC. For me solving a puzzle was an end in itself and a good way to deal with too much time.

Less than a year after I began my own four-year tour, Jim got orders sending him to Vietnam. He departed from an Army post in North Carolina, stopping in the Mohawk Valley before heading to the west coast and then to the war zone in Southeast Asia. His diversion from Army life had consisted of reading Ayn Rand. Having read a few of her books, he asked me to find and send him the others. Shortly after his departure, I found a bookstore in Syracuse that carried all of Rand's books – her novels and her collected essays on the philosophy of Objectivism. I bought two of each. Over the following weeks, I would send Jim a Rand book and then read the copy I'd bought for myself.

Objectivism is strong medicine, especially for people with a background in engineering. I had spent my college years avoiding courses in the social sciences because of the apparent lack of structure and reason. But Rand's *Capitalism: the Unknown Ideal* (1967) was full of structure and reason, and it provided a moral foundation for a free society. This collection of essays by Rand and others came with a list of recommended readings, including a number of books on economics. Rand identified the economists of the Austrian School as the most capable of showing just what is – or ought to be – sitting on her philosophical foundation. I soon discovered that Austrian economics is appealing to an engineering mind: basic principles, law-like propositions, unequivocal conclusions – all grounded in logic and applicable to the world as we know it. Among the authors flagged for further study were Eugen von Böhm-Bawerk and Ludwig von Mises as well as such popularizers as Frédéric Bastiat and Henry Hazlitt.

The Rand volume itself contained two articles by Alan Greenspan, one exposing the fallacies of 'Antitrust,' the other establishing the connection between 'Gold and Economic Freedom.' And in an article by Nathaniel Branden dealing with the economics of depression, a memorable metaphor was attributed to Greenspan: putting the government in charge of the money supply is like putting a penny in the fuse box. As recounted in a recent biography by Justin Martin (2000), Alan Greenspan was a member of Ayn Rand's inner circle.

All this was heady stuff to me. Just what was the role of gold in the economy? And what was the purpose of a central bank? Were depressions inherent in the nature of a market economy, or were they the result of ill-conceived stabilization policy? For me, these questions had the makings of a new puzzle. And this puzzle had a special significance because of my awareness of the lingering effects of the Great Depression on my family. My parents were just reaching adulthood when the depression came. Their experiences in coping with deprivation during the 1930s set their attitudes about economic matters for life. They strongly distrusted banks, but they were always big savers – even though there was little income out of which to save. A large portion of my extended family (mostly on my mother's side) left Missouri in the 1940s and 1950s for California. (The economy-wide depression had gotten compounded in southwest Missouri by the depletion of quality ore in Missouri's lead belt.) I remember hearing an older cousin quip that many in our family were so poor they had nothing to lose by starting over in California and that the rest were so poor they couldn't afford the trip!

There was no coherence in political attitudes in my extended family – my father's family being Republican and my mother's family Democratic. I remember an aunt expressing her political views in an impish ungrammatical sing-song fashion: 'Roosevelt was for poor people; I'm a poor people; so I was for Roosevelt.' But I also remember the contempt in my father's voice when he recited the campaign slogan that had emerged in Roosevelt's 1936 reelection campaign: Spend, spend, spend; elect, elect, elect!

In my immediate family, my father's political gene was dominant. My mother showed no signs of a cross-party marriage and even did duty, along with my father, as a grass-roots committee chairperson for the Republicans. They were comfortably on the right side of the issues of the day – but not on the religious right. In fact, my father's Ayn Rand was Robert Ingersoll, a prominent nineteenth-century free thinker. The touchstone for my parents'

Republicanism was self-reliance. In my father's eyes, Barry Goldwater personified the party's ideals.

I began reading from Rand's list of recommended books and soon came across *America's Great Depression* (1963) by Murray Rothbard, another erstwhile member of Rand's inner circle. I found Rothbard's account of boom and bust compelling and especially significant in light of the stark contrast between the views of the Austrian economists and those of my engineering cohorts. With a monopoly on money creation, the government could artificially cheapen credit and orchestrate an economic expansion – an artificial expansion that eventually and inevitably would collapse. Policies commonly defended in the name of stability and growth led instead to instability and decay. In later years, I would attach even more significance to this view of boom and bust – when I compared it to the curious and implausible accounts of the business cycles offered by other schools of thought.

During the second half of my military career, I immersed myself in economics – Austrian and otherwise. My brother had returned safely from Vietnam and regained his status as a civilian. He was beginning a career in graphic design in New York City. We had a number of opportunities to bounce ideas off one another, and on a couple of occasions, we met in Boston to hear Ayn Rand's annual Ford Hall Forum Lecture.

Though I was sympathetic to Rand's philosophy, I felt that I might actually have something to contribute on the economics front. The puzzles of boom and bust had an enduring appeal. Times were good in the 1920s and bad in the 1930s. How could times in general be either good or bad, and just what made them so? I jumped into the middle of the ongoing battle of ideas by reading Henry Hazlitt's *Failure of the 'New Economics'* (1959). The first few chapters of this critique of Keynes's *General Theory* (1936) were enough to persuade me that I could not read Hazlitt's book with profit unless I first read Keynes's. I had no idea at the time what actually lay in store for me.

In his own preface, Keynes does warn the reader that his arguments are aimed at his fellow economists, but he invites interested others to eavesdrop. As it turned out, even the most careful reading of the *General Theory*'s 384 pages and the most intense pondering of its one solitary diagram were not enough to elevate me much beyond the status of eavesdropper. But Keynes made me feel that I was listening in on something important and mysterious. The ideas that investment is governed by 'animal spirits' and that the use of savings is constricted by the 'fetish of liquidity' do not integrate well with more sympathetic treatments of the free-enterprise system. Keynes's notion that the rate of interest could and should be driven to zero seemed puzzling, and his call for a 'comprehensive socialization of investment' served as a red flag in more ways than one.

With Keynes's mode of argument – though not the full logic of his system – fresh in my mind, Hazlitt's book was intelligible, but his virtual page-by-page critique came across as the work of an unreceptive and hostile eavesdropper. Keynes's vision of the macroeconomy – in which the market tends toward depression and instability and in which the government assumes the role of stimulating and stabilizing it until social reform can replace it with something better – was never effectively countered. Not surprisingly, Hazlitt did point to the Austrian economists as the ones offering the most worthy alternative vision. There was a double handful of references to Hayek's writings and twice that many to Mises's.

After a diet of Keynes, contra-Keynes, and then Austrian economics, I returned to my old principles text to see how I had failed to come to any understanding at all during my undergraduate experience with macroeconomics. In Samuelson's chapters on the macroeconomy, I found a total eclipse of the most fundamental issues. The questions of whether, how, and in what institutional settings a market economy can be self-regulating were crowded out by a strong presumption that self-regulation is not possible. The vision of an economy adrift was reinforced by simplistic exercises showing how in a failure-prone circular flow the extent of labor and resource idleness is related to the leakages from (and injections into) the economy's streams of spending.

IV. FROM ENGINEERING TO ECONOMICS

The engineering market was glutted in 1971 when Vietnam was winding down and I was making my exit from the military. Electrical Engineering was second only to Aerospace in terms of the difficulty of making the transition from guns to butter. An electrical engineer with four years' experience in warfare electronics could not compete effectively with an entry-level applicant with a fresh degree. One option popular among my peers was to work on an MBA degree while waiting for better times. An EE/MBA was considered to be a very marketable combination. I chose to pursue a masters in economics instead, knowing that the course work would be more interesting and thinking (erroneously) that an EE/MA combination would also be marketable. I applied for admission into the masters program at the University of Missouri at Kansas City. Attempting to compensate for having very little formal undergraduate training in economics, I attached to my application a list of books I had read in preparation for graduate school. The books ranged from Ludwig von Mises's *Theory of Money and Credit* (1912) to Shirley Schiebla's *Poverty is Where the Money Is* (1968). It is a wonder that I was admitted into the program.

At UMKC the most revered economists were the Institutionalists – Thorstein Veblen and Clarence Ayers. But the courses in macroeconomics offered heavy doses of Keynesianism. Direct references to Keynes's *General Theory*, however, were rare. Instead, his analytical framework was presented in the conventional form of IS–LM analysis, those interlocking diagrams that jointly determine the equilibrium values for the economy's income and its interest rate. Gardner Ackley's *Macroeconomic Theory* (1961) was the assigned text. The substantial investment involved in mastering the diagrammatical technique seemed to give professors and students alike a special interest in defending Keynesian views. Further, the only alternative mentioned was the trumped-up classical model devised by Ackley himself as a foil for understanding and appreciating the revolutionary character of the Keynesian system.

I vividly remember reporting to my brother on the state of macroeconomic pedagogy. I explained how the Keynesians had a virtual lock on macroeconomics. The interlocking graphics yielded up answers to macroeconomic questions, and if the students didn't give those answers, they had no answers at all to give. Hayek was a genuine alternative to Keynes in the 1930s. Forty years later there was a glaring need, Jim and I agreed, for a genuine alternative to the Keynesian graphics.

In late 1972 I began to devise an Austrian counterpart to the Keynesian diagrams. Rothbard's *Man, Economy, and State* (1962) provided the primary source material. In the end, I was able to draw together individual diagrams taken from or inspired by Rothbard, Mises, Hayek, Böhm-Bawerk and Wicksell and show that they all fit together into a coherent story about boom and bust. I wrote a term paper titled 'Austrian Macroeconomics: A Diagrammatical Exposition.' My graphics were three-dimensional: the Austrian view was represented in one plane, the Keynesian view in another, orthogonal plane. This construction allowed me to show the definitional connections between the two views as well as the key substantive differences.

The professor gave me a high mark on the paper but confessed that he hadn't actually worked through the graphical analysis and wasn't familiar with Austrian economics. To my surprise, though, he offered to arrange for me to present the paper at the Midwest Economic Association meetings to be held in Chicago in April 1973. With some urging from this professor, I agreed to go to Chicago. I soon realized, however, that neither he nor anyone else had provided me with critical feedback. No one had actually read the paper. And I was to present it to a professional audience in April! The one action item that occurred to me was to send the paper to Rothbard. Maybe he would respond in time to give me some confidence about Chicago – or to allow me to renege on my agreement to go.

About a week after mailing the paper, I got a phone call from Rothbard. He was clearly enthused about the diagrammatical exposition; he saw it as beating the Keynesians at their own game. 'Would you be coming to New York anytime soon?' he asked. Although I had no plans whatever to go to New York, I managed to announce: 'I'll be there during spring break,' at which point he invited me for dinner and further discussion of the diagrams.

Dining with Murray and Joey Rothbard in their book-lined upper westside apartment was a pleasant and memorable experience. After dinner more guests arrived for a lively discussion of the paper. There were lots of good suggestions for revision and further development. In the short period between my March trip to New York and the April meeting in Chicago, I was able to make some improvements and gain some confidence.

The presentation in Chicago was a virtual non-event, which, as I soon learned, is typical of sessions at professional meetings. But that disappointment was overshadowed by the fact that Rothbard had invited me to attend a week-long conference on twentieth-century American economic history sponsored by the Institute for Humane Studies and scheduled in the summer at Cornell University. He and Forrest McDonald (now of the University of Alabama) were to lecture for a week to an audience consisting mainly of student historians.

With that conference, which came at the end of my studies at UMKC, I became comfortable with the fact that I had left engineering forever. I had spent the summer of 1972 – the Watergate summer – as an intern at the Bureau of Labor Statistics in Washington, DC. But on finishing the course work for the masters degree, I applied for employment in engineering as well as in economics. In the same week I had interviews with the Bendix Corporation and with the Federal Reserve Bank of Kansas City. I discovered that an MA in economics was a poor substitute for an MBA in the eyes of engineering firms. With some philosophical reservations, I accepted the job at the Kansas City Fed, delaying my start date until after the Cornell conference. I learned much from the Rothbard–McDonald lectures, but more importantly, my name was added to the invitation list for subsequent conferences.

In June of the following year (1974) I spent a week at South Royalton, Vermont – at an IHS conference that came to be widely recognized as the take-off point for the Austrian Resurgence. There, Murray Rothbard, Israel Kirzner and Ludwig Lachmann gave lectures dealing with method, theory and policy, all published in due course as *The Foundations of Modern Austrian Economics* (Dolan, 1976). Henry Hazlitt and Bill Hutt added much insight and perspective to the discussions. Milton Friedman was there for the opening banquet. His now-famous remark that 'there is no Austrian economics – only good economics and bad economics' had a certain (but unintended) galvanizing effect on the conference. The list of participants, most meeting one another for the first time, now reads like a Who's Who in Austrian economics: Dom Armentano, Walter Block, John Blundell, Richard Ebeling, David Henderson, Jack High, Randall Holcombe, Don Lavoie, Larry Moss, Gary North, Gerald O'Driscoll, Mario Rizzo, Joe Salerno, Sudha Shenoy, Karen Vaughn. One purpose of that conference was to persuade Lachmann that there was sufficient interest in Austrian economics to justify his coming out of semi-retirement and teaching at New York University. By week's end, the interest was not in doubt, and Lachmann soon began teaching at NYU.

There were two follow-on conferences held in successive years – with Hayek joining the original South Royalton faculty. In 1975 the Austrians met at the University of Hartford in Connecticut; in 1976 they met in England at Windsor Castle. At both conferences, papers by South Royalton participants were presented and discussed. The Windsor Castle papers, among which was my newly revised 'Austrian Macroeconomics,' were eventually published as *New Directions in Austrian Economics* (Spadaro, 1978). My diagrammatical exposition has had a limited but enduring success. It was published separately as a monograph by IHS and was excerpted extensively in Duncan Reekie's *Markets, Entrepreneurs and Liberty: An Austrian View of Capitalism* (1984). It continues to appear on Austrian economics reading lists, was the basis for some discussion in an interview published in Snowden et al. (1994), and tends to get mentioned in histories of the Austrian school, such as in Vaughn (1994), and in survey articles, such as in Kirzner (1997).

V. INTERLUDE: THE FEDERAL RESERVE

Spending time at the Federal Reserve was an important part of my education. But apart from occasionally being on 'burn detail' – destroying soiled or torn currency – I was not directly involved with monetary matters. I was in the Division of Bank Supervision and Structure, where applications for the acquisition of banks by bank holding companies were processed. In play here were the issues of industrial organization. The Federal Reserve, in effect, was serving as trust buster for the banking industry. The focus in each case was on market share – although there was no benchmark market share according to which some actual market share could be judged harmless or worrisome. And the numbers quantifying the change in market share were very sensitive to the definition of the market area, a definition that itself was almost wholly arbitrary.

Suppose that Missouri's largest bank holding company, whose lead bank is in Kansas City, wanted to acquire a small bank in nearby Blue Springs. The holding company would press for a definition of the relevant market area that minimizes the impact of the proposed acquisition. It would argue one of two extremes – that there would be no change in the market-share figures because the relevant market areas were so small that the Kansas City bank and the Blue Springs bank were in two different market areas; or that there would be only a minuscule change in the market-share figures because the lead bank and the target bank were located in a very large market area (the whole state of Missouri) in which many banks competed. The Federal Reserve would usually opt for some middling market-area definition – using rivers (despite bridges), county lines, and even highways as market-area boundaries. But I don't recall a case where the change in market share was judged to be significant. The Fed didn't bust many trusts.

Evaluating an application always entailed interviewing the CEOs of other small banks that competed with the target bank. Tellingly, the reactions of the target banks' competitors were either grave concern or seeming indifference: 'How are we supposed to compete with the largest bank holding company in the state?' Or, quite often: 'The acquisition is fine with us; we'll compete' – which really meant that this bank was currently in the negotiation phase with the second largest bank holding company in the state. While traveling around the Federal Reserve's tenth district for on-site visits (mostly in Missouri and Colorado) I was also reading Israel Kirzner's *Competition and Entrepreneurship* (1973) in preparation for attending the South Royalton conference. I had trouble, to say the least, trying to reconcile what I was reading with what I was doing.

In between applications, I had time to pursue my macroeconomic interests. Did the boom during the 1920s have a significant policy-driven component? There was no dispute that there was significant real growth during that decade. But what about money growth and its effects on prices and on interest rates – and hence on resource allocation? I juxtaposed two key books giving contrasting answers to these and related questions, both published in 1963: Friedman and Schwartz's *Monetary History of the United States (1867–1960)* and Rothbard's *America's Great Depression*. It became clear that, with minor variation, both books relied on the same data: Friedman and Schwartz reported the annual growth rate of the money supply for the 1920s and took it to be consistent with macroeconomic stability. Rothbard reported the cumulative growth of the money for an eight-year period (1921–29) and saw it as alarmingly high.

Clearly, the difference between Friedman and Rothbard lay in their contrasting interpretations of Federal Reserve behavior during the 1920s. Friedman took the constant or near-constant price level that characterized the decade as evidence of monetary stability. Money creation was accommodating real growth. Rothbard looked at the effect of this accommodation on interest rates and hence on the intertemporal pattern of investment. In his judgment, the credit expansion resulted in widespread intertemporal disequilibrium. I would later learn that Hayek (1994, Introduction), who was watching the Fed in the early 1920s, began work on an NYU PhD thesis on the question 'Is the function of money consistent with an artificial stabilization of purchasing power?' – a question that could only be puzzling to the monetarists.

The difference between these two books was a reflection of their competing analytical frameworks. But in each case the analytical framework was not well defined. Friedman (1970) had attempted to set out the differences between himself and the Keynesians by expressing these two sets of ideas in the IS–LM framework. Was this Keynesian framework also the monetarist framework? If not, then just what – beyond the equation of exchange plus a money-demand equation – was the monetarist framework? The Austrian analytics seemed to revolve around the intertemporal structure of production as depicted by the Hayekian triangle, whose changing shape reflects marginal adjustments in the roundaboutness of the economy's production activities. Though vital, this little piece of pedagogy, by itself, hardly passed muster as an analytical framework.

Dating from the South Royalton conference, my interests in the analytical framework of Austrian macroeconomics grew. Lectures at that conference by Ludwig Lachmann, though somewhat cryptic, further convinced me that it was capital theory that made the difference between the Austrians and mainstream schools. And having listened to the lectures by Israel Kirzner, my interests in market areas and market shares were decidedly on the wane. Besides, with only a masters degree, I did not have a bright future with the Federal Reserve. It was time for me to go. I had been reluctant to continue my graduate studies mainly because I did not know which doctorate programs might be worthwhile. But I now knew of three possibilities – all suggested to me by Rothbard: New York University, UCLA and the University of Virginia.

Other events and opportunities at the time spurred me on. Sudha Shenoy, whom I had met at South Royalton, arranged for me to attend the Hayek-led Mont Pélerin Society meetings in September of that year. Those meetings were held in Brussels, just three months after South Royalton. And in the following month, Hayek was awarded the Nobel Prize for his early work in industrial fluctuations. In November I attended the Southern Economic Association meetings in Atlanta in order to discuss with George Pearson a possible fellowship arrangement. If I was inclined to leave the Federal Reserve and resume graduate studies, the Institute for Humane Studies, then in Menlo Park, California, would accept me as a resident fellow during the summers. With that opportunity, I became a short-timer in Kansas City. I did not search for other graduate programs beyond the three that Rothbard had mentioned. But having no strong desire to live in either New York City or Los Angeles, I headed for Charlottesville.

VI. VIRGINIA: PREPARING FOR AN ACADEMIC CAREER

Virginia's economics department in the mid-1970s was in decline. Jim Buchanan and Gordon Tullock had left. Warren Nutter had fallen ill, and the few others to whom the University owed its good reputation (for its adherence to the principles of classical liberalism) were on the political outs. The department was beginning to turn towards mathematical economics – though not as much so as was the general trend in those years. In the field of macroeconomics, there wasn't much sympathy for Keynesianism, except in the first-semester core course. That course was taught by a visiting professor who was so inept and narrow-minded as to make Keynesian constructions monumentally unappealing. Monetarism and its offshoots (new classicism and rational expectations) were considered to be the mainstream and the cutting edge of monetary theory.

The propensity to mathematize was eroding the Virginia tradition. The math never got in my way, thanks to my engineering background, but I had no inclination to take a purely mathematical approach to economics. Having learned Lagrangian multipliers and the like separately from the substantive content of economics had a definite payoff. That training sequence keeps the mathematics in perspective – which, in many cases, is to say that it keeps the math at bay. In macroeconomics, what often matters most are the institutional arrangements, such as the fact that new money enters the economy through credit markets and hence impinges in the first instance on interest rates. And changes in the interest rate have a predictable effect on the pattern of investment – as can be demonstrated by those present-value calculations I learned in Engineering Econ.

For me the shining light at Virginia was Leland Yeager, whose monetary disequilibrium theory (Yeager, 1997) derives from the pre-Friedman monetarism of Clark Warburton. Yeager taught a course in monetary theory using Don Patinkin's *Money, Interest, and Prices* (1965), a book well anchored in name and in spirit to Knut Wicksell's *Interest and Prices* (1898). It was the Wicksell–Patinkin connection that inspired my dissertation. Wicksell had called attention to the 'cumulative process' that is set into motion by a bank rate of interest held below the market, or natural, rate. I could trace the Wicksellian insights in two different directions – to Patinkin and to Hayek – showing how one direction of development emphasized the sense in which money is neutral while the other emphasized the inherent non-neutrality of the process through which the economy adjusts to a monetary expansion. The key difference between the two different directions of development was capital theory – its wholesale neglect in Patinkin's framework and its centrality in Hayek's.

While in residence at the University of Virginia, I had the good fortune to serve as a teaching assistant to Kenneth Elzinga and Bill Breit, a peerless duo who taught Virginia's two-semester sequence of microeconomics and macroeconomics. Their performances in the undergraduate classroom, together with Yeager's performance at the graduate level, were a virtual how-to course for budding academics who themselves would soon be teaching.

Of course, making the transition from graduate student to professor required actually completing the dissertation. I was able to work on mine at the Institute for Humane Studies in 1977 and 1978 when, as luck would have it, Hayek was in residence there, too. After having been occupied with the broader issues of political science for more than three decades, Hayek was beginning to think again about the issues of money and macroeconomics. He had just published his *Choice in Currency* (1976) and had expanded it into the *Denationalization of Money* (1976).

Participating in the UCLA Oral History Program, Hayek had reaffirmed his early views about the nature of business cycles. And he wrote an inspiring Foreword to Gerald O'Driscoll's *Economics as a Coordination Problem: The Contributions of Friedrich A. Hayek* (1977). O'Driscoll, a UCLA graduate and IHS resident fellow, had demonstrated in his dissertation the unity of Hayek's work. Hayek found the demonstration satisfying and even moving:

> That it seems in principle possible to recast a great part of economic theory in terms of the approach which I had found useful in dealing with such different problems as those of industrial fluctuations and the running of a socialist economy [is] gratifying to me ... Professor O'Driscoll has almost persuaded me that I ought to have continued with the work I had been doing in the 1930s and 1940s rather than let myself be drawn away to other problems which I felt to be more important.

Hayek was an inspiration for me to finish the dissertation and to press on with the research agenda that had occupied him during his early LSE years.

IHS provided opportunities to teach Austrian macroeconomics. Starting the year of the Windsor Castle conference, IHS ran a teaching conference almost every year – at the University of Delaware (1976), Mills College of Oakland, California (1977), the University of Colorado (1978–80), and Marquette University (1982, 1984 and 1986). I was a Teaching Assistant at the Delaware conference and was on the faculty at all the others – along with Israel Kirzner, Jerry O'Driscoll, Mario Rizzo and a number of guest lecturers.

VII. AUBURN: A BASE OF OPERATIONS

In the late 1970s the Department of Economics at Auburn University was in a building phase. The strategy was to attract low-tech market-oriented economists. The department attracted me in 1978. 'Market orientation,' it turned out, got translated into 'not much macroeconomics.' The department proudly described itself as a place to learn low-tech applied microeconomics. In my early Auburn years I taught Principles of Microeconomics and History of Economic Thought as well as Business Conditions Analysis in the MBA program. But soon enough, as one of the few macroeconomists on the faculty, I saw my teaching repertoire narrow to macroeconomics at all levels – principles, upper-level undergraduate and graduate.

In 1981 I took leave from Auburn to spend a semester at New York University as a Visiting Fellow. The attraction there was the weekly Austrian Economics Colloquium, the active participants including Israel Kirzner, Ludwig Lachmann, Jerry O'Driscoll and Mario Rizzo. It was during that visit that I began writing an article that eventually appeared as 'Time and Money: The Universals of Macroeconomic Theorizing' (1984). Capital-based macroeconomics integrates capital theory, which captures the critical time element in the macroeconomy, with monetary disequilibrium theory, which identifies the source of macroeconomic problems. Precisely because of the time element, disequilibrium affecting the economy's capital structure can persist. Problems can fester until the disequilibrium begets a crisis and downturn. An aphorism emerged that captures the idea: 'Capital gives money time to cause trouble.' The article is widely cited (in Austrian circles) and has been reprinted in various volumes of collected essays.

The Ludwig von Mises Institute attached itself to Auburn University in 1983 and soon enticed Leland Yeager to leave Virginia to become Auburn's Ludwig von Mises Professor. Though critical of those very aspects of the Austrian theory that I have always found most attractive, Yeager has been a continuing and significant force in shaping my ideas. My research and writing in the 1980s and 1990s can be characterized as a piecemeal approach to resolving the key issues separating the various schools of macroeconomic thought.

In one instance, I collaborated with an Auburn colleague to pit Hayek against Friedman. Don Bellante, who was also my immediate successor as an NYU Visiting Fellow, is a labor economist with a macroeconomics orientation. He and I had similar views about the disruptive effects of monetary expansion. Our separate strengths were very much complementary – his in critically expositing the dynamics of the Phillips curve, mine in expositing the dynamics of the Hayekian triangle. We conspired to write an article titled, 'Phillips Curves and Hayekian Triangles: Two Perspectives on Monetary Dynamics' (1988). In terms of both logic and implications, we found Austrianism to be superior to monetarism. (This publication represents one of the few instances where co-authoring seemed to work for me. Generally, I prefer to work on my own, my aversion to co-authorship being similar to my aversion to teamwork in the undergraduate engineering labs at the Missouri School of Mines.)

Some years later, I put the dynamics of the Hayekian triangle in play in my 'Comment on Friedman's "Plucking Model"' (1996). Curiously, Friedman (1993) had taken the observed temporal pattern of total output to be a basis for declaring irrelevant all theories that suggest a cause-and-effect connection between boom and subseqent bust. His critical remarks, explicitly directed at the Austrian theory, would be equally telling, of course, against his own short-run/long-run Phillips curve analysis.

In another critical article, 'The Persistence of Keynesian Myths: A Report at Six Decades' (1995b), I employed a production possibilities frontier (PPF) to highlight the essential difference between Keynesian and Austrian constructions. I discovered later that Abba Lerner (in Colander and Landreth, 1996) had made the same distinction early on: for Keynes, consumption and investment are magnitudes that move up and down together, their path of possible movements intersecting the PPF; for the classical economists, including Hayek, those two magnitudes can be traded off against one another – as can be depicted as movements *along* a PPF.

In an encyclopedia entry on the Austrian theory of the business cycle (Garrison, 1997a), I focused on the market for loanable funds to make the key Austrian distinction between sustainable and unsustainable growth. An increase in saving shifts the supply of loanable funds rightward, lowers the rate of interest, and sets the economy off on a steeper growth path. By contrast, credit expansion pads the supply of loanable funds, drives a wedge between saving and investment, and sets the economy off on an unsustainable growth path.

These three simple graphs – the Hayekian triangle, the production possibilities frontier, and the loanable-funds market – all came together for me in the classroom at Auburn. They jelled into a capital-based macroeconomic framework that was much superior to my earlier diagrammatic exposition. The 1984 article lends its title to my book-length treatment of the issues: *Time and Money: The Macroeconomics of Capital Structure* (2001). The analytical framework of interlocking graphs, first assembled to demonstrate the logical coherence of Hayek's business cycle theory, turned out to have much broader application – in analyzing the fiscal issues such as deficit finance and tax reform and in sharpening the contrast between the Austrian's capital based theory and Keynes's labor-based theory.

VIII. CAPITAL-BASED MACROECONOMICS ON TOUR

I took a sabbatical in the fall of 1997 to speed the progress on the book.

Coincidentally, I was invited to deliver the Ludwig Lachmann Memorial Lecture at the University of the Witwatersrand in Johannesburg, South Africa in late August of that year. The trip to South Africa quickly developed into a lecture tour with stops at the University of Capetown and the Reserve Bank in Pretoria. I used the Lachmann lecture to deal with the issue of expectations in macroeconomics. This was always Lachmann's favorite topic – and in light of the dominance of rational-expectations models in mainstream theorizing, one that had to be addressed head on. That lecture (Garrison, 1997b) became Chapter 2 in my book. At Capetown, I presented the capital-based framework to a very receptive and appreciative audience and put it through its paces in the context of boom and bust.

The visit to the central bank in Pretoria, which was arranged by South Africa's Free Market Foundation, was an occasion to make the distinction between a Fed-led boom and a debt-led boom. The economic expansion that began during the Reagan administration was spurred on by a Treasury that was borrowing money rather than by a central bank that was creating money. Still, the boom was an unsustainable one, though the dynamics were different. Investments had become excessively speculative rather than excessively roundabout. The Free Market Foundation asked me to write up the lecture for publication as a monograph. My *Chronically Large Federal Budget Deficits: The American Experience* (1998) appeared in print just as the Clinton administration's Fed-led boom turned the budget from deficit to surplus. The timing dampened interest in the monograph, but the arguments were incorporated into Chapter 6 of my book.

For me, the most satisfying experience came by way of an invitation to be the first Hayek Visiting Fellow at the London School of Economics. The visit, during May/June 2003, was arranged by Toby Baxendale, a London businessman, and was sponsored by LSE and the Mises Institute. The highlight of that five-week visit was a well-attended public lecture in LSE's Old Auditorium. Seventy-two years after Hayek gave the lectures that became *Prices and Production*, I was able to give a lecture that was inspired by that book, telling the story of the business cycle with the aid of a capital-based analytical framework and putting Keynes and Hayek head to head in a way that had not been done before.

IX. PROSPECTS AND PERSPECTIVE

The Mises Institute has given me many opportunities to fine-tune the pedagogy in presenting the Austrian theory of the business cycle and, more generally, capital-based macroeconomics. Starting in the mid-1980s with a pilot program in Auburn, the Institute has organized teaching conferences –

first at Stanford University and Claremont University in California and, since the mid-1990s, at Auburn University. Those conferences, as well as the Institute's annual Austrian Scholars Conference, have been – and, undoubtedly, will continue to be – important in developing the theory and pedagogy that appears in *Time and Money*. Similar benefits have come from my participation in the teaching conferences organized by New York University and, more recently, by George Mason University and held each year at the Foundation for Economic Education in Irvington-on-Hudson, New York. On the research front, the Society for the Advancement of Austrian Economics (SDAE) has increased the professional respectability of work in the Austrian tradition by its strong presence at the Southern Economic Association meetings.

Time and Money continues to be a source of ideas for development for me and for others. I note with some satisfaction that the term capital-based macroeconomics seems to have found its way into the lexicon of macroeconomics as a more substantive name for analytical framework that was once identified only by its country of origin. I have become intrigued with the puzzles of the associated doctrinal history, such as reconciling the concepts of 'Forced Saving and Overconsumption in the Mises–Hayek Theory of the Business Cycle' (2004). And currently I am spending my time editing the business cycle volumes for the Collected Works of F.A. Hayek, an ongoing project of the University of Chicago Press.

The story told in this essay, though involving a roundabout progression, seems to entail a greater linearity and singularity of purpose than was ever actually evident along the way. And although it is true that, when in an academic frame of mind, my thoughts are dominated by time, money, capital and interest, these macroeconomic concepts and the theories we can build with them are kept in perspective by more worldly matters – by the memory of my parents, by conversations with my brother, and by spending time with my 12-year-old son Jim and with my wife Karen, who is also my best friend.

BIBLIOGRAPHY

Ackley, Gardner (1961), *Macroeconomic Theory*, Toronto: Macmillan.

Bellante, Don and Roger Garrison (1988), 'Phillips Curves and Hayekian Triangles: Two Perspectives on Monetary Dynamics,' *History of Political Economy,* **20**(2), 207–34.

Böhm-Bawerk, Eugen von (1959 [1984, 1989, and 1909]), *Capital and Interest*, 3 vols, South Holland, IL.: Libertarian Press.

Caldwell, Bruce J. (1998), 'Why Didn't Hayek Review Keynes's General Theory?,' *History of Political Economy*, **30**(4), 545–69.

Cohen, Ali J. and G.C. Harcourt (2003), 'Whatever Happened to the Cambridge Capital Theory Controversies?,' *Journal of Economic Perspectives*, **17**(1), 199–214.

Colander, David and Harry Landreth (1996), *The Coming of Keynesianism to America: Conversations with the Founders of Keynesian Economics*, Brookfield, US: Edward Elgar.

Dolan, Edwin (ed.) (1976), *Foundations of Austrian Economics*, Kansas City: Sheed and Ward.

Friedman, Milton (1970), 'A Theoretical Framework for Monetary Analysis,' in Robert Gordon (ed.), *Milton Friedman's Monetary Framework: A Debate with His Critics*, Chicago: University of Chicago Press, 1–62.

——— (1993), 'The "Plucking Model" of Business Cycle Fluctuations Revisited,' *Economic Inquiry*, **31**(2), 171–7.

Friedman, Milton, and Anna Schwartz (1963), *A Monetary History of the United States, 1867–1960*, Princeton: Princeton University Press.

Garrison, Roger (1978), 'Austrian Macroeconomics: A Diagrammatical Exposition,' in Louis M. Spadaro (ed.), *New Directions in Austrian Economics*, Kansas City: Sheed, Andrews, and McMeel, 167–204.

——— (1979), 'Comment: Waiting in Vienna,' in Mario J. Rizzo (ed.), *Time, Uncertainty, and Disequilibrium*, Lexington, MA: D.C. Heath and Co., 215–26.

——— (1984), 'Time and Money: the Universals of Economic Theorizing,' *Journal of Macroeconomics*, **6**(2), 197–213.

——— (1995a), 'Murray Rothbard,' in *Murray N. Rothbard: In Memoriam*, Auburn, AL: Ludwig von Mises Institute, 13–18.

——— (1995b), 'The Persistence of Keynesian Myths: A Report at Six Decades,' in Richard M. Ebeling (ed.), *Economics Education: What Should We Learn About the Free Market?*, Hillsdale, NJ: Hillsdale College Press, 109–36.

——— (1996), 'Friedman's "Plucking Model": Comment,' *Economic Inquiry*, **34**(4), 799–802.

——— (1997a), 'Austrian Theory of Business Cycles,' in David Glasner (ed.), *Business Cycles and Depressions: An Encyclopedia*, New York: Garland Publishing, 23–7.

——— (1997b), 'The Lachmann Legacy: An Agenda for Macroeconomics,' *South African Journal of Economics*, **65**(4), 459–81.

——— (1998), *Chronically Large Federal Budget Deficits*, FMF Monograph 18, Sandton, South Africa: the Free Market Foundation.

——— (2000), 'An Austrian Economist: An Interview with Roger W. Garrison,' *Austrian Economics Newsletter*, **20**(4).

——— (2001), *Time and Money: The Macroeconomics of Capital Structure*, London: Routledge.

——— (2004), 'Forced Saving and Overconsumption in the Mises–Hayek Theory of the Business Cycle,' *History of Political Economy* (forthcoming).

Hayek, Friedrich A. (1967 [1935]), *Prices and Production*, 2nd edn, New York: Augustus M. Kelley.

——— (1976), *Choice in Currency*, Occasional Paper No. 48, London: Institute for Economic Affairs.

——— (1976), *Denationalization of Money*, Hobart Special Paper No. 70, London: Institute for Economic Affairs.

——— (1994), *Hayek on Hayek: An Autobiographical Dialogue*, S. Kresge and L.Wenar (eds), Chicago: University of Chicago Press.

Hazlitt, Henry (1959), *The Failure of the 'New Economics'*, Princeton, NJ: D. Van Nostrand.

Hicks, John R. (1967), 'The Hayek Story,' in J. Hicks, *Critical Essays in Monetary*

Theory, Oxford: Clarendon Press, 203–15.

Keynes, John M. (1936), *The General Theory of Employment, Interest, and Money*, New York: Harcourt, Brace and Company.

Kirzner, Israel M. (1973), *Competition and Entrepreneurship*, Chicago, University of Chicago Press.

——— (1997), 'Entrepreneurial Discovery and the Competitive Market Process: An Austrian Approach,' *Journal of Economic Literature*, **35**(1), 60–85.

Leijonhufvud, Axel (1998), 'Three Items for the Macroeconomic Agenda,' *Kyklos*, **51**(2), 197–218.

Martin, Justin (2000), *Greenspan: The Man Behind the Money*, Cambridge, MA: Perseus Publishing.

Mises, Ludwig von (1953 [1912]), *The Theory of Money and Credit*, New Haven, CT: Yale University Press.

O'Driscoll, Gerald P., Jr (1977), *Economics as a Coordination Problem: The Contributions of Friedrich A. Hayek*, Kansas City: Sheed, Andrews, and McMeel.

Patinkin, Don (1965), *Money, Interest, and Prices*, 2nd edn, New York: Harper and Row.

Rand, Ayn (1967), *Capitalism: The Unknown Ideal*, New York: New American Library.

Reekie, W. Duncan (1984), *Markets, Entrepreneurs and Liberty: An Austrian View of Capitalism*, New York: St Martin's Press.

Robinson, Joan (1975), 'The Unimportance of Reswitching,' *The Quarterly Journal of Economics*, **89**(1), 32–39.

Rothbard, Murray N. (1962), *Man, Economy, and State*, Princeton, NJ: D. Van Nostrand.

Samuelson, Paul A. (1967), *Economics*, 7th edn, New York: McGraw-Hill.

——— (1971 [1966]) 'A Summing Up,' in G. Harcourt and N. Laing (eds), *Capital and Growth*, Harmondsworth: Penguin Books, 233–50.

Schiebla, Shirley (1968), *Poverty Is Where the Money Is*, New Rochelle, NY: Arlington House.

Snowden, Brian, Howard Vane and Peter Wynarczyk (1994), *A Modern Guide to Macroeconomics: An Introduction to Competing Schools of Thought*, Aldershot, UK and Brookfield, US: Edward Elgar.

Solow, Robert (1997), 'Is There a Core of Usable Macroeconomics We Should All Believe In?,' *American Economic Review*, **87**(2), 230–32.

——— (2000), 'Toward a Macroeconomics of the Medium Run,' *Journal of Economic Perspectives*, **14**(1), 151–8.

Sraffa, Piero (1960), *The Production of Commodities by means of Commodities*, Cambridge: Cambridge University Press.

Spadaro, Louis M. (ed.) (1978), *New Directions in Austrian Economics*, Kansas City: Sheed, Andrews, and McMeel.

Vaughn, Karen (1994), *Austrian Economics in America: The Migration of a Tradition*, Cambridge: Cambridge University Press.

Wicksell, Knut (1962 [1898]), *Interest and Prices: A Study of the Causes Regulating the Value of Money*, trans. by R. Kahn, New York: Augustus M. Kelley.

Yeager, Leland (1997) *The Fluttering Veil: Essays on Monetary Disequilibrium*, Indianapolis: Liberty Fund.

12. My life philosophy*

Eli Ginzberg

The title of this essay was assigned to me. Perhaps I would have declined the editor's invitation if I had remembered that my recently published book, *The Skeptical Economist*, embodies quite a bit of personal history, so much in fact that my wife wanted me not to publish it.

Let me explain why I accepted the editor's invitation. I have had only tenuous connections with my fellow economists since the mid-1930s when I began to teach at Columbia University and even less after 1939 when I went my own way to pursue empirical research in the borderline between economics and psychology in the new field that later was designated as 'manpower' or 'human resources.' I have attended only two conventions of the American Economic Association since the mid-1930s and my total contributions to the AER, *The Proceedings* and the *Journal of Economic Literature* consist of a very few pieces.

The fact that I, such a distant and outlying member of the profession, was asked to write a piece in a series to which a number of the nation's leading economists had earlier contributed was a form of flattery that I could not resist no matter how skeptical I have been, and remain, about the contributions of even our most distinguished contemporary economists.

It may help the reader to understand how much of an outlier I am if I list what I failed to learn during my undergraduate and graduate years, all of which were spent at Columbia University (1927–33) except for the eventful year 1928–29 when I was enrolled at the University of Heidelberg. I never had a course in microeconomics, either in college or in graduate school. In fact there was no competent course in microeconomics taught at Columbia until the late 1930s, when I convinced the Chair of the Economics Department, Roswell McCrea, to invite Milton Friedman to give such a course, and Friedman was followed by Moses Abramovitz. Abramovitz has told me more than once that I was lucky because I didn't have to spend years unlearning the microeconomics which he and other well-trained economists at Harvard, Chicago and elsewhere had mastered until it became their principal tool of analysis.

*This chapter first appeared in *The American Economist*, **32**(1), Spring 1988, 3–9.

My quantitative skills were at the same low level as my command over the formal apparatus of economics. I had a single course of old-fashioned descriptive statistics. My teacher, who was also my PhD examiner, said that I was a much better philosopher than I was a statistician. Since I had stopped taking courses in mathematics early in my undergraduate years, I was unable to attend Harold Hotelling's or Abraham Wald's classes that were opening up new frontiers in statistical analysis.

Readers may find it hard to believe that Columbia in the late 1920s–early 1930s was an economics desert; they may ask whether I was even then an outlier. The answer to the second question is that I was not an outlier with respect to my course of studies or in terms of my achievements. Upon the completion of my doctorate in 1933, I was awarded a Cutting Traveling Fellowship, the most prestigious award the University had to offer.

And economics at Columbia was not a desert. Wesley Clair Mitchell and John Maurice Clark were the two luminaries and they were recognized by the American Economic Association as the first and second winners of the prestigious Francis A. Walker medal. Neither held mainline economics in high regard. Mitchell, the founder of empirical economics, was busy directing the National Bureau of Economic Research and took his Columbia teaching duties lightly; Clark, not an outstanding classroom teacher, spent most of his time in his home in Westport attempting to turn the inherited doctrines on their head, convinced that they were more relevant when they were turned upside down.

I also studied with E.R.A. Seligman in the last year he taught public finance. Seligman is generally credited with having played a critical role in the passage of a federal income tax. The other teacher who made a lasting impression on me was H. Parker Willis, the chief adviser to Senator Carter Glass, the architect of the Federal Reserve System. Mitchell once remarked that Willis had not changed his views about money and banking since they were fellow students at Chicago in the early 1890s. But Seligman and Willis provided me with the prototype of the scholar–activist which I found congenial. Leo Wolman, who joined the faculty in 1931 as Professor of Labor Economics, after long service with the Amalgamated Clothing Workers' Union, further reinforced this prototype.

In Heidelberg in 1928–29, I had studied with Emil Lederer who gave a seminar on rationalization in German industry and its effects on the labor force. My current research funded by the Ford Foundation focuses on 'technology and employment.' Plus a change …!

My two semesters in Heidelberg and my 17-month sojourn in Europe which enabled me to travel as far south as Sicily had a much stronger influence on me than any course on economics. From my courses in philosophy, history, sociology and law – the ghost of Max Weber still dominated Heidelberg – I came to the unshakable conclusion that the German economy, in fact all economies, were subsystems of a larger societal matrix in which race, religion, politics, class and, in Europe, above all nationalism, played determining roles in how production was organized and who got what.

When I returned for what was ostensibly my junior year at Columbia, I studied with leading scholars in the fields of anthropology, sociology, political science, economic history and philosophy. The committee for my oral examination for the PhD in economics included Robert Morrison MacIver. Columbia may have been skeptical about *laissez-faire* economics but the economics department followed a *laissez-faire* approach. It was assumed that good students would learn something useful between time spent in the classroom and in the library, and it really didn't matter much what happened to the duller students.

I wrote my doctoral dissertation on a reinterpretation of Adam Smith's *The Wealth of Nations*, the first book-length study of Smith in English! I had access to the recently acquired Seligman collection of rare books which gave me a unique opportunity to reconstruct the world in which Adam Smith lived and to which he reacted. In my view, Smith was a reformer interested in demolishing mercantilism which, he concluded, exploited both farmers and laborers and enriched only the manufacturing and mercantile groups. Having lived at close quarters with the mind of Adam Smith for the better part of two years, I accepted and tried to emulate the prototype of the scholar–activist. I could not loosen its hold had I wanted to, but never, from that day to this, have I had the slightest inclination to jettison this model.

I started this essay by discussing my teachers, to make at least some contact with the economists who can still remember the names of Mitchell and J.M. Clark, even if Seligman, Willis, Wolman and Lederer are unknown to them. But now I want to talk briefly about my parents before I flesh out some of the other highlights of my own life and philosophy.

My parents were each strong and had quite distinct personalities. My father was a scholar of Judaica of world renown, whose books attested to his mastery of both law and lore. He wrote in eight languages. While he had a lively interest in the world of affairs, his own life was largely confined to the four walls of his library. He left home twice a week to lecture at the Jewish Theological Seminary where he was the senior professor for a half century. My mother was an individualist in the best sense of that term. She had no fear of anybody or anything. I recall that in my youth she insisted on singing German Lieder while walking in the streets during World War I, not because she admired the Germans, which she didn't, but because she saw no reason to conform to silly jingoistic prejudices. At 88 she went on a safari. A few years earlier, when she returned from a visit to the USSR she called the Russian Consulate to tell them what she liked and what she didn't like about her visit!

When my dean and mentor came to dinner at my parents' home my mother asked him what he did. He said he was an economist to which she commented, 'Oh, another faker like my son!'

She loved my father and respected his work, which was totally beyond her ken but she had little respect for most writers of books, including her son. She always asked whether this or that book would help the poor, the sick, the disadvantaged. Since I could not give her an affirmative answer, she felt entitled to go her way and concentrate on pursuing good works.

I have reflected on occasion that my genetic endowment could have resulted in my becoming a schizophrenic with strong pulls in opposite directions – one of ideas and the other action – but I was lucky, although I did have to live with the basic tension between ideas and action all of my adult life.

In 1935 I started to teach at the School of Business at Columbia; assisted Mitchell in a graduate seminar; finished (1939) my *Illusion of Economic Stability* book; and spent most of my time exploring how to work on the borderline between economics and psychology, the field that had attracted my attention as offering the best prospect of making economics more relevant.

With Mitchell's encouragement and help, my research career was launched in 1939 when I received my first grant to study long-term unemployed in New York City and in the coal-mining areas of South Wales. My collaborators were a psychiatrist and three psychiatric social workers. Milton Friedman helped me to construct the New York City sample. Since my principal aim was to develop a realistic theory of human behavior in the economic marketplace, I knew that I had to find sophisticated investigators in other disciplines who would be willing to work in an interdisciplinary mode. From that day to this, my research associates have been drawn from all the social sciences as well as from history, psychology and health sciences research.

The study of the long-term unemployed had led us to establish close contacts with the Department of Welfare and the WPA in New York City in order to draw our sample. Our basic instrument was a structured interview; when the preliminary results became available we had extended discussions with those in policy positions to elicit their responses and thus deepen our findings. We wanted our results to be useful in the world of action as well as to contribute to the advancement of knowledge. I was pleased when Brigadier General William C. Menninger, the Chief Psychiatrist of the US Army during World War II, told me that he had relied heavily on our book *The Unemployed* in testifying in 1945 on behalf of the Full Employment Act.

World War II proved to be a watershed for me as for so many others both in and out of uniform. Again, profiting from the good advice of Professor Mitchell, I took the risk of staying out of uniform in order to function effectively in the higher reaches of the Army Services Forces (ASF), which was my work arena. The most important assignment that I carried out for Lieutenant General Brehon B. Somervell, the Commanding General of the Army Services Forces, was to remove 180000 civilians from the payroll and transfer 60000 servicemen from service duties to the Army Ground Forces both within a period of 90 days.

My second assignment was that of Director, Resources Analysis Division in the Office of the Surgeon General of the Army. I became the chief logistical adviser to the Surgeon General with responsibility to provide the requisite personnel and other resources to care for, at their peak, 600000 patients who were hospitalized worldwide, drawing on a pool of 45000 physicians, 100000 nurses and 600000 ward personnel. It was a formidable assignment and of the rewards I received none pleased me more than the gold medal I was awarded by the Army for 'exceptional civilian service.'

In the spring of 1946, while still on the Army's payroll, I was the US Representative to the Second Reparations Conference (for non-repatriable refugees). As a result of this Conference, the Jewish Agency and the American Jewish Joint Distribution Committee received tens of millions of dollars to help relocate thousands of displaced persons, most of whom were Jews who would not return to Germany or Austria. This was accomplished primarily because of the pressure exerted by the US government that justice be done.

As a result of my four-year stint in the Pentagon, I had proved to myself that I could operate in the halls of power without difficulty, but when I had to make a decision between a most attractive offer in industry, at seven times the salary that Columbia would pay me on my return, and my job at Columbia, I did not hesitate for one moment and headed back to the University. I knew that continuing my research into human resources was my first, but not my only, priority. I wanted to continue in a consulting relationship with the federal government; I did not want to sever all relations with the medical arena, and I had a deep and abiding interest in matters affecting the Jews and particularly their establishing a homeland in Palestine.

It has been my great good fortune that I have been able to pursue these four objectives over the last four and a half decades. Since I placed a high value on a continuing role in Washington I eschewed playing an active role in politics and adopted the stance of a non-political consultant who was willing to assist whoever was in power. I had an opportunity to serve every president from Roosevelt to Reagan, although in December 1981 Reagan dismissed all the members of the National Commission for Employment Policy, of which I was the chair since its inception as well as the chair of all of its predecessor bodies since 1962. Beginning in 1982, for the first time in almost forty years I no longer had to commute on a weekly basis to Washington, a change that proved to be most welcome.

The combination of being an active director of a research group at Columbia – The Conservation of Human Resources – and my Washington consulting made it difficult – in fact, impossible – for me ever to go on sabbatical. I have completed 52 years of uninterrupted teaching on the faculty of the Graduate School of Business except when I was on wartime leave between the fall of 1942 and the spring of 1946.

In addition to the formative influences of my father and Wesley Clair Mitchell on the shaping of my life and career, I must call attention to one other – General Eisenhower – who, when he became president of Columbia University (1947), took the initiative to expand my research base and encouraged me to pursue the systematic analysis of the military manpower experiences of the nation in World War II. A series of studies culminating in *The Ineffective Soldier: Lessons for Management and the Nation*, three volumes (1959), mined the rich repository of military and civilian (Veterans Administration) records.

If I may adapt Feuerbach's observation that 'Man ist was Man esst' – 'one is what one eats' – to read 'one is what one writes,' I believe that my life's philosophy is embedded in my books. Today I think that I may have written too many books, since I have had an opportunity to look back on them with the perspective that comes with time and distance. I will call attention to some of the better ones to illustrate the values that I have pursued in the different stages of my attenuated writing life, which began with my first publication in 1932 – *Studies in the Economics of the Bible*.

Roswell McCrea, who gave me my first job at Columbia in 1935, once told me that I was like an 'exploratory surgeon,' getting my jollies by opening people up and looking for the causes and cures of their problems with little patience for the more tedious closing-up procedures.

Our initial studies of the long-term unemployed impressed upon all of us the centrality of work in human life. We traced what unemployment does to people not only in terms of the male breadwinner who loses his job and can't find another, but also the impacts of his lack of employment on his wife, his children and his community.

In shifting from unemployment to work, we selected the arena of 'occupational choice' for exploration. Several points soon became clear: occupational choice is not a one-time decision but is, rather, the outcome of a long developmental process. Further, one's choice is greatly influenced by family connections and societal forces – racism, sexism, subsidized higher education, etc. Our book, *Occupational Choice: An Approach to a General Theory* (1951), is recognized as the first broad conceptual approach to a theory.

One fall-out from the Eisenhower studies of the manpower experience in World War II was *The Negro Potential* (1956) in which my colleagues and I demonstrated the enormous costs which segregation and discrimination inflict on blacks and also the adverse externalities which they inflict on the nation. It was the first post-World War II book that focused on the wasted potential of blacks and it became a rallying point for the National Urban League and other black organizations dedicated to reform.

A few years later I wrote *The Troublesome Presence: American Democracy and the Negro*, the culmination of my interest in finding the answer to the question of how it happened that the United States, which had succeeded in absorbing a great number of different immigrant groups, had choked on integrating the free Negro. The answer appeared to lie in fears of miscegenation, economic exploitation, and the politics of keeping the United States open for 'our cousins in Europe,' as Lincoln put it.

In the mid-1950s the National Manpower Council, a Ford Foundation-funded policy group of which I was Director of Research, published *Womanpower*, the first extended analysis of the rapidly changing role of women in the labor force. When we presented a copy of the report to Eisenhower in the White House, he commented, 'Yes, women were very important in World War II in communications, clerical support, and transport services.' In the mid-1960s the Conservation Project published two in-depth studies of women and work entitled *Life Styles of Educated Women* and *Educated Women: Self Portraits*.

The unemployed, the uneducated, the ineffective soldier, blacks, women were major research targets that engaged me early on and have continued to be subjects of my continuing concern. In 1963 I was able to assist Senator Joseph Clark to expand the Civil Rights bill to include a section on employment, and I have been active in both the public and private sectors by seeking to broaden educational and employment opportunities for groups that have suffered from discrimination. During the 19 years I served as chair of the manpower advisory committees of the federal government, I was involved in the oversight of $100 billion of federal training and job creation efforts. My assessment (*Employing the Unemployed*, 1980) was that the federal outlays contributed to the well-being of the beneficiaries but that relatively few made it into permanent jobs as a consequence of these federal efforts.

I was also continuously involved with the Pentagon in an advisory capacity in the ongoing formulation and reformulation of the military manpower policies until the early 1970s. At that time I completed (as chair) a Task Force report for the Department of Defense which concluded that during peace outsiders could not significantly affect the shape of the personnel policies of the Armed Services except to the extent that the White House and Congress set limits on what they could spend.

As a result of my wartime experience and my major study of the hospitals in the State of New York for Governor Dewey in 1948–49, it would have been very easy for me to have a lucrative career as a hospital consultant. But again, weighed against the advantages of my academic career, that held little attraction. However, once Medicare and Medicaid were passed in 1965, I realized that in light of my continuing interest in health affairs, it would be desirable for me to allocate more of my research time to the area which is the nation's third largest employment sector (eight million) after government and retail sales and which in 1987 accounted for $497 billion in total expenditures, or 11.2 percent of GNP.

I found the arena of health affairs particularly challenging since the conventional competitive market model has so little applicability, the enthusiasts – from Enthoven to Reagan – notwithstanding. In 1977 I wrote in considerable haste *The Limits of Health Reform* for the explicit purpose of moderating President Carter's enthusiasm for national health insurance, but by the time he received a copy of the book from a member of his Cabinet his ardor had cooled because of the additional costs of such an initiative.

Since 1959 I have fought an almost solo rear-guard action to moderate the enthusiasm that most politicians, the public and economists have had for increasing the supply of physicians to improve access to care and to reduce its costs. I have argued that no matter how ample the supply, physicians will avoid establishing practices in the ghetto and that improved access for the poor requires linking them to institutional structures.

Furthermore, I believe that more physicians might result in lower fees but higher total costs. Only within the last year has the American Medical Association finally shifted its position in favor of policy changes aimed at reducing the inflow of new physicians, turning its back on its long-term support for 'market-determined' outcomes.

Having found a way of combining empirical research with public policy issues, especially those that were first appearing on the horizon, and an active involvement in the world of affairs, I did not have the time, the energy, or even the inclination to grapple with larger macro problems. A quarter of a century separated the *Illusion of Economic Stability* (1939) in which I provided an explanation of the boisterous twenties and the depressed thirties in terms of the interactions among technology, the money supply, and expectations and my next foray into the macro arena.

In *The Pluralistic Economy* (1965) my colleagues and I argued that the US economy could not be understood in terms of a two-sector model – private and governmental – it required a third sector – nonprofit. Further, the conventional wisdom that the private sector dominated the economy had to be modified because the not-for-profit sector (government plus nonprofit) accounted for at least a third of all jobs and a quarter of the GNP. A decade later, under the prompting and with the assistance of my associate, Alfred Eichner, I tried my hand at integrating what I had learned about human resources in the United

States as well as from extended consulting assignments abroad for the Department of State and other organizations.

The Human Economy (1976) rested on four foundation stones: values, government, the economy, and manpower development institutions. The book had a broad sweep, encompassing both developed and developing countries and it dealt with job creation and manpower utilization at both macro and micro levels. It represented a distillation of what I had learned over more than four decades but it made little impact on my academic colleagues, many of whom were deeply into the human capital approach, the methodology of which provided such powerful assistance to those who needed to publish, irrespective of whether the findings had relevance for policy. It has never been clear to me, especially in a post-Freudian world, how the maximizing principle could do anything but confuse the analysis of such emotionally charged avenues of human life as marriage, childrearing, crime, divorce and discrimination. But then, I was a student of Veblen, once removed via Mitchell, not of Frank Knight or Henry Simons.

Another decade had to pass before I could try my hand, not once but twice, at dealing with larger themes. In *Beyond Human Scale: The Large Corporation at Risk*, which I wrote with George J. Vojta, the Executive Vice-President of Bankers Trust, we formulated a simple thesis, one whose origins I trace back to my postgraduate fellowship year when I visited 20 of America's largest corporations. I learned then, and had much reinforcement in the intervening decades, that large for-profit organizations are almost as handicapped as the Armed Services and other large organizations in making effective use of their human resources. Planning and control systems block the exercise of initiative and the incentive that drives most managers is to move up the hierarchy without calling undue attention to themselves, for with the spotlight comes risk.

I have been discomfited all these years with the increasing mathematization of economics and its growing preoccupation with methodology, neoclassical and general equilibrium. But I had found my niche and have been comfortable in it. My concern and regret were related to the impact of these trends on young people who were first entering the field and what seemed to me to be the growing irrelevance of most, though fortunately not all, of the world of the academy. One Sunday afternoon several years ago a younger, well-trained (MIT) associate told me his concerns about the directions that academic economics had taken and his sense of frustration that the establishment could not be moved out of its groove. I listened and sympathized but later, on reflection, I decided that I had to do more. *The Skeptical Economist* (1987) is my modest contribution. I took a close look at all the Stockholm award addresses given by US Nobel Laureates in economics (up to Buchanan) and raised a question about the relations between their central contributions and the world of policy. Some might say that the question is irrelevant. My answer is that an economics increasingly disconnected from the realities of economic life is irrelevant.

I plan and have recently begun one more macro book which has the working title *The Viable Economy*. My point of departure is that all economies are subsystems of the larger society, that the values and goals that people pursue are critical determinants of their behavior in the marketplace, as are the capabilities and limitations of governmental systems. Also of transcendent importance are family structures and the educational-training systems in a world in which competences and skills become ever more important determinants of who gets the good jobs and the higher incomes.

I have no way of knowing at this early stage whether my current writing will be successful. I know it will persuade only those few members of the academy who are already persuaded, for the others, as George Stigler has repeatedly made clear, have no intention of actively participating in the destruction of their capital. But I retain the hope and expectation that it may have some influence on other members of an increasingly well-educated society both at home and abroad.

One can never tell what happens to one's children or to one's books. Years ago in the late 1950s, Saburo Okita, at that time the Chief Economist of the Prime Minister's Office in Japan, came to talk with me about the future of the Japanese economy. I had a simple formulation: Japan would go nowhere if it did not undertake a major reform of its educational system and insure that most of the population finishes high school and a much larger proportion goes on to the university. He translated my *Human Resources: The Wealth of the Nation* into Japanese; soon thereafter the educational reforms were carried out with efficiency and speed but the womanpower issue still remains on the agenda. But Japan has not done badly. I have no illusions about the influence of my book but it surely provided a thrust in the right direction. What more can a writer of books expect?

BIBLIOGRAPHICAL NOTE

My complete bibliography is contained in *Understanding Human Resources* (Lanham, MD: University Press of America, ABT Books, 1985). The book most relevant to the present effort is my latest, *The Skeptical Economist* (Boulder, CO: Westview, 1987).

13. Reflections of a policy economist*

Edward M. Gramlich

> The ideas of economists and political philosophers, both when they are right and when they are wrong, are more powerful than is commonly understood. Indeed, the world is ruled by little else. Practical men, who believe themselves to be quite exempt from any intellectual influences, are usually the slaves of some defunct economist. Madmen in authority, who hear voices in the air, are distilling their frenzy from some academic scribbler of a few years back. (Keynes, 1936)

In this time when so many are questioning the value and relevance of doing economics in the policy domain, the above quote from Keynes bears rereading. I first noticed it as a graduate student back in the early 1960s; it resonated (to use a modern term) then, and it still does.

I have been practicing in the interesting field that might be called policy economics for three decades now. As is probably true for anybody in the field, there have been high points and low points, cases where my struggle was right and my side lost the battle, cases where my struggle was right and my side may have won the battle, cases where I still believe now what I believed then, and cases where I have changed my mind. But one point on which I have not changed my mind involves the overall value of the effort. Three decades ago I ventured forth in the idealistic hope that some time, in some way, what I might be doing would pay off. After all that has happened, I still retain this faith.

A lot has happened, some of it depressing. Comparing the field of policy economics now and then, there has been a noticeable change. In the 1960s there was a view (not always acted upon, to be sure) that policy should be far-sighted towards the future and generous towards those on low incomes. Policy research was viewed as an important link in both chains. Today, it is harder to make all arguments – harder to argue for far-sighted, high-saving policies; harder to argue for generosity towards low-income people; harder to defend policy research. Certainly there are reasons that these arguments are harder to make – some of the predictions of beneficial effects of anti-poverty programs have not been borne out, and some of the presumed values of policy research have not materialized. At the same time, I personally feel that now we

*This chapter first appeared in *The American Economist*, **41**(1), Spring 1997, 22–30.

have replaced too much optimism with too much skepticism on the other side of these arguments. But this is not the only domain of life where we are sadder but wiser, and sadder but wiser we still push on.

Two other points bear mentioning at the outset. One is that policy economics has always been interesting and challenging. The problems that come along are new and complicated, often involving large changes in either the allocation of resources or the welfare of particular individuals. The outlets for one's efforts are diverse – not only does one try to publish articles in journals, but often one actually tries to influence legislation. This in turn can involve legislative testimony, advisory board reports, discussions with reporters, and even garden variety lobbying.

The second point is that doing one's economics in the real world puts one in contact with a rich and varied set of colleagues and adversaries. There are sympathetic and unsympathetic economists, political scientists, sociologists, politicians, reporters, business executives, lawyers, social workers, teachers, students, and on down the list. It is usually not sufficient to invoke some theorem that *everybody* may have had in graduate school. Everybody may not have had the theorem, and one must often find ways to explain things in simple terms, to be persuasive to people from many different persuasions. The values of this requirement are obvious.

This essay reviews some of the personal high points of my career in this interesting field.

EARLY DAYS

We are all strongly influenced by our early background, and I am no exception. I was born in Rochester, NY, in 1939, just ahead of the baby boom cohort. My father was an engineer at Eastman Kodak. My mother had her hands full raising four children, of whom I was the oldest.

Most of my childhood was consumed with an intense preoccupation with sports – playing every sport imaginable, wasting (so others would say) thousands of hours trying to hear faraway games on the radio, learning how to compute batting averages at roughly the time I learned to read. If there is a holdover from those days, it is that both then and now I have been on lots of teams – then as player, sometimes as captain, and sometimes even as coach; now often in similar roles.

There were at least two significant values my family tried to pass along, and that I have tried to absorb. One was the importance of family. My family was extremely close-knit – my parents and siblings have always been very supportive, we still get together a lot, and I have always spent much time with various cousins, aunts, uncles, and even more distant relatives. The second

was the importance of public service. While my parents were strongly devoted to their own children, they both found the time and energy to give to charity work. They continue in these efforts even now, when both are in their eighties.

My first contact with economics did not come until I was a student at Williams College. I loved economics from the day I walked into my first class. Looking back on it, it seems almost impossible for me *not* to have become enchanted with the policy side of economics. Those were the Camelot days of the Kennedy Administration, an inspirational time for young economists with a nascent public service bent. My main teachers – most prominently John Power and Paul Clark – were strong advocates of real-world policy economics. There were even role models among my fellow students – the class ahead of me included Keith Griffin, Stephen Lewis and Lester Thurow. I graduated from Williams in 1961, majoring in economics, and went off to graduate school at Yale, where I came under the spell of two even more inspirational policy economists, Arthur Okun and James Tobin. By this time my interest in real-world policy economics was nailed down beyond any doubt.

MACROMODELLING

I never studied much econometrics at Yale, but as I got into my thesis – under the direction first of Okun and later Tobin – I found that I had to build a simple macroeconometric model to complete my task, which was to determine the aggregate demand impact of fiscal policy. The idea was first suggested by Okun, but by the time I got anywhere on the project, Art had moved down to Washington to chair the Council of Economic Advisers and most of the supervising was left to Tobin. As large numbers of Yalies have testified over the years, Jim was a fantastic role model. Even now I still wonder what he would think about this or that, and I sometimes even call him to find out.

My thesis experience led to a job at the Federal Reserve Board of Governors, beginning in 1965. The Fed was at the time initiating a much larger econometric modelling project. The in-house project leader was Frank de Leeuw, another very inspirational role model and another person I still occasionally consult. There was also an outside group of university economists under the direction of Franco Modigliani and Albert Ando. One of these outside economists was Harold Shapiro, later to achieve some distinction in the field of university administration.

Work on the Fed project was very exciting. While we had outstanding computer facilities for the time, the method of operation today would be considered quite primitive. If we needed a time series we looked it up, copied it down, and had the numbers punched on cards. We submitted regressions to be done overnight, on a mainframe computer. We solved the model by an iterative procedure that probably took a million times longer than now and cost much more.

In the end we developed a 100 stochastic equation model that forecast reasonably well, though many of the equations had to be 'adjusted' to do out-of-sample forecasts. Whether models should have been so adjusted, and if so, could be used to forecast better than more judgmental procedures was in doubt then, as it still is today. But in many ways I thought then and still think that the forecast accuracy debate missed an important point. Even if econometric models could not forecast better than judgmental techniques, one could still *calibrate* the model and then use its multipliers to examine the impact of policy changes. We used to do that often at the Fed in the late 1960s.

There were at least two lively exchanges in those days. The first was inspired by Milton Friedman and his numerous disciplines, many of whom were then at the Federal Reserve Bank of St Louis. The question was in the short run whether monetary or fiscal policy had the greater impact on nominal and real GNP. One could run reduced form regressions and show things either way, as I tried to point out in one paper. One could also simulate a macro model, as de Leeuw and I did on several occasions, and find that both monetary and fiscal policy could exert fairly powerful short impacts – again the question of which was more powerful seemed beside the point. There were hundreds of pages written on what was known as the 'radio station' debate (AM, for Ando–Modigliani (1965), vs FM, for Friedman–Meiselman (1963)).

Since exchange rates were fixed then, a more complete knowledge of international economics, or open economy macroeconomics, would not have helped resolve the radio station debate. But still as I look back on it, I cannot remember what today would be viewed as the key theoretical issue ever coming up. In teaching this material today one stresses the critical behavior of exchange rates – if rates are fixed, fiscal policy is likely to be powerful and monetary policy weak; if flexible, the reverse. In those days these open economy implications were not given nearly the attention they deserved.

The other lively debate involved defense spending. In 1967 defense spending for the Vietnam War was accelerating rapidly. But the budget information coming from the Johnson Administration never showed much escalation. Another young economist at the Board, Harvey Galper, and I discovered a time series of defense contracts that proved a good leading indicator of defense spending. We fit equations, made forecasts, and sure enough showed rapid growth in defense spending, much more rapid than was forecast in the budget document. Our paper received some attention in official Washington and, of course, subsequently was thoroughly vindicated. Thirty years later, after Watergate, Irangate, and various other governmental credibility difficulties, the fact that the Administration merely fudged its budget document a bit seems like small potatoes, but at the time it was big potatoes to Galper and me.

I left the Board in 1970. While the modelling work continued to be challenging, there were new issues coming along that intrigued me more. One was the War on Poverty being conducted at the newly created Office of Economic Opportunity (OEO). Geographically, I moved my place of employment only a few blocks up New Hampshire Avenue, but intellectually I gave up macro-modelling and joined OEO's fight against poverty.

FIGHTING POVERTY

At OEO I again had the pleasure to work alongside outstanding people. I was the Director of about thirty professionals – economists, sociologists, political scientists and statisticians – in what was known as the Policy Research Division. My boss was a superb government economist named Thomas Glennan, and we worked very closely with the Institute for Research on Poverty at the University of Wisconsin, in those days under the direction of Harold Watts and later Robert Haveman.

A central concern of the office, and the one I spent much of my time on, was social experimentation. This was a time when if the government wanted to find out how social policies might work in the real world, it actually tried them out in a controlled setting. Such was done for the income maintenance experiments, under the direction of Watts and Glen Cain, and also for another social experiment on the impact of health insurance, co-insurance and deductible provisions on health spending and health status, under the direction of Joseph Newhouse,

These projects were among the proudest achievements of our office. In welfare we did the analytics pretty well, but I now think, and have written since, that we misunderstood the politics. In those days our common belief was that the government should get off the back of the poor and just give out income transfers on the basis of need. The experiments were to measure work reduction, which proved to be rather small. The political misunderstanding was in our failure to see how even small work reductions would appear to taxpayers, many of whom could not reduce work effort to pay their cost of the transfers. By today's standards, in particular the current political attacks on welfare, whether the work reduction from an income maintenance plan with no work requirements was 5 or 10 percent seems of minor import. But just completing the income maintenance experiments taught poverty analysts much about the state of living conditions among the poor and difficulties in measuring poverty, conducting surveys, and administering transfer programs.

There were some other areas of work on income maintenance that proved to be very relevant over the years. A colleague at OEO, Larry Orr (1976), wrote a paper that brought up the migration issue – since states set welfare benefits and welfare recipients are free to migrate from state to state in search of higher benefits, there should be some utility loss from *not* having common national base standards. I have since done much work on this issue, often using another OEO-initiated project, the Panel Survey of Income Dynamics (PSID), and often co-authored with Deborah Laren. The upshot of all this work is that even though migration flows are rather small, they are largely one way – from low- to high-benefit states – and they can influence state benefits – though they are not the main reason for the vast disparity in these state benefits. There indeed is a utility loss in not having national standards. Regrettably, in 1996 US policy seems poised to go exactly the wrong way from this perspective – converting the present matching grants to block grants that would raise the cost of welfare in all states, particularly in states that now pay very low benefits. This should indeed put a downward pressure on all state benefits, and spark what is known in the press as a 'race to the bottom' for welfare benefits.

There were many other interesting projects from the OEO research. I have already mentioned the health insurance experiment, which Newhouse and others have used to sharpen knowledge on the response of health care usage to price and income incentives. The PSID was initially set up as a five-year longitudinal survey that was to have ended in 1972. Our OEO group decided to extend it then, and the survey has proved so useful that it is still being extended and modified, taken into new areas, and it has been responsible for hundreds of studies in labor economics. The office also did some education experiments – most notably one in educational performance contracting – that can still be examined to predict how more contemporary programs such as charter schools might work.

While these were all significant achievements for a tiny office, the larger political world was moving in a different direction. By now it was 1972 and the famous Watergate election in which Nixon swamped McGovern. After the election Nixon offered to slim down the Executive Office of the President, which just happened to be where OEO was located. The agency was killed early in 1973, with some of its functions given over to the department that is now called Health and Human Services. I did not make that switch, but instead moved a few more blocks up New Hampshire Avenue to the Brookings Institution.

CIGARS AND FLYPAPER

At Brookings I was involved in several projects. Alice Rivlin and Michael Timpane had organized a large project on social experimentation and I continued some of the experimentation work, writing on performance contracting with first Irv Garfinkel and later Patricia Koshel. Orr and I also fended off an attack on the ethics of experimentation. I co-authored Brookings' annual budget analysis for two years with Barry Blechman and Robert Hartman. But the issue that ended up preoccupying me most regarded the behavior of state and local governments in a federal system, often involving the structure of grants from the federal government. I had done some early work on this topic at the Fed, continued with a large project with Galper, and kept on with the issue after moving to Michigan in 1976, then working with Paul Courant and Daniel Rubinfeld (CGR, or Cigar, as we were known).

One interesting debate of these years involved the so-called 'flypaper' effect. Making some standard theoretical assumptions, it can be shown that state and local governments should spend the same marginal fraction of block grants as they should if income rises in their community. If for every dollar's rise in state income, a state devotes \$.10 to public goods and \$.90 to private goods, for every dollar of block grants the state should raise spending by \$.10 and *cut* taxes by \$.90. As a digression, this simple idea is why many economists fear converting federal government programs to block grants. But as Galper and I were working on our state and local spending paper, we never got this empirical result. Block grants appeared to stimulate about \$.40 of state-local spending and about \$.60 of tax reduction. When we showed these results to Art Okun, by then our editor for the *Brookings Papers on Economic Activity* series, he said – 'Oh, you mean like flypaper' (money sticks where it hits). The metaphor appealed to us, perhaps I should say stuck, and a new term was born.

In a way the debate illustrates the half-empty, half-full problem that often arises in economics. To me, the important policy question was, and remains, whether to convert matching grants to block grants. If matching grants are open-ended, most estimates would put their impact on state and local spending in the neighborhood of \$.75 on the dollar, give or take a bit. Converting these grants to block grants should lower spending significantly, whether or not there are flypaper effects. But what seems to have intrigued the profession more is the difference between the impact of block grants and the impact of income. There have been many attempts to rationalize flypaper, often involving some sort of misperception, even including some attempts by the Cigar team. Nowadays flypaper has become a standard term and flypaper effects are being found in many other areas of economics as well.

As time went on, my concerns in this area broadened from simply how grants worked to how a federal system should be constructed – what governments should be responsible for what functions. In contrast to many others, I have been a proponent of a mixed role for states and the national government in each of Musgrave's three important areas of governmental concern – allocation, distribution and stabilization. Many other economists who have studied the issue would agree with me on allocation but part company on either distribution or stabilization. My distribution argument involves shared responsibilities – I favor basic national standards with optional, perhaps subsidized, state supplementation. Among other things, states should be free to experiment with different ways of establishing support services and work training requirements. My stabilization argument involves the fact that states, not the national government, are likely to be facing fixed exchange rates, so it is more logical for states, not the national government, to be responsible for discretionary fiscal stabilization measures.

These federalism concerns also have a practical side. Many other countries are now grappling with how and what functions to centralize and how and what functions to decentralize. In my case I became involved in federalism consultations in Australia, Canada, Germany, Spain and Sweden. It is always fascinating to go to new countries and see the same old problems crop up. It can also be a heady experience, because American economists have a higher scarcity value in other countries.

NATIONAL SAVING

In 1976 I finally moved off New Hampshire Avenue and to the University of Michigan, where I had a joint appointment with the Economics Department (by then chaired by Harold Shapiro) and a unit that has since become the School of Public Policy. Over time my responsibilities have gradually waned in economics and grown in public policy, though I do confess to serving a term as chair of the Economics Department. My public policy teaching responsibilities were in two areas. There was a course in benefit–cost analysis that I taught and for which I later wrote a textbook. I also taught a course in macroeconomics for which I did not write a textbook (the world is not exactly short of macro textbooks!). But the macro teaching did get me into some interesting public policy work. I learned what university economists have discovered over and over – that a faculty position still enables one to play a role in real-world events.

The first time this happened involved budget deficits. It was the early 1980s and I just knew the large-scale budget deficits then beginning under the Reagan Administration could be quite dangerous. But in looking around for an article to assign to my macro students, I could not find anything that did more than simply assert that large-scale budget deficits were bad, while small-scale deficits were all right. This did not sound very convincing to me, and I knew it would not sound very convincing to my public policy students, who have always been extremely good at forcing their professors to come up with clear and convincing arguments.

This was the time when personal computers were first coming out, and I sat down to try to develop a simple Solow growth model that would show why deficits were bad, in terms of consumption per capita now and later. The result, not surprisingly, was that budget deficits actually raised consumption for about twenty years. Eventually the loss of national saving implicit in budget deficits (this was a non-Ricardian model) would result in lower consumption levels, but not for a long time. Some later work has indicated I may have overestimated the adjustment time, but the general point remains valid. The deficit issue then sets up a clear tradeoff, or conflict between the interests of present generations and future generations. Intellectually, I remembered all of this from Tobin's course in the 1960s, and now in the 1990s the argument has become commonplace. But I could find very little on the issue in the early 1980s when it was important. I worked out my model, presented it to my class, and later presented a paper on it to the Urban Institute project on Reaganomics.

The paper was noticed at the Congressional Budget Office (CBO), then engaged in a similar exercise of trying to explain why large budget deficits could be harmful. The CBO Director at the time, Rudolph Penner, called, invited me to Washington, and the next thing I knew I had accepted a two-year appointment as Deputy Director of CBO.

My two years at CBO were 1986 and 1987. By this time everybody in Washington recognized that the large-scale tax cuts and defense spending increases of the early Reagan years were damaging, and people were even beginning to see why, though to this day official Washington focuses far too much on federal budgets and far too little on national saving, which should be the measuring rod for policy changes. This was the time of the famous, or infamous, Gramm–Rudman–Hollings (GRH) deficit reduction act, and much of my time at CBO was spent writing about or otherwise refereeing GRH. GRH did indeed inspire budget gimmickry, but I thought then, and have argued since, that it also was responsible for some real fiscal austerity, or increases in national saving. It of course never was a substitute for honest and specific deficit reduction plans.

As for CBO itself, this was my third government job and, as with the others, I thoroughly enjoyed the experience. The idea of a Congressional budget office probably would not work in a parliamentary system of government, where the administration is a creature of the legislature. But it does, I think, work in a Congressional system that features checks and balances between the administration and the legislature. These checks and balances cannot operate very well on budgetary issues if the administration has all the expertise, which basically was the case before CBO was established in the mid-1970s. The agency is small by Washington standards, a little over 100 professionals, sometimes PhDs but often graduates of public policy schools, and everybody there is an expert on at least some aspect of government policy. The agency tried to strike a non-partisan political stance, and phrases like 'on the one hand, on the other hand' were common in CBO reports. So common, indeed, that the CBO softball team was called 'The Other Hands.' But Penner and I did agree, along with our Congressional sponsors, that when writing about budget deficits, we could forget the other hand and just try to say why, not budget deficits as such, but large drops in national saving could be dangerous.

My most recent experience with policy, and national saving, involves social security. In 1994 I was appointed Chair of the Quadrennial Advisory Council on Social Security, a group of 13 social security experts that has met monthly for the past two years and as I write is just now lurching toward its final report. There are many social security issues in hot dispute within the Council, but there is one area where we have arrived at a consensus, and it involves national saving.

For workers of different characteristics one can compute money's-worth ratios. These consist of the expected present value of benefits over the expected present value of taxes paid by the worker and employer, for various different groups of workers. When these money's-worth ratios are plotted by birth cohort, one finds that for those born early in the twentieth century all money's worth ratios were well above 1, indicating that social security was a very good deal for all broad population groups. For groups retiring nowadays some money's worth ratios are above 1 and some below, but since social security does give protection against inflation, disability, and very long lives that is not available privately, social security is still a pretty good deal for many groups of retirees. But as time goes on, because of the maturing of the system *and* the fact that the internal pay-as-you-go rate of return has now fallen well below the bond rate, money's-worth ratios will continue to drop, threatening the long-standing popularity of the system.

Our Council is now debating three very different approaches for turning around this drop in money's-worth ratios. The macroeconomics of these approaches are similar, but the social security implications are quite different. Macroeconomically, each approach involves a measure to raise national saving, and a device for getting some of this new saving invested in the equity market where returns have been higher, at least for the last century. One approach involves very little change in the benefit formula, some rise in taxes, and some investment of social security's assets in the equity market. The problem with this approach is that there could be significant political problems in having one investment board allocate what could be a huge amount of funds in the stock market. Another approach is to replace the present benefit system with large-scale pre-funded individual accounts. These could be invested in equity index funds if individuals so chose. The problem with this approach is that the present system is by and large not pre-funded, implying that large transition taxes and/or borrowing would be necessary. The third approach, my favorite, involves some modest changes in the benefit schedule combined with mandatory small-scale individual accounts that could also be invested in equity index funds.

BASEBALL

From the somewhat important – protecting retirement income for all living Americans – to the absolutely critical – protecting major league baseball.

In 1991 I was heading up the public policy school here at Michigan (more on this below). It was commencement time and we hold elections among the graduating class to choose a commencement speaker. The winner this year was my friend from Brookings days, Henry Aaron. I called Henry, he agreed to come, he gave a very nice commencement speech that I have borrowed from often, and I took him out to dinner as his consultant's fee (our school is a bit weak on the endowment side).

He mentioned a new project he was involved in and asked me if I would like to join up. The then Commissioner of major league baseball, Fay Vincent, was distressed that in the 1990 negotiations about the baseball salary framework the owners and players could not seem to agree on the economic facts. Some owners felt they were getting killed by the free agency that had recently come to major league baseball, while the players felt that the owners were doing just fine. Vincent was a lawyer, not an economist, and he may have had an inflated view of the extent to which economists' pronouncements could lead warring parties with millions of dollars at stake to bow down and accept the economists' advice. Whatever the case, he set up the Economic Study Commission (ESC) on Major League Baseball, co-chaired by Bud Selig, owner of the Milwaukee Brewers and for three years now the Temporary Commissioner, and Donald Fehr, the chief lawyer of the Players' Association. Henry was on the Commission, and being the careful economist he is, he realized that there was lots of necessary statistical work that would not get done in, say, monthly meetings of the Commission. The Commission needed a staff, and he asked me if I'd be interested in leading it. I won the bid and got Charles Brown and Gary Solon from our own economics department – both serious econometricians and baseball fans alike – to do some baseball econometrics.

Our work involved two questions. The first was whether competitive balance on the field had worsened since the advent of free agency. Theory actually predicts it would not worsen, Brown and Solon showed pretty conclusively that it had not. The second, and harder, question was whether free agency made it too difficult for small market clubs to make a profit – really the question of whether baseball should go to the salary cap that all other pro sports now have. Here the answer was in the fine old tradition of CBO. On the one hand, if one looked at income statements, free agency did seem to imply persistent income deficits for small market clubs. On the other hand, if one looked at investment rates of return, even small market clubs did quite well, getting returns that the social security system would be delighted with, to take one example.

We made our report and the ESC tried very hard to come up with a consensus statement. There were agreements on some small points, but not on the big point of a salary cap. But whether we outside economists agreed on anything was also of small moment in the negotiations that followed between players and owners. If we had declared in favor of one group or another, that group might have used our findings, but our middle-of-the-road findings were largely ignored by both sides. Vincent himself did not even last as Commissioner until we made our report in late 1992. The ESC did some good work but it was not able to lessen the bargaining hostilities on either side – hostilities that eventually led to the 1994 cancellation of the World Series.

PUBLIC POLICY

Aside from occasional sorties into professional baseball and social security, my main business these days is to try to continue improving our public policy school. Apart from the two years on leave at CBO, I have been teaching in the program since 1976. Over the years I have often been the program director, and just last year, in July 1995, we got the program upgraded and renamed as the School of Public Policy. For nearly three decades Michigan had one of the strongest public policy programs around, but this 1995 action was a deserved affirmation of the importance of public policy and the contributions of our school by the University Regents.

The school now consists of about 140 students, most of them highly committed to improving social conditions, earning their Master's Degrees in Public Policy. On the faculty side, we have joint appointments with 25 faculty members at Michigan, mainly from the Departments of Political Science and Economics, but some from the Schools of Business, Law and Social Work. In the early days, a large share of our graduates went into government work, but as government employment growth has been cut back, and as other policy schools have entered the competition, we are nowadays placing many more graduates with consulting firms, international agencies, and not-for-profit institutions.

It turns out that many of the issues we confront in trying to build up the School of Public Policy are the same ones that have been coming up in my whole career. One involves the split between theory and real-world policy applications. Compared to most other public policy schools, Michigan's school is quite analytical. Our main appointment mode is the joint appointment with an academic department. The vast majority of our faculty have made tenure in academic departments. Our courses stress rigorous analysis, often quantitative. Most of us here, faculty and students alike, feel that this analytical model has worked well over time and continues to work well. But the issue comes up again every time we consider making a faculty appointment, and for me every time I decide how to present some course material.

A second issue involves the public service question that my parents first put on my plate. I feel our school has an excellent record here. It has been one of the leaders in minority education. We have a number of courses on the topic, we have a diverse faculty, we have a model summer training program, and we have one of the highest shares of minority students of all public policy programs. Student study groups seem to be well integrated and harmonious, and friendships seem to cut across racial lines. We have also been a leader within the University in developing a program involving community service learning and nonprofit management. The challenge is to continue to use and harness the idealism of our students and faculty toward this worthwhile end.

FINAL THOUGHTS

In writing this autobiography it is hard to avoid the feeling that one is wrapping things up. I do hope that is not the case – I have enjoyed my career and want to keep on trucking. Right now I would like to see some favorable outcomes from our social security work, and I hope we continue to improve our public policy school. I also hope and expect that some new challenges will be coming along.

I have mentioned various colleagues and co-workers along the way. I have been blessed in being able to work with all of those mentioned, and many who were not mentioned. I have also been blessed in having a wonderful family to share the journey with. My wife, Ruth, is at least an amateur policy wonk. Her day job is in human resources with the Ford Motor Company. In recent years as I have gotten more into management she has helped on the numerous delicate issues that always seem to be arising. She is also every bit as demanding as my students in forcing me to have clear and comprehensible policy arguments. On the social security issue, for example, she accepts the money's-worth argument and she accepts the national saving argument, but she is very skeptical that my mandated individual accounts will fly, say among her colleagues at Ford.

Our children are now grown and as it turns out they too have both become policy advocates or analysts. Our daughter Sarah received a Master's Degree from Michigan's School of Natural Resources and the Environment, and now works as a project coordinator in the county's environmental office. Our son Robert received a Master's Degree in Public Policy from Berkeley (he might have come here but that was viewed as unwise within the family), and now is deregulating electricity with the Federal Energy Regulatory Commission. His daughter, and our granddaughter, Rachel, also shows a strong policy interest (at the age of six months!). Ruth, the kids and I have had many dinner table policy debates, and sometimes we even agree! Like any father, I would be proud of my children whatever they decided to do, but it is particularly gratifying to see them trying to make an impact on the world in their own way.

REFERENCES

Ando, Albert and Fanco Modigliani (1965), 'Velocity and the Investment Multiplier,' *American Economic Review*, **55**, 693–728.

Friedman, Milton and David Meiselman (1963), 'The Relative Stability of Monetary Velocity and the Investment Multiplier in the United States, 1897–1948,' in *Stabilization Policies*, Commission on Money and Credit.

Keynes, John Maynard (1936), *The General Theory of Employment, Interest, and Money*, New York: Harcourt and Brace.

Orr, Larry L. (1976), 'Income Transfers as a Public Good: An Application to AFDC,' *American Economic Review*, **66**, 359–71.

14. My life philosophy*

Everett E. Hagen

The sum of what one does in life reveals one's life philosophy, and reveals it more clearly than does one's own description of it, though of course all that one does is seldom known. In any event, in this essay one's own description is called for, and one must do the best one can.

The choice of academic life as one's career, and, within academic life, economics, tells us something, but unfortunately we are not all agreed on what it tells, or what the causes of the choices are. Economists' philosophies differ. Paul Samuelson suggests that one's economic philosophy may reflect more of one's total philosophy – political, ethical, moral – than one knows. But will *my* discussion of myself reveal hidden secrets? Of course not. Not mine. I accept the assignment with pleasure.

More than is true of any other economist writing in this series, I have found it necessary to incorporate noneconomic analysis not merely in explaining myself but in the analysis of many economic problems that interest me. In part this is because my field within economics is economic growth, which has its own logic, but this is not the total explanation, for many other development economists do not think it necessary to step beyond the boundaries of economics. Because the sources of this deviance, as a case in point, may interest other economists and perhaps also any noneconomic readers, one aspect of this brief autobiography will be an attempt to explain how I have come to differ.

Karl Brunner writes that he became an economist because the 'human animal and his society' attracted him. But if one is interested in the human animal, why economics rather than literature? or philosophy? or sociology? or psychology, defined in one way or another? or anthropology? or personality theory, or specifically psychiatry? One may choose economics, I suggest, because one has an interest in humans, but a guarded interest. Without realizing it one feels unease at looking too closely at one's own behavior or that of other humans, so one chooses a discipline that enables one to be fruitfully empirical and yet keep one's distance. If one is drawn to academic life, but even economics is too close, one may choose physics. I am not

*This chapter first appeared in *The American Economist*, **35**(1), Spring 1991, 10–18.

derogating physics by this comment. I know of no reason to deride a desire to understand the universe in which one lives but to avoid pondering closely oneself or one's relationships with one's fellows.

Samuelson states that he turned to economics because he found it to be easy and interesting. Easy, yes. It is easier to make order out of assumed or observed economic behavior than out of any of the other aspects of human behavior. But interesting, as a reason for choice? You beg the question, Paul. What academic, in whatever field, has not found his field interesting?

Let us then, as Erik Erikson once wrote in a different context, begin at the beginning – not at the beginning of the universe but at one's individual beginning.

I begin with a discussion of certain influences of my parents on me. Both were born in the same region of rural Norway, my mother in 1862 and my father in 1864. They lived in Norway until they were in their twenties but met each other not there but on an immigrant ship steaming toward the United States, in 1888.

Both were moderately well educated by what I assume to have been the standards of rural Norway in their time. My father attended public school until he was 15 years of age, then a private 'high school' for two years. I assume that a 'private school' was one to which one paid tuition. After graduating from the school, my father served as deputy sheriff for two years, then clerked in a general store for five years, by which time he had accumulated enough savings to finance the voyage to the United States, and in the United States to Minnesota, an agricultural state to which other Norwegians had gone before him.

The community in which my mother spent her childhood was apparently less prosperous than was my father's; it provided only four years of public schooling, whereas my father seemingly obtained six or seven. After her public schooling, my mother attended a private high school for two years, then after taking a short teacher training course perhaps similar to American post-secondary-school teacher training short courses of the early twentieth century, taught school for one year, but for only one year. Either she did not like teaching or was unsatisfactory. After clerking in a dry goods store for a time she became a maid ('hired girl') for a well-to-do Oslo (then Christiana) family. That family was acquainted with one that had migrated to Minneapolis; the Minneapolis family financed my mother's trip from Norway to that city, perhaps to employ her as a maid there, certainly to offer her a home in the New World.

My father migrated beyond Minneapolis, first to work on a farm in western Minnesota, then to rent one, and after succeeding in contracting a rental returned to the city briefly in 1890 to marry Marthea and take her back with him to his farm. They lived on that farm for 14 years, during which six children were born. In 1904 my father accepted a position as operator of a grain purchasing station ('elevator') of a Minneapolis 'commission firm' that bought grain in villages along the railroad line and sold it to millers in Minneapolis or points east. He moved to the small town in which the 'elevator' was situated (a very small town; population about 300). There a seventh child was born in 1904 and the eighth and last, me, in 1906. During that two-year period my father had left his position with the commission firm to become manager of the local farmers' cooperative grain elevator company, in which position his salary was increased steadily until by 1920, if my memory is correct, it had reached the level, locally thought to be munificent, of $180 per month. Perhaps his urge to increase his income betrayed him into moving too often; by 1920 he might have been earning higher income farming. In 1920 he bought (with a bank loan) an elevator in a larger town (population 1700) seven miles away and at the age of 56 entered upon the grain-buying business for himself.

My origins, then, were 'humble.' So were those of several other economists writing in this series; 'humble' seems to be a not uncommon starting point for the lives of American economists. Mine differed from the others whose accounts in this series I have read in that their mental horizons, even if limited, were urban; mine, as I grew up, remained rural. When I entered college, and, for that matter, when I was graduated from college, I knew less of the variety of life available to an American college graduate than did fellow composers of these essays.

I was graduated from secondary school in 1922, just before my sixteenth birthday. My parents then delayed my entry into college for one year in order that my next older brother might finish high school and enter college with me. It was hoped that I would 'steady' him.

We entered St Olaf College, a liberal arts college in Minnesota sponsored by the Norwegian Lutheran Church. At St Olaf, to encourage each student of Norwegian descent to retain or gain at least a minimum knowledge of his or her cultural background, each student of that descent (a large majority) was required to take one year of Norse (that is, of Norwegian). For many, like me, it was their first acquaintance with the language (despite the joke that circulated around Carleton College, which is just across the river from St Olaf, about the St Olaf student who was asked whether he spoke Norwegian. He replied, 'Oh, enough to get around the campus.'). In the required course I read in Norwegian a poem by, I think, Bjornstjerne Bjornson whose opening lines were 'Out! I want to go out. Over the high mountains.' As I read it I realized that my father not only had wanted to 'go out' but in Minnesota had wanted his children to be able to 'go out' also, beyond the parochial village life he knew, to lives that he did not know. By the time I existed and I think for some years earlier he subscribed to three 'metropolitan' English language daily newspapers, the morning and evening Minneapolis papers and the one St Paul daily paper and to no Norwegian-language newspaper or magazine. By the time I was born Norwegian had also disappeared from speech in the family.

Traces of the accent, vowel sounds, or pronunciation of their native tongue remain in the English speech of even some present-day immigrants to the United States who have gained prominence in American life. A psychiatrist would say, I think, that, immigrants of whom this is true were afraid to sever completely their roots with their past. No such touch of the past remained in my father's speech and none in my mother's except that she used a few English words incorrectly.

I cite these various petty facts as indication of attitudes of my parents and especially my father. Further evidence is provided by the life history of the siblings. All of us but one of my two sisters who taught rural school near the town and married a farmer left the village for adult lives elsewhere with modestly wider horizons. (Another sister died in childhood.) This parental encouragement, however, is only partial explanation of my reaching out to an academic life. Parts of the explanation that I believe are more important relate to what may be called the 'family drama.' My mother's life exemplified the saying 'Women's work is never done.' I am sure that each of her children craved more of her attention than she was able to bestow. The brother next older than I gained the admiration of both of our parents by his handiwork – work as varied as building bird houses that won first prizes at the county fair, repair of a defective chimney on our house, even before he was in his teens, etc. My attempts at competition with his handiwork were hopeless. But I learned to read the letters of the alphabet from packing boxes before I entered school, was promoted from first grade to third as soon as I did enter school (no kindergarten in that school), and skipped a grade later. My parents were proud. In this competition I was secure.

This was the brother who later entered St Olaf College with me. He did no studying and dropped out before the end of his first year, when he surely would have flunked out. My parents admired his handiwork, but he also behaved in ways that caused our mother great pain. In adolescence he was a petty thief. In one instance his thievery was discovered (by the local constable) and made public. I realized that he was probably the unknown thief in elementary school who had stolen coins from the pockets of coats hanging in the school cloakroom, and I wondered whether our mother feared this as well. He associated with the 'wrong' persons – male and female. Sometimes he stole out of the house after our parents were asleep; sometimes he was detected leaving or returning. Often, to my knowledge, he lied about his activities. I knew of more of these episodes than I think our parents did. It pained me to lie to our mother about them, but in this one respect I was not completely honest.

I have no doubt that this behavior in his younger years was, in part, an added desperate attempt to draw his mother's care to him from his younger, smarter brother. Nor do I have any doubt that my meek obedient complete pre-adolescent honesty was a tool in my competition with him.

I wanted to know why my brother behaved as he did. In secondary school I gained an awareness that there are explanations, even logical causes, of human behavior that scholars have studied. The principal of the school in the village of 1700 subscribed to the *New Republic* and left his copy in the school library when he had read it. The school committee, if it had known of this, would probably have censured him severely for exposing the students to this radical magazine, quite different from the *New Republic* of today. I read it eagerly. One article of some length particularly excited me. It argued that the slovenly and antisocial behavior of several generations of two families well known to sociologists, the Jukes and the Kallikaks, was probably due to environment, not heredity as was the assumption at the time. The argument began with the observation that the antisocial generations, who had the same heredity, also had the same family environment. The writer proceeded to attack the stress placed on heredity throughout early twentieth-century sociological theory. That evil arises from something outside oneself rather than being in one's blood seemed to give me relief. Moreover, the article expanded my world. It opened a door to something new.

At St Olaf I took the usual menu of small college liberal arts courses. My parents had no notion of choosing among schools to follow a specialized course of study; they were merely sure that their church school was a good one to go to (and indeed St Olaf is and was an excellent liberal arts college); and I had little more notion of selection than did my parents.

I was graduated from St Olaf in 1927, with a major in history. I do not know why I chose that major. For eight of the next nine years I taught social science in Minnesota and Wisconsin public secondary schools. I did not feel that this was a vocation; I felt that my life was at a standstill. Worse, I was young, no more mature in appearance than many of my students, unable to maintain good discipline, and, like many school teachers, miserable. I continued nevertheless. I did not yet know what to do with my life. I am sure that my inertness was related to the meekness of my earlier years, but I am not able to spell out the connection.

As I have noted, my college major was history. In 1931–32 I interrupted my teaching to do graduate work in American history at the University of Wisconsin, where two distinguished professors of American history, Frederick Logan Paxson and Carl Russell Fish, taught. At Professor Paxson's suggestion, I chose as a seminar topic the panic of 1907. Paxson's interest in it was as the event that led to the formation of the Federal Reserve System. I produced a seminar paper, full of charts and tables, that seemed fully satisfactory to Paxson, but I felt that I understood the causes of the 'panic' no better than when I had begun to study it.

I financed the year's study from my meager savings; I had no fellowship or scholarship. In 1932 I returned to high-school teaching, but the need for more knowledge or more understanding of life kept gnawing at me. At some time during the next two years I decided to quit high-school teaching and to get a PhD in Economics and seek a college teaching position. During the summers of 1934 and 1935 or 1935 and 1936, I took courses in economics or statistics at the University of Wisconsin, and in 1936 I applied for and received a teaching assistantship in economics, effective for the 1936–37 school year.

ACADEMICS, ETHICS, ECONOMICS

Let me sum up to this point. I believe that I became an academic for two reasons. One was that I had a problem to solve, and out there somewhere there seemed to be an answer. I believe also that in choosing an academic life – in any academic field – I felt the security that I had felt in reading letters of the alphabet on packing boxes. I do not know why I chose economics. I surely did not expect to find the answer to my problem in economics. However, in economics I did feel that sense of security even though not a sense that I was solving my problem. Perhaps the panic of 1907 still intrigued me, but that hardly explains the choice of a career field. Perhaps the problem of the Great Depression burdened my mind, though I had no conscious conception that I could solve that problem. My comments earlier in this essay about why an individual may choose economics as an academic field do not apply unqualifiedly to me, for as I shall note presently I did not flee from closer analysis of the human animal.

The explanations in the preceding paragraphs do not purport to be complete. I am aware of other influences that could be adduced; I will not use more space to present them. Moreover, the total influences were more complex, I am sure, than I understand. But I would make the point that the factors that I have cited that influenced me were of the same general nature as those that affect all choices of career. It is a safe assumption, that is, that, whether or not they have realized it, the career choices of other economists were influenced by factors of a nature similar to the nature of those that influenced me.

On the causes of the influences that affected my code of ethics I have less to say. I pay my taxes, including income taxes on fees for consulting abroad that could hardly be traced by the Internal Revenue Service even in these days of computers and computer records. I contribute modestly well to United Way, and make modestly large political contributions, concentrated on one effective organization that provides technical political aid to liberal members of

Congress of either party who are up for a close election – the National Committee for an Effective Congress.

I do not believe that most or even many individuals who have done poorly in life's economics are responsible for their misfortune and should be left to the workings of the free market. Rather, I believe in governmental intervention to modify the distribution of income – the more so in the present days of lust for money that has made income inequality in the United States even greater than it was 20 years ago. In short, I am a typical liberal in the American sense of that word.

My transition from graduate study to a faculty position occurred more rapidly than I had anticipated. During the summer of 1936 I became engaged to be married. My fiancée was a teacher in the Springfield, Illinois school system. During the depression, Illinois, like many other states, in order to spread income as widely as possible, had enacted a statute that only one member of a married couple should be employed in Illinois schools. My fiancée and I decided to become married in June 1937 and to keep the marriage secret from the Illinois authorities while she continued to teach and I continued graduate study during the 1937–38 year. Springfield and Madison were, after all, not far apart by train. This sort of dishonesty did not trouble my conscience.

We were married on 4 June, but the rest of the plan failed, for surgery on my wife in July to explore a problem that seemed to be appendiceal revealed not the expected inflamed appendix but a rather rare tubercular infection in the pelvic area. I had anticipated another year's full-time study, supported by my wife. After the surgery I decided that full-time study would not come again, and instead sought full-time employment. I found a position at Michigan State University (then Michigan State College) effective in September of that year. Under Wisconsin's generous provisions of social welfare, my wife was placed in a state tuberculosis sanatorium near Madison for care; I was expected to pay the expense at some future time if possible.

The next date for general examinations in economics at the University of Wisconsin was in November. The head of the sanatorium thought that by November my wife would be able to travel by Pullman berth. (Today she might have been ousted from the sanatorium in three weeks.) Before the Michigan State school year began in September, and during the time not occupied by teaching after the Michigan State year began, I read furiously, and during a week's leave from teaching in November I travelled to Madison, took four written general examinations successfully on successive days, and brought my wife back to Lansing with me.

The graduate courses I had taken in economics were a required two-semester seminar in micro theory (then simply titled theory), a lecture course and seminar in what would now be called macro theory, a lecture course in institutional economics, and a summer course (presumably a semester course but in fact less) in labor relations. The quality of the microseminar is illustrated by the fact that the professor offering it, chairman of the department, introduced it by observing that in any action one or more of three types of cost are present: pain, labor time and opportunity cost. The courses in macro theory were remarkable. The lecture course, offered by that odd, brilliant, 'grand old man' of the department, John R. Commons, with assistants substituting during a few weeks of the second semester while he warmed his old bones in Florida, covered whatever topics seemed to him of interest in any given year. I remember nothing specific about the course except the lectures on Wicksellian economics. The seminar in Keynesian economics was remarkable in that it was surely one of the first offered in an American institution. Harvard's fiscal policy seminar, for example, was first offered two years later. Keynes's *General Theory* was published in 1935. Professor Walter Morton of Wisconsin had spent the year 1935–36 in England on a sabbatical, came home filled with the excitement that Keynes's book had aroused in England, and offered the seminar immediately on his return to Wisconsin.

I also had taken two solid courses in statistical method – solid even though much more limited than comparable courses today. One cost of ending my course work so abruptly was that I had no formal work in international economics, the history of economic thought, except bits that were present in Commons's lectures, or monetary theory or 'money and banking.'

THEORY AND CAREER

During the late 1930s Frank Knight and Nicholas Kaldor were engaged in controversy concerning capital theory. My doctoral dissertation took off from the controversy. The dissertation proceeded only slowly, but I completed it and received my PhD in 1941. My first published article, derived from my thesis, was on 'Capital Theory with No Agents Fixed in Quantity.' I submitted it to the *Journal of Political Economy*. Knight, who was then editor of the *JPE*, stated in a letter to me that he thought there had been too much of this stuff, but that if his colleagues thought the article worth publishing he would publish it. Apparently they did, for he published it (in 1942). On re-reading the article now I agree with Knight.

In 1941 came also a somewhat more important event, America's entry into war. I knew that the armed forces would not want me; I had a thyroid deficiency, and the device used a number of times later of applying for a commission and assignment to Washington or other post at which medications were dependably available did not occur to me. In any event I think that I would have seen no superior virtue in performing service in a military rather than civilian uniform. I went down to Washington, in civilian garb, to find a wartime job.

My first wartime employer was the National Resources Planning Board, where I was interviewed and my employment recommended by Paul Samuelson, who was a consultant to NRPB.

GNI and GNP data had come into full use in government by the end of the 1930s, but they had not come fully into the mental awareness of all economists. A small and unofficial part of my work in Washington in 1941 and 1942 consisted of explaining GNP concepts and analysis to some older economists who found some of the concepts baffling.

I aided Paul in the writing of a pamphlet that analyzed the effect of military and economic demobilization after World War I (during 1918–20) on employment and income, and drew deductions concerning difficulties that might arise during demobilization after World War II. The pamphlet, *After the War: 1918–1920*, was published in 1943. Also, with Nora Kirkpatrick I wrote an article, published in the *American Economic Review* in the same year, on 'The National Output at Full Employment in 1950.' The forecast proved remarkably accurate, but for a reason that few economists would wish to duplicate. We appreciably underestimated the size of the labor force in 1950 and equally overestimated what the level of productivity would be in that year.

The long-range work of NRPB, dear to the heart of Franklin Roosevelt, was not closely related to the war effort. NRPB was soon to be terminated, and I moved to one and then another agency that were doing work that in principle was important. In practice, however, both were marginal to the prosecution of the war, and I was delighted to be drafted (figuratively) to the small staff of Jimmy Byrnes at the Office of War Mobilization, the 'domestic presidency.' Byrnes had been asked by President Roosevelt to resign his seat on the Supreme Court to head the agency.

My functions were varied, some important, some unimportant. The Office of War Mobilization presently became the Office of War Mobilization and Reconversion. Among various pieces of work concerning reconversion to peace let me mention one general one. I asked economists of five other agencies to estimate the likely level and duration of unemployment as the war ended. Though my own unemployment estimate, for OWMR, was the lowest of the six, it too was considerably too high; OWMR found it possible to abandon programs tentatively considered. We had greatly underestimated the speed with which the country's industrial corporations would be able to turn from war production to production for the peacetime market. In a few cases, it seemed certain, the conversion was so speedy because the companies involved had violated the governmental injunction to devote no resources to preparation for peacetime production while their production was still wanted for war, but in the main we had simply underestimated the agility of the American industrial system.

During the war, state governments, to curb consumer expenditures somewhat, had maintained their tax rates at prewar levels even though expenditures required for social welfare and a number of other state functions had greatly shrunk. By the end of the war almost every state government had accumulated a large treasury balance. Many a state had plans to use the balance to place various state programs and agencies at the nation's forefront. To make the state university one of the nation's greatest was a frequent aim. Illinois had such an aim, and had asked Howard R. Bowen, an economist of some note in wartime Washington, to become dean of the School of Business and Economics to accomplish the purpose. Bowen offered me a professorship, and I moved to Urbana in 1948. In the 1949–50 school year he asked me to become chairman of the Economics Department.

Even though members of the old guard were assured equality with the new faculty members in salaries and salary increases, they resisted encroachment, as they viewed it, by new young faculty members from the East and West coasts with ideas, as the conservative Champaign newspaper put it in an editorial, not attuned to the black soil of Illinois.

The trustees of the university were elected by state-wide popular vote. Traditionally the two political parties had agreed on a slate of trustees to avoid political contest. Now, however, the downstate Republicans chose a competing slate with the avowed aim of purging the university of the corrupting influence of the out-of-state ideas. Their slate was elected.

In the tension within the Economics Department, in a bit of mental fog I authorized circulation of a statement concerning the School, brought to me by the vice chairman of the department, a member of the old guard, that seemed innocuous, but in a normal frame of mind I would have realized could be used deceptively. It was circulated by the vice chairman, and responses counted, without identification of names of the persons responding; this permitted many persons who had no current connection with either the Department of Economics or the School of Business (for example, were long since retired) to respond as if they were members of the Economics Department petitioning against the dean. The result, adverse to the dean, was publicized. I still feel ashamed when I recall the incident.

To digress briefly: when Fritz Machlup, ideologically a conservative, chaired a program at the December 1950 convention of the American Economic Association and introduced Bowen, a speaker on the program, as a man who was being crucified for trying to change a trade school into a university, a newspaper report stated that Bowen had received an eight-minute standing ovation. Though the time period reported may have been exaggerated, as such periods often are, the ovation was impressive; it indicated the attitude of a large share of the academic economists of the country. I had earlier asked Milton Friedman to propose an investigation of the University of Illinois situation by the American Economic Association. He did not think it appropriate.

George D. Stoddard, who had been made president of the university at the war's end, was ousted by the new trustees, and Bowen was removed from the deanship. He soon accepted a professorship at Williams College, was shortly asked to become president of Grinnell College, and a very few years later was chosen president of the University of Iowa, whose trustees apparently had their own view of the Illinois action.

With six other of the new Economics Department faculty members, including ones who had brought the department a national ranking it had not known previously, I resigned. I accepted a job in the United States economic aid administration that would take me to Burma as adviser to the government of the country. The country called itself socialist. The *Chicago Tribune* editorially denounced this 'socialist globaloney.'

I went to Burma in 1951. There I worked for a year with half a dozen engineers who were planning specific projects, then during a second year headed a staff of five economists who worked with 15 to 20 engineers. My continuing tensions concerning relationships with other persons prevented me from doing a good job, but the talent of the Angel Gabriel would hardly have achieved much, for in Burma no political official soiled his hands and none who headed any operating agency felt responsibility for its performance. To cite only one example: a governmental tile and brick factory was created. The first act of the directors was to have homes for themselves built on a hill which happened to be the one excellent clay deposit in the country. It was then necessary to build a road across a swamp to obtain clay, inferior clay, from which to make brick and tile.

After my thoughtless action within the University of Illinois Economics Department, I had entered into psychotherapy to clear my mind and relieve my tensions. Some time after returning to the United States two years later I resumed psychotherapy. The gradually increased understanding of myself and of cultural, that is, psychological factors that affect economic development considerably influenced my later analysis of economic growth, as will be noted.

I had returned to the United States to accept a five-year research professorship at the Massachusetts Institute of Technology, which had been invited by the Ford Foundation to submit an application for a large grant to study problems of the economic development of the low-income countries. Some of the funds were used for four such professorships. Before the end of the five-year period, the MIT Economics Department decided to offer two of the four men permanent positions. I was one of the two.

From the time when I went to Burma until the present, under various auspices, I have labored briefly or at some length to do research or to give advice, on specific topics or the general problem of growth, in Burma, Singapore, Malaysia, Japan, El Salvador, Colombia, Brazil, Argentina and Saudi Arabia. From Burma at one end of an array, where, I think, no amount of advice would have created attitudes conducive to development, to Singapore and Japan, where no advice except on certain specific projects was necessary, the cases provided a remarkable variety of situations. In Saudi Arabia, a special case with no shortage of economic resources, men with only political experience displayed a remarkable ability to plan, and engage experts to manage, the construction of infrastructure and other economic development projects.

UNFINISHED BUSINESS

I have written one book that I think is of some importance: *On The Theory of Social Change: How Economic Growth Begins* (1962). Economic growth requires labor with one's hands – grubby labor – and technical creativity (even today, though technically advanced methods already exist). In the Middle Ages, a student of the period has noted, gentlemen did not engage in economic production. Neither do gentlemen in preindustrial low-income countries. The book deals with the historical cases. It notes, first, that economic growth begins in a derogated group within a country, whose members are striving to advance economically to improve their status in the society and are willing to engage in grubby work to do so, since they are barred from advancing by traditional means. It notes, also, that a derogated family takes special pleasure in the petty achievements of its infants and children, and that that pleasure tends to breed technical creativity in these children. The book uses recent advances in the study of infants and children to make this point.

Economists have been little interested in this theorizing about how economic growth begins. In his book *Capital and Growth* (1965) Hicks notes that growth theory has nothing to do with 'underdeveloped countries.' In his noted article 'Economic Development with Unlimited Supplies of Labor' (1954) Lewis notes that growth begins when men who save and invest appear in a country, but he has nothing to say about how they happen to appear. But the question is of interest to anthropologists and students of personality theory, and a survey that I think covered the 1970s showed my name (presumably because of this theory) among the more frequently cited in articles in social science journals as a group. The theory has not been extended to the lower-income countries as derogated nations within the world, but the extension would not be difficult. More difficult, and a problem for anthropologists and personality theorists, would be to note the cultural factors that deter growth in some countries (such as Burma), which thereby remain the world's lowest in income.

Every discipline should have its iconoclasts, and I have attacked a few sacred cows of development theory, in articles on the contribution of protectionism to real income in certain circumstances (1958), the reality of technological unemployment (1965, 1966, and correction of an error in 1987), and, in an unpublished manuscript, the virtues of rapid population growth. The qualified anti-free trade argument has not always seemed obvious. Kindleberger, who apparently did not read the article carefully, thought that I was reviving the Manoilesco thesis of the inherent superiority of manufacturing.

Let me conclude this essay by noting part of the argument concerning population growth.

The argument that rapid population growth retards economic growth is based explicitly or implicitly on diminishing returns to labor plus the need to use some of the country's investment funds for capital widening to accommodate the population growth and some of its current funds to provide services such as education to the added people.

However, the Ricardian–Malthusiam argument is pertinent only to agriculture; secondary and tertiary industry need only land on which to stand. In a technically advancing economy added capital widening may not burden the economy; it may merely absorb labor disemployed by labor-augmenting (labor-saving) technical advance. Moreover, in a technically advancing economy 'demographic' investment is not merely capital-widening. It permits the introduction of technically advanced methods sooner than would otherwise be possible except by discarding existing capital, and economically sufficient capital will be discarded only in a condition of perfect competition. With rapid population growth, then, the product per unit of capital in use will always – that is, at any given time – be greater, *ceteris paribus*, than if the population were growing less rapidly.

It does not follow from these considerations that more rapid population growth will always yield an increased rate of economic growth. The added costs, for example for housing and education, may exceed the added benefits. But they may not; the added benefits may exceed the added costs. There is no presumption one way or the other. To determine the conditions in which the one rather than the other result will occur is one of the bits of unfinished business of social scientists.

REFERENCES

Hagen, E.E. *On The Theory of Social Change*. Homewood, IL: Dorsey Press, 1962.

———. 'An Economic Justification of Protectionism.' *Quarterly Journal of Economics*, November, 1958.
———. 'Reply.' *Quarterly Journal of Economics*, February, 1961.
———. 'Technological Disemployment and Economic Growth.' *Journal of Development Economics*, **10**(2), April 1982.
———. 'More on the Employment Effects of Innovation.' *Journal of Development Economics*, **17** (1986).
———. 'More on the Employment Effects of Innovation: A Correction.' *Journal of Development Economics*, **23** (1986).

15. Political economy, politics and religion: intertwined and indissoluble passions*

G.C. Harcourt[†]

I

When I returned to Cambridge at the end of August 1997 after two terms of leave in my native Australia, I was delighted to find waiting for me a letter from Professor Szenberg asking me to contribute to his ongoing series on the life philosophies of economists. In recent years I have written a number of essays which circle around this theme. His request gave me the opportunity to bring the various strands together and, it is hoped, into focus.

II

Let me begin at the beginning. I was born in Melbourne, Australia on 27 June 1931 at the height of the Great Depression, the younger of twin sons of Marjorie and Kenneth Harcourt. According to family lore, I was not expected. The doctor had packed his bag after delivering my brother, John, in the double bed of the home in which John still lives, when the midwife alerted the doctor to my presence, a presence he initially was reluctant to accept. Following a breach birth I spent my first minutes with no clothes on, until my grandmother was contacted to bring some spares. This experience may have something to do with my hedonism in later life.

Both my parents were Jewish. At the time when we were born, they were agnostic and assimilationist in religion, right-wing in politics, especially my mother. Both were born in Australia. My father's father[1] probably came from

*This chapter first appeared in *The American Economist*, **42**(2), Fall 1998, 3–18.

†I thank most sincerely but in no way implicate Stephanie Blankenburg, Jeremy Butterfield, Philip Gaudoin, Joan Harcourt, Rebecca Harcourt, Robert Harcourt, Tim Harcourt, Wendy Harcourt, Prue Kerr, Suzanne Konzelmann, Julie McKay, Peter Nolan, Terry Roopnoraine, Bob Rowthorn, Claudio Sardoni, Giles Slinger and Hugh Stretton for their comments on a draft of the essay. I also thank the editor for his positive response and support.

Transylvania (then Romania, now Hungary); his mother came from Poland. My mother's father came from Germany; her mother's parents were English Jews in origin, who had already been in Australia for a generation. They were rather posh and I often say that my mother married my father as she was going down in the world and he was coming up – his parents were itinerant shopkeepers in New South Wales. My father was brought up as an orthodox Jew but what he came to see as the hypocrisy of religious people of all faiths led him to an agnostic position by his twenties. When I was born he was a leather merchant, working with my maternal grandfather. His mother was dead and he was estranged from his father who previously had left his mother and their four children. My mother had little if any religious sense. She viewed religious affiliations as tags to signal where people stood in the pecking order of society – Melbourne in those days was stuffy, snobby and sectarian. She entered us as Church of England (C of E) at our primary and secondary schools. Being C of E was then regarded as highly respectable, even upper class, certainly much above Methodism, probably on a par with Presbyterianism. This ranking system must have stayed with us. I subsequently became a Methodist, my brother a Presbyterian (after I had paved the way, as it were) and, in the last years of her life, my mother also became a Presbyterian. My father resolutely remained an agnostic to the end of his life.

As I said, Melbourne was a sectarian place. The principal fights were between the Roman Catholics, many of whom were of Irish origin, on the one hand, and all manner of Anglicans and Protestants, on the other. Nevertheless, these warring groups cheerfully formed a united front when ganging up on the Jews – thoughtless, British-style, anti-Semitism was very much alive and well when I was young. Indeed, as a child I heard much of it in my own home. I shall never forget the trauma that engulfed me when as a four- or five-year-old – I may even have been younger – I repeated some anti-Semitic sentiments I had heard at home, expecting approval but instead being told sternly by my father that I was a Jew myself. This was a fundamental landmark in my psychological and philosophical development. From then on I was conscious of being an outsider, a feeling that was confirmed during my boyhood by several episodes which were traceable, directly or indirectly, to the prevailing anti-Semitic attitudes (I described some of these in Harcourt, 1960).

At our primary school our Jewishness was the basis for much of the (verbal) bullying and ostracism we received. It was behind the breakup of a close friendship with another boy. Another incident from this period concerns a holiday my brother and I spent in Ballarat with a family we had previously met on a holiday at Torquay, a Victorian seaside holiday town. A son of the family began acting strangely, he seemed embarrassed to have us there. The next-door neighbors had objected to having Jews staying next to them, principally, it seemed, because Jews had no homeland of their own (this was before Israel had been founded), were anyway generally undesirable, mean and money-grubbing and, I suspect, Christ-killers into the bargain. I tried to explain to him that it was not the Jews' fault now that, centuries ago, they had been driven out of their original homeland, that, while they were often associated with business and money, often through necessity, they were neither necessarily mean nor money-grubbing. As for the Christ-killing charge, I mentioned the Romans; I hope I also tried to point out the irony expressed in the rhyme:

How odd of God
To choose the Jews
But not so odd
As those who choose
A Jewish God
And scorn the Jews.

I do not think I had much success with him, or with others in later instances.

These experiences heightened my interest in religion, in the existence or not of God, while, at the same time, reinforcing the skeptical attitudes concerning religion and religious persons that I took over uncritically from my father. I went to divinity classes at both my schools and learnt a lot about the Old and New Testaments; indeed, I won the Divinity Prize at least once at my secondary school. (I must say that now I have embarked on a two-year stretch of reading the Bible, courtesy of the Cambridge Bible which rearranges the readings so that they are relatively interesting and the reader is not bogged down in chapter after chapter of 'begats,' I realize that we were given highly selective readings at school, especially of the Old Testament. The portraits of God and the behavior of his People that I now find emerging are ambivalent, to say the least.)

III

As I mentioned, my parents' political views were conventionally right-wing, on the whole uncritical and, indeed, adulatory in their support of the views of R.G. Menzies and his, inappropriately named, Liberal Party (which was started after the end of World War II. Before that he had been the leader of the United Australia Party (UAP)). Their support partly reflected their bourgeois background – both my grandfathers were business people, albeit my mother's father had a much larger business until he went broke in the late 1930s. My father continued in his own business until he was well into his seventies.

It also reflected their desire to belong to the Australian, especially Victorian (state and variety), middle class and its way of life. For over 50 years, they were the only Jews at their golf club, for example. I do not wish to suggest that they were unprincipled or expedient. They were only too aware of what was happening in Europe – some of our relatives were still in Germany – and they took the steps they thought best to protect us.

My father especially had all the old-fashioned virtues in great abundance and his care during his entire eighties of my mother when she had a terrible stroke in 1972 was heroic. He was an honest, selfless, warm, kind and witty person. He could be stubborn and inflexible, and was prone at times to mild depression. But he was much loved and respected by all who knew him. One woman who had known him since she was a small child wrote after his death that it was always a pleasure, never a chore, to drop in to see him in his old age. (He was 96 when he died.) I should also say that the death of our older sister, Robyn, in her fourth year (she was a blue baby) meant that a sense of grief and sadness pervaded our home though our parents rarely spoke of Robyn herself. My mother was efficiently caring and warm-hearted, and basically kind. But she was also most insecure, with the result that she had little sense of proper boundaries in relationships with her children, other relatives, or friends. This was a continuing source of friction and ill will. She mellowed after her stroke when she realized, at last, that people really did care about her and were fond of her.

I had tremendous rows with my parents when I was growing up – so what is new? – and especially when I went to university. Ostensibly these were mostly about politics (I quickly became a democratic socialist at university) and religion, but, especially in my mother's case, it was basically about independence and letting go. My father understood that there are two equally important parts to parenting – love and support and guidance when children are young, love and letting go, coupled with a dependable fall-back position, if needed, when children are grown.

The profession of Christian principles combined with anti-Semitic behavior (and Catholic and/or Protestant bigotry) were the major stumbling blocks in the way of me accepting belief in God and joining a religious group when I was a schoolboy. In the matter of faith as in my then political views, I was a carbon copy of particularly my father's views, even up to my sixth form (university entrance) years. I remember writing an essay on the illegality of coal miners striking (because coal was an essential commodity for us all), clearing the arguments with my father, and getting a very rude shock when it was returned with a low mark because the teacher wrote, correctly, that it was so intolerant and one-sided – the beginning of wisdom indeed!

My politics then were therefore rather like those of Margaret Thatcher – a belief in 'free enterprise' and the supreme importance of competitive markets as institutions, in the businessman as hero coupled with a dislike of trade unions and of their leaders as obstructionist bully boys, usually Communists (in those days Communism and Unionism were regarded as virtually synonymous by my parents and their friends); a suspicion of the role of government and a dislike of public servants – bureaucrats who were lazy, good-for-nothings lacking initiative and manners, wasting 'taxpayers' money' through their actions and by their salaries, purveyors of enormous numbers of useless forms and likely as not Roman Catholics into the bargain. Labor Party politicians were suspect both as citizens and as people, virtually non-Australian and non-British in attitudes, too often of Irish origin and therefore suspect as far as loyalty was concerned. We, though, were extremely patriotic, almost jingoistic, and pro-British (my formative years took in World War II); we were lost in admiration for Winston Churchill (and shocked at the 'injustice' and 'ingratitude' of the British electorate in turning him and the Conservatives out in 1945). All told, it was admiration for a never-never-land composed from Noël Coward's wartime films, Vera Lynn songs, together with 'There'll always be an England,' 'Rule Britannia,' 'Land of Hope and Glory,' and 'God Save the King,' all of which we sang and listened to with bursting chests and much emotion: so much so that even today, I cannot watch the Last Night of the Proms without a resurgence of these emotions, though my rational self detests and disowns the sentiments and sentimentality involved.

IV

So we start with a small boy who became increasingly conscious of feeling an outsider, especially at my secondary school where I had the misfortune to be in forms, the form captain of which was the most rabid Jew-baiter at the school. I countered by trying hard at my school work (a risky strategy because being a 'swot' and too friendly with teachers led to accusations of 'greasing,' of 'sucking up') and even more at sport, where the enthusiasm (if not the skills) of my cousin Richard and myself were legendary. At this time – the mid- to late 1940s – I wanted to be a vet (I had always been mad on animals and birds) and so I struggled with natural science subjects at which I was no good at all. I took economics as a 'fill-in' subject but it was not until I left school, having at last passed the dreaded physics (a prerequisite for veterinary science), that I decided to do economics at university and become a secondary school teacher. The latter decision allowed me to get a scholarship to go to university, to save my parents paying for me – 1950 was just before a generous system of Commonwealth Scholarships was introduced.

Going to the University of Melbourne (to do the B.Com. degree) in 1950 was a revelation; it was, as I have often written, a 'paradise on earth' after school. It was possible to be friendly with lecturers (my first mentor was Joe Isaac). Religious intolerance at a personal level (sectarianism still bugged the Labor Party) as opposed to political intolerance – it was the start of the cold war – was virtually absent. I revelled in the atmosphere and loved all lectures (except those on commercial law, a subject which I found to be a nightmare). In particular, economic principles and economic geography were most admirable complements (Paul Krugman please note). As I have explained elsewhere, the lectures on economic geography – it was in effect a course on comparative economic systems – were responsible for me quickly becoming a democratic socialist. Especially crucial was the account of the development of Californian oil fields by 'free enterprise' and the consequences of this, the large permanent losses of natural gas and oil. This alerted me to the irrationality of unfettered competitive capitalism. I felt that any vital resources which were meant to serve the needs of both present and future generations should be developed by organizations with suitably long horizons and so I argued for the nationalization of all such resources. I still believe my basic reasoning to be correct but I accept that I was naïve to expect that politicians and managers of nationalized industries would *necessarily* have longer time horizons and more enlightened attitudes than their counterparts on boards of private enterprises.

I was also shocked by the descriptions of the disparity in incomes and wealth in many different economic systems, which seemed to me unjust and irrational. I put 'unjust' first because my own experiences of intolerance and of the blatant racism against our indigenous people which was widespread in the middle-class circles in which my parents moved (and not *only* there) often filled me with impotent rage. Sometimes this was expressed in slanging matches with my uncle Sam who, though basically a good and kindly man, was also a very prejudiced one. I still experience these powerful emotional feelings. I cannot, for example, reread *The Ragged Trousered Philanthropists* (Tressell, 1914, 1962), nor, especially, listen to Paul Robeson singing 'Joe Hill' without anger, and, often, tears.

Of course, to start economics at university in 1950 was still to be in an environment enthused by the first flush of *The General Theory* and of the successful application of its principles in both the UK and Australia during World War II. The Commerce Faculty at Melbourne was most Cambridge-oriented. We were quickly introduced to Keynes himself (*The Tract* in the first year, *The General Theory* itself in the second), Marshall, of course, and Pigou's *Economics of Welfare*,[2] Joan Robinson's *Economics of Imperfect Competition*, Sraffa (1926), Maurice Dobb on *Studies in the Development of Capitalism* and *Political Economy and Capitalism* (one of my favorite books), and Richard Kahn on the multiplier. In addition, we had Kaldor on the equilibrium of the firm and imperfect competition generally (also the trade cycle), Chamberlin and Triffin, Kalecki on the macroeconomic theory of distribution, Boulding's *Economic Analysis*, Hicks on *Value and Capital*, Hayek on *The Pure Theory of Capital*, Samuelson on *The Foundations*, and Wicksteed's *Common Sense*. All this was heady stuff for someone who was amazed to find himself at university, let alone doing well at his subject.[3]

In my third year I took history of economic thought as one of my two specializations for the third and fourth honors years (my other specialization was mathematical economics). HET entailed reading many of the greats in the original. The exception for me was Marx – after reading 100 or so pages of Vol. I of *Capital* of which I could make neither head nor tail – I am basically a simple soul – I turned with relief to Paul Sweezy's *Theory of Economic Development* for enlightenment. It was not until I had three brilliant scholars of Marx as research students in the 1970s and 1980s – Prue Kerr, Allen Oakley and Claudio Sardoni – that I was able to make sense of Marx himself.[4] I also browsed long and read widely and haphazardly in the library of the University of Melbourne. Of the many journal articles I read, the single most influential one was Kurt Rothschild's classic, 'Price Theory and Oligopoly' (1947). These experiences provided much of the base on which I erected the structure of economic theory I have used ever since.

With this foundation in economics was allied, very early on, my democratic socialist beliefs. I used then to be much more gung-ho about nationalization, especially of the financial sector and of essential (for present and future generations) industries such as steel and coal than I am now. But overriding all was the need to create a fair distribution of income and wealth and especially to avoid absolute (and relative) poverty amongst the disabled, the disadvantaged and an inevitable hard core of the inadequate. Of course, then, we took for granted the commitment of governments of all shades of opinion to full employment, regarding achieving it as a necessary characteristic of a just and equitable society (not to mention one claiming to be civilized). Though I was familiar with accounts of the price mechanism and its workings – I had read a lot of Hayek's work on this as well as on capital theory – I was also convinced that the typical market structure in advanced capitalist economies was an oligopolistic one, not a competitive one, so that the blueprints of people such as James Meade and Abba Lerner did not seem to me to be practical, idealistic and appealing though they otherwise were. (Meade idolized Keynes but I do not think they ever saw eye to eye on the efficacy of the price system and competition, and especially on the place in the pecking order of priorities which free trade should take in an ideal world.) Belief in God, any God, took longer to come. It was a prolonged and difficult process.

V

I had no trouble in reconciling the precepts of Christianity with democratic socialist economic principles – indeed, I could not and cannot see how any other conclusion could logically be reached. I was held up by problems of personal faith, and those observed inconsistencies between the practices of many Christians and their professed ideals and beliefs.

Once I convinced myself that, despite my associations with Wesleyanism (my secondary school, Wesley College, and university college, Queen's, were Methodist institutions), I did not need to have a warm feeling somewhere near the pit of my stomach before I could believe, I coupled my democratic socialist beliefs with a decision to regard belief in the Christian God (all Three) as a working hypothesis: let us suppose it to be true and see how we go from there. I took that step in 1953. I still regard it as a correct decision – my working hypothesis has not let me down.

It seemed to me irrational that capitalist institutions should push the exploitation of human selfishness (often called freedom of choice to make it sound better) so far to the front; while simultaneously stunting the development of the Christian (and humanist) virtues of altruism, cooperation, tolerance, compassion, and striving for consensus, not to forget forgiveness. I believe that the only essential difference between socialist humanists and Christian socialists is that the former think that people can bring about desirable reforms by their own unaided efforts. By contrast, Christians believe that it is only by the workings of the Holy Spirit in and through individuals and those individuals in turn working in and through secular and religious groups, that people may be able to achieve what the humanists think people can do unaided. Maybe Philip Wicksteed, a hero from my undergraduate days, put it too strongly: 'If there is no descent of the Holy Spirit there can be no Kingdom of God, in spite of the most perfect and ideal social machinery' (quoted in Steedman, 1994, p. 87). But then, maybe not.[5]

The Holy Spirit works in at least two ways. First, the Holy Spirit removes the intolerable pressures associated with the impossible task of achieving and maintaining personal perfection (think of poor Wittgenstein). This was a preoccupation of Evangelicals in Melbourne during my youth, to my mind, a perverse and unhealthy obsession with gazing at their own navels. Second, the Holy Spirit helps believers to work vigorously and with some chance of success, or at least optimism, within the social and political institutions of their societies. I explicitly rejected the view that religion is related to individual but not to group or social behavior. I was never under any illusion as to the chances of complete success. That a cause or course of action is right and just does not guarantee that it will succeed. But I do believe that to strive for the Kingdom of God on earth is both correct and feasible for committed democratic Christian socialists even if I am also bound to accept that a just and equitable society is unlikely ever to be fully realized. At one stage on the way I was tempted to become a Roman Catholic but a crucial sermon in which the preacher set out the characteristics of the Roman Catholic, Evangelical and Protestant versions of Christianity led me inexorably towards the last. So I was baptized in 1953 in Queen's College Chapel just before I joined the Australian Labor Party (ALP) (a lagged relationship, my political beliefs having been formed by mid-1950) and when I took up my first lecturing post in Adelaide in 1958, I began to call myself the only Jewish Methodist in that fair city.[6]

VI

So, by the time I graduated in April 1954, I had formulated a working political and religious philosophy/hypothesis and an embryo's, perhaps even an infant's approach to economics from which to proceed. My main interests in economics had also been formed;[7] there were six: first, the links between the behavior of firms and systemic performance, as illuminated by Keynes's great work, over the trade cycle and beyond – this was the topic of my undergraduate dissertation in 1953. In it I tried to put the arguments of Rothschild's paper on the warlike behavior of the decision-makers in oligopolistic firms who desired secure as much as maximum profits into the framework of *The General Theory*. My aim was to examine a particular issue: Keynes's argument that 'financial prudence,' whereby firms wrote off the book values of their durable assets well ahead of the need to replace them, was a contractionary force in the economy as a whole. I conjectured that this might not be so in a world of Rothschild's oligopolists acting according to Clausewitz's *Principles of War*. I looked at the reserve policies of a number of Australian companies over the years of the 1930s depression by examining their profit and loss accounts and balance sheets and constructing their funds statement, in order to see whether any of my inferences were confirmed by their experiences. The overall verdict was the Scottish one of 'not proven.'

Second, a fascination with theories of the trade cycle generally. In my second year as an undergraduate I read the two volumes of Schumpeter's *Business Cycles* (and spelt his name without a 'c' all through an essay I wrote on the trade cycle in the United Kingdom in the nineteenth century). In our honors years we had lectures on Hicks's *Trade Cycle* and read Kaldor and Swan's review articles of it. A desire to understand the nature of cyclical growth in capitalist economies has remained with me ever since.

Third, the beginning of a lasting love for the analytical history of our subject, as well as an insatiable curiosity about the main players over the years in economics – I read Harrod's life of Keynes in 1951. This gave me an abiding taste for intellectual biography (which was not confined either to biographies of economists or, eventually, only to reading what others wrote. Since the early 1970s I have written essays in intellectual biography myself. Intellectual biography allows us to begin to see the link between the historical settings of its subjects – their class, their racial, religious and philosophical backgrounds – and the issues of the day on which they write or have written. By analyzing these intertwinings, we may hope to understand better their contributions, to recognize both the achievements and limitations of the particular forms which their analyses take and, it is hoped, to be inspired to carry on from where they left off.)

Fourth, a desire to understand and do mathematical as well as theoretical economics (they were not explicitly split then as they are now). This has been a continuous source of frustration, for my desire greatly outran my proficiency. I am a poor mathematician and I have only rarely found collaborators who are mathematically gifted (the exceptions are Jorge Araujo and Mohammed Dore).[8]

This had not been for lack of trying. For example, my own favorite theoretical paper is the two-sector model of employment and income distribution in the short period which I published in 1965. I wrote it while on leave from Adelaide in Cambridge in 1963–64. It was meant to be the first of a series of papers I wanted to write on these themes: I asked the young Jim Mirlees and, when he said 'no,' the even younger Joe Stiglitz, to collaborate with me on the extensions. Joe lasted a week, a long time in the intellectual life of J.S., before he too said 'no.' So the sequels have never been written by me – Jorge Araujo built on my base in parts of his PhD dissertation. My use of mathematics in articles peaked in 1968 in a paper on investment-decision rules, investment incentives and the choice of technique, though I continue to use simple mathematics and, especially, simple diagrams now and then. My views on mathematics as a good servant but bad master are to be found in an essay in a 1995 selection of my essays.

Fifth, a desire to contribute to down-to-earth, realistic and humane policy based on theoretical developments and applied work. I have done this both through journals and through many years as a back-room boy in the Australian Labor Party where my most important contribution was as the economist on the late 1970s National Commission of Enquiry into the Party's poor performances in the second half of the 1970s. There, I wrote the first draft of the economic policy discussion paper, drawing together the most progressive strands of thinking of people in the Party and of its supporters in the profession at the time. I like to think that it had some influence on the policies of the Party when it was returned to power in the early 1980s; for an independent, rather depressing assessment, see Battin (1996, pp. 103–6).

Sixth, capital theory and distribution theory generally. As I said, I read a lot of Hayek's work when an undergraduate and, of course, the capital bits of *Value and Capital*, as well as Boulding and Schumpeter's writings. But it was going to Cambridge in 1955 which first brought my interest in these issues into sharp focus. My years as a PhD student coincided with Joan Robinson's lectures on what became *The Accumulation of Capital* in 1956. This was another watershed in my development, for it provided, more comprehensively than ever before, the framework within which I have worked. If there is anything original in my PhD dissertation (apart from the empirical work), it is the coupling of the pricing models of Russell Mathews and John Grant, and Trevor Swan, with Joan Robinson's macroeconomic model, in an attempt to analyze the implications of historical cost accounting procedures for measuring incomes for dividend and taxation purposes and for setting prices in a period of inflation. Kaldor (who had been my first supervisor before he went on leave and I went to Ronald Henderson) was then working on his models of distribution and growth and Meade (who succeeded Robertson in 1957 in the Chair of Political Economy) had begun his work on growth theory.

VII

When I took up my first lecturing post at Adelaide in March 1958, I had a number of strokes of good fortune. First, dominating all else, I met Eric Russell for the first time. He became my mentor as well as greatest friend; his influence on me as an economist and as a university person was massive (see Harcourt, 1977a, 1977b). Second, I was able to work directly with John Grant and Russell Mathews as I wrote my PhD dissertation virtually from scratch (I quickly jettisoned all but one chapter of the very rough first draft I brought with me). Third, Peter Karmel, our Head of Department, asked me to review Wilfred Salter's 1960 classic for the *Economic Record*; doing so greatly expanded my understanding of the microeconomic and macroeconomic processes associated with technical progress, and their links to economic policy.[9]

Fourth, Karmel asked me to take over the first year macro course (it was called 'Outlay'); it was essentially an introduction to the economics of Keynes in an Australian setting. The lectures, first given by Karmel, then by me, and subsequently by Bob Wallace, my greatest friend from Melbourne days who was then at Adelaide, were the basis of my first book, *Economic Activity* (1967) (it was written jointly with the other two givers of the lectures).

Fifth, Harold Lydall, Karmel's successor in the Adelaide Chair (Karmel had asked me to take over the Outlay course from him because he had been appointed the foundation vice-chancellor of the new Flinders University of South Australia) asked me to work with him on a puzzle that he had found in some arithmetical examples. The values of the accounting rates of profit he had calculated did not tally with the corresponding values of the economic rates of profit (internal rates of return). This led me to formulate the analysis that became 'The Accountant in a Golden Age' (1965). The principal reason for the discrepancies between the two measures has to do with the difference in the ways in which accountants and economists respectively calculate depreciation allowances.

VIII

When I returned to Cambridge in August 1963, the burst of productivity that ensued, first in the year of study leave from Adelaide and then during my time as a university lecturer in economics and politics and Fellow of Trinity Hall,[10] had its main source in the experiences of the preceding years in Adelaide. Trying to understand Sraffa's *Production of Commodities by Means of Commodities* in tandem with Vincent Massaro led me back to undergraduate studies of Ricardo and Marx, at first through a glass darkly but now, I hope, more clearly. While in Adelaide, I had given lectures on Kaldor's postwar contributions to the theory of distribution and growth. This resulted in an article (1963) which criticized aspects of his theory. With my interest in the theory of the firm, especially pricing policies, it was natural to ask what were the pricing policies of Kaldor's businesspeople, or rather, what would they have to be in his theory of distribution if the economy was constrained to be at full employment in *both* the short period and the long period, a proviso which was emerging explicitly in his writings on growth and technical progress in the late 1950s. As I have often remarked, hearing Solow's 1963 Marshall Lectures on a mythical creature called 'Joan' and another called 'Nicky' stimulated me to cease being negative, to accentuate the positive, by developing the two-sector model to which I referred above, in which the ideas of Keynes, Kahn, Kaldor, Kalecki, Joan Robinson, Salter, Solow and Sraffa's recent contributions all came together.

At much the same time, Robin Matthews asked me to review for the *Economic Journal* Minhas's 1963 book on the CES production function and factor reversals in international trade. Writing the review, in which I combined insights from Salter with those I was obtaining from writing 'The Accountant in a Golden Age,' led eventually to my one excursion into the *Review of Economic Studies* (see Harcourt, 1966), a paper which has often been misunderstood. For example, one referee of the *Review* thought it a woefully inadequate exercise in discovering biases in econometric procedures and Bob Solow in his chapter in my *Festschrift* volumes called it an 'atypical paper' (for me), attributing to me when writing it a subtlety of mind which I could never claim, then or now. I thought its purpose was pretty straightforward, that it was an ironic paper designed to answer the question: suppose we grant the neoclassicals everything except their abstraction in early aggregate production function exercises from the existence of vintages; then, will the methods used in the initial work on CES production functions allow unbiased estimates to be made of the values of a key parameter, the elasticity of substitution of capital for labor of the Salter 'best-practice' isoquant? I tried to show by using a series of, I hoped, plausible growth scenarios with vintages, that large and unpredictable biases emerge.

While I was not explicitly conscious of it, I was in fact moving into a post-Keynesian mode of reasoning when at this time I wrote a number of papers on the choice of technique, investment-decision rules and investment-incentive schemes. For in them I contrasted the results obtained from models which came straight from the world as it was, i.e., I used the actual decision-making rules of businesspeople, with those obtained by standard economic theory. Subsequently, Kaldor was to provide a pithy description of this procedure, not least because he was an outstanding pioneer of its design and use, and of the limitations of standard economic theory, in the first chapter of *Economics without Equilibrium* (1985).[11]

IX

I now come to the two single most important events of my political/academic life. The time is the early to mid-1960s. The wider political background of that time for me was a growing realization of the immorality of the war in Vietnam and of Australia's disgraceful role in it as one of the US's few 'respectable' allies, a role adopted in order to secure political positions at home and some ill-defined, long-term insurance policies abroad. The details of the background to the war itself were provided for me by Martin Bernal and Ajit Singh in particular. The Faculty at Cambridge and its visitors were, like most other communities then, torn in two: they were either doves or hawks, especially in the early 1960s. For example, in 1963–64, Ken Arrow was a dove, Bob Solow was still a hawk and many of the Faculty were too. But by the end of 1966, when I left for Australia there had been a marked increase in the number of doves, including Solow, who courageously spoke out for his changed position.

I had been a member of the ALP since 1954, President of my local sub-branch in the late 1950s and early 1960s and also active in penal reform as Secretary of the Howard League for Penal Reform (SA Branch). But I was very much a political animal operating within normal channels. This changed when I came home, scandalized by the war and Australia's role in it, including the immoral conscription by birthday ballots of 18-year-old males. I was soon radicalized by the emerging student and anti-war movements of which I immediately became a part in 1967 – a founding member of the Executive Committee of the Campaign for Peace in Vietnam in South Australia and subsequently, for two spells, its chairman (as it was called in those less 'politically correct' days).

The two most intellectually important influences on me articulating my new position on direct action and involvement were Noam Chomsky's essay 'The Responsibility of Intellectuals' (1967) and Hugh Stretton's *The Political Sciences* (1969); the practical influences were the day-to-day experiences of helping to organize a protest movement. My economic analysis started to change as well; not only was my personality intruding more into my writing, but also, as I no longer accepted that ideology and analysis could be separated, I made the former explicit in my writings and my teaching, especially by the end of the 1960s.

As to direct action itself, I thought it was justified if the cause itself was really fundamental and all other avenues had been tried seriously and found wanting. Of course, 'favored nation treatment' could not be claimed for those taking direct action, especially university professors with tenure, though fairness of treatment by police and courts alike when the law was broken could be. That is to say, all the legal consequences of breaking the law had to be accepted but the person involved did not have to accept being bashed up by police, or false accusations – set-ups – such as happened then, especially in the early days of the anti-war protests when the protesters were a small and much-reviled minority whose views were generally unacceptable to the population at large.

I have described elsewhere (see Sardoni, 1992, pp. 5–6) my experiences of those years and those of Joan and the children, now four (Rebecca, our fourth child, was born – when else? – on 10 May 1968, the day the French riots started), with the attendant death threats, potential and, on one occasion, an actual attempt, and so on. Here I want briefly to describe the events which were to change my academic life.[12]

In August 1968 I heard a mysterious rumor that Mark Perlman, the founding editor, wanted me to do a 'Hahn and Matthews' on capital theory for the newly formed *Journal of Economic Literature*. Sure enough, Perlman arrived in Adelaide to ask me to do just this – evidently, the person he initially commissioned had pulled out and Perlman was left in Australia with a new journal to edit and no author for the survey article of the second issue.

Following a day's 'hard sell,' I said 'yes.' I partially separated from the anti-war movement (with my comrades' blessing), closed a door which was usually open and wrote the first draft in four months. Having to do so wonderfully concentrated the mind, for while I was aware of the issues in a vague, general way, I did not fully understand them, especially the details of the reswitching and capital-reversing debates. Reading the literature more closely, I wrote 'A Child's Guide to the Double-Switching Debate' as the first of five working papers, each on a different aspect and issue, because I found that this was the only way to avoid being overwhelmed by the massive volume of literature to be surveyed. I sent the first paper to about 30 friends ranging from Joan Robinson to Bob Solow and Jim Mirrlees. The favorable feedback emboldened me to keep on and the first draft of the survey was duly sent to Perlman in time for him to have it refereed.

The then economics editor of Cambridge University Press saw the working papers and asked me to write the book of the survey. It would never have been written had I not been invited by Masao Fukuoka to spend three months at Keio University in Tokyo on a Leverhulme Exchange Fellowship. I describe in the Preface (p. ix) of Harcourt (1972) how I lived the selfish life of a scholar and wrote the first draft in two months. There were two main themes: the critique of the conceptual basis of price as an index of scarcity in the theory of value and distribution, and the methodological critique emanating from Joan Robinson of the error of using differences to analyze changes, which became her dominant critique of neoclassical economics. I think she went too far in playing down the first theme – the conceptual basis of an approach *is* a legitimate target for criticism – but was spot on with her insistence on the second critique, one with which Hicks increasingly was to agree and which Kaldor always stressed. His 1984 Raffaele Mattioli Lectures (which were only published in 1996) are replete with examples of analysis which avoids the error, and one of his first papers (1934) already contained the seeds of doubt. Moreover, the best mainstreamers – e.g., Ken Arrow, Franklin Fisher, Frank Hahn – were simultaneously developing path-dependent models.

I wrote a number of commissioned papers on these issues in those years. In one of them, Harcourt (1975, 1982), I began to draw out some policy implications of the capital theory controversies and the post-Keynesian approach more generally. When I returned to Australia in 1973 after a year's leave at Clare Hall in Cambridge, inflation was soon to take off in a major way and the Golden Age of capitalism came to its end. Australia was about to go through an (unintelligent) Thatcherite experiment several years before Thatcher came to power in the UK as the Fraser government from 1975 on cumulatively introduced monetarist policies combined with an ugly confrontationist approach between government, capital and labor. Eric Russell, Barry Hughes, Philip Bentley and I, in support of Ralph Willis, who subsequently became Treasurer in the Keating ALP government, but who was then a lone voice crying in the ALP wilderness, started to develop a package deal for ridding the system (slowly) of inflation while trying to maintain high levels of employment and external balance. This appealed to my continuing interest in policy constrained by *Realpolitik*. With Australia's history and tradition of centralized wage fixing through the Arbitration Commission (sadly – and unwisely – now abandoned),[13] this involved arguing for, amongst other things, indexation combined with restraint on the rate of increase of money wages. My thinking at the time is most fully to be found in the 1982 John Curtin Memorial Lecture, 'Making Socialism in Your Own Country.'

In essence, it involved redistribution through the public sector as the *quid pro quo* to wage-earning groups for accepting incomes policies directed at limiting the rate of increase of money incomes, using the traditional Australian institutions of indexation and the Arbitration Commission. Fiscal and monetary measures were to be directed towards the level of activity, the rate of growth and the post-tax distribution of income. Nationalization of certain key industries including financial intermediaries was put back on the agenda for discussion and I sat on the fence concerning the tariff, i.e. leave it much as it is and concentrate on export promotion. (The act in my professional life I most regret in retrospect is that I publicly supported, as did most other Australian economists at the time (no excuse, of course), the cut in tariffs by the Whitlam ALP government in the early 1970s. Both the economic reasoning and the timing were-wrong.) I opted for a fixed exchange rate, with the proviso that in an economy like Australia's, a change might have to be contemplated from time to time.

X

The final major trauma in my life (to date, and apart from four brushes with death between September 1992 and September 1994) occurred when I was near 50. I – we, for it was a joint family decision, an extraordinarily selfless one by Joan, the children, my father and Joan's parents, I hope a not too selfish one by me – decided to return to Cambridge to try to document the approach and contributions of Joan Robinson and her circle, to see if there was a coherence in their version of the Cambridge tradition, something worthwhile to try to preserve by telling its and their intellectual histories. I would not have done this had I not believed, passionately, that there was. I still do; if anything, even more so. Of course, I had other reasons as well, that I was too old to play Australian Rules Football (I retired when I was 47), that the cricket club was making me play on matting and I wanted to get back on turf. Life cannot be real and earnest all the time, or, at least, our reaction to it should not be. I am not by nature an overly solemn person and I believe it is tactically sensible (even wise) often to speak true words in the form of jests.

If ever the unfolding of events served to reinforce the need for what I have been trying to do, it is the happenings of the last 20–25 years or so. A great irony of our times is that Marx and Keynes would have had no trouble in explaining their characteristics in terms of their approaches and their theories (suitably modified and updated, of course) – the shift in the balance of economic, social and political power from labor to capital, the emergence of sustained mass unemployment in many advanced economies, the destruction of capacity so that Marxian unemployment has now been added to deliberately induced Keynesian unemployment, the shameful growth of inequality in income and wealth, the smashing of labor unions and the social protection of wage-earners generally in order to create cowed and quiescent workforces, the re-emergence of homelessness and poverty, and, most fundamental as the main cause of instability, the dominance of industrial and commercial capital by domestic and global finance capital. In stark contrast, the mainstream now uses a Fisherian, sometimes even a normative Ramsey representative agent model of lifetime utility maximization (with all other major real-world institutions and players in society acting merely as *its* agents) to discuss these same characteristics and events: with the result that the concerned young are leaving economics in droves for the more relevant and satisfying social sciences, or even prefer to be hired prize fighters, by choosing to do business studies and to go to business schools instead of economics departments 'proper.'[14]

Even so, I still find it disquieting that so little interest has been shown in mainstream classrooms in the concepts of 'capital' and 'profit,' not only when the capital theory controversies were raging alongside the anti-war movements and student revolts generally but also now, when the events I described above dominate our everyday experience.

As to my major project, sadly, virtually all the major figures have now died, starting with Joan Robinson and Piero Sraffa in 1983, ending – to date – with Austin Robinson in June 1993 and James Meade in December 1995. As I nearly joined them myself, I am rather lagging in getting it altogether in book form. But there are now well over 30 separate essays which provide the essential background to the project and so I do not entirely despair of getting it finished before I call it a day. When I retire in September 1998, I shall be able to spend more time in King's Modern Archives where most of the papers of these economists are housed. While I shall draw mostly on what is in the public domain – I am not a fan of the modern 'tell it all' biography – I do think it necessary to provide evidence on what was going on behind the scenes when their articles and books were being written.

XI

I must confess to having been side-tracked on occasions and in different directions. Since 1992 I have returned to policy on a large canvas, following the invitation to give the Second Donald Horne Address in Melbourne in February 1992, on 'Markets, Madness and a Middle Way.' It spawned further papers, one on macroeconomic policy for Australia in the 1990s (1993, 1995), another on 'A "Modest Proposal" for Taming the Speculators and Putting the World on Course to Prosperity' (1994, 1995). In 1997 I published a paper on economic policy, accumulation and productivity and gave the Seventh Colin Clark Memorial Lecture on 'Economic Theory and Economic Policy: Two Views' (Harcourt, 1997b).

The other major 'side-track' was collaborating with Peter Riach on *A 'Second Edition' of The General Theory*. Peter had a bright idea based on the well-known fact that composers have often died before they could finish certain works which others then took up and completed. Keynes had thought of writing at least 'footnotes' to *The General Theory* soon after it was published, but his severe heart attack in 1937 and then World War II and his death in early 1946 prevented him from doing so. Peter's project, which he asked me to join, was to ask a number of Keynes scholars, ranging from Golden Oldies to the up-and-coming, each to write an essay of 6000 words or so on, first, what they thought, based on whatever evidence there was in the *Collected Writings* and other sources, Keynes might have written and, second, why and what they have done on particular aspects of *The General Theory* in the postwar years. It is a most opportune time to have done this, for Keynes is surely rising again from the grave. The book was published in two volumes by Routledge in January 1997, just over 60 years on from the publication of *The General Theory*. (Some of the contributors write, in the first sections of their essays, 'as J.M. Keynes.') The second volume contains an overview (by James Tobin), essays on extensions and new developments since *The General Theory* was first published, and essays on predecessors and successors. Riach and I wrote a long introduction setting the chapters in context and, between us and the contributors, we accumulated a 50-page bibliography.

XII

I mentioned above my continuing interest in policy questions. Increasingly, as a result principally of the influence of Richard Goodwin, Kaldor, Kalecki and Joan Robinson on my thinking, I have come to realize that the efficacy of single and package deal policy proposals depends vitally on whether individual markets and systems as a whole are best characterized as equilibrating mechanisms, at least as long-term tendencies, or as cumulative causation processes. As I also think that the latter underlie the operations of most major markets and systems, the policy recommendations that I have made explicitly reflect this link. These considerations have especially affected what I have proposed for dealing with the harmful systemic effects of speculation in the markets for foreign exchange, financial assets and property. The same realization also lies behind my arguments over the years (I first learnt of these from Eric Russell) for tailor-made, permanent incomes policies based on the adjustment of nominal incomes for effective productivity (at least as the starting point). Finally, following the arguments of Keynes and Kalecki in particular, and, more recently, Paul Davidson, I have argued for the recreation of institutions which, while modified for new economic conditions and a changed political environment, nevertheless have the same ultimate rationale as those which came out of Bretton Woods: to wit, to offset the inbuilt contractionary forces in the operation of the world economy. There is also a need for a re-examination of buffer stock schemes for internationally traded primary products, both to protect the real incomes of their producers in the developing countries and to eliminate the potential in the unstable prices of these products for setting off chains of inflation (or deflation) in substantial areas of the world economy as a whole.

XIII

I want to conclude by highlighting three fundamental things. First, though I have only mentioned my students in passing, I want to stress that I regard teaching undergraduates and supervising research students as the most responsible and rewarding tasks university teachers are privileged to have. The achievements and the friendships of students, past and present, are amongst the greatest pleasures and satisfactions of this life.

Second, it may fairly be asked: are my Christian democratic socialist flames still burning as brightly now as when first lit in the early 1950s? The answer is 'yes.' While the going was tough in the 1970s and late 1980s, recent events, e.g., the publication of *Reclaiming the Ground* (Bryant, 1993), the election of, first, John Smith and then Tony Blair as leader of the British Labour Party, the accompanying return to basics (in a non-Majorite manner) cheered me up no end, as have the elections (and re-elections) in Australia of ALP governments in the 1980s and early 1990s, for all their faults and limitations. (Most annoyingly, just as the UK returned a Labour government (1 May 1997), Australia was in its second year of an extremely unpleasant, narrow, ruthless, little-minded conservative government, laughingly called a coalition of the Liberal and National Parties.) Moreover, I am experiencing a sense of *déjà vu* as the Blair Labour government (January 1998) seems to be making many of the mistakes that the Whitlam, Hawke and Keating Labor governments did – do they *never* learn?[15] Of course, the agendas have changed; the proposals are now more modest, more basic – jobs, homes, schools, hospitals, trains, the environment(!) – than in those heady days immediately after World War II. But they still make up a worthwhile agenda for the creation of just and equitable societies, for middle ways which are tailor-made for each country's history, sociological structure and inherited institutions. And they ought to be supported as more and more citizens recoil from the excesses and horrors of both command and market, free-for-all, economies.[16] I hope to play some role in securing these aims.

In a comment on a draft of the essay, Giles Slinger noted that only one of the six aspects of economics cited on pp. 255–7 above – policy proposals – seemed 'to be clearly connected to my religious beliefs.' He asked whether my beliefs had altered '*the way* [I would] have done economics otherwise?' I think the answer is 'no' though I am sure my beliefs affected what I found most vital in economics itself and how I approached our subject. Omar Hamouda once asked me to record what I thought the purpose of political economy is. Perhaps my answer then (Harcourt, 1986) may help to answer Giles[17] now. Evidently I said that the purpose is: to make the world a better place for ordinary men and women, to produce a more just and equitable society. In order to do that, you have to understand how particular societies work and where the pockets of power are, and how you can either alter those or work within them and produce desirable results for ordinary people, not just for the people who have the power. I see economics as very much a moral as well as a social science and very much a handmaiden to progressive thought. It is really the study of the processes whereby surpluses are created in economies, how they are extracted, who gets them and what they do with them. All economies have created surpluses in one way or another. Capitalism does it in a particular way and that is the process in which I am most interested because I live in capitalist economies. At the same time, I would like to help to create a society where the surplus is extracted and used in a way quite different from that of a capitalist society.

Third, and most fundamentally, I have been blessed with an exceptionally happy marriage and family life. So I end this account of my life philosophy by expressing my thanks to Joan, to our four children, Wendy, Robert, Tim and Rebecca, to Claudio and Jo and to our *numero uno* grandchild, Caterina, for their unstinting love and support.

NOTES

1. Israel Harkowitz. In the 1920s, my father and his brother, Sam, changed the family name to Harcourt, a fine old Norman name, as I tell everyone!
2. Because we also read Graaf and Little, I was soon disillusioned with welfare economics.
3. I had been overshadowed by the brilliance of my twin at our schools. Moreover, as was

common in those days, we 'jumped' classes, so that we were soon over a year younger than the average age in our class, a handicap for me intellectually and for both of us socially, especially when you consider the extra baggage we had to carry anyway.

4. So I am rather proud of having written, with Prue, the entry on Marx in Malcolm Warner's Encyclopaedia for managers – all managers need and want to know of Karl; see Harcourt and Kerr (1996)!
5. In a wonderfully perceptive comment, Hugh Stretton (7 March 1998) describes his '"agnostic" working hypothesis [as] a humanism [related to] something in our human nature – much influenced but not created by our upbringing – [which] allows us to figure out our individual versions of *both* the Theory of Moral Sentiments *and* the Wealth of Nations, and the better and worse relations that we may conduct between them' (emphasis in original).
6. Now that the Methodists have ceased to exist in Australia (they have been absorbed into the Uniting Church), it is only in the UK that I may refer to myself as a Jewish Methodist Democratic Christian Socialist; it is always good for a laugh.
7. The prelude to the most fundamental event of my life had also occurred – on the day John and I graduated (he in dentistry), Joan Bartrop (who graduated on the same day in Arts) and I announced our engagement. We had met in our respective final years (1953) at the University of Melbourne, we had an idyllic courtship, and in December 1953 I proposed in the kitchen of her aunt and uncle's house while we were baby-sitting their two children. The proposal was accepted in early 1954. We married in July 1955, just before leaving for Cambridge where I was to do a PhD at King's.
8. After the paper which Dore and I wrote was published in *Economic Letters* in 1986, I received a letter from a Norwegian economist. He said that up till then he had admired my economics and my mathematics. He then pointed out in great detail the awful hash I had made of both in the paper. Since Dore had done the math (they were beyond me; I had merely conjectured the economic approach we might take and Dore most kindly made me a joint author), I asked Bob Rowthorn to adjudicate. He said we were all wrong!
9. I have just finished (January 1998) reviewing Bob Solow's Arrow Lectures on learning from learning by doing and examining a dissertation on evolutionary economics and the role of technical progress in evolutionary processes. In the policy papers which I wrote in 1996 and 1997 I coupled the insights of Salter and Kalecki in a discussion of attaining and then sustaining full employment without inflation. In all these pursuits. Salter's influence remains as fresh and as illuminating as when I first wrote about *Productivity and Technical Change*.
10. These appointments were completely unexpected – I no more thought of having a post at Cambridge, then probably the outstanding center for economics in the world, than of flying to the moon (indeed the latter was more on the cards at the time). Because I was on leave from Adelaide when I was offered the posts, I decided to take them for three years only, on unpaid leave from Adelaide, because I felt I had a moral responsibility to return there.
11. *Economics without Equilibrium* arose from the first Okun Memorial Lectures at Yale. Okun was a person very much after Kaldor's heart (mine, too), both because of his methods and his rationale for doing economics.
12. Perhaps I could add that in the anti-war activities, I tried to follow the practices of a liberal academic and a Christian. That is to say, I tried to present arguments and critiques fully and fairly rather than as one-sided advocacy, and I tried to remember the essential humanity of those to whom I was opposed, no matter how angry and distressed I was about what they were doing and supporting.
13. Tim Harcourt reminded me that the Industrial Relations Commission (formerly the Arbitration Commission) is still the institution whereby an annual safety net for low-paid wage-earners who cannot bargain collectively is maintained.
14. I was delighted to find that Paul Samuelson (1997, p. 6) in his ninth decade is so far off the mainstream regression line as to describe the American economy now as having two outstanding characteristics: it is 'a ruthless economy' with a 'cowed workforce.' Karl, that you should have lived to see this day!
15. Tim Harcourt thinks I have been too hard on the Hawke and Keating ALP governments. He reminded me that on social issues, they had a creditable record as they did with regard to employment for much of the 1980s. It was their uncertain handling of powerful business and

media moguls (always a fiendishly difficult task for Labor politicians and governments), together with the over-enjoyment of the trappings of power (this was especially true of some members of the Whitlam government) that I had in mind.

16. In a wonderfully supportive and wise letter (17 March 1998), Hugh Stretton cited Christopher Hills's *The Experience of Defeat*, 'about the retrospective reflections of the English revolutionary leaders who survived the Restoration.' He asked me 'to recall that the whole of the Leveller program was in force within a couple of centuries … ,' so that, today, we may hope that even a 'cumulative causation on the Right track' may come to an end, be reversed.
17. Giles also wanted me to be more explicit about when, where and why I had done various things, written certain articles and books. May I refer him (and others) to a companion piece to the present essay, my chapter in Volume IV of Arnold Heertje's series. *The Makers of Modern Economics* (Harcourt, 1998)?

REFERENCES

Arestis, Philip, Gabriel Palma and Malcolm Sawyer (eds) (1997a), *Capital Controversy, Post-Keynesian Economics and the History of Economics. Essays in Honour of Geoff Harcourt. Volume One*, London: Routledge.

Arestis, Philip, Gabriel Palma and Malcolm Sawyer (eds) (1997b), *Markets, Unemployment and Economic Policy. Essays in Honour of Geoff Harcourt. Volume Two*, London: Routledge.

Battin, Tim (1996), *Abandoning Keynes. Australia's Capital Mistake*, Basingstoke: Macmillan.

Brennan, H. Geoffrey and A.M.C. Waterman (eds) (1994), *Economics and Religion: Are They Distinct?*, Boston, Dordrecht and London: Kluwer Academic Publishers.

Bryant, Christopher (ed.) (1993), *Reclaiming the Ground: Christianity and Socialism*, London: Hodder and Stoughton.

Chomsky, N. (1967), 'The Responsibility of Intellectuals,' in T. Roszak (ed.), *The Dissenting Academy*, New York: Pantheon Books, 1967, 254–98.

Dore M.H.I. and G.C. Harcourt (1986), 'A Note on the Taxation of Exhaustible Resources under Oligopoly,' *Economic Letters*, **21**, 81–4.

Harcourt, G.C. (1960), 'The Early Verdict,' *Nation*, 3 December, reprinted in K.S. Inglis (ed.) (1989), *Nation. The Life of an Independent Journal of Opinion 1958–1972*, Melbourne: Melbourne University Press, 45–6.

Harcourt, G.C. (1963), 'A Critique of Mr Kaldor's Model of Income Distribution and Economic Growth,' *Australian Economic Papers*, **2**, 20–36.

Harcourt, G.C. (1964), 'Review of Minhas (1963),' *Economic Journal*, **74**, 443–5.

Harcourt, G.C. (1965a), 'The Accountant in a Golden Age,' *Oxford Economic Papers* (n.s.), **17**,66–80.

Harcourt, G.C. (1965b), 'A Two-Sector Model of the Distribution of Income and the Level of Employment in the Short Run,' *Economic Record*, **41**, 103–17.

Harcourt, G.C. (1966), 'Biases in Empirical Estimates of the Elasticities of Substitution of C.E.S. Production Functions,' *Review of Economic Studies*, **33**, 227–33.

Harcourt, G.C. (1969), 'Some Cambridge Controversies in the Theory of Capital,' *Journal of Economic Literature*, **7**, 369–405.

Harcourt, G.C. (1972), *Some Cambridge Controversies in the Theory of Capital*, Cambridge: Cambridge University Press.

Harcourt, G.C. (1975), *Theoretical Controversy and Social Significance: An*

Evaluation of the Cambridge Controversies, Edward Shann Memorial Lecture, University of Western Australia Press.

Harcourt, G.C. (1977a), 'Eric Russell, 1921–77: A Memoir,' *Economic Record*, **53**, 467–74.

Harcourt, G.C. (1977b), 'Eric Russell, 1921–77: A Great Australian Political Economist,' the 1977 Newcastle Lecture in Political Economy. Reprinted in Sardoni (1992), 344–56.

Harcourt. G.C. (1982), *The Social Science Imperialists. Selected Essays. G.C. Harcourt*, Prue Kerr (ed.), London: Routledge and Kegan Paul.

Harcourt, G.C. (1986), *Controversies in Political Economy. Selected Essays of G.C. Harcourt*, O.F. Hamouda (ed.), Brighton: Wheatsheaf Books.

Harcourt, G.C. (1992), 'Markets, Madness and a Middle Way,' *The Second Annual Donald Horne Address*, Melbourne: Monash University, also published in *Australian Quarterly*, **64**, 1–17.

Harcourt, G.C. (1993), 'Macroeconomic Policy for Australia in the 1990s,' *The Economic and Labour Relations Review*, **4**, 167–75.

Harcourt, G.C. (1994), 'Taming Speculators and Putting the World on Course to Prosperity: a "Modest Proposal,"' *Economic and Political Weekly*, **29**, 2490–92.

Harcourt, G.C. (1995), *Capitalism, Socialism and Post-Keynesianism. Selected Essays of G.C. Harcourt*, Cheltenham: Edward Elgar.

Harcourt, G.C. (1997a), 'Economic Policy, Accumulation and Productivity,' in Michie and Grieve Smith (1997), 194–204.

Harcourt, G.C. (1997b), 'Economic Theory and Economic Policy: Two Views' (The Seventh Colin Clark Memorial Lecture 1997), *Economic Analysis and Policy*, **27**, 113–30.

Harcourt, G.C. (1998), '"Horses for Courses." The Making of a Post-Keynesian Economist,' in Arnold Heertje (ed.), *The Makers of Modern Economics*, Vol. IV, Cheltenham: Edward Elgar.

Harcourt, G.C. and P. Kerry (1996), 'Marx Karl Heinrich (1818–83),' in Warner (1996), 3388–95.

Harcourt, G.C. and P.A. Riach (eds) (1997), *A 'Second Edition' of The General Theory*, 2 vols, London: Routledge.

Kaldor, N. (1985), *Economics without Equilibrium*, Armonk, NY: M.E. Sharpe.

Kaldor, N. (1996), *Causes of Growth and Stagnation in the World Economy*, Cambridge: Cambridge University Press.

Michie, Jonathan and John Grieve Smith (eds) (1997), *Employment and Economic Performance. Jobs, Inflation and Growth*, Oxford: Oxford University Press.

Minhas, B.S. (1963), *An International Comparison of Factor Costs and Factor Use*, Amsterdam: North-Holland.

Robinson, Joan (1956), *The Accumulation of Capital*, London: Macmillan.

Rothschild, K.W. (1947), 'Price Theory and Oligopoly,' *Economic Journal*, **57**, 299–320.

Salter, W.E.G. (1960), *Productivity and Technical Change*, Cambridge: Cambridge University Press, 2nd edn, 1966.

Samuelson, Paul A. (1997), 'Wherein do the European and American Models Differ?' Address delivered at the Bank of Italy, 2 October .

Sardoni, Claudio (ed.) (1992), *On Political Economists and Modern Political Economy. Selected Essays of G.C. Harcourt*, London: Routledge.

Solow, Robert M. (1997), 'Thoughts inspired by reading an Atypical Paper by Harcourt,' in Arestis et al. (1997a), 419–24.

Sraffa, Piero (1926), 'The Laws of Returns under Competitive Conditions,' *Economic Journal*, **36**, 535–50.
Sraffa, Piero (1960), *Production of Commodities by Means of Commodities. Prelude to a Critique of Economic Theory*, Cambridge: Cambridge University Press.
Steedman, Ian (1994), 'Wicksteed: Economist and Prophet,' in Brennan and Waterman (1994), 77–101.
Stretton, Hugh (1969), *The Political Sciences. General Principles of Selection in Social Science and History*, London: Routledge.
Tressell, Robert (1914, 1962), *The Ragged Trousered Philanthropists*, New York: Monthly Review Press.
Warner, Malcolm (ed.) (1996), *International Encyclopedia of Business and Management*, London: Routledge.

16. Some ethical and methodological convictions*

E. Malinvaud

The essays published here are sorts of autobiographies by academic economists about their scientific motivations and their professional life. This will also be the case in my contribution. I shall make an honest attempt at taking a philosophical stance and considering economics from the two standpoints of ethics and methodology, the only realms of philosophy about which I have definite ideas on how to apply them in my field. I shall try to avoid as much as possible repetitions of details, reported in what I wrote not so long ago about my main contributions to our discipline for a series of 'recollections on professional experience' (Malinvaud, 1987). This essay is not the place for lengthy arguments for my ethical or methodological positions, which a philosopher would find neither original nor deeply rooted in anything other than the environments in which I was born, grew up, and worked. Thinking that these environments may be unfamiliar to readers, I shall briefly characterize them when necessary.

INITIAL MOTIVATIONS

At the age of 13, I was taking the regular curriculum, along with Latin and Greek, at the 'lycée de Limoges,' the public high school of Limoges, a provincial, somewhat industrial town in a mostly rural area. A good deal of my spare time was spent as a Christian boy scout, sharing the enthusiasm about the movement that was frequent in those years. My family was loving and secure. My father was a lawyer with socialist ideas, who married late because of the premature death of his own father, the ensuing lack of resources during his beginnings as an independent attorney, and World War I. Limoges was well known in labor movements because it was the place where was instituted the very active union CGT whose leaders later had joined the Communist Party. The local industry had been hit badly by the Great

*This chapter first appeared in *The American Economist*, **45**(1), Spring 2001, 3–16.

Depression. I could directly see strikes as well as hardship resulting from unemployment. My curriculum and teachers totally ignored the social sciences. Social phenomena appeared only occasionally and indirectly in our courses involving French, Latin and Greek literature, or history.

During those years as a teenager, I became conscious of a main ethical principle which was underlying the visions and projects I formed about my future: since I was so fortunate, I had to accomplish something which would be useful to those less fortunate. I was certainly eager to know and to understand, but before anything else I had to serve.

When I reached the age of 21 in 1944, I was living at 'Ecole Polytechnique,' learning mathematics and its application in the physical world. I had already decided to somehow specialize in the study of economics. How did this come about? Graduating from high school in 1940, I had chosen to enter the special classes to prepare for the competitive examinations selecting students admitted to the scientific 'Grandes Ecoles.' This was a choice of reason rather than inclination. I felt I was performing better in sciences than in letters or philosophy. But I had kept open the option of becoming a lawyer. I had registered as a student in law, which I could do without attending classes, simply by taking the summer exams in whatever year I would feel ready after independent study of the manuals. The curriculum of each of the three years leading to the BA degree included economics. The manuals in economics were descriptive rather than analytical, but immediately attracted my interest, as they dealt with phenomena that I knew were important in people's lives.

In addition to Limoges industrial workers, many small poor farmers were still populating the countryside, and refugees had flown from Alsace in 1939 after forced evacuation of their villages neighboring the German border, as decided by the French military authority. In subsequent years, the disorganization of the economy in occupied France, food shortages and the like added to my direct experience underscoring the importance of the economy. Those were also years during which I had to organize my own thoughts concerning more general social and political issues. Information about what had been happening under the totalitarian regimes of Germany and the USSR was very far from complete for a young man (not to speak of current news, which was censored). But discrimination against Jews could be seen everywhere nearby, and we knew progressively more and more about the reality of mass deportation. I am glad I had at this time an experience of a different kind, namely being sent as a manual worker to a huge forest for a year. This is where I confirmed the idea that all human beings are very similar, reacted most often in the same way, and shared many common moral values. I could even realize that, contrary to what I had often heard and would later often hear, individual liberty has as much value for the poor as for the rich; my fellow workers coming from poor families praised it as much as I did.

There was more to my attraction to the study of economics. Not only were economic conditions important, but I also felt intuitively that they could be improved by intelligent management, and moreover, that I could contribute to this improvement. The fact that I held onto those intuitions during my first years studying economics is still a bit of a mystery to me; it probably reflects how stubborn I can be. In law, I limited my reading to what was required of students, but this was not the case in economics. I went from one manual to another, then to books that were quoted, without the direction of any teacher or even advice from anyone. I was a pure autodidact, discovering almost haphazardly what was available in French in the early 1940s. It is hard for me to be precise about what I really learned then. Certainly the basic concepts, the main historical facts, a sense of what writers were up to, and probably a good knowledge of partial equilibrium theory, several other bits of theory and, more importantly, an understanding of the respective roles of observation and reflection in economics. I remember I was particularly interested in books where some data were discussed and that I found too few of them.

To give a proper account of my initial motivations and the way in which they marked my career, I must report other steps, involving experiences and personal choices during my twenties. I shall try to be brief, however, dividing the period in three sections: 1944–46, 1947–49 and 1950–53.

After the landings in Normandy and on the Mediterranean coast in the spring of 1944, German troops withdrew from most of France and we had a new government headed by de Gaulle. I was sent on army training for a year, part of which took place in Germany, but with no direct participation in fighting. The following year was devoted to completing my studies at Ecole Polytechnique. I kept passing law exams and reading economics, basically in the same way as I had done during the preceding years.

Admission to the Ecole Polytechnique meant that my studies and subsistence were publicly financed, and that I would subsequently be assigned to civil service. When school ended, I had the choice of the 'grand corps' in which to serve, at a high level of competence, after two more years of specialized studies. My main concern was then to select where I could be guaranteed later work as an economist. I was led into accepting the idea that the newly created INSEE (Institut National de la Statistique et des Etudes Economiques) was *de facto* offering this guarantee. INSEE was the French central statistical office, and it had an important branch devoted to the study of economic conditions and prospects. I had no reason to later regret this choice I made in 1946, all the more so as I soon discovered that working at creating or improving social and economic statistics was quite an interesting job.

An important part of the curriculum at the INSEE school was mathematical statistics, which would later be useful for following the progress of econometric methodology. More crucial in my case was the section on economics because it gave me what I was lacking, namely a structure for the organization of knowledge. By that time it had already become clear to me that I needed to read English, which I had not learned earlier. I then made the required effort to be at least able to use the scientific literature published in English.

The most significant event during these two years was meeting Maurice Allais, who became one of my teachers in the fall of 1947. Allais had recently completed his two major books in economic theory (Allais, 1943 and 1947), working alone far ahead of anyone in France. He was eager to promote his inspirations, formalizations and results, as well as to confront them with those contained in books available in English such as Hicks (1939) or Samuelson (1948). His grand general equilibrium approach immediately impressed me as giving order and perspective to what I had earlier learned.

In the fall of 1948, I was assigned to the INSEE unit in charge of setting up household budget surveys and consumer price indices. Simultaneously, I joined an informal group of young economists who were meeting around Allais at lunchtime (which could then mean a long break in the French working day) or in the late evening. The group included Marcel Boiteux, Gérard Debreu, and others gifted with enthusiasm and imagination. At the age of 25, it was the first time I had been placed in a true research environment. My first three publications appeared in 1950. Two of them came from contributions I had made at Allais's informal seminar; one discussed price elasticities in international trade, and the other was a survey of the then raging dispute among English economists about the value of socialism and the feasibility of planning. The third publication came out of my work as an official statistician and concerned how best to define a price index for fresh fruit and vegetables, which in those days were an important part of household budgets and the prices of which were subject to wide seasonal fluctuations. I owe to Allais an introduction to the Rockefeller Foundation, which granted me a fellowship to study at the University of Chicago in 1950–51. I also owe to INSEE a simultaneous one-year leave.

This took place at the Cowles Commission for Research in Economics, which was an ideal environment for a young mathematical economist and statistician. The main work on the econometrics of simultaneous equations had recently been completed, but extensions, applications, or better presentations were still explored. Research on activity analysis and general equilibrium theory was in its most active phase. I worked on how to connect it to capital theory, on which I had already touched, advised by Allais. My main debts at the Cowles Commission are first to Tjalling Koopmans, but also to others, particularly to Jacob Marschak and to my French friend Gérard Debreu, who had moved from Paris.

This experience in the Cowles Commission was opening academic opportunities for me, which were made more or less explicit in subsequent years. It may be wondered why I was not really tempted to seize these opportunities. There are two reasons. First, they were not in France. Having chosen the channel of Ecole Polytechnique and taken my law degree, I was not in the competition. Also, the large majority of influential French professors in economics kept expressing objections to the idea that mathematical economics could make any valuable contribution to their discipline. But I had chosen to serve among my people. Only a political regime hostile to personal liberties would have forced me to emigrate from France (until the end of the Algerian war in 1962 I did not consider the risk as negligible). Second, I was reluctant to gamble that, if devoted mainly to research, my life would really be useful. I had a very clear vision of what I could contribute with my participation in INSEE and more generally in the French public administration. Notwithstanding the enthusiasm I had witnessed with Allais and at the Cowles Commission, I feared that the prospect of a socially fruitful career in research could turn out to have been a mirage.

As is well known, in the immediate postwar years many French intellectuals were attracted to the Communist Party. This was indeed the case of quite a few of my best colleagues and friends. I was protected from the contagion because I had no guilty feelings that would have come from being born into a bourgeois family. I had a sense of duty, yes, but of guilt no, because of the exemplary life led by my father and mother. But I know so many for whom adherence to a left-wing party was a form of purification. I was also protected by good judgement. I did not discard as false the testimonies about the reality of liberty in the Soviet Union; moreover, I knew how people with the best ethical principles could forego them when talked into believing that the supposedly superior interest of the party so required. I had seen that, of course, on a quite minor scale, within the boy scout movement, which I did not quit, however.

APPEAL OF ECONOMICS AS A NORMATIVE SCIENCE

In my environment during the 1950s and 1960s, economics was viewed mainly as a normative science, to be used for public policies and public management. My older equivalents, who had entered professional activity before the war, had developed an acute sense of the need to conduct economic affairs more rationally.

This was the case of engineers serving in public utilities or in the ministries controlling transport, mining, and the like. Allais was one of them. Others, actually more influential on the French scene, were promoting the use of economic principles in the pricing of public services and in the choice of investment projects. Some of them had a good perception of the need for more appropriate foundations of the criteria to be used then. Pierre Massé had imagined the technique of dynamic programming for such a purpose. Marcel Boiteux was recruited by Electricité de France to restructure the tariff. And so on.

A similar concern existed among authorities of the Ministry of Economy and Finance, to which INSEE was attached. Reforms of the fiscal system were discussed, with economic considerations being given great weight. The value added tax was invented in this spirit, so as to make taxes on goods and services neutral with respect to the allocation of resources. Receptive to new trends in economic thinking, particularly to the Keynesian approach, those in charge of monetary and budgetary policies were taking steps in order to develop national accounts and other macroeconomic tools, on which I personally worked.

This activity was only gradually reflected in French academia. Various reasons underlay the resistance, including prejudice against mathematical economics practiced by engineers and modelers, nationalistic feelings against acceptance of 'Anglo-Saxon theories,' and ideological opposition to capitalism and to the mixed market economy context in which the development was taking place. Personally, I did not pay attention to these various attitudes, except when I had to teach bright young students at the INSEE school, who were sensitive to surrounding ideologies and had received little basic training in economics.

In contrast, I felt at home in the European meetings and workshops where I was regularly finding Ragnar Frisch, Jan Tinbergen, Richard Stone, and others with similar backgrounds. Although technical issues were being discussed, most of us agreed on the ultimate aim of our work, namely to improve economic management in our democratic societies. Thinking in terms of economic planning was viewed at the time as appropriate.

I believe that a good history of this postwar European planning movement is not available now and should be constructed. Certainly the movement did not gain unanimous support. Allais, for one, stood as an opponent among quite a few others. But we had a good framework for the simultaneous analysis of public policies and public participation in the economy. It helped in a close study of rational public action in the macroeconomic and microeconomic domains.

The fact is, however, that we tended to underestimate the difficulties of the tasks within this framework. Of course we were well aware of market failures. We even knew that most of the reasons explaining market failures make proper public management difficult. But we remained too optimistic. We insisted on the information needed by public agents in order for them to improve efficiency and equity. But we did not pay sufficient attention to the generation of appropriate private incentives. If the now existing microeconomic theory of incentives under asymmetric information had been available at the time, we would probably have often been more circumspect. In any case, increased complexity and international globalization of our economies were making some features of our conceptual framework progressively less adequate. Indeed, we realized this in the late 1960s, so that more and more among us gave up the hope of actually applying planning procedures for which we had elaborated blueprints.

This does not mean that I am now fully satisfied with the turn taken by economic teaching on the issues that were then concerning us. Neither am I satisfied with what I see around about the actual management of infrastructures, collective services and the environment. I have no objection to the phrase 'government failures,' which is now common. I have experienced quite a few such failures, but the proper diagnosis of them was most often different from what is being taught. When a so-called 'public choice theory' is arguing as if public decision makers and their staff were moved only by self-interest, this may be building a theory of corruption, but not much more. Actually the main government failures in our countries are due either to mistakes in knowledge and judgment or to failures of the political democratic process.

The point deserving some attention in this essay is that there is an ethic of public service, which is widely shared and breaches of which are widely disapproved. This ethic leads many to resist the temptation to follow what the pursuit of selfish interest would imply. Ignoring or, worse, disparaging this ethic when teaching to students is misleading them and is not healthy for the future of democracies. I know that we economists have to study economic incentives, because private business has to achieve economic results and because it would be dangerous to expose citizens and civil servants to situations in which economic incentives were too strong and too often conflict with ethical incentives. But when teaching courses on the economics of incentives, we ought to explain what is really at stake, without unduly propagating a vision of human beings and of a world where economic incentives would exclusively dominate.

Success of the drive towards instilling more rational conduct of economic affairs in France, and in Europe more generally, reached a climax in the late 1960s. This is true not only of the macroeconomic stabilization branch of public economics but also of the allocation branch concerned with infrastructures, collective services and the environment, the branch on which I am now focusing. I must recognize that excessive dogmatism had prevailed in the diffusion of methods to be applied in project evaluations, pricing of services or identification of externalities. Valid criticism of this dogmatism was raised. Unfortunately it considerably weakened the drive and the enthusiasm of those who were still involved. Progressively the quality of the staff declined. Starting in the mid-1980s, privatization of the large public enterprises was undertaken. There were very good reasons for this, including mismanagement of some of these enterprises, often after recent political appointments of managers or as a result of a prolonged personnel policy that was too facile, international competition in industries in which public enterprises were handicapped, the competition policy of the European Union, and globalization of markets. This naturally led to shift the focus of attention from the proper management of public firms to the regulation of natural monopolies and public utilities. Overall, the menu of the main issues to be tackled was completely changed.

It is probably too early to judge whether it was for the better. However, I venture to say that, in my environment and at the present stage of reconsideration of what public economics ought to recommend in its allocation branch, there seems to be a good deal of confusion. In my view, the old practical rules for cost–benefit analysis and its implications in pricing and in the choice of projects have been downgraded. Ample room is now left to operators for anything that can improve their market shares, for instance as between alternative means of transportation. Tariffs are uncertain, because they are so frequently revised. The weight of political considerations increases again, to the detriment of economic rationality.

I must not end this section without turning to a different subject and saying how I interpret the scope and problems of the theory of welfare economics. I am not referring here to the main body of this theory, which concerns the correspondence between a Pareto-efficient allocation of resources and the general equilibrium of prices and quantities in a market economy. Rather, I am referring to the question of knowing how to extend this theory so as to make it relevant to comparative assessments between actual or hypothetical situations differing by levels of living, rates of unemployment, economic inequalities and, indeed, other social inequalities, personal liberties and so on. I am referring also to calculations of 'the welfare cost' of alternative tax or regulatory systems, this being given in a monetary equivalent. Let me simply say that I feel uneasy about such extensions, and let me clarify, if possible, the background of this uneasiness.

At the most philosophical level, I was convinced since my youth that 'l'argent ne fait pas le bonheur' (money does not make happiness). I had so many opportunities to see the truth of this old dictum, both for individuals and for societies. In somewhat more academic terms it means that there are values which are, almost incommensurately, more valuable than economic affluence. For instance, take France in 1965 and France in 1995. Real per capita GDP doubled in between, but some features other than the volumes of production and consumption worsened, in particular for the most important age group in any society (15–25-year-old) that had very gloomy expectations in 1995, when the overall unemployment rate was 12 percent (from less than 2 percent in 1965) and when it could witness the problems experienced by so many older couples. As an economist with such a philosophical conception, I am very circumspect in each case before accepting any normative assessment, in particular if it is based on comparisons between welfare monetary equivalents.

On the other hand, I do not belong to the group of extremists who, as a matter of principle, object to any interpersonal comparison of welfare. Since it is common practice in our societies to weigh the gains of the winners in any exchange against the losses of the losers, we must find ways of putting as much rationality as possible into such comparisons. On this, as well as on a number of ethical choices, I agree with Amartya Sen and, in fact, with many others.

But my uneasiness remains when I see the risk of oversimplification to which we are exposed in aggregate assessments. For instance, I feel uneasy when consulting the tables of the 'human development index' and other similar indices, published by UNDP.[1] Real GDP per capita is certainly not a good indicator of human development. But, to obtain a good indicator, is it enough to combine GDP per capita with very few other indices (such as life expectancy at birth, adult literacy, an index of enrolment in schools)? Which formula should be used for the combination? Even more fundamentally, is it conceivable that we all agree on a definition for a valid all-purpose 'human development index'? Rather, my philosophy would be that we proceed modestly, avoid rash aggregations, and adopt in each case, depending on the purpose, the set of qualitative or quantitative indicators that seem to be the most appropriate. We may hope to progressively learn how to work better as economists, to be more useful in decision-making, and to raise the level of knowledge of our students and country citizens.

RESEARCH IN MICROECONOMIC THEORY

In retrospect, it appears that research on the theory of prices and resource allocation took a sizable part of my time, even though it was most often not at the forefront of research and during some periods it may have been hardly more than a hobby. In my first years at the INSEE school, at the Cowles Commission, or in the rank and file of the Econometric Society, I was attracted to the search for solutions to well-posed and relevant logical problems. The same motivation held when I encountered similar problems in my early teaching or in the French environment of the 1950s and 1960s. It is how my best-known articles were produced in capital theory, in the theory of planning, particularly for public goods, in the theory of risk (Malinvaud, 1953, 1967, 1969, 1971, 1973). Of course, interchange with others played a part in the maturation of each one of these articles, particularly about the scientific or real-world context in which it could be meaningful. Incidentally I may note that, at about the same time, the search for the solution to logical problems motivated what may have been original in my teaching contributions to econometric methodology (Malinvaud, 1966).

Some may think that my interests shifted away from microeconomic theory in the early 1970s, in order to concentrate on macroeconomic issues. There is a bit of truth in that. It is also true that I never felt quite at home within the theory of games and its teachings about interactive rationality, which were influential in the 1970s and 1980s, particularly in the industrial-organization literature. Nevertheless, I kept being interested in the new developments of microeconomic theory.

This may be the place to comment on how I interpret the methodological conviction that science has to, above all, be relevant to the real world. The theory of the allocation of resources is illustrative in this respect. In the middle of the twentieth century it seemed to be on the verge of reaching unity and perfection. The elegance and clarity of the emerging structure impressed many of us. But it was at the cost of playing down the role of the productive sector and its messy structures. This was a high cost because, as everyone can see, the actual allocation of resources depends much on what firms do.

In fact, my strongest interests in microeconomic theory during the 1970s and 1980s concerned the microeconomic foundations of macroeconomics, but not quite the kind of foundations that were at times claimed. To be precise, an archetype of methodological perversion emerged when proponents of the real business cycle theory claimed that their theory had sound microeconomic foundations in the now well-known aggregate, intertemporal, market-clearing model of a unique representative agent. This may have been a respectable academic reference, but certainly not a valid microeconomic foundation when the microeconomic business-cycle facts experienced by many firms and workers were market disequilibria and when the model was so cavalier in its ignorance of the difficulty of aggregating heterogeneous microeconomic behaviors.

It is convenient to distinguish three groups in the research projects that are necessary for consolidating the microeconomic foundations of macroeconomics. The third group concerns aggregation and may be considered to belong to macroeconomic theory rather than to microeconomic theory. I shall say a little more about it later. But the first two groups are best seen as belonging to microeconomic theory. The first one concerns individual behavior of agents with respect to the kinds of choice which play a major part in the determination of the macroeconomic equilibrium and of its change through time, saving, investment, wages and markups, and so on. Since I became an economist more than fifty years ago, I have seen important progress in the knowledge of individual behavior and of the laws that characterize it. This was achieved by a sound combination of improvements in models representing this behavior and of econometric investigations from increasingly rich bodies of data. This progress continues, and there is indeed much to gain still, with respect to accuracy in particular. I tried to convey a good idea of the progress and of its methods in *Macroeconomic Theory* (Malinvaud, 1998–2000).

The second group of research projects required to consolidate the microeconomic foundations of macroeconomics concerns the characterization of the structures within which agents actually operate and of the kind of interdependence that results. Such research naturally focuses on deviations from the general competitive equilibrium model. Since there are in fact many deviations, we cannot expect to build a model incorporating all of them simultaneously. But looking at a variety of models and at their respective properties, we shall progressively better understand the foundations of our macroeconomic assessments. The literature contains a number of such models, notably all those which have been imagined in order to explain variations in involuntary unemployment between periods or countries. I consider that the theory of the fixed-price general equilibrium is particularly enlightening in this respect (Malinvaud, 1977).

I taught for six years at the Collège de France (1988–93). The course for the two first years discussed the methodology of macroeconomic research (Malinvaud, 1991). During the four remaining years I explained recent developments in microeconomic theory, which were not covered in my textbook (Malinvaud, 1972, revised 1985). The main part of the 1990–91 course was published and concerned general equilibrium developments, in particular with overlapping generations models, markets for financial assets, and decisions of firms in the market equilibrium framework. The main focus in 1992 and 1993 was on asymmetric information, incentives and contracts. Part of this last course will no doubt be incorporated into a new edition of my lectures on microeconomic theory, if I can complete it.

Thinking in general equilibrium terms about current problems is also at times a motivation for some investigation of my own. For instance, I am presently trying to clarify a point occurring in the analysis of policies targeted at the least skilled and least employable people in industrial countries. Unemployment of these people is substantial, particularly where a minimum wage exists and is not so low. A policy now frequently adopted in Western Europe consists of changing the schedule of labor taxes so as to reduce the rates on low wages, hence to lower the corresponding labor costs and to stimulate the demand for unskilled labor. Econometricians are asked to estimate the effects expected from such a policy. The main point is to make a correct assessment of the importance of substitutions between inputs, in favor of unskilled labor. Estimates exist of the microeconomic elasticity of the demand for labor with respect to the labor cost, this depending on the skill level. But relying on these estimates only is overlooking the fact that substitution between inputs may also come indirectly. The relative prices of the goods and services whose production is unskilled labor intensive are likely to decrease, hence the consumption of those goods and services will increase. It is natural to conjecture that neglect of this indirect effect leads to an underestimation of the increase in the demand for unskilled labor. Validation of the conjecture requires a model in which relative prices are endogenous, substitutions occur both in production and in consumption, and finally, production functions of the various goods and services are heterogeneous with respect to the use of unskilled labor. It turns out that the conjecture is not valid in full generality. But the main implication of the research should be to show how to combine, for the problem at hand, estimates of elasticities of substitution between primary inputs in production units with estimates of other elasticities of substitution, between consumptions and between intermediate inputs broadly understood.

THE CHALLENGE OF ECONOMICS AS A POSITIVE SCIENCE

From my early study of economics on, I always paid attention to empirical approaches in our discipline. This inclination could only be reinforced by my work as an official statistician and by my teaching of econometrics, starting in the mid-1950s. With respect to methodology, that is, to how empirical approaches contribute to our knowledge and how they should proceed, I am holding an intermediate position.

I fully accept the point made by Lionel Robbins (1935) insisting on a major difference between economics and the natural sciences. Experimentation in economics can only have a limited scope, but economic phenomena result from the activity of human beings and from human institutions. Hence, much of what we know comes from our direct acquaintance with the rules chosen for the functions and operations of various institutions and from our direct understanding of the constraints and motivations shaping individual economic behaviors. Modeling this direct knowledge has an important part in the construction of our science. But in many cases the results would remain too qualitative and limited if we were not taking advantage also of the existence of statistical data and other observations on the manifestation of economic phenomena, data and observations thanks to which we can make our models progressively more precise.

For this inductive process, the best guide and rationalization is what was called 'the probability approach' at the Cowles Commission and is normally taught in econometrics, as well as more generally in mathematical statistics. Each inference on a sample of data takes place within a stochastic model, which is believed to provide a good representation of what is known *a priori* about the generation of these data. I do not doubt the value of the methodological principle that is so defined. But discussions may concern the question of knowing how to apply the principle in the practice of research, or even whether in all circumstances the principle is appropriate.

With respect to this last question I never shared the dogmatism expressed by some. I recognize the value of exploratory data analysis, which for instance searches for regularities in time series, for concordances or discordances between time series, and looks at how to contribute to theories from such facts, rather than rushing to tests and estimations within a pre-selected model. At the exploratory stage, eclecticism is often wise. Such is the conclusion I drew from the methodological dispute between the Cowles Commission and the National Bureau of Economic Research after publication of an important book by A. Burns and W. Mitchell.[2] Indeed, a significant part of my work at INSEE was devoted to exploratory data analysis.

This open attitude was also revealed by the fact that I reacted positively in 1962 when I was asked by Moses Abramovitz to take part in a joint project of parallel studies on modern economic growth in each one of the main developed countries. The project assumed acceptance of the quantitative methodology initially promoted by Simon Kuznets, who was long associated with the National Bureau of Economic Research (see Carré et al., 1975).

This being said, I am also aware of the strict limits of data analysis as sometimes practiced by critics of methodologies developed within the probability approach paradigm. For instance, I was not really impressed when, in an influential article published in 1980, Christopher Sims attacked macroeconometric structural models while introducing his own approach (the vector autoregressions, now known as VARs). The objection to structural models was the existence, in their specification, of identifying restrictions stating that such and such exogenous variables of the model were not appearing in the structural equation meant to represent at the aggregate level the behavior of some agents with respect to a particular type of operation. Sims claimed that such restrictions were 'incredible' because, for practically any exogenous variable, we could find an argument explaining its presence in any structural equation. But the weight he gave to this objection was clearly misleading.

In the first place, the specifications of our models do not have to be strictly exact; ignoring a restriction which we know to be approximately valid would be neglecting a useful piece of information. Moreover, it is by now well recognized that no firm conclusion could be drawn from purely empirical VARs, since identifying restrictions are also required for interpreting the statistical fits in a meaningful way. Indeed, the later developments of the VAR methodology recognized the value of the hybrid 'structural VARs.'

A philosopher would probably say that methodological eclecticism is not a respectable position because it is too easy. I accept this, or rather I should say that such an eclecticism requires lucidity and discipline because it is exposed to the risk of permitting sloppy or even perverse practices.

Discipline in the treatment of data by economists has greatly improved since the 1920s. This was the result of efforts made by official statisticians, research teams such as those of the National Bureau of Economic Research, the econometric movement, and so on. Discipline was promoted in concordance with measurement of an ever-increasing number of abstract concepts, with collection and organization of richer and richer macroeconomic and microeconomic databases, with definition of procedures for data analyses, and with characterization of econometric methods and of their properties. Overall, this progress goes along with those of rigor and ethics in our non-experimental science. Awareness of this progress explains my irritation when I occasionally see practices of which the diffusion would be regressive, according to me. I shall not deny that this occurred when I perceived in the writings of some promoters of the real-business-cycles movement cavalier attitudes with respect to serious econometric tests, selection bias in ignoring facts which did not fit their theory (such as fluctuations in unemployment) or misleading statements about the accuracy of estimates available in the literature for such parameters as intertemporal elasticities of substitution.

The difficulties of economics as a positive science are widespread. Being interested in macroeconomics, I was particularly concerned, since my early years as an economist, with difficulties arising from aggregation of economic relationships. In 1956, I wrote an article on the subject. But it was long (78 pages) and published in French, and therefore not widely read. I regret now that I did not submit at the time a short article (in English) to a journal which would have presented the main message, namely, that it was often possible to bypass the difficulties of aggregation thanks to a statistical approach and to a search for statistical invariants.[3] The idea was not really new, but its potentials were not widely perceived until the 1980s. These potentials are now sometimes even overestimated, for instance when 'exact aggregation' is claimed in some applied macroeconomic works where exactitude ought to be understood as fairly imperfect (irritation may arise from seeing abuses of rhetoric).

TEACHING MACROECONOMICS

I taught courses on macroeconomics from the late 1950s to the early 1980s, and again for two years at Collège de France. My students had good training in mathematics, but most of them knew little about economics. They were living in an intellectual environment where, until the 1980s, the Marxist vision of the world and the Marxist approach to philosophy or social sciences was influential, often even predominant. Positioning themselves with respect to Marxism was a main concern of these students, whether they were adepts, adversaries, or, for most of them, still in between. Before all else, I had to know how to deal with this concern.

I had enough sense to realize that I should refrain from responding to it. Whatever I could have said would have damaged the reception of my economic teaching. Keeping distance from the concern was also recommended by the rather touchy secular ethics implying that religious questions or political proselytism be ruled out in French public education. This did not prevent me from presenting how nineteenth-century economists, Karl Marx included, analyzed the functional distribution of incomes or economic growth, but in a way that implied no necessary link with the class struggle. Ideological neutrality appeared wise in retrospect when some of my students were later working at INSEE on macroeconomic issues and peacefully collaborating with each other notwithstanding their ideological diversity.

Rather, the main difficulties in the conception of macroeconomics teaching concerned the balance to be established between various parts of the theory and, still more difficult, between various sources, expressions and applications of our knowledge, the basic notions and their conceptualization, the facts, the theories and their models, the interpretations given of these theories and models, and the applications to economic policy. I knew from experience how difficult it had been for me to reach a usable understanding of macroeconomics. How could I best convey such an understanding to the students?

This is a proper place to now explain how I think I learned macroeconomics. It was a slow process. Some fifteen years were required before I thought I was mastering enough of the subject to be able to teach it. Also, for the young autodidact I was for a number of years, it was in part an unconscious process. However, the following short presentation of my recollections should be accurate.

I had no difficulty with descriptive approaches, i.e. the history of economic facts and the elementary techniques for time-series analysis that practitioners were using in order to characterize short-run or long-run trends. This meant that I could also easily grasp the bits of theoretical structures which supported rather natural extensions of such data analyses toward interpretative schemes, for instance why it was interesting to consider trends in the productivity of labor, and subsequently trends in global factor productivity. I could well understand the sense of such simple and partial theories as the accelerator or the quantity theory of money. I was then interested in realizing that these clear theories did not fit the data as well as I had thought was claimed in the writings of their proponents.

In contrast, I well remember my difficulties with books that I had seen quoted as important. After difficult reading in French, including some translations, or later in English, I could not make any sense of them, being unable to select from the text what the main structure of the theory argued for was. This applied, I must say, to my first reading of Keynes's *General Theory*, but in many other cases also. Still today, some of this experience occasionally comes to mind, such as when I see the Austrian writings of the first half of the twentieth century being praised as containing a useful macroeconomic theory.

Then, in the late 1940s and early 1950s came a period during which things were progressively sorted out, thanks in part to my work on macroeconomic data in a national accounting framework and on macroeconomic projections, but mainly thanks to some enlightening theoretical writings. The first one was probably Gottfried Haberler's book *Prosperity and Depression* (available in French since 1936). Then I benefited from various presentations of Keynes's *General Theory*, toward which my spontaneous readings happened to be guided, presentations by Joan Robinson (1937), Lawrence Klein (1947) and, of course, John Hicks (1937). A clarifying introduction to the approach of the Swedish school was provided by Erik Lindahl (1939). I had no difficulty fitting Wassily Leontief's work (1941) within my macroeconomic approach.

A complete survey of what I remember having learned from others during this period would be much too long. I then became an adept of the 'neo-classical synthesis,' according to which, in the short run, movements in economic activity are dominated by those in aggregate demand whereas, in the long run, the economy tends to move along a steady growth path, well analyzed by the market-clearing assumption. I do not remember when or how that came about. It may even have been progressive and long unconscious.

My present conception on how to best organize macroeconomics teaching certainly owes to my personal experience in first learning macroeconomics, and second, teaching it to students who had a good background in mathematics but little prior knowledge of economics. However, I do not think that this personal bias suffices to explain my dissatisfaction with the way in which the subject was taught during the 1980s in some academic quarters. It is hardly a caricature to say that a number of courses in macro then started with a set of dogmatic, and invalid, methodological slogans, went on with long mathematical developments on what the teacher liked, and ended up with the display of a few so-called stylized facts, selectively chosen so as to appear to provide empirical support.

I shall refrain from repeating here the three pages I wrote in Malinvaud (1987) about my choice of a program for the organization of macroeconomics teaching. I should have only minor revisions to make; moreover my book (1998–2000) exhibits the result of this program. Rather, I shall consider how we, as teachers, ought to respond to the pedagogical challenge posed by the dissatisfaction of many of our students. Our courses are then found too academic, hence inadequate for answering the concerns of students about the macroeconomy and the way it impacts on our societies.

The best response, according to me, lies much more in our attitudes than in the content of our courses. We should better show that we understand, and to a large extent share, the concerns of students. We should recognize from the beginning that macroeconomic knowledge is far from perfect. We should often say that each theory provides a very simplified representation of the results to be expected from the functioning of a very complex system. We should admit that a long familiarity with theories and their applications is required before one can correctly evaluate the scope of each particular theory. We should be persuasive in explaining that there are no other ways for improving macroeconomic knowledge than those followed by the research, the results of which we are reporting. These recommendations may appear trivial, but I suspect that in many cases they are overlooked by teachers too busy exposing models and their mathematical treatment (such expositions are, of course, part of what teachers have to do, but it should not be too exclusive).

To these general recommendations, I shall just add two comments based on personal conviction: economists often tend to underestimate the real importance of macroeconomic disequilibria, and macroeconomic knowledge is at present eclectic and cannot really be otherwise.

Speaking of macroeconomic disequilibria at this point I do not mean to refer to the distinctions that were discussed when some of us were working on what was called 'disequilibrium economics.' I am more concretely pointing to cases of mass unemployment, cases of high inflation, or cases of huge deficits either in the balance of payments or in the consolidated account of public administrations. When they occur, such disequilibria are commonly perceived as serious evils, whereas some economic evaluations of the costs imposed have been found to be small. I should recommend teachers of macroeconomics to be careful when speaking about such mismatches between public perception and economic evaluation of costs, because the students may have the good sense to think that the public perception is more significant than are available economic evaluations. Indeed, these evaluations are given in monetary units and neglect non-pecuniary costs, such as the loss of social status which comes along with long unemployment of persons seeking to work, or the effective breaches of the rule of law following from an unexpected inflation with respect to the implementation of standing private contracts, or still the increased uncertainty about the future economic environment resulting from large deficits. Moreover, available economic evaluations take poor account of great inequities and inequalities that usually occur, even in pecuniary terms, as a consequence of macroeconomic disequilibria. Distributive aspects are wholly neglected when evaluations use the fiction of a unique representative agent. They are also most often underrated in the standard ways of allowing for changes of the statistical distribution of welfare, because after macroeconomic disequilibria these changes are very skewed when they mean important hardship concentrated on a small fraction of the population, which is the common case.

Since each theory gives a very simplified, hence inaccurate, representation of the actually complex macroeconomic phenomena, mature macroeconomists draw their knowledge from a large body of facts and theories. Each theory isolates some facts and neglects the rest in order to focus attention on one aspect of phenomena. Mastering the knowledge embodied in several theories is like having various pictures of the same complex object taken from different perspectives. These theories complement each other, in the same way as the different pictures do. Good transmission of knowledge to students requires that they be led to study various theories, even when these theories have the appearance of somewhat conflicting with one another. Hence, eclecticism in teaching must be recommended.

ECONOMICS IN THE SOCIAL SCIENCES

All throughout my professional life I was confronted with the problem of knowing how to view the relationship between economics and other disciplines within the social sciences. Over and over again I had difficulties in trying either to dissuade those engaged in the vain quest for a grand interdisciplinary synthesis, which would wholly renew economics, or to persuade them that there was no fundamental conflict between ethics and economics. This frequent exposure to difficulties coming from my environment contributed to forging some of my ethical and methodological convictions.

Before I explain this I must, however, report that I had no real difficulty at the French central statistical office, INSEE, which would have come from conflicts on how to develop jointly the observation of social and economic facts. We all shared basically the same sense of our mission, to extend objective knowledge of all social realities that mattered and could be approached by intelligent gathering and processing of public statistics. In reports on how to interpret statistical results, the proper formulation was at times difficult to find. But memory of our common experience contains no substantial problem of the sort that would have remained long unsolved. This proves that we have in social sciences a solid factual base from which we can work and no part of which should be dismissed out of hand on the grounds that it would be fundamentally false. No statistician could deny that improvements in the accuracy of this factual base are feasible. But the existence of such possible improvements does not much affect the overall value of what is available. Moreover, there is no conflict between the two parallel developments of economic and social statistics.

Criticism of the mainstream trends in economic research and of its relative isolation from other social sciences was, however, widespread in my French environment. During the early decades it reflected reluctance to follow the mathematization of economics, a mathematization often presented as 'having no scientific future.' It also reflected fears that dominant trends would deter the humanistic Christian vision of society, or even ideological choices in favor of a Marxist approach. It is revealing in this respect to remember that, when in May 1950, at the initiative of influential professors of Paris University, the *Revue économique* was launched, two objectives were assigned to the new journal: (1) 'to produce a vigorous effort ... in order to give to French economic thought the opportunity not only to assume its part in the common work, but also and mainly to assert its own specific identity,' and (2) 'to firmly anchor political economy within the whole social sciences and research.' The editorial committee expressed the will 'to devote the main part of its efforts to organizing exchanges between the various social disciplines and economics, to promote joint meetings and common surveys.' Typical of the research stimulated by such intentions was the project devoted to 'the realistic study of income distribution,' which designated the distribution between social groups as preferable to the functional distribution of incomes, which was dismissed as irrelevant.

The environment changed greatly in the subsequent decades, as the enlightening influence of engineers and civil servants made an impact on academic quarters, as the value of new developments in economics abroad, including mathematical economics, was better recognized, as new techniques of microeconomic and macroeconomic analysis were learned, and as new generations of students were forming their own judgments. However, the difficulties I mentioned at the beginning of this section definitely went on more vividly than elsewhere. Still today we frequently hear in France that there are fundamentally different approaches to economics from the ones usually taught, approaches which, if systematically followed, would lead to a more human economic and social order. Still today we frequently hear that the alleged failure of economics is due to its neglect of the other social sciences.

A larger part of the intelligentsia in France than elsewhere thus may be stubborn in how it looks at economists as responsible for mischief. But my readers know that this attitude exists in many other places also. I have witnessed it often during the past few years, as I had a new experience in my life. In late 1993, I was asked not only to join but to chair the newly created Pontifical Academy of Social Sciences, which aims at 'promoting the study and progress of the social sciences, primarily economics, sociology, law and political science. The Academy … thus offers the Church the elements which she can use in the development of her social doctrine' (article 1 of the statutes). The few economists who are members of this small academy (eight economists, out of 33 geographically dispersed members) are often challenged to explain any among the unpleasant features in national economies or in the world economy, features that some systematically consider as due to the 'glorification of the market,' this glorification being thought by some to be the main function of economists. Misunderstandings between economists and other social scientists are obvious, beginning with the principle that normative science is in vain unless it first specifies the list of feasible alternatives between which to choose.

After these snapshots of my environment I must briefly characterize my attitudes to the division of the scientific work between economics and other social disciplines. In the first place, fruitful collaborations exist on well-specified issues. For instance, the field of labor economics overlaps at various points with that of sociology, for the study of industrial relations, of people's work experience, and of poverty. On many relevant issues concerning either pure knowledge or policies, combining the two viewpoints of sociologists and economists is fruitful. Similarly, the empirical study of economic growth by economists was often found to be complementary to the study of history. Experimental economics has interesting joint projects with psychology or social psychology. In all such cases collaborations are welcome. They show in particular that the boundaries of our discipline are a bit fuzzy and flexible.

Looking deeper into the core of economics, we can also see increasing interest in contributions from other disciplines. After decades during which we fruitfully investigated the many forms and consequences of economic rationality, with respect to time, uncertainty, information and its asymmetries, and with respect to the difficulties of interactive behavior, we feel the need to better account for bounded rationality, for the role of reciprocity and trust in mutual relations, and for the importance of social norms and behavioral routines. We realize that psychology, cognitive sciences, sociology and history may help us to achieve a better command of these features, which look somewhat unfamiliar in the main core of our teaching. We should not ignore this possibility. But we should not entertain unrealistic expectations as to its impact on our economic theories. As Amartya Sen wrote:

> It will not be an easy task to find replacements for the standard assumptions and rational behaviour – and related to it of actual behaviour – that can be found in the traditional economic literature, both because the identified deficiencies have been seen as calling for rather divergent remedies, and also because there is little hope of finding an alternative assumption structure that will be as simple and usable as the traditional assumptions of self-interest maximization, or of consistency of choice. (Sen, 1987)

This being said, our scientific ethics must give realism precedence over convenience or beauty.

More delicate is the question of knowing what to think of the various cases in which, during the past decades, some economists have extended their domain by deep entries into territories that were formerly considered to belong to others. The common characteristic in these cases was to see economists study how economic incentives would play in domains that were not viewed as specifically economic. Beyond the economics of the household, the latter being working, earning, consuming and saving, the economics of the family discussed how you marry, have children, care for them, educate them, divorce … Who ought to judge the scientific value of this development? I submit that economists are not well placed for that. Rather, it belongs to demographers, psychologists and sociologists.

I feel still more uncertain about the law and economics movement as presented in particular by Richard Posner (1987). Perhaps I ought to be silent about it, because I did not study the writings of the school. But with this reservation, presenting my initial reaction fits well into the present essay. I see the sense of the research, namely to try to explain how laws and their interpretation by judges might aim at efficiency in the functioning of societies. I am ready to accept the idea that the approach is appropriate for the study of laws ruling economic operations. But, how about all the rest? In which domain will lawyers really gain from introducing a concept of efficiency when dealing with the implementation of private contracts, of justice in criminal affairs, of human rights and of human values?

Dealing here with the interface between economics and political science would require much more space than I can devote to it. This interface is made up of so many different parts, some of them in common with law or philosophy, and some more specific, such as the theories of social choices, of votes, of public choices, and there is, of course, 'political economy' more or less widely defined. The most relevant comment, on my part at this point may appear minor. But it is based on my long practice as an economic policy adviser. I then had my own, almost ethical, rule to leave the politics entirely to political advisers. When reading the economic literature that closely or remotely dealt with economic policy making I never found any valid reason to regret having abided by the rule. This also reflects my frequent doubts about the value of what economists write when they venture outside their natural field of competence.

Ending this long essay, I shall still say a word about my thesis that there should not be any fundamental conflict between ethics and economics. I need not stress that it is a normative thesis. Neither do I need to elaborate on the idea that the actual teaching of economics or conducting economic research runs the risk of sometimes being ethically objectionable. In this essay I have not refrained from hinting at the existence of cases in which this occurred. But I shall add that economists have, in modern societies, a responsibility for the progress of ethics. Viewed as a normative discipline, ethics is the science of how conduct ought to be directed. When approaching such a question, we economists immediately react in thinking not only of choice criteria but also of feasibilities. For this reason, we are in fact often more advanced in understanding the issues than are philosophers and other social scientists. We should therefore not shy away from exhibiting and discussing ethics. We must do it within economics,[4] but even somewhat beyond, for instance when we meet sociologists or political scientists to discuss reform of the welfare state.

NOTES

1. See: United Nations Development Programme (UNDP), *Human Development Report 1999*, New York, 1999.
2. For reprint of the dispute, see *Scientific Papers of Tjalling C. Koopmans*, 1970, pp. 112–63.
3. Of course the idea is presented in my now available macroeconomics textbook, which actually discusses aggregation at many places (Malinvaud, 1998–2000; for the general theory see pp. 107–26).
4. In this respect see in particular the work of Serge-Christophe Kolm.

REFERENCES

Allais, Maurice. 1943. *Traite d'économie pure*, 3rd edn, Clément Juglar, Paris, 1994.

Allais, Maurice. 1947. *Economie et intérêt*, Imprimerie Nationale, Paris.

Carré, Jean-Jacques, Paul Dubois and Edmond Malinvaud. 1975. *French Economic Growth*, Stanford University Press, Stanford, CA.

Hicks, John. 1937. 'Mr. Keynes and the Classics: a suggested interpretation,' *Econometrica*, April.

Klein, Lawrence. 1947. *The Keynesian Revolution*, Macmillan, London.

Kolm, Serge-Christophe. 1996. *Modern Theories of Justice*, The MIT Press, Cambridge, MA.

Koopmans, Tjalling, C. 1970. *Scientific Papers of*, Springer-Verlag, New York.

Leontief, Wassily. 1941, *The Structure of the American Economy*, Harvard University Press, Boston, MA.

Lindahl, Erik. 1939, *Studies in the Theory of Money and Capital*, Alien and Unwin, London.

Malinvaud, Edmond. 1953. 'Capital accumulation and efficient allocation of resources,' *Econometrica*.

Malinvaud, Edmond. 1956. 'L'agrégation dans les modèles économiques,' *Cahiers du séminaire d'économetrie*, no. 4.

Malinvaud, Edmond. 1966. *Statistical Methods of Econometrics*, North-Holland, Amsterdam.

Malinvaud, Edmond. 1967. 'Decentralized procedures for planning,' in Malinvaud. E. and M.O.L. Bacharach (eds), *Activity Analysis in the Theory of Growth and Planning*, Macmillan, London, pp. 170–208.

Malinvaud, Edmond. 1969. 'First-order certainty equivalence,' *Econometrica*.

Malinvaud, Edmond. 1971. 'A planning approach to the public good problem,' *The Swedish Journal of Economics*.

Malinvaud, Edmond. 1972. *Lectures on Microeconomic Theory*, North-Holland, Amsterdam, last edition 1985.

Malinvaud, Edmond, 1973. 'Markets for an exchange economy with individual risks,' *Econometrica*.

Malinvaud, Edmond. 1977. *The Theory of Unemployment Reconsidered*, Basil Blackwell, Oxford.

Malinvaud, Edmond. 1987. 'The challenge of macroeconomic understanding,' *Banca Nazionale del Lavoro*, no. 162.

Malinvaud, Edmond. 1991. *Voies de la recherche macroeconomique*. Odile Jacob, Paris.

Malinvaud, Edmond. 1993. *Equilibre general dans les économies de marché*. Economica, Paris.

Malinvaud, Edmond. 1998–2000. *Macroeconomic Theory – A Textbook on Macroeconomic Knowledge and Analysis*, North-Holland, Amsterdam, vols. A and B, 1998; vol. C, 2000.

Posner, Richard. 1987. 'The law and economics movement,' *American Economic Review*, May.

Robbins, Lionel. 1935. *An Essay on the Nature and Significance of Economic Science*, Macmillan, London.

Robinson, Joan. 1937. *Introduction to the Theory of Employment*, Macmillan, London.

Sen, Amartya. 1987. 'Rational behaviour' in J. Eatwell et al., *The New Palgrave Dictionary of Economics*, Macmillan, London.

Sims, Christopher. 1980. 'Macroeconomics and reality,' *Econometrica*, vol. 48, January.

UNDP (United Nations Development Programme). 1999. *Human Development Report 1999*, Oxford University Press, New York.

17. Trains of thought*

Harry M. Markowitz

My essay will be concerned principally with some philosophical views I have held for much of my life. After recounting the sources (for me) and the nature of these views, I will conclude with some brief personal reflections.

These philosophical views are on a few related topics. My views on any one topic did not spring instantly to mind, but were the results of a train of thought to which I would return many times over weeks, months and years. It was also important to me that the train of thought on one topic did not contradict that on another.

WHAT DO WE KNOW?

The first topic to occupy me, among those reviewed here, concerned what do we know and how do we know it. Until I was 13 or 14 I read comic books and *The Shadow* mystery magazines, then I read (I cannot remember why) Darwin's *Origin of Species*. I was especially fascinated with how Darwin marshalled his facts, argued his case and considered possible objections. Subsequently I read popular accounts of physics and astronomy, from the high-school library, and original accounts by philosophers, purchased from wonderful big, old, musty used-book stores then in downtown Chicago.

The philosopher who impressed me most, who became 'my' philosopher, was David Hume. He argued that even though we release a ball a thousand times and each time it falls to the floor, we are not thereby provided proof with certainty that the ball will drop when released a thousand-and-first time. On reflection, one modification to Hume's views seemed necessary. Hume spoke in terms of cause and effect. I release the ball, then it drops to the floor. I eat a substance with a particular appearance and then I feel nourished. I see or do A and then B occurs. At least it always has; but there is no necessary proof that it will. The reason that Hume's view needs modification – really amplification – is that science does not merely catalog cause and effect. Rather it develops

*This chapter first appeared in *The American Economist*, **37**(1), Spring 1993, 3–9.

theories, what I would now refer to as models, sometimes mistakenly thought to be inevitable universal laws.

Consider the ball once more. What do we mean that it will fall down if I release it? Which way is down if I stand in Australia? Or in space a thousand miles from the earth? The 'universal truth' which was observed over and over – as any eighteenth- or nineteenth-century physicist would tell you – is that the ball attracts, and is attracted to, each other object by a force which is proportional to the product of their mass and inversely proportional to the square of their distance. But this universal law of gravity did not hold universally. In particular it failed to accurately explain the path of the planet Mercury. Einstein's general theory of relativity presents a quite different model of phenomena which the older Newtonian model failed to explain as well as phenomena which the latter has succeeded in explaining. But, as Hume tells us, the fact that the theory of relativity had succeeded in all instances in the past does not prove that it will continue to do so in the future; and, as Einstein himself said, in this case we would have to seek a new theory. For a statement of this view, amply illustrated, see Einstein and Infeld, *The Evolution of Physics*.

Some readers may feel that Hume's views may be true in principle, but of little applicability to economics or finance. But if the reader has attended economics seminars for a few years, he or she can probably supply examples of empirical economic relationships which held in one decade and not in the next; or which held for the preceding 20 years, but not last year.

Better still, the reader should try the exercise which Descartes undertakes in his first meditation, to distinguish between what is known and what is conjecture; in the present instance, however, seeking this distinction in financial or economic matters. The reader might reflect on the fact that much of our information on economic and financial matters come from newspaper, radio and television accounts. But we know from our experience as teachers or students that even good, college-level students have difficulty in relating more than 80 or 90 percent of any material correctly. This, in itself, is a source of a 10 or 20 percent error rate. In addition, we frequently learn from later accounts of events that earlier accounts were falsified. Even if all participants in events tried to inform reporters accurately, we know that participants and witnesses see and believe different things; and who knows who is correct.

Thus our primary facts delivered to us by newspapers, radio and television are the output of a process full of noise. In addition, we know that different people receiving essentially the same primary facts can fit these into radically different belief structures. Again, who knows who is correct?

Further, databases have errors, programs have bugs; most facts are brought to mind from our memories, and you know how faulty memories can be. Sometimes we dream, and then anything can happen. Perhaps now is a dream.

I do not assert that everything we believe is wrong; rather, that much we take as fact is only hypothesis.

PROBABILITY, UTILITY AND QUADRATIC APPROXIMATIONS

When I was a student member of the Cowles Commission at the University of Chicago, Karl Brunner and I worked through parts of von Neumann and Morgenstern's *Theory of Games and Economic Behavior*, including the appendix on expected utility. At first I was skeptical of expected utility as a maxim for rational behavior in the face of risk. But a conversation with Herman Rubin when he visited the Cowles Commission and a reading of Marschak's article on expected utility convinced me that this was a plausible maxim. Not long afterward I was convinced in a course by Leonard J. Savage, that one should act under uncertainty as if one assigned probability beliefs to events for which there are no objective probabilities, and should update probability beliefs according to Bayes's rule. At first, I considered questions of expected utility and probability beliefs in the context of economic action in the face of risk and uncertainty. After reading F.P. Ramsey's pioneering essay, and further reflecting on Savage's arguments, I decided that the subject was the older one of 'what do we know and how do we know it?' As explained above, I previously concluded that models of the world are never known with certainty. But we are more willing to give up some hypotheses than others. I agreed with Ramsey and Savage that degrees of belief should be formalized in terms of the actions of a rational decision maker, i.e., a decision maker who is not omniscient, but makes no mistakes in logic or arithmetic.[1]

Another train of thought began while reading John Burr Williams's *Theory of Investment Value* as background for my PhD dissertation at the University of Chicago. Williams asserted that the value of a stock should be the present value of its future dividends. But since the future is uncertain, I interpreted this to be the expected value of future dividends. But if one is concerned only with some expected value for each security, one must be concerned only with expected value for the portfolio as a whole. In this case, the investor would place all his funds in a single security – that with maximum expected return; or he or she would be indifferent between any combination of securities, all with maximum expected return, if there were two or more which tied for maximum. In no case would the investor prefer a diversified portfolio to all undiversified portfolios. But common sense, as well as prior examination of Wiesenberger's *Investment Companies*, showed that diversification was a common and sensible aspect of investment practice. The reason, obviously, was to reduce risk. Thus the investor was, and should be, concerned with risk and return on the portfolio as a whole.

As a student in the Economics Department it was natural to think of Pareto optimality. More specifically, as a student of Tjalling Koopman's course on activity analysis, it was natural to distinguish between efficient and inefficient risk–return combinations; and to draw, for the first time, what is now referred to as the efficient frontier, then with expected return on the horizontal axis. Standard deviation, or variance, came to mind as the measure of risk. I did not know, off hand, the formula for the variance of a linear combination of random variables. This was supplied by a copy of Uspensky's *Introduction to Mathematical Probability* on the library shelf. I was delighted to see that portfolio variance depended on the covariances between securities as well as the variances of the securities held in the portfolio.

I left the University of Chicago for the RAND Corporation in 1952, having completed all but my dissertation. At the invitation of James Tobin, I spent the 1954–55 academic year at the Cowles Foundation at Yale, on leave from RAND, writing a book that would be published in 1959 as Cowles Foundation Monograph 16, *Portfolio Selection: Efficient Diversification of Investments*. Much of the time during this period was spent writing drafts of chapters explaining the elements of mean–variance analysis. A parallel activity involved attempting to reconcile mean–variance analysis and expected utility theory. Rather than consider the mean and variance of the present value of future dividend, as I first thought after reading J.B. Williams, I now considered a many-period game, and assumed that securities were perfectly liquid. Under certain assumptions, each period the rational investor maximizes the expected value of a single-period utility function which depends only on end-of-period wealth, as explained by R. Bellman. It seemed natural then to approximate this single period utility function by a quadratic, and approximate expected utility by the function of mean and variance which results from taking the expected value of the quadratic. This approach was illustrated by a few examples in my 1959 book, and more extensively by Young and Trent (1969), Levy and Markowitz (1979), and others. For most utility functions reported in the literature, and for probability distributions such as historical returns on portfolios, the quadratic approximation does quite well.

It is important to distinguish between the assumption that the investor has a quadratic utility function, and the use of quadratic approximation to a given utility function. For example, Levy and Markowitz show that the Arrow and Pratt objection to a quadratic utility function does not apply to an investor who uses a quadratic approximation to a given utility function. In particular, the latter, quadratic approximation maximizer, has exactly the same risk aversion in the small, in the sense of Pratt, as does the expected utility maximizer whose utility function is approximated.

Markowitz (1959) also notes that under other assumptions the single-period utility function may depend on state variables in addition to end-of-period wealth, and that maximizing the expected value of a quadratic approximation to this function of several variables leads to a mean–variance calculation. However, such quadratic approximations to utility functions of several variables were not explored in Markowitz (1959).

SIMULATION AND SYSTEMS DESCRIPTIONS

In the 1950s Alan S. Manne and I at the RAND Corporation, and others at RAND, UCLA and elsewhere, tried our hand at building industry-wide and multi-industry 'activity analysis' models. The first thought was to build models like Leontief's input–output model, except allowing for alternate methods of producing the output of any one industry. Examination of the inverse of a large input–output matrix revealed anomalies that would not be cured by alternate activities, nor by better data. What was required was a more radical departure from the Leontief format; namely, a model in which aggregates of production equipment and aggregates of producer and consumer products were the building blocks of the analysis, as opposed to the Leontief model whose building blocks are 'industry capacities' and 'interindustry flows'. Our reason for departing from the Leontief model, and the results of our collective work, are presented in Cowles Foundation Monograph 18, A.S. Manne and H.M. Markowitz et al., *Studies in Process Analysis: Economy-Wide Production Capabilities*.

Various people provided industry models for this 'process analysis' effort. For example, Alan Manne provided a petroleum industry model; Tibor Fabian, a blast furnace, iron and steel industry model; Alan J. Rowe (then at UCLA) and I developed a metalworking industries model, etc. As a by-product of this work, I became interested in manufacturing planning and scheduling in the metalworking industries.[2] I soon agreed with those who argued that typical realistic manufacturing planning problems were too complex for analytic solution, or for optimizing algorithms such as linear programming. Simulation techniques were needed for advanced analysis, i.e., to give greater insight than provided by the static analysis of the day. One of the things I did at RAND, after returning from leave at Yale, was to supervise the programming of the computer simulation portion of a large man/machine logistics system simulation. This experience reinforced for me the potential usefulness of simulation techniques and illustrated the difficulty of programming detailed simulation models. These two points had already been illustrated by a previous simulation that had been programmed for me, and large and small simulations programmed by others at RAND. (Programming at the time was done in Assembler. FORTRAN was about to make its appearance.)

Not long afterwards I resigned from RAND to accept a tempting offer at the General Electric Computer Department. Soon after I moved from the Computer Department to General Electric's Manufacturing Services, where my friend and colleague Alan Rowe was developing a 'general purpose' job shop model. It took two or three years for Rowe and one or two programmers to complete the model. Then, when one applied it to a factory other than the one for which it was developed, it turned out to be less 'general purpose' than had been hoped. My own theory at the time was to seek 'flexibility' rather than generality. This flexibility was to be achieved by building a simulator out of 'reusable' FORTRAN modules. The first such General Electric Manufacturing Simulator (GEMS) was built in nine months. This shorter time to program was probably due to the use of FORTRAN rather than Assembler language as used in Rowe's job shop simulator. As it turned out, my flexible subroutines were not all that flexible, except for some that performed basic actions such as that of creating or destroying some entity in the simulation (such as a job in the job shop) or inserting an entity into a collection of entities, such as the queue awaiting some resource.

I decided that these basic actions would be more conveniently placed at a programmer's disposal by making them part of a programming language rather than leaving them as subroutines as in GEMS. I decided that I would like to develop such a programming language at a place whose mission and environment were like those I had known at RAND. I let my interests be known to a small number of organizations and, in the end, returned to RAND. Bernard (Bernie) Hausner was assigned to me to implement the new language. Later, Herb Karr was hired as a consultant to write a programming manual. Bernie, Herb and I spent many hours together designing the language which we called SIMSCRIPT (now referred to as SIMSCRIPT I).

Our objective in designing SIMSCRIPT was, insofar as we could, to allow the user to describe the system to be simulated, as distinguished from having the user describe the actions which the computer must take to accomplish the simulation. The status of the system to be simulated was described in terms of *entities* of various *entity types*. Each individual entity was characterized by the *values* of its *attributes*, the *sets* to which it *belonged* and the members of the *sets* it owned. Status changed at points in time called *events*. Subsequently, Ed Russell introduced the notion of a *process* into SIMSCRIPT, which he borrowed from SIMULA, a later simulation programming language. During an event or process, status changes as entities are created or destroyed, attribute values are changed and entities gain and lose set memberships. The SYSTEM as a whole is an entity which can have attributes and own sets. Compound (Cartesian product) entities are also represented.

The SIMSCRIPT programming languages (including the original

SIMSCRIPT I and following I.5, II and II.5 versions) have been applied to a wide variety of fields such as manufacturing simulation, from which it evolved, logistics analysis at RAND, and other applications such as to computer systems design, war games, transportation problems and the effects of trading systems on stock price behavior. SIMSCRIPT II.5 continues to have a large number of simulation application users.

The Entity, Attribute and Set (EAS) view of system description has also proven useful for other than simulation programming. For example, the SIMSCRIPT I.5 and SIMSCRIPT II Translators were themselves written in SIMSCRIPT, based on an EAS description of the entities encountered in the translation process. The SIMSCRIPT II Translator was 'bootstrapped' from a SIMSCRIPT I description of the translation process, then recompiled in terms of a SIMSCRIPT II description of its own compilation.

When SIMSCRIPT II was designed in the mid-1960s it was planned that it should be a database as well as a simulation language. A database would consist of the EAS description of the entities of the world represented within the database. In other words, the thought was that not only could entities be represented within a simulation, but also 'real' entities could be represented within a database in EAS terms. Because of miscellaneous events, not related to the applicability of the EAS worldview, an implementation of the EAS view of database management, bootstrapped from the SIMSCRIPT II translator, was not completed until the work of Malhotra, Markowitz and Pazel. We argue that the performance of the EAS-E system, including its use in internal IBM applications, prove the technical success of the approach. However, we were not able to persuade IBM to support EAS-E as a product. In part at least this was because IBM had just announced its support for the relational database methodology, after many years of supporting the hierarchical view of IMS. IBM seemed unlikely to be persuaded to change again in the short run. In the long run I was elsewhere; i.e., after building EAS-E at IBM and seeing that it would be a very long process to sell it internally, I was delighted to accept the offer of the Marvin Speiser Chair at Baruch College, where I am now located.

The EAS concepts of system description are described in an article on SIMSCRIPT in the *Encyclopedia of Computer Science and Technology*. This includes a proposal for using this view in managing the entities of a computer operating system as well as those encountered in simulation, compilation and database management. The thought is to provide a uniform method of interacting with the entities encountered in computer systems, whether user defined or defined by the developers or the computer system, whether simulated or real, transient or database, etc. I have not succeeded in persuading the software development profession of the desirability of this approach. On the contrary, 'object-oriented' programming has emerged as the chief contender for the role which I had hoped for EAS programming. It is not only that I speak of 'entities' and they speak of 'objects.' There is also a difference in the paradigms by which my entities and their objects are manipulated.

Perhaps if I took the time to work with object-oriented programming with an open mind on a variety of applications I would conclude that it is at least as good as the EAS approach. As it is, the largest item in my queue of things to do, someday, remains to demonstrate the efficacy of the EAS view of system description.

PERSONAL REFLECTIONS

Life has afforded me many pleasurable activities, such as enjoying a fine meal, walking with Mrs Markowitz on new-fallen snow on the path through the woods near our home, flying kites with one or more grandchildren, listening to music, especially J.S. Bach, and the like. But no activity sustains my interest as long as does struggling with some technical or philosophical problem, sometimes alone, sometimes with colleagues. From one point of view these struggles may be classified as 'work', since I sometimes get paid for such efforts. From another viewpoint they are play – part of a game like chess or amateur cryptography which I have also enjoyed. Often in my work–game, part of the objective is to produce something that someone will use. It is not only that sometimes someone pays me for such creations. It is also the fact that for a long time I have been primarily concerned with the theory of rational action, especially rational action under uncertainty. One measure of one's success in achieving a useful understanding and techniques for rational action is to have theory and techniques tried, accepted and endure. I have also spent time applying theory and techniques. For example, I currently spend half-time as Director of Research of Daiwa's Global Portfolio Research Department (GPRD), which has money management responsibilities in conjunction with other branches of Daiwa Securities. Previously I was President of Arbitrage Management Company. Such alternating between theory and practice is not uncommon among financial theorists. Sharpe, Rosenberg, Roll, Ross, Black, Vasicek, Leland and Rubinstein are a few of those who are both theoretician and practitioner. Sometimes they develop the theory of practice, and other times the practice of theory. I find that these two activities reinforce each other.

Some economists report that they entered economics to better mankind's state (e.g., see Szenberg, *Their Life Philosophies: Eminent Economists*). I have never thought it in my power to much improve the human condition generally. Much of human ill is due to violent aggression, political suppression, ancient hatreds and the like. These are not matters I know how to deal with, either from my training as an economist or with the decision-making techniques I have developed. Together with my wife, I try to be a good neighbor, contribute moderately to charities, try to help my children, grandchildren, students and colleagues when I can be of service, and the like. That done, I feel that I have paid my dues and may indulge myself in life's pleasures, including the struggle with interesting problems and questions of philosophy.

NOTES

1. The question of what it means to 'make no mistake in logic and arithmetic' raises further questions which have been extensively explored, without universal agreement, by generations of mathematicians concerned with the foundations of their own discipline. See for example Kleene, *Introduction to Metamathematics*.
2. Another byproduct of the process analysis research was methods for solving large, sparse systems of equations i.e., large systems with relatively few non-zero elements. See Markowitz, H., 'The Elimination Form of the Inverse and Its Application to Linear Programming,' *Management Science*, 1957. Variants of these methods are now part of large, production linear programming codes.

REFERENCES

Arrow, K. (1965), *Aspects of the Theory of Risk Bearing*, Helsinki.

Bellman, R.E. (1957), *Dynamic Programming*, Princeton University Press, Princeton.

Darwin, C.R. (1968), J.W. Burrow (ed.), *The Origin of Species by Means of Natural Selection*, Penguin Books.

Descartes, R. (1961), *Meditations on First Philosophy*, 2nd edn, Liberal Arts Press, New York.

Einstein, A. and L. Infeld (1938), *The Evolution of Physics; the Growth of Ideas from Early Concepts to Relativity and Quanta*, Simon & Schuster, New York.

Hume, D. (1927), *Enquiries Concerning Human Understanding & Concerning the Principles of Morals*, reprinted from the posthumous edition of 1777, L.A. Selby-Bigge (ed.), 2nd edn, The Clarendon Press, Oxford.

Kleene, S.C. (1950), *Introduction to Mathematics*, Van Nostrand, Princeton.

Koopmans, T.C. (1951), 'Analysis of Production as an Efficient Combination of Activities,' in T.C. Koopmans (ed.) (1971), *Activity of Production and Allocation*, 7th edn, Yale University Press, New Haven.

Levy, H. and H.M. Markowitz (1979), 'Approximating Expected Utility By a Function Mean and Variance,' *American Economic Review*, June.

Malhotra, A., H.M. Markowitz and D.P. Pazel (1983), 'EAS-E: An Integrated Approach to Application Development,' *ACM Transactions on Database Systems*, Vol. 8, No. 4, December.

Manne, A.S., H.M. Markowitz, et al. (1963), *Studies in Process Analysis: Economy-wide Production Capabilities*, John Wiley and Sons.

Markowitz, H.M. (1952), 'Portfolio Selection', *The Journal of Finance*, Vol. 7, No. 1, March.

Markowitz. H.M. (1957), 'The Elimination Form of the Inverse and Its Application to Linear Programming,' *Management Science*.

Markowitz, H.M. (1959), *Portfolio Selection: Efficient Diversification of Investments*, John Wiley and Sons; Basil Blackwell, 1991.

Markowitz. H.M. (1979), 'SIMSCRIPT,' *Encyclopedia of Computer Science and Technology*, Vol. 13, Belzer. J., A.G. Hoizman and A. Kent (ed.), Marcel Dekker, Inc.

Markowitz, H.M., A. Malhotra and D.P. Pazel (1984), 'The EAS-E Application Development System: Principles and Language Summary,' *Communications of the ACM*, Vol. 27, No. 8, August.

Marschak, J. (1950), 'Rational Behavior, Uncertain Prospects, and Measurable Utility', *Econometrica*, Vol. 18, April.

Pazel, D.P., A. Malhotra and H.M. Markowitz (1983), 'The System Architecture of EAS-E: An Integrated Programming and Data Base Language,' *IBM Systems Journal*, Vol. 22, No. 3.

Pratt, J.W. (1964), 'Risk Aversion in the Small and in the Large', *Econometrica*, January.

Ramsey, F.P. (1931), *The Foundations of Mathematics and Other Logical Essays*, Harcourt Brace and Company, New York.

Savage, L.J. (1954), *The Foundations of Statistics*, Wiley, 2nd edn, Dover, 1972, New York.

Szenberg, Michael (ed.) (1992), *Eminent Economists, Their Life Philosophies*, Cambridge University Press, Cambridge.

Uspensky, J.V. (1937), *Introduction to Mathematical Probability*, McGraw-Hill, New York.

Von Neumann, J. and O. Morgenstern (1944), *Theory of Games and Economic Behavior*, 3rd edn, Princeton University Press, 1953, Princeton.

A. Wiesenberger and Company, *Investment Companies*, New York, annual editions.

Williams, J.B. (1938), *The Theory of Investment Value*, Harvard University Press, Cambridge, MA.

Young, W.E. and R.H. Trent (1969), 'Geometric Mean Approximation of Individual Security and Portfolio Performance,' *Journal of Financial Quantitative Analysis*, June.

18. My life philosophy*

Allan H. Meltzer

If 'life philosophy' suggests an articulated set of tastes or beliefs that I apply repeatedly to give direction to my life, I cannot set out a life philosophy. In fact, I don't believe that it is useful much of the time to describe, even after the fact, whether one's choices are the result of initial or acquired beliefs (or tastes) or the result of constraints. Clearly, both operate and both tastes and constraints change. Choices are observable; beliefs are not. Moreover, my beliefs are not static. They are shaped not only by where I came from but by what happened to me along the way.

The latter is important. Much of what happened to me, but not only to me, is the result of chance rather than of plan, belief or philosophy. A different experience would have given me different beliefs and imposed different constraints. Discussion of my life philosophy is a narrative with four or five main events that seem to me to have been important for shaping my beliefs and my later decisions in one area. Events did not always work by building on the past; some modified the influence of past experience and caused me to accept beliefs that I had rejected earlier or widened my perspective by introducing new elements. I illustrate this process by highlighting the changes in my beliefs about the role of government.

CHANCE EVENTS

The first of several chance events that had a major influence on my beliefs had a very unhappy beginning. My mother died just before I was six years old, so most of what I believe about her influence probably reflects what I was told later rather than what I learned from her. It is not the same. From six to ten, my sister and I lived with our grandmother, a stern disciplinarian and a strong personality. The first word I think of is matriarch, and she was that. But she was much too wise to depend only on her power to influence. She exerted influence in the way that other people chew gum; she didn't have to think about it. Looking back I believe she internalized a set of rules. She was

*This chapter first appeared in *The American Economist*, **34**(1), Spring 1990, 22–32.

strong-willed, but she had a sense of humor and, though she could be fierce when angry, she was usually thoughtful, perceptive and kind.

I learned both by observing her in action and by listening to her. Itinerants and peddlers came regularly. None was refused. There were no lectures on the virtues of charity or social responsibility and no need for them. The example was far more powerful. I like to believe that, in this as in other ways, she greatly influenced my beliefs and attitude toward others.

Her most important influence on my career and my outlook was her strongly held belief that, in America (and only in America), there were no real limits other than ability to what one could achieve by personal effort. Prejudice and restrictions were real; one would have to work a bit harder or be a bit smarter to overcome them. She must have been disappointed when, at eight, I gave up the violin, but she accepted and perhaps secretly agreed with my conclusion that I had little talent for that instrument. Despite this bit of contrary evidence, I grew up with a positive view of challenges and a desire to accept them. The moral was not that winning is good; it was to live up to your potential, expand your horizon and develop your skills.

Grandmother had been a successful businesswoman earlier. Looking back, I believe that it was her discussion of this experience, especially the emphasis on the satisfaction she got from producing and selling a good product, that strongly influenced me to look for satisfaction in the work I do. This should not suggest that rewards and recognition are unimportant, but they are not the sole or even the most important reason for choosing one's activities. While I grumble as much as anyone about the pressures of deadlines and commitments, I enjoy much of what I do. At times, I cannot distinguish between 'work' and 'recreation,' as those terms are used conventionally.

I cannot begin to sort out and set down all that I learned in the four years spent in my grandmother's house. One strong effect was on my early social views. She was a Franklin Roosevelt Democrat, as were all of her family, neighbors and friends, committed to the idea that the government was a big brother or sister with responsibility for helping people with their problems just as she helped people who came to her door.

Grandmother was not very active in the practice of religion, but she faithfully followed the Jewish laws and orthodox traditions. At six I was sent for what now seems a large dose of daily religious and cultural training. I did not object at the time, and I continued the training for several years after I left her household. By the mid-teens, I tired of the disputatious arguments over narrow points of doctrine that could not be resolved. Man's fate could not depend on such small differences. Further, there was, for me, too much emphasis on rules and prohibitions relative to ends or objectives, on form rather than substantive outcomes, on authority instead of personal choice. There seemed to be a wide gap between professed beliefs and practices. Later,

I became convinced that these problems were not unique to Judaism or for that matter to religion. My religious training heightened my interest in issues such as these. My interest in institutions, in the way they work and the gap between objectives and outcomes, began with this experience.

Like many teenagers, I was eager to leave home. I applied to colleges that were out of Boston and chose Duke. If there was a reason for the choice from among schools that took me away from home I do not recall it. At Duke, I learned some of what it meant to be in a segregated society. The Duke campus was completely segregated. I was appalled by the racial laws and by segregation. I joined various activist groups concerned with equality and in 1948, though not yet old enough to vote, helped to organize the Progressive Party of North Carolina. As a delegate to the party's national convention in Philadelphia, I voted to nominate Henry Wallace and Glen Taylor for President and Vice President and to pass resolutions, many of them obscure items in the leftist political program of that day. No one explained the issues; we were told how we ought to vote. Only later did I learn what some parts of the platform meant. Others were so obscure, I could not find out what they meant and learned only that many delegates were as ignorant as I. I found much in the experience that reminded me of the religious orthodoxy I had rejected earlier.

The convention was in July. In August I completed my undergraduate work and moved to Los Angeles where my family had relocated. I went to work for the family business and, despite some concerns about my experience at the convention, continued working in the Wallace campaign. To my regret and surprise, the Los Angeles branch of the campaign had a very narrow view of the issues. They were not much interested in segregation and civil rights. Their focus was on defeating the Marshall Plan, which they denounced as an imperialist effort by the United States to establish hegemony in Europe. Although the number of active workers was not very large, my efforts to change the focus were futile. Somewhat disillusioned, I left the campaign by October.

The experience did not fit well with the view of government and government's role acquired in my grandmother's house. My associates were not much interested in working to achieve equality of opportunity and what I thought was self-evidently a better world. They not only had their own agenda, but they dismissed the benefits the Marshall Plan would have for the Europeans and for trade and development.

The experience was disconcerting for a believer in the goodwill theory of government according to which a responsive government acts to improve society's performance and increase justice. It was not that I recognized then how much is hidden by the words 'improve society's performance and increase justice.' Here were 'good people' interested in pursuing their own objectives in much the same way as the people in power. I believed, then, that justice was a state or condition. Although one might not be able to describe the state in full detail, it was possible to describe changes as movements toward or away from the ideal of equal justice. The problem was that self-interested people used government for personal ends. 'Good people' were not supposed to do that.

Writing this after 40 years, it seems totally naive. Yet it is close to what I believed at the time. I do not think that these ideas were mine alone. They are common in the press, in journals of opinions and elsewhere, and they reappear in discussions with many academic colleagues.

By all the usual standards, I had been a good undergraduate student of economics, but I did not begin to think like an economist or think about institutions, incentives and their roles in society until I met Karl Brunner.[1] Brunner has been my teacher, collaborator and lifelong friend. We have worked together, and talked about so many things that it is not surprising that we often think alike. What is surprising is that we often think differently. The benefits of collaboration come in no small measure from ability to use what we agree upon to resolve many of our disagreements. We have also learned to use, and rely on, each other's comparative advantages to gain from exchange.

When I first met Brunner, he was in his second year as an assistant professor at UCLA. I came to UCLA by chance. I was married and living in Los Angeles. I don't recall that my wife and I discussed moving, and I know that I did not reopen the graduate admissions to larger and older schools that had been offered when I completed my bachelor's degree, nearly five years earlier.

At the time, UCLA's PhD program was small and relatively new. I learned, or relearned, price theory as a teaching assistant in classes for William Allen and Warren Scoville and by talking with fellow graduate students, especially Walter Oi and Ted Balbach, after taking Armen Alchian's course. Alchian later became an outstanding classroom teacher but, at the time, he showed little interest in teaching graduate students. He did manage to stimulate us with his questions, but he did little to help us learn to think about the answers. Perhaps that was his method. His questions drove the student toward fundamental issues about the price system and institutional arrangements. Like most graduate students, we were more interested in analytic technique. We did not know until later that he relied on Milton Friedman's (then unpublished) notes on price theory. All we knew was that there was little relation between his lectures and the assigned readings, so it fell to the graduate students to try to understand his lectures by pooling our very incomplete knowledge of economic analysis. That was how we learned. It may not have been efficient, but learning rarely is.

Brunner was the very opposite of Alchian. He would stop by the room where all the teaching assistants had desks and invite us to join him for coffee. These invariably became sessions devoted to some question to which we applied economic analysis. One had to make the analysis explicit. These sessions and the coursework taught me to analyze first and apply value judgments or preferences later. It sounds simple, but it is rare and requires discipline. Much easier and far more common is to find arguments that support a conclusion one likes for other reasons.

At the time Brunner was more or less a Keynesian, and his graduate class developed versions of that model and taught us to squeeze out implications and compare them to the facts that we could assemble. It was not so much what he taught as his dedication, enthusiasm and the repeated demonstrations that economic analysis is applicable to real-world problems that attracted me. When some students became interested in working through Paul Samuelson's *Foundations of Economic Analysis*, Karl ran a night seminar to help us. With his remarkable and indefatigable wife, Rosemarie, he welcomed the students and encouraged them to think analytically about a wide range of problems. History, logic and philosophy were of particular interest to him, but Rosemarie's interests included dance, art, religious beliefs, psychology and much more. To this day, he remains open to new ideas, willing to reexamine old ones and thoroughly committed to economics as a discipline and as a policy science. I learned much more from him than monetary theory and macroeconomics.

Karl urged me to begin systematic study of mathematics, and he laid out a program that would have kept me studying at UCLA for years. That was not my plan or program. I saw a PhD degree as a license to learn on my own. What other way can one learn? In two and a half years I completed the economics courses, language and minor requirements and comprehensive examinations, applied for and received a Fulbright scholarship and a grant from the Social Science Research Council and left for France with wife, infant son, a pile of books and a thesis topic.

Brunner had become interested in the theory of the supply of money, and I had a strong desire to spend a year in France, so we combined the two into a thesis topic on the determinants of the stock of money during the wartime and postwar inflation in France. I had no idea whether I liked research and was somewhat vague about how to go about it. Research began only after one completed coursework, an odd and inefficient way to train researchers. Later, at Carnegie, I helped to develop a different model in which training for research begins early. This way students have a better idea about what an academic career entails and faculty have some information about whether a student has an aptitude for research.

Chance worked for me again. I enjoyed the problem-solving aspect of the thesis, the search for data, and seeing the hypothesis prove to be fruitful. By choosing monetary theory and developing an interest in inflation, I had chosen a specialty that soon became an important research topic and a major policy issue. My interest in money and inflation, both as areas for research and as policy problems, continued for many years.

During my investigation, I learned about some incidents that, though unimportant for my thesis research, affected my views about government and about the uses of discretion. Early postwar French prices were controlled, and wages were indexed to prices. On occasion the government of the day would remove items from the price index or make large imports of items that rose in price to reduce the increase in prices and hence in wages. Payments for the imports were financed by printing money. To my surprise socialist ministers not only did not object to these schemes; often they proposed or implemented them. (Years later, the Brazilian government made a similar effort to control wages by controlling the reported price index instead of choosing policies to control inflation. Perhaps this practice is more common than I know.)

This experience, and several others, reopened issues about institutions and incentives. I did not have a compact way of thinking about issues of this kind, but I believed they were important and I was intrigued by them. I began to look for ways to structure problems of this kind. Among the books I read, much later, Hayek's *Constitution of Liberty* and Popper's *The Open Society and Its Enemies* helped me most to appreciate the importance of institutions or rules that restrict arbitrary actions of government. I came to believe that the large difference between rhetoric and reality which I had encountered in the Wallace campaign, in France and elsewhere was not accidental and, unfortunately, not a rare occurrence.

An early consequence of this way of thinking was that I did not develop much interest in that part of economics where the market is the only institution. I recognize the value in formal analysis of an Arrow–Debreu economy or other efforts to develop axioms. Standard price theory produces implications that are useful, indeed indispensable, for predicting observable outcomes. Yet neglecting institutions must have some cost.

The University of Pennsylvania offered me an entry-level job while I was in France. The Penn Economics Department was then in the Wharton school, but the department's mission did not include macroeconomics. That course or subject belonged to the Finance Department. I was hired to teach nine hours a week of principles and money and banking. To supplement my modest salary, I was given a night course to teach.

The Penn Department was an unexciting place. Most of the faculty had graduated from the school, and several had never been anywhere else. The department was long on pretensions about being part of the so-called Ivy League and, with a few exceptions, short on research or a desire to excel. My experience at Penn convinced me that it is a good rule to diversify by restricting the hiring of your own students at least until they have established their independence.

Grandmother's lessons and an extremely supportive wife helped me through the years. I worked hard to finish my thesis, grinding out regressions every night on a home calculator. The computer had been developed at Penn, but it was not yet widely used to process data, so I (and everyone else) inverted matrices and computed coefficients by hand. The department had two hand calculators, mainly used by the chairman and his assistants. I rented my own and worked at home whenever possible, a habit I have retained ever since. When my thesis was far enough along to be described as 'almost finished', I wrote letters to other schools offering my services.

This time good fortune came in the form of a telephone call from Lee Bach, then the Dean of the Graduate School of Industrial Administration (GSIA) at (then) Carnegie Tech. By the end of summer 1957, I had defended my thesis and moved to Pittsburgh.

The move was a good one. At the time, GSIA had a lively and stimulating atmosphere and I believe it has remained that way. I have visited schools where faculty do not exchange ideas until they are ready to be published. GSIA was not (and is not) one of them. There are schools where faculty have to have the 'right' view to be promoted. GSIA has not been one of them. Sometimes junior faculty have to apprentice to senior faculty in their field. GSIA has largely avoided both fields and apprentices. When I came, the atmosphere was open; you were expected to be enthusiastic about what you were doing and to be able to explain it to others. With rare exceptions, seminars were not trials by combat or efforts to show off. They were intended to be – and often were – efforts to help the author improve his paper. Several young faculty, who later became distinguished professionals, have told me that it was this atmosphere that attracted them to GSIA when they were interviewed at the start of their careers. I know it helped me to develop my ideas.

The original conditions owed much to the young Herb Simon and Bill Cooper. Their direct influence waned long ago, but the tradition continues. The remarkable record of achievement by faculty and students who have come, and in many cases gone elsewhere, speaks to the stimulus that others have found in the GSIA environment and that they, in turn, helped to foster. The small size of the school and the school's commitment to interaction across disciplines probably contributed to the stimulation. Some rather unique and time-consuming procedures for faculty review and promotion helped to maintain high quality. Now that the school is larger, and cross-disciplinary research has declined in relative importance, the valuable local public good – the outstanding research environment – may not survive as in the past. The tradition is well established, however, so some of the tradition is likely to remain for a long time.

The contrast between GSIA and Penn was so marked that I can recall after more than 30 years my heightened sense of excitement. The school was relatively new – less than ten years old – when I arrived and very conscious of its 'Mission.' By reciting achievements of the school and the faculty, Lee Bach communicated that the aim was excellence, that the small faculty of 25 or 30 was to be innovative in education for business and economics and in research, that the tiny school in a small and not very distinguished technical university was going to change management education. With some help from the Ford Foundation, he managed to do just that. It fitted well with some of grandmother's teachings and my personal objectives.

Some of the excitement vanished long ago, perhaps the inevitable result of the professionalization of management education that the school set out to achieve, perhaps the result of increased size and the influence of professional disciplines, as Herb Simon insisted in the early days of the school. In my experience as a visiting faculty member at Harvard, Chicago and other universities, I have never found an atmosphere that matched my early years at GSIA.

A RESEARCH PROGRAM

Research, like other types of learning, is mainly an individual activity. Perhaps that is why the author is often the one who learns most from research. Even collaborative research, of which I have done a lot, requires that someone write out the results and someone revise what is written. Often this is the time when I understand most fully the implications of what I (or we) have done and the price paid to get the result.

When I was a graduate student, I wondered about how people decided what was a researchable topic. This concern must have stayed with me early in my career because I would write down and file potential topics. I don't recall ever looking in the topics file, and soon I stopped adding new material. Years ago, I threw away the contents.

Much of the appeal of academic life to me comes from the large amount of freedom to work on subjects that interest me. There is no apparent limit to what people can convince themselves to believe. I enjoy finding out whether data support my hypotheses or whether a conclusion follows from established hypotheses without too many restrictions or auxiliary assumptions. Mostly, I am interested in work that has some bearing on the way the world works. I am, unashamedly, part of the generation that was attracted to economics as a discipline that can be used to improve welfare. Over the years, experience and research – my own and others' – has altered my view about the role that economists can play, but I have never changed my belief that economics is a policy science, not a branch of applied mathematics. Economics will be poorer if it does not include institutions and the incentives embodied in the rules, institutions or arrangements that we call society. Economics as a policy science includes both formal models and the analysis of institutions and their effects.

Much of what passes for research and fills the journals, even the quality journals, seems remote from the development of economics as a policy science. One person gets a result. Another finds that it does not hold under some change in assumption. Neither may have much to say about the world we inhabit. It is a poor excuse, though probably correct, to point out that much of what appeared in journals in the past did not contribute to the development of economics as a policy science. Economists are not the group to defend inefficiency.

Concern for policy does not mean that every piece should carry its own message. Foundations are necessary in any discipline. Economists have done much good work to strengthen the foundations of the discipline by working out the conditions under which standard propositions hold. Part of being an expert is knowing more than others about the qualifications and restrictions on the realm of application. At one time, economists often included in their papers statements about what happened when one 'relaxed the assumptions' used to obtain sharp implications, but the practice has gone out of fashion. It is a pity; 'relaxing the assumptions' should include taking into account institutions and the types of incentives that a policy proposal generates or neglects, and the effects of assuming that it is costly to acquire information.

Looking back, I cannot be certain when these ideas began to affect my research program. By the mid-1960s, Karl Brunner and I had written about the gap between economic analysis and policy actions and, by the end of the 1960s, we were thinking more formally about the role of institutions and costs of information. Some of these ideas eventually found their way into a paper on 'The Uses of Money.'

That was not where I started, however. At first, I tried two different ways of doing empirical work combining institutions and economic theory without examining why the institutions developed their form. One proved to be more fruitful for me than the other, again partly a result of chance.

The less fruitful path, for me, was stimulated by the work at GSIA on the behavioral theory of the firm. With a graduate student, I took protocols – detailed, step-by-step notes – on how an experienced professional investor made his decisions. Then we simulated his decision by writing down his rules of thumb. Although we published a paper explaining the method and giving the results of our simulation, and my collaborator, Geoffrey Clarkson, later won an award for the work he expanded into a dissertation, I was not attracted either by the method, or its possibilities in finance, or by the subject matter.

The other approach started with an empirical study of the way trade credit changed the allocation of loans. Critics of monetary policy had used banking data to show that banks denied loans to smaller firms when credit contracted. I was skeptical. The banking data did not take account of the allocation by the borrowers. I found that lending by large firms to small, through the use of trade credit, was one important, though perhaps costly, means of reallocating the outstanding stock. This paper influenced my thinking about financial markets, institutional arrangements and the many, at times important, aspects that could not be captured in standard models such as IS–LM. The paper helped to persuade Eli Shapiro, then working with Bert Fox to organize research at the Commission on Money and Credit, to support some additional work and, more importantly, to recommend me later to Senator Paul Douglas, then Chairman of the Joint Economic Committee, as the person to lead a study of the dealer market for government securities.

The study of the dealer market (1960) gave me and my colleague Gert von der Linde, whom I invited to join in the study, a valuable introduction to market institutions. We interviewed many of the dealers and learned a great deal about the market for government securities and the first steps in the execution of monetary policy and other Federal Reserve operations. The study attracted the attention of Robert Roosa, then a vice president at the New York Fed who soon after became Under Secretary of the Treasury for Monetary Affairs in the (new) Kennedy administration. Roosa invited me to be a Treasury assistant. It was my understanding that I would attend policy meetings to find topics on which research could be helpful to the Treasury. I had the foresight to ask him to agree that I would not answer letters or do other routine tasks.

When I arrived in June, full of enthusiasm, energy and anticipation, I found that either there was a misunderstanding about my job or a change in the (unwritten) contract. My first assignment was to respond to a letter from a Congressman. Roosa declined to invite me to policy meetings. I resigned at the end of two weeks. Lee Bach supported my decision, urged me to leave on good terms, and welcomed me back to GSIA. The Treasury made me a consultant. For several months I commuted to Washington for a few days every other week to work on the taxation of municipal bond interest. David Ott was doing a complementary analysis at Brookings. We joined our two studies in a book published as part of the Brookings study of taxation. After a while, I stopped going to the Treasury.

My experience in government lasted long enough to raise the issue about why governments act as they do. The Kennedy Treasury had 'positions' that it did not choose to examine, including the importance of defending the dollar. None of my superiors wanted to consider whether it was good policy to 'defend the dollar' by raising interest rates during a recession. The US had large reserves relative to its trade deficit. Why not let reserves flow out during the recession and return during the next expansion to maintain money growth and moderate the recession? Nor did they wish to analyze whether efforts to use debt management to raise short rates and lower long rates had any effect on either the rates or the economy. I cannot claim that I understood why these issues could not be analyzed or even discussed, but I recognized that the Treasury was a much more restricted environment than the staff of the Congressional Joint Economic Committee, where I had worked on the study of the dealer market in my previous experience in government. It was clear that 'political constraints' restricted not only the choice of policies but even discussion. I tried to think about what the constraints were, where they came from and how they affected the choice of policies.

Congressman Wright Patman had been the force behind the study of the dealer market. Although our conclusions about the market did not confirm his prior beliefs, he invited me to undertake another study of the dealer market for the House Committee on Banking and Currency. I persuaded him that the problems that interested him lay not in the dealer market but in the Federal Reserve's method of conducting policy. He agreed that the study should concentrate on the Federal Reserve.

A few months earlier, Karl Brunner had suggested that we begin to work together to write a textbook. I had published enough independently to be able to work as a colleague. We agreed that we would not write a textbook until we had done much more to fill in some of the empirical gaps in monetary economics. I began work on the demand for money and Brunner continued his work on money supply. We never wrote the textbook.

Patman's invitation struck me as an exciting opportunity to learn more about the supply of money and the Federal Reserve's methods of controlling money and making decisions. I invited Brunner to join me, and he agreed immediately. He was still at UCLA, so many of the interviews with dealers, bankers and Federal Reserve officials in Washington and New York fell to me and to David Meiselman, who had joined the staff of the Banking Committee. During the summer Brunner and I conducted interviews on the West coast and began work on the study.

I was surprised at how little research the Federal Reserve had done on the monetary mechanism. Many of our questions were about basic issues such as what they controlled, how they decided to act, or how their actions affected economic activity and prices. Many of their answers came as analogies with different analogies favored by different governors. A set of questions about operating procedures and regular policy actions required a system-wide committee to agree on the answers. In its first 50 years, the Federal Reserve appeared to have done little to learn about its mission and the effects of its actions. The focus was, or seemed, dominantly short-term and did not get beyond the money market to study the effects on economic activity and prices.

The study and what we learned in the process greatly influenced the work that Brunner and I did on targets and indicators, on monetary control and monetary policy, on money and intermediation and on the relation of money and debt to income and prices. In our view, research on money that would be useful for policy decisions had to be rich enough to be able to answer questions about institutional structure and regulation. We saw our work as fitting between the large-scale econometric models, with their emphasis on details and concern for aggregative effects of allocative patterns, and standard macro theory in which money was a given denoted M. I think we made the right choice, but I am convinced that we did not persuade most of the profession. Discussions of intermediation and monetary policy most often still use models with one asset or use a large-scale econometric model to simulate the responses. Discussions of Federal Reserve actions typically assume that the Federal Reserve's objective is to maximize social welfare.

Two of the main conclusions of our study were that the Federal Reserve relied on unreliable control procedures and that they had made no effort to achieve better control procedures. The Federal Reserve staff detected turning points in the economy, but the process used to control money was so inadequate that policy actions were only loosely related to the objectives of full employment without inflation. Typically, money growth rose (relative to trend) in periods of economic expansion and declined (relative to trend) in recessions. Monetary policy was procyclical, adding to problems of inflation and recession in the economy.

The study produced little response from the Federal Reserve. Internal memos commenting on the study did not refute the main conclusions; a seminar on the study at the Board drew a large audience but not much comment or criticism. Later, when the Federal Reserve changed procedures, it did nothing to eliminate procyclicality; the change was from control of free reserves, which we had criticized, to control of a short-term interest rate. A consequence of the short-term focus and reliance on interest rates as an indicator of the current policy stance is that the Federal Reserve produced the inflation of the 1960s and 1970s not by design but by misinterpreting the degree to which policy was expansive. They did not give up reliance on interest rates as an indicator of policy stance until 1979 when, under pressure from foreign governments, they finally adopted and maintained a policy to reduce inflation. They shifted to a measure very similar to free reserves and, in 1982, with inflation reduced, shifted back.

The Federal Reserve study and subsequent events had two lasting effects on my attitudes toward government. First, the Federal Reserve had made major contributions to two debacles – the Great Depression of the 1930s and the Great Inflation of the 1970s. Both were costly to the US and the rest of the world. Yet there was no public outcry. Neither the Congress nor successive administrations seemed concerned about the Federal Reserve's role in these failures. Congress and the public did not consider alternative arrangements to reduce errors in the future. Second, my skepticism about discretionary policy increased. If an agency of government that I knew well performed as poorly as we had found, why would other agencies be different? Subsequent experience with regulation Q, the management of deposit insurance and housing programs increased my skepticism about activities with which I was most familiar and, of course, about other areas as well.

Governments often seemed to commit human and material resources without a clear long-term objective. When short-term objectives were not met, additional resources were often committed to avoid the appearance of failure. During my brief stay in the Treasury in 1961, a small incident left a deep impression. A businessman, serving as an intern in the public service, was studying the drug problem, part of the Treasury's responsibility at that time. He was amazed that there was no long-term program to achieve some set of objectives. He found neither the program nor the objectives. All planning was tied to the short-term budget cycle. Later, I realized that much the same could be said about the lack of objectives and of strategies to achieve objectives in actions to prevent or reduce inflation, the so-called war on poverty and many other activities including, apparently, waging war.

This absence of long-term objectives and operating strategies characterizes many activities, private as well as public, civilian as well as military. The private sector has more effective corrective mechanisms and, therefore, greater incentive to correct errors. One reason is that more of the costs of private mistakes are borne privately by those who undertake the risk or those who make the mistakes. Can these costs be incorporated when comparing the two sectors?

At the time of the Federal Reserve study, many views about limiting discretion were not well formed. I knew about proposals for rules and had read some of the literature on rules and discretion. Although we were critical of the way discretion was used, I don't recall any discussion with Karl Brunner about a proposal for a monetary rule as part of our study.

The skepticism that grew out of my limited experience with government was reinforced by some main implications of the literature on public choice that was emerging at about the same time. Lingering early beliefs about the role of government withered. I did not become an anarchist; I recognized that there must be a role for collective action. What was that role? What should it be? The standard literature on public goods did not give satisfactory answers. Governments engaged in many activities that could not be described as public goods without removing all meaning from that term. Theories of optimal taxation seemed to be divorced from actual tax systems. Theories of optimal tariffs and regulation and much of welfare economics, whatever their other merits, do not explain either what modern governments do or how they choose policies. The gap between research and practice is much too wide.

In the social sciences, it is said, ideology or beliefs influence the problems people choose to study, or the way in which they proceed. This is at most a partial truth but difficult to reject since we observe decisions and can only speculate about motives, beliefs or philosophy. However, I don't believe that I began work on the size of government to support any normative view.

A number of different influences, in addition to those I have mentioned, combined to shift some of my interest from monetary theory and policy to forces determining the size of government. Data on the growth of public expenditure or tax revenues showed that these measures of the size of government had increased faster than broad measures of aggregate output in all developed countries during the postwar years. Why was this so? Discussions with political science colleagues suggested that there were only a few papers but no generally accepted answer. In the early 1970s, Brunner started the annual Interlaken Seminar on Analysis and Ideology where broad issues of this kind were discussed. In 1974, I was invited to give a lecture at a law school as part of a series on the role of government. My first effort was, in fact, an attempt to work out my own normative view. In the process of writing, I realized that there was nothing I would say that had not been said, probably better, many times, so I tore up the draft and tried a positive approach. Since transfers or redistributions had become the largest part of government spending, I concentrated on that.

The main idea in the explanation I offered is that benefits are concentrated and taxes diffused. My colleague Scott Richard later criticized that idea from a rational expectations view. It relies on myopia to a degree. Voters can know or learn that benefits will be concentrated and costs diffused even if they do not know the details of a particular program. What prevents them from learning that the taxes they pay are more or less than the value of the services they receive? What prevents them from learning that the difference between the costs and benefits to the individual of most spending programs rises with income?

I found the questions hard to answer. Together, we developed what we called 'A Rational Theory of the Size of Government.' Voters are not myopic. The size of government is determined by a median voter who recognizes that taxes reduce effort. He compares the loss he experiences because taxes reduce his own and others efforts to the benefits he gets from redistribution.

'A Rational Theory …' explained the size of government as a result of voter choice and the difference between the uniform distribution of votes and the skewed distribution of income. Earlier work often invoked special interests or institutional arrangements in particular countries. These explanations do not give a common explanation for the increased size of government common to many countries after the war. They do not explain the failure of conservative parties to reduce government spending relative to broad measures of output when they are in office or why voters do not learn about the redistributive pattern.

Research opens new issues to analysis. A puzzling issue of long standing is why the public chooses to have governments engage in providing services that can be produced competitively. I have never encountered a claim that governments produce health services, education, or other services more efficiently than a private market. The aim is nearly always redistribution of opportunity or cost. Redistribution of the cost of purchasing these services can usually be achieved without having government involved in production or distribution. Much the same can be said about housing. Yet governments own and operate rental housing in most countries. Why do voters not oppose these programs? If voters choose to redistribute income in kind, why not give cash or vouchers to be used for payment? Richard and I extended our work to explain in-kind transfers. Later, Alex Cukierman and I extended the model to explain intergenerational redistribution and other commonly observed patterns.

Some of the implications of this work affected my beliefs and actions. If, as our work implies, the size of government depends mainly on the distribution of income and the voting rule – modified majority rule with universal suffrage – there is not much reason to believe that a few individuals would have much effect by serving in government. They may be able to change a few details, but major changes are unlikely. Politics is mainly about income distribution – who pays and who receives. One party will talk about equity and justice; in practice, they will seek more redistribution for their constituents and higher taxes on upper income groups. The other party will talk about incentives; in practice, they will favor less redistribution and lower taxes. An equilibrium that appeals to the median voter keeps the tax share fixed. Efforts to achieve a particular agenda by working in government will not have large effects unless there is a change in the distribution of income, the voting rule or some other relevant determinant of the process. I lost much of my early enthusiasm for trying to improve policy or increase efficiency by working in government.

My interest declined also in the normative question that excited me earlier: what should governments do? Countries have established institutions or arrangements to answer that question. I became more interested in research about how arrangements such as voting rules influence the choices that voters or officials make and how the institutions are chosen or evolve. Economic analysis applied to these problems seems far more powerful than the ideas I learned from Grandmother, or the goodwill theory of governments or the fiction that government is mainly engaged in supplying public goods. When we understand better the consequences of various arrangements, and why the arrangements persist, we may be able to address broad issues about optimal arrangements in economies with individuals who vote and spend.

INFORMING THE PUBLIC AND IMPROVING POLICY

Although my interest in normative questions has declined, it has not vanished. Academic research can contribute to the policy process by analyzing existing rules and procedures and proposing improvements. The improvements may not be the ideal point chosen in a free election by informed voters, but they may increase welfare.

Voters are not fully informed about the consequences of alternative rules or procedures. Neither are economists or officials. Acquiring information is costly. Every teacher who grades exams learns that there is a difference between providing and acquiring information. Surely, the same problem arises in society, where the incentives to acquire information about public policy are weak. Economists who have studied an issue can contribute information about alternatives.

There are times when policy changes can be made. Major changes in policy often occur in periods of 'crisis.' A crisis, within government, often means little more than a strong belief that prevailing methods or rules do not work or have become costly. The public may have lost confidence in a program or a governing party, or Congress may complain about the side effects of a policy and want some change, so there is a perceived need for change.

The breakdown of Bretton Woods, public criticism and avoidance of the military draft, and rising inflation are three examples of perceived crises. In each case, previous research and discussion had made a case for an alternative. Objections and criticisms had been answered, if not completely, at least in a way that clarified the problem and increased understanding of the choice.

When the perceived crises came, the options were understood. Instead of exchange controls and trade restrictions, the US and other countries adopted fluctuating rates. The volunteer army replaced the draft instead of a lottery or some other scheme. The Federal Reserve allowed interest rates to rise substantially and partially changed procedures. Thus research influenced practice and the choice of rules. No one can be certain that the outcome would have been different without years of research and public discussion, but I believe the research and discussion changed the outcome for the better in these cases.

Some economists are critical of efforts at public education carried on by those of us who speak in public forums and write in the public press. I am not one of them. It is true that one must leave out qualifications and possible exceptions when addressing public issues in a public forum. This involves making a judgment about the main conclusion and the importance of the qualifications. Some feel exposed and uncomfortable making these judgments.

I respect the need for care and not overstating the case. The risk that anyone will persuade by overstatement seems small, however. Responsible officials seek not one, but many, views. There is a competitive market in ideas and recommendations. Officials often use this market to delay or avoid change by finding 'experts' on different sides, thus showing that opinion is divided or making a case for their policy or for their views.

Critics usually have the advantage of hindsight. With others who share some of my views about the role of experts, I have joined to organize groups like the Shadow Open Market Committee and the Shadow European Economic Policy Committee to criticize policy actions and to propose alternative policies in advance. There is a discipline that comes from choosing policy actions after considering the facts, the uncertainty about what has happened and about what the future may bring. There is always much relevant information that we do not have, and cannot know, about the duration of shocks, the reasons for observed changes and their future consequences. I have learned that even the best forecasts of economic variables are subject to errors that are large and, on average, not very different from the average change. The relatively large errors of forecast, and the realization that the errors cannot be reduced using the methods or models, have been more persuasive for me than any theoretical arguments about rules and discretion.

In the present state of knowledge, I have become convinced that activist, discretionary policies are more likely to increase than to reduce variability and uncertainty and lower welfare, so I have become a proponent of policy rules that do not rely on forecasts. My beliefs about the appropriate role of government evolved out of experience, in response to research findings and by looking at evidence. In this area, as in others, it is difficult to understand fully why I accepted the views I once held. The account I have given is almost certainly incomplete, but it may convey why I find it difficult to set out a 'life philosophy.'

NOTE

1. Karl Brunner died in May 1989, long after this was written. I have not altered the text to reflect this sad fact.

19. Following the indicators*

Geoffrey H. Moore

My life's work, and the philosophy behind it, has been deeply affected by two developments. One is my acquaintance with two economists who guided my work for many years, Wesley C. Mitchell and Arthur F. Burns. The other is the principles and practices of the institution where I spent most of my working life studying business cycles and inflation, the National Bureau of Economic Research.

The concern for human welfare that was at the root of Mitchell's and Burns's interest in business cycles continues to motivate those of us who have followed their path. However, both Mitchell and Burns saw no contradiction between this objective and their adherence to the proposition that economic analysis can and should be conducted on a strictly objective basis. And there is none. The National Bureau, which was founded in 1920, was based on this proposition and Mitchell directed its research program during its first 25 years. That was long enough to establish a pattern and set a standard for the rest of us.

What are the chief characteristics of this type of research? It is quantitative, in that it deals with statistical data, often on a massive scale. It is concerned with problems that are important in the economic life of the nation, such as the problems of the business cycle and of inflation. The research blends theory and empirical fact, not going very far with one without checking against the other. Is there a rational explanation for the relationship that appears in the data? Are the implications of hypothesis X consistent with actual observations? Affirmative answers to both questions help to establish confidence in the findings.

The kind of research that Mitchell's work exemplified emphasized findings. Appropriate methods had to be developed and explained so that results could be understood, but they were not the end that was sought. The end was the finding. What had been discovered that was worth reporting, so the result could be put to use? Many of the results of National Bureau studies were eventually incorporated in the regular statistical work of governmental agencies. The estimates of national income, of productivity, the flow of funds,

*This chapter first appeared in *The American Economist*, **39**(1), Spring 1995, 15–19.

and the leading indicators are examples. This outcome made the research more broadly useful. But it would not have come about unless the research itself had commanded confidence, and confidence is not attained overnight.

One basic ingredient upon which this confidence depends is the careful review of each of the studies. A fundamental characteristic of the research procedure established at the National Bureau was careful review of the findings before publication. No matter how expert the author, others are likely to find errors, oversights, obscurities, or unnoticed implications in his or her work. A review procedure, which included reviewers whose outlook on economic matters diverged from one another, was part of the research process itself. It lengthened the process, but the firm belief was that the delay was worth the cost when measured against the likelihood that the results would command confidence and be of lasting value.

How far could the finding be relied on? The last question points up another characteristic of the research – testing the findings against other data not used in the original work. It was largely for this reason that Mitchell was not satisfied with limiting business cycle research to the United States or to a recent period. Business cycles had been experienced in many countries, and the historical record for each country provided a laboratory for testing findings on a broad scale.

Findings could also be tested by attempting to apply them to contemporary developments. It is one thing to show historically that downturns in series A occurred before those in series B; it is quite another to demonstrate this while it is happening. Revisions in the data; erratic movements due to strikes or embargoes; legal or political events; and knowledge about new factors that might have altered the previous relationship are apt to disconcert the contemporary user of the historical finding. But studies conducted with contemporary data can reveal whether the historical finding is powerful enough to overcome these difficulties.

While he was a student at Columbia University, Arthur Burns met and studied with Mitchell, who hired him to work at the National Bureau in 1930. At that time, Burns was still working on his graduate studies, which he completed in 1934. At the same time, he was also teaching full-time at Rutgers University, and I met him there in 1937 when I was a graduate student in agricultural economics.

My original career plan was to work in the field of poultry husbandry, and my BS degree at Rutgers in 1933 was in that field. Shortly thereafter I switched to agricultural economics. Then in 1939, Burns invited me to work at the National Bureau for one year as a research associate. This proved to be the beginning of a long association both with the Bureau and with Burns. His influence on my knowledge of economic analysis and policy, and how one's life should be conducted, left a lasting imprint. We remained in close touch with one another during the 50 years of our friendship. For many years, we shared nearby offices, and our summer residences in Vermont were only three miles apart. These contacts led to many discussions with other economists about the validity of certain research findings and the need for further research. The visible benefits from such discussions helped to establish them as part of my life philosophy.

At the Bureau in 1939, I met Mitchell and devoted most of my initial research, upon his request, to a review of his writings on agricultural cycles. W. Allan Wallis, who was also a research associate, and I developed a test which would help to determine whether fluctuations in time series were random or systematic. Mitchell had carried out such a test himself, but Wallis and I thought his methodology was wrong. We applied our test to Mitchell's agricultural data. It took little effort to persuade him that crop yields per acre fluctuated randomly from year to year. This was confirmed by similar analyses of fluctuations in rainfall and temperature. Acreage harvested, which is more controlled by farmers and influenced by economic conditions, did not move randomly, and neither did business cycles. It should be observed, also, that in recent years yields per acre have become less random, evidently because of greater control by farmers through the use of fertilizer, irrigation and other practices. Here then is another illustration of Mitchel's, Burns's and my philosophy regarding the need to keep watching in case structural or other changes affect the basic features of economic cycles and lead to changes in the behavior of particular indicators.

Although the original invitation was to spend one year at the Bureau, somehow I managed to extend it to about fifty years. In the early years, I was learning the methods of business cycle analysis that Mitchell and Burns had developed and applied to many economic indicators. The study of these indicators became the focus of my economic interest for many years thereafter.

In 1953, Burns, responding to President Eisenhower's call to serve as Chairman of the President's Council of Economic Advisers, left the responsibility for directing research at the Bureau in the hands of Solomon Fabricant and me. We decided on a special publication of the NBER. It would consist of Arthur's reports on the work of the National Bureau during his tenure as research director. We entitled the volume *The Frontiers of Economic Knowledge* and in our Foreword we characterized the work of the NBER as 'a venture into the unknown …' We wrote that it was a book about the National Bureau and 'about the adventure of economic research, and particularly about one organized expedition's explorations in economics.' I like to believe that I was part of that company of explorers bound together in a pact of mutual assistance in which collegiality really meant something.

Among the various strategies adopted by the National Bureau to promote scientific analysis was the use of empirical data to test theoretical propositions. To be sure, this did not mean dropping theory entirely, as some suggested; rather it meant to be always ready to supplement theory with empirical tests. The National Bureau approach to the study of business cycles was subjected to serious criticism. One well-known critique described it as 'measurement without theory,' a sobriquet used by many to describe this research to this day. It was argued that this was an ineffective and inefficient approach to economic research.

This criticism focused on the Bureau's methodology of cyclical analysis, rather than any of its substantive findings. The principal criticism was its inefficient approach to economic research. But would Burns and Mitchell ever have suggested, any more than any other true scientist, that they had used any of their limited knowledge in the most efficient way?

Locating the appropriate empirical data is not always easy and we spent much time and effort on developing the relevant statistical information. My own work focused on this to a large extent, especially in the development of leading, coincident and lagging indicators. Contrary to general belief, the selection of these indicators was based on economic theory. The economic relationships that explained the systematic leads or lags were often rather obvious. It does not require a very profound or elaborate theory, for example, to realize that orders for durable goods tend to lead the production of those goods because the orders facilitate decisions to produce, but the decisions take time to be carried out. Finding the data to test and make use of this proposition can take much effort. Nonetheless, the idea induced me to find such data for numerous industries and in many regions or countries.

Another simple hypothesis, which underlies the selection of the average workweek in manufacturing as a leading indicator, is that many firms react to changes in demand, real or anticipated, by changing the amount of labor used in production in the easiest and cheapest way possible. Often this is accomplished by increasing or reducing the amount of overtime hours worked or by shifting part-time employees to full time or vice versa. Mitchell and Burns, in their 1938 study for the Secretary of the Treasury, noted this property of the average workweek and pointed out that it usually led revivals in the economy by a few months. This simple hypothesis has survived repeated tests on new data for over fifty years and is still going strong.

Similar stories could be told about the hypotheses underlying the studies of the cyclical behavior of inventories by Abramovitz and Stanback; of national income and its components by Kuznets and Creamer; of construction by Burns and by Lipsey and Preston; of the money supply by Friedman, Schwartz and Cagan; of consumer credit by Haberler, Kisselgoff and Klein; of consumer spending by Friedman, Mack and Juster; of interest rates by Conrad, Kessel and Cagan; of costs and profits by Epstein and Hultgren; of prices by Mills and

Cagan. No one of these studies started from or ended with a comprehensive model of the business cycle, but all have enhanced our knowledge of how business cycles come about.

My own work, the reader will by now surmise, has not been fitted into the framework of a comprehensive business cycle model either. For example, in my studies of security markets and business cycles, I start with the hypothesis that stock prices are largely determined by movements in profits and interest rates. I've sought to learn the degree to which the extensively observed tendency for stock prices to move early in the business cycle can be explained by a similar tendency on the part of profits and an opposite tendency on the part of interest rates.

Throughout his studies of business cycles, Mitchell emphasized the central importance of the pursuit of profits. He plainly stressed in his 1913 treatise, *Business Cycles*, that the prospects for profits is the controlling factor among the economic activities of those who live in a market economy. He re-emphasized this insight in his 1927 *Business Cycles: The Problem and Its Setting*. However, the statistical evidence needed to support his central insights on these matters was sketchy during the course of his lifetime. The studies by Thor Hultgren on price–cost–profits relationships did, of course, provide some provisional support for his hypothesis.

One of the ironies of fate is that it was not until 1971, nearly a quarter-century after Mitchell died, that the definitive quarterly data were published that showed the essential validity of his hypothesis. In 1969, I left the National Bureau to become Commissioner of Labor Statistics in the US Department of Labor. The task of constructing comparable quarterly data on prices, costs and profits per unit of output for all nonfinancial corporations had been one of the items on my research agenda. By 1971, the Bureau of Labor Statistics had completed this work and it started to publish these quarterly figures. The data began in 1947 and now cover nine business cycles. In every one of these cycles, unit costs, prices and unit profits follow essentially the course that Mitchell had described.

Another compilation, undertaken by the BLS at about the same time, which became known as the employment cost index, also facilitated wage and price comparisons. From this quarterly index one can tell whether wage and benefit payments are advancing more rapidly or more slowly than prices. Such discrepancies are important factors in business cycles and I hoped the new data would contribute to our knowledge here.

In 1968, I had the honor to be elected President of the American Statistical Association and in my address to the members, I suggested a number of efforts which could improve the performance of economic forecasters. First on my list was the recommendation that we needed to accumulate and analyze the record of forecasts. This recommendation was implemented by an agreement between the American Statistical Association and the National Bureau. The program was initiated in 1968 and continued into the early 1990s under the direction of Victor Zarnowitz. This effort led to a number of important findings. One well-known finding is that over a period of time, the average forecast by a group of forecasters tends to be more accurate than the individual forecasts of the majority of the group.

After leaving the Bureau of Labor Statistics in 1973, I returned to the National Bureau and commenced work on an International Economic Indicators Project with Philip Klein. The concept of the project was to develop a system of leading, coincident and lagging economic indicators for the major industrial countries which would be comparable to those already developed for the United States. In this effort, we received considerable cooperation from the Organization for Economic Cooperation and Development (OECD) and statistical agencies for the major industrial economies.

In 1978, when retiring from the National Bureau, I decided to continue the work on international business cycles by establishing with the aid of John Cullity, the Center for International Business Cycle Research (CIBCR). At the Center over the past 15 years, leading and coincident economic indicators for 11 major industrial economies have been constructed. In addition, we have pursued numerous other studies dealing with inflation cycles around the world. We like to believe that the research at the Center has benefited from its healthy working habits, which include a sense of social responsibility, precision of thought and expression, a repugnance for shoddy work, the ability to profit by criticism, and a passion for objective evidence.

We learn from each other, and the function of a research program or a research institution is to facilitate this learning process. If we continue to organize our affairs so that this function is focused on the larger problems of national concern, we will continue to make our contribution to the development of a useful economic science.

REFERENCES

Burns, Arthur F. (1934), *Production Trends in the United States*, National Bureau of Economic Research.

Burns, Arthur F. (1953), *The Frontiers of Economic Knowledge*, National Bureau of Economic Research.

Burns, Arthur F. and Wesley C. Mitchell (1946), *Measuring Business Cycles*, National Bureau of Economic Research.

Burns, Arthur F. (1952), Wesley Clair Mitchell, *The Economic Scientist*, National Bureau of Economic Research

Klein, Phillip A., (1990), *Analyzing Modem Business Cycles*, M.E. Sharpe, Inc.

Mitchell, Wesley C. (1913), *Business Cycles*, University of California Press.

Mitchell, Wesley C., (1951), *What Happens During Business Cycles*, National Bureau of Economic Research.

Mitchell, Wesley C. and Arthur F. Burns (1938). *Statistical Indicators of Cyclical Revivals*, National Bureau of Economic Research, Bulletin 69.

Moore, Geoffrey H. (1947), *Harvest Cycles*, PhD Dissertation, Harvard University.

Moore, Geoffrey H. (ed.) (1961), *Business Cycle Indicators*, National Bureau of Economic Research.

Moore, Geoffrey H. (1969), 'Forecasting Short-term Economic Change,' *Journal of the American Statistical Association*, **64**, No. 325, March 1969.

Moore, Geoffrey H. (1983), *Business Cycles, Inflation, and Forecasting*, 2nd edn, National Bureau of Economic Research, Ballinger Publishing Company.

Wallis, W. Allen and Geoffrey H. Moore (1941), 'A Significance Test for Time Series and Other Ordered Observations,' National Bureau of Economic Research, Technical Paper 1.

20. A view from the Midway*

Walter Y. Oi

1. DRIFTING

People with foresight plan their careers at an early age. At UCLA, I decided to enroll in economic statistics taught by Armen Alchian because I enjoyed my first course in the business school. I did not learn about the measurement of the national product or the cost of living. I was led instead through the intricacies of the problem of the lady tasting tea.[1] I chose to major in business statistics and economics because I could not do the lab work in the physical sciences. I took a variety of courses. Joseph McKenna, a young buck from Harvard, came to Los Angeles and taught a summer session course in which the text was a monograph on the dynamics of automobile demand.[2] The econometric model was way above our heads. I resolved to save the text, hoping that I might learn enough later to understand the model. But like so many resolutions, I failed to keep it and lost the book. A production function applicable to education, transportation, and retail trade differs from that for the goods-producing firms in at least one important respect, namely the consumer/customer supplies an essential input. My education at UCLA was uneven, but I cannot tell you how much was due to the uneven quality of the instruction and how much to the attentiveness of the student.

What does one do with a baccalaureate in business statistics? One professor suggested that I might do well in quality control. The Department was offering positions as teaching assistants for graduate students. The latter path looked to be a familiar one for a risk-averse person. I quickly learned that this was not so.

Those with knowledge and foresight develop and follow a plan of action. W. Allen Wallis left his friends and professors at Chicago in the late 1930s to study under Harold Hotelling at Columbia. I learned last year that Robert Basmann traveled to Norway to be trained by Trigvi Haavelmo. We who were less informed and organized drifted in an almost random search for a lifetime pursuit. It could not be elevated to the status of a calling. Chance seemed to play an important role. Aaron Director remarked that he had never heard about the University of Chicago before an accidental meeting with a sociology

*This chapter first appeared in *The American Economist*, **43**(2), Fall 1999, 13–18.

instructor at Reed College in Portland, Oregon. This sociologist told Aaron that Chicago was the place to study economics. He took the advice, earned a PhD degree, wrote a book on unemployment (with Paul Douglas), and was appointed to the faculty. After a stint in Washington, Edward Levy appointed Aaron to the faculty of the Law School. This was indeed a fortuitous event that took place in the early 1920s when a sociology instructor pointed Aaron toward Chicago. A conference held at UCLA in 1982 honored Aaron Director and Ronald Coase as the individuals who began the field of specialization called Law and Economics.[3] The accidental meeting of a Reed College undergraduate and a sociology instructor produced other externalities. Aaron's sister, Rose Director, followed him to the University of Chicago, where she met and wed Milton Friedman nearly 60 years ago. The union produced two offspring, many ideas, and a monograph, *Free to Choose*, which has, in my opinion, significantly influenced the worldwide swing away from socialism to free enterprise over the last 20 years.

The chance event in my life was not initiated by a sociology instructor but by a labor economist, Professor George Hildebrand. I was on my way to proctor an exam; he was looking over a bulletin board. He asked if anyone might be interested in applying for a fellowship at Chicago. We had heard about Friedman and the people at the Cowles Commission. The thought of transferring to another university had not crossed my mind. I discussed the matter with my professors and fellow students. Chicago, Johns Hopkins and MIT were unknown places that were both frightening and exciting. I wrote off for catalogues and applications. I had been drifting and following the path of least resistance, but in April 1954, the drift made a quantum leap. In September 1954, my brother Sam accompanied me on the Union Pacific bound for Chicago.

2. THE MIDWAY

The streetcar on Cottage Grove Avenue provided the transport mode that conveyed us from the Loop to the southside. We walked the short blocks to 1005 East 60th Street, Burton–Judson Court, which would be home for two years. The University was built at around the same time that a national commission was deciding on the site for the Columbian Exposition of 1893, the Great Chicago World's Fair. Both were located some eight miles south of downtown Chicago.

> Jackson Park was a murky swamp, 586 acres extending for a mile and a half, bordered on the west by the Illinois Central. A narrow strip of land, 600 feet wide and nearly a mile long called the Midway Plaisante, connected Jackson Park to Washington Park on the west.[4]

My dormitory was a five-story stone building which with its tall iron gates looked very much like a prison. It, along with the Quonset huts housing married graduate students and the offices of the American Bar Association, was on one side of the Midway. The main campus and the social science building were on the other side. In late September, the Midway was a park. People were strolling, babies were pushed in perambulators and, occasionally, one could see unicyclists pedaling down the sidewalk from the pond in Washington Park to the Museum of Science and Industry in Jackson Park. The austerity of the dormitory was muted by the beauty of the Midway. Later, when the winds blew and the temperature plummeted, I would have preferred a narrower Midway.

In the fall of 1954, I was introduced to the Department. The physical layout was probably about the same as it was when J.L. Laughlin and Thorstein Veblen were on the faculty. I sat in a classroom on the first floor of the social science building at a very large round table, probably the same table where Paul Douglas lectured before he left to become a US Senator. Douglas allegedly climbed upon the table, crawled across its dusty middle and questioned a student seated across from him. At 3 or 4 o'clock, coffee and cookies were served on the second floor. It was an excellent place to eavesdrop on a lot of interesting conversations and learn a fair amount of economics. This must have been the place where the oral tradition was born. Books, equipment and structures are important, but the critical inputs in the education production function are the faculty and students. A strong department is one that can replace its superstars. Jacob Viner had left for Princeton, and Frank Knight was nearing the end of a brilliant career. Lloyd Metzler, Milton Friedman, Ted Schultz and the Cowles Commission had been added to the staff. The new assistant professors included Al Harberger, Carl Christ and Gary Becker. H. Gregg Lewis and Margaret Reid were not as well known, but both would be recognized when they were made Distinguished Fellows of the American Economics Association. It was an imposing staff for the incoming class of 1954. Size bestows some obvious agglomeration economies. One has a better chance of finding a compatible professor and helpful classmates. Some forty years later, in October 1994, thanks to the efforts of Claire Friedland, Meyer Burstein and Zvi Griliches, we reconvened on the Midway for a reunion of 'seasoned' economists.

3. THE PUBLIC FINANCE WORKSHOP

The first year was a shakedown cruise as we enrolled in the price theory and money courses. Once we got by the qualifying examinations, we could begin the search for a dissertation. Some enrolled in the Money Workshop. Others were actively recruited, some might even say proselytized, by Al Harberger to attend his Public Finance Workshop. I went to listen to the papers prepared by the students ahead of me, Lester Telser on the term structure and the futures market, Gregory Chow on the demand for used cars, Marc Nerlove on adaptive expectations, Larry Fisher on risk premiums, and Richard Muth on housing demand. These were enthusiastic guys with exciting ideas. I wanted to emulate them and signed up along with Meyer Burstein, Zvi Griliches, Yehuda Grunfeld and Bill Niskanen. The seminars were sometimes combative. I spent long hours at my desk in the basement of the social science building where we learned how to invert a matrix using Frieden calculators via the Doolittle method. Very late one night, Marshall proudly announced that everything checked on the inverse of his 4×4 matrix. He lit up, laid his cigarette down, and burned a hole in his worksheet. The investment in training on the Frieden depreciated very quickly as the mainframe and later the desk top calculators came down in price.

Mike Mussa remarked that going to a second-rate undergraduate college might not be good, but it was rarely fatal. However, enrolling at a bad graduate school was almost sure to be ruinous. Chicago and the Public Finance Workshop proved to be a godsend. The Midway was the site at which I spent three of the most formative years of my life.

4. LABOR ECONOMICS

My first research effort, if it can be dignified by that label, dealt with an extension of the inventory model due to Lloyd Metzler.[5] I pursued this avenue by estimating short-run labor demand equations for selected 3-digit manufacturing industries. Using monthly data spanning the Great Depression, I regressed manhours M on the Federal Reserve index of output X and an industry specific real wage rate (W/P).[6] I had not read the notes to the *Federal Reserve Bulletin* which explained that the monthly output indexes were interpolated from monthly variations in manhours. Albert Rees pointed out this fact to me. It was with much sadness that I packed away this project in which I had invested so much time and effort. The regressions fit well as they should when nearly the same variable appeared on both sides. I lost this paper in my moves across the country.

In his essay on the Chicago School, Melvin W. Reder wrote:

> The expansion of Chicago economics beyond the traditional boundaries of the discipline began in the middle and late 1950s. Two early examples were H.G. Lewis's application of price theory to the demand and supply of unionism and Gary Becker's dissertation on racial discrimination.[7]

I was interested in the cyclical behavior of the labor market and the uneven burden of unemployment. The textbooks assumed that in the short run, capital was the fixed input, and labor the variable input. I chanced upon a study by the International Harvester Company which tried to estimate the costs of labor turnover. The cost of hiring and training a worker was a sunk cost that had to be amortized over the expected period of employment. These fixed costs were proportionally higher for more skilled workers, and their presence could explain the cyclical employment variations evident in the data. I articulated this idea in 1956 to my colleagues who attended the Public Finance and Labor workshops, thinking that it was an original idea. At around this time, Gary S. Becker came across the same idea in his development of a theory of human capital.[8] It was during this period that I learned to appreciate the ability of H. Gregg Lewis, the economist.[9] Gregg raised some hard questions both about the theory as well as the empirical analysis. I rationalized that the pressure of work prevented me from allocating the requisite time to complete the research. The gestation period from the idea in 1956 to the dissertation defense in April 1961 and publication in 1962 could have accommodated an enormous elephant. A very large part of the value-added over this period was contributed by my main thesis supervisor.[10] The Chicago approach to labor economics put price theory in a prominent place and relegated the importance of institutions. It has shaped the way in which I think about labor.[11]

5. PRICE THEORY

The theory sequence was required of all, two in price and two in money. The theory of joint product in Alfred Marshall's *Principles* was familiar, but it had not occurred to me that this theory could be extended to the tying of cards to IBM mainframe computers. This was one of the many problems and applications that were interspersed in the courses at UCLA and Chicago, some obviously borrowed from antitrust cases.[12] Friedman was one of the few economists who explicitly analyzed the relation of the firm to the industry and the atomistic consumer in a market of many consumers. The representative firm and the representative consumer are useful ways to simplify the analysis. However, the economy is not a collection of identical firms and homogeneous consumers. Economic agents are different, and the theory that I learned from Alchian and Friedman enables us to explore the implications of this heterogeneity.

6. CONSCRIPTION AND PUBLIC POLICY

I had troubles in landing my first job because I was legally blind. Karl Fox, who was the Chairman of the Department of Agricultural Economics and Rural Sociology, offered me a one-year contract as an instructor. Meyer Burstein drove me to Ames to find an apartment. I did not stay long and resigned in March 1958, when Yale Brozen offered me a job at the Transportation Center located at Northwestern University. I worked on the economic value of the United States Merchant Marine, private trucking, and urban travel demands. I also taught the undergraduate course in statistics, which was originally taught by Bob Strotz. It met at 8:30 a.m. because Strotz believed that the best time to think was from 2 to 6 p.m. One ought not to waste 'quality thinking time' on teaching undergraduates, a position that I suspect that he reversed when he later became President of Northwestern. I had first-rate colleagues and was beginning to get stuff published, but I wanted an academic post.[13] Douglass North hired me at the University of Washington in 1962 where I spent five years.

In January 1964, Bill Sharpe and I were figuring out how to get research money for the summer. A gentleman from Honolulu asked me to submit a proposal for an urban travel study. Bill was negotiating with the RAND Corporation to spend his sabatical in Paris. He landed his deal in April while I was still waiting to hear from Honolulu. Bill Gorham, a Deputy Assistant Secretary of Defense, called me in May 1964 and asked if I would serve as Director of the Economic Analysis section of a Military Manpower Policy Study. Since I had not heard from Honolulu, I accepted and flew to Washington DC in early June to be briefed and to obtain security clearance. When I got back around 6 June 1964, a letter from Honolulu was waiting for me. As Aaron Director says, chance and luck are terribly important.[14]

The year that I worked on the Pentagon study turned out to be a valuable investment. Harold Wool taught me a great deal about the institutional structure of the Armed Forces. I supervised a research staff including Harry Gilman, John Hause and Stuart Aultman, who assisted me in estimating a supply curve of recruits to the Army in the absence of a draft, a military service obligation. The Vietnam War was getting hotter. The Secretary of Defense had no interest in our econometric estimates. In July 1965, we delivered our study whose bottom line was that the *cost* of ending conscription was between 5.5 and 17 billion dollars a year, a sum that the nation could not afford. I objected to this conclusion. I managed to insert the distinction between a budgetary cost and the social cost of securing manpower via a draft rather than through a free labor market. Our report was shelved. It eventually surfaced in the Hearings before the House Armed Services Committee in August 1966.

The escalation of the Vietnam War raised draft calls and fueled an opposition that moved onto the college campuses. Sol Tax, an anthropology professor, organized a draft conference which was held at the University of

Chicago in December, 1966.[15] At the start of the conference, a poll was taken. A majority endorsed the continuation of conscription as a necessary obligation of citizenship. On the second day, Arnold Weber chaired a session at which Milton Friedman, Bruce Chapman and I presented the case for ending the draft. At the close of the second day, Professor Sol Tax took another poll. We had persuaded the people at the conference that conscription was indeed antithetical to the Constitutional liberties applicable to a democratic society. A majority now voted to end the draft. It was a sign of things to come. It was a very nice December evening at the Center for Continuing Education on East 60th Street.

Conscription is the taking of labor services without the payment of just compensation. It places a hidden tax on those who are coerced into uniform. The Johnson administration established a Presidential Commission chaired by Burke Marshall whose report, 'Who Serves When Not All Serve?' recommended a lottery to achieve a 'more equitable' draft. One cartoon depicted several generals rolling dice and muttering, 'What kind of Army is it going to be when it is filled with losers?' Candidate Richard M. Nixon argued, 'It is not so much the way they are selected that is wrong, it is the fact of selection' (radio campaign speech, 23 October 1968). W. Allen Wallis, the President of the University of Rochester, expressed his opposition.

> My objections to the draft are of two kinds. First, it is immutably immoral in principle and inevitably inequitable in practice. Second, it is ineffective, inefficient, and detrimental to national security.[16]

Following the election, Wallis was instrumental in establishing the President's Commission on an All Volunteer Force chaired by Thomas S. Gates. Allen did not have to conscript the Dean of his Graduate School of Management, William H. Meckling, to serve as Director of the staff. Harry Gilman and I served as senior staff economists. I was getting married to Marjorie Robbins while simultaneously estimating the supply price needed to attract sufficient numbers of recruits, projecting manpower requirements and turnover rates in an all-volunteer force, and analyzing the optimal mixes of reserves and civilians to support the uniformed forces. The Report of the Gates Commission which was delivered to President Nixon in the Cabinet room on 20 February 1970, played a significant role in the abolition of the military draft.[17] It was in the tradition of the Chicago School which Mel Reder described as follows:

> In a nutshell, the two main characteristics of Chicago School adherents are (1) belief in the power of neoclassical price theory to explain observed economic behavior and (2) belief in the efficacy of free markets to allocate resources and distribute income.[18]

Freedom of choice to serve in the Armed Forces was certainly the right policy.

7. UNDERSTANDING ECONOMIC BEHAVIOR

A belief in the power of neoclassical price theory to explain observed economic behavior is a hallmark of the Chicago School. I am a believer and know many others. George J. Stigler was surely a believer; some might even call him a zealot. I got to know the man, his philosophy and his research when I was a Fellow at the Hoover Institution in 1970–71. Over the next two decades, I spent many hours talking to him, being entertained by his anecdotes, and studying his continuing development as a contributor to the literature.[19] I try to apply the research strategy implicit in the writings of Stigler, Alchian, and others. The Census data revealed only one-third of working-age adults with a work disability belonged to the labor force, an outcome that was often attributed to discrimination and functional limitations. A simple theory of labor supply implied that the decision to work depended on the person's market productivity proxied by her wage rate, the preferences for income versus leisure, and her endowments of nonwage income and discretionary time. I directed attention to the fact that disability steals time. The onset of a disabling condition (the loss of hearing, sight, or a limb, a heart condition, respiratory problems, or mental illness), was almost always accompanied by the need to allocate more time to sleep, and to personal and medical care. The result was that a disabled person had a smaller endowment of discretionary time for work and leisure. The utility-maximizing choice often entailed a voluntary withdrawal from the labor force. Price theory is a powerful analytic tool.

Karl Brunner said that economics was the queen of the sciences. It is the key to understanding the behavior involved in producing wealth. The brand of economics that I learned was produced by people who honed their tools on the Midway, a long narrow strip of land, 600 feet wide and nearly a mile long.

NOTES

1. J. Neyman, *First Course in Probability and Statistics* (New York: Henry Holt and Company, 1950).
2. Charles Frederick Roos and Victor Spartan von Szeliski, *The Dynamics of Automobile Demand*; a portion appeared in *Journal of the American Statistical Association*, 34 (December 1939), 652–66.
3. The spirit of the oral tradition was captured in the edited transcript of the conference, which extends over 70 pages. See Edmund W. Kitch, 'The Fire of Truth: A Remembrance of Law and Economics at Chicago, 1932 to 1970,' *Journal of Law and Economics* (April 1983),

163–233.

4. Reed Badger, *The Great American Fair, The 1893 Columbian Exposition* (Chicago: Nelson Hall Inc., 1979), p. 53.
5. Lloyd A. Metzler, 'Factors Governing the Length of Inventory Cycles,' *Review of Economics and Statistics*, **29** (Feb. 1947), 1–15.
6. I constructed a price index from the price relatives from the producer price index weighted by the 3-digit industry's output mix. I thus developed a product price index for each of some four or five 3-digit industries. In this way, I obtained a real wage rate applicable to the firms in each industry.
7. Melvin W. Reder, 'The Chicago School,' *The New Palgrave*, ed. John Eatwell, Murray Milgate and Peter Newman (New York: The Stockton Press, 1987), 413–18.
8. There is little that is truly new. The gist of the idea can be inferred from the work of Magnus Alexander, 'The Cost of Labor Turnover,' Bulletin No. 227 (Washington, DC: US Bureau of Labor Statistics, 1918), pp. 13–28.
9. A short review of the man and his work was prepared by Gary S. Becker for the 'Essays in Honor of H. Gregg Lewis,' 'Prefatory Note,' *Journal of Political Economy*, Vol. 84 (Supplement, August, 1976), sl–s3. The reader is also referred to the citation on the occasion of Lewis being named a Distinguished Fellow of the American Economics Association, *American Economic Review* (September 1982).
10. The core of the thesis appears in W.Y. Oi, 'Labor as a Quasi-Fixed Factor,' *Journal of Political Economy*, Vol. 70, No. 6 (December 1962), 535–56. It was not unusual to send Gregg a manuscript of 20 double-spaced pages and to receive in return, some ten days later, comments squeezed into 15 single-spaced pages. I must acknowledge the considerable assistance provided by my other committee members, Arnold C. Harberger and Albert E. Rees.
11. See W.Y. Oi, 'On Working,' Presidential address at the Western Economics Association meetings, June 1992, printed in *Economic Inquiry*, Vol. 31, No. 1 (January 1993), 1–28.
12. The tying example motivated the path-breaking article by M.L. Burstein, 'The Economics of Tie-in Sales,' *Review of Economics and Statistics* (Feb. 1960), 68–73 as well as my piece, W.Y. Oi, 'A Disneyland Dilemma: Two-Part Tariffs for a Mickey Mouse Monopoly,' *Quarterly Journal of Economics*, **85** (Feb. 1971), 77–96.
13. Stan Warner, Herb Mohring and Steve Sobotka were members of the Transportation Center staff. I also had contact with Meyer Burstein, Bob Strotz, Bob Clower and, for a short time, Franco Modigliani in the Department of Economics.
14. William Gorham, who is now the President of the Urban Institute, told me that his first choice for Director was H. Gregg Lewis. Gregg evidently had an earlier commitment and suggested me for the job. Chance surely smiled upon me and gave me the opportunity to participate in one of the most important policy issues.
15. The papers presented at this conference as well as a roster of those attending can be found in Sol Tax (ed.), *The Draft* (Chicago: University of Chicago Press, 1967). See especially pp. 200–51.
16. His speech, 'Abolish the Draft.' appears in W. Allen Wallis, *An Over Governed Society* (New York: The Free Press, 1976) pp. 43-51; see p. 47.
17. The transition from conscription to the All Volunteer Armed Force can be found in W.Y. Oi, 'Historical Perspectives on the All Volunteer Force: The Rochester Connection,' in *Professionals on the Front Line* edited by J.E. Fredland, C. Gilroy, R.D. Little and W.S. Sellman (Washington, DC: Brassey's, 1996), pp. 37–54.

    In 1966 and again in 1969, a fear was voiced that if the draft were replaced by an all-volunteer force, the Army would be filled with blacks. At that time, blacks made up around 40 percent of the infantry and combat arms branches of the Army. The prediction of an all-black infantry was never realized. The statistics reported by Thomas E. Ricks revealed that in 1996, blacks accounted for only 9 percent of the infantry and combat arms (*The Wall Street Journal*, 6 January 1997, p. 1).
18. Melvin W. Reder, 'The Chicago School,' at p. 413.
19. When George was visiting me in my office, I asked him to autograph my copy of his text, *Theory of Price*. He observed that I had a third edition, printed during the Korean War on

cheap paper and that the binding would never hold up. It might not, but it is still on my shelf. Unlike him, I do not collect books and do not intend to sell my autographed copy, whose low quality assures that it won't fetch much even with the signature of a Nobel Laureate.

21. What makes my mind tick*

Mark Perlman

Doubtless there are many purposes for editing a collection of one's essays, particularly when the span of time of their preparation covers more than 40 years. In the end perhaps the most obvious purpose is to describe what one did with those decades and begin to explain why. I will come to the description a bit later, but here I focus on why. Many academics believe that their thoughts were responses to ideas and even to the influences of ideas as propounded by their teachers and other great persons. Yet, while I am more than willing to admit that my life has been shaped by others, including great teachers handling great ideas, in looking back what has principally shaped my adult life was a series of institutional questions which I perceived sometimes conventionally, but more than occasionally idiosyncratically.

I have always been as interested in *how to teach* – that is, in how to influence others – as I have been in *what I was trying to put across*. This trait I share with Adam Smith, who was more of a rhetorician than either an economist or a philosopher. To teach, one has to understand the constraints in the other person's mind. Many of these constraints are institutional, by which I mean (to paraphrase John R. Commons) collective thought shaping individual choices. This introductory essay, accordingly, is my own analysis (buried in the narrative) of what has made my mind work.

PHYSICAL SURVIVAL AND EMOTIONAL SHAPING

Surely the dominant institution which shaped my conscious thinking and my life was the fact of Hitler's Germany. Although I was born and largely raised a native of Wisconsin, I was living in Cardiff, Wales in late 1938 and early 1939, and the Munich Agreement exacerbated the all-too evident insecurities which a Jewish faculty child living in a semi-hostile Madison, Wisconsin had. Whatever, I recall the unanticipated feeling of profound relief when I heard

*This essay is a slightly abridged version of the opening essay in Mark Perlman, *The Character of Economic Thought, Economic Characters, and Economic Institutions: Selected Essays by Mark Perlman*. Ann Arbor: The University of Michigan Press, 1996. It appeared in *The American Economist*, **39**(2), Fall 1995, 6–27.

shortly after one o'clock the special news bulletin on the radio of the attack on Pearl Harbor. Up to that moment I had lived with an immense fear that nothing could stop the Nazis. Of course, my analysis was, as we say these days, macro; from the micro standpoint I still felt doomed, since I assumed correctly that I would soon be in the Army and incorrectly, what with my size and physical ineptitude, that I would probably be killed. That I was not killed I ascribe to the bombing of Nagasaki; contrary to current revisionism, the reason that the Japanese surrendered was neither their economic exhaustion nor the bombing of Hiroshima. It was the second bomb that did it, contemporary and later apologists notwithstanding.

MY FAMILY BACKGROUND

I eschew most discussion of my childhood, which was then more than now clearly atypical. I was the second child (both sons) of my parents. My father, Selig Perlman, was a major figure on the academic world scene. My mother, Eva Shaber Perlman, died in her 36th year. She left a strong positive impression in both the Jewish and non-Jewish Madison community. My father then married a younger sister of my mother, and there were two children (both girls) from that marriage. My older brother, later a research biochemist, was at ten better prepared to handle the death of our mother than I was at six. He appreciated and could articulate the dimensions of the loss; the event of her death took me before I could define where my own interests had to be protected, and I grew up in my father and aunt/stepmother's home feeling not only that I was unfortunately complicating their lives, but that I owed them something for taking care of me. My brother resisted feeling the same way – he believed that his rights were prior to my aunt/stepmother's, a view he did not hesitate to proffer. But for reasons that do my insight little credit I never availed myself of his line, 'if Mother hadn't died, I could have had …' Instead, I tried to ingratiate myself with my father, for whom I became briefly something of an alter ego.

Thus a second factor in my development was my mother's premature death and my trying to become close to my father. He was a superb teacher, but also someone insulated with an observable layer of self-concern, albeit usually termed by him as *Weltschmerz*. But however he chose to define it, it was still used by him to place his emotional needs up front, center stage. In my boyhood I must have spent a minimum of three hours each week in one-on-one sessions listening to him discuss the way as well as the substance of how he interpreted events. It was an overwhelming, if European-Jewish-style intellectual relationship – a brilliant father and an admiring son; and neither ever forgot who was the teacher and who was the student. While he was quick to identify whatever originality I may have had, there was little equality in the debating. His way of teaching me was to ask me what I thought, listen to my reply without interruption, consider my answer, and then go on to show either how that answer could be reinforced or be negated. He exhibited an infinite patience in leading me through historical databases, analytical routines and discussions of appropriate rhetoric. By the time I was his teaching assistant at the University of Wisconsin we talked on professional matters well over two hours every day. He was a historian, not only of the labor movement (which was the basis of his fame), but also of philosophy, political science and literature. A one-time medical student, he remained interested all of his life in the evolution of biological science, a discipline which stressed the process of mutation, not equilibration, as its principal analytical mode. This combination of interests in history and mutation was characterized by him as an *institutional* or *organic* approach to thinking. His data bank seemed all but inexhaustible. For him analysis or theory was not in and of itself something aesthetically elegant. Rather, it was merely a step to understanding pressures for change juxtaposed to pressures for continuity.

In his twenties, John Stuart Mill came to regard his father's domination of his mind with anger and repugnance. I was clearly far less prescient than the younger Mill, and all that I can truly say is that I was well into my late thirties before I even began to realize that unlike his explanation of external events, my father's interpretation of personal events was not necessarily to be my own. Unlike John Stuart Mill, I was never as strong in mind to be able to detach myself that completely from the impact of my father's influence. He died when I was 35.

Life in his household was intellectually exciting, but only if a child were prepared to listen and participate as an adult. Few of his many visitors (academic and occasionally political) were so awe-inspiring as to make me mute (not infrequently to my parents' articulated embarrassment); my siblings chose to be not only mute, but generally absent. Given my set of interests, the nine years I spent in *his* home between my 12th and 24th year (I was in the Army between 1943 and 1946) are a good part of my lifetime's intellectual treasure.

MY GENERAL EDUCATIONAL PREPARATION AND THE IRRATIONAL RUSH TO COMPLETE IT

The formal facts of my academic life included a preliminary education in the school systems of Madison, Wisconsin (with one intellectually splendid year at the Cardiff, Wales High School for Boys), baccalaureate and master's degrees in 1947 from the University of Wisconsin, and a doctorate in 1950 from Columbia University. I enlisted in the United States Army in late 1942 and was called up early in 1943. I returned to civilian life in March 1946. During the Academic Year 1947–48 I taught full-time at Princeton University.[1] Thus, if one considers this period from the calendar standpoint, between 1941 when I entered the University of Wisconsin as a freshman and 1950 when I was awarded my doctorate, a span of nine and a half years, I spent three in the Army and one as a full-time teacher at Princeton; the three degrees were accomplished in five and one half years, all but one year of it being periods when I was also an undergraduate and then a graduate teaching assistant – much too short a time to do properly what I set out to accomplish. But I was of the World War II academic cohorts, and we hustled with time and took unnecessary and unwise intellectual chances.

I decided early on that I would become a professor and would try to succeed in my father's field. Even more, I became more imbued than I realized, until towards the end of my teaching career, with the importance of a high-pressure undergraduate education, one involving considerable contact with very capable thinkers. My father was unwilling to educate his children anywhere but at Wisconsin (his university), and it was only after I took both a baccalaureate and a master's degree under him that even he agreed that the time had come for me to study elsewhere. But, while I was at Wisconsin I had some magnificent personal (one-on-one) tuition; from Merle Curti (the social historian), from John Gaus (the political scientist), from Ed Witte (father of the American Social Security System), Willard Hurst (the legal historian), Ruth Wallerstein (the preeminent seventeenth-century English literature scholar), and Roberto Lopez and Charles Edson (both first-rate historians with marvelous gifts for generalization).

My two Wisconsin degrees were awarded in 1947, and in the autumn of that year I went to Princeton where I had taken a position as a full-time instructor, but where in fact I learned a fair amount from the lectures given by Jacob Viner,[2] somewhat less from Frank Dunstone Graham, and no small amount from conversations with two much younger men, Ansley Coale and Harvey Leibenstein.[3]

Princeton, with its emphasis on style and form, was clearly not to my academic taste. The Dean of the Faculty for whom I served as a preceptor, J. Douglas Brown, put the matter best when he said, 'Perlman, you are not prepared to learn anything in the labor field besides what your father believes in. Get out of his field or go away,' and I transferred to Columbia in the autumn of 1948 where I taught half-time (one course each semester) and managed to zip through a year of studies in residence before I left to do my dissertation abroad. The details of that year in New York are unimportant except to report that I began the courtship of Naomi Waxman and that as part of the post-World War II veterans' rush, I spent far too little time absorbing the intellectual atmosphere associated with graduate student fellowship.

There were many major events which dominated thinking in the late 1940s. Of course, the advent of the cold war explains why I, myself, wanted to get on with life – few of us ex-GIs had much confidence that peace would last, and unlike later generations who questioned their personal responsibility for making America militarily successful, my generation saw military service as not only patriotic, but something we somehow personally owed our chums who had been killed in World War II.

America was in a kind of turmoil associated with what in retrospect now seems hard to explain. The GI Bill had initially been viewed as a simple boondoggle (like the much-maligned 'Hoover' Veterans' Bonus), but by 1948 it was evident that post-war America, in part fueled by legislation, was 'flying.' We believed that the growth in economic output, no doubt associated with a disciplined skilled labor force and the availability of considerable capital, would run, in real terms, around 4 to 6 percent per year, and of that amount no less than two to four percentage points could be associated with a partly inexplicable 'residual productivity growth.' So magnificent a phenomenon led most working people to expect regular and marvelous annual wage rate increases. Given everything, their expectations were almost regularly realized, but not without a stately minuet of strikes in the basic industries, the convening of 'fact-finding panels,' and the finding of such facts as would justify wage rate increases.

MY DISSERTATIONAL PROJECT: APPLYING A THEORY OF JUDICIAL NOTICE

Doubtless influenced by my training in labor economics and one aspect of law, the judicial interpretation of the legislative process, at Wisconsin (Selig Perlman, Edwin E. Witte and Willard Hurst) and by Carter Goodrich and Paul Brissenden at Columbia, I chose to do my dissertation on an Australian labor relations topic. My motive was shaped by my wanting to work with Goodrich (who had done a major seminal article on Australia some 20 years earlier) and with Brissenden (who was something of a saintly figure). I applied for and was given a research training grant by Paul Webbink at the Social Science Research Council; my sponsors were Goodrich, Brissenden, Arthur Frank Burns, and John Maurice Clark, as well as Witte and Curti from Wisconsin. I mention Webbink because he has been far too easily forgotten; he was the person who was Simon Kuznets's impresario in the development of the American social accounting system as well as the administrative figure behind Kuznets's later work on economic growth. When I was interviewed by

Webbink, I had no idea of his own historical significance; but I remember telling others how impressed I was with his capacity to listen, to absorb what I was trying to say, and then helping me clarify and assign priority to my thoughts. I told him that I wanted to compare the Australian labor relations system (depending upon compulsory arbitration) with the American free-wheeling system which eschewed judicial interposition.

As I knew almost nothing about Australia when I got there in early November 1949, I gave myself an intensive but extremely brief reading course on Australian history and then turned to looking at the way that the Arbitration Court operated. Subtlety was never my long suit, and I found myself asking the Court's judges what I now realize were such grossly impertinent questions as to what personal reservations caused each to disagree with his brethren-on-the-bench, and what did each think kept the others from seeing the appropriate point? Usually I had prepared myself well regarding the facts of the cases, and to my continuing amazement I found the judges ready, even eager, to talk. In particular I knew the facts of the cases in the pastoral (wool-raising and shearing) industry, the metal trade (metal working) industry, and the stevedoring industry. What I learned from the judges was that each of those industries was significantly different. In the first (the pastoral), the employers were in bitter competition and the union was greatly divided between the interests of the elite shearers and the unskilled sheep station workers. In the second (metalworking), each side of the industry was tightly organized – the monolithic Amalgamated Engineering Union faced the tightly organized Metal Trades Employers' Association. And, in the last (the stevedoring), the union was tightly controlled by its leadership (politically Communist, but insofar as the Court was concerned that was pretty much of an irrelevance), while the employers were divided between coastal shippers (who faced competition from the railroads and truckers and for whom Australian stevedoring charges could determine firms' survival or bankruptcy) and overseas shippers (who faced no competition from Australian railroad and truckers, and for whom Australian stevedoring charges were trivial compared to their need to get their ships in and out of Australian ports quickly and who were willing to give the union pretty much anything if time in Australian ports could be minimized).

In studying legislatures and courts, perceptive students become aware that no one ever really asks where legislatures come on their ideas, but courts are supposed to derive their information from five sources: (1) the examination and cross-examination of witnesses; (2) constitutional authorizations pertaining to judicial powers; (3) positive legislation which meets judicial standards for clarity and constitutionality; (4) legal precedent as defined in the Common Law and through *stare decisis* as seen in each court's own jurisdiction; and, (5) a nebulous thing that the judges, themselves, define as common knowledge. That last is called *judicial notice*, and Willard Hurst had suggested in several of his lectures that it was a Pandora's box which clever judges used to twist a clearly 'the-law-is-an-ass-situation' into something truly appropriate.

I appropriated his point to 'explain' when and how the Arbitration Court was successful.[4] When the parties were both disunited the judges actually seemed to use a vastly expanded *judicial notice* to establish the facts – in other words a judge would replace testimony and cross-examination with the product of his own reading and thinking (a kind of procedure which Louis Brandeis had advocated). A judge's sanction was that if he were challenged he would expose the contestants to questions showing their own organizational frailty.

By contrast, when each of the parties did have its act together, the judge minimized the insinuation of his own views and gave opinions based on the other four sources. His sanction was to threaten the parties with the usual legal obstacle course – 'take what comes from your testimony, etc. and accept it, or go ahead and appeal and see what all of the litigation will give you.' (In one wonderful case, Mr Justice O'Mara, usually a clever practitioner of this ploy, tried to get judicially over-tough and in the end had to admit from his bench that it was apparent that the Arbitration System needed the Amalgamated Engineering Union more than the union seemed to need the Court.)

In the instance where each of the litigants preferred different approaches (the shipowners wanted the judge to find the facts for himself because they could not agree on what they really wanted) and the stevedores wanted conventional testimony and cross-examination, the Court repeatedly foundered.

In the course of my extended talks with the Arbitration Court judges, one, Mr Justice Alfred William Foster, invited to our lunch his close friend and mentor, Mr Justice John Vincent Barry (later Sir John Barry) of the Supreme Court of Victoria. Barry and I left Foster after eating sandwiches in his chambers and spent the rest of the day talking – I recall arguing with him that private monopolies were more responsive to corrective criticism than public monopolies (*Quis custodiet ipsos custodes*). That he was impressed (and, incidentally, had never heard of my father) doubtless I found flattering. Anyway, from that chance luncheon there developed the great intellectual friendship of my life. Barry, then a widower with two adolescent children, was an indefatigable letter writer. He matched me letter for letter. He had a historical sense which equaled anything that I had ever seen; his awareness and feeling for nuances in words reflected his Irish cultural heritage; his ideas on penology were not merely intellectual fantasies coming from his voracious reading, but many of them had actually been experimentally tried by him from his bench. His views on the relationships between biological advances and equity law were eventually taken both to the High Court and appealed to the Law Lords in the London Privy Council (initially he was overruled, but by now his views are canon). A marvelously organized and brilliant man, Barry was a wonderful challenger of most of my conservative views. In the early 1950s he was an advocate of abortion on demand; I thought that it was too profound a cultural question to admit of easy dispensation. He was an early advocate of environmentalism; I thought it a trendy enthusiasm. He was the preeminent civil libertarian in Australia; I had and still have reservations about the dangers of expression of hateful comments (the English legal maxim, 'the greater the truth the greater the libel' always made sense to me, and I share the British view that the test for libel is the intent to harm, not the falsity of the statement). Barry sharpened my thoughts more than he dominated them, however. In truth it was a wonderful relationship because while I was always ready to give him an opportunity to lay out systematically his thoughts (as I should have been), he took my objections seriously, and in virtually every one of our contacts I came away consciously wiser than I had been.

He remarried in 1951 (we had met in 1950) and I tended to regard myself (no doubt presumptuously) as what the Jews call *Ben Bayit*, 'son of the household.' Never lacking much in the way of brashness when it came to doing something I thought socially useful, upon my return from Australia in April 1950 I visited the Carnegie Corporation and proposed that it finance a trip to America for him. It did, he came, and his Australian reputation stretched to his becoming world-famous as a criminologist. From 1950 until his death in 1969 I participated in a weekly debate with what I truly believe was the best-read man, quite probably the man with the most catholic knowledge, and one of the most generous of souls I had ever met.

Barry sponsored the publication of my dissertation. He proposed as readers, both lawyers, Richard Eggleston KC (later Mr Justice Sir Richard Eggleston and longtime university chancellor) and Professor Zelman Cowan (later Sir Zelman Cowan, Governor General of Australia, Provost of Oriel College, Oxford, and President of the British Press Council). These two brilliant men were unbelievably generous; Eggleston offered to write an introduction for the book, and Cowan did for a complete stranger what I still cannot comprehend – he offered to and did edit the manuscript to get rid of its legal errors, ambiguities *and* many of its stylistic *gaucheries*.

Later (in 1954) Eggleston was instrumental in having the 1904 Act creating the Arbitration System declared *ultra vires* (unconstitutional). In the 1954 *Boilermakers' Union Case* the Australian High Court overwhelmingly (7 to 1) bought Eggleston's point; he handled the brief of the President of the Boilermakers' Union, who had been jailed by Justice Foster for well-documented contempt-of-court offenses. Eggleston argued that the Arbitration Court, since its inception in 1904, had unconstitutionally mixed the legislative and the judicial roles, a view which clearly paralleled what I had originally noted in my dissertation. I was later told *second-hand* (that is, by someone who had been present) that Chief Justice Latham, when questioned about my work – the product of a hardly mature economist – reacted so violently to this parallelism that it seemed apparent to all at that dinner save him that I had 'discovered' the law even before he had. The Menzies Government took the case on appeal to the Privy Council (that avenue then existed) and Eggleston passed through the United States on his way back to Australia after arguing before their Lordships. The Privy Council accepted his view, and I was briefly infamous in Australia. But, I am getting away from my story.

In due course (December 1950) I defended my dissertation. My examining committee included Carter Goodrich (my nominal supervisor), David Truman (the political scientist), Leo Wolman, Arthur R. Burns, some historian whose name I have mercifully forgotten and George J. Stigler.[5] The defense went swimmingly, although the historian said all too pompously, 'Perlman, you write in the tradition of Adam Smith, but not as well.' Before I could think of what to reply, Professor Truman, who had previously assessed the dissertation in superlatives, remarked dryly, 'Yes, he also writes in the language of Shakespeare, but not nearly so well.' A few days later I deposited the manuscript in the Columbia University Library and even asked (personally, it turned out) General Eisenhower, then about to leave Columbia University to set up NATO, to sign my diploma. He did.

GETTING ALONG ON THE JOB

Upon receiving my doctorate I taught for 12 months (starting in January 1951) at the University of Hawaii[6] and then went to a temporary position at Cornell. That initial one-semester appointment was extended over no small amount of opposition from within the faculty (the issue was a desire to have an avowed socialist on the faculty) to a three-year assistant professorship. I have always taken lecturing very seriously in that I believe that one lectures not only to convey data and constructs but also to show why and where one applies both. A lecture should reflect the organic nature of the lecturer's thinking process. At Cornell I gave a couple of courses, one of which was on the literature describing labor unionism.

What evolved was my second book, *Theories of Labor Unionism*, which was neither the panegyric to nor the bitter dismissal of my father's *A Theory of the Labor Movement*, which I suppose that my sponsor and my critics really wanted. For the most part the book was well reviewed, although I did note two lines of criticism which I had not really anticipated. One line was that the literature I reviewed was, itself, not 'close to the level of historical fact,' a view which my father had known from the beginning would be his reservation. The other, coming from an economic historian with a personal history of conversions from one truth (Marxism) to another (neoclassical economics), offered the judgment that I really did not know what a theory was. Of course, he was right; no one knows what a theory is, if by knowing what a theory is gives you a key to truth such that you can unlock everyone's mind. When I read his review I wondered just how my colleague Fritz Machlup (to be mentioned below) would respond. Machlup's reaction was reassuring: 'The man's a fool; indeed, the very worst kind, a wise fool,' he said. 'There are numerous irrelevant interpretations of what a theory ought to be; the real issue is what a theory is supposed to do. Moreover, your book provides a taxonomy, and that is where most thinking and then theorizing has to start.' But that was several years after I had left Cornell.

My Cornell experience involved me in a problem which, drawing upon von Gierke's idea called *Genossenschaft*[7] ('fellowship or brotherhood'), came to fascinate me. What constitutes and who determines a group's boundaries? Being both overconfident of my views of things and insensitive to what I was doing to the interests of others, I learned about *Genossenschaft* the hard way. It was clear that among the assistant professors I was probably the most respected teacher, and I certainly published more than the others put together, but it also became apparent even to me (and that unwillingly) that at Cornell I 'just did not fit in.' That was reason enough for our leaving. 'Fitting in' or becoming a member of the *Genossenschaft* is very much the 'name' of any social struggle, and although one who 'holds property' may buck the system for a time, 'fitting-in' whether it is a religious, political, or even a cultural test, has long been the active bugaboo of social success. It is *the* general academic problem, with the actual terms of membership in the *Genossenschaft* varying – sometimes one is inadmissible because of the wrong race, the wrong sex, the wrong politics, the wrong age, the wrong jargon, the wrong value system, or even the wrong level of mediocrity.[8] At Cornell I failed the 'level of mediocrity test.'

Harvard's John Dunlop (later an unusually conscientious Secretary of Labor who resigned when President Ford found it politically expedient to annul a moral commitment to him) came to my rescue and arranged for a comfortable stipend for me to write a history of the International Association of Machinists. And George Heberton Evans, Jr hired me as Assistant Professor of Political Economy at Hopkins.

About Dunlop I will say that he had all of the qualities of Ed Witte – he was indefatigable as a teacher and, as a public servant, he was thoroughly well informed, and he was totally committed to his work and to the institutions which supported him. In addition, he was thoroughly trained as an economic theorist, with *inter alia* 'credentials' coming from the great Maynard Keynes.

I always found him straightforward, well informed and kindly. My personal acquaintanceship with my father's teacher, John R. Commons, was slight, but John Dunlop seems to me to have been cut from the same cloth. True, he may lack some of Commons's complex spark of originality and genius, but neither is he burdened with Commons's neuroticism nor with Commons's inability to turn brilliant generalizations into forceful abstractions. Commons's *forte* was a knowledge of history; Dunlop's is of sociology. Commons read German fluently; from my standpoint, it is unfortunate that Dunlop does not read Italian, because were he able to, like John Hicks, he could have chosen Pareto as an intellectual mentor, and ridden that line of genius to even greater fame as an economic theorist. As it is, he knows Pareto's translated works well, and is one of the few American economic theorists to have begun to mine the treasures in *Trattato de Sociologia Generale* (translated as *Mind and Society*). Dunlop's interest in economics focused on what gave labor institutions their stability and what worked to destroy them. Whenever I have talked to him, I have marveled at how much my father and he set up their analysis in the same way.[9] Both saw labor movements as conservative (when the workers had anything real to lose). Both were true pragmatists – among the various tests to be applied before judgments were made was the test of workability. Both embraced nominalism (going from the specific to generalizations), rather than the method of medieval realism (applying abstractions to concentrate situations). Both were students of the uses of language to highlight or to shade meanings.

But it was my experience at Hopkins which reshaped my thinking more. After our move to Baltimore (1955), I became devoted to two quite different men, both historical luminaries – Fritz Machlup and Simon Kuznets. Each was conscious of the sensitivities of the other, and each used me to 'test' the other's reaction to proposals before they were publicly put. As I wrote several essays concerning the work of these great and dear friends, I shall not give attention to their magnificent perceptions of economics in this essay. Suffice it to say that the happiest academic years of my life were the few when they were together at Hopkins, and that their intellectual guidance and subsequent personal–professional friendship I greatly treasure. My appointment to Hopkins had been made in Machlup's absence from Baltimore, and I suspect that much of his warmth for me was his discovery that I had great eagerness to learn about the Austrian economic tradition – he had supposed that I was 'anti-theory' only to learn that I was all for the subject, providing it was not advanced as a religion. Machlup was a Hayekian, and like Hayek he had his own reservations about economic theory as 'scientism.' While Fritz lacked Lionel Robbins's patrician lordliness, the two men were much alike – they were aesthetes, compulsively hardworking, and above all else curiously tolerant and generous.

Kuznets was only in some senses their type. Also an aesthete with regard to art and music, Simon had fantastic breadth of historical and literary knowledge, grasp of the principles underlying statistical technique, and general economic imaginativeness. Like my father, he had had a tsarist *Gymnasium* education, had turned as a high school student to *Bundist*[10] Socialism as a definition of problems, and had emigrated to America where, fortuitously, he had been chosen by a great empiricist (Wesley Clair Mitchell) as his special student. I saw a fair amount of Kuznets even after he went to Harvard. Listening to Simon was a joy. Moreover, he and I often differed in interpretations. I recall once when he was arguing that the modern world was the result of technological changes in the cotton weaving and iron industries, I argued that it was more likely the extension of the market (a point I discovered much later that Viner had made in his Earlham Lectures). He and I were each holding tight when he asked me why I was so adamant. Embarrassed, I answered that he argued just about on a par with my father, but that he didn't put me down as my father did; and, I still entertained a hope that I could persuade him.

It is in the essay on his work on national economic accounts that the magnificence of his genius comes across. In my judgment, he and his student, Robert Nathan, did measurably more to shape the world's destiny before and during World War II than any other economist in history has ever done. Men like Smith, Malthus and Keynes did much to shape ideas; but Kuznets truly caused epochal history.[11] I have met a great many wonderful and a great many truly brilliant men, but, in terms of makers of history, none was like Simon Kuznets.

MY INTEREST IN PUBLIC HEALTH AND ECONOMIC GROWTH

Some time late in the winter of 1959–60 Hopkins was asked to staff a team investigating the record of a wartime US–Brazilian agency, the *Servicio Especial della Saudia Publica*, which had sought to foster improved public health (largely preventive medical) services. The team's leader was Abel Wolman, a legendary individual who had done most of the work in establishing a sanitary engineering academic profession in the world. Kuznets had initially been asked to join the team, but he had little or no interest in the travel, indeed in the questions, involved. These questions were whether expenditure on public health investment programs could be justified on economic grounds. Absent Kuznets, then me. And that is how I came to consider the bases for investment in public health. I spent about a month traveling with Wolman, from whom I learned a great deal about the actual methods of epidemiology, about the facts of disease transmission, and about the problems of intercultural communication. After that, I traveled in Brazil for about another month alone, but with a vast sum of money put aside for my education. I recall chartering small airplanes to fly me about the Amazon Valley and to one or more points in the state of Minas Gerais.

Ours was an energetic and friendly team; beside Wolman the other members were Timothy D. Baker, MD and Margaret Bright, a sociologist. I drafted much of the report; in it I presented my own 'theory' of economic development, with the health of entrepreneurs being in some senses the most fragile variable. Later, Baker and I did a book on the supply and demand for health services in Taiwan in which we actually collected a stratified random sample of household consumption data, which we then used as the principal economic independent variable. And after I left Hopkins and went to the University of Pittsburgh, Baker and I tried to collaborate on a further study of the relationship between health and economic development, but I had lost my faith in our earlier results and had begun to argue that health was a final, not an intermediate, product – or to put the matter in its worst light, investment in health programs really could not be justified in terms of speeding economic growth.

This eventual conclusion likely soured my colleagues, who preferred to think that virtue and success should be constant companions. Nonetheless, early on (as those things go) I was writing in the health economics field; indeed I wrote numerous articles and edited three books on the topic. For the most part, my interest was not in the popular question of how to improve health care delivery but in broader economic questions such as when and how to invest in public health (including particularly preventive disease) facilities. Nevertheless, it was my experience in Brazil which was key, and it led me to wonder about the mechanism of economic growth. I fancied that economists handled the mechanism too abstractly; from a macro standpoint almost anything could be considered *abstractly* as either a simple fixed or variable factor. My view was that studying the economic process required a set of foci on several *concrete* factor markets: (1) *land and other natural resources*, (2) the availability of *water and power*, (3) the cost of *transportation*, (4) the availability and spectrum of *labor skills*, (5) the sum of *capital*–control of scale and production time, including technology, (6) *managerial talent*, and (7) effective *markets*.

In recent years my reading has led me to wonder about the meaning of economic growth. I now conclude that it is a murky concept quite capable of four different definitions, involving rising per capita consumption, rising national gross domestic product, falling levels of unemployment, and higher levels of national domestic investment. But in 1960 I was quite fired up with what the team had been doing, and was pleased, nay overjoyed, when Ernest

Stebbins, Dean of the Faculty of the School of Hygiene, offered me a supplementary appointment (with summer pay) on his faculty. He told me that when queried about my credentials he explained to the School's Advisory Board that I was the most 'Compleat Hypochondriack' that he had ever known – not only do I know the symptoms of diseases that he had never heard of, but I had personally experienced them!

I returned from Brazil to Hopkins in September 1960 just delighted with life. I became interested in urban economic problems, just then emerging as an important focal point. Harvey Perloff of Resources for the Future and its Committee on Urban Economics asked me if I would do an essay on defining urban problems. I presumed what he had in mind was doing for that emerging discipline what economists had done for the study of labor institutions – something which was academically known as 'labor problems.' I prepared such an essay, and it was used to stimulate a group to undertake separate essays. In retrospect, I think that Perloff erred; while he may have wanted a study of urban problems, what the profession wanted was econometric studies which offered positive and measurable criteria for policy choices. My tie with Resources for the Future was of limited duration; I enjoyed the association. Perloff's eventual choice was to sponsor econometric studies, something more numerical and seemingly scientific. Yet, for all of their appearance of numerical accuracy, we are still at the point of not really having defined the sources of, much less the cures for, urban malaise – of which blight is only the most obvious frustration.

During the ensuing academic year 1960–61 the Hopkins Department of Political Economy quickly disintegrated. Evsey Domar had already left, and Richard Musgrave had replaced him. Kuznets, who had turned down a Harvard offer in 1959–60, accepted it when it was renewed. And Musgrave, believing that Machlup's brand of economic theory, focused as it was on separate theories (each with its own methodology) of relative prices, incomes and employment, was conceptually out of date, counseled Evans (by this time Dean of the Faculty as well as departmental chairman) to encourage Machlup to leave.

When Machlup was suddenly offered the sucessorship to Viner at Princeton (Ragnar Nurkse had already accepted the post, but died suddenly before he could take it up), Evans did as Musgrave counseled; and I, by going to the Provost saying that Evans's decision was flawed, probably fouled my own nest.[12] Anyway, the events played out. Kuznets went to Harvard; Machlup to Princeton, and then after a bit, Musgrave also went to Princeton. Evans brought in a new team, with Carl Christ as impresario. The criterion for membership in the new *Genossenschaft* was econometric analysis and presentation – quite possibly again the wrong level of mediocrity or to be interpreted as the wrong religion (numeracy can be a religion).

THE PITTSBURGH YEARS

I looked around for alternative offers, and the one that I took was a professorship at Pittsburgh, where I have remained until now. I had asked and had been granted an appointment specifying that I could teach economic history as well as labor economics. I should mention here that upon my arrival in Pittsburgh, there was a sudden need to staff an advanced course in the history of economic thought. As it was easier to replace me temporarily in the labor field, I concentrated on the other two. But I was unwilling to leave the labor field, and I had what I thought was an inspiration. I had agreed to work with Edgar M. Hoover on a research project involving the relationship between fertility control programs and economic development, and I proposed to Hoover that if he would give a lecture course on demographic economics (which I could take more or less as a student), I would prepare myself to take it over in a year or two. Thus, in the autumn of 1964 I began an intensive reading course in demographic economics, and by the autumn of 1965 I was teaching American economic history, demographic economics (with Hoover) and the history of economic thought. I will say more later about my own academic work during the 30 years I was at Pittsburgh, but here I turn to two major responsibilities I undertook in the 1960s.

By 1965 the University of Pittsburgh's administration was in deep financial trouble, and Benjamin Chinitz, the departmental chairman who had hired me and a long-time collaborator of Hoover's, despaired of his program surviving. He resigned suddenly to take a political position in the Johnson Administration. In the absence of anyone presumed to be a fitter candidate, I became chairman, a position I retained for about five years – also resigning suddenly when the newly appointed Dean of the Faculty of Arts and Sciences found my hard-line administrative posture (it was the era of anti-Vietnam radicalism) unacceptable. However, in 1969 I was appointed University Professor of Economics, a title which was supposed to indicate breadth of interest spanning two or more disciplines – in my case it was economics, history and public health.

What Should an Economics Department Be?

As a departmental chairman I thought that my principal duty was to build a teaching department, one which taught undergraduates how to think and express themselves in serious economic terms and graduates how to do responsible, competent research and express it in terms if possible simultaneously understandable both by college graduates and holders of doctorates in economics. I favored each faculty member handling three moderate-sized classes (with quiz sections to supervise writing and testing), and I used the argument that as a department we were generating sufficient 'shadow-revenue' for all of us to have what was then an uncommon amount of money for faculty research assistance as well as seminar speakers. Thus I sought generous administrative support for my colleagues' professional development, and I wanted the senior administrators to know and to appreciate just what each person was doing. One such effort involved my drafting a congratulatory letter, summarizing the principal findings, which was then sent from the Vice Chancellor every time a significant article or book was published. I recall that my most perceptive colleague accused me of some minor duplicity in these efforts, saying, 'Mark, do you think me so naive as to not realize that the letter from the Vice Chancellor was really written by you?' My reply was that as the Vice Chancellor was a contracting officer he had the habit of reading very carefully only what he signed; accordingly, the one best way to get him to grasp just what was going on in the department was to give him something to sign.

When I became chairman I put in place my version of a system based on tenure and as much merit and mature judgment as was civilized and possible. I started by trying to get those already on the scene to focus attention on the departmental and personal aspects of their own performance. As I have noted, I assumed, really without thinking much about it, that professors should teach a lot. Their 'bread and butter' came from teaching undergraduates; they had a duty to teach research methods and supervise research efforts of advanced students; whatever creative research they wanted to undertake should generally be done only after their teaching responsibilities had been met. When it came to new hires (and in those days chairmen and deans usually made most of the decisions), my plan had an equal opportunity aspect, and since there was still institutional prejudice against blacks and women, we managed to hire *and promote* some exceptional people.

Yet, among those I hired were several whose perception of what economics was about as well as priorities with regard to academic responsibility differed markedly from mine. Differences in their ideas regarding economics I will come to later, but here I focus on our differences regarding academic responsibility. I came eventually (less quickly than should have been the case) to realize that many of my colleagues believed in the 'marketing of their own careers,' seeking to pursue policies intended to maximize their alternative offers. They pointed out that research, *and surely not undergraduate teaching* (as seen in the output of articles), was what 'paid off.' And, insofar as teaching was concerned, most were prepared, if required to teach at all, to teach only graduate courses, courses which employed the going 'professionalese' (shades of Molière's *Les Précieuses Ridicules*) and were more concerned with what was abstractly stylish than studying directly just how men went about earning their livings. For many of them (to quote Viner), 'Economics is what economists do,' which, in practice, meant that whatever they chose to do was accordingly economics. In the 1960s production functions enjoyed *le succès fou*. Later it was the Quantity Theory of Money, followed after a few years by Rational Expectations. More recently, Game Theory (in its third or fourth incarnation, including Experimental Economics), has become all the rage. I do not wish to suggest that my perception of economic theory involved no more than organizing the presentation of a mixture of Marshall–Joan Robinson–Chamberlin and Keynes and Musgrave–Ackleyan macroeconomics plus Hicks–Samuelson general equilibrium into a quasi-integrated set of ideas, which ideas could then be rather loosely jammed into what Clapham had originally noted was simply a 'box of tools,' a box containing intellectual implements to be applied selectively to policy problems and historical materials, sometimes referred to applied subfields. Indeed, shortly after I became chairman I invited G.L.S. Shackle, whose interpretation of Keynesianism was non-Hicksian, to spend a semester with us 'to teach us [the faculty] about uncertainty,' then emerging as a fashionable focal point. He came and gave two superb sets of lectures – one achieved fame as *The Years of High Theory*.

Thus began my relationship with him, which flowered over the remaining years of his long life. I count him as one of my most insightful mentors, and I have selected here a single, but very meaningful to me, piece, referring to his work and to him. It is my review of his *Economics and the Imagination*, a book which he undertook, he notes in the introduction, at my suggestion. I also thought that the links between economics and such disciplines as epidemiology, operations research, philosophy, political science and sociology ought to be explored. In retrospect, I did not see the fascination of linkages between economics and very advanced mathematics (like chaos theory), which was particularly blind of me since I had had some awareness of the work done in mathematical statistics – but it surely did not register as it should have. In a tribute to Shackle, I confessed that what I knew of uncertainty I had originally gotten from reading Knight; I was far less aware of Maynard Keynes's work on subjective probability (to say nothing of Savage's major contributions) than I should have been.

How to Create a Journal

When I first arrived at Hopkins I discovered that the Department, which was with but a single exception composed of mutually admiring colleagues, lunched together almost daily, but on Wednesdays we spent part of the time discussing annotations of books prepared by Edith Penrose, a Machlup *protegée* as well as something of a literary stylist. Machlup had managed to get funds to publish the *Economics Library Selection Lists*, which originally paid for and evaluated the books that the editor (then Dr Penrose) selected. In time the funds grew thinner, and the books were donated by publishers seeking listings. After Dr Penrose left Hopkins to take a readership at the University of London School of Oriental Studies, the publication had several fine editors, including Eileen Springer. About the time I left Hopkins, interest in it ceased, and the new chairman offered the publication to me as part of my 'dowry' in my new 'marriage.'

During the period when I was departmental chairman, I had some discussions with Milton Friedman, then President of the American Economic Association, about the founding of a new type of academic economics journal, the *Journal of Economic Literature*. Insofar as I am aware, my name had been brought to Friedman's attention by both Fritz Machlup and George Stigler.

Friedman asked me what I thought should be included, and my plan involved commissioned survey articles on the broad developments in subfields, commissioned essays reflecting personal thoughts about the development of the academic economics profession and its literature, book reviews of about 200 to 225 books, and annotations of about 1200 to 1400 new books each year (the last being an expansion of the ideas explicit in the *Economics Selection Lists*). Friedman wanted the new journal also to offer reference to the contents of around 200 academic economics journals in a four-tiered classificatory matrix as well as author-presented brief (100-word) abstracts of about one quarter of the journals. The two ideas were merged, and my wife, Naomi, and I undertook the task jointly. Of course, we had the help of a small staff (including specifically a copy editor as well as help from two of my then junior colleagues who supervised graduate students handling the classification of journal articles).

I had my own views about journal editing and remained managing editor for something just over 49 issues; these opinions were summarized in my valedictory issue. But it is pertinent to add to what I mentioned there. First of all, it was a splendid opportunity to get good scholars to undertake the kind of *refereed* expository studies which I relished.[13] It was a way to learn the high points about areas which I had no time to study. Many ideas about topics were my own, some came from the eventual authors, and I was ever alert to suggestions, particularly from professional colleagues like Machlup, Wilfred Prest, James Tobin and William Fellner. One of my first ideas when I was taking up the editorship was to approach Anne Krueger about an article describing the going issues on balance of payment theory. And, when I was telling Wilfred Prest about Anne's willingness, he suggested that I seek out Geoffrey Harcourt in Adelaide to explain the lines of argument in the Reswitching Controversy between Cambridge-on-the-Cam and Cambridge-on-the-Charles. Others whom I contacted were: Jacob Mincer to explain what he saw as the potential of the human capital approach to studying the operation of labor markets; Bruce Johnston on structural transformation of agriculture in developing countries; Eirik Furubotn and Svetovar Pejovich on recent adaptations of the theory of property rights; Raymond Mikesell and James E. Zinser on the savings function in developing countries; Gerald Goldstein and Leon Moses on urban economics as a field; Robert Ferber on consumer economics as a field; Robert Stern on international trade policy as it was actually developing; Edwin Burmeister on the neo-Austrian theories of capital; Ray Marshall on the economics of racial discrimination; Morton Kamien and Nancy Schwartz on innovation and market structure; Michael J. Greenwood on the literature on migration; E. Roy Weintraub on the tie between micro- and macroeconomics as seen in the literature; George M. von Furstenberg and Burton Malkiel on government and capital formation; Helmut Frisch on inflation theory; Ewald Nowatny on inflation and taxation; Gian Singh Sahota on theories of personal income distribution; Anthony M. Santomero and John J. Seater on the inflation–unemployment tradeoff in the literature; Robert Clark, Juanita Kreps and Joseph Spengler on the economics of an aging population; Robert Ferber and Werner Z. Hirsch on systematic social experimentation with economic policy; Amartya Sen on the literature about the welfare basis of real income distribution; William S. Comanor and Thomas A. Wilson on advertising and competition; Jack Hirshleifer and John G. Riley on uncertainty and information; Ryuzo Sato and Rama Ramachandran on the impact of technical progress; Todd Sandler and John T. Tschirhart on the economic theory of clubs; and Bela Gold on size, scale and returns. This list is not complete, but it does offer a good example at the kind of things which intrigued me.

I also commissioned a large number of personal reaction articles. Among these I remember with particular vividness two articles by Allen Meltzer (one on intermediation and the other on Keynes), two by Harvey Leibenstein, three by Paul Samuelson, one by Abram Bergson; one on Japanese Marxism by Thomas T. Sekine; one on disequilibrium and coping with uncertainty by Theodore W. Schultz, several on Keynes by Abba Lerner, G.L.S. Shackle, Alan Coddington, Walter S. Salant and Richard Kahn; two by William Fellner on macroeconomic policy; one on rational expectations by Robert E. Lucas Jr, and another by Brian Kantor; one by Joan Robinson giving her second thoughts on a personal research agenda; one by Gary Becker on altruism; one by Richard Stone commenting on Dennison's accounting for the growth slowup; and above all else two by Oskar Morgenstern – one on his complaints about modern economic theory and the other about his collaboration with John von Neumann. Perhaps the one I best remember for the tone it set was 'A Curmudgeon's Guide to Microeconomics' by Martin Shubik.

Of course I enjoyed reading the annotations of virtually every economics book printed in English as well as the reviews of about 15 percent of them which I commissioned. Choosing which book to review (as well as the reviewer) bothered me a great deal. I told Friedman from the start that one advantage of the annotation process was that books which were not reviewed at length would still be described.

When we started the journal, the American Economics Association's Secretary–Treasurer was Harold F. Williamson of Northwestern University. He had 'inherited' the job from George Washington Bell, who as Treasurer had invested the Association's funds most wisely. Williamson was a Harvard PhD, an economic historian of note (also the author of a popular text on American economic history), and he ran the American Economic Association's office with diplomatic skill. The Association has a fascinating history. Founded in 1885, in its first incarnation its self-defined task was to stress the disadvantages of *laissez-faire* and the advantages of the responsible state. The early founders were strongly influenced by the Bismarckian Hohenzollern German experience. For their troubles, they were shunned by several of the leading American theorists. However, peace was made in the 1890s, and it was agreed that the Association might discuss, *but would never endorse*, any legislative course of action. During the Vietnam War years the progressive wing repeatedly sought to get Association endorsement for its anti-US government position, but because of that phrase in the Charter, no vote could ever be taken – not that there was any reluctance on the part of the 'peace-niks' to spend hours in useless debate at the annual meetings.

Over the years, the Association experimented with publications, and starting in 1910 it brought out the *American Economic Review*; in 1969 it brought out the much larger and more expensive-to-produce *Journal of Economic Literature*, and more recently it has produced a third journal, the *Journal of Economic Perspectives*. After World War II the Association expanded considerably. By the early 1960s it was operating with a large surplus. The old political division still could be seen and there was a tendency to alternate as President someone of a conservative and someone of a progressive persuasion. By and large the crucible of conservatism was the University of Chicago; and the crucibles of progressivism were Harvard and Columbia Universities. (I use the term *crucible* to indicate where the people tended to be trained – not necessarily where they taught. Tobin, one of the major progressives, taught at Yale, albeit he was Harvard-trained.) Michigan, Wisconsin and Berkeley tended to be 'progressive.'

Of the various presidents of the Association with whom I dealt as the journal's managing editor there were a couple who, although distinguished scholars in one way or another, were simply difficult persons, many who were interesting and often quite helpful (Friedman, Leontieff, Galbraith, Arthur Lewis and Ackley – to name several who come easily to mind), quite a few who seemed to me to be intuitively brilliant (Arrow, Friedman, Klein and

Tobin – to mention but only four), and one who simply 'wowed' me. That was William Fellner, a man with whom whenever I spent an hour I came away with an insight that I believed that I would never otherwise have acquired. It was a quality I found in my father, in John Vincent Barry, in Richard Eggleston and Zelman Cowan, in Fritz Machlup and Simon Kuznets. Others who have had it, and whom I have not yet mentioned, were G.L.S. Shackle, Arthur Frank Burns, Shigeto Tsuru, Joan Robinson, Herbert Giersch, Harvey Leibenstein and Alan Coddington.

Being a journal editor, particularly a journal with a circulation well in excess of 23 000 copies, gave me a kind of entrée which was like a dream. My correspondence with different authors and reviewers was only a part of it;[14] the discussions about content and style often spilled over into all sorts of fields and interests. I enjoyed the job thoroughly, but I was always worried that I was having too much fun, and that my liking for the personal contacts was numbing my editorial sensitivities. I decided that ten or eleven years was the maximum that a founding editor should have (presumably non-founding editors should stay less long). George Borts, managing editor of the *American Economic Review*, and I had both been appointed at the same time by Milton Friedman, and the other, more progressive, wing of the Association may have wanted its turn. In any event, we both resigned (I stayed on until Moses Abramovitz (my own chosen successor as managing editor) had completed his term as President of the Association).

There were several personal spinoffs from my editorship of the *Journal of Economic Literature*. During the early 1970s I organized (with the help of a Pitt colleague, Dr Arnold Kroner) a 'prestige give-away' publication for the United States Information Agency, the *Portfolio on International Economic Perspectives*, which contained reprints of articles from a myriad of American magazines and journals as well as selected reprinted book reviews. In the late 1970s Dr Colin Day, then of the Cambridge University Press, asked me to edit (I suggested Professor Phyllis Deane as co-editor) the Cambridge Surveys of Economic Literature, which drew on many of the authors who had written survey articles for the *Journal of Economic Literature* as well as others. The list of that series' books comes to over twenty. And I particularly recall talking with Mark Blaug about a book on methodology in economics, which I correctly predicted would be a 'best-seller.' In recent years the Cambridge University Press has launched a second, companion, series, the Cambridge University Surveys of Economic and Political Institutions, with the first three books being a splendid review of the postwar German economy, *The Fading Miracle: Four Decades of Market Economy in Germany* by Herbert Giersch and two young associates (Karl-Heinz Pacqué and Holger Schmieding); a brilliant interpretation of the postwar Japanese experience, *Japan's Capitalism: Creative Defeat and Beyond*, by Shigeto Tsuru; and, a speculative view of the US economy as it enters the twenty-first century by Nicholas Spulber. I also took up editing for the Joseph A. Schumpeter Intellectual Society and the *Journal of Evolutionary Economics* as well as the series, Great Economists of the Twentieth Century, for Edward Elgar, Publishers.

MY RESEARCH INTERESTS IN RECENT YEARS

Demographic Economics

I have already mentioned my work for Harvey Perloff of the Resources for the Future. He had asked me to write an essay on my perception of urban economic labor problems. From it there stemmed a conference at which a number of papers were presented. My essay was included as an appendix in that volume. Perloff then asked that I write a second essay outlining a policy prescription. Insofar as I can infer, that essay was a bust. Presented in the autumn of 1962, it had several themes which were seen more as wrong than they were as premature. For one thing, I thought that structural unemployment was becoming a major concern, and that the federal government was going to be forced into becoming 'the employer of last resort.' For another thing I was critical of the way jobs were classified, arguing that pigeon-holing by the kinds of skills involved overlooked a much more basic problem facing the unemployed – what to do in order to maintain not skill classification, but wage-group classification. While there were other points relating to the relationship between economic and sociological categories, what I most remember was the misery I felt when Neil Chamberlain in November 1962 in kindly but firm terms dismissed my effort as a set of pipe-dreams; Perloff did not publish that essay. Of course, by November 1963, Lyndon Johnson had become President and he labored to create governmentally Wallas's Great Society, something which envisioned the government as the employer of last resort. But from the experience I concluded that my trying to do work in urban labor problems, particularly relying upon my knowledge of market institutions, was not going to be easy.

Much worried about the future of my research interests, I consulted Simon Kuznets, by that time already at Harvard. Simon's advice was somewhat Delphic, but I decided that he thought that my having a better knowledge of demographic analysis would stand me in good stead were I to want to do work in public health or in urban economic analysis. Fortunately I found at Pitt a congenial colleague, Edgar M. Hoover, who offered to tutor me (in the guise of our jointly giving a course) in demographic economics. As a consequence my interest in labor moved from industrial relations to the institutional determinants of labor supply and the demand for aggregate product. He and I collaborated on several projects (the terms of intellectual trade made me the great recipient). Initially we were supported by a grant from the Planned Parenthood Association, and although we were assured of complete freedom in terms of the results we discovered, the Federation leaders were clearly disappointed when our final report suggested that a diminution in the number of births would not be without serious economic consequences. After that, he and I undertook a study for the Agency for International Development concerning some hypotheticals as applied to Pakistan, where we purported to find that a reduction in the number of births could make Pakistan able to generate enough capital to meet its own developmental needs. Insofar as I recall, the Pakistanis were thrilled with our results – not because they had any intention of relying on their own capital for economic development (meaning increased per capita consumption); rather they saw a hope that they could spend more on their military.

Hoover and I differed slightly on one important assumption. He believed that fertility control programs would work in all sectors of the population; I thought that such programs, if officially favored, might well work best in just that portion of the population from which future entrepreneurs would come. My concerns about inadequate natality among the educated and social leadership probably were self-generated. The Holocaust gave me profound emotional fears that certain cultures, not committed to large families, would easily disappear, and that to the disadvantage of civilization as I knew it. This was also the view of Simon Kuznets, Harvey Leibenstein and Julian Simon. In recent years when the burden of an aging population seems to be upon us, there is more tolerance for the position that we took than before. But, our fears for refugees and our concern for having enough skilled workers has made all of us enthusiastic about easy immigration policies.

My work in demographic economics tended to focus more on the facts of increasing life expectancy than on the problems of reducing natality. I wrote several papers reflecting this concern. One point which stands out is that intellectuals have always seemed to have a predilection for encouraging the 'unwashed' to limit their procreative propensities, a point which I made in several different contexts.

What About Macroeconomic Problems?

During the mid-1970s one of my colleagues at Pitt, Marina von Neumann Whitman, had seen considerable government service, and eventually became one of the Council of Economic Advisers. When it came time for her to return to academia, I (probably along with many others) urged the appointment of William Fellner as her successor. I recall telling her sometime around 1972 that I had the impression that the Nixon Administration was going to need someone with the reputation for probity, and that that was Fellner's long suit. (Fellner had known Marina from her infancy, and when the time came that I had to decide whether or not to print Oskar Morgenstern's essay on his own role in the creation of game theory, Fellner was the critical referee – particularly after he told me that he and John von Neumann had been engineering students together in Zurich, had disliked the lectures and had between themselves decided to attend the economics courses. He offered the view that he, more than anyone else, knew von Neumann's span of interest in matters economic, and that 'Johnnie would have granted every point *and more* that Oskar had claimed.') Whatever else, Fellner exuded personal integrity, broad scholarship, imagination and careful generosity. And when he went to the American Enterprise Institute (after his White House service) he offered me a regular spot as a contributor to his annual book of essays on macroeconomics.

In all, I wrote five essays for him before he died. The first was a survey of the debate about productivity measurement and change in which I sought to integrate my understanding of what productivity change involved on the micro level with demographic changes. The second described the principal demographic changes which had been occurring since 1957 or so and which were all but unrecognized as late as 1980. The third dealt with popular expectations about the delivery of medical care, productivity gains in that sector, and why costs could really not be contained. The fourth dealt with expectations, tax policy and regional (state) economic growth. And the last dealt with what had been happening in the area of labor relations.

One theme which can be found in these essays was my view that the federal government usually achieved its policy objectives but generally was blind to the problems its success engendered. Shades of Willard Hurst's lectures – 'what was the problem, what was the solution, and what problems did the solution engender?' Another theme was that certain forces, usually tied to personal expectations, could really not be thwarted for very long. One was the immigration of the ambitious poor from areas of stagnation to areas of opportunity; another was the desire for good-quality, inexpensive goods and services.

Coming from the progressive State of Wisconsin I had been taught since childhood that central governments could and should exercise protective responsibility for those unable to handle the uncontrollable economic vicissitudes of their lives. To effect this purpose, governments had to have control over their tax base. And for that reason, as a student I had great doubts about the long-run implications of free trade policies. But, during the 1980s it began to seem to me that the taste for good-quality, inexpensive goods and services had become so general and so strong that trade restrictions were no longer politically feasible. My consequent worries about what to do about the tax base clearly emerged. The first instance was in a paper, deemed unpublishable at the time, on what Giersch and others had been advocating, and the other was a series of books which bear my name as co-editor, but which really bear the organizational genius of Claude Barfield and Christopher DeMuth of the American Enterprise Institute. I should add that when in 1988 the University of Pittsburgh sought to celebrate its 200th anniversary I asked Arthur Frank Burns, Lewis Branscomb (then the Chief Scientist of the IBM Corporation), Yotaro Kobayashi (President of Fuji-Xerox), and Jagdish Bhagwati (Columbia University), to prepare formal papers on the world integration of factor markets, and I was not only pleased with the result (also published by the American Enterprise Institute), but came to the conclusion that for political, but not necessarily for macroeconomic reasons, the urge for free trade of both factors and products was proving to be irresistible. I still do not begin to fathom how national states can finance their social welfare programs if they have no control over the location of industry within *and particularly without* their borders. But, true to the principles laid out for me by Shackle, the real measure of the greatness of man is his inventiveness, and I do not completely despair.

The History of Economic Thought

At Pitt on the first day of classes in 1963 Asher Isaacs (whom I had never met) died suddenly in his office; I agreed to pick up immediately his 'required course' in the history of economic thought in addition to my course on American economic history and my course in labor economics. Over the years I gave this two-semester course many times, not only because it seemed desirable to have the material taught to PhD candidates, but also because I thought that all undergraduate students seeking economics honors degrees ought to know something about the crucibles of their cultural legacy.

In 1977 I began to be active in the History of Economics Society (I had been a founding member, but had taken no role). I had helped Helmut Frisch organize an international meeting in Vienna honoring Joseph A. Schumpeter, and we agreed that I would present a paper on the evolution of Schumpeter's thinking about economic analysis. And when I became President of the Society, I used the opportunity to suggest that the study of what underlay the evolution of various types of economic thinking was a companion topic to the study of economic methodology. In general my views have been that one can compare various approaches to the study of economic thought – among these are approaches which build on differences in the Aristotelian–Aquinas legacy and the Talmudic–Aristotelian–Maimonides legacy; the former seeing scarcity of goods and services as the unique assumption of economic analysis, the latter seeing scarcity of goods, services, *and information* as the assumption at the core of the topic. I have also been interested in three modern approaches to the topic, using the methods of Karl Pribram, Wesley Clair Mitchell and Joseph Schumpeter as exemplars.

There is a story that Clare Luce Booth, a convert to Catholicism, while serving as American Ambassador to Rome, once lectured Pope Pius XII on the evils of communism; it is said that he replied with patience, 'Madam Ambassador, I have always been a Catholic.' The relevance of this anecdote is that I have always been a student of history, including the evolution of ideas, of cultures, and of institutions. I recall being asked whether I was a Schumpeterian or an institutionalist, and while I aver in an essay that the differences between the economic sociology of Schumpeter and of the Commons institutionalists are more talked about than real, I recall Richard Arena (of Nice), also in the company saying, 'But you are a historian of thought. You are not allied with any school.' As I was pondering, I realized that he was correct. I was raised in an environment which was both interested in and skeptical of the assertions made by any Prophet preaching Salvation-by-School; at times, however, I have inevitably envied 'Born-Again Economists.' Like George Schultz I have always wanted (but failed) to be as sure of anything as some economists are of anything. I recall telling some academic colleagues that as I am a rather conventional conservative Jew (a middle path between the Orthodox who seek to preserve the customs of the Middle Ages and the Reform Jews who find most of the tribal identification rituals arcane and too quaint to be observed) I find my identification in my[15] religious and national identification, I don't look for my significance in either my politics or even my professional alliances. I repeat: I recognize that, in truth, I accept myself as a historian of economic thought and institutions and I eschew generalizing and then defending ideologically what I find in my studies.

Perhaps it follows that my inability to identify my professional economic alliances is accompanied by a skepticism about just how truth is (or should be) identified. Even before Donald McCloskey summarized his position stressing that economics was not scientific truth so much as it was rhetoric, that is the art of persuading, I had written in a review (actually cited by McCloskey), that economists were advocates, not true scientists (or I might add in retrospect) nor real evangelists. As advocates we tailor our arguments to the minds of our clients – for some empirical observation works best; for others it is the test of immanent criticism. For me the test which carries most weight is some kind of congruity with my patristic (cultural) legacy, a legacy combining a traditional Jewish view that man should be compared to animals, not to God; that the historical accounting unit is even more the family than it is the individual; that the greatness of America has been not so much its material wealth as the openness of its social structure; and that personal indifference is the greatest of human failings.

THE SUMMING UP: THE IMPORTANCE OF TEACHING

My upbringing was in an academic household – one which stressed that the teacher has not taught until the student has learned. Early on the problems of teaching became involved in the framework of most of my value systems, systems which depended upon the concentration of the mind.[16] With this background I have had a profound respect for the places of memorized data bases in one's mind. Indeed, much of the problem of early education is how to use the memorizing ability efficiently. One must memorize language, dates, philosophical concepts, theological truths, and even most emotional references. I was similarly impressed with the need to learn how to analyze. This was done by imitation – one memorized theorems and then tried them out on corollaries. One memorized others' efforts at generalizing and then experimented both on generalizing and on abstraction on one's own. In the end, one seeks to emulate neither Bacon's ant nor his spider, but Bacon's bee, 'which selects its nectar carefully and processes it into sweet honey.'

Another factor in my analytical process was a basic belief that one could not anticipate the uses to which one's teachings and writings would or could be put. Someone once wrote that a rational author would gladly trade 1000 readers at the year of publication for 100 readers ten years later, and a mere ten readers 100 years later. Thus when my dissertation produced an idea that ended up in a major Australian High Court Case, then appealed to the Law Lords of the Queen's Privy Council, I was flattered, but I hardly believed that my having a star, much less a rising star, was certain. It is perhaps for this reason that much of my teaching and written work strived to be no more than 'my level best' (to use the phrase of my Cardiff headmaster, getting 'your level best' out promptly took priority over endless revision with a hope for the achievement of perfection).

It is within this context that I have become agitated about what we are teaching our best students. This is the concern expressed in the opening essay of this collection [*Selected Essays by Mark Perlman*], drawing upon the topic (and criticizing the conclusions) of Charles Snow's Reid Lecture on 'The Two Cultures.' Where Snow thought that science was the key to the future and that study of the past was a sort of dilettantism, I believe that one studies science to learn about things, but one must study the humanities to learn how men think and derive their conclusions from both the cultural legacies and their scientific and nonscientific observations. Of course, underlying my view is the conviction that economic principles are not in the Lavoisier/Priestly tradition paradigmatic foundations. About virtually all economic propositions reasonable men can differ, largely because those propositions rest on empirical rather than purely logical foundations. These days physicists are not as sure about their 'laws' as they once were.[17] I have always thought that economists were advocates, not 'true scientists,' whose work would always stand the test of truth. Some of my writings anticipated the direction, but not the integrated evidence and analytical beauty, of Donald McCloskey's views about rhetoric.

I have been a university teacher for almost fifty years, and in that time universities have seemingly shed their commitment to explaining value systems in terms of civilizations. Such moves have seemed to me to be pedagogically a disaster. I have never believed that a student had to accept a system, but he surely had to grasp it. When I was younger, English departments were guardians of the culture. I always felt that the English culture was quite warped in several critical areas – indeed, pedagogy in the French Lycées and the German *Gymnasia* was better. But the English experience was the foundation of much American law; Protestantism and the Old Testament were the foundations of much American political theory; and Shakespeare was the architect of much of our language. In any case, these were the things which should be stressed in an undergraduate liberal education, and any education was incomplete if the student was inarticulate both in writing and in speech.

During my three decades at Pitt I supervised well more than three dozen dissertational students. After a bit, I developed a system. Generally, each student took about six months to discover his/her topic, and thereafter he/she was to present about ten pages every fortnight for group criticism. The critics were required to say something, and it became apparent that blood drawn by any of them would be reciprocated when they had their turns to present something. Consequently, there was much behind-the-scenes mutual preparation, and the critics usually explained why they thought the author was on to something good. And, since the author had already incorporated many of their better points, he/she usually was. The system worked, and I not only enjoyed those seminars immensely, but the speed with which dissertations were completed was unusual. As I recall, only one student never finished his dissertation. My view was that a dissertation was to be a professionally competent research job. If it managed to offer something truly original and correct it was to be published; otherwise not.

I was also stimulated by my undergraduate Honors students. Undergraduates, particularly Senior Year Honors students, put up with relatively little cant and even less useless repetition; boredom was shown by absence from class.[18] As time went on, however, I came to feel that my students were coming less and less well prepared. Eventually, I took to giving them my typed-up lectures just before the previous lecture so that they would be ready for discussion. In the discussions I tried to point out how my 'potatoes' were cooked, and even if they were small they were still fresh (my father's phrase).

For over 45 years I was ready to join battle and argue that while there was likely some excellent reason to see just what was involved in 'how people went about their daily lives making their living' by examining the problem from a wide variety of perspectives, that the professional eye should never wander far from that 'ball,' and when I no longer felt the fight either winnable or worth the candle, I realized that my retirement time had come. I retired at 70 with no significant regrets.

All of which brings me back to my opening thoughts. Why should one want to bring together a collection selected from over forty years of writing? Let me eschew the obvious and shallow reasons. But, as I have noted, we study the past in order to study the evolution of the mind of man. And, if it is true as Protagoras wrote that man is the measure of all things, and it is one's own mind that does the initial measuring, then how better to see the spark of one's own thought within the context of one's own patristic legacy than by tracing for oneself what one has believed – insights and blunders together?

NOTES

1. I served as a preceptor for David A. MacCabe (labor economics), Ansley Coale (probability statistics), J. Douglas Brown (social security), and Paul Strayer (introduction to economics). I sat in on courses with Jacob Viner, who in his aggressive way was really very kind to me, and Frank Dunstone Graham. My memories of Princeton vary: on the one hand Paul Strayer (a wonderful man who died young) used as one textbook in an elementary course Hicks and Hart, *The Social Framework*, at a time when national accounting was still all but unknown to academic economists. On the other hand, I recall having a brief romance with a young lady at the Institute for Advanced Study and discovering its cafeteria. The romance quickly paled, but my love affair with that cafeteria (its menu and its prices) persisted. I found myself occasionally eating with a somewhat hard-to-understand scientist, whom others seemed to treat with self-imposed distance. I, however, found him delightful, and one time after arguing with him about how few atom bombs it would take to destroy the American chemical industry, largely centered in Northern New Jersey, and after I had assured him that Ansley Coale, whose dissertational research on the subject contained such a calculation, was a very careful workman – even with wartime experience at the MIT radiation labs (!!), I decided to introduce myself and inquire his name. He was a mumbler, and I had to ask him to repeat it twice. When that proved inadequate I asked him to spell it. B-O-H-R – Nils Bohr, he said. I was so humiliated by my chutzpah, that I did not return to that, my favorite, cafeteria until 1981 when I was a Member of the Institute.
2. Viner made an indelible impression on all of his students. In 1992 a review of mine regarding some of Viner's last essays was published in which I wrote:

   > Jacob Viner, long-time co-principal economist (with Frank Knight) and contending polymath (with almost everyone) at the University of Chicago (off and on from 1916 until 1946) and thereafter Princeton resident–guru to the scholarly learned in academia until his death in 1970, wrote well and much. Trained first at McGill and then at Harvard under Taussig, Viner was the teacher of economic price theory and international economics at Chicago, advisor to the Treasury, specifically, and to the federal government, generally, during the 1930s and 1940s, and scholar *par excellence* for all of his professional life. He was a man of indefatigable energy, unlimited curiosity, amazing self-confidence, and what seemed (at least to his students) witty and cruel bumptuosity.
   >
   > Those of us who remember Viner both as a teacher and as friend are wont to wonder

how anyone who could be so devastating in the classroom could be so warm and charming in the salon. My judgment is that Viner, contrary to most current pedagogic practice, believed in the efficacy of adrenalin – his own and particularly his students. A truly compulsive talker, Viner believed in true competition for the leadership of every salon – and he was indefatigable in preparing for each opportunity and for exercising his considerable wit in capturing the podium, real or imagined.

Viner liked to tease me (clearly not much of a match) about whether American Institutional Economics with its emphasis on time and place made any noticeable contributions to economics; if I had had the wit I would have asked him if he was really above contextual analysis, why did he spend so much time studying context. But, as it was, I could do no better than cite the old fashioned welfare economics, which he told me was not much in the way of *economics*, as such. (Review of *Essays on the Intellectual History of Economics*, by Jacob Viner. *Journal of the History of Economic Thought*, vol. 14, pp. 116–18)

3. Harvey Leibenstein was one of the few authentic near-geniuses of my cohort. He did important work in development economics, demographic economics, and in microeconomic theory. His professional career was abruptly ended in an auto crash which effectively destroyed his mind, although the body lingered on for almost a decade.
4. The gist of these distributions is explained with the actual case material, in *Judges in Industry: A Study of Labour Arbitration in Australia*, Melbourne: Melbourne University Press, 1954.
5. Stigler had earlier (October 1949) given me a very rough time in my economic theory field examinations; the examiner was to have been John Maurice Clark, but the new chairman, James Waterhouse Angell (who had replaced Goodrich), decided to experiment, and I was the first and only victim. After that first bitter examination (Stigler had voted against my being passed) I recall actually saying to Stigler, 'What do I have to do to get past you, memorize your god-damned text?' Stigler replied imperturbably, 'That should do for starters, but you will probably have to do even more.' Yet, during my defense (December 1950) Stigler and I developed a mutual regard for each other. Many years later, when writing a memorial about Stigler for the *Economic Journal*, I observed that it was my opinion that he suffered fools more gladly than those he did not consider fools, but ill prepared. People like me got 'the treatment,' but I was surely the better for it, and my appreciation of his focus on catallactics was greatly sharpened.
6. During my year in Hawaii I wrote several essays. I was able to use papers from my students in a class in labor history to ferret out the references for me. What impressed me most was how more concerned the workers were with *Genossenschaft*, membership grouping, in this instance ethnic, than in a real economic class struggle. I do not recall ever being able to use undergraduates for such purposes after that. I discovered in 1951 what is now generally known, the children of immigrants from the Orient (then as now) combine occasional brilliance with almost invariable careful, hard work.
7. Otto von Gierke, an historian of German government, explores this as an evolutionary idea. His research, based on medieval and later data, saw informal groups, which started as voluntary associations, eventually developing internal rules and in time becoming the effective political government. These internal rules often specified who was eligible for membership. The medieval guilds were one example of this kind of organization. They had complex rules for admission to membership. On one of my travels I was told, for example, that the reason that Jews in Amsterdam went into diamond-cutting and book-printing was simply because the technology came after the period of guild hegemony, and Jews were accordingly not subject to the usual guild exclusionary rules.
8. When I once remarked to my father that David Hume claimed that the basic sense was the sense of smell, he replied that while that may have been true of eighteenth-century Edinburgh (about that, he said that he knew not), in twentieth-century Madison, he had found it to be the sense of envy – one failed entry into the *Genossenschaft* if one were too able.
9. Of course their ways of looking at the American labor movement were somewhat different.

My father's fascination was with the craft unions; Dunlop, coming to maturity in a later period, studied both craft and successful industrial unions.

10. The *Bund*, the translation of its full title being, 'The General Jewish Workers' Union in Lithuania, Poland and Russia,' at the time these men were youths was a political movement in tsarist Russia. It was part of the group making up the *Menshevik* (that is, the anti-Bolshevik) wing of the Marxian spectrum. The *Bundists* were secularists (anti-Jewish religious orthodoxy) seeking political recognition of Jews as full citizens (albeit with recognition of their Jewish national status) and were passively, and more often actively, anti-Zionist; they wanted democratic reforms to replace the official autocracy of the tsarist system. What is more important than the details of their projected reforms was their outlook. They believed that capitalism set worker against worker; that great inequalities of wealth and income set class against class; that the tsarist government's official anti-Semitism exacerbated anti-Jewish feelings, themselves largely caused by the Orthodox and Roman Catholic Churches and particularly by the vicissitudes of the business cycle. After World War I the *Bund* became a major Jewish political party, particularly active in combating the official anti-semitism of the Polish government during the 1930s. The Party was disbanded by the Communists after World War II.
11. From 1933 to 1935 Nathan, under Kuznets's general direction, designed the basic national income accounts of the United States. Then Kuznets turned to studying gross capital formation in the United States, particularly in manufacturing industry. After Pearl Harbor, Nathan, by then Director of Planning for the War Production Board, brought Kuznets to Washington. Their collaboration resulted in a completely new concept of ordering war material – in about four years military output went from a mere 4 percent to a gigantic 48 percent of the nation's gross national product. Their wartime collaboration was initially resisted by the Army General Staff, and they resigned in disgust. But, Ferdinand Eberstadt, the investment banker, managed to persuade Henry Stimson, the Secretary of War, of the correctness of their system. It was adopted.
12. Machlup was long unaware of my presumptuous intervention. Several years later (1982, the last time we talked – his wife, Mitzi, and he stayed with me in Vienna) I mentioned it to him. He said nothing in immediate response, but the next day he mentioned to me *en passant* that he felt that he owed me no thanks – I did what I did not for him, but because I had moral principles. One respects (and does not thank) those whose principles motivate their actions, he commented. I felt his compliment could not have been improved upon. During that visit he insisted upon telling me and a visitor he had never previously met the 'these days not so unusual' story of his birth and upbringing, saying that the editors of the *New Encyclopedia of the Social Sciences* had foolishly bowdlerized John Chipman's article about him.
13. Sir Zelman Cowan (mentioned earlier), when Governor-General of Australia, was asked to give a tremendous number of speeches. Like mine, his interests are catholic, and I well recall his telling how pleased he was to be able to use the talent of the Commonwealth Scientific Industrial Research Organization as his tutors. I was pleased to tell him that I had had a similar set of experiences, albeit not as preparation for my own speaking engagements.
14. My professional correspondence, of extreme bulk (my diligent secretaries found the filing system so useful that they were loath to throw any letter out if they thought that at some time it could be retrieved (that took two minutes) and referred to), is in the special collections unit at the Duke University Library; it is divided between letters as the *Journal of Economic Literature* editor and all other professional letters.
15. To have one's behavior compared to an animal's is among the least flattering things that can be done within the Jewish context. This point is particularly subtly made in Genesis xxii 5, where a line is drawn between the moral levels of different kinds of men:

    [Abraham] said to his [two accompanying servants], 'Stay here with the Ass while I and the boy go [to the top of Mount Moriah where the drama of the sacrifice of Isaac was to take place].'

    The principal Jewish perception of sin is that the target appropriate for humans has been missed, rather than some venal or mortal offense has been posted to the individual's divine credit balance.

16. I am wont to tell my students who doubt that nothing can be better for children than gentleness about my strongest memory of my mother (who died five months after the incident involved in this story). I recall coming home from first grade on a Tuesday in October 1929 and her asking me how well the reading was coming. I replied that I found it too hard – the other children could read the word on the card that Miss Scarseth (the teacher) held up, but that I couldn't. She then said, 'There are those who read with their eyes and those who read with their ears; you read with your ears and by Friday you will be able to read.' I remember that Tuesday to Friday as a period of real horror. I was scolded; I was shaken; I was spanked; I was sent to my bedroom; but by Friday I could tell Miss Scarseth, when she asked me why I could read 'phone' while no else in the class could,' 'Because *ph*, *gh*, and *f* all make the same *f sound*.' Mother, an experienced first-grade teacher, had no doubts about the need to make students governable before you could make them take pride in achievement. The conclusion is that with adrenalin one learns; with enough adrenalin one may well learn what had been impossible on Tuesday could become routine by Friday.
17. During my time at Princeton University I had a brief interchange at a party with von Nemann. He remarked that we had met once before, and in the course of our pleasantries he asked me what my 'field' was. When I replied, 'Economics,' his reaction was to comment that it really was quite an advanced subject,' 'more so, than physics, [perhaps].' I responded that his assessment ran contrary to common thought. And, as I recall, his final point, really before turning to some other guest, was that economists realized how little they really knew about the foundations of their theories – not so the physicists, who thought little about such things.
18. My father used to say that bravery was so rare among his colleagues that its exhibition was always perceived as historic; students, however, spoke out. Towards the end of my years at Pitt, I became convinced that real bravery among my colleagues was still very rare, but that students no longer spoke out. I tried to encourage the latter to pursue the advocacy of their interests, but to no avail. It was not so with me; I recall in my senior year at high school my math teacher told me that I was the most arrogant student she had ever had, and she had been teaching for nearly 30 years. My reply, as I have been recently reminded by a classmate who was there, was, 'Mrs Cowles: for a guy who's chosen last for every sports team and who hears those who have to carry him on their team groan, I tell you that my problem isn't arrogance; that just is not the word you're groping for.' Perhaps my generation was not easy to handle, but we were diligent and articulate. (Indeed, I do not recall that my answer was treated as *chutzpah* so much as it was taken as an acceptable, sharp retort to an out-of-line aside. As I recall, Mrs Cowles, aunt of my closest friend, had no trouble giving me the only B+s I got in senior high school; her nephew was grateful for the C she gave him.

22. To push and to be pushed*

Kurt W. Rothschild

In his collection of life philosophies of eminent economists, Michael Szenberg (1993) quotes a passage from Karl Popper which opens with the following sentence: 'We all have our philosophies, whether or not we are aware of this fact, and our philosophies are not worth very much.' Since I cannot but agree with this opinion of an outstanding philosopher it is perhaps frivolous to accept the invitation to write about my own life philosophy – something of which I am hardly aware and which anyway is not worth very much. That I nevertheless accepted the invitation should be excused by the fact that it offered a provocation to think about this question. And to spend some thoughts on provoking questions is or should be a characteristic of scientists (economists included).

But before I try to outline some ideas about my life philosophy, its background and development (as I see it), let me first ask a naughty question. The question is whether it makes sense to ask *convinced* neoclassical economists (to whom I do not belong!) what their life philosophies are. If by life philosophy we think – in contrast to philosophizing about the universe, about 'last things' etc. – of the basis for the deeper reasons of our being, why one is what one is and why one does what one does, we have to look at the thoughts, the motives and the norms which lie behind a person's behavior. But the neoclassical economic paradigm offers already a ready-made assumption about what makes human beings tick. Given preferences and maximizing utility are the behavioral characteristics of – at least – *homo œconomicus*. The life philosophy then boils down to a description (genetical or otherwise) of the given preferences of a given individual and from these his future 'rational' behavior could be – given the various external constraints – objectively derived. This would of course also have to include his choice to become an economist, to specialize in monetary economics, to recommend anti-inflationary policies and so on. Such a perspective does not leave much room for considering a life philosophy which can change and develop, which creates doubts and normative demands. Indeed, acknowledging that the question about a life philosophy makes sense implies doubts about the adequacy of the

*This chapter first appeared in *The American Economist*, **43**(1), Spring 1999, 1–8.

strict behavioral axioms of *homo œconomicus* even when they are restricted to the market sphere. *Homo sociologicus*, who is partly guided by norms, and *homo psychologicus* with his emotions should also be considered and with them the emergence of changeable viewpoints and evolving attitudes. With these – in relation to myself – I shall now be concerned.

The first question coming up when one searches for one's life philosophy is the age-old question of 'Nature or Nurture.' How far is it the genes, how far the environment which have shaped our eventual attitudes? It is obvious that both play a role. But we can neglect the genes because biology with all its stupendous progress cannot yet tell me with what the genes provided me as far as character, motivations, insights etc. are concerned. The same, by the way, goes for possible Freudian influences originating in my babyhood of which I can remember very little. So the story must concentrate on the environmental influences during the course of my conscious life. And it begins in Vienna in the interwar period.

PRE-WAR VIENNA, OR WHY I WANTED TO BECOME AN ECONOMIST

Vienna, the city into which I was born (accident No. 1), was in the interwar period a rather exceptional phenomenon (of which I was of course not aware at the time). In a recent campaign for tourism the Viennese municipality created the slogan: 'Vienna is different.' I doubt whether this statement has much meaning today, but it certainly could be applied to pre-war Vienna. At that time it still had the trappings of the (former) capital of a big multi-ethnic empire with its magnificent appearance and its cultural diversity, while at the same time presiding over a small country which had lost self-confidence and slid into extreme poverty in the depression years when the effective unemployment rate rose to almost 25 percent in 1932. This resulted in a sharp cleavage between an attractive and lively cultural scene on the one hand and a deeply divided and unstable political environment on the other. This was the milieu to which we young Austrians were exposed and which provided a strong challenge to take sides even if one grew up in rather unpolitical and 'normal' families as was the case with me where a devoted mother (first together with a father and then alone, after he had left her) tried on a rather small and insecure financial basis to enable her two children to obtain a decent education.

As far as the cultural side is concerned, Vienna could still offer – in spite of restricted financial possibilities – a rich spectrum of high-class and original activities which had their roots in pre-World War II foundations which could persist and be developed in the economically more difficult postwar years.[1]

Without trying to give a full account of the richness of the cultural life, one can point out among other things the lasting tradition of Vienna as a musical center with her opera house continuing to belong to the world's leading stages; the influential developments and lively debates in the fields of psychology and sociology characterized by such names as Freud, Adler, Lazarsfeld, Jahoda; the 'Viennese Circle' of philosophy which with people like Neurath, Schlick, Kari Menger, Popper, Carnap and others provided – partly after their emigration – an important impetus to modern philosophical developments; and last not least the remnants of the special perspective of economic (marginal utility) theory contained in the so-called 'Austrian or Viennese School' founded by Menger which were kept alive and kicking for some time after 1918 by people like Mises, Haberler, Hayek, Machlup. That most of these Austrians, together with their ideas and traditions, were gradually transferred to other countries, and particularly to the US, was caused mainly by Austrian and German fascism, but also (to a lesser extent) by Austrian poverty and political neglect. They nevertheless left their imprint on the Viennese interwar period.

As far as the present writer is concerned, the most lasting influence which emanated from this background was perhaps – apart from the generally stimulating climate of an active cultural life (which had to compete with the allurements of sports and entertainment) – the intensive and often bitter discussions between Freudians and Adlerians. Without becoming a fervent partisan of one side or the other (as was the fashion at the time) there grew an interest in the complexities of human behavior and the intricacies of psychological motives. An interest in *individual* action and motivation, their motor and their effects on the 'happiness' of the person, was awakened and has remained as a constant reminder that individual circumstances in all their complexity matter, both analytically and ethically. This was later to some extent fortified by the individualistic perspective of Menger's brand of marginal utility theory (with which I was later indoctrinated at the University of Vienna). On the whole it made me later critical and impatient with the thoughtless and dogmatic use of the neoclassical theory of choice, i.e. with the *homo œconomicus*. By neglecting other motives and explanations and rejecting them *generally* as *ad hoc* or unscientific, this has hampered theoretical insights and has biased policy debates.

Let me now turn to the political background. Here the decisive specialities were partly Austrian in general, partly Viennese in particular. The dominating feature of the Austrian political scene until the downfall of democracy and the establishment of Austro-fascism in 1934 was a very deep polarization between a ruling reactionary, Catholic-oriented right-wing party (the 'Christlichsoziale Partei') and a strongly left-wing Social Democratic Party with nothing worth speaking of in between. The polarization and the bitter fights between the two parties, leading ultimately to civil war and dictatorship, meant that one either abstained from taking any interest in politics or was induced to become strongly attached to one side or the other.[2] For most young people the second alternative was the most obvious one when faced with the social and economic problems of the country. As far as I was concerned this meant an early sympathy with the left, driven partly by personal experience of economic worries in my lower middle-class family, but later increasingly by a strong revolting feeling (coming from where?) about the injustices and inequalities suffered by the working class (in whose district I lived) which slid more and more into unemployment and poverty while the right-wing party stood one-sidedly for the interests of the employers. This partisanship of mine was supported by strong anti-Semitic tendencies on the right which for me – as a Jew – could not prove attractive.

To feel attracted by the Social Democratic movement in Austria and particularly in Vienna meant, however, more than, for instance, voting for Social Democrats in Germany or for Labour in Britain. Austria's Social Democratic Party had – irrespective of its daily policies and political controversies – a program strongly influenced by Marxist ideas which were not only used as a sort of traditional prop but were taught, discussed and further developed with the aim to adapt them to the changed conditions of the twentieth century. 'Austro-Marxism' became a special branch of Marxist studies and the leaders of the Social Democratic Party – in particular Otto Bauer and Kari Renner – took a prominent part in it, being theoreticians as well as politicians. Thus in my early times as a school attendant I came into contact with the Marxist 'vision.' Without reading *Das Kapital* (let alone understanding it!) I learned to see the world and its economic aspects not just as a harmonious progress of mankind (which so obviously it was *not*) but as a dynamic process of interacting interests and conflicts, of power and exploitation. This influence could and has been maintained and colors my perspective far beyond Marx's class war approach.

This awareness of and alertness to conflict and change was strengthened by the *practice* of the Viennese Social Democrats who always had – until the downfall of democracy – a comfortable majority in the town council. By making extreme use of the legal and budgetary possibilities open to a municipality they created, against the background of a hostile government, the famous 'Red Vienna,' which through taxation of luxuries and other means financed generous housing policies and a whole lot of social and educational institutions, thus achieving a certain redistribution which alleviated the worst effects of inequality and poverty. This experience supported a viewpoint that in economic, political and social affairs things do not just 'happen' and are not predetermined by 'iron economic necessities' (as the opponents of the Viennese experiment continually argued). It has remained as a permanent reminder that activism and interventionism are possible and useful when conditions are regarded as unjust or undesirable, particularly in regard to basic human needs and extreme inequalities. This was a perspective which I could to some extent detect again in the postwar years. It inspired the idea of the welfare state, but is being lost in the present neoliberal climate.

The 'philosophical' ideas emerging in my youth which persisted into later years did, however, not immediately influence my career plans. Neither did I want (quite apart from possibilities) to become a politician, nor did I consider studying politics, economics or any other social science. My preferred studies would have been mathematics and/or physics, the interest for which had been kindled by an excellent teacher in my secondary school (Gustav Kürti, who later worked as a physicist in the US), who managed to turn these two subjects into an exciting adventure. But times and circumstances prevented me from taking this road. Austria was at the depth of its crisis, which not only affected my personal conditions but also the general outlook. Since I had to earn some money (through tutoring) in order to finance my extended education, it seemed unwise to choose a long and demanding study and – more importantly – a subject which at the time seemed to offer no chances of subsequent employment, be it in teaching (as I would have liked) or in industry. But the wish (supported by my mother) to continue studies at the university remained. The subject chosen was the study of law mainly because the Austrian tradition of employing graduates from the law faculty in industry and government on a fairly large scale (in addition to the obvious employment in the legal professions) seemed to offer the best chances for finding some sort of a job in spite of widespread academic unemployment.[3] In addition, the idea (nourished by romantic impressions from literature and films) that I might be able to become a lawyer defending innocent people against a reactionary judiciary also played a role.

In those days the Austrian universities had no social science faculties.[4] In line with older traditions the final section of Law Studies was reserved for a study of economics, public finance ('Finanzwissenschaft') and aspects of political science. It was this 'niche' in the law curriculum in which Menger, Böhm-Bawerk, Wieser and the other heroes of the Austrian School had been brought up and where they taught later generations. This was the place where I made my first acquaintance with the subject of (non-Marxian) economics. And became fascinated by it. And this for several reasons.

The first was – just as in the case of mathematics in school – the influence of a 'sparkling' teacher. Hans Mayer, a former assistant of Wieser and one of the last prominent representatives of the 'old' Austrian School, was an exciting teacher. Though he was rather lazy and did little research (he was proud of never having written a book), he was able to create interest and curiosity in the way he posed theoretical questions and their analytical treatment. That alone would have sufficed for a growing interest on my side. But it was fortified by my not-forgotten love for mathematics and physics, because here I found – for the first time in my studies after the not uninteresting but tiresome casuistic treatment of legalistic matters – the sort of theoretical and analytical approach which resembled the methods of the natural sciences. Thus I was attracted by the *methodological* qualities of economic theory (or the glimpses of it which I obtained). In this connection Menger's passionate attack on Schmoller and the Historical School (Menger, 1883) was an important influence and has left a lasting interest in methodological questions. It was not, however, only the methodological side which attracted me but also and particularly the *subject* of economics. In addition to the fact that it afforded the promising luxury to deal with interesting problems and intellectual challenges, it also offered the hope that with a better understanding of the economic mechanisms a contribution to a more satisfactory economic and social society could be achieved. The differences between the university-taught marginal utility theory and what I had picked up about Marxism earlier on did not worry me. They seemed (and still do) to have their main applicability in rather different spheres of the complex socioeconomic environment: the microeconomic, short-run mechanisms of current economic activities on the one side, the macroeconomic long-term dynamics of the socioeconomic interplay of powers and interests on the other. That both theories (and others as well) have their weaknesses and often try to move into fields for which they are not suited is regrettable, but also understandable in view of the complexity and interdependence of the economic processes. This provides the basis for continuing research and controversy.

After I had fallen in love with economics – a side-subject in my studies! – I realized that I would prefer to be able to switch from law to economics in my active life, be it in research, teaching, or in some useful advisory or administrative capacity in a public or private institution. But though I was sure that this was what I wanted, I was also sure that under the desolate economic and political conditions in Austria the chances to follow such a course were nil. At best, I hoped, I might perhaps be able to keep an interest in economics as a hobby.

SCOTLAND, OR HOW I BECAME AN ECONOMIST

The question whether there could be any chance to choose a career in economics rather than in less preferred fields ceased to be relevant in 1938 after Hitler had invaded Austria. With Austria incorporated into Nazi Germany, my chances as a Jew to obtain *any* job – preferred or not – were nil.

But there were good chances to be sent to a concentration camp. To leave the country as quickly as possible became an urgent target. In August 1938 I fled – after marrying the girl I liked (and still like) – to Switzerland (where I was permitted to stay in Basle) in the hope of finding an opportunity to go to Paris where my sister lived. Before leaving Vienna I had tried without success to find legal ways to emigrate from Austria. Among other things, I had applied for a scholarship which the Scottish branch of the International Student Service had advertised as open to two endangered students in Austria. I got an interview with an ISS representative in Vienna but left – because conditions became increasingly threatening – before a decision was taken. That decision reached me in Basle. My application to be accepted for a continuation and completion of my economic studies (my knowledge of Austrian law had become obsolete) was granted and I was offered a two-year scholarship to study economics at Glasgow University. I hardly need to explain what this decision meant for me and my future.

After the decision had reached me, it still took about three months of administrative and visa arrangements until I could finally move from Switzerland to Scotland. In the meantime the ISS contacted me in the person of a young Scottish economics lecturer with the – now well-known – name of Alec Cairncross (later Sir Alec Cairncross). Though my direct personal contact with Cairncross lasted only less than two years (he left Glasgow in 1940 to take up wartime work for the government), we became rather close friends even though communication was at first inhibited by the clash of highly developed Scottish and Austrian accents. He and my subsequent 'boss' at Glasgow University, Alec Macfie, became – each in his own way – a lasting influence on my interests and life philosophy. In those early days when I was still in Basle, Cairncross urged me to use my time there to study a recently published book which – as he stressed – decisively influenced theoretical discussions in Britain. The recommended book was Keynes's *General Theory of Employment, Interest, and Money*. It is today difficult to realize the shock which I experienced when I tried to come to terms with this book. Quite apart from language problems, which were not negligible, I was suddenly confronted not only with a 'revolutionary' approach which startled even experienced Anglo-Saxon economists, but I also came to it with only a relatively narrow introduction to the Austrian brand of marginal utility choice and price theory where I had not even heard of monetary theory, let alone had any understanding of it. I was so desperate that I played with the idea of abstaining from accepting the scholarship which had been such a hoped-for event.

But then I happened to get hold of Joan Robinson's slim introduction to Keynes (Robinson, 1937) and the ban was broken. I managed to enter a new world which I should never leave, but again seeing it not as the final heaven but as an extremely important supplement, modification, and also critical correction of the theoretical bases which I had acquired earlier. The decisive influence and attraction which Keynesian economics provided for me was that it offered better and more direct theoretical approaches to the socioeconomic aspects which I regarded as important but not sufficiently embedded in the traditional theories (be they Austrian, Marshallian, or Walrasian). The most important characteristics in this respect are the immediate access to macroeconomics, which points the way to considering state and political action; the stress on uncertainty and decisions under uncertainty (a bridge to psychology and away from the 'mechanic' rationality of the *homo œconomicus*); and the shift in emphasis towards the analysis of the socially most pressing economic problem,[5] viz. unemployment, instead of starting with and concentrating on price formation and equilibrium conditions in more or less perfect markets. These characteristics appealed to me not only because of my special biases (or 'philosophy'?), but also because they force one to pay more attention to realism and relevance than some other types of economic analysis.

What I have just said about Keynesian economics and its meaning for me was of course not suddenly apparent but grew gradually in my two years of finishing my MA studies in economics and political philosophy at Glasgow University and in subsequent years when I held a job as assistant lecturer in economics. It was in those years that I got the chance – assisted by constant encouragement and criticism from Cairncross and Macfie – to delve deeper into the intricacies and diversity of economic theories and their relation to real-world problems. The openness and unbiased atmosphere of research and teaching in the economic faculty and also in neighboring faculties[6] greatly strengthened my feeling that a plurality of paradigms in economics and in social sciences in general is not only an obvious fact but also a necessary and desirable phenomenon in a very complex and continually changing subject where abstract general theories (and abstract they have to be) can only cover a comparatively narrow and extremely simplified section of the totality of interdependent connections and developments. Depending on circumstances and the problem to be tackled, different approaches or a combination of them have to be used in order to be able to get nearer to the far-away 'truth.' This 'box of tools' idea had – through my training in Glasgow – obtained a more solid basis and had opened the door for my old wish to become a 'proper' economist.

The tolerance and openness to various theoretical approaches, i.e. the ecclecticism which tries to see what different theories have to offer, was however not only a result of my experiences in university life, but had also to do with general effects of my transfer to Scotland. The Austrian democracy of the twenties with its sharp divisions and conflict orientation and its brutal extinction through Austro-fascism had created a general feeling that one has to adhere strictly and without compromise to one side or the other in order to reach one's chosen targets. In the democratic period that meant the uncompromising use of majority power; in the dictatorship the suppression of rights. In Scotland I found democratic attitudes which had grown in centuries of democratic institutions and which were intensified by the fact that the Scots saw – not completely without reason – certain injustices in the way they were treated by the London governments. Here democracy was normally not *only* seen as the victory of one side or the other in elections with subsequent majority rule, but *also* as discussion, consensual reforms, attention to minority rights etc.; in short, a differentiated and differentiating view in political matters and tactics was accepted. This openness towards other opinions and the readiness to cooperate with 'other' sides when the situation seems opportune impressed me and has not only left its marks on my views on politics and political action but probably also contributed to my eclectic leanings in theoretical matters.

POST WAR: CONFORMIST AND DISSENTER

In 1947 I left – not without regrets – Glasgow University and Scotland and returned to Vienna. My subsequent professional career happened to be divided into two periods of almost equal length, roughly twenty years each. In the first period I worked as a senior research worker in the Austrian Institute of Economic Research which – founded by Mises and Hayek in the 1920s – held and still holds a central position in the empirical analysis of the Austrian and international economy. The fields with which I was mainly concerned were (1) problems of the labor market, and (2) international trade. In 1966 I moved to the newly founded University of Linz, which was created simultaneously with the installation of social science faculties (separated from the law departments) in the Austrian universities. Linz University was planned as a special center in this sphere. Here my activities were once again turned more to theoretical research and teaching with which I had been concerned in Glasgow.

If by 'philosophy of life' one means the ways in which one looks at life, work and values, I do not think that these later years led to any *fundamental* changes in the views and attitudes which had been formed in my younger years, though of course they were modified by changing experiences, impressions and personal contacts. The work in the Institute of Economic Research sharpened my awareness of the complexity and changeability of economic processes and the fragility of economic data which in turn underlined my former feelings that one cannot expect any single theoretical paradigm or model to cover everything, and that great care must be taken to find relevant bridges between theory and policy applications. These and some other deliberations were greatly stimulated by the presence of Josef Steindl, who had returned to the Institute from the Oxford Institute of Economics and Statistics where he had worked alongside Kalecki with whose ideas he acquainted me.

The work at Linz University, which was exciting and stimulating because it demanded the establishment of a new curriculum in a new department in a new university without (helping or obstructing) traditions, also had some effects. In fact, one of the weaknesses of the situation proved, in my view, to have its good sides. The weakness was that the relatively small size of the university and the budgetary restrictions meant that we had to start with a rather small staff. This involved not only a considerable teaching load; it also meant that one had to cover – in addition to one's own special fields (in my case macroeconomics, the labor market, international trade) – several subjects which were outside one's 'normal' studies and interests. The positive side of this shortcoming (which robbed one of time for further intensification of my chosen research area) was that I was forced to remain in touch with a wider sphere within the rapidly narrowing specializations in economic theory. This has contributed to a lasting recognition of the relativity of special theories and approaches and also to an openness *vis-à-vis* non-economic (sociological, psychological, social etc.) facts and theories. It also broadened and stimulated personal contacts and discussions with colleagues (who worked under the same demands and constraints). I benefited particularly from lively discussions and seminars with Hajo Riese (who later moved to the Free University of Berlin), who developed interesting and original post-Keynesian and monetary models, and with Kazimierz Laski, who had come to Austria from Poland where he had worked with Kalecki.

All this, as I said before, did not lead to fundamental changes in my 'philosophical make-up,' i.e. in my 'values' and 'views,' which continued to consist in an intellectual attraction to economic theory combined with a methodological understanding that multiparadigmism and 'openness' are unavoidable if realistic insights and relevance to practical affairs are to be achieved, and an ethical and social 'bias' that economics should contribute to a 'better' world with less unemployment, less poverty, or – to formulate it more pathetically – to a world that is guided by the utopian battle cry of the French Revolution: 'Liberté, Egalité, Fraternité.'

While I thus changed very little as far as my basic outlook is concerned, the world around me did change quite considerably. Let me digress for a moment. I know a man in Bratislava, the present capital of Slovakia, who observed that during his lifetime he had been a citizen of Austro-Hungary, Czechoslovakia, Germany, Czechoslovakia again, and finally Slovakia, but had never left his native town Bratislava. The analogy to my case is not difficult to find. When we look at the Western European postwar period we can distinguish two distinctly different basic forces behind the main socioeconomic trends. From the end of the war until the mid-1970s the outlook and the consensus in most countries were influenced by the memory of the interwar depression years and by the needs for reconstruction and the reestablishment of decent living conditions for the population. There existed an openness for economic and social reforms. Social aims like full employment and a 'fair' income distribution were confronted and compared with economic aims like price stability and balance of payments requirements. The need for political action and consensus in these matters was recognized. From the 1970s onwards, under the influence of inflation and balance of payments problems, but also because of a restored influence of business interests, there was a shift to a one-sided 'free market' policy. The former socioeconomic consensus was abandoned and the priorities were shifted from social and employment targets to the predominance of price stability and reduced state interference.

This change in societal conditions and priorities caused by changed technological conditions ('microelectronics,' 'information society'), power and interests ('globalization,' 'transnational companies'), and also by emerging cases of 'state failure' (in contrast to 'market failures,' which had triggered state action before) had repercussions on economic theory, both by influencing it and being influenced by it. When one shares the view that a multitude of theoretical approaches (the 'box of tools') combined with situational and interdisciplinary supplementary considerations (McCloskey's 'rhetoric' – see McCloskey, 1985) is at least helpful if not essential to interpreting real events, then one finds that this whole postwar development can be explained by such combinations. Very roughly and primitively speaking, one can derive from a Marxian perspective the influence of changes in productive relations and group conflicts on the shifts in market and political power; Keynesianism and post-Keynesianism are helpful to see what possibilities interventionism may offer, and neoclassical theory can work out the intricacies of various new market mechanisms. All this is of course interrelated and – alas! – often contradictory, but it permits at least an attempt to do justice to the dynamics and high complexity of events.

The picture looks, however, different when one adheres rather strictly and dogmatically to one theory (paradigm) as the only road to 'true' knowledge. This leads first of all to difficulties for cognitive reasons. The problem is, however, intensified by the fact that the theories are not just toys for theoretical debates but are used normally in extremely simplified forms and excluding alternative perspectives for legitimatory purposes. Thus a vulgar Marxism was misused as a legitimation for the Soviet economic system, a vulgar Keynesianism supported the idea of the welfare state, and a vulgar neoclassical theory is supposed to justify free markets and deregulation. In all these cases the reliance on 'one eye' only and blindness of all other eyes (of which there should be many) lead to a very uneven distribution of weights and interests regarding various theoretical approaches which is not independent of the ruling 'Zeitgeist.' This is particularly true in political debates. But it has its reflections in the theoretical scene. From the times when a famous saying was 'We are all Keynesians now' we have moved to a situation where neoclassical equilibrium theories 'are in.' Yet equilibrium theorists with their horizon were not useless 30 years ago and Keynes is not 'dead' today. An eclectic perspective need not be abandoned. But being a human being with a 'philosophy' of my own, I was of course more in sympathy with a period of welfare state targets and its need for a predominantly Keynesian tool-box than with a period of neoliberal ideology and its concentration on neoclassical tenets. I could be a conformist with ruling tendencies then and have become a dissenter now. But I have never left Bratislava.

NOTES

1. See on this, for instance, Janik and Toulmin (1973).
2. In no other democratic European country could parties count on such high membership numbers as in Austria.
3. A well-known play in those days (written by the Austrian playwright Karl Schönherr) carried the title: *Haben Sie zu essen, Herr Doktor?* (*Have you anything to eat, Doctor?*).
4. There existed a 'Hochschule für Welthandel' (High School for World Trade, now called the Economic University) in Vienna, in which economic studies could be chosen. But they were mainly centered on 'Betriebswirtschaftslehre' (business economics) rather than on 'Volkswirtschaftslehre' (economic theory).
5. This applies to the developed world. In some developing countries the basic needs of food and health are of course more important. They are also connected with unemployment but not restricted to it.
6. With, for instance, the stimulating Alee Nove and Rudolf Schlesinger in the Department of Soviet Studies.

REFERENCES

Janik, A. and Toulmin S. (1973), *Wittgenstein's Vienna*, Simon & Schuster, New York.
McCloskey, D.N. (1985), *The Rhetoric of Economics*, Wheatsheaf, Brighton.
Menger, C. (1883), *Untersuchungen über die Methode der Socialwissenschaften und der politischen Oekonomie insbesondere*, Leipzig.
Robinson, J. (1937), *Introduction to the Theory of Employment*, Macmillan, London.
Szenberg, M. (1993), *Eminent Economists. Their Life Philosophies*, Cambridge University Press, Cambridge.

23. An accidental Schumpeterian*

F.M. Scherer

My research program as an economist has emphasized two intersecting themes: the causes and consequences of technological innovations; and how business firms' behavior varies with the structural environment (e.g., competitive, oligopolistic, or monopolistic) within which they operate. In commencing this agenda I was powerfully influenced by the writings of Joseph A. Schumpeter (whose death coincided with my senior year in high school). Although the insights I have attained were often at odds with Schumpeter's teaching, I continue both substantively and methodologically to be a Schumpeterian.

BLUNDERING INTO ECONOMICS

How I came to be a Schumpeterian economist and indeed an economist at all is a chronicle of accidents. My formal graduate studies in economics commenced only when I was 29 years of age – at the close of life's third decade, which, Schumpeter insisted, is the most creative period in the typical economist's career.

I was born in 1932 and grew up in Ottawa, a central Illinois farming and glass-producing community whose population was approximately 16000. My father sold coal and ice at retail – commodities with relatively low income elasticities, so we were not traumatized by the Great Depression. (My maternal grandfather, however, was forced to liquidate his department store and become an insurance salesman.) My childhood hero was Thomas Alva Edison, and if I had distinct career hopes in my early years, it was to become an inventor–chemist. Half of grade school and all of high school were spent in local Catholic schools, strong on Latin and English, weak on mathematics.

My father had attended the University of Michigan and was elected senior class president. I chose to follow in his footsteps. Much of my time was taken up by extracurricular activities, leading among other things to the hoped-for repetition of a Scherer family class presidency. But somehow an intellectual

*This chapter first appeared in *The American Economist*, **40**(1), Spring 1996, 5–13.

seed was planted in my dormant soil. Chemistry bored me, so for a while, having been editor of my high-school newspaper and a part-time reporter for Ottawa's daily newspaper, I turned to journalism. But I am not a night person, and my work on the *Michigan Daily* student newspaper, requiring frenzied page-closing activity until 2 a.m. two or three nights a week, led me to consider alternative career paths. Since it was expected that I would ultimately take over the family business, studying business administration seemed the obvious step. But my fraternity brothers – an extraordinarily intelligent and studious lot – persuaded me that an economics major was equally useful but much more interesting intellectually. So I blundered into economics.

Several experiences in Michigan's economics department nurtured the seed. The geometric model-building approach pursued in my intermediate micro-theory course was for me a new and strange way of analyzing human behavior, and at first I found it very difficult. Consultations with the course's teacher were of little help, so I timidly approached Professor Kenneth Boulding, the author of *Economic Analysis*, one of the textbooks we were using. Boulding's kindly, patient guidance led me to appreciate the power of economic theory and the quality of an extraordinary human being. I was encouraged also by taking his course on the economics of agriculture, especially when he appended to my term paper, 'A Report on Agricultural Policy to the President of the United States,' a note, 'I nominate you for Secretary of Agriculture.' Boulding had each of his students conduct the class for an hour. Any interest I might have had in being a teacher was quelled when I observed that a good third of my classmates were asleep during my lecture. Another formative experience was the comparative economic systems course I took with Professor Z. Clark Dickinson. My term paper, 'Social and Individual Motivation in the Soviet Union,' kindled a life-long fascination with how economic and noneconomic incentives affected individual and organizational performance. That interest was reinforced by electing courses in Michigan's psychology department, including a course on the psychology of management.

By far my most formative experience, however, was the senior honors seminar offered by Shorey Peterson. We read widely in and discussed the classics. Schumpeter's *Capitalism, Socialism, and Democracy* (1942) captivated me. His assertion that technological changes were the principal source of economic growth seemed wholly plausible, given my prior fascination with inventors and chemistry, and an exciting break from the statics of price theory. Equally stimulating to me as a prairie-bred 'agin-er' was his argument that giant monopolistic corporations were the most powerful engines of technological advance, and that, in stressing the beneficence of competitive market structures, neoclassical economists and policy makers had overlooked the main wellspring of economic progress and backed the wrong policy horses. As the seminar proceeded, the US Congress passed the Atomic Energy Act of 1954, clearing the way for private-sector development of nuclear power. My honors thesis, on 'The Atomic Energy Patent Laws and Economic Progress,' applied monopolistic competition theory to the economics of technological innovation and explored the role that patent grants play in encouraging high-cost, high-risk innovations. It was the beginning of my career. Yet that was far from evident at the time.

Initially, Uncle Sam had other plans. It was almost impossible for college students who had enjoyed Korean War draft deferments to escape post-baccalaureate military service, especially in my home town, where my aunt's hard-nosed husband chaired the draft board. So I was inducted into the Army in 1954 and, after basic training, was selected to attend Counter-Intelligence Corps School in Baltimore. A three-day pass allowed me to visit friends at Harvard Law School and attend a class taught by the person on whom Professor Kingsfield in the hit movie, *The Paper Chase*, was modelled. The unalloyed nitpickingness of that class quenched any simmering thoughts of becoming a lawyer. Because 'CIC' trainees were considered an elite group, we were allowed to request our next duty theaters. Most of us who were unmarried elected Europe and were sent to Germany. The married members of our class almost all chose the Continental United States and were sent to Korea. For a smalltown kid from Illinois, military duty in Germany was a marvelous eye-opener, ending forever my predilection as a *Chicago Tribune*-bred isolationist. I was fortunate to be sent to the Army Language School in Oberammergau, where I learned to speak German fluently. Two months later I was assigned to an Iron Curtain border outpost in Coburg, where on Christmas eve of 1955 I met Barbara Silbermann, who two years later became my long-suffering (thus far, nearly four decades) spouse.

MEANDERING THROUGH GRADUATE SCHOOL

Having ruled out law school, I applied for graduate studies in business administration and, after appealing an initial rejection, was accepted into the Harvard Business School (HBS). There the lightning of chance struck again – repeatedly.

During the 1957 summer break between academic years, I returned to Ottawa to work for the interstate trucking branch of the family business, whose head was my favorite uncle. Over the years I had worked part-time in a variety of jobs for Scherer Freight Lines, but now I was considered mature enough to become sales representative for the central Illinois territory. My selling efforts were successful, but I also learned something important. Under Interstate Commerce Commission regulation, all common carrier trucking companies charged the same rates, and the quality of their service on any given route was largely indistinguishable. With competition on key dimensions stalemated, rivals sought other ways of getting ahead. Investigating why competitors were securing most of the freight from some leading local shippers whose owners were friends of my family, I discovered that the rivals' sales staff were plying decision-making traffic managers with gifts of liquor, golf excursions and the services of prostitutes. I discussed the matter with my uncle Alex Scherer, a thoroughly moral individual, who assured me that no matter what the consequences were, we would never use prostitutes to solicit business. Yet the experience set me to wondering whether I wanted to be in an industry where the dimensions of competition were so thoroughly suppressed by governmental regulation.

Upon my return to Boston in September 1957, my first assignment in the mandatory second year business policy course was to write a paper on my career aspirations. Ruling out life as a trucking company executive was an easy decision. Given my long-standing interest in technological innovation, I decided that if I went into business at all, it would be with a high-technology company. But for the first time, the idea of being a scholar entered my mind. Almost simultaneously, the head of the Business School's doctoral program invited me to pursue a Doctorate in Business Administration (DBA). The soil had been prepared, and now the seed began to take root.

One of the options I elected during my second year at HBS was General Georges Doriot's course called simply 'Manufacturing.' Doriot, who moonlighted as president of the first US high-technology venture capital firm, American Research and Development Corporation, required us to form groups of roughly nine, which conducted two field projects with companies and wrote a major 'topic report' (some of which helped Doriot identify new lines in which ARDC would invest). Our group developed a cost accounting system for a small manufacturer of electronic sensors, researched new markets for a job-shop lithographer, and wrote a monograph, *Patents and the Corporation* (1958), which we subsequently self-published in two editions. The monograph was my idea, inspired by the *Wall Street Journal*'s prediction that dire consequences for technological progress would follow antitrust consent decrees accepted by AT&T and IBM in January 1956, under which tens of thousands of patents were subjected to wide-open compulsory licensing at zero royalty rates. Members of our group fanned out across the nation, querying R&D executives and patent attorneys of 22 companies about the role patents played in their research and development investment decisions and the impact patent compulsory licensing actions had on investment incentives. We secured mail questionnaires exploring the same questions from 69 companies, analyzed statistically how patenting trends for companies subjected to compulsory licensing differed from those of other US corporations, and read extensively in the literature on the management and economics of R&D. Much to our surprise, we found patents to be unimportant in the investment decision making of most companies. This discovery has been reaffirmed in studies by Taylor and Silberston (1973), Mansfield (1986), and Levin et al. (1987), among others.

While our student group was conducting preliminary interviews for the patent study and I was contemplating Harvard's DBA program, the Soviet Union in October 1957 launched its first satellite. *Sputnik I*. Citizens of the United States were shocked. We were palpably behind in space technology, and we appeared also to be lagging in missile technology. What had gone wrong? And around the Harvard Business School, the question echoed, how had the American business system failed? To secure answers, the Business School initiated a Weapons Acquisition Research Project, headed by Professor Paul W. Cherington, an air transport expert. I was invited to join as research assistant and, given my preconditioning, did so enthusiastically, simultaneously progressing toward the DBA degree. Returning to Ottawa during the Christmas break, I dreaded telling my father that I planned to become a scholar rather than joining the family business. Much to my astonishment, he replied, 'I think that's a good idea.' The transition from student to full-time researcher was swift, since at the time I received my MBA in June 1958, my wife and I had exhausted our finances and were expecting our first child (Tom) that month. Starting work the Monday after my last examination was a necessity.

Our research team, which included economist M.J. Peck, a former Navy supply captain, the erstwhile chief counsel to Lyndon Johnson's Senate Democratic Policy Committee, and (as consultant) economist David Novick of the RAND Corporation, prepared 12 book-length historical case studies of weapon systems development programs and seven shorter case studies of civilian sector research and development projects. (The case studies, alas, have not been published, although some circulate in *Samidzat*.) For me, conducting interviews at companies and government agencies, being immersed in the complex details of real-world R&D projects, some ongoing, and struggling to make sense of what we learned, was the most exciting and formative learning experience of my professional career. The project's work assignments turned out to follow the inverted pyramid principle. Peck, with the second-lowest seniority of the project team, and I, as junior member, wrote a majority of the case studies. Peck and I together wrote the first book analyzing and integrating our findings, *The Weapons Acquisition Process: An Economic Analysis* (1962). I was sole author of the project's other major published work, *The Weapons Acquisition Process: Economic Incentives* (1964), which also served as my doctoral dissertation. It is not excessively immodest to say that both books are still considered classics.

As I worked with 'Joe' Peck, who was trained at Harvard's economics department, I realized that I really wanted to be an economist, not a DBA-holding professor of business administration. My DBA program adviser, John Lintner, suggested that I contact Wassily Leontief, who taught the second-year graduate theory sequence in the economics department. I called him, and what took place next has probably never happened again at Harvard. He invited me to tea at his home, and before I knew it, I was enrolled in his 1960–61 theory course. I simultaneously continued my weapons research and honed my mathematical skills through Barbara Bergmann's course on mathematics for economists. A formal transfer to the economics PhD program followed in the fall of 1961.

During the 1961–62 academic year, I struggled to complete my PhD course requirements, among other things taking my first graduate industrial organization course (taught by visitor Jesse Markham) while making final revisions on the book with Joe Peck, who had left Harvard to take a position with Robert McNamara in the Pentagon. Two weeks after passing my general examinations in the fall of 1962, I handed in the draft of my dissertation – the second book from our project. Richard Heflebower, who replaced Markham as Visiting Professor of Industrial Organization, chaired a hastily assembled thesis committee. My approach to the theory of contractor behavior had been influenced by the writings of Herbert Simon and colleagues, so I modelled companies as managerial utility maximizers and not as profit maximizers. Heflebower suggested that by incorporating a 'user cost' function to capture the long-run consequences of short-run cost choices, the problem could be reformulated as one of long-run profit maximization. The power of this change influenced my subsequent thinking about the objectives of modern corporations. The theoretical article (1964) emerging from my dissertation was probably the first fully worked-out mathematical treatment of principal–agent contracting relationships, although the 'principal–agent' terminology had not yet been invented, so it is seldom recognized as a part of that literature.

TEACHING AND FURTHER CAREER CHOICES

Thus, after many false starts and swerves, I became a full-fledged member of the economics profession in 1963, at the ripe old age of 31. For my first 'real' job, I followed Jesse Markham to Princeton. My first teaching assignment was the microeconomic analysis course for second-year Woodrow Wilson school master's candidates. Except for the miserable hour in Ken Boulding's course, I had never taught. I had no idea what one had to do to motivate students, and I assumed that graduate students in a public administration program would share my love for economics. I spent the first nine hours of class writing equations of general equilibrium on the blackboard. The theoretical pitch modulated only slightly thereafter. It was a disaster. The students complained bitterly, and I was fired from the Woodrow Wilson faculty. Since my appointment was joint, I retreated to a refuge in the economics department. My first assignment there was to share the teaching of microeconomic principles with W. Arthur Lewis. In addition to being an outstanding economist (who eventually won the Nobel Prize), Arthur was a marvelous teacher of both students and teachers. From him I began to learn how to teach (a lesson continued in industrial organization courses co-taught with Jesse Markham) and also, through our weekly teaching staff seminars, filled in many of the serious gaps in my knowledge left by too swift a progression through graduate studies in economics. One result of that experience was a pedagogical paper on general equilibrium theory published in the *American Economist* (1966).

Although I continued to teach microeconomic principles and my applied field specialty, industrial organization, my favorite course at Princeton was one I inherited from colleague Robert Kuenne, on the economics of national security. At Harvard I had participated in Thomas Schelling's seminar on game-theoretic models of international conflict. The first half of my Princeton national security course extended what I had learned at Schelling's feet, exploring the rationale of deterrence, compellence, escalation and arms races. The second half taught what I had gained from my research on the economics of military research, development and contracting. It was an exciting time to offer such a course. The Vietnam War was escalating, and the theoretical concepts we explored in class were being played out week by week in the real world.

My own view of the world had evolved over time into that of a thoughtful peacenik. Brainwashed in my youth by the *Chicago Tribune*, I went to Michigan as a Fortress America isolationist. I recall giving a speech in class one day expositing those views and provoking a classmate to remark in wonder, 'You really believe that stuff, don't you?' The first twinges of doubt intruded when I took a political science course at Michigan on international politics, using a book by Hans Morgenthau as text. A more decisive step came during my Army service in Germany. At a training session, we were shown a film on US tactical doctrine for repelling a feared Soviet invasion into Western Germany. As Soviet troops stormed through the Fulda gap and the (less well-known) Neustadt–Coburg gap (my duty station), tactical nuclear weapons would be fired at the confined military hordes. The simulated motion pictures were so beautifully antiseptic, yet I could not avoid exclaiming, 'My God, don't they know there are 100000 civilians living in this valley?' From that time on, I was distrustful of military doctrine. I became even more distrustful at Harvard. From our research on weapons programs our team learned that the United States did not in fact lag behind the Soviets in missile technology, yet presidential candidate John F. Kennedy made the alleged 'missile gap' a key talking point of his election campaign. Torn by doubts, I questioned in the preface of my 1964 book the basic efficiency-enhancing goal of the Weapons Acquisition Research Project:

> Given the pervasive pressures for added arms spending, however, it seems likely that efficiency gains would lead more to increases in our already formidable arsenal than to the reallocation of resources into applications yielding greater social benefit. An efficiency-induced increase in U.S. military strength would in turn, if recent history can be extrapolated, spur the Soviet bloc to intensified efforts in forging new and more powerful countervailing weapons. And I believe that continuation of this arms race will not reduce and probably will increase the already grave risk of nuclear war due to accident, escalation, miscalculation, or madness.

Why then, I asked, did I write the book?

> I am not proud of what seem to be my principal motives – intellectual fascination with a complex and challenging problem, the desire to be recognized for proposing an improved analysis of and solution to the problem, and the well-known need in academic circles to publish or perish ... The scientist, by tradition reserving judgment on the moral implications of his work, will continue to publish, and perhaps we shall all perish.

Senior Business School faculty members tried to dissuade me from publishing these thoughts, but I was adamant. Their advice was correct in one sense; I became a pariah in Pentagon circles. But if a choice must be made, it is better to state one's beliefs honestly than to be a major factotum in the Defense Department.

Despite these beliefs, I tried hard to teach my national security economics course objectively, assigning readings that represented all the widely differing viewpoints. I believe I succeeded; one student from the course's second iteration became a RAND Corporation analyst (who later collaborated with Daniel Ellsberg in disseminating the Pentagon Papers) and another a professional peacenik.

In the fall of 1965, with a zero probability of tenure at Princeton, I faced another, perhaps more crucial, career choice. I had come to believe that controlling the spread of nuclear weapons was the most important problem confronting humanity. James Schlesinger of the RAND Corporation (later Secretary of Defense) invited me to join him and work on arms control problems. We spent a day by the swimming pool of a Washington motel talking about what we might do together. At the end of the day, I decided that I could not accept Jim's proposal. For him, the probability to be minimized was Russian and Chinese cheating on arms control agreements; for me, the probability of unabated nuclear weapons spread. If we could not agree on the objective function, we were unlikely to work together fruitfully. From this came another decision. Curbing the arms race was vitally important, but the probability that my exertions would have any impact was infinitesimal. The classic industrial organization problems of monopoly, regulation and antitrust were vastly less important. But there was a high probability that I could have some influence on their solution, so I would concentrate my professional efforts on them. Since then, I have worked only sporadically and casually on questions of weapons, war and peace. Despite occasional regrets, I cannot say that I reached the wrong decision.

My three years at Princeton were highly productive in terms of new research. From essentially completed work on weapons research, development and contracting, I turned in new, more Schumpeterian directions. One branch was theoretical. From our weapons project research, Joe Peck and I had discovered that within certain limits, progress toward completing R&D projects could be accelerated by investing more resources. There was a time–cost tradeoff. From our case studies, we saw also that the intensity of competition among rivals racing toward similar R&D results affected how the tradeoff was resolved, with more intense competition seeming to induce more rapid progress. At Princeton I turned in earnest to modelling this problem theoretically. From the successful completion of that effort came what I still consider to be my most significant contribution (Scherer, 1967), initiating a research tradition in which there have been scores of subsequent articles, mostly by other scholars, see Reinganum (1989). The other research branch was empirical. I put together a large data base on 448 US corporations' size, growth, profitability, market shares, R&D, employment and patenting. With those data, I was able to conduct the most thorough tests to that date of Schumpeterian hypotheses concerning the most favorable industrial environment for rapid technological progress; see Scherer (1965). The results suggested that Schumpeter's assertions in *Capitalism, Socialism, and Democracy* were more wrong than right. Giant monopolistic corporations were not uniquely efficacious engines of technological advance.

Although these contributions were sufficient to win an associate professorship with tenure at my undergraduate *alma mater*, the University of Michigan, I was not satisfied with my professional progress. My work on weapons acquisition, the theory of R&D rivalry, and structural influences on R&D was of interest to only a small fraction of economists in my chosen specialty, industrial organization. I needed to write something that would be received more broadly. Dissatisfied with existing industrial organization textbooks, I decided to write a new kind of text. The role model for my effort was the treatise by my Princeton colleague, Richard Musgrave, *The Theory of Public*

Finance (1959). Work was begun during a terminal sabbatical semester at Princeton in the spring of 1966 and culminated in the publication of *Industrial Market Structure and Economic Performance* in 1970. The effort was more successful than I could have imagined. More than 100000 copies were sold over the course of the book's three editions. Many budding industrial organization economists were introduced to the field by it before the book was overtaken by changes in fashion. It had three distinguishing characteristics. It was encyclopedic, attempting to encompass and footnote most of the important theoretical and empirical contributions to the field of industrial organization. This trait repelled many students, but pleased others. Second, unlike previous textbooks, it was avowedly behaviorist, assembling a rich theoretical apparatus (mostly geometric) to explain what happened in real-world industries. Third, although this point is denied by some who appear not to have read the book, it makes market structure explicitly endogenous – i.e., resulting not only from scale economies and chance but from the strategies chosen by firms vying for position in the marketplace.

RESEARCH PHILOSOPHY

Much of my research since 1970 has continued to pursue from diverse angles Schumpeterian paradigms. However, it has been Schumpeterian in another sense too. In his monumental *History of Economic Analysis* (1954, p. 12), Schumpeter asserts:

> What distinguishes the 'scientific' economist from all other people who think, talk, and write about economic topics is a command of techniques that we class under three heads: history, statistics, and 'theory.' These three together make up what we shall call Economic Analysis.

Schumpeter went on to say that if he were forced to choose only one of the three, he would choose economic history. But there is no need to choose. My own strong belief is that one must command and use all three to do economics well. Although it is hard to combine the three in individual articles, this is evident in my articles viewed as a collection (e.g., Scherer, 1984) and also *within* my principal research books. My two books on weapons acquisition, the three editions of my industrial organization text, a completely new (1996) text, my study of scale economies (Scherer et al., 1975), my book with David Ravenscraft on mergers (1987), and my book on international high-technology competition (1992) all blend historical research, often done through on-the-site field interviewing, with econometric analysis and systematic theorizing. I have chosen this methodological approach not because Schumpeter advocated it, but because in my bones I have always sensed that it was right. The three-pronged approach is visible in *Patents and the Corporation* and the first *Weapons Acquisition Process* volume, both written before I became familiar as a PhD student preparing for qualifying examinations with Schumpeter's *History of Economic Analysis*. In this approach, I have departed grievously from Wassily Leontief's definition, in one of his 1961 lectures on economic theory, of an industrial organization economist as 'a person who has never been inside a factory.'

It is no doubt a sign of encroaching senescence when scholars scold about the divergence between how research is currently done and their own methodological ideals. I claim no immunity to the syndrome. I love economic theory – geometric, algebraic and numerical. I have witnessed few things more beautiful during my career than a series of lectures at the University of Michigan by Hugo Sonnenschein (now president of the University of Chicago) 'proving' the existence of competitive general equilibrium using a fixed point theorem attributable to Kakutani – unless it was the lecture on the theory of random walks by Professor Kakutani himself at Swarthmore College during the 1980s. Yet I believe there is in industrial organization economics a distressing imbalance between theorizing on the one hand and historical and statistical research on the other.

In my first published attempt to disclaim on matters methodological (1986), I recounted the history of Johannes Kepler. Convinced that the Copernican view of the heliocentric universe was correct, but lacking rigorous theoretical support, Kepler constructed numerous mathematical models. But none corresponded with well-known evidence on the way the planets moved across the earth's field of view, because Kepler assumed incorrectly that the planetary orbits were circular. Not until Kepler joined Tycho Brahe in Prague in 1600 and (later) obtained access to Brahe's unprecedently detailed astronomical observations did he realize that the orbits were elliptical, not circular. Once he had the right data, he derived his famous laws of motion, which (combined with the results of Galileo's experimentation) led to the Newtonian system. Those who sit at their desks constructing industrial organization models without the essential supporting evidence, I argued, are like Kepler, fitting circular orbits within circular orbits. A long footnote recited similar examples form the histories of nuclear physics and microbiology.

We economists like to think of our science as akin to physics in its mathematical rigor. Quite by accident, while pursuing some research on stochastic processes, I obtained in 1995 a detailed description of the research being done by tenured and tenure-track members of the Harvard University physics department, ranked that same year in a National Research Council survey as the top physics department in the United States. Analysis of the research summaries indicated that ten of the 41 active faculty members were working exclusively on theoretical inquiries, six on a combination of theory and experimentation, and 25 on essentially experimental projects (which, of course, might have implications for theory). This set me to wondering: how does the pattern in physics compare with what one might find in my own economics specialty? To find out, I examined all the articles published in volume 12 (1994) of the *International Journal of Industrial Organization* – a high-quality journal in whose founding I played an indirect role. Of the 31 articles, five were exclusively empirical–statistical, one was a mixture of theory and econometrics, one was a case study, and 24 consisted of theory alone with no more than anecdotal real-world foundations. Thus, Harvard physics research and research in the economics of industrial organization, at least as reflected in the not atypical *IJIO*, are almost mirror images of one another – physics preponderantly empirical, industrial organization preponderantly theoretical.

This, I am persuaded, is not a good basis for improved understanding of economic phenomena. The situation persists because it is hard to conduct well-controlled experiments in economics; because analyzing data from 'natural' experiments is time-consuming, costly and prone to the confounding of effects; and because one can generate tenure- and plaudits-winning articles much more rapidly through purely theoretical research than through empirical grubbing.

RECAPITULATION

I have devoted much more of my career to statistical and historical grubbing than to theorizing. Since my first dismal experience at Princeton, I have also tried, with decent success, to teach as well as I was able, among other things not allowing the temptations of Washington and conferences at exotic locations but inconvenient dates to interfere with teaching obligations. (My sole full-time plunge into the business of government was as chief economist of the Federal Trade Commission from 1974 to 1976 – a time when the FTC was at its activist zenith. It was a memorable and gratifying experience, but it was frustrating later to see the Reagan Administration dismantle much of what we struggled to accomplish.) All this has been hard work – perhaps too hard. It has been hard among other things on family life. My wife Barbara and my three children – Tom (an environmental consultant), Karen (a mother of six, artist and musician), and Christina (a molecular biologist) – have received short shrift. That I regret, but all have borne my frequent absences from the hearth and even my several job changes with reasonably good humor. We are united among other things by a love of music – for my wife, teaching piano professionally; for my children, occasional performance on the clarinet, violin, or piano; for me, listening (especially to J.S. Bach, Mozart and Haydn).

When my business policy paper assignment in 1957 triggered the first recognition that I might become a scholar, my maximum aspirations from such a career were slight. I have accomplished much more than I could have expected. And although there have been intervals of depression (usually cured by listening to Brahms symphonies played very loud), life in academia has been good. In hindsight, I would not trade it for anything, and certainly not for the standard Harvard Business School ideal, in Samuel Johnson's words, of 'wealth beyond the dreams of avarice.'

REFERENCES

Levin, Richard, Alvin Klevorick, Richard R. Nelson and Sidney Winter. 1987. 'Appropriating the Returns from Industrial Research and Development,' *Brookings Papers on Economic Activity*, no. 3:783–831.

Mansfield, Edwin. 1986. 'Patents and Innovation: An Empirical Study.' *Management Science*, (32): 173–81.

Richard Musgrave. 1959. *The Theory of Public Finance*. New York: McGraw-Hill.

Peck, M.J. and F.M. Scherer. 1962. *The Weapons Acquisition Process: An Economic Analysis*. Boston: Harvard Business School Division of Research.

Ravenscraft, David J. and F.M. Scherer. 1987. *Mergers, Sell-offs, and Economic Efficiency*. Washington: Brookings.

Reinganum, Jennifer. 1989. 'The Timing of Innovation,' in Richard Schmalensee and Robert D. Willig (eds), *Handbook of Industrial Organization*, vol. I. Amsterdam: North-Holland: 849–908.

Scherer. F.M. and eight others. 1958, 1959. *Parents and the Corporation*. Boston: privately published.

Scherer, F.M. 1964. *The Weapons Acquisition Process: Economic Incentives*. Boston: Harvard Business School Division of Research.

———, 1964. 'The Theory of Contractual Incentives for Cost Reduction,' *Quarterly Journal of Economics*, (78): 257–79.

———, 1965. 'Firm Size, Market Structure, Opportunity, and the Output of Patented Inventions,' *American Economic Review*, (60): 1097–123.

———, 1966. 'General Equilibrium and Economic Efficiency.' *The American Economist*, (10): 1–17.

———, 1967. 'Research and Development Resource Allocation under Rivalry,' *Quarterly Journal of Economics*, (81): 358–94.

———, 1970. *Industrial Market Structure and Economic Performance*. Chicago: Rand-McNally.

———, 1984. *Innovation and Growth: Schumpeterian Perspectives*. Cambridge: MIT Press.

———, 1986. 'On the Current State of Knowledge in Industrial Organization,' in H.W. de Jong and W.G. Shepherd (eds), *Mainstreams in Industrial Organization*, Book I. Dordrecht: Kluwer: 5–22.

———, 1992. *International High-Technology Competition*. Cambridge: Harvard University Press.

———, 1996. *Industry Structure, Strategy, and Public Policy*. New York:

HarperCollins.
———, Alan Beckenstein, Erich Kaufer and R. Dennis Murphy. 1975. *The Economics of Multi-Plant Operation: An International Comparisons Study*. Cambridge: Harvard University Press.
Schumpeter, Joseph A. 1942. *Capitalism, Socialism, and Democracy*. New York: Harper.
———, 1954. *History of Economic Analysis*. New York: Oxford University Press.
Taylor, C.T. and Z.A. Silberston. 1973. *The Economic Impact of the Patent System*. Cambridge: Cambridge University Press.

24. Philosophy and my work life*

Julian L. Simon

I

As a 17-year-old starting college, I was anxious to study what the great philosophers taught about how to conduct our lives well. My second (and last) course was a selective gallop through Western thought. I enjoyed it and did much of the extensive reading. But though some of the philosophy of science made sense, much of the rest seemed meaningless to me. Most especially, the pompously unreadable school of Hegelian German philosophy seemed a fraud on the public; pure obscurantist nonsense, I concluded. When much later I read John Locke's and David Hume's similar judgments about the bulk of academic philosophers, they fortified my doubts.

The exam for the philosophy course was the last of five, so I let it slide. Then the night before the exam I could not find my class notes, which were unusually important in that course. Naturally, I panicked.

A philosophy major upstairs lent me his notebook for a few hours, but it didn't help much. I then had the inspiration to ask him to teach me some impressive-sounding German words that I could insert into my exam essays. He did so. And the next day, for the first and last time in my life, I faked the answers on an exam.

The result? During my first three semesters I had not received even an A minus. This time I got a straight A, and my phil major friend upstairs – who had been doing very well in all his classes and understood the material thoroughly – got a C. Lest one put the incident down to the inadequacies of a third-rate institution, this happened at Harvard College. If I had drawn the obvious lesson from that experience, and applied it by fancying up my work instead of trying to keep it simple, perhaps my entire work life would have had a different course.

The Navy ROTC (which sent me to college) had a system whereby at the end of each semester we returned our used textbooks; they constituted a pool from which students would draw books the next semester. The book room was administered loosely, and we were not discouraged from taking books that

*This chapter first appeared in *The American Economist*, **40**(2), Fall 1996, 22–36.

might only be 'relevant' to a course. Nor was there strict monitoring about book return. So it was not unusual for one of us to take a book on 'extended loan'.

Triggered by a stray remark in the philosophy course, the title *Positivism* by Richard von Mises piqued my interest, so I liberated the book and neglected to return it. When I got around to reading it after college, it greatly influenced my thinking, perhaps because von Mises was not doctrinaire to the point of considering poetry and religion simply metaphysical nonsense, as did some Positivists.

Questions about how one may best live one's years – such as what to choose as goals in life for one's own sake as well as for others', and how much of one's efforts should be allocated between self and others – these questions are still as puzzling and almost as little understood as when people first thought and wrote about them 'philosophically.' And the questions about how research work may best be done still belong mostly to the philosophy of science because they have yet been little studied by the sciences. Philosophy has entered my work life in both those ways: in deciding what I shall try to accomplish, and in the methods I employ to achieve those goals.

The best idea I got from the philosophy of scientific methods is the concept of the operational definition. It focuses on what can be observed and measured, and it battles against vague concepts that cannot be pinned down. I luckily learned about the operational definition in my undergraduate major of experimental psychology, a field in which the concept has greatly helped clarify such concepts as morale and intelligence. More about that later.

II

Underlying my choice of work goals is the belief – based on observation, data and 'philosophic' speculation – that there can be progress in human affairs; if I did not believe in progress, I would be condemned to think of my work and the rest of science as the game that many others consider it to be. That is, I believe that the states of material and non-material human well-being are not static in the long run. People nowadays have more of the most important material elements of welfare than in centuries past, notably life itself. That life is the highest value, and that all have an obligation to cherish life and good health in others and in themselves is an idea that I attribute to Judaism even if I did not derive it therefrom.

There also has been improvement in all the secondary material aspects of life: food; shelter and privacy; mobility; communication; and, most important, education. I have recently spent much time pulling together the data that document this proposition, much of it published in an edited collection called

The State of Humanity, and in the greatly expanded 1996 edition of *The Ultimate Resource*. One of my dreams is to compile a much larger compendium of the most important time series on the human enterprise, going back as far into the centuries and millennia as possible. But this project requires institutional backing and the cooperation of many individuals; whether I will achieve this dream is an open question.

Most of the material progress has suddenly occurred in just the past few centuries, following tens of thousands of years of near-stasis in 'consumer' welfare even though the base of knowledge that led to these momentous changes was building gradually for thousands of years. I conclude that the speed of this process up to the take-off point (with respect to consumer welfare, and not with respect to the capacity to produce) was the result of growth in population and in knowledge, and that population size was the ultimate determinant of knowledge growth; this work is embodied in a yet-unpublished book entitled, *What Governed The Speed of Human Progress?*

III

There is a great difference between me and most other economists that Professor Szenberg has invited to write essays here: they have been honored by their colleagues with Nobel Prizes, election to the presidency of the American Economic Association, and similar marks of distinction. In contrast, I have never had a single mark of professional respect (let alone honor) in my academic professions. I've never held an office (not even membership on the committee that nominates *other* people for offices and honors, or the committee that counts the ballots for the candidates), never been asked to give a to-be-published paper at an annual AEA meeting, and – any scholar must be amazed that any one could publish a huge pile of books and papers over many years and yet compile this particular record – never been asked to referee a paper for the major 'official' journals in my three fields of economics, demography, or statistics, or by almost any other top journal. These implicit judgments by the professions accurately reflect my lack of success in achieving what I most sought to achieve – that my research would induce further work by my colleagues.

Why, then, did Professor Szenberg ask me to join this group? Most probably because I have had a peculiar kind of success outside the economics profession. This success is indicated most clearly by the invective directed at me by non-economists; curiously, they often denounce me as being quintessentially an economist. (Here it is interesting to note that I never studied economics, a matter we will come back to later.)

IV

Roy Pascal wrote that the key question for the autobiographer is how s/he became what s/he became. The answer inevitably needs much more than an article, of course. But I can at least try to answer a more limited question here: how did I become the kind of *economist* I am?

My father and mother were both born in Newark, New Jersey, in 1895 and 1900 respectively. Their parents were Jewish immigrants who arrived impoverished in the previous decade, but who had by then saved money and opened small stores. In both cases, the women were the driving forces. My mother's mother had in 1900 opened a hardware store measuring about 100 square feet in an Italian neighborhood in Newark, New Jersey. From that store eventually sprang a hardware 'empire' in Newark, in the 1920s totaling 21 stores and a wholesale operation, and in the 1950s including a chain of stores. Each new operation was started by a new-immigrant relative who came to live with my grandparents for a while, learned the business, and then opened up on his or her own in an area of the city that as yet had no Goodstein family store.

My father's mother opened a 'dairy store' that sold no meat and therefore avoided the many problems of food being certified kosher.

My parents grew up working in their parents' stores. Dad quit high school around the end of his junior year, ostensibly because he was needed in Grandma Simon's store. My mother was valedictorian of her class in high school, her greatest pride in life. Her father having died, she then went to work to help support the family, and she took some night courses in accounting at NYU.

I was born on 12 February 1932 – Abraham Lincoln's birthday, which accounts for my middle name being 'Lincoln.' My first clear memory is of being downstairs in Grandma Goodie's old-fashioned hardware store and being given a small box of nails of assorted sizes to sort – probably nails that had spilled in the process of weighing them by the pound for customers. That was a wonderful task to give to a child to occupy him and make him feel that he was 'working' and doing something useful.

I remember with pleasant warmth the first nine years of my life. Our block in the gritty, working-class Weequahic neighborhood of Newark was composed of two-story, two-family houses; we lived downstairs at 124 Grumman Avenue. All the people on the street were Jews except for the Greek family that had a nice one-family home at the corner with garden; they owned a restaurant. Son Jimmy-the-Greek was my age. It was a neighborhood of nicknames. The kid across the street was Bupkiss (Yiddish for 'beans') Barnhart.

I swam like a fish in water in Newark. I felt a part of the group, never like an outsider. I may even have been pampered by the older kids and grown-ups;

this certainly is the impression given by a photograph of my gang, taken when I was about six. I remember a tribal-like arrangement in which the gang made allowances for the kids' various ages and physical capacities (I was the youngest), but I may be romanticizing. The 17-year-old in the picture was like an older brother to me; it was the last time in my life I experienced having a protector.

There was always something to do on the street, ranging from A (apple-crate scooters mounted on worn-out steel skate-wheels) to Z ('zip-guns' made from orange-crate corners and rubber bands that shot tiny squares cut from shirt cardboards). When I was six, seven, eight and maybe nine years old, we scaled the baseball and 'Horrors of War' series of picture cards that came with bubble-gum against the house wall in the alley (that is, the driveway between two houses), with the closest toss being the winner of all the cards played on each round. This game illuminates a central point in my nature.

There were two styles of throwing: (a) holding the corner of the card between the second and third fingers, or between thumb and forefinger, and flipping the card from the back of the hand; and (b) propelling it by bending it between the thumb and the index finger and using the spring of the bend, plus the thumb, to snap it forward. The latter was the 'big kids' way – sophisticated and macho. Little kids did it either way. I well remember experimenting to see which worked best for me, and reflecting that the backhand method was more efficient, in considerable part because it was simpler – no moving parts and no need to have a properly springy new card to flap. So I opted for the backhand method because of its efficiency, despite its lower 'little-kids' status.

That decision foreshadowed many decisions in my life – simplicity over sophistication, efficiency over style. I have always wanted to do well what I was doing, even when the choice is between doing the task skillfully and impressing other people. The interesting part about the picture-cards story is how clearly I remember making the decision on those grounds even at that young age.

I like to win, but winning is usually less important than doing it well. To win a squash game when the opponent errs on the last point, rather than my scoring a nice winning shot, leaves me unsatisfied. And playing in tournaments has never mattered a lot to me. I don't get a special rush out of competing. And I almost never had a sense of competition against other students in my school work.

My introduction to duopolistic price competition came when, about age ten, I overheard my father on the phone fixing prices with his competitor. Dad owned a tiny business selling sal soda – crystallized sodium carbonate, also known as 'washing soda' – mainly for use as an industrial water softener.

National Crystal Company – it sounds rather grand – was located next to a railroad siding in Irvington. Dad's 'factory' was four sideways concrete steps up from the railroad track, through a heavy tarpaper door that slid sideways, then onto rough wooden tracks on which barrels were rolled up and down. The main equipment was a crude mixing vat that combined water and the central input, potash; the technology was vintage 1830s [*sic*] except that it was driven by an electric motor rather than an overhead belt powered by steam or water power. There was also an 'office' – a walled-off desk and telephone, my father's desk chair with a ripped horsehair seat, and a pile of burlap bags for another seat in case anyone else came in. The establishment had no heat in the winter other than a kerosene stove in the office.

Besides potash, the main input was my father's labor – shoveling the potash from the railroad cars (with which half-time laborer Willie helped), mixing the potash with water (and perhaps other materials), packing the crystals into wooden barrels, and finally loading the barrels onto a customer's truck. The business employed only my father and Willie, but it provided the family perhaps $50–$100 a week (say, $500–$1000 in 1996 prices) during the depression – very respectable.

There was one other sal soda firm in the New Jersey area, at the other end of Newark. From my parents' comments I'd guess it was about the same size as my father's business. And I remember my father's side of the worried phone conversation – we may have already moved to Millburn, in which case it would have been after June 1941 – in which he and the competitor agreed to hold prices at something above a cut-throat level. Afterwards there were discussions between my father and my mother about whether or not the competitor would keep the agreement. (This is the stuff of industrial economics that gets lost in the equations we write.) Here George Stigler's theory of poly-poly, with its emphasis on firms making price-fixing agreements and then cheating on them, resonated with me. (None of this is inconsistent with my belief that, taken as a whole, the world of commerce induces people to act more honestly and cooperatively than does any other system of economics.)

We moved to Millburn, a New Jersey suburb a few miles north of Newark, in the summer of 1941. The move produced a crack in my life, though not an earthquake. I never again felt like an insider. The picture of the gang in Newark with me as the littlest kid in the center was my last such experience.

Though I had no brothers or sisters, I do not remember wishing for siblings until we lived in Millburn. But then the phrases 'my sister,' and especially 'my brother,' became for me the sweetest words in the English language.

About 1942 or 1943, National Crystal Company shut down for war-induced lack of raw material. For the rest of his life my father worked only for two periods of about 18 months each, until I could hire him part-time in 1961 when he was 66. My mother would not allow him to take the jobs he could easily get during the war – such as driving a bus, and working as a semi-skilled laborer in war industries – because of status considerations; his not working on the sabbath was mostly an excuse because during the war, there were jobs galore. My mother then went to work as an office manager, and the wolf lurked behind the door thereafter. Ensuring the future economic well-being of my parents became a constant element in my thinking for the next 25 years.

I was a pretty good student up through high school, and a fairly good athlete. I tried not to stick out in any way, and succeeded in doing so. I did not think of myself as different or special in any way. Socially, I was always a bit marginal, perhaps in part because I was Jewish in a mostly non-Jewish town, and perhaps because of some aspects of personality such as my feeling that there was nothing especially desirable about me; after all, I was just another guy trying to find a place in the world. Also, there always lurked inside me some irreverence for authority and for orthodoxy, and that probably contributed to my being at the edges. I never had any interest in socialism, and I remember joking that I was against communism because I would be one of the first people they put up against the wall and shot – because I would not be properly reverent.

I remember nothing of what happened in classes except a few bizarre events such as the students – including me – cruelly torturing teachers. I remember lots of sports, hanging around, and telling jokes outside the classrooms. I also have no memories of classes in elementary school and very few in college. And I had no personal relationships with teachers.

I took a test for the Navy ROTC scholarship program, and wound up at Harvard; the scholarship, plus jobs after I got back from cruises in the summer, enabled me to get along without any money from my parents. College years were fruitful and enjoyable. Majoring in experimental psychology was a good choice for me, and my senior honors thesis on concept formation was the high point of the four years; I felt that I was obtaining new knowledge unknown to anyone in the world, an exhilarating feeling. It turns out that I really was making a considerable discovery in cognitive psychology, but my adviser had left Harvard for a sabbatical and no one in my behaviorist department was interested. Later when I was aboard ship I sent an article on the subject to a psychology journal, but my lack of proper formalism – references, etc., – was abysmal, and that is all the referee saw; as I re-read that referee's report now, I see the herald of much of the rest of my life.

For almost two years I served aboard a destroyer as a deck officer. I loved my job as 'First Lieutenant' – the title for the officer in charge of the decks and sides and all seamanship. But I got fired because we failed an inspection. (We were short of personnel, and I did not know how to 'fight' for more.)

Serving as the ship's defense counsel at captain's mast and lesser courts-martial for sailors accused of minor offenses perhaps inevitably fell to my lot. I did not realize that I was supposed to act my part in a court-martial drama whose script was informally written in the wardroom over coffee. Giving one man a spirited defense that got him off on appeal to higher authority got me in trouble because it was a black mark for the ship. My stupidity about organizational realities like this has persisted throughout my life.

After the Navy I came within two weeks of going to medical school. But I had a vision of my brain being fossilized as I passed through the gate of the school. I also worried about the give-'em-a-pill mentality of the medical profession at that time, as if the body could safely be dealt with a part at a time. So I took a leave of absence, and never looked back. (Tufts Medical School will be surprised if I write them that I plan to matriculate next fall.)

So I went into business: cost accountant at Prudential Insurance Company for four days, until the extraordinary regimentation did me in. Technical writer of instruction manuals for a week, until I was terminally bored. *Encyclopedia Britannica* salesman for a month, until the lies became impossible and I found another job. Then advertising copywriter in a pharmaceutical drug agency for six months, and advertising promotion writer for a complex of magazines for six months. Halfway through that year I decided to learn the theory of business, so I went to the University of Chicago for an MBA. That took a year, and – hungry for bodies at the time – associate dean Jim Lorie recruited me for the PhD program, telling me that it would only take another three months of class work, plus a thesis I could do in six months. I stayed because I had a girlfriend, and I was enjoying the university and university life, though I had no intention of becoming a professor; I thought I had no special talent for it.

My career at the School of Business was distinguished by having been the only PhD candidate in living memory, before or after, to have failed his/her PhD orals. I had studied so little economics that when asked a question about consumer surplus I put price on the horizontal axis and quantity on the vertical axis, and never could get untracked after that; I had a fugue, the only such happening in my life; it was as if I was gliding through the air in a Chagall painting. The committee mercifully reexamined me a couple of months later, and I passed.

After a total of three years and a thesis on the storage operations of a university library (I took a job directing the project to make money, with no thought to the academic importance of the work), my new wife (sociologist) Rita James Simon and I moved east to start a mail-order business in Hoboken, New Jersey, where I could employ my parents and provide them a source of income.

After a year and a half in business, I realized that the writing of a correspondence course I then sold – naturally entitled *How to Start and Operate a Mail-Order Business* – was what I most enjoyed doing. And because of something wrong I did, I fell into a deep depression that lasted for years until I found a new theory of depression that cured me in a week (see my *Good Mood* book). On a fluke I also gave a lecture at Columbia that I enjoyed. Hence I decided to become a professor.

The better of the two opportunities in a thin market for my services was teaching advertising in the College of Journalism at the University of Illinois. There I started doing the economics of advertising; I think I was born an economist. After a year and a half I was offered the opportunity to be put up for tenure, but readily acceded to the department head's suggestion that I wait a year. A year later he wrote me a letter saying that I could expect never to receive tenure in that department, despite two books in publication, a flock of articles, etc.; I did not fit into the head's vision of what the department should be. This freed me to go across the street and solicit a job in the Department of Marketing in the College of Commerce. Three years later, in 1969, I was also given a joint appointment in economics. But I always wanted to remain half-time teaching business because I liked teaching practical subjects even though they had almost nothing to do with my research.

V

This essay is addressed to economists and therefore focuses on my life as an economist rather than my private life. But my family life has more influence on me emotionally. I am enormously lucky to have a wonderful wife who has had an extraordinarily productive and valuable professional life as a sociologist, plus three grown children who are healthy and who have their feet firmly planted on roads that lead to useful, productive lives; indeed, they already are doing so. I can shake off a letter or a newspaper article that calls me 'the Devil Incarnate', or even the rejection of a technical article, in a relatively short time. But a family unpleasantness can throw me into the pit of despair for days, and the feeling that something good has happened to one of my children can buoy me up for days or weeks; this is a measure of the relative importance of family life for me.

VI

Though I only had three MBA courses in economics, years ago I stopped feeling like a pretender and a fraud when I referred to myself as an economist. And I have thought from time to time that my lack of socialization in the field may have helped me be open to some ideas that graduate study might have closed off, or to use tools that we did not easily revert to because we had never learned them.

VII

The subject here is my philosophy and not my work. Yet my life philosophy is not understandable without a bit of information about the professional work I have done. I'll mention the main topics briefly here, and many of the topics will reappear later as I discuss some of their aspects in particular contexts.

After three years of work on the economic and managerial aspects of advertising, I ended that study because, as I wrote at the end of a book of my technical articles and essays on the subject (badly titled as *Issues in the Economics of Advertising*; it sounds like an edited collection): '[T]he economic study of advertising is not deserving of great attention except for special problems ... (As the reader may realize, this is not a congenial point at which to arrive after spending several years working on the subject)' (1970, p. 285).

The main subject of my professional life has been the economics of population, and the effects of size, density and growth on the standard of living, availability of resources (including such human resources as the amount of education), cleanliness of the environment, and other phenomena that may be related to the demographic variables. Both my empirical and theoretical studies have mostly confirmed the prior discoveries by Colin Clark, Simon Kuznets, Harold Barnett and Ester Boserup (and the speculations by Alexander Everett, Friedrich Engels and Henry George) showing that first-edition Malthusianism does not fit various sets of relevant long-run data (as Malthus himself published in his second and subsequent editions); models that allow for human adaptation to physical conditions through increases in knowledge fit the facts much better in the long run.

The economics of immigration is a sub-topic that has some special twists and professional surprises. For example, immigration is not at all analogous to trade because the 'pure' Ricardian gains to trade go to consumers whereas the 'pure' gains to immigration (in equilibrium) go to producers (the immigrants themselves, if one abstracts from capital effects). On the other hand, the larger is the government sector in a country, the larger the one-time windfall contribution made by immigrants through their excess of taxes over services used (because they typically arrive when just starting their labor-force years).

Population economics also led to large-scale gathering of data on the important material aspects of human life over as many decades, centuries, and even millennia as possible.

Another main topic has been the development of ways to do statistical inference by simulation rather than Normal-based and non-parametric formulas. This has come to be known as resampling. Among other devices, I introduced the bootstrap method in 1969, and developed a computer language and program in 1974 to perform the Monte Carlo simulations efficiently but still with such simplicity that the user understands every logical step. This line of work – which I went back to with renewed vigor in 1989 – threatens much of the intellectual capital of mathematical statisticians. My main interest, however, is in presenting workaday tools to statistics users rather than investigating the properties of complex variations of the method.

Simulation of duopoly and triopoly is another topic that I worked on around 1970 and then again in the 1990s, with the same colleague: Carlos Puig, who was an undergraduate when we began collaborating. And I have also allowed myself to get interested in a wide variety of empirical questions ranging from the effect of smoking on life expectancy to the relationship of media coverage to public opinion.

VIII

More and more as I have gotten older, and consistent with my belief that progress is not only possible but inevitable, and probably irreversible by now, the crucial philosophical element in my work life has been the desire to be useful. The sage Rabbi Tarphon enjoined, 'One may not neglect the work.' I am comforted, however, that he added, 'but one is not required to finish it, either.' Here I consider 'work' to be that which aims to produce something useful to others or to oneself.

The value of doing something useful led me to stop working on the economics of advertising, my first major topic.

I may have succeeded in being of some use to the larger society. My reverse-auction 'volunteer' scheme to resolve the problem of involuntary bumping of passengers from oversold airline flights, and the lengthy and strenuous promotion of the scheme, has been a complete and unmitigated success starting the very first day it was inaugurated – after 12 years during which everyone (except economists, I'm proud to say) asserted that it was ridiculous in principle and could not possibly work in practice. My studies of immigration may have had some effect on federal legislation regulating the volume of immigration into the United States – at least Senator Rudy Boschwitz (the only immigrant then in the Senate) told me so, and the anti-immigration organizations have paid me the tribute of calling me a liar and a profiteer. And maybe my work on population and resources has had some salutary effects. But it is very easy to fool yourself that you have been more important than you really have been in such matters where causal influence is so indirect.

I judge, however, that I have failed abysmally in what I have spent 90 percent of my work effort trying to do – being useful to my fellow economists and statisticians and social scientists by providing to them theoretical ideas, frameworks, data and methods that would help them in doing more advanced work.

When I say I have aimed to do work that is 'useful' to *economists*, I do not mean work that other economists would simply *consider* valuable, but rather work that would advance other economic work that would be useful to *society*. In a memorable interchange in their 1960s presidential addresses to the American Economic Association, Paul Samuelson and Kenneth Boulding proposed very different tests of the value of economic work. Samuelson stated his criterion to be the approbation of one's peers: 'In the long run the economic scholar works for the only coin worth having – our own applause' (1962, p. 18). Boulding then replied that 'I did not become an economist for anybody's applause; I became an economist because I thought there was an intellectual task ahead, of desperate importance for the welfare and even the survival of mankind' (1966, p. 13).

Boulding's criterion appeals to me, and I suspect that it appeals to Samuelson, too. But Samuelson's criterion is much more easily measurable – with citations, for example, or speaking invitations or salary offers – than is Boulding's criterion, which helps Samuelson's criterion to dominate the profession. And many of those who espouse Samuelson's criterion say that the acceptance of the profession is in fact the best available proxy for Boulding's criterion of usefulness.

IX

Turning to the role of philosophy in actually doing my work: one does not need the philosophy of science for run-of-the-mill research circumstances. But one does need it for tough questions that arise in unusual circumstances.

Even before I intended to become a professor, I realized that I was interested in research methods. And when I first began to teach and was scheduled to teach a course in research methods, I was delighted. Because I thought I had a new way of looking at the subject – viewing research methods as devices to overcome obstacles to knowledge – I wrote a textbook, *Basic Research Methods in Social Science*. I read a lot of philosophy of science while doing so. I realized that any text on research methods – especially mine – bootlegs a working philosophy of science. That is, a text is almost an operational definition of the subject.

I have sought to do work so that the methods would be effective in producing useful information rather than 'finding' an abstract 'truth.' And along the way I have concluded that general principles of research laid down by philosophers, most of whom have never done any empirical research, are worth little. Consider, for example. Popper's assertion that a proposition is never confirmed but can only be disconfirmed. The plain fact is that the weight of evidence matters; if there is a lot of evidence for, and little evidence against, a proposition, people will *act as if* it has been confirmed, and the acting as-if is what matters. Another example is the hypothetico-deductive 'method' that for quite a while ruled the roost in the philosophy of science, and even within economics. This principle condemns all rooting around in the data for plausible hypotheses, and insists that hypotheses be deduced from theory. That was a helpful corrective against the danger that if you conduct many tests of statistical significance, you will surely arrive at some apparently significant findings as artifacts. And it was a handy device to help referees condemn papers they do not like. But the hypothetico-deductive 'method' is an intellectual straitjacket, and no sensible researcher pays much attention to it. If philosophy runs too much against standard practice of the most competent workers in a science, one should consider that the philosophy must be wrong, rather than the practice.

An early foray into philosophy was into the question of whether one should refer to smoking as a *cause* of lung cancer. That problem roiled the medical and statistical communities after the *Surgeon General's Report* in 1964. And R.A. Fisher came down on the side of 'unproven.' Having read that *Report*, I thought that the aggregate of the evidence – the proper way to consider the matter, in my view – constituted an open-and-shut case, so I wrote a letter to that effect to *American Statistician*.

Then chance intervened in a convoluted fashion, as it so often does, leading further into the concept of causality. In New York I had done some consulting work for a liquor trade association. A key issue in liquor-tax hearings is the extent to which liquor sales are affected by a change in price. Looking over the available studies, I was struck by their lack of solidity; none of the many methods tried, many of them extremely complex, seemed persuasive. It occurred to me that with a simple set of adjustments, the sales volumes observed before and after state changes in liquor-tax laws should yield a reliable answer. Later in Urbana I did the calculations for the liquor study, and after writing them up I sent the study to *Econometrica*. To my surprise and delight, the article was accepted for publication. This was amazing because the article contained not a single equation in algebra (though it did contain an equation in plain English), probably the first time in the history of *Econometrica* that such a 'mathematically unsophisticated' article had been published.

The explanation for the happy accident of the article being accepted is that the referee was Herman Wold, far too capable a man to be put off by lack of mathematical dazzle. And he requested the editor to put me in touch with him because he wanted to tell me about a related piece of work he had done in Sweden with postal rates.

Now finally causality: in the course of our correspondence in 1964, Wold enclosed a draft of a paper about causality in statistical investigations. Flattered by the thought that he sought my comments, I read the paper carefully. Try as I would, however, I could not figure out just what the term 'causality' meant in the context of that paper.

After I had grappled for some time with the concept of causality, I realized that the concept of the operational definition provides a key to the matter. What is needed is not a definition of causality with respect to the *properties* of the concept, but rather an operational definition which in practice is a set of criteria. And that in fact cracks open the conundrum.

This is the criteria set I proposed: a statement shall be called 'causal' if (a) the relationship correlates highly enough to be useful and/or interesting; (b) it does not require so many side-condition statements as to gut its generality and importance; (c) enough possible 'third factor' variables must have been tried to give some assurance that the relationship is not spurious; and (d) the relationship is deductively connected into a larger body of theory, or (less satisfactorily) is supported by a set of auxiliary propositions that 'explain' the 'mechanism' by which the relationship works. This checklist constitutes the definition of criteria. Whether a given relationship meets the criteria sufficiently to be called 'causal' is not automatic or perfectly objective, but rather requires judgment and substantive knowledge of the entire context.

Another application of the operational definition: because I had learned as an undergraduate that psychology dealt with such difficult concepts as morale and intelligence by recourse to operational definitions, it occurred to me that the concept of utility and interpersonal comparisons should be treated in similar fashion. It is necessary simply to find one or more measures that are relevant to a particular context of discussion; one can then abandon the debilitating idea of the 'properties' of utility. Thought of this way, the 'problem' of interpersonal comparisons simply disappears. Questionnaire measurements of happiness, and rates of suicide and mental illness, are obvious candidates as measures. Utility is then simply defined as, say, a score on a questionnaire, just as Einstein defined time as what is read on a clock. So I organized and presented data on these and other matters and showed how they could help make sense of problems in taxes and transfers.

Hand in hand with the operational definition goes the analysis of language that the Vienna Circle taught. For example, when I examined closely the usages of Chamberlin's term 'product differentiation' I found that they usually are tautological, and it is impossible to give consistent meaning to the term and the concept. This – together with George Stigler's demolition of Chamberlin's concept of 'the group' – shows that the concept of monopolistic competition is without value as an analytic tool.

Another example: what is the 'true' effect of income on fertility? In a short book I wrote in the 1970s showing different relationships between income and fertility in different times and places, I concluded that the 'true' relationship even at a single moment in a single country is impossible to state meaningfully. Rather, the relevant statement about the relationship must depend upon one's larger purposes – a theme concerning the need for judgment that runs through all my methodological work.

It is quite amazing how many concepts that seem to be pillars of economic theory crumble like sand upon close examination. For example, the capital–output ratio turns out to be meaningless for most or all long-run and inter-country comparisons because the value of capital is a function of the price of the output it is used to produce, rather than having any meaningful independent valuation. (Original cost is not meaningful in such contexts.) This assertion is perfectly analogous to the value of farmland, which Colin Clark showed is about 3.5 times the value of the average year's gross output all throughout history and in all countries, apart from temporary bubbles or depressions. Deviations from average capital–output ratios therefore say nothing fundamental about the state of an economy. Naturally, it is not easy to convince capital 'theorists' of this point of view. I published this idea in an appendix to a book, but after 20 years I am still looking for a journal to publish it.

Off and on for about 20 years I have spent many hours on sabbaths trying to understand special relativity intuitively. I devoted several happy years to the early chapters of Einstein's own little book intended for pre-university students(!). I understood Einstein's critique of the concept of simultaneity because of my prior understanding of the operational definition, and in turn that critique sharpened my understanding of operational definitions and helped me apply it to such problems as the theory of natural resource supply; with respect to the latter, the operational definition helped me formulate the view – mind-boggling to many – that the supplies of natural resources are not finite because the definition of 'finite' implies measurability, and there is no way – even in principle – to measure those future supplies because of the very real possibility of new substitutes being invented and new sources being discovered in the cosmos.

X

The dispute was about payment for the rent of some beach umbrellas. I was perhaps seven years old, and it was early in the day in Bradley Beach, New Jersey. One well-muscled, suntanned lifeguard had the beer-bellied truck driver's arms pinned behind him and another muscular lifeguard was smacking him with his fists in the midsection. It didn't go on long, I suppose;

I don't have an end to the recollection. But the memory has remained vivid.

All my life I have identified with individuals and groups in the truck driver's situation. For myself, too; having someone attack me in print when I can't obtain the opportunity to reply is a bit like the situation of the umbrella man. Somebody is getting hit and is denied the opportunity to fight back.

XI

I noted earlier that my professional history is different from the other persons whom Michael Szenberg has invited to write essays in this series: they have been successful in the eyes of their colleagues, and their work has been fruitful in inducing their colleagues to build their work. And they have mostly taught in university departments of high prestige, and have been honored with offices in their professional associations. None of this is true for me. This is not a statement of modesty about my work, which I believe to be powerful, sound and important. It is rather a statement about how my work has been received (or to be more accurate, not received). Nor is this a lament, because this result was almost inevitable, given the nature of the work and of my own professional habits. It is just a fact that the reader must recognize in order that the rest of what I write here will make any sense.

Naturally, I've speculated a lot over the years about why the corpus (corpse?) of the work I consider my best has not been attended to and built upon by other economists. The simplest and most obvious hypothesis is that the work is no good. But by now there has been enough confirmation of the results of my work, both in practice (the airline oversales auction system), and in the non-appearance of work showing me to be in error (as well as the same work being done later by others and received well), that that hypothesis does not explain the whole. Therefore I have cast around for other explanations.

For a while I thought that it was my mode of presentation that was at fault – too staid, or not well-enough organized, or too lengthy. Another early hypothesis was that I have worked in too many areas, spreading myself too thin and weakening my credibility. But now I can't believe either of these is the main explanation.

Still another hypothesis is that I have not been a member of a group of people working in a shared tradition on a related set of problems in which the profession at large is interested. Maybe. Yet the successful innovators do not confine themselves in such a fashion, and they manage to get their ideas across anyway. Perhaps such successful innovators have greater force of personality than I do, and are supported by more confidence in themselves and their ideas, which shows up as infectious enthusiasm. But this can't be the whole answer, either.

My social relationship to my professions certainly has been dysfunctional. Michael Szenberg wrote that 'There is increasing recognition of the significance of face-to-face interaction, interpersonal communication, and cooperation among scientists' (1992, p. 2). But because of a combination of the circumstances that have constituted my opportunity set, my shifting of interests from subject to subject, and my own bashfulness at seeking instrumental relationships, I have almost no professional friends among economists, demographers and statisticians. How important this element has been I cannot estimate.

Friends have speculated that I may have evoked damaging resentment by having participated in public debate on various issues in newspapers and television. Scientists are not 'supposed to' speak in blunt terms and be seen in the media. But this hypothesis is too self-flattering; resentment could hardly explain the fates of my writings in the years before 1980 when I stuck completely to my academic grindstone.

And ideology is not the explanation. Joan Robinson may or may not have been correct when she wrote that 'Economics has mixed its ideology into the subject so well that the ideologically unconventional usually appear ... to be scientifically incompetent' (1977, p. 1319). But my economic and social ideology is quite in the mainstream of Anglo-Saxon economics, and hence cannot explain the fate of my work.

My approach to the craft of science, and my philosophical approach to scientific method, however, are out of the mainstream. It is true that, on grounds that *seem* ideological, some economists and almost all demographers disagree vigorously with the conclusions about population growth that I (though not I alone) arrive at. But my work on subjects other than population – including on advertising, long before I was at all notorious – also evoked chilly reactions, with no ideological explanation.

Certainly my reluctance to employ the framework of the optimizing allocation decision – with full mathematical regalia – in those situations where I consider that framework unnecessary or inappropriate has not helped. And much of my work deals with very long run economic development, a context in which the creation of new technology is the most important element. That process often is best not treated with the logic of profit maximization.

The pro-technique tendency of the profession is a disaster for me professionally because I have a distaste (irrational because counterproductive) for unnecessary flourish. As an outgrowth of how my mother's need for status kept my father from taking available jobs, as I mentioned earlier, I grew up seeing how the desire for proper front can destroy a person's self-respect, and keep a family from getting a living; therefore I hated it. Nowadays I no longer actively hate front and flourishes, but only despise them that that attitude shows through.

My methodological philosophy of simplicity certainly is in some part responsible for my failure to win the attention of my economist colleagues, though I still believe in its essential soundness. For a long time I was taken (or better, taken in) by the notion that simplicity is an ideal in science. (I even titled two of my early articles 'A Simple Method' ...). It took me years to appreciate that T.S. Eliot's remark about poetry applies also to scientific writing, to wit: it must be easy enough to understand, but hard enough so that it cannot be understood immediately. Simplicity fails because, as Stigler puts it, 'The form of work takes on a value independent of its content: a scholar should be literate, and his work should be pursued with non-vulgar instruments' (quoted by Fisher, 1986, p. 78). And as Goodwin (quoted by Fisher, 1986, p. 80) put it, 'It is the essence of a profession that the skills required therein are not possessed by those without.' This has led my work to take some lumps. For example, I wished to compare the areas between two empirical curves showing sales responses to advertising over time, and I simply counted the squares under the curves on graph paper. A referee was horrified at the 'primitiveness' of this mode of integration, and at the ignorance of the author.

To a considerable extent, however, the content of my best ideas is inseparable from a mode of presentation that damns them; hence using other than my unacceptable style of work was not within my power, and negative effects were inevitable. Here are some examples:

1. My article on the price elasticity of the demand for liquor that appeared in *Econometrica*, mentioned earlier. The very essence of the work was showing that a very simple method – the 'quasi-experimental' study of a large set of controlled before-and-after comparisons – can be more powerful than standard or even 'elegant' non-standard methods of the sort that had been tried before, and this method is more flexible and easier to interpret.
2. Applying the Monte Carlo method to the entire range of problems in statistics – including the bootstrap technique – and also to simple and complex problems in probability, may have enormous practical advantages. But it is the very antithesis of the highest value of the mathematically minded persons who are the gatekeepers: it foregoes all of the esthetic quality of the deductive formulaic proof-based methods of mathematics. Hence it encounters resistance from those who prefer formulae. Even as a method of teaching and doing probability and statistics, the Monte Carlo simulation arouses hostility despite the experimentally demonstrated success in the classroom.
3. Simulations of duopoly and triopoly competition produce novel propositions about the effects on the results of various changes in

conditions, such as the number of competitors and the cost of capital. But this is from a July 1995 referee's report to the *American Economic Review*: 'The bottom line after all of this is that I am of the strong opinion that this paper should not be published – anywhere, anytime.' The referee's main criticism is that the model is 'of the sort that no one has been interested in for at least 15 years.'

4. The book *Applied Managerial Economics* shows that with only a simple spreadsheet – either on paper, as I first showed it, or wonderfully better with a computer spreadsheet – one can get perfectly sound answers to all of a firm's decision problems concerning control variables. The spreadsheet is incomparably more flexible than the standard marginal analysis conducted with the calculus, because the spreadsheet handles multi-period analyses – which are at the core of all difficult firm decisions – with perfect ease; it does not require simple equational forms, as does the calculus. But to people raised on the calculus who have invested much professional capital in learning how to surmount and enjoy its intellectual difficulties in conquering these problems, the simple tabular system has all the intellectual charm of hammer, handsaw and manual screwdriver.

A close friend who is a very imaginative and productive student of finance, and an astute observer of the academic world, chides me with 'Why don't you do things the way other people do them?' That simply isn't possible in the sorts of cases mentioned just above.

Also, like engineers and business-persons, I intend my studies to fill needs and do jobs, rather than to be works of art. This inevitably makes it more difficult to attract the interest and attention of colleagues in the knowledge 'game.'

Along with engineers and business-people, I focus on the independent variables rather than on the dependent variable. That is, economists (and scientists generally) usually want to know the causes of the variation in the dependent variable – for example, the birthrate, and the movements of the stars. In contrast, business-people and engineers want to know how a particular independent variable – say, income or education – changes a dependent variable such as consumption of alcohol or the birthrate.

The subjects I have worked on were not well chosen for success. I did not choose topics that were 'hot;' I had little sense of what hot topics were, and I would not have liked the sense of competition to publish first; also, I have believed that if lots of people are already working in a subject area, I am not needed (unless I think that the field is pointed in the wrong direction). Instead, I chose topics where I saw big lacunae of knowledge that I often came upon because I went looking for published results and did not find them; this was the case in 1974 with estimating the effect of amounts of smoking on life expectancy, and it was often true in population and immigration economics. I also chose theoretical and empirical topics that seemed important because of public policy discussions – again, especially population and immigration economics. I did not have the knack of choosing those topics that other researchers would like to build on because they are a natural forward extension of the main stream; by contrast, George Stigler was a master of doing so. My work in endogenous growth theory with respect to population was an exception in this respect, but I did not impress it upon the consciousness of the profession, and my work therefore was bypassed.

The most self-flattering speculation is that I fail because my ideas run against common beliefs. I believe that, as information theory teaches, information contributes most to knowledge if it is dissimilar to other information presently in the system (and, of course, if the information is correct). As it is said, 'If the two of us agree, one of us is unnecessary.' Indeed, much of what I write does not simply bill itself as new, but begins by saying that the conventional view is wrong. Still, I can't convince myself that this is a major explanation of my outcomes, much as I would like to so believe. Others also offer unpopular or unconventional ideas, and yet they manage to get people to pay attention to those ideas.

XII

Why did this person Julian Simon arrive wherever I got to, rather than lots of other young kids who were indistinguishable from me in high school or in college or in the Navy?

I started out in life quite close to the main stem of the tree from which I grew, closer than many other young persons. But unlike many others, I kept growing away from the main stem, rather than closer to it. One reason may have been that I was not afraid to get further away from the main stem – further and further out into the uncharted forest, a greater and greater distance from the shelter of the community. In adulthood I grew more and more comfortable with being away from the main stem.

Later on I knew I was a bit eccentric, particularly in my irreverence for authority. But I always thought that there were plenty of others a lot more eccentric than I – in fact, downright weird, which I did not think myself to be. When I was young I did my best to hide whatever eccentricities I had.

My working life has been a curious blend of discipline and indiscipline. I have been very disciplined in the regularity of my work habits and the length of my work day; even at the pit of my prolonged depression I managed to work from morning to night, in part because I could partly escape the depression by working. And my research seems to me to always have been careful and comprehensive. But in the larger picture of what I chose to work on, and whether I continued to work on topics even though every sign pointed to the outcome being fruitless for one reason or another, there was no disciplined thought at all; I simply followed my nose into imprudent and sometimes haphazard pursuits.

I have simply followed my nose in two senses [*sic*]. First, I have gone where I have sniffed possibly interesting new discoveries, without worrying too much about the dangers of pursuing those scents to their sources. Second and more important, there has been a very random quality to the path I have followed wherein my brain has followed behind my nose and my feet, rather than my planning faculties directing my nose.

Indeed, even on those occasions when I did analyze and plan my future – as when I decided to work on population economics in order to help lower the world's birthrate (that's how I began) – my plans often were negated and my direction eventually became the opposite of what I had planned it to be. That is, I wound up working in a field that was very good for me only because I chose it for entirely the wrong reasons, based on a completely backwards analysis of what I would find myself thinking and doing.

Another element in my development is my curiosity about almost every human enterprise. Perhaps I started out with just an ordinary kid's curiosity, but it never got stamped out of me the way that institutions (including schools) and other individuals seem to squeeze the curiosity out of most people.

It would be easy to conclude that my sense of being an outsider after I left Newark had great influence on my intellectual development and led to my ideas that have been outside the mainstream. But I think that if I had decided when at college or in the Navy to be an academic, and perhaps a psychologist rather than an economist, and if I had gone to a mainstream graduate school after getting out of the Navy, I think that I might have gone on to a rather conventional academic career. Or at least it would have been quite a few years before my thinking began to deviate from the main stream. Given the peculiar route I followed in becoming an economist, it is not surprising – if not inevitable – that I would find myself doing studies of far-out topics using unconventional methods.

Sooner or later I probably would have begun to take a radical approach to various issues because of what I now consider the key element in my thinking: skepticism. This element would have been present whether we remained in Newark or moved to Millburn. Whether or not I had begun in a more conventional educational path than I did, eventually I might even have addressed some of the same issues, such as the influence and role of IQ, which were not at all logically connected to other topics I have worked on.

But what was the cause of my skepticism? It would be easy to attribute it to my encounters with my father, who was a very unreliable authority; one was wise to be skeptical about every statement he made. But I am inclined to think that there were other important roots as well, some of them perhaps congenital. My inclination to first think concretely rather than abstractly about problems is relevant here. I remember a conversation with a cosmologist who had concocted models of the future extending far beyond the extinction of our sun seven billion years from now. I said to him that I compared some of his conclusions about 'human' life at that time with my observations about human nature now, as I always begin with the most concrete elements of information and build upwards and more abstractly from there. He responded that his thinking mode is exactly the opposite: start at the abstract top and work downwards.

This inclination for the concrete impels me to want to see data on a phenomenon before I discuss or theorize about it, lest I find myself discussing something that does not exist. And I always ask myself what I have seen with my own eyes or heard with my own ears that does or does not fit with the generalization or theory under discussion. When reading a technical article I look first for the empirical data (if any), and then if I believe the data I am inclined to make up my own theory rather than fight my way through long algebra-laden abstractions.

Another element: I enjoy the tussle of hard learning, in exactly the same spirit that Hume describes the pleasures of philosophy being like the pleasures of the hunt and the chase (Hume, 1739–40/1969, p. 498).

Still another element in the courses my life has taken – a complementary element to all the others, but perhaps also the dominant element – is just plain chance. After I got out of the Navy and decided to postpone going to medical school for a year, I decided to look for a job in the advertising business simply because a close friend was working in an advertising agency, and I could imagine myself being a copywriter. In the course of our discussing the advertising industry I asked him – while hanging from straps in the New York subway one afternoon – about the effects of advertising on the society. He told me the little he had learned in a course at college. So when I decided to become a professor, I parlayed my experience into a job teaching people how to do advertising, and I decided to study the economics of the subject because my casual question to my school friend was the only open research question in my mind. That's a very chancy sequence of events, with very little design in it.

As noted earlier, the only reason I came to write my deepest theoretical paper – on causality – is because Herman Wold happened to send me a couple of his preprints on the subject when we corresponded about an unrelated article that he refereed. This elicited my curiosity, aroused by an idea I could not understand: my enjoyment of trying to crack a tough intellectual nut, and a willingness to follow my nose into professional work on a topic that was completely unrelated to my 'fields' – that is, outside the subjects I had been working on and that were within the boundaries of the department (advertising) and college (journalism) in which I was then teaching.

The work on causality also typified the pattern of my seeing an open door and an interesting subject, and walking through the open door even though I knew that it was not prudent to do so.

XIII

I wondered one day: if asked who among economists might make good models for a young person, whom would I recommend? Theodore Schultz and Milton Friedman came quickly to mind for the following reasons:

1. Hayek and Kuznets, whose work I learned most from, and whom I revere as economists, seem too far from American tradition to serve as models.
2. A young person can at least *begin* on the same path as Schultz and Friedman, even if he or she does not get to the same places they did. That is, one can start with workmanlike empirical studies in important areas of the economic domain, even if the work does not evolve into the kinds of theoretical advances that Schultz and Friedman achieved. And *one can tell a student where to put her or his feet to start on such a path*. But one cannot tell anyone where to put his or her feet to start on the path of an Irving Fisher, an Alfred Marshall, or a Hayek (though Marshall would recommend that one begin by reading a trade paper from any one industry).
3. There are many important economists who have done important work with the aim of impressing their colleagues, as Samuelson explicitly recommends as a criterion. I would want as models economists whose work is fueled by moral fervor, as is Schultz's and Friedman's, and that is marked by an unswerving devotion to choosing topics and publishing results without reference to funding agencies or the opinion of various publics. I also would not want for a model someone who believes that economists should not recommend governmental policies, as George Stigler so often said about himself.

XIV

The brief assessment of my life as a whole: I have lived an extraordinary lucky life.

REFERENCES

Bondi, Hermann, *Relativity and Common Sense: A New Approach to Einstein* (Dover, 1961/1964).

Boulding, Kenneth E., *Economics as a Science* (New York: McGraw-Hill, 1977).

Markowitz, Harry M., 'Trains of Thought,' in *The American Economist*, Vol. 37, No. 1 (Spring 1993).

Rumelt, Richard P., Dan Schendel and David J. Teece, 'Strategic Management and Economics,' *Strategic Management Journal*, Vol. 12, 1991, pp. 5–29.

Samuelson, Paul, 'Economists and the History of Ideas,' *American Economic Review*, vol. LI, 1, March 1962, pp. 1–18.

25. Life and philosophy*

Hirofumi Uzawa

In 1928, I was born in the provincial town of Yonago in Tottori Prefecture. Tottori is located in the western part of Japan, in the scenic region officially referred to as the Region in the Shadow of the Mountains. Although it is now among the poorest in terms of per capita income, it used in ancient times to be one of the most advanced in Japan. Being located at the shortest distance across the Japan Sea from the Korean Peninsula, its culture was the finest and the most sophisticated. But it was allegedly destroyed by the more brutal and barbarian culture of the Yamato Dynasty, supposedly the ancestors of the present-day emperor.

In my family, my brother and I were the first male children in many generations. In prewar Japan, only male children (the first sons, for that matter) could inherit family estates. As far as I can trace back my family lineage, either no sons were born or none survived beyond adolescence, and husbands from neighboring areas had to be adopted. To be adopted into a family of small fortune must have been most humiliating. My father was a school-teacher, but this sense of humiliation seemed to have remained all through his life.

To have been born in the Region in the Shadow of the Mountains in a family of adopted males seems to have had a lasting influence upon my life, even though my family moved to Tokyo when I was four years old. My childhood was quiet and peaceful; I hardly remember any incident of importance, except for one rather unpleasant experience. It occurred when I must have been a third or fourth grader in the elementary school. My school-teacher proudly taught us the long lineage of the family of the emperor, tracing back from the legendary Emperor of Jinmu 2600 years ago, up to the present emperor, all directly and linearly related. I then raised my hand and asked him the question which I thought was most natural: what would they do if the first son of the emperor turned out to be an idiot? I do not recall what punishment I received, but the teacher's stunned white face which turned to a flush angry one is still vivid in my memory.

The Pacific War broke out in the year when I entered the middle school. The

*This chapter first appeared in *The American Economist*, **35**(2), Fall 1991, 8–15.

school was called the First Middle School in the District of Tokyo and it was reputed to be the best in Tokyo, or in Japan for that matter. My own experience there, however, sowed in me the seed which would develop into the full-fledged critical view I now have about the quality of the Japanese educational system in general.

The school was located near the official residence of the Prime Minister and next to the school there was a Japanese restaurant called Kohraku where the leaders of the 26 February incident were headquartered. The incident took place on 26 February 1936, when a group of young army officers led a rebellion and attacked the official residence of the Prime Minister and other strategic posts, killing several members of the Cabinet (the Prime Minister himself miraculously escaped the attack). They occupied the official residence of the Prime Minister, the Diet, the Headquarters of the Ministry of Army, and other strategic buildings for several days until they were crushed by a contingent of the Navy and other divisions of the Army. Although all the leaders of the rebellion were executed, the 26 February incident led Japan irreversibly into military expansion and war.

Since the school was located in the center of the rebellion, our teachers often talked about their personal experience during the 26 February incident. By the time I was in school there, however, every attempt was made to conceal the nature of the incident, and I was not able to find out what it was about. None of my teachers could provide me with an adequate answer and I vainly went to a number of public libraries to find material on the mysterious 26 February incident.

The school had had a rather liberal tradition, but the Pearl Harbor attack had changed the atmosphere. Right after the Pacific War broke out, our art teacher assigned us to draw posters to encourage our war effort. Art was the subject I felt most deficient in and I painted a poor picture with a caption, 'Remember Pearl Harbor!' Naturally, I did not know at that time that the phrase was popular in the United States. The teacher was so angry with me that I was severely reprimanded by him as unpatriotic and unworthy of studying in that reputable institution. Later on he volunteered for the Army and was killed in action in the Southern Pacific.

In 1944, we were all sent to the war factories to supplement the shortage of skilled labor. My class worked in a factory which was making speedometers for submarines. I was assigned the job of assembling the parts into a final product and then testing its accuracy. However, I was so bad at manual skill; most of the speedometers I was assembling were so deficient that indicators did not show any sign of moving when the machines were put in the testing device. I had to use a heavy hammer to hit them so that their hands would move at all. Out of frustration, a close friend of mine and I often scaled the fence of the factory to escape to the River Tama to ride on a Japanese-style racing shell. Thus I could master the delicate art of sculling a boat, the only manual skill I have mastered to this day. The friend of mine later died in one of the air raids on Tokyo.

In my class, there was a brilliant student who had a maturity not comparable with his contemporaries. I was much influenced by him and gradually became concerned with the role of militarism and the supporting industrial power in entrapping Japan into the war with the Great Powers. We decided to organize some of the students to stage a strike on the pretense that the factory management abused and treated us inhumanely. We then locked the factory manager in a room and forced him to promise us better and more humane treatment. I remember it was in the summer of 1944. The school authorities found out what we had done and our parents were summoned to school to receive a harsh warning. How this friend of mine and I were not found out to be the ringleaders, I do not recall. This friend later became an economic historian, noted for his excellent contributions to the detailed and unique analysis of the economic conditions during the Edo Period.

In the spring of 1945, I entered the First High School. In the prewar Japanese educational system, there were three years of high school before we entered the university. There were about twenty high schools in all Japan at that time, all boarding schools, with a few exceptions, where students supposedly received an elitist education. The First High School, located in Tokyo, was the first such school; thus it was regarded as the most revered one. Those who were able to pass the severe entrance examination were regarded as the cream of Japanese youth. My own experience, however, convinced me that its reputation was based on a mirage. It is true that the alumni of that high school comprise a distinguished roster, ranging from several prime ministers and the leaders of the bureaucratic and industrial as well as academic communities to the leaders of the Japanese Communist Party. I suspect, however, that the political and social backwardness the Japanese society has been suffering up to this day, in spite of rapid economic growth, may be not unrelated to the educational system where such an institution as the First High School was revered.

Despite these criticisms, in the First High School I was able to grow beyond the immediate confines of my own personal experience. The first experience which substantially changed my historical, social and political vista was my close acquaintance with a contingent of Chinese students. When the Japanese Army began the invasion of China in 1937, it encountered a persistent and strong resistance by the Chinese people. The Japanese Army then had a brilliant idea; as part of the Pacification Program, they would pick up promising Chinese students and bring them to Japan to educate them in the Japanese way of life. They chose the First High School as the institution which, they thought, was best qualified to educate these Chinese students. One of the dormitories on the campus was exclusively assigned to Chinese students. By the time I entered the school, around April of 1945, there must have been close to fifty Chinese students there. Contrary to the wishes of the Japanese Army, they were actively engaged in converting us to their cause. As I found out later on, Chinese students were at first divided between a group who stood for Mao Tse-tung and another in favor of Chiang Kai-shek. After a bitter argument, the Mao group persuaded the Chiang group, and together they began to convey to us the basic messages of Mao Tse-tung. Many years later, in 1976, I visited the old headquarters of the Eighth Route Army in Sian, and with deep nostalgia I looked at the pamphlets written by Mao Tse-tung during the Anti-Japan Resistance War, some of which were exact replicas of those pamphlets which were passed to me by my Chinese friends in the First High School during the darkest days towards the end of the war. The irony was that the influence of the Chinese students upon us was so great that, right after the war, the First High School became the center of an intense leftist student movement which produced a large number of leftist leaders who played a prominent role in the resistance movement during the Occupation Era. The Japanese Army thought they would educate young Chinese students in the Japanese way of life and thinking, whatever it might have been, but it was the Chinese students who succeeded in educating Japanese students in the Chinese way of life and thinking.

At the First High School, I was enrolled in the premedical course, the graduates from which mostly went to the School of Medicine. But as the years passed, the idea of entering the medical profession was pushed to the farthest corner of my mind. I was torn between pursuing an academic career and engaging more actively in political and social activities. I finally decided to choose mathematics and took the entrance examination to the Department of Mathematics in the University of Tokyo. The Department of Mathematics was a small institution with a dozen professors and a student body of only 15 new students per year. It was at that time, and still is, one of the most distinguished institutions in the world, and its professors were all renowned mathematicians, who were extremely modest and courteous to us. Upon my graduation, I was fortunate in being chosen as a Special Research Fellow to pursue my studies in the department. To this day, I occasionally wonder why I decided, at a later date, to leave such a splendid academic atmosphere.

While I was preparing myself to become a professional mathematician, my field of speciality being that of algebraic number theory, I was not able to extinguish my passion for social issues. At this time Japan had not yet recovered from the ruinous conditions of the war, and poverty, starvation and inflation were the order of the day. My concern with social issues gradually became focused upon economics. I began to read books on economics, particularly those of Marxian economists. I was a member of a small reading group where we tried systematically to study the basic contemporary literature on Marxian economics, from Marx, Engels, Lenin, down to Stalin. I had trouble with Stalin, particularly with his *Essays on Languages*. I was not able to decipher what Stalin was trying to say, and I felt that my mind was blocked by the mere utterance of his name. Later, when I heard that Khrushchev made a severe attack on Stalin in 1953, I felt greatly relieved.

I began to entertain seriously the idea of becoming a member of the Japanese Communist Party, the most fashionable thing to do among us at that time. But a friend of mine, who was the theoretical leader of our group and later to become a leading member of the Communist Party, advised me that, with my scant knowledge of Marxian economics, I would hardly be able to pass the entrance examination for the Party. Hearing this advice from someone whose intelligence and judgment I greatly admired, I decided that it was time to quit mathematics and devote myself exclusively to studying economics, so that one day I might accumulate enough knowledge in Marxian economics to pass the entrance examination for the Communist Party. Since then, however, my interest in economics has turned in an entirely different direction, and I have not taken that examination. To this day, I do not know whether I should thank my friend for his advice.

To quit mathematics was not as easy a matter as I expected, particularly because most of the professors I sought out for advice thought mathematics was the only subject in which I had a talent and they were eager to persuade me to reconsider. I remember, with a feeling of regret, that I told the main professor under whom I studied number theory that, with the poverty and chaos the Japanese society was suffering at that time, it was almost a crime to continue to do research in pure algebraic number theory. This professor was instrumental in helping me whenever I had difficulties in my life later on. I do not know what words I should say or what I should do to adequately express my gratitude.

With the help of this professor, I obtained a job with the Institute of Statistical Mathematics in the Ministry of Education and later with a life insurance company as a statistician in the actuarial department. But I could not stay in any of these jobs; somehow my urge to concentrate solely on economics overcame any practical consideration.

At about this time, I joined a small group of young economists in the Faculty of Economics at the University of Tokyo. The leadership was shared by the late Professor Hiroshi Furuya and Professor Ryuichiro Tachi. Professor Furuya was on a leave of absence at Harvard University and it was Professor Tachi who was the organizer. Thus Professor Tachi was the first living economist with whom I was personally acquainted and who was to have a lasting influence upon the direction in which my studies in economics were to turn. In retrospect, it seems that by then, my enthusiasm for Marxian economics had begun to wane as I began to question the logic of some of its basic theoretical premises. Under the tutelage of Furuya, Tachi, and others, I had been drawn into what turned out to be neoclassical economics, almost an antithesis to Marxian economics.

Working with Professor Everret Hagen seemed to have accelerated this tendency. At that time, the Japanese government was planning to build the first automobile highway, one between Nagoya and Kobe, and applied to the World Bank for loans. The World Bank sent the Watkins Mission to investigate the feasibility of the plan. Professor Hagen was in charge of the macroeconomic analysis and I was hired as an assistant to him. During the six-month period when I was working with him, I was able to learn a great deal, in particular with respect to the practical implications of the Keynesian theory of economics.

I was also fortunate in participating in the seminar conducted by Professor Hendrik Houthakker, then of Stanford University. Each year, the University of Tokyo and Stanford University ran a joint seminar; during the summer of 1954, Professor Houthakker came to Tokyo to organize a seminar on demand analysis. Not only was Professor Houthakker the author of one of the most original concepts, that of the Strong Axiom of Revealed Preference, but also he was one of the most profound teachers I had ever met.

My encounter with Hagen and Houthakker, together with my association with the Furuya–Tachi seminar, had a great influence on my parting with Marxian economics. Up to this time Marxian economics had been the most fascinating and penetrating guide for me through the maze of economic issues. Through these new stimuli, Marxian economic concepts began to recede into the background and modern economic theory became my main concern. The most decisive moment came when I read Professor Kenneth Arrow's *Social Choice and Individual Values*. In fact, I had read the book a few years earlier, around 1952, just after it was published under the tutelage of Professor Ken-ichi Inada, but it took me a couple of years more to digest the import of the conceptual framework of Arrow's theory and I had begun to formulate my decision to leave mathematics for research in economics. I was then reading anything Professor Arrow wrote, published or unpublished, and devoured the content just like the sand on a summer beach. Later on, several American friends of mine even told me that my English resembled that of Professor Arrow; what a great honor!

Among the works of Professor Arrow, I was particularly fascinated by the contributions he was making jointly with Professor Leonid Hurwicz on the feasibility and stability of the allocative mechanism in a socialist economy. The topic itself was immensely appealing to me, but I was attracted by the way higher mathematics could be used to solve problems of substance. This train of thought was new to me, who came to economics through the door of Marxian economics.

It was some time in 1955 that I received an invitation from Professor Arrow to come to Stanford University to do research on his project. Stanford then was a Mecca for mathematical economists and I was so thrilled by the prospect of working with Professor Arrow that I could hardly wait for the time when the appointment would begin the next year.

My Stanford years were the happiest and the most productive. The Economics Faculty was composed of a harmonious group of economists, producing an ideal atmosphere for research and teaching. It was there that I was able to concentrate upon the enlargement of the frontier of economic theory.

I was particularly concerned with the problems of economic growth and development and with formulating theoretical models which would capture the essential aspects of the economic system in question, either capitalistic or socialist. The two-sector model of capital accumulation, which I was able to construct and work through to understand its implications for the process of economic growth, was an attempt to transplant the content of Marx's *Das Kapital* into a coherent mathematical model in such a manner that Marx's intentions would be more clearly brought out. However, I became more concerned with the problems of short-run fluctuations in a capitalist economy and began to work with Keynes's *General Theory*.

Although my first initiation into economic theory was the reading of Keynes's *General Theory* under the tutelage of Professor Tachi and my earnest endeavor as a professional economist began when I worked with Professor Hagen on the macroeconomic implications of the construction of a highway system in Japan, it was at the beginning of the 1960s that I finally came close to the core of the *General Theory*. At this time I had a particularly close association with Nicholas Kaldor and Joan Robinson, both of whom were occasional visitors to Stanford and Berkeley. They convinced me that the neoclassical interpretation of the *General Theory à la* Hicks's IS–LM analysis might miss some of the more important and subtle aspects of the Keynesian theory. As I worked through the labyrinth of the *General Theory* and put some of the more salient aspects of the theory into a number of mathematical models, I began to be bothered by the suspicion that the *General Theory*, if one read it superficially, might not coherently represent the theoretical framework of the work done by the young group of economists in Keynes's circle. I then was drawn into the subject of dynamic disequilibrium, where the instability of the price mechanism in an advanced capitalistic economy is emphasized, and the role of stabilization policy became important.

Although my association with Professor Arrow was close and rewarding, I began to feel so inferior and small in his presence, both from intellectual and personal points of view, that I had to be away from him in order to restore my own identity. At the same time, I felt that the physical and climatic atmosphere at Stanford was too languorous an environment in which to bring up my children (what a pity for them!). I moved from Stanford to Chicago to meet the new challenge and to seek an opportunity for myself and my children to grow more vigorously. In Chicago, I could enjoy relative autonomy and intellectual independence, and at the same time, I began to develop new acquaintances with my colleagues at the University of Chicago. Particularly rewarding was my association with the late Professor Lloyd Metzler, whose intellectual depth and personal charm have left a permanent imprint upon me.

By 1965–66 the United States had seriously escalated its military involvement in Vietnam. I was greatly disturbed by the moral, political and economic implications of American military escalation in Vietnam and its brutal, savage military tactics, together with the serious damage the Vietnamese people were suffering. I was particularly concerned that I, as an Asian, stood by silently while my neighboring people were suffering at the hands of the country in which I was living, not by birth, but out of my own choice. After a relatively calm year at Churchill College in the University of Cambridge in England, I thought that it was about time for me to return to Japan.

In 1968, I returned to the Department of Economics in the University of Tokyo. Although I was not an alumnus, I could feel at home with the faculty there because of my close association with a number of faculty members. However, the University was then at the height of a student revolt, the harshest of its kind anywhere in the world. For almost two years, the teaching and research at the University ceased to function. The nature of the student revolt movements at the University of Tokyo and elsewhere showed that higher education in Japan was in real trouble. The trauma left by the student revolt caused a deterioration in the academic atmosphere in the universities and the Japanese Ministry of Education took advantage of the confusion to gain effective control of academic affairs, thus shattering the academic structure of the august body of the once great Japanese national universities.

The Japanese economy had experienced a process of rapid economic growth, from the mid-1950s to the end of the 1960s. During this period all the economic indicators such as gross national product grew at unprecedented rates. The social and natural environments, however, showed no sign of improve-ment. To the contrary, they had deteriorated to such an extent that the real living standard of the Japanese people had gone down during this period of rapid economic growth, and this became my main concern upon my return to Japan.

The social implications of the allocative mechanism in the Japanese society, which had made such a rapid growth possible, may be best illustrated in terms of the incident concerning the Minamata disease. Not only is this incident one of the most serious and most publicized events in the postwar period, but also it reveals the basic characteristics of the social and political system which still dominate Japanese society today.

The Minamata incident is one of the most extensive and serious incidents in the whole history of poisoning due to the residual emittance of industrial pollution. It was caused by the mercury contained in the industrial refuse emitted from one of the largest chemical factories in Japan.

This situation is indicative of the nature of the economic and social disturbances associated with the process of Japanese economic growth, even though it actually antedates the decade of most rapid economic growth.

Industrial and other economic activities have been performed without taking proper account of the preservation of natural and social environments and they have victimized the inhabitants who have had no choice other than to continue to live in a region which has been heavily contaminated by poisonous wastes.

If one were to visit the Minamata region today, one would be struck by the poverty that still prevails in a country which takes pride in being one of the largest industrial producers in the world and by the agony and suffering which the Minamata disease has left upon the victims and their relatives.

One often wonders if economic growth is desirable when it is associated with such a miserable effect upon human life and the surrounding natural environment.

It may be possible to characterize the basic institutional arrangements of postwar Japanese society as those of a market-oriented economy in the broad sense of the word. It has two distinctive features. The first feature of a market economy is related to the process of allocation of scarce resources. Such a system presupposes that the resources which are limitational in the processes of production and consumption are privately owned, and their disposal is done in such a manner that private benefits, either in the form of private profits or utilities, are maximized from this point of view. Market institutions are those which resolve possible conflicts between various members of that society without resorting to regulatory measures.

The second feature of the market economy is concerned with the distributive aspect; namely, in such a system each individual is entitled to receive rewards, to be based upon the values established by the market, for the scarce resources one owns, and nothing more or less. Thus, if an individual's own resources are relatively scarce and highly appreciated in the market, then the income from those resources will be larger, otherwise one has to be satisfied with whatever income one gets, and this is one of the factors that is responsible for the effectiveness of the market mechanism in attaining efficient resource allocation. But it has a rather significant impact upon the distribution of real income from the welfare point of view. In particular, such a rewarding arrangement has a tendency to increase the degree of inequality, particularly from the viewpoint of the intergenerational distribution of income. This tendency, inherent in a market economy, toward a more unequal income distribution has long been recognized. Various measures such as progressive income taxes and inheritance taxes have been adopted by most contemporary societies in an attempt to counterbalance such unstable tendencies. However, it may be noted that such arrangements do not have any visible impact upon the probability that each citizen may drop below the poverty line in terms of his or her income. The main impact of counterbalancing measures is to rescue those who have dropped out of the society, at least from the economic point of view.

It is one of the most basic propositions in economic theory that such a market mechanism brings about an efficient allocation of scarce resources. But this proposition crucially depends upon the institutional arrangements whereby all the resources are to be privately owned. In most market-oriented societies, however, a very significant portion of scarce resources are not privately appropriated or owned, either for the reason of technological nature or from the point of view of social justice. Instead they are owned by the society as common property resources, and the construction and the management of such resources are delegated to the government. It is in general the case that such social resources are used by the members of the society, either free of charge or with a nominal price. Such social resources are often called social overhead capital and they play a very important role in the processes of resource allocation and income distribution in any contemporary society. But the role of social overhead capital has not been properly recognized in economic theory and its analysis has not been fully explored, so that it is not easy to see the extent to which the management and regulations concerning the use of such capital are related to the allocative mechanism in a basically decentralized market economy.

This social overhead capital constitutes what may be called the environment in the very wide sense of the word and the role of such overhead capital has been increased as the process of economic growth takes place and the level of living standards has been increased.

In a sense, the phenomenon of environmental pollution may be regarded as an outcome of mismanagement of social overhead capital, but in a purely market economy, there is very little incentive to bring about the effective measures in regularizing the use to be made of such social overhead capital.

Thus, in the market economy, the intrinsic tendency of the adverse effect upon the income distribution, combined with the redistributional effect due to the social costs associated with environmental pollution, has been aggravated during the process of economic growth in the last decade. The resulting social and economic problems have now forced us to reexamine the basic institutional arrangements underlying such a market economy, and to gradually adopt social and economic policies which put a priority on the economic welfare of the members of the society and try to restore social stability in the allocative mechanism.

If I take the case of the Japanese economy again, during the last two decades the Japanese government has adopted various policy measures such as credit expansion, export subsidies and so forth, and in addition to these measures it has also allocated a fairly significant portion of public investment to be spent on the construction of industrial infrastructure. According to one estimate, about 80 percent of public expenditures have been spent on the construction and maintenance of industrial infrastructure and only a very small portion of public investment has gone into the maintenance of social overhead capital directly concerned with the health and living standards of the people. Such a pattern in the allocation of public investment is justified usually only if the policy objectives were to ignore the non-market aspects of economic performance. But, in a welfare state, the primary objective of the government is to ensure the harmonious development of economic welfare, which takes account not only of the level of personal income, but also the amount of services people would obtain from social overhead capital. This will imply a significant shift towards public expenditures for the maintenance of social capital directly involved with living standards and preservation of the natural environment, and investment and infrastructure for industries will have to be to a large extent slowed down, resulting in an overall increase in manufacturing costs. Such an investment pattern would have an adverse effect on the rate of price increase in general, and, indeed, would have some inflational effect in the short run, but from a longer point of view it is possible to attain a more stable pattern of price increase.

Also public provision of services to ensure the basic rights of the citizen imply an increase in the total public expenditures and a shift in the allocation of public expenditures. The first effect of such a shift would be to lower the probability that an average person's income may drop below the poverty line, thus trying to restore social stability, and also it would entail a significant shift in the management of the natural environment. The use of services and destruction of the natural environment would be strictly regulated, either in the form of effluent charges, or in the form of ambient standards more directly concerned with the preservation of the environment. Such regulatory measures have adverse effects upon the process of economic growth and alter the composition of the gross national product. But again, such adverse effects are of a short-run nature and when the economy is fully adjusted to the new regulatory measures, it becomes possible to maintain a stable and relatively high rate of growth, even in terms of the conventional national income account. This phenomenon is primarily due to the fact that natural and social environments constitute a vital factor in the processes of production and consumption, and only by taking proper measures to reflect their scarcity in the use of their services is it possible to achieve a long-run stable path of economic growth.

Thus the optimum policy structure and objectives for Japan are not very much different from those which are now regarded as desirable in many countries. But it will be extremely difficult to implement such measures in the foreseeable future.

26. A life philosophy*

Sir Alan Walters

I was astonished to be asked to contribute to this series. Who on earth anyway, would be interested in my 'philosophy'? I would bring an entirely unnecessary attention upon myself in exposing my ego and my errors. Indeed, unlike Mr Jourdain, who discovered that for all his life he had been speaking prose and had not realized it, I suspected that, having professed a deviationist economics all my life, I was now expected to expose it. But the temptation was too enticing. I agreed to write this portentous 'life philosophy' partly, of course, due to ego, but also partly because I believe that my life has been rather unusual and may be useful in illustrating some surprising aspects of the alleged rigidity of British society and the development of ideas and economic policy.

Born in 1926 of working-class parents in a Leicester slum, I was unpromising material. My father was then a clerk in a grocery chain store. He had left school at the age of 13, but he was, as we would say nowadays, both numerate and literate. From 1917 until 1937 or 1938 he was a communist, but, unlike many others, he was revolted by Stalin's terror, in particular the massacre of the POUMS in Spain. He remained a staunch ultra-left-wing socialist until the end. My early intellectual domestic diet was one of romanticized revolutions righting the capitalist exploitation of the working class, etc.

In the 1930s, schools, even in such slums, were well structured and disciplined. Corporal punishment was administered firmly and fairly. The pupils learned or else. School was highly competitive – and a good preparation for life. One was rewarded for performance and punished for perfidy and laziness, but not for failure. The critical test came at the age of 11. Then all pupils were set an examination, the outcome of which decided whether they were to win a scholarship and be sent to the superior 'secondary schools' to be educated to the age of 15 or 16 (and even to the age of 18), or to the 'senior schools' for the 70 per cent who did not qualify for the secondary schools. The senior schools were intended as the last rung on the educational ladder for those who would not repay further training beyond the age of 14.

*This chapter first appeared in *The American Economist*, **33**(2), Fall 1989, 18–24.

Since I was thought to be one of the better pupils, I was expected to pass this examination and qualify for secondary school. Indeed, I thought I would pass and the secondary school would prepare me for a skilled job in one of the light engineering factories which were a very fount of prosperity in 1937. Disaster struck, however. Not only did I fail the examination, but I failed in arithmetic! My ambition to be a skilled worker, such as a draughtsman, was largely dashed by that failure.

The senior school which I then attended was, however, staffed by some of the most selfless, dedicated schoolmasters who regarded their pupils, with their demonstrably modest abilities, as worthy of enormous effort and application. Both my mathematics and English masters were convinced that I had the right stuff for higher things. Through various negotiations, I know not what, they managed to get me transferred to a well-respected secondary school – Alderman Newton's – at the age of 13. The first step up, and the first year of World War II. For me a fortunate conjunction. My father had lost his job in 1936 or 1937, and had been on the dole for about two or three years. He could ill afford to keep me at school beyond the statutory age of 14. But 1939 saw my brother, another grocery store clerk, mobilized, and my father stepped into his shoes. So he had the means, however slender, to give me the opportunity 'to better myself' by an additional year or two at a worthy school.

Again I was extraordinarily lucky. My mathematics and English teachers identified me as a suitable pupil for the stream which did two year's work in one year (called the 'remove'). I repaid their faith with a very good matriculation result at the early age of 15. This meant that I *could* be enrolled as reading for a degree in a recognized university in the United Kingdom – if they would have me. But in 1940 and 1941, no such thought ever crossed my mind. The seemingly endless war was the only concern and, with the impetuosity of my years, I wanted to join the forces as quickly as possible. Meanwhile, with the objective of making as much money as possible, I went to work first as an errand boy in a surveyor's office and then as a machine operative in a munitions factory. At the age of 17, I volunteered for the Army.

After three years of uneventful service as a private, the war was over and I was soon to be demobilized with no clear idea of my prospects. Everyone thought that unemployment would return, and so job security loomed quite large. I believed that the best job I could hope to get was that of school-teacher. I was particularly attracted by the long holidays, the high steady incomes and the easy life of the school-teaching profession. I saw my old schoolmaster and I told him of my assessment and my ambition. He insisted, however, that I should aim higher and apply to read for a degree at a university since, he said, 'they are taking anyone now' – meaning that they may take someone who had only a school education limited to matriculation. When we discussed the subject of the proposed degree, he was quite blunt. Since I had forgotten what I had learned at school, and since I had learned nothing in the Army, clearly I knew virtually nothing, so, he concluded, the only subject for me was economics.

Fortified by the belief that for the study of economics, knowledge was no asset – perhaps even a liability – I applied for admission to many universities; for very good reasons, all sent rejection letters except, almost as an act of local charity, University College, Leicester accepted me as an external student for the London BSc degree. In those days, Leicester had a very limited range of courses, compared with London, whose faculty set the crucial examinations. But I was a beggar and no chooser. Because of my alleged mathematical aptitudes, however, I elected to read statistics, rather than economics, as my major. This decision was based also on the vague feeling, which has persisted to this day, that, for obvious reasons, the bottom might well drop out of the market for economists. But, as the age of chivalry dies, there would always be a demand for statisticians and accountants.

Since there was only one elementary statistics course at Leicester, this meant that I was left largely to find my own way in the library with the aid of a primitive barrel-type calculating machine. A most damaging handicap, you may think. But not if one judges, as scientists do, by the results. After three years (and much part-time work to eke out an ex-serviceman's grant), I came out first in the thousands of hopefuls, external and internal students, who sat the London BSc (Econ.) examinations in 1951.

From thence my future prospects moved to another level and place. In Britain this meant that, without master's or doctorate, I could become a tenured university teacher within a period of two or three years. (Incipient university teachers in the United States, I have found, see much virtue in this short cut to the groves of academe; I would now argue strongly against it for reasons other than my obvious self-interest! There is a need to ensure that the university teacher has a basic knowledge of the discipline; I believe that the PhD system does, albeit inefficiently, provide the assurance of that basis.) The presumption was that my baccalaureate had equipped me adequately to pursue research. And so I spent an academic year at Nuffield College, Oxford supervised by David Champernowne and attending the famous seminars of Sir John Hicks.

Oddly enough, I learned much more from my fellow students (there were about half a dozen in economics) than I did from the various luminaries on the faculty. But my fellow students eventually became most distinguished economists, and many, such as Robert Clower, Peter Newman and Hugh Rose, remain friends to this day. I did not attempt to write a thesis for a D.Phil degree – mainly because I thought it would not pass the rather fitful standards of the examiners. In fact, I do not recall any of that most distinguished band of students receiving a D.Phil (Oxon), although many tried and failed. You may draw the conclusion that there was something wrong, not with the students, but with Oxford.

My real piece of luck came when Terence Gorman and Gilbert Walker offered me a job teaching statistics at the University of Birmingham in 1952. With a shrewdness that belied his bohemian façade, Gilbert Walker – a distinguished scholar of transport economics – had gathered together a veritable galaxy of boundless young talent. At the very pinnacle was a man whom I continue to regard as the only obvious genius I have ever encountered in the economics profession – Terence (W.M.) Gorman. His vaulting imagination combined with an analytical sharpness and sophistication was rounded out by a very broad knowledge of the social sciences, history and culture. Just below this pinnacle was Frank Hahn, who pursued economic ideas with an infectious ebullience and a talmudic delight in following through an argument wherever it may lead. In applied economics, Birmingham boasted the young Michael Beesley, Esra Bennathan and David Rowan. For good reasons the students were also a distinguished fraternity – including Maurice McManus, Sig Prais and Ed Mills. In Birmingham one was driven not merely to learn economics in order to join in the fierce and often hilarious debates, but also one had to be sharp and incisive, otherwise one lost the day. Competition was exhilarating. In this intellectual ferment the fittest not only survived but, in a few short years, that is by the end of the 1950s, they were recognized internationally as a fount of new ideas, even new standards in British economic theory and econometrics.

During the discussions of the 1950s, most of that Birmingham vintage developed the basic approach and ideas which would carry them through the next two decades of their professional lives. For example, the astonishing insight of Terence Gorman into the aggregation problem was developed around a lake in Birmingham in 1952. My work at Birmingham changed focus. Hitherto I had worked in the traditional areas of mathematical and economic statistics. But at Birmingham, I discovered the efficacy of free markets first in 'getting prices right' and in allocating resources efficiently, but also as the key freedom in a liberal (I use that term in the European sense) society. And that peculiar mixture of analysis, interpretation of evidence, and imaginative invention – so characteristic of policy analysis and prescription – seemed to me to be enormously attractive. (Incidentally, I cannot understand why such pursuits are so out of favour in modern departments of economics in the United States.) The fantastic follies and the egregious errors of past policies made the targets quite irresistible. And, whatever nit-picking one may do on the carcass of theoretical welfare economics, the application of the most simple analysis, provided it was carried out in a sophisticated way, seemed to pay handsome dividends.

The presence of Gilbert Walker at Birmingham gave me my first field of application – transport economics. My first major contribution was in the field of public utility pricing – and, in particular, in the pricing of road services. Conventional wisdom in the track costs debate was that in order to charge people the appropriate price for road (or railroad) usage, one should measure the additional costs of building the road and then divide those costs up among users according to some criterion – such as the value of the damage inflicted by use, or according to 'what the traffic can bear' (a sort of Ramsey rule). A formal development of a long-run-marginal-cost pricing rule was developed eventually by the Harvard group – Meyer, Peck, Stenason and Zwick.

But these methods generated results which were clearly absurd. They produced road user prices for underutilized roads which were considerably greater than the prices for obviously highly congested roads. In my 'Track Costs and Motor Taxation' – a paper written in 1952, but not published until 1954, I argued that price theory, properly interpreted, gave us exactly the opposite result. There should be tolls on congested roads in urban areas, while the uncongested intercity and rural roads should have only low user fees. More generally, the argument was that *short-run* not long-run marginal costs were the principles which should guide utility pricing policies.

After more than 35 years I am still involved in these arguments – still, as it were, battling for the application of sensible policies. Although I believe that, after many articles (I think the most influential was in *Econometrica*, 1961) and books (particularly *The Economics of Road User Charges*, 1968), the *principle* has been largely conceded, the applications are much more timorous and messy. Perhaps my greatest reward was Singapore's adoption of a pricing policy to enter a congested downtown area. This area pricing scheme of 1975 was very similar to the model I had outlined more than 20 years before. The scheme turned out to be not only a considerable economic success but also, which I did not foresee, a great political success. But Singapore was an exception: in general, rational road pricing has been elsewhere treated as a political hot potato. However, I do not retain a faith that, because it is so rational and liberal a solution, ultimately it will be widely adopted.

Congestion was not restricted to roads. It had become a desperate problem at the world's major airports, and apparently was quite acute in London. In 1968 I was appointed as a member, the only economist, of the Commission on London's Third Airport (known, after the chairman, Lord Roskill, as the Roskill Commission). After two and a half years, during which the commission's research team carried out the largest cost–benefit study in history, the commission wrote what I believe was a good report and a sound recommendation. Although Mr Heath rejected the recommendation and instead started to lay out an airport off the coast of Essex (Maplin), I believe subsequent analysis and events justified the commission's views, particularly on the fact that one could use existing capacity much more efficiently. This took the form of the first introduction of congestion pricing in the use of airport facilities. Heathrow started charging high prices for peak slots, and it worked.

In working on the congestion problem, I had discovered that I had a relative advantage in what appeared to be a new school of applied economics. My knowledge of statistics and econometrics gave me the formal tools for handling data, but it was evident to me that what was much more important was, first, to be able to distill all the empirical implications of a theoretical principle – in effect to show how the process produced observable data; and second, to seek data, of various kinds and with varying provenance, to bring to bear on the propositions at hand. (The model for this approach – Friedman's *Theory of the Consumption Function* – appeared in the mid-1950s and greatly boosted my confidence in what was possible.) Thus, as an example of this approach, I believe that I was the first to use the data collected by traffic engineers to measure the marginal social costs and estimate the best congestion tax.

It seemed also then quite natural to extend my interests to the econometric exploration of cost and production functions, not only in utilities but also in manufacturing industry. After a number of papers, I wrote a survey article for *Econometrica*, 1963. Although such exercises were interesting and instructive in using various forms of data and in wringing seemingly surprising implications from theory, I found them fundamentally unsatisfying, largely because the policy implications were quite remote. I found that I did my best work when I had my teeth into a policy proposal that challenged conventional wisdom. From the free spirits at Birmingham in the 1950s, I had acquired a taste for being an *enfant terrible*.

Thus I was a natural candidate for the vanguard of the monetarist revolution in the United Kingdom. I had been fascinated by the institution of money even as a wet-behind-the-ears undergraduate, and I wrote what I thought at the time was a devastating critique of Hicks's *Contribution to a Theory of the Trade Cycle* (1950) for his cavalier treatment of such an important aspect of business fluctuations. My interest however was riveted by, first, the Conservative government experiments with monetary policy in the mid-1950s, and second, the Chicago essays, *Studies in the Quantity Theory of Money* (1956). By 1959, after a spell as visiting professor at Northwestern and some peripheral contact with Friedman, I was convinced that the view prevalent among British economists, and confirmed by the *Radcliffe Report* – that the quantity of money was of little consequence because of the (Radcliffe) *infinite* variability of the velocity of circulation – was dangerously wrong. And so from 1960, with a small group of young hopefuls at the University of Birmingham, we started research on money in the United Kingdom. But first we had the monumental job of preparing the historical series on money and credit supply, etc. I applied for a modest research grant to the Bank of England. The Bank refused to support such research since, it said, the quantity of money was of little consequence and there would be few people interested in such statistics! Such was the wisdom of the day.

Nevertheless, I can claim that the empirical and particularly the statistical analysis of money was substantially pioneered in the University of Birmingham in the first half of the 1960s. We challenged the conventional wisdom of the primacy of fiscal policy and the need for an accommodating monetary stance. Our analysis revealed substantial monetary multipliers and more dubious reactions to fiscal stimuli. Unfortunately, this monetary work at Birmingham lapsed as I left for a visiting professorship at MIT en route to the Sir Ernest Cassel Chair of Economics at the London School of Economics in 1967. At that time, LSE seemed like a reincarnation of the 1950s Birmingham, with Terence Gorman and Frank Hahn, but with the added weight of Harry Johnson and his Chicago ideas. The unique contribution of my move to LSE, however, was my association with one of the most distinguished scholars, Peter (now Lord) Bauer. I learned to appreciate his sceptical and reflective attitude and his pure intellectual integrity. I believe that my work and friendship with Bauer gave a maturity and a greater integrity to my work, particularly on policy. Location in London was important for my work on monetary economics and policy. I was brought into much closer contact with the City, which was developing as one of the great international financial centres, and Westminster, where a factious House of Commons and socialist government were providing endless opportunities for illustrating the fallacies of ideas and the follies of policy.

The election of the Conservative government in 1970 was, I thought, a great opportunity to restructure economic policy. I had been involved with that most influential think tank, the Institute of Economic Affairs and IEA's ebullient director Ralph (now Lord) Harris, for many years in framing a new economic policy based on monetary stability, fiscal rectitude and free and unfettered markets. We imagined that this policy had been largely accepted by the Conservative leadership both in its election manifesto and in a famous meeting at Selsdon. With great hopes, I accepted a job in the cabinet office as part-time adviser (that is, at one remove, to the Prime Minister, Mr Edward Heath) on macro policies.

I think I can say that I was utterly ineffective. In the second half of 1971, in pursuing an elusive goal of 'full employment', the Heath government began a massive fiscal stimulus and tripling of the monetary growth rate. Virtually all economic advisers and commentators thought that there would be such an expansion of employment and real output that there would be a *reduction* in the rate of inflation. My view was quite the opposite. I forwarded to Mr. Heath a memorandum entitled 'Inflation, Devaluation and More Inflation', where I predicted that by 1974 the inflation rate would be at least 10 and possibly as high as 15 per cent, that there would be a current deficit of as much as one billion sterling, and that he would be driven to reimpose prices and incomes controls. My advice was rejected and I was relieved of my part-time job. The Heath policy, pursued with increased vigour in 1972, came to grief in 1974 when the inflation rate reached 14.7 per cent, the current account deficit was more than 3.3 billion sterling, and prices and incomes controls had been reimposed. I published my memorandum in July 1972, so my Cassandra-like performance was in the public record. In retrospect, it seems no big deal to have made and persisted with such predictions, yet the pressures to conform were considerable; but all the arguments made me even more convinced that I was correct.

In 1974 the electorate, in two elections, threw out Heath and elected Harold Wilson and his curious band of expropriating socialists. In the words of one of Wilson's ministers, Mr Douglas Jay, 'the man from Whitehall really does know best.' Then I decided that Britain, facing alternatives of Wilson and Heath, had a choice between the devil and the shallow blue sea. Whatever the political outcome, Britain was in for a pronounced decline into the absurdities of controls, planning and dirigism. In 1974, I decided to leave Britain and, after a year at the World Bank, to join the department of political economy of Johns Hopkins in 1976. Meanwhile, what I thought was politically impossible had happened: Heath had lost the leadership and by a series of split votes and accidents, the party had elected a woman who was regarded as an upstart – a mere housewife and junior minister – Margaret Thatcher.

I knew Mrs Thatcher as an ardent student of economics on the various occasions I had talked to her over the past few years. I confess that I had not thought of her as a leader at all. But right from the beginning, she began to display those traits that have become so much her own: the strong belief in the morality of individual responsibility, the government's duty to restore and protect freedoms, the need to secure financial stability and a non-inflationary environment, the belief that, freed from government's constrictions, Britain could become an enterprising, prosperous nation – and a firm linchpin in the Alliance. Of course we had heard the same sort of thing from Edward Heath, so, even when the Thatcher government came to power in 1979, one reserved judgment. But right from the beginning it was clear that Mrs Thatcher was no Heath. In contrast to Heath, who disliked ideas and hated people who went on about them, Margaret Thatcher passionately, and with complete commitment, devoted her every hour to furthering the idea of a liberal society and to the permanent demise of socialism in our land.

By 1980 I had been at the Bank and Hopkins for four years, working in deregulation, financial reform, monetary policy, exchange rate policy, tax reform and housing finance, as well as in the familiar fields of transport.

Although Bank employment brought with it many inhibitions, these were compensated by being able to observe the breadth of experience of many countries and the consequences of many policies. But in 1979–80 my attention was riveted on Britain, and all the evidence suggested that Mrs Thatcher really did mean to reform the nation – and I surmised that there was a good chance (but I recall thinking that the odds were less than even) that she would pull it off.

In response to the invitations extended by Sir (now Lord) Keith Joseph and (now Sir) Alfred Sherman, I decided to return to London in 1980 as personal economic adviser to the Prime Minister for a period of two years. My appointment was greeted with protests, partly about the salary (£50000) and partly because I was thought to be the rigid monetarist whom Mrs Thatcher would use to clobber the more pragmatic officials and ministers in the Treasury and the Bank of England. There was much pressure to put me in the cabinet office or in the Treasury, but the Prime Minister and I agreed that I would be most effective at her elbow in No. 10. The job was unique. My role was defined by the Prime Minister with the words: 'you know what you can do best and you know what needs doing'. Thus began what I believe was the apogee of my career. I had the best job anyone could devise. Since I soon earned Mrs Thatcher's trust, I acquired a considerable influence on economic policy.

Yet the first months were most difficult as I worked to bring about immense changes in monetary and fiscal policy. First, in 1980, I had become convinced that monetary policy, as measured by the narrow aggregates, had drastically tightened from mid-1979. (The growth rates had fallen from some 15–17 per cent to virtually zero by 1980). High real interest rates and a massive (circa 45 per cent) real appreciation of sterling together with the rapidly escalating recession corroborated this diagnosis (later confirmed by my old colleague from Hopkins, Jurg Niehans). Second, as the fiscal situation unfolded in the first weeks of 1981, I believed that, contrary to all conventional wisdom both in and out of government, it was essential to cut in half the borrowing requirement of the public sector (PSBR). I proposed the biggest budgetary squeeze in peacetime history – a reduction of more than 2.5 per cent of GDP – and that during a time when output was falling faster than in any year since World War II and when the monthly unemployment figures were soaring. After much fierce debate, Mrs Thatcher became convinced and, with characteristic courage, adopted this fiscal squeeze.

Professional judgment was swift and virtually unanimous. In a letter to the *Times* on 31 March 1981, signed by Frank Hahn and 364 economists including all living ex chief economic advisers to the government, the policies were said to 'deepen the depression, erode the industrial base of our economy and threaten its social and political stability'. It was clear that they had been looking for an *increase* in the PSBR as a countercyclical measure against the recession. My argument, per contra, stressed the unsustainability of yet another large PSBR (estimated at about 6.5 to 7.5 per cent of GDP) following a decade of such deficits, the soaring effect on real interest rates, and the need for a consistent and, above all, *credible* fiscal–monetary policy before there could be any hope of sustained recovery. So the deficit was cut and interest rates fell some 500 basis points below their peak.

The results appeared in the summer of 1981. Contrary to the dire predictions of the 365, the economy turned sharply *upwards*. Nor was it a flash in the pan, as it was so confidently asserted by many of the 365. From 1981 to this day (a still continuing boom in 1988), Britain has grown for the longest expansion on record. For the first time since World War II, Britain has been at the top of the OECD growth league instead of its usual place at the bottom. Furthermore, inflation was reduced from an ambient 15 per cent in the 1970s to less than 5 per cent from 1983 on. It became the accepted view, except among academic economists, that the budget of 1981 together with the adjustment of monetary policy was the foundation of Britain's economic renaissance.

After this auspicious beginning, I acquired a considerable reputation at the Treasury and the Bank of England, and I received their full cooperation during the next three and a half years. We managed to produce a fairly stable monetary policy (the growth rate of Mo remained in the 3–6 per cent range). And from 1981 onwards the British could look forward to tax reform and steady but sizeable yearly reductions in tax rates, at least as long as Mrs Thatcher remained in office. And such tax reductions combined with the transformation from an unmanageable deficit to a budgetary surplus in 1987–88.

In my role as adviser, there was one other major controversy where I found myself in a beleaguered but rather select minority. The issue was exchange rate intervention and in particular the advisability of Britain joining the exchange rate mechanism (ERM) of the European Monetary System. For more than 35 years I have been convinced that the various forms of pseudo-fixed exchange rates, dignified by various names such as crawling pegs, reference zones, etc., had only deleterious consequences – especially encouraging overvaluation and repression (on the part of dependent currencies such as sterling, the French franc, etc.) and massive capital flight or inflow when the 'realignment' was imminent, which would in turn give rise to proposals for more exchange controls and trade barriers. The pressure from Europe and the British establishment to conform and join the ERM has been enormous. But the arguments have never attained even a minimum level of plausibility. My advice has been for Britain to retain its system of flexible exchange rates and to stay out of the present arrangements of the ERM. So far Mrs Thatcher has concurred. (Of course I would not be opposed, at least not on economic grounds, to the development of a proper European currency administered by a European Central Bank preceded by absolutely fixed exchange rates *and* appropriate monetary institutions to support that fixity. But that is another story.) It would not be in Britain's or, I believe, Europe's interest to join the present half-baked system.

CONCLUSION

So far, that is my life. My final reflection must be on my extraordinary luck. My life has been one lucky break after another – although I am reminded of Pasteur's dictum that 'luck visits the prepared mind'. I am reminded that to many people, it seemed positively foolhardy for me to join Mrs Thatcher at No. 10 in 1980 when the chattering classes were confidently predicting that she and her policies were finished. Events did not turn out that way. It was my great privilege to serve as trusted adviser to one of the greatest political leaders who would thrust Britain into the renaissance of the 1980s. As so often the case in Britain, my working-class origins were no handicap in attaining one of the most influential jobs that any economist could wish. This surely is evidence that discredits the widespread notion that, in important respects, Britain is dominated by rigid class barriers. I suspect that Britain is one of the most mobile societies in the world today, and that mobility has been much enhanced by the reforms of Thatcherism.

I have learned one important lesson in the last nearly four decades. Virtually all economists too readily accept received opinion, especially if it is thought to be fashionable and being propagated by clever and influential minds. Yet most of the most serious errors perpetrated by the most eminent economists, particularly in the analysis of policy, have resulted from, on the one hand, the neglect of the simplest and most basic principles of economics, and, on the other hand, of the merely causal and partial examination of the evidence. It is often difficult and sometimes painful to face reality; frequently it reminds us how wrong we have been or how we must regard as redundant much of what we thought we knew. But it is also a great liberator.

Finally, one should never give in to pressure – to be popular or fashionable or in the mainstream. One should concede only if the argument and evidence win the point or the day. 'To thyself be true'.

Index